קונטרס העבודה

LOVE LIKE FIRE AND WATER
A Guide to Jewish Meditation

Essay on the Service of the Heart
by the Rebbe Rashab נ"ע

With translation and commentary
by Rabbi David Sterne

Jerusalem Connection Publishing
New York / Jerusalem

Love like Fire and Water
Kuntres Ha'avoda

©
All rights reserved
Copyrighted by the author, Sept. 2005
Second Edition 2011

POB 28186
Jerusalem, Israel
jerconn@netvision.net.il

Printed in Israel

Dedicated to all the beautiful souls,
students, new immigrants and others who pass
through the Old City of Jerusalem, looking
for knowledge and inspiration
May this book help you find your way!

Credits

To Rabbi Alek Friedman
for checking the initial draft for accuracy

To Rabbi Imanuel Schochet
for making invaluable scholarly suggestions

To Rabbi Nissim Mangel and Rabbi Simon Jacobson
for offering encouragement

To Ms. Uriela Sagiv for editing

To Ms. Barbara Sopkin
for editing and proofreading

To Rabbi Yosi ben Shachar and Rabbi Moshe Kaplan
for typesetting

To my parents
for inspiring within me commitment to Torah and Judaism

TABLE OF CONTENTS

Table of Contents composed by the Lubavitcher Rebbe, ztz'l	i
Foreword by Rabbi Dr. J. Immanuel Schochet	iii
Author's Note	vii
Introduction	ix
Chapter 1 - Soul Levels	3
Chapter 2 - Guarding our Senses	38
Chapter 3 - Meditating to attain fear of G-d	62
Chapter 4 - Meditating to attain love of G-d	86
Chapter 5 - Advanced meditative techniques	123
Chapter 6 - Detailed Meditation	157
Chapter 7 - Things to be avoided	203
Endnotes	221
Appendix I - Letter from the Previous Rebbe	233
Appendix II - Notes of the Lubavitcher Rebbe	249

TABLE OF CONTENTS

(COMPOSED BY THE LUBAVITCHER REBBE,
R' MENACHEM MENDEL SCHNEERSON, ztz'l
in the original printed edition of Kuntres Ha'avoda)

Kuntres Ha'avoda

Chapter 1
Prayer is about uniting the G-dly soul with G-d, as well as purifying the animal soul. Both take place through [the medium of] love of G-d. Service of [the various levels of the soul] *nefesh, ruach, neshama* and *chaya*. The inclusion of *nefesh* in *ruach*, and both of them in *neshama*, and all of them in the essence of the soul. Acknowledgment of G-d, within the *avoda* of the emotions and of the intellect. *Kavana* (intention) and speech within prayer.

Chapter 2
Eyesight and [the necessity of] guarding it. Guarding the senses. Acceptance of the yoke of G-d, fear of transgression, fear of G-d. The reasons for foreign (un-spiritual) thoughts. The nature of weakness of the G-dly soul, and advice for dealing with it.

Chapter 3
Factors that bring about fear of G-d. Love of G-d does not occur naturally from birth, but fear does. Love is associated with revealed spirituality, fear with the essence of G-dliness. Dimensions of fear - fear that is inferior to the service of prayer, and fear that surpasses prayer.

Chapter 4
Love like water, love like flames of fire, and their various aspects. The meditation associated with each of them. Their effect upon the animal soul, whether weakness or nullification. Love versus *tshuva* (return to G-d). Meaning of offering the "fat and blood" in service of G-d.

Chapter 5

The will of the [soul level of] *yechida*. And of *chaya*. Love that is dependent upon something, and two kinds of love that are not dependent on anything. The effect of the *chaya* and *yechida* upon the animal soul. Whether or not *mesirat nefesh* (self-sacrifice) is associated with the natural soul. The spiritual arousal of the ten days of *tshuva*, and one's service during the course of the year.

Chapter 6

General meditation, its effects and its drawbacks. "Engraving" from the outside, "engraving" from the inside. The reasons for indifference that may occur after initial meditative excitement. Everyone has their particular character trait(s) to rectify.

Chapter 7

Service that surpasses one's true spiritual level. Spiritual excitement detached from the animal soul, and how it comes about. Step-by-step *avoda*. The generation of Jews that wandered in the desert, and those that entered the land of Israel, and what we have to learn from them.

FOREWORD

When R. Shneur Zalman of Liadi, founder of Chabad Chassidism and known as the "Alter Rebbe," turned eighteen, he was already a renowned scholar with vast knowledge in all subjects of the Torah. Nonetheless, he felt a need for a special mentor. Considering several options, he decided on R. Dov Ber, known as the Maggid of Mezhirech, the major disciple of the Baal Shem Tov and his successor as leader of the Chassidic movement. At a number of occasions the Alter Rebbe explained this choice in slightly varying ways:

Proficiency in Torah-knowledge and methodology in the study of Talmud and Halachah study he had mastered already, but "as for *tefilah* I hardly knew anything."[1] At another time he expressed it in terms of "I was not aware how to serve G-d (*avodah*)."[2] And at a third occasion he said that elsewhere one learns how to master the Torah; in Mezhirech one learns how to let the Torah master you, i.e., "how the Torah teaches man to become a Torah himself."[3]

Torah-study is the comprehensive core of Jewish life: *"Talmud Torah keneged kulam* – Torah-study is equivalent to them all."[4] On the one hand it is a *mitzvah* on its own, thus a meritorious end by itself. On the other hand it is also a means towards another end: the practice of the Divine precepts and the spiritual perfection of man, which are impossible without prior study and knowledge of Torah - as Hillel taught: "A boor cannot be fearful of sin, nor can an unlearned person be a *chasid* (a person of scrupulous piety)."[5] Torah-study, in spite of its unique and superior quality on its own,[6] may never be divorced from its application on the practical level. He who claims to have nothing but Torah – he has not even Torah, for one must be occupied with Torah and the performance of *chassadim*[7] (lit. acts of kindness, which include not only kindness to fellow-beings but also, as it were, to G-d, i.e., the performance of *mitzvot* and the worship of G-d[8]). The Torah is but the gateway to *yirat Shamayim* (the fear of, or reverence for, G-d).[9] The superiority of Torah, therefore, lies in the fact that "Torah-study leads to practical observance."[10]

Thus Torah must lead to *avodah*. It will do so when studied *lishmah*. *Lishmah* means (a) for its own sake, as opposed to ulterior motives of personal benefits (which include the objective of becoming a renowned scholar), as derived from the verse "to love G-d and to obey His voice and to cleave unto Him" (Deuteronomy 30:20).[11] (b) *Lishmah* also means literally "for its name's sake." The "name" Torah is an idiom of *hora'ah* - teaching, instruction, guidance.[12] This "name," then, implies that the Torah instructs, guides and counsels man to be wholehearted with his Maker and Master who, by means of revealing the Torah, "seeks to benefit man in this world and in the world-to-come."[13] In this sense, therefore, learning Torah *lishmah* means to absorb and internalize this guidance and counsel, to generate *ahavah veyirah*, love and fear (reverence) of G-d[14] - "oneself to become a Torah."

Man was created to serve his Maker by means of Torah and *mitzvoth*.[15] His mission on earth is to manifest to himself and others the concealed G-dliness that pervades all of creation - "I fill the heavens and the earth" (Jeremiah 23:24) and there is no place devoid of His Presence even in the physical realm.[16] Thus one must breach the barriers of mundane illusions and bring about a full consciousness of the reality of Divine Presence.[17] This *avodah*, service of G-d, cannot be perfunctory "as a commandment of men learned by rote" (Isaiah 29:13). Without *kavanah*, encompassing intent and concentration, the heart and the mind, it is lifeless, a "body without soul." Torah, *mitzvot* and *tefilah* that lack *ahavah veyirah* will not achieve their goal of ascending.[18] True *avodah* means the consciousness of "Now, Israel, what does G-d, your G-d, ask of you but to fear G-d, your G-d, to go in all His ways and to love Him, and to serve G-d, your G-d, with all your heart and with all your soul!" (Deuteronomy 10:12)

This fundamental principle is the major focus of Chassidism. It applies universally, equally to scholar and layman, to each according to his or her capacities. The Alter Rebbe once said: "I received from the Maggid of Mezhirech, and he had received that teaching from the Baal Shem Tov: the *mitzvah* of *ve'ahavta* (you shall love [G-d]) means to 'thrust' one's thought and mind (in Yiddish he said *men zol zich arajn tohn* - to immerse oneself) in those subject-matters that will stir that love,[19] while the resulting effects are not of the basic precept."[20]

Much has been taught by the Chassidic masters throughout the generations to emphasize this principle and to motivate its application. In this context, the fifth Rebbe of Chabad, R. Sholom Dov Ber of Lubavitch, known by the acronym "the Reshab," composed a special treatise *Kuntres Ha'avodah*, as a primer for those seeking guidance in *avodah* to explain "the principle of *avodah shebalev* (service of the heart), i.e., prayer, to draw near and cause one's soul to cleave unto G-dliness..."

This treatise touches upon many basic ideas of Chassidism, but its inspiration is not lessened by its profound scholarship. A proper study of its contents will most assuredly affect the student with new insights, a proper understanding of the issues, and above all result in the true and enhanced *avodah* it sets out to achieve.

Rabbi David Sterne deserves much credit for undertaking the arduous task of translating *Kuntres Ha'avodah*, thus making this treasure available and accessible to the English-speaking public. Moreover, he added numerous explanations for complex concepts as well as most helpful diagrams to ease the student's journey. His work is most certainly a tremendous achievement. Unfortunately, the restraints on my time did not allow me to review the translation. The few passages I did manage to scan, however, were sufficient to impress and to evoke admiration for the great effort Rabbi Sterne must have put into this labor of love, of which it may be said with confidence that he has the zechut that his work will cause many to attain merit. Hopefully he will use his blessed talents for further contributions.

Toronto, Tishrei 5766
J. Immanuel Schochet

1. Likkutei Diburim, III:p. 966
2. Ibid., IV:p. 1324
3. Ibid., II:II:p. 492
4. Pe'ah I:1
5. Avot II:5
6. See Tanya, ch. 5-6
7. Yevamot 109b, and see there 105a. Note the Rebbe's glossary comment in Sefer Hama'amarim 5708, p. 266, note 7. Cf. Zohar III:119a, and the references cited there in Nitzutzei Zohar. Tanya, Igeret Hakodesh, sect. 5.
8. Zohar III:281a. See also Zohar II:214b and III:222b; Tikunei Zohar 1b.
9. Shabbat 31b; Yoma 72b and Rashi ad loc.
10. Kidushin 40b
11. Sifre, Eikev, end of sect. 48. Nedarim 62a
12. Zohar III:53b. Redak on Psalms 19:8. Maharal, Gur Aryeh on Genesis 1:1; Netivot Olam, Netiv Hatorah, ch. 1, and Netiv Ha'emunah, ch. 2.
13. Zohar II:82b. See also ibid. I:11a, II:96b. Cf. Avodah Zara 17b; Sifre, Ha'azinu, end of sect. 322. Rambam, Hilchot Shechitah 14:16, and Hilchot Temurah 4:13.
14. Maggid of Mezhirech, Or Torah, sect. 317. See there also sect. 453.
15. Kidushin 82a
16. Tikunei Zohar 57:91b; ibid. 70:122b. Shemot Rabba 2:9. See Tanya, Igeret Hakodesh, sect. 25. Note also Tanya, ch. 41.
17. See Tanya, ch. 32
18. Zohar I:24a. Tikunei Zohar 10:25b. See also Zohar II:121a.
19. See Rambam, Hilchot Yessodei Hatorah 2:2 and 4:12; Hilchot Teshuvah 10:6.
20. Keter Shem Tov, Hossafot, sect. 38. See the Rebbe's glossary comments on Sefer Hama'amarim 5701, p. 116.

Author's Note to the Second Edition of
LOVE LIKE FIRE AND WATER
(*Kuntres Ha'Avoda*)

Five years have passed since the publication of the first edition of LOVE LIKE FIRE AND WATER, translation of the *Kuntres Ha'Avoda* ("Tractate on Divine Service") in 2005. In the ensuing years, the original edition has passed the "test of time." It has found acceptance among wide swaths of readership, among people who are thirsty to learn and practice the meditative path of spiritual connection inherent in Judaism. This path is implicit within Chasidic literature, and finds its most explicit expression in the Chasidut of Chabad and especially in the *Kuntres Ha'Avoda* of the Rebbe Rashab (1860-1920). It is perhaps for this reason that the English translation has found its way into so many houses and libraries. For some time, there has been an unfulfilled demand for a second printing, and that is the purpose of this new edition of the work.

However, it would be inappropriate to produce a new edition of the translation without adding something to its content and depth. Just as a live person grows continuously, striving for new horizons, so his/her breadth and depth of knowledge must expand as well.

Anyone who takes the trouble to examine the footnotes of the Lubavitcher Rebbe (R' Menachem Mendel Schneerson) that appear in the Hebrew edition of *Kuntres Ha'Avoda* will see that they "open up worlds." The notes that the Rebbe appended to *Kuntres Ha'Avoda* illuminate many of the roots and antecedents from which the Rebbe Rashab drew his teachings and system. Thus, they shed more light on how to climb the ladder of spirituality and cling to the One Above. But, they do far more than that. Sometimes, by simply quoting another text, the Rebbe points us in a new direction, showing how a particular principle of meditation may equally apply to another aspect of connecting on high, for example, through the process of *tshuva*, or "return" to the One Above. At other times, the Rebbe's notes elucidate an otherwise obscure spiritual process, letting us know that it is equivalent or similar to something that we have read or learned elsewhere. In these and all other cases, the Rebbe's notes allow us to take the teaching of the Rebbe Rashab and apply them to new contexts and situations in service of the One Above.

For this reason, we are happy to present this new, expanded edition of LOVE LIKE FIRE AND WATER, which includes translations of the reference notes of the Lubavitcher Rebbe, appended by him to the original Hebrew edition of *Kuntres Ha'avoda*. In this way, we hope that the reader will not only strive to adopt the meditative approach to Jewish prayer that is found in *Kuntres Ha'Avoda*, but will also discover how it is an integral part of *avodat Hashem* and of Judaism in general.

                        Rabbi David Sterne
                        Jerusalem Connection in the Old City of Jerusalem
                        Chodesh Shvat, 5771 – January, 2011

INTRODUCTION TO
"LOVE LIKE FIRE AND WATER" - *KUNTRES HA'AVODA*

Some twenty-six years ago, I was present when the Lubavitcher Rebbe *ztz'l* spoke of the necessity of responding to the hunger for meditation techniques that would be compatible with Jewish sources. As a beginning yeshiva student at the time, I thought to myself that it should be easy to search Jewish sources and find out exactly what Jewish meditation is, or should be. However, it would take me years of learning and practice before I could integrate it and explain it to others. As a rabbi, I have had the opportunity, thank G-d, to gain the experience necessary in order to begin passing on some of that information to others. Through the Old City of Jerusalem, where I live, pass many of the most spiritually inclined Jews of this generation (and in truth, all Jews are spiritually inclined). It is my privilege to have contact with them, and it is to them that this translation and commentary is dedicated.

One of the distinguishing characteristics of our generation is the search for spirituality. Jews are especially active in this regard – we seem to be in the vanguard of almost every spiritual movement that exists. Yet, when we look for the spiritual well-springs of our own heritage, they're not necessarily easy to find. While *Shulchan Aruch* the Code of Jewish Law, provides the essential framework within which a Jew is supposed to live his life, in order to find the spiritual connection with the One Above and strive to be more G-dly, our generation needs the inner dimensions of Torah – explained in Chassidic and Kabbalistic literature. It is here that we find the intellectual meaning of G-dliness and spirituality, as well as the emotional excitement leading to love and fear of the One Above. But, that only comes about when we embark upon a path of learning combined with meditation. And the latter is an essential which most Jews don't even know exists.

In the 12th century, long before the advent of the Chassidic movement, Maimonides, the first codifier of the Jewish law, wrote that the way to achieve love and fear of G-d is through meditation on the creation and the amazing wisdom that goes into it. First, he said, one will be overcome with love. Then, upon further contemplation, he will be overwhelmed with fear and awe. He then proceeded to describe succinctly the nature of the spiritual and physical realms of the universe (*Hilchot Yesodei HaTorah*, Chapter 2, Halacha 2 and onwards). It is clear that he intended meditation to cover the abstract and spiritual as well as the physical creation. Following Maimonides, in the 16th century, Rabbi Yoseph Karo authored the *Shulchan Aruch* which is universally accepted by all Jews today (with amendments for the Ashkenazi community); he wrote, "...the early pietists and men of action would go off on their own and work on their spiritual intentions to the point of abstraction from the physical world and devotion to the spiritual on a level which was close to prophecy." To which the *Ramah* (Rabbi Moshe Isserles) added, "and one should think of the greatness of G-d and the lowliness of man" (*Shulchan Aruch Orach Chaim* 98:1). Clearly, Jewish meditation is no latter day augmentation of Judaism. It is a vital and integral element of Judaism that no Jew should be without.

In our own generation, since the 18th century, it is the Chassidic movement that has developed Jewish meditation into a technique. In Hebrew, it's called *hitbonenut*. The etymological source of the word is *boneh*, meaning "build." To practice Jewish meditation, you "build" a spiritual structure inside of yourself. Also implicit in the word *hitbonenut* is the word *bina*, "understanding" or intellectual analysis. The structure that you build consists of G-dly concepts and ideas that you must understand thoroughly and deeply. They become the framework and girders of your inner "building." When you properly understand a series of G-dly concepts and put them together in your mind, you are building your own inner spiritual structure. When you actively dwell in this inner structure for a certain period of time each day (usually before morning prayers), exploring its nooks and crannies and reinforcing its girders while building it ever higher, you are practicing Jewish meditation, or *hitbonenut*. The sages of the Talmud (mentioned above) used to do this three times a day, for an hour before each set of prayers. Additionally, they would spend an hour "coming down" after each set of prayers. In our own generation, by studying and meditating upon the infinite concepts and G-dly ideas contained in contemporary Chassidic literature, we gain the proper understanding that allows us to build a spiritual edifice inside of ourselves, climb all the way to the top of it, and cling to the One Above.

***

The purpose of this free translation and commentary is to serve as a handbook, an instruction booklet, if you will, of Jewish meditation for the serious person who knows next to nothing about Judaism, but wants to be convinced that there is something seriously spiritual in his or her heritage. Such a book could have been written as a simple, direct set of instructions. However, it makes much more sense to show how a true spiritual master, a Chassidic Rebbe, whose very life was dedicated to G-d and other Jews, explained the subject. From him, we can glean the basics of the technique and hopefully pass it on and explain it to others in terms that they understand.

***

The years 1909-1910 (when *Kuntres Ha'avoda* was written) were tumultuous years in Russia. These were the twilight years of the czarist regime, and the forces of Communism and Bolshevism were on the rise. As always when there is strife, the Jews were the scapegoats. The pogroms and physical suffering were great, and yet somehow the spiritual lives of Russian Jewry not only continued, but in some cases thrived. Such was the case with the Jews of Lubavitch. Under the leadership of the fifth Lubavitcher Rebbe, Rebbe Shalom Dov Ber Schneerson, they managed (in 1896) to establish a yeshiva dedicated not only to the study of Jewish law, but to the inner dimensions of Torah, as well. Under the leadership of the Rebbe Rashab, as he was called, the yeshiva (called Tomchei Tmimim), grew and developed. Its goal was to cultivate not only rabbis who knew the legal texts of the Jewish tradition-the Talmud and code of Jewish law-but also to develop *ovdei HaShem*, true "servants of God," pious and learned Jews who knew how to meditate and pray, using the wellsprings of Chassidic literature.

The *Zohar* predicted that the opening of the "wellsprings" of the inner dimensions of Torah would be accompanied by a corresponding development in the secular disciplines. The period indicated by the *Zohar*, the sixth millenium (from 5500 to 5600, or roughly 1740 to 1840) saw not only the revelation of the Chassidic movement, but the beginning of the scientific, and soon after, the industrial revolution. But, the prediction wasn't restricted to the scientific disciplines. As the Rebbe Rashab was writing his longest Chassidic dissertations (discourses of the years 5666 -5608, or 1906-1908, and also 5612- 5616, or 1912-1916, but written earlier), Russian novelists (such as Leo Tolstoy, *lehavdil*, died 1910) were penning their long novels. It was a period that was well-suited to long, detailed, and nuanced literature, and since this was expressed first of all in the G-dly discipline of the Rebbe's Chassidus, it was expressed in secular literature as well.

In addition, the Rebbe penned four *kuntresim*, or shorter tractates for the specific purpose of guiding the students of Yeshivat Tomchei Tmimim in *avodat HaShem*, "service of G-d." One of them – *Kuntres Ha'avoda* – deals with the subject of meditation. The *ovdim*, the pious students of Lubavitch were guided in their service by the Rebbe's Chassidic discourses and his instructions on how to lose their *yeshut* (ego), while praying and getting closer to G-d. However, the vicissitudes of the time, including the Bolshevik revolution and with it the uprooting of the yeshiva, nearly caused this meditative approach to disappear from the world. The Rebbe Rashab's son, Harav Yoseph Yitzhak Schneerson *ztz'l*, continued to teach his father's tradition and *avoda*, first in Russia, then in Poland, and ultimately in New York during the awful years of World War II. However, the Holocaust decimated the ranks of the Chassidim, and the *ovdim* of yesteryear are no longer to be found among us. Nevertheless, by reading and studying the *Kuntres Ha'avoda*, and focusing on the study of other Chassidic texts, we can try to reconstruct the *avoda* of the Chassidim who lived roughly one hundred years ago.

It was the previous Rebbe, HaRav Yoseph Yitzhak Schneerson (son of the Rebbe Rashab and director of Tomchei Tmimim) who foretold the necessity of this reconstruction. He wrote in his introduction to his father's work:

"The days will come and a young generation will arrive with a claim from the depths of their souls against all of their leaders, and in particular toward the directors of the yeshivas and their heads, saying:

WHY DIDN'T YOU REBUKE US FOR OUR CONDUCT?

WHY DIDN'T YOU TELL US THE TRUTH, THE TRUTH OF THE LIVING TORAH OF G-D, IN ITS COMPLETENESS?

WHY DIDN'T YOU INSTRUCT US IN THE PATH OF LIFE AS IT IS LIVED IN DAILY LIFE, TELLING US:

HOW WE SHOULD PRAY EVERY DAY BEFORE OUR FATHER ABOVE, THE KING OF KINGS, THE HOLY ONE BLESSED BE HE...

HOW WE SHOULD LEARN HIS TORAH, AS COMMANDED "IN FEAR AND AWE, TREMBLING AND SWEAT"...

HOW WE SHOULD FULFILL HIS COMMANDMENTS, AS COMMANDED "IN HAPPINESS AND A GOOD HEART," -WHICH ITSELF IS A TREMENDOUS SERVICE OF THE ONE ABOVE...

And what will we say and how will we justify ourselves on that day?

It is incumbent upon all of us, and especially upon the administrations of the yeshivot to organize our service and to make the schedule and conduct of the yeshiva such that it doesn't only teach the 'sterile' professions of becoming a scholar, rabbi, rosh yeshiva, and the like, but imparts the guidance necessary for the student to become a complete Jew in his body (mitzvot), in his soul (prayer) and in his Torah [learning]. Anyone looking at the student should recognize that in him are combined the three levels of "Israel, Torah, and G-d [are one], all three of them both hidden and revealed..."

That day is upon us, but it is certainly not only the students of the yeshivot who are asking the questions. Every Jew with a G-dly soul in his or her body is asking, "how can I serve G-d?" Sometimes the question is concealed deep inside, and sometimes (especially among those who make their way to Jerusalem, and to the Old City), the question is obvious and on the tips of their tongues. It is also for them that the Rebbe Rashab wrote the *Kuntres Ha'avoda,* and I hope that I have succeeded in bringing his words to them in a way they can understand and internalize.

Rabbi David Sterne
Chodesh Tammuz and Av, 5765/August
2005
Old City of Jerusalem, Israel

Kuntres Ha'Avodah - **Essay on the Service of the Heart**

An explanation of the service of the heart - prayer - with which
we approach and attach our soul to G-d, while also purifying
and refining our natural (animal) soul. About this subject, it is written,
"And you should know today and take it to heart ... "
leading to love (*ve'ahavta*) with all our heart,
including both our divine and natural inclinations ...

Essay on Service of the Heart - Love Like Fire and Water

CHAPTER 1 — פרק א

The *avoda* (service/worship) of the heart in prayer is a labor leading to love of G-d. As such, it serves two purposes. The first is to cleave to G-d, in order to unite our [divine] soul with G-dliness [and the second is to purify and refine our animal soul].

הִנֵּה כָּל הָעֲבוֹדָה וְהַיְגִיעָה שֶׁל עוֹבְדֵי ה' בִּתְפִלָּה הוּא לָבוֹא לְמִדַּת הָאַהֲבָה. כִּי הַתְּפִלָּה כְּלָלוּת עִנְיָנָהּ הוּא ב' דְּבָרִים, הָא' לְקַשֵּׁר וּלְדַבֵּק נַפְשׁוֹ בֶּאֱלוֹקוּת,

Prayer is a labor of love that unites our soul with its infinite source.

> All Jews are endowed with two souls or spiritual dimensions: a G-dly soul that imparts spirituality, and a natural soul that enlivens the physical body.

In the [first] case, we understand prayer — *tefila* in Hebrew — to mean "joining," as in *tofel*, "joining pieces of ceramic." This definition of prayer refers to joining our divine soul with the One Above. In this case, prayer

וְזֶהוּ מַה שֶּׁתְּפִלָּה הוּא לְשׁוֹן הִתְחַבְּרוּת וּכְמוֹ הַתּוֹפֵל כְּלִי חֶרֶס דְּהַיְנוּ הַתְקַשְּׁרוּת וְהִתְחַבְּרוּת נַפְשׁוֹ בֶּאֱלוֹקוּת, וְעַל שֵׁם זֶה נִקְרֵאת הַתְּפִלָּה סֻלָּם וּכְמוֹ שֶׁכָּתוּב סֻלָּם

COMMENTARY

In Chassidic meditation *(hitbonenut)* — whose purpose is to unite the intellect with the heart — there is no such thing as going "up" without going "in." When the Chassidic masters took the secrets of Kabbalah from the plane of spiritual space and revealed how they can be understood via the psychological dimension — that is, the dimension in which the soul operates in this world— they also established the concept that we must delve inward in order to go upward, spiritually. Going inward means stripping away layers of perceived reality in order to expose the true kernel of G-dliness inside ourselves and in creation.

Chassidic literature defines five different levels of inner consciousness (*p'nimiyut*) within the soul, corresponding to five levels of spiritual reality in the outer world, the macrocosm. There are infinite nuances within each of the five, and the divisions among them are only general rather than clear-cut.

For purposes of clarity, we will give English names to each of the five levels which correspond very roughly to the experience of each level, as described in Chassidic literature.

מַצָּב אַרְצָה וְרֹאשׁוֹ מַגִּיעַ הַשָּׁמַיְמָה וְאִיתָא בַּזֹּהַר סֻלָּם דָּא צְלוֹתָא שֶׁעַל יְדֵי הַסֻּלָּם דִּתְפִלָּה מִתְעַלִּים נֶפֶשׁ רוּחַ וּנְשָׁמָה שֶׁבְּנַפְשׁוֹ עַד שֶׁרֹאשׁוֹ מַגִּיעַ הַשָּׁמַיְמָה,

is also called a "ladder," as in the verse [in Genesis 28:12] which describes a "ladder placed on the earth, with its head reaching into the heavens." The *Zohar* says that "the ladder represents prayer," since by way of prayer, we elevate [our lower soul-levels], our *nefesh*, *ruach*, and *neshama*, [which are en-clothed in the body] until our head reaches into the heavens.

The divine soul has five levels; the lower three (1, 2, and 3) are en-clothed in the body, while the higher two (4 and 5) connect the essence of the soul with its source in the infinite light of G-d, as follows:

1.	*Nefesh*	"Enlivening soul"	Action Consciousness
2.	*Ruach*	"Spirit"	Emotion consciousness
3.	*Neshama*	"Intellectual Soul"	Intellect consciousness
4.	*Chaya* or *Nishmata d'Nishmata*	"Living one"	Transcendent consciousness
5.	*Yechida*	"Single one"	Unity consciousness

הַיְנוּ הִתְקַשְּׁרוּת עַצְמוּת הַנְּשָׁמָה בְּחִינַת נִשְׁמָתָא לְנִשְׁמָתָא בִּמְקוֹר חוּצְבָהּ בְּעַצְמוּת אוֹר אֵין סוֹף בָּרוּךְ הוּא בִּתְפִלַּת שְׁמוֹנֶה עֶשְׂרֵה, שֶׁגַּם הַנֶּפֶשׁ רוּחַ וּנְשָׁמָה עוֹלִים וְנִכְלָלִים בְּהִתְקַשְּׁרוּת זֹאת לֶאֱלֹקוּת

This means that we unite the essence of our soul — the *nishmata d'nishmata*[1] [equivalent to the *chaya*] — with its source in the infinite light of the essence of the Holy One. We achieve this in the course of praying the *Amida* [which is the pinnacle of prayer], when the *nefesh*, *ruach*, and *neshama* ascend and are included in this supernal unity.

i) See footnote of the Rebbe on page 249

The elevation of the soul starts with acknowledgment of G-d.

ii) See footnote of the Rebbe on page 258

(וַעֲלִיַּת וְהִתְקַשְּׁרוּת הַנְּשָׁמָה הוּא עַל יְדֵי הָעֲבוֹדָה בְּכָל מַדְרֵגָה שֶׁבָּהּ בִּפְרָט. תְּחִלָּה הָעֲבוֹדָה דִּבְחִינַת נֶפֶשׁ בִּבְחִינַת הוֹדָאָה וּכְמוֹ שֶׁכָּתוּב בְּמָקוֹם אַחֵר עִנְיַן הַבִּטּוּל דְּהוֹדָאָה. וְכֵן קִיּוּם הַתּוֹרָה וְהַמִּצְווֹת בְּפֹעַל

The elevation and unity of the soul require effort on all its levels.[i] It begins with the *avoda* on the level of *nefesh*, when we acknowledge the existence and presence of G-d.[ii] On this level emphasis is placed on adherence to the commandments — both the positive and the negative *mitzvot*. This constitutes *avoda* of the One Above in the World of *Asiya* [the World of Action, the lowest of the four worlds].

מַמָּשׁ בְּסוּר מֵרַע וַעֲשֵׂה טוֹב, שֶׁזֶּהוּ הָעֲבוֹדָה דִּבְחִינַת עֲשִׂיָּה כַּנּוֹדָע.

G-d created existence by means of a number of worlds. In this discussion we are concerned with the following four (from lowest to highest):			
1.	*Asiya*	"World of Action"	Particular existence; individual creatures
2.	*Yetzira*	"World of Formation"	General existence; archetypes, species
3.	*Bria*	"World of Creation"	Potential existence; formless substance
4.	*Atzilut*	"World of Emanation"	Awareness of God only; no self-awareness

With this *avoda*, we rise to [the next world], the World of *Yetzira* [the World of Formation], where we serve the One Above on the

וְעַל יְדֵי זֶה עוֹלֶה לִבְחִינַת הַיְצִירָה הַיְנוּ שֶׁיַּעֲלֶה וְיַגִּיעַ לְהָעֲבוֹדָה דִּבְחִינַת רוּחַ בְּחִינַת הִתְפַּעֲלוּת הַמִּדּוֹת, וְגַם בְּחִינַת נֶפֶשׁ מִתְעַלָּה

The elevation proceeds to a more emotional level of acknowledgment.

COMMENTARY

The English names bear little or no relationship to the corresponding Hebrew names of the levels of the soul, but will help us to understand what is meant by each level. These levels are:

#	Soul level	Experience	World	Morning Prayer
1.	*Nefesh* "Enlivening soul"	Action consciousness	World of *Asiya* "World of Action"	*Modeh Ani* until *Baruch Sh'amar*
2.	*Ruach* "Wind/spirit"	Emotion consciousness	World of *Yetzira* "World of Formation"	*Baruch Sh'amar* until *Barchu*
3.	*Neshama* "Soul/breath"	Intellect Consciousness	World of *Bria* "World of "Creation"	*Barchu* through the *Shema*
4.	*Chaya* "Living one"	Transcendent consciousness	World of *Atzilut* "World of Emanations"	*Shmoneh Esreh* or *Amida*
5.	*Yechida* "Single one"	Unity consciousness	Beyond worlds	Beyond prayer, Level of Prophecy

בָּזֶה וּכְעִנְיַן הִתְכַּלְלוּת הָעֲשִׂיָּה בִּיצִירָה, וְהַיְנוּ דְּהַהוֹדָאָה הִיא בְּמַדְרֵגָה עֶלְיוֹנָה יוֹתֵר וּבִידִיעָה בְּיוֹתֵר אֵיךְ שֶׁצָּרִיךְ לְהוֹדוֹת. וְהַיְדִיעָה בְּהַמַּדְרֵגָה שֶׁמּוֹדֶה בְּזֶה וּבִבְחִינַת הֶרְגֵּשׁ פְּנִימִי יוֹתֵר –

soul-level of *ruach*, the level of emotional excitement. Our *nefesh* also rises in the process, just as the World of *Asiya* rises to the World of *Yetzira*. This means that our acknowledgment of the One Above takes place on a higher soul-level, that is, on a higher plane of consciousness. Here, we have a better understanding of how we must acknowledge G-d's Presence, and we have a deeper understanding of the divinity we are acknowledging. In addition, our understanding is imbued with more feeling.

The worlds, together with *Keter*, the infinite light transcending the World of *Atzilut*, correspond to the five levels of the soul:			
1. *Asiya*	Particular creations	Action consciousness	*Nefesh*
2. *Yetzira*	General creations, templates	Emotion consciousness	*Ruach*
3. *Bria*	Possibility of creation	Intellect consciousness	*Neshama*
4. *Atzilut*	*Sephirot*, emanations	Transcendent consciousness	*Chaya*
5. *Keter*	Infinite light	Unity consciousness	*Yechida*

We differentiate between general and specific acknowledgment of G-d's presence.

(גַּם יֵשׁ לוֹמַר דְּיֵשׁ הוֹדָאָה כְּלָלִית וּכְמוֹ מוֹדֶה אֲנִי לְפָנֶיךָ כו' שֶׁהוֹדָאָה זוֹ אֵינָהּ בְּמַדְרֵגָה פְּרָטִית בֶּאֱלֹקוּת כִּי אִם הוֹדָאָה כְּלָלִית לֶאֱלֹקוּת וְכֵן הַבִּטּוּל וּנְתִינַת עַצְמוּתוֹ בְּהוֹדָאָה זוֹ אֵין בָּזֶה אֵיזֶה עִנְיָן פְּרָטִי כִּי אִם מַה שֶּׁבִּכְלָלוּת מְצִיאוּתוֹ הוּא נוֹתֵן אֶת

(There is a difference between *general* acknowledgement, as when we rise in the morning and say *Modeh Ani* — "I am thankful," that is, "I acknowledge the One Above" — [and *specific* acknowledgment of G-d's Presence on a particular spiritual level]. General acknowledgment en-

---
COMMENTARY
---

1. *NEFESH*

First of all — and lowest of all — is the level of "action consciousness." On this level, one acknowledges that G-d exists, while experiencing little or no emotional or intellectual awareness of Him. It is on this level as well, that emphasis is placed on fulfilling the commandments (*mitzvot*) which connect us to Him. When performing an action, it is not necessary to feel or understand (although it is often beneficial). The main thing is the action itself, and that is why this level of G-d awareness is called "action consciousness." In Hebrew, its name *nefesh* means

tails no recognition of any specific levels of spirituality. Rather, it is an overall affirmation of G-d's existence and also general nullification of our ego, a giving over of ourselves to Him in totality. There is no reference to any specific soul-level of self-nullification in this acknowledgment; we simply deliver ourselves into G-d's hands.)

עַצְמוֹ לֶאֱלוֹקוּת בְּהוֹדָאָה זוֹ

> "Acknowledgment of G-d" — *hoda'ah* in Hebrew — means consciously affirming G-d's existence and living with an awareness of Him. *Generally*, this entails thanking G-d at every step for the gifts He constantly bestows on us, especially the gift of life, and giving over this life to the *avoda* of the One Above. *Specifically*, this means acknowledging G-d while meditating on particular spiritual levels.

(The advantage of this general/overall acknowledgment is that it is usually more sincere than an affirmation of His presence on any specific level. [Understanding] particular levels of spirituality may be beyond us, but the ability to give ourselves over completely to G-d is well within the capability of every Jew. There's another advantage to this general acknowledgement, and that is that we give ourselves over in totality and in all our essence. Therefore, general acknowledgment is a foundation and cornerstone of serving the One Above all day long, as explained elsewhere.)

(וְיֵשׁ בָּזֶה יִתְרוֹן מַעֲלָה בְּעֶצֶם נְתִינַת עַצְמוּתוֹ שֶׁהִיא אֲמִתִּית יוֹתֵר מֵהַנְּתִינָה בְּאֵיזֶה עִנְיָן פְּרָטִי, וְהוּא לְפִי שֶׁהָעִנְיָן הַפְּרָטִי הוּא לְמַעְלָה מִמַּדְרֵגָתוֹ מַה שֶּׁאֵין כֵּן הַנְּתִינָה לֶאֱלוֹקוּת בִּכְלָל (שֶׁלְּמַעְלָה מִמַּדְרֵגָה פְּרָטִית) זֶה קָרוֹב מְאֹד לְכָל אֶחָד מִיִּשְׂרָאֵל. וְגַם יֵשׁ בָּזֶה יִתְרוֹן מַה שֶּׁהַנְּתִינָה הִיא בְּכָל מַהוּתוֹ, וְלָכֵן בֶּאֱמֶת הוֹדָאָה זוֹ הִיא יְסוֹד הָעֲבוֹדָה דְּכָל הַיּוֹם וּכְמוֹ שֶׁכָּתוּב בְּמָקוֹם אַחֵר.)

General acknowledgment is the foundation of daily avoda.

———————— **COMMENTARY** ————————

"enlivening soul" and refers to that aspect of the soul which enlivens the physical body. "Action consciousness" corresponds to the World of *Asiya*, the "World of Action." It is the lowest of the worlds, but it is "where the action is," where G-d wants spiritual revelation and revolution to take place. It is the world that most conceals anything spiritual and G-dly, but which G-d nevertheless seeks to transform into a world permeated with spirituality.

וְזֶהוּ הָעֲבוֹדָה דַּעֲשִׂיָּה בִּבְחִינַת נֶפֶשׁ שֶׁהִיא בְּחִינַת הַהוֹדָאָה כְּלָלִית לְבַד (וּבִפְרָטִיּוּת בַּתְּפִלָּה הוּא עַד בָּרוּךְ שֶׁאָמַר).

This [overall affirmation], then, is the spiritual *avoda* of the World of *Asiya*, on the soul-level of *nefesh*. It constitutes a general acknowledgement of G-d's Presence alone. (In the [morning] prayers, this level extends from the beginning of *Hodu* until *Baruch She'amar*.)

Specific acknowledgment extends to the highest levels of G-dliness.

אָמְנָם יֵשׁ הוֹדָאָה פְּרָטִית הַיְנוּ בְּמַדְרֵגוֹת פְּרָטִיּוֹת כְּמוֹ בְּעִנְיָן יִחוּדָא עִילָּאָה אֵיךְ שֶׁכּוֹלָּא קָמֵי' כְּלָא חֲשִׁיבֵי, דַּאֲמִיתִּית הַשָּׂגָה זֹאת הִיא רַק בִּנְשָׁמוֹת גְּבוֹהוֹת אֲשֶׁר עֲבוֹדָתָם הִיא בִּבְחִינַת הַבִּטּוּל דְּיִחוּדָא עִילָּאָה,

It is true that acknowledgment of the One Above may also occur on specific levels of spiritual awareness, such as the level known as *yichuda ila'ah* [2] [supernal unity]. On this level, we become aware of the ephemeral nature of creation in light of His true Presence. However, [this is such an elevated level that] real understanding is only achieved by lofty souls who reach [total] self-nullification, corresponding to *yichuda ila'ah*.

> *Yichuda ila'ah* (literally "higher unity") is a state of mind in which our primary awareness is of G-d and G-dliness, while the creation and universe are in the background. It takes place when we have achieved total nullification of our self — known as *bitul b'metziut*.

אַךְ בְּכָל אֶחָד מִיִּשְׂרָאֵל צָרִיךְ לִהְיוֹת בִּטּוּל זֶה וּכְמוֹ שֶׁכָּתוּב בְּקוּנְטְרֵס עֵץ הַחַיִּים פְּרָק ז', רַק שֶׁבְּדֶרֶךְ כְּלָל הוּא בִּבְחִינַת הַהוֹדָאָה לְבַד וּמִכָּל מָקוֹם בְּהוֹדָאָה זוֹ יֵשׁ בְּחִינַת יְדִיעָה וְהַשָּׂגָה וּבְחִינַת הֶרְגֵּשׁ פְּנִימִי כוּ' וּכְמוֹ שֶׁכָּתוּב שָׁם פְּזוּ"ח. וְעִם הֱיוֹת שֶׁהַיְדִיעָה הַזֹּאת אֵינָהּ אֲמִתִּית כִּי אֲמִתִּית הַיְדִיעָה

Of course, it is true that all Jewish people should strive to achieve this level of total self-nullification, as is written in *Kuntres Eitz Chaim*, chapter 7. While generally speaking, *yichuda ila'ah* implies only acknowledgement of G-d's existence, it also includes dimensions of knowledge and intellect as well as deep feeling, as written in *Kuntres Eitz Chaim*,

———————— **COMMENTARY** ————————

In prayer, the time for experiencing "action consciousness" is from the time we wake up, saying *Modeh Ani* — "I am thankful" or "I acknowledge the One Above" — until *Baruch she'amar* ("Blessed is He who spoke"), the beginning words of *P'sukei D'Zimra* ("Verses of Praise"). During that time, we dress, say

Essay on Service of the Heart - Love Like Fire and Water

chapters 7-8. The knowledge associated with *yichuda ila'ah* isn't full and true [spiritual] awareness. [True awareness] arrives only via *hitamtut* [confirmation of one's spiritual level from Above], which involves seeing G-dliness in the mind's eye. Or at the very least, it [comes cloaked] as the profound knowledge of *p'nimiyut bina*[4] [the inner abstract understanding that remains after we have stripped away our "outer garments" of perception and reasoning]. That is why *bina* is sometimes called the "Supernal Bride"[5] (*kalah*) — the one who "consumes" the [external] physical realm.[iii] If our comprehension is only superficial, utilizing the "outer garments of understanding," we do not gain true knowledge of the subject. Nevertheless, [even our shallow understanding] contains elements of inner knowledge and deep feeling.

דִּבְחִינַת יְחוּדָא עִילָאָה הִיא שֶׁבָּאָה בִּבְחִינַת הִתְאַמְּתוּת דַּוְקָא שֶׁזֶּהוּ עִנְיָן רְאִיַּת עֵין הַשֵּׂכֶל כַּנּוֹדָע, וְעַל כָּל פָּנִים בִּבְחִינַת הַשָּׂגָה פְּנִימִית דִּבְחִינַת פְּנִימִיּוּת בִּינָה (דְּעַל שֵׁם זֶה נִקְרֵאת בִּינָה כַּלָּה עִילָאָה בְּחִינַת אִישְׁתֵּיצֵי גּוּשְׁמָא כו' וּכְמוֹ שֶׁכָּתוּב בְּמָקוֹם אַחֵר) אֲבָל מַה שֶּׁיּוֹדֵעַ וּמַשִּׂיג הָעִנְיָן בִּבְחִינַת חִיצוֹנִיּוּת הַהַשָּׂגָה אֵין זֶה הַשָּׂגָה אֲמִתִּית בָּעִנְיָן הַזֶּה, מִכָּל מָקוֹם הֲרֵי זֶה בָּא בִּבְחִינַת יְדִיעָה וְהֶרְגֵּשׁ פְּנִימִי

iii) See footnote of the Rebbe on page 261

(Therein lies the advantage of specific acknowledgment over the general acknowledgment described above. Specific acknowledgment [implying inner understanding and feeling] is a stage of progress in serving the One Above, while general acknowledgment is not a stage but a foundation and beginning.)

(שֶׁבָּזֶה יֵשׁ יִתְרוֹן בְּהוֹדָאָה זוֹ לְגַבֵּי הַהוֹדָאָה כְּלָלִית הַנַּ"ל. וְהִיא דַרְגָּא בַּעֲבוֹדָה מַה שֶּׁאֵין כֵּן הוֹדָאָה כְּלָלִית הַנַּ"ל אֵינָהּ בְּחִינַת דַּרְגָּא עֲדַיִן כִּי אִם הִיא יְסוֹד הָעֲבוֹדָה וְרֵאשִׁיתָהּ כו')

Specific acknowledgment is a stage of progress in avoda, not the foundation.

Specific acknowledgment may be described as an elevation of the level of *nefesh* and its inclusion in the level of *ruach*, or even higher.

וּבְחִינַת הַהוֹדָאָה זוֹ יֵשׁ לוֹמַר שֶׁזֶּהוּ עֲלִיַּת מַדְרֵגַת נֶפֶשׁ וְהִתְכַּלְלוּתָהּ בְּמַדְרֵגַת הָרוּחַ אוֹ גַּם לְמַעְלָה מִזֶּה).

--- **COMMENTARY** ---

morning blessings and also recite the details of the services in the Temple, all of which are physical and action-oriented. [Other things corresponding to "action consciousness" include the final *hey* of four-letter Name of G-d (the Tetragrammaton), the tenth and final *sephira* — *malchut* ("sovereignty") — and the mineral world within creation.]

1. *Nefesh*	World of *Asiya*	General Acknowledgement
2. *Ruach* (*nefesh* within *ruach*)	World of *Yetzira*	Specific Acknowledgement
3. *Neshama*	World of *Bria*	Intellect

Intellectual love and fear of G-d are on a higher level than natural fear and love in the heart.

וְעַל יְדֵי אֲמִתִּית הָעֲבוֹדָה בִּבְחִינַת רוּחַ הֲרֵי הוּא עוֹלֶה כָּךְ אַחַר כָּךְ לְעוֹלָם הַבְּרִיאָה, וְהַיְינוּ שֶׁיַּעֲלֶה וְיַגִּיעַ לְמַדְרֵגַת נְשָׁמָה שֶׁהִיא הָעֲבוֹדָה דִּבְחִינַת הַמּוֹחִין וְגַם בְּחִינַת רוּחַ עוֹלֶה וְנִכְלָל בָּזֶה כְּהִתְכַּלְלוּת הַיְצִירָה בְּעוֹלָם הַבְּרִיאָה כו'.

וְהָעִנְיָן הוּא דְּהִנֵּה בְּסֵפֶר שֶׁל בֵּינוֹנִים פל"ח ול"ט מְבֹאָר דְּהָעֲבוֹדָה בִּבְחִינַת דְּחִילוּ וּרְחִימוּ טִבְעִיִּים עוֹלָה בְּעוֹלָם הַיְצִירָה וּדְחִילוּ וּרְחִימוּ שִׂכְלִיִּים הֵם בִּבְרִיאָה, וְלִכְאוֹרָה נִרְאָה דְּהַיְינוּ הָאַהֲבָה וְיִרְאָה שֶׁבְּהִתְגַּלּוּת הַלֵּב הַבָּאָה עַל יְדֵי הִתְבּוֹנְנוּת כו', אַךְ בֶּאֱמֶת נִרְאָה הַכַּוָּנָה שָׁם דִּדְחִילוּ וּרְחִימוּ שִׂכְלִיִּים הֵמָּה נַעֲלִים הַרְבֵּה יוֹתֵר מֵאַהֲבָה וְיִרְאָה הנ"ל, וְהֵמָּה מַה שֶׁבָּאִים בְּדֶרֶךְ מִמֵּילָא מֵהִתְבּוֹנְנוּת בִּגְדֻלַּת אוֹר אֵין סוֹף בָּרוּךְ הוּא כו', וּמִמַּה שֶׁכָּתוּב שָׁם בפל"ט "אַךְ הַיְנוּ דַוְקָא נְשָׁמוֹת מַמָּשׁ שֶׁהֵן בְּחִינַת מוֹחִין דְּגַדְלוּת אֵין סוֹף בָּרוּךְ הוּא אֲבָל בְּחִינַת הָרוּחַ שֶׁל הַצַּדִּיקִים וְכֵן שְׁאָר כָּל נִשְׁמוֹת יִשְׂרָאֵל שֶׁעָבְדוּ אֶת ה' בִּדְחִילוּ וּרְחִימוּ הַמֻּסְתֶּרֶת בְּלֵב כְּלָלוּת יִשְׂרָאֵל כו'",

Through true *avoda* on the level of *ruach*, we rise to the World of *Bria* [the World of Creation], ascending to the soul-level called *neshama* and *avoda* of the intellect. Our soul-level of *ruach* also rises and is included on this level, just as the World of *Yetzira* is included in the World of *Bria*.

To make things clearer, let us refer to *Tanya*, chapters 38-39. There, it is explained that *avoda* that is motivated by "natural fear and love" of the One Above [the innate fear and love of G-d in our hearts] is associated with the World of *Yetzira*, while [the *avoda* motivated by] "intellectual fear and love" is associated with the higher World of *Bria*. At first glance, it would seem that "intellectual fear and love" become revealed in the heart by meditation [on G-d as He fills creation]. [Upon further investigation], it becomes clear that the "intellectual fear and love" referred to here are far superior to this level of emotion in the heart. True intellectual fear and love flow spontaneously from the mind as a result of meditation on the infinite light of G-d [as He transcends the universe]. *Tanya* states in chapter 39:

Essay on Service of the Heart - Love Like Fire and Water

"This [intellectual love and fear] is only among souls that are blessed with **"mature mindfulness"** capable of meditating upon the Infinite One, may He be blessed, but the **ruach** of *tzadikim* and also the **rest of the Jews** who serve G-d with **love hidden** in the collective hearts of the Jewish people…"

This statement defines *neshama* as "mature mindfulness" and differentiates between the levels of *ruach* of *tzadikim* and the *avoda* of hidden love and fear — synonymous with "natural love and fear" — of the rest of the Jews. Thus, there are three levels, corresponding to the three soul-levels of *nefesh*, *ruach*, and *neshama*. The hidden love — about which it says in *Tanya*, chapter 16, that it is the love that G-d "deserves" — is on the level of *nefesh* alone. It doesn't involve true desire [for Him], but rather "acquiescence" [so that we should worship Him with love]. (Even the intellectual comprehension which causes this acquiescence is not true comprehension.) This acquiescence is not the same as the "agreement" that remains after we experience love of G-d during prayer. After prayer, this agreement only leaves an impression that enables us to conduct ourselves properly all day long. The acquiescence to love G-d, though, because He deserves it, includes more spiritual energy and feeling, though it remains only acquiescence and not true desire.

הִנֵּה מִמַּה שֶּׁאָמַרְנוּ גַּבֵּי נְשָׁמָה שֶׁהִיא בְּחִינַת מֹחִין דְּגַדְלוּת וּמִמַּה שֶׁכּוֹתֵב בכ' חֲלוּקוֹת בְּחִינַת הָרוּחַ שֶׁל הַצַּדִּיקִים וְהָעֲבוֹדָה דִּשְׁאָר כָּל נִשְׁמוֹת יִשְׂרָאֵל בִּדְחִילוּ וּרְחִימוּ הַמְסֻתֶּרֶת דְּהַיְנוּ דְּחִילוּ וּרְחִימוּ טִבְעִיִּים, נִרְאָה בִּפְרָטִיּוּת הַמַּדְרֵגוֹת דְּנֶפֶשׁ רוּחַ וּנְשָׁמָה, דְּהָאַהֲבָה הַמְסֻתֶּרֶת אֲשֶׁר כָּךְ יָאֲתָה לָהֶן כו' הַמְבֹאָר בְּסֵפֶר שֶׁל בֵּינוֹנִים פט"ז הִיא בְּחִינַת נֶפֶשׁ לְבַד לִהְיוֹת שֶׁהָאַהֲבָה אֵינָהּ מַה שֶּׁחָפֵץ בֶּאֱמֶת כִּי אִם בִּבְחִינַת הַסְכֵּם לְבַד (וְגַם הַהַשָּׂגָה הַמְבִיאָה לָזֶה אֵינָהּ הַשָּׂגָה גְּמוּרָה) (וְהֶסְכֵּם זֶה אֵינוֹ כְּמוֹ הַהֶסְכֵּם הַנִּשְׁאָר אַחַר הָאַהֲבָה בַּתְּפִלָּה שֶׁהוּא בִּבְחִינַת רֹשֶׁם לְבַד הַשַּׁיָּךְ לְקִיּוּם בְּפֹעַל כָּל הַיּוֹם, מַה שֶּׁאֵין כֵּן הַהֶסְכֵּם דְּכָךְ יָאֲתָה לוֹ הוּא בִּבְחִינַת חִיּוּת וְהַרְגֵּשׁ יוֹתֵר וּמִכָּל מָקוֹם הֲרֵי זֶה רַק בִּבְחִינַת הֶסְכֵּם לֹא שֶׁחָפֵץ בֶּאֱמֶת כו').

"rest of the Jews…with love hidden"	Acquiescence	*Nefesh*
"*ruach* of *tzadikim*"	Natural love and fear	*Ruach*
"mature mindfulness"	Intellectual love and fear	*Neshama*

As for what is stated there [in Ch. 16 of *Tanya*] — "and also his *nefesh* and his *ruach* that are within him..." — this would seem to indicate inter-inclusion of the two lower levels of *nefesh* and *ruach*. But this inter-inclusion is not similar to the one mentioned above, in which the level of *nefesh* rises to that of *ruach*. Here, it refers to the combination of the two different levels [as opposed to one rising to the level of the other].

וּמַמָּה שֶׁכָּתוּב שָׁם וְגַם נַפְשׁוֹ וְרוּחוֹ אֲשֶׁר בְּקִרְבּוֹ כו' נִרְאֶה שֶׁזֶּהוּ הִתְכַּלְלוּת מִבְּחִינַת נֶפֶשׁ וְרוּחַ (וְלֹא כְּעִנְיַן הִתְכַּלְלוּת הַנַּ"ל דְּהַיְנוּ שֶׁהַנֶּפֶשׁ נִכְלַל בִּבְחִינַת רוּחַ וְכָאן הוּא הִתְכַּלְלוּת מַדְרֵגָתָן,

During the inter-inclusion described earlier, the level of *nefesh* remains associated with acknowledgment. Since the person is operating on the level of *ruach*, or even higher, the acknowledgment also takes place on a higher level. Here, however, the inter-inclusion of *nefesh* and *ruach* means they become one level. That is, they become a higher level within *nefesh* itself, similar to [but not on the true level of] *ruach*, and this constitutes their inter-inclusion. Although we are speaking of *nefesh* [as it rises to *ruach*], it nevertheless remains *nefesh*. However, [it attains] the level of *nehy* [acronym for *netzach-hod-yesod*, the lower three instinctual *sephirot*].[6]

רְצוֹנוֹ לוֹמַר דְּבַהִתְכַּלְלוּת הַנַּ"ל הַנֶּפֶשׁ הוּא בְּחִינַת הוֹדָאָה, רַק לִהְיוֹתוֹ עוֹמֵד בַּעֲבוֹדָתוֹ בְּמַדְרֵגַת רוּחַ, אוֹ גַם לְמַעְלָה מִזֶּה, לָכֵן הַהוֹדָאָה הִיא בְּמַדְרֵגָה נַעֲלֵית כַּנַּ"ל, וְכָאן הַהִתְכַּלְלוּת הוּא שֶׁהַנֶּפֶשׁ וְהָרוּחַ הֵן בְּמַדְרֵגָה אֶחָת, וְהַיְנוּ שֶׁזֶּה מַדְרֵגָה גְּבוֹהַּ יוֹתֵר בְּמַדְרֵגוֹת הַנֶּפֶשׁ שֶׁהוּא כְּמוֹ בְּחִינַת רוּחַ (אֲבָל אֵין זֶה אֲמִתִּית בְּחִינַת הָרוּחַ) וְזֶהוּ הִתְכַּלְלוּת מַדְרֵגָתָן) וּמִכָּל מָקוֹם הוּא בְּחִינַת נֶפֶשׁ, רַק שֶׁזֶּהוּ בְּחִינַת נֶצַח הוֹד יְסוֹד

> The process of "inter-inclusion" allows different *sephirot* and soul-levels to interact. Every *sephira* and soul-level incorporates within it something of all the others. In this way, creation reflects its underlying "holographic" unity, demonstrating that it is the handiwork of one G-d. This can only take place when the *sephirot* or soul-levels are sufficiently nullified to accept and interact with one another.

(*Nehy* is also called *nefesh* and is considered one of the three "governors" — the mind, the heart,

(שֶׁנִּקְרָא גַם כֵּן נֶפֶשׁ כַּנּוֹדָע בְּעִנְיַן תְּלַת שַׁלִּיטִין אִינוּן מוֹחָא לִבָּא וְכַבְדָא שֶׁהֵן חָכְמָה בִּינָה וְדַעַת חֶסֶד

and the liver, which correspond to *chabad*, *chagat*, and *nehy*. [In the structure of the *sephirot*,] *nehy* is situated just above the [lowest] level of *malchut*, which itself corresponds to the level of acknowledgment.)

גְּבוּרָה וְתִפְאֶרֶת נֶצַח הוֹד יְסוֹד) שֶׁלְּמַעְלָה מִבְּחִינַת הַמַּלְכוּת (שֶׁזֶּהוּ בְּחִינַת הוֹדָאָה).

The structure of the *Sephirot* (emanations)		
	Keter "crown"	
3. Intellectual *sephirot* CHABAD	*Bina* "understanding" *Da'at* "knowledge"	*Chochma* "wisdom"
2. Emotional *sephirot* CHAGAT	*Gevura* "strength/restraint" *Tiferet* "beauty"	*Chesed* "loving-kindness"
1. Instinctual *sephirot* NEHY	*Hod* "acknowledgment/thanksgiving" *Yesod* "foundation"	*Netzach* "victory"
	Malchut "kingdom"	

The love and fear — which become revealed in the heart as a result of meditation on the greatness of G-d, and which cause us to truly cleave to Him with heartfelt desire — are called *ruach*. The meditation that brings us to this level focuses on G-dliness that can be grasped intellectually [even

וְהָאַהֲבָה וְיִרְאָה שֶׁבְּהִתְגַּלּוּת הַלֵּב שֶׁבָּאָה מֵהַהִתְבּוֹנְנוּת בִּגְדֻלַּת ה' שֶׁאוֹהֵב אֶת ה' וְחָפֵץ בֶּאֱמֶת לְדָבְקָה בּוֹ בִּתְשׁוּקָה מֻרְגֶּשֶׁת בַּלֵּב זֶהוּ בְּחִינַת רוּחַ, וְהַהִתְבּוֹנְנוּת בָּזֶּה הוּא בְּמַדְרֵגָה בֶּאֱלֹקוּת שֶׁשַּׁיָּךְ בָּהֶם הַשָּׂגָה וְהוּא בָּאוֹר וְחַיּוּת אֱלֹקִי הַבָּא בִּבְחִינַת

Ruach meditation relates to the G-dly illumination within the universe.

——— COMMENTARY ———

2. RUACH

Going in and up the spiritual ladder, we come to the level known as "emotion consciousness." Here, we discover our own natural love and fear of the One Above through meditation on the "garments of G-d" — that is, creation itself. Just as we get to know a person by the effect he has upon the world, so we begin to get to know G-d by considering the variation,

הִתְלַבְּשׁוּת בָּעוֹלָם לִהְיוֹת וּלְהַחֲיוֹת אֶת הָעוֹלָמוֹת וּבְדֶרֶךְ כְּלָל בִּבְחִינַת מְמַלֵּא כָּל עָלְמִין שֶׁבְּכָל זֶה שַׁיָּךְ בְּחִינַת הַשָּׂגָה גְמוּרָה כְּמוֹ שֶׁכָּתוּב בְּלִקּוּטֵי תוֹרָה דִּבּוּר הַמַּתְחִיל וְיָדַעְתָּ דְּרוּשׁ הָרִאשׁוֹן,

though *ruach* is associated with the emotions]. That is, this meditation focuses on the G-dly light and energy that is en-clothed in the universe in order to create and maintain it. In general, it is called *ohr memalle* ("immanent light"), which is well understood by the human intellect (as related in *Likutei Torah*, *Vayadata*, in the first discourse).

> *Ohr memalle* ("inner/immanent light") is the spiritual energy within the creation. *Ohr makif* ("transcendent light") is the spiritual energy beyond creation (and the source of *ohr memalle*).

Ruach meditation demands "labor of the soul and labor of the flesh."

וְהָעֲבוֹדָה בָּזֶה הוּא לִיגַע אֶת עַצְמוֹ בִּיגִיעַת נֶפֶשׁ וִיגִיעַת בָּשָׂר בַּהֲשָׂגָה וְהִתְבּוֹנְנוּת זוֹ לֵידַע וּלְהַשִּׂיג הָעִנְיָנִים הֵיטֵב לֹא בִּידִיעָה כְּלָלִית לְבַד כִּי אִם בִּידִיעָה פְּרָטִית וַעֲמֻקָּה בְּעוֹמֶק וַאֲמִתַּת הָעִנְיָנִים הָאֵלּוּ וְיִתְקַע וִיקַשֵּׁר דַּעְתּוֹ בְּחֹזֶק בָּזֶה לִהְיוֹת הָעִנְיָן נִרְגָּשׁ הֵיטֵב בְּמוֹחוֹ וְלִבּוֹ וְעַל יְדֵי זֶה יִתְעוֹרֵר בְּאַהֲבָה אֲמִתִּית לַה' יִתְבָּרֵךְ וּבִתְשׁוּקָה מֻרְגֶּשֶׁת בְּהִתְגַּלּוּת לִבּוֹ לְדָבְקָה בּוֹ יִתְ'.

The *avoda* on this level requires "labor of the soul and the labor of the flesh." It necessitates intellectual acumen in order to properly grasp and internalize G-dly concepts through meditation. We must not be satisfied with a general, superficial knowledge alone, but must develop a deep and detailed comprehension of these topics. [In order to do so], we must focus our concentration on the subject, so that it becomes clear in our minds, and it is felt in our hearts. By doing so, we will arouse true love of G-d within ourselves, and [then] a strong desire will be revealed in our heart to cling to the One Above.

וְהִנֵּה עִם הֱיוֹת דַּעֲבוֹדָה זוֹ הִיא בִּבְחִינַת הַמֹּחִין בִּבְחִינַת הַשָּׂגָה וְהִתְבּוֹנְנוּת טוֹבָה כנ"ל מִכָּל מָקוֹם

Even though this requires intellectual acumen and as such is an "*avoda* of the mind," it still takes place

─────────── **COMMENTARY** ───────────

complication, and sheer beauty of His creation. Humanity is a mere speck in the scheme of things, and when we recognize this, the natural result is fear of the One who created the whole thing, together with love of Him over the wonder of it all. This meditation reveals the natural love and fear in the heart of the meditator. It was there all along, but it takes an outside

on the level of *ruach* ["emotion consciousness"]. This is because the main objective is to arouse the [G-dly] emotions of the heart, and this intellectual meditation does indeed lead to the arousal of [G-dly] feelings. Although deep concentration is involved here, all of the intellectual activity is still "external." The meditation engages the intellect as it is associated with the emotions [as opposed to pure intellect, which is devoid of emotions]. (See what is written in the *Siddur* of the *Alter Rebbe* regarding the verse, "The heavens tell of His honor..." and in the book of Chassidic discourses of the year 5670, *Parshat Trumah*.⁷) The nullification associated with this level involves letting go of our [natural, unG-dly] emotions. It is called *ego*-nullification. The higher level, associated with pure intellect, is called *self*-nullification.

הֲרֵי זֶה בְּחִינַת רוּחַ לִהְיוֹת שֶׁהָעִקָּר כָּאן הוּא הִתְעוֹרְרוּת הַמִּדּוֹת שֶׁבַּלֵּב, וְהַהִתְבּוֹנְנוּת הִיא לְעוֹרֵר אֶת הַמִּדּוֹת. וְהָגַם שֶׁהוּא בְּהַשָּׂגָה גְמוּרָה וּבְהַעֲמָקַת הַדַּעַת מִכָּל מָקוֹם כָּל זֶה הוּא בְּחִינַת חִיצוֹנִיּוּת הַמֹּחִין כְּמוֹ שֶׁהֵן בִּלְבוּשֵׁי הַשָּׂגָה שֶׁיֵּשׁוּ בְּחִינַת הַמֹּחִין הַשַּׁיָּכִים אֶל הַמִּדּוֹת. וְעַיֵּן מַה שֶּׁכָּתוּב בַּסִּדּוּר בְּשַׁבָּת בְּרָכוֹת * בְּפָסוּק הַשָּׁמַיִם מְסַפְּרִים וְעַיֵּן מַה שֶּׁכָּתוּב בְּדִרוּשׁ תִּקְעוּ עת"ר דִּבּוּר הַמַּתְחִיל וְזֹאת הַתְּרוּמָה. וְהַבִּטּוּל בָּזֶה הוּא הַבִּטּוּל שֶׁמִּבְּחִינַת הַמִּדּוֹת דְּהַיְנוּ בִּטּוּל הַיֵּשׁ לֹא הַבִּטּוּל דְּמוֹחִין שֶׁלְּמַעְלָה מִבְּחִינַת בִּטּוּל הַיֵּשׁ לְבַד כו'

The objective of ruach meditation is to arouse the emotions of the heart.

Nullification" — *bitul* in Hebrew — refers to getting our self-centered concerns out of the way of our encounter with G-d. Different levels of *bitul* lead to different levels of *da'at*, consciousness of G-d's presence in the universe. Here we are concerned with two: ego-nullification and self-nullification.	
1. Ego nullification (*Bitul hayesh*) ⇓	**2. Self nullification** (*Bitul b'metziut*) ⇓
Nullification of one's pride and ego (effecting emotions but not intellect)	Nullification of one's whole self (effecting intellect as well as emotions)
Associated with: ⇓	**Associated with:** ⇓
Da'at tachton or *Yichuda tat'ah* "lower awareness"	*Da'at elyon* or *Yichuda ila'ah* "elevated awareness"
Our primary awareness is of creation, with G-d in the background	Our primary awareness is of G-d, with the creation in the background

All that has been discussed here is the "service of the heart" about which the verse states, "And you should know today and put it in your heart..." in your heart specifically, since the love and fear of G-d, which become revealed in our heart, are the fulfillment of the Biblical commands to love and fear G-d. These are the emotions associated with fulfilling the commandments of the Torah, the 248 positive and 365 negative *mitzvot*, as discussed in *Tanya*, chapters 4 and 40, and in other places. It is precisely through these emotions of love and fear that the animal soul becomes purified and refined. Therefore, we all must know G-d and appropriately labor at meditation, while focusing our concentration with determination, in order to arouse love and desire to the extent that it becomes felt in the heart. Then, our heart will truly yearn for G-dliness, and this yearning will bring about the purification and refinement of the animal soul, so that we will desire to cleave to G-d through fulfillment of the Torah's commandments.

(וְזוֹ הִיא עֲבוֹדָה שֶׁבַּלֵּב שֶׁעַל זֶה נֶאֱמַר וְיָדַעְתָּ הַיּוֹם וַהֲשֵׁבֹתָ אֶל לְבָבֶךָ דַּוְקָא, דְּאַהֲבָה וְיִרְאָה שֶׁבְּהִתְגַּלּוּת הַלֵּב הֵן מִצְוֹת אַהֲבָה וְיִרְאָה שֶׁנִּצְטַוִּינוּ עֲלֵיהֶם. וְהֵן הַשַּׁיָּכִים לְקִיּוּם הַתּוֹרָה וּמִצְוֹת רמ"ח מִצְוֹת עֲשֵׂה וְשְׁס"ה לֹא תַעֲשֶׂה כְּמוֹ שֶׁכָּתוּב בְּסֵפֶר שֶׁל בֵּינוֹנִים פ"ד וּפ"מ וּבְכַמָּה דּוּכְתֵי, וּבָהֶם וְעַל יָדָם דַּוְקָא הוּא בֵּרוּר וְזִכּוּךְ הַנֶּפֶשׁ הַבַּהֲמִית, וְהוּא מִדַּת כָּל אָדָם אֲשֶׁר כָּל אֶחָד מְחֻיָּב לֵידַע אֶת ה' לִיגַּע אֶת עַצְמוֹ בְּהַשָּׂגָה וְהִתְבּוֹנְנוּת כְּדִבְעֵי לְמֶהֱוֵי וּלְהַעֲמִיק דַּעְתּוֹ בְּחֹזֶק וּלְהִתְעוֹרֵר בְּאַהֲבָה וַחֲפִיצָה וּתְשׁוּקָה מַרְגֶּשֶׁת בַּלֵּב לִהְיוֹת לִבּוֹ חָפֵץ בֶּאֱמֶת בֶּאֱלֹקוּת (וְעַל יְדֵי זֶה הוּא בֵּרוּר וְזִכּוּךְ הַנֶּפֶשׁ הַבַּהֲמִית כו') וּלְדָבְקָה בּוֹ עַל יְדֵי קִיּוּם הַתּוֹרָה וְהַמִּצְוֹת כו').

———— *COMMENTARY* ————

inspiration — "impression from the outside," meaning meditation on the garments of the Creator — to bring it into revelation. "Emotion consciousness" is called *ruach* in Hebrew. *Ruach* means "wind/spirit" and corresponds to the World of *Yetzira* ("World of Formation") in the macrocosm. The World of *Yetzira* is the world of general archetypes and templates of creation, also known as angels. Here in the World of *Yetzira*, there are only spiritual creatures (angels), each one corresponding to and including details of many specific creations of the lower World of *Asiya*.

The level known as *neshama* corresponds to *mochin* [8] ("spiritual intellect"), as it is written (Job 32:8), "The breath [*nishmat*] of G-d gives understanding." At this level, through meditation, we can grasp the essential G-dliness that is the "soul" of the concept, stripped of its outer garments. What is left is essential G-dliness, and it becomes revealed in our mind. It shines with a tremendous light, riveting our attention and causing us to cleave mightily to this illumination in our mind. (The sign of this occurring is that we completely lose awareness of anything physical because of our intense connection to the G-dly light revealed in our mind.) This level of intellectual understanding is beyond anything emotional.[9]

אָמְנָם בְּחִינַת נְשָׁמָה הִיא בְּחִינַת הַמֹּחִין וּכְמוֹ שֶׁכָּתוּב נִשְׁמַת שַׁדַּי תְּבִינֵם, וְהוּא הַהַשָּׂגָה וְהַהִתְבּוֹנְנוּת בִּבְחִינַת פְּנִימִיּוּת הַמֹּחִין דְּהַיְנוּ בִּבְחִינַת הַפְשָׁטָה מִלְּבוּשֵׁי הַהַשָּׂגָה כִּי אִם בְּעֶצֶם הָעִנְיָן הָאֱלֹקִי כְּמוֹ שֶׁהוּא שֶׁמֵּאִיר הָעִנְיָן הָאֱלֹקִי בְּגִלּוּי בְּמוֹחוֹ בִּבְחִינַת גִּלּוּי אוֹר רַב וּמִתְקַשֵּׁר וְנִדְבַּק מְאֹד בְּמוֹחוֹ בְּהָאוֹר הָאֱלֹקִי (וְהָאוֹת עַל זֶה הוּא שֶׁמִּתְבַּטְּלִים אֶצְלוֹ כָּל חוּשֵׁי הַהֶרְגֵּשׁ הַטִּבְעִיִּים מֵחֲמַת הַדְּבֵקוּת בָּאוֹר הָאֱלֹקִי הַמֵּאִיר בְּגִלּוּי בְּמוֹחוֹ כוּ') וְהַשָּׂגָה זוֹ הִיא לְמַעְלָה מִבְּחִינַת הַמִּדּוֹת

Neshama meditation penetrates to the 'soul' of G-dliness in the world, and rivets our attention.

COMMENTARY

In prayer, the stage in which we experience "emotion consciousness" begins from *Baruch sh'amar* and continues until we say *Barchu* ("Bless Him") which begins the introduction to the *Shema*. This gives us sufficient time during recitation of *Pesukei D'zimra* to meditate upon the creation *ex nihilo* ("from nothing") and to produce wonder and amazement in our souls. [Other things corresponding to the soul-level of "emotion consciousness" include the *vav* of the four-letter Name of G-d, the lower six *sephirot* which are active in creation (*Chesed* through *Yesod*) and the vegetable world in creation (plants grow, as do emotions).]

3. NESHAMA

Finally, we reach the highest of the three soul-levels that are en-clothed in the body (two higher levels are not en-clothed in the body). It is called "intellect consciousness," or *neshama*. In Hebrew, *neshama* means "soul," and it is on this level that the meditator penetrates to the "soul" of creation and finds there the spiritual essence and enlivening power that brings creation

Neshama emotions respond spontaneously to the G-dly light; the meditator cleaves automatically to G-dliness.

→ iv) See footnote of the Rebbe on page 262

(וְהִיא הָעֲבוֹדָה בִּבְחִינַת הַמֹּחִין בִּבְחִינַת הַהִתְאַחֲדוּת וּבִבְחִינַת דְּבֵקוּת בְּהָאוֹר הָאֱלֹקִי, וְהַבִּטוּל בָּזֶה יֵשׁ בּוֹ חִלּוּקֵי מַדְרֵגוֹת כְּמוֹ שִׁית' בְּסָמוּךְ. מִכָּל מָקוֹם הֲרֵי זֶה לְמַעְלָה מִבְּחִינַת בִּטוּל הַיֵּשׁ לִהְיוֹתוֹ בְּחִינַת פְּנִימִיּוּת הַמֹּחִין כוּ'),

רַק שֶׁהָאוֹר מִתְפַּשֵּׁט וּמֵאִיר גַּם בַּלֵּב (דְּכַאֲשֶׁר הָאוֹר הָאֱלֹקִי מֵאִיר בְּגִלּוּי אֵינוֹ בִּבְחִינַת הַגְבָּלָה לִהְיוֹת דַּוְקָא בַּמֹּחִין וְלֹא בַּלֵּב וְאֵינוֹ מִתְעַלֵּם בְּמֵצַר הַגָּרוֹן לָכֵן מֵאִיר גַּם בַּלֵּב כוּ' כְּמוֹ שֶׁכָּתוּב בְּמָקוֹם אַחֵר) וְגַם הַלֵּב מִתְפַּעֵל בָּזֶה בְּדֶרֶךְ מִמֵּילָא שֶׁאֵין צָרִיךְ לַעֲשׂוֹת הַהִתְפַּעֲלוּת וְהָאַהֲבָה בַּלֵּב כָּל אֶחָד בָּא מִמֵּילָא מֵהַגִּלּוּי אוֹר, וְהִיא גַם כֵּן בִּבְחִינַת דְּבֵקוּת לֹא בִּבְחִינַת הִתְפַּעֲלוּת כָּל כָּךְ. וְהוּא בִּבְחִינַת גַּדְלוּת הַמֹּחִין וְגַדְלוּת הַמִּדּוֹת כוּ'

18 — Kuntres Ha'Avoda - קונטרס העבודה

(This *avoda* [of the *neshama*] leads to unity with the G-dly light. There are differences in the levels of self-nullification associated with this spiritual level, as will be explained shortly. In any case, the level of nullification here is beyond ego-nullification alone, since it involves pure intellect.)

The illumination spreads from the mind and illuminates the heart as well. (Since when the G-dly light shines, it shines without limitations, and is not confined to the mind; it does not become trapped in the "narrow straits of the throat" — that is, in the inability of the mind to express itself in emotions — and, therefore, it is able to illuminate the heart as well.) The heart responds spontaneously.[iv] There is no need for us to bring ourselves to feel the excitement of the heart through meditation, since the G-dly light is revealed spontaneously in the heart. It is a state of cleaving [to the One Above], rather than excitement [about Him]. This state is called [in the Kabbalistic literature], a spiritually "mature intellect/mind" and "mature heart."

COMMENTARY
---

constantly into existence. Creation didn't just happen during the six days and then remained in existence. Constant input of spiritual energy from the Creator is required in order to sustain it. This spiritual energy, conveyed by the letters of the Hebrew alphabet, is embedded in each and every aspect of creation, according to its individual needs and nature.

When we penetrate the "outer garments" described above and discover the "soul" of creation — the spiritual energy that keeps it going — we arrive at the level of *neshama*, or "intellect

Essay on Service of the Heart - Love Like Fire and Water

In general, what is being described here is the complete structure — that is, the ten *sephirot* — of the spiritual intellect. In this condition of full intellectual and spiritual maturity, the emotions are similar to the intellect. The emotions are neither felt nor expressed as excitement, but rather as unity with the One Above. In chapter 39 of *Tanya*, this love of G-d is called *reuta d'liba* ("will of the heart").[10] To put it simply, it is the state in which our heart truly desires G-d [and so ignites] a love which is then revealed in the heart. (See *Likutei Torah* on "Song of Songs," regarding the verse, "Behold, you are the most beautiful..." about *rayayoti*.[11]) However, it is possible to explain *reuta d'liba* as the spontaneous will of the heart, rather than as the love which is ignited in the heart as a result of meditation.

(וּבִכְלָלוּת זֶהוּ צִיּוּר קוֹמָה דִּבְחִינַת מֹחִין לִהְיוֹת שֶׁגַּם הַמִּדּוֹת הֵן כְּמוֹ הַמֹּחִין דְּהַיְנוּ לֹא בִּבְחִינַת מַרְגֵּשׁ וּבִבְחִינַת הִתְפַּעֲלוּת כִּי אִם בִּבְחִינַת אַחְדוּת וּדְבֵקוּת כו') (וּבְסֵפֶר שֶׁל בֵּינוֹנִים פּל״ט כ׳ שֶׁאַהֲבָה זוֹ נִקְרֵאת רְעוּתָא דְלִבָּא. וְעַל פִּי פְּשָׁט הוּא מַה שֶׁלִּבּוֹ חָפֵץ בֶּאֱמֶת כו׳ וְהִיא הָאַהֲבָה בְּהִתְגַּלּוּת הַלֵּב כו׳ וְעַיֵּן מַה שֶׁכָּתוּב בְּלִקּוּטֵי תוֹרָה שה״ש בְּדִבּוּר הַמַּתְחִיל הִנָּךְ יָפָה בְּעִנְיַן רַעְיָתִי. אָמְנָם יֵשׁ לוֹמַר דְּפֵי׳ רְעוּתָא דְלִבָּא הוּא מַה שֶׁהַלֵּב חָפֵץ מִמֵּילָא וְלֹא הָאַהֲבָה הָעֲשׂוּיָה בַּלֵּב עַל יְדֵי הַהִתְבּוֹנְנוּת בִּבְחִינַת חִיצוֹנִיּוּת הַמֹּחִין שֶׁזֶּהוּ הָאַהֲבָה שֶׁעַל פִּי טַעַם וָדַעַת כו׳ וּכְמוֹ שֶׁכָּתוּב בְּדִבּוּר הַמַּתְחִיל זָכוֹר בְּתוֹרָה אוֹר פּ׳ תְּצַוֶּה).

In neshama meditation, the emotions cleave to the mind. They are not felt as excitement, but as rapture and awe.

In the latter case [of meditation], the meditation takes place in the outer garments of the intellect, and it produces love which is commensurate with that level of intellect (as is written in *Torah Ohr, Parshat Tezave*, beginning with *Zachor*....)

───────── **COMMENTARY** ─────────

consciousness." Why "intellect consciousness?" Because at this point, the intellect is dominant. Although emotions are aroused as a result of "intellect consciousness," they are not the same as the natural love and fear that were present in the heart at the lower level of *ruach*. Here, the spiritual experience is so powerful that the resulting emotions are lifted up to the level of the intellect itself. In fact, we don't even feel the emotions, as they are nullified and "caught up" within the intellectual experience. We know this is happening in our meditation when we lose contact with the physical world. We are so enraptured with the spiritual essence of our experience that we don't know what is going on around us.

Sometimes we need meditation on the outer "garments" in order to reach the inner soul.

וְהִנֵּה נת' דְּהָעֲבוֹדָה בִּבְחִינַת פְּנִימִיּוּת הַמֹּחִין דְּהַיְנוּ הַהִתְבּוֹנְנוּת בְּעֶצֶם הָעִנְיָן הָאֱלֹקִי הִיא בְּחִינַת נְשָׁמָה. אָמְנָם יֵשׁ בָּזֶה חִלּוּקֵי מַדְרֵגוֹת, דְּכַאֲשֶׁר הַהַשָּׂגָה בְּעֶצֶם הָעִנְיָן הָאֱלֹקִי בָּא לְאַחַר הַהַשָּׂגָה תְּחִלָּה בִּלְבוּשֵׁי הַשָּׂגָה, דְּהַיְנוּ שֶׁאֵין בִּיכָלְתּוֹ לִתְפֹּס וּלְהַשִּׂיג אֵיזֶה עִנְיָן אֱלֹקִי כְּמוֹ שֶׁהוּא בְּעַצְמָם, כִּי אִם כַּאֲשֶׁר מִתְלַבֵּשׁ תְּחִלָּה בִּלְבוּשֵׁי הַשָּׂגָה דְּהַיְנוּ שֶׁבָּא הָעִנְיָן אֱלֹקִי בְּעִנְיָנִים הַמַּצִּיּרִים אוֹתוֹ בִּדְבָרִים הַמֻּשָּׂגִים (כְּמוֹ בְּחִינַת זְעֵיר אַנְפִּין בְּעִנְיָן הַמִּדּוֹת הַמֻּשָּׂגוֹת וּבְחִינַת חָכְמָה וּבִינָה בְּעִנְיָן יְדִיעָה וְהַשָּׂגָה וּבְחִינַת מְמַלֵּא כָּל עָלְמִין כְּמוֹ הַנְּשָׁמָה שֶׁמְּמַלְּאָה אֶת הַגּוּף וְסוֹבֵב כָּל עָלְמִין בִּבְחִינַת רָצוֹן וִידִיעָה כְּלָלִית כו' וּכְהַאי גַּוְנָא) וּבְעִנְיָנִים הַמְבָאֲרִים אֶת הַדָּבָר הַמֻּשָּׂג (כְּמוֹ מְצִיאוּת עִנְיַן הַמִּדּוֹת וְעִנְיַן הַיְדִיעָה וְכוּ')

We have explained that the *avoda* of "pure intellect" (*pni'miyut hamochin*), involving meditation on the spiritual essence of G-d, constitutes the level of *neshama*. Within this level, several approaches exist. One may arrive at the "soul" (*neshama*) of the concept only after a lengthy meditation on its outer garments. This approach can be used when it is beyond our ability to directly grasp the inherent G-dliness of the concept, without first en-clothing it in outer garments. We are capable of grasping the inner spiritual "kernel" only when it comes "packaged" in images and examples that we understand. (For example, when we want to understand the Kabbalistic concept of *zeir anpin*,[12] we associate it with emotions that we feel, and we describe *chochma* and *bina* [13] as "intellect" and "understanding." [To explain] *memalle kol olamim*,[14] or "immanent G-dliness," we use the simile: "as the soul permeates the body." [To explain] *sovav kol olamim*,[15] or "transcendent G-dliness," we use the example of will, or general knowledge, and so forth...)

─────── **COMMENTARY** ───────

In prayer, we experience "intellect consciousness" from *Barchu* through the reading of *Shema*. This section of prayer speaks of higher spiritual creations which we can only comprehend through our intellects. The effort to appreciate that there are higher levels of creation makes an "impression from the inside" on us. If these very high spiritual creations are nullified before the One Above and would not do anything without His consent, all the more so that we, with our limited minds and intellects, must be nullified before Him.

The "packaging" enables us to understand the G-dly concept with all its details. For, it is impossible to grasp the concept without its details. This understanding comes as a result of the explanations and analogies, through which the concept becomes clear. Afterward [upon achieving intellectual understanding], we must negate, abstract and strip away all of the packaging, through which we initially understood the concept, in order to penetrate to the spiritual essence. In this way, we arrive at the essence of the G-dly concept to whatever extent we are able to grasp it, using the "tools" mentioned above. We remove the concept from its physical shrouds (the image which enabled us to comprehend it). We then come to understand that this is a G-dly concept, whose essence cannot be depicted by the image that we had formerly evoked. After we realize that, in general, G-dliness is beyond anything that we can grasp, we can come to understand the concept in G-dly terms.

שֶׁבָּהֶם מֵבִין וּמַשִּׂיג אֶת הָעִנְיָן הָאֱלֹקִי אֵיךְ וּמַה הוּא, וּבִפְרָטֵי הָעִנְיָנִים שֶׁבּוֹ, דְּאִי אֶפְשָׁר לִהְיוֹת הַשָּׂגַת דָּבָר מִבְּלִי שֶׁיְּפָרֵט אוֹתוֹ לִפְרָטִים שֶׁהֵמָּה מְבָאֲרִים אֶת הָעִנְיָן, וְכָל זֶה בָּא בְּהֶסְבֵּרִים וְגַם בִּמְשָׁלִים שֶׁבָּהֶם וְעַל יָדָם מֵבִין וּמַשִּׂיג אֶת הָעִנְיָן הֵיטֵב, וְאַחַר כָּךְ שׁוֹלֵל וּמַפְשִׁיט וּמֵנִיחַ אֶת הָעִנְיָנִים שֶׁבָּהֶם הוּא מַשִּׂיג אֶת הָעִנְיָן וּבָא אֶל עֶצֶם הַדָּבָר הַמֻּשָּׂג אֵיךְ שֶׁהוּא מֵבִין אוֹתוֹ מִכָּל הָעִנְיָנִים הַנַּ"ל, וְהַיְנוּ שֶׁבָּא אֶל עֶצֶם הָעִנְיָן הַמֻּשָּׂג אֵיךְ וּמַה הוּא וּמַפְשִׁיט אוֹתוֹ מִגַּשְׁמִיּוּתוֹ (הַיְנוּ מֵהַצִּיּוּר הַמֻּשָּׂג) שֶׁהֲרֵי זֶהוּ עִנְיָן אֱלֹקִי שֶׁאֵינוֹ כְּלָל בְּאֹפֶן וְצִיּוּר כָּזֶה בְּעֶצֶם הַמַּהוּת, וְאַחֲרֵי הַיְדִיעָה אֵיךְ שֶׁבִּכְלָל הָאֱלֹקוּת מֻשְׁלָל מֵעִנְיָנִים הַמֻּשָּׂגִים לָנוּ, יְצַיֵּר הָעִנְיָן הַמֻּשָּׂג אֵיךְ שֶׁהוּא בֶּאֱלֹקוּת

Afterward, we must negate, abstract and strip away the "garments," in order to penetrate to the spiritual essence of the concept.

COMMENTARY

The soul-level of "intellect consciousness" corresponds to the World of *Bria* ("World of Creation"). This world was the first to be created in which there is awareness of the "self," as opposed to the higher worlds in which there is only awareness of the One Above. The subjective experience of the World of *Bria* is not one of direct contact with the One Above; rather, we feel that we have some existence, or at least possibility of existence as an entity separate from the One Above. But, *Bria* is still close enough to the One Above that we cannot feel ourselves to be entirely independent. We are very much aware of the One Above,

We must always remember that we're involved in a G-dly process, not an intellectual exercise.

(וְגַם בְּהָעֲבוֹדָה בִּבְחִינַת חִיצוֹנִיּוּת הַמּוֹחִין צָרִיךְ לִהְיוֹת הָרְגֵשׁ זֶה שֶׁהִתְעַסְּקוּת שֶׁלּוֹ הוּא בְּעִנְיָן אֱלֹקִי הַיְנוּ שֶׁמֵּבִין וּמַשִּׂיג עִנְיָן אֱלֹקִי, וְלֹא כְּמוֹ בְּלִמּוּד שֶׁהוּא טָרוּד בְּהַשֵּׂכֶל רַק לְהָבִין אֶת הָעִנְיָן וּלְהַשִּׂיגוֹ. וּבְהִתְבּוֹנְנוּת הִנֵּה עִם הִשְׁתַּדְּלוּתוֹ לְהָבִין אֶת הָעִנְיָן הֵיטֵב שֶׁיּוּנַח בְּמוֹחוֹ בַּהֲנָחָה טוֹבָה יְהִי' אֶצְלוֹ הַרְגָּשָׁה זוֹ תָּמִיד (הַרְגָּשָׁה קְרוֹבָה בְּמוֹחוֹ) שֶׁהִתְעַסְּקוּתוֹ הוּא בְּעִנְיָן אֱלֹקִי, וּמִכָּל מָקוֹם אֵין לוֹ מֻשָּׂג עֲדַיִן כְּלָל בְּעֶצֶם עִנְיָן הָאֱלֹקִי אֵיךְ שֶׁהוּא רַק כְּמוֹ שֶׁהוּא בִּלְבוּשֵׁי הַשָּׂגָה שֶׁזֹּאת הִיא הַשָּׂגָתוֹ וַעֲבוֹדָתוֹ וּכְמוֹ שֶׁנִּתְבָּאֵר לְעֵיל

שֶׁזּוֹ הִיא עֲבוֹדָה שֶׁבַּלֵּב וְשֶׁהִיא מִדַּת כָּל אָדָם כו', וּמַה שֶּׁנִּת' כָּאן הוּא שֶׁמִּתּוֹךְ הַהַשָּׂגָה הִנֵּה עַל יְדֵי הַהַפְשָׁטָה וְהַשְּׁלִילָה בָּא אֶל הַמֻּשָּׂג בְּעֶצֶם הָעִנְיָן הָאֱלֹקִי אֵיךְ וּמָה הוּא. וְזֶה מוּבָן שֶׁאֵין הַכַּוָּנָה כָּאן עַל עִנְיַן יְדִיעַת הַשְּׁלִילָה הַמְבֹאָר בְּמָקוֹם אַחֵר).

When the approach of the outer garments is used, there must be a feeling that, as we are meditating, we are involved in a G-dly process. That is, we are delving into a G-dly matter, [which cannot be compared with] something that we seek to learn intellectually. Even as we strive to grasp the concept with our minds in such a way that we understand it well and are able to internalize it, we must never lose the feeling (in our consciousness) that the concept is a G-dly one, and that we have no real understanding of the essential G-dliness, except through the intellectual garments that correspond to our own *avoda* of the One Above.

This, as we mentioned before, constitutes the "service of the heart," and it is demanded of every Jew. What is being established here is that intellect — through a process of negation and abstraction — leads us to comprehend the G-dliness at the very core of the concept. We gain an awareness of just what it is and how it exists. (It is understood that this is not referring [to the *avoda* of G-d that is called] *yediat hashlila* [circumscribed knowledge couched in negative terms, since positive terms are inapplicable when describing G-d, as explained by the Rambam].)[16]

--- **COMMENTARY** ---

and therefore the Chassidic masters described *Bria* as the world of "possibility of existence." [Other things corresponding to "intellect consciousness" include the first *hey* of the four-letter Name of G-d, the *sephira* of *bina* ("understanding"), and the animal kingdom within creation (animals move, and the intellect also moves us from one plane of comprehension to the next).]

Essay on Service of the Heart - Love Like Fire and Water

With the approach of the "garments," the essence of the G-dly light still does not illuminate fully.

After all this — wherein by way of intellect we strip away the garments and arrive at the essential G-dlliness of the concept at the level known as *neshama* — the essence of the G-dly light still doesn't shine in a fully revealed manner. Since we came to the G-dly "kernel" of the concept only by way of the outer garments of the intellect, even when we have succeeded in stripping them away, they are never completely gone. We find the concept still clad in a thin, refined intellectual garment. Even after we have negated the image with which we grasped the concept, our understanding remains tainted with a residue of our own imagination. (In truth, it is not within human power to hold onto a G-dly concept without some kind of garment.) For this reason, even though our intellectual grasp is of the inner essence of the concept (*p'nimiyut hamochin*), nevertheless, it has a connection to the emotions [as opposed to pure intellect, which has no connection whatsoever to the emotions]. (That is, our meditation is still "tainted" by some sense of emotional excitement, even if only a little. It is not to the same extent as when we were meditating on the outer garments of the intellect, but nonetheless, we still have not left the realm of excitement and feeling behind.)

וְאַחַר כָּל זֹאת מֵאַחַר שֶׁעַל יְדֵי הַהַשָּׂגָה בִּבְחִינַת הִתְלַבְּשׁוּת בָּא אֶל עֶצֶם עִנְיָן הָאֱלֹקִי הִנֵּה עִם הֱיוֹת שֶׁזֶּהוּ בְּדַרְגוֹת דְּמַדְרֵגַת נְשָׁמָה, מִכָּל מָקוֹם אֵינוֹ מֵאִיר בָּזֶה עֶצֶם הָאוֹר בְּגִלּוּי מַמָּשׁ, דִּלְפִי שֶׁבָּא לְזֶה עַל יְדֵי לְבוּשֵׁי הַהַשָּׂגָה הִנֵּה גַּם כְּשֶׁמַּפְשִׁיט אוֹתוֹ אֵינוֹ מַפְשָׁט לְגַמְרֵי וְהוּא מְלֻבָּשׁ עֲדַיִן בִּלְבוּשׁ דַּק מִלְּבוּשֵׁי הַשָּׂגָה. וְהַיְנוּ שֶׁגַּם לְאַחַר הַהַפְשָׁטָה וְהַשְׁלִילָה מֵהַצִּיּוּר הַמֻּשָּׂג הוּא מִכָּל מָקוֹם מַשִּׂיג וּמַרְגִּישׁ אֶת הָעִנְיָן בַּאֲחִיזָה קְצָת בְּהַצִּיּוּר הַמֻּשָּׂג (כִּי בֶּאֱמֶת אֵין בִּיכָלְתּוֹ לִתְפֹּס וּלְהַשִּׂיג עִנְיָן אֱלֹקִי בְּלִי שׁוּם לְבוּשׁ) וְעַל כֵּן גַּם הַשָּׂגָה זוֹ הֲגַם שֶׁהִיא בְּמַדְרֵגַת פְּנִימִיּוּת הַמֹּחִין יֵשׁ לָהּ שַׁיָּכוּת אֶל הַמִּדּוֹת (הַיְנוּ אֶל חוּשׁ הַמִּדּוֹת בִּבְחִינַת הִתְפַּעֲלוּת וּמַרְגָּשׁ קְצָת, וְלֹא כָּל כָּךְ כְּמוֹ בִּבְחִינַת חִיצוֹנִיּוּת הַמֹּחִין אֲבָל מִכָּל מָקוֹם אֵינוֹ יוֹצֵא עֲדַיִן מִבְּחִינַת הִתְפַּעֲלוּת וּמַרְגָּשׁ)

The same is true of the emotions. Although they arise spontaneously, this is not because the G-dly light illuminates the heart as it does the mind, but because the heart feels the light and revelation that is in the mind

וְכֵן בְּעִנְיַן הַמִּדּוֹת עִם הֱיוֹת דְּהִתְפַּעֲלוּת הַמִּדּוֹת בָּאִים בִּבְחִינַת מִמֵּילָא מִכָּל מָקוֹם אֵין זֶה שֶׁהָאוֹר מֵאִיר בַּלֵּב כְּמוֹ בַּמֹּחַ כִּי אִם מַה שֶּׁהַלֵּב מַרְגִּישׁ אֶת הָאוֹר וְהַגִּלּוּי שֶׁבַּמֹּחַ וְנִמְשָׁךְ אַחַר הַמֹּחַ כו׳,

and is drawn to it. As a result, the emotions are not truly "mature" in a spiritual sense and don't cleave strictly to the One Above, since the G-dly light isn't shining directly into them from above. It is only that the emotions respond to the G-dly light [as something separate that they are drawn toward] and become excited. [As this happens], the emotions rise to the level of the intellect (that is, to the true dimension of intellect, which will be explained shortly). It is possible that this is the level described as *ruach*, as it ascends to and is included in the level of the *neshama*, in which case the *ruach* becomes equal, in a way, to the *neshama*.

וּמִמֵּילָא הַמִּדּוֹת אֵינָם בִּבְחִינַת גַּדְלוּת מַמָּשׁ לִהְיוֹת בִּבְחִינַת דְּבֵקוּת מַמָּשׁ אַחַר שֶׁאֵינוֹ מֵאִיר בָּהֶם הָאוֹר מַמָּשׁ רַק מַה שֶׁנִּרְגָּשׁ כוּ' הֲרֵי הוּא בִּבְחִינַת הִתְפָּעֲלוּת קְצָת וְרַק שֶׁמִּשְׁתַּוִּים קְצָת אֶל בְּחִינַת הַמּוֹחִין כוּ' (רְצוֹנוֹ לוֹמַר אֶל אֲמִתִּית בְּחִינַת הַמּוֹחִין שֶׁיִּתְבָּאֵר בְּסָמוּךְ). וְיֵשׁ לוֹמַר שֶׁזֶּהוּ מַדְרֵגַת רוּחַ הָעוֹלָה וְנִכְלָל בְּמַדְרֵגַת נְשָׁמָה הַיְנוּ שֶׁמַּדְרֵגַת הָרוּחַ מִשְׁתַּוֶּה קְצָת אֶל מַדְרֵגַת הַנְּשָׁמָה כוּ'.

On the true level of neshama, we sense G-dliness. We grasp a G-dly concept in its essence, without need of intellectual garments.

However, when we are [truly] on the level of *neshama*, we are able to sense G-dliness. We grasp a G-dly concept in its essence, without need of intellectual garments [to clothe and describe it].

אָמְנָם מִי שֶׁהוּא בְּמַדְרֵגַת נְשָׁמָה הוּא שֶׁיֵּשׁ לוֹ בְּעֶצֶם חוּשׁ בֶּאֱלֹקוּת וְתוֹפֵס וּמַשִּׂיג עִנְיָן אֱלֹקִי כְּמוֹ שֶׁהוּא בְּעֶצֶם לֹא עַל יְדֵי לְבוּשֵׁי הַשָּׂגָה

(וּבְחִינַת זוֹ הִיא גַּם כֵּן כְּמוֹ שֶׁהָאוֹר הָאֱלֹקִי יָרַד לְהָאִיר בִּבְחִינַת צִמְצוּם כְּדֵי שֶׁיּוּכְלוּ שְׂכָלִים נִבְרָאִים לְקַבֵּל מֵהֶם חָכְמָה בִּינָה וְדַעַת לֵידַע אֶת ה' וּלְהָבִין וּלְהַשִּׂיג כוּ' כְּמוֹ שֶׁכָּתוּב בְּסֵפֶר שֶׁל בֵּינוֹנִים פל"ט, וּמִכָּל מָקוֹם הִיא הַיְדִיעָה וְהַהַשָּׂגָה בְּעֶצֶם הָעִנְיָן כוּ')

(This level is also associated with the G-dly light that descends to illuminate creation after contracting, in order to allow mortal minds to receive it — with their wisdom, understanding, and knowledge [*chochma, bina,* and *da'at,* i.e., *chabad*]. They are enabled to know and understand G-dliness, as is written in Tanya, chapter 39, and their knowledge and understanding is of the essence of the G-dly concept.)

וּמֵאִיר אֶצְלוֹ הָאוֹר הָאֱלֹקִי בְּגִלּוּי מַמָּשׁ בְּמוֹחוֹ בְּאֹפֶן שֶׁהוּא לְמַעְלָה מִבְּחִינַת הַמִּדּוֹת מִצַּד הָאוֹר וְהַגִּלּוּי שֶׁבַּזֶּה כוּ', וְהָאוֹר מֵאִיר בַּלֵּב גַּם כֵּן

[When we are able to grasp G-dliness without garments], the G-dly light is completely revealed in our mind in a way that is above and

Essay on Service of the Heart - Love Like Fire and Water

beyond emotions, due to the spiritual illumination within us. The G-dly light shines into and permeates our hearts as well, and arouses in them a powerful love and desire. This is not a love and desire of excitement and feeling. It is a mighty attraction to the One Above. It is an expression of spiritually "mature emotions" that rise to equivalence with [and are possibly transformed into] the intellect. Even though, in general, the nullification associated with the Worlds of *Asiya*, *Yetzira*, and *Bria* is ego-nullification alone, the type of nullification associated with the soul-level of *neshama* is one that results in total unity, rather than emotional excitement.

וּמִתְעוֹרֵר גַּם בְּלִבּוֹ בְּאַהֲבָה וּתְשׁוּקָה נִפְלָאָה אֲבָל אֵין זֶה בִּבְחִינַת הִתְפַּעֲלוּת וּבְמַרְגָּשׁ כִּי אִם מַה שֶּׁנִּמְשָׁךְ וְנִדְבָּק מְאֹד בֶּאֱלֹקוּת כוּ' וְהוּא בְּחִינַת גַּדְלוּת הַמִּדּוֹת שֶׁמִּשְׁתַּנִּים אֶל הַמֹּחִין. וְהַבִּטּוּל בְּזֶה עִם הֱיוֹת דִּכְלָלוּת הַבִּטּוּל דִּבְרִיאָה יְצִירָה עֲשִׂיָּה הוּא בְּחִינַת בִּטּוּל הַיֵּשׁ לְבַד מִכָּל מָקוֹם הַבִּטּוּל דִּבְחִינַת נְשָׁמָה הוּא בִּבְחִינַת דְּבֵקוּת וּבִבְחִינַת יִחוּד יוֹתֵר לֹא בִּבְחִינַת הִתְפַּעֲלוּת וּמַרְגָּשׁ,

This is not the case at the soul-level of *ruach*. Even on the high level mentioned above, *ruach* produces some feeling in the heart, but nothing like the strong excitement associated with meditation on the outer garments of the intellect. It is possible that just as the World of *Bria* does not imply existence but only the possibility of creation,[v] (meaning that it only "makes room" for existence, while the next world down, *Yetzira*, implies actual existence [but not yet physical which comes into being in the World of *Asiya*], as written elsewhere), so also is there a corresponding difference in their levels of nullification. The nullification of the soul-level of *neshama* [corresponding to the World of *Bria*] is not noticeable and conscious. It allows room for the self to be experienced. It isn't total self-nullification. Total abnegation is

מַה שֶּׁאֵין כֵּן בְּחִינַת רוּחַ גַּם בַּמַּדְרֵגָה הָעֶלְיוֹנָה הַנַ"ל הוּא בִּבְחִינַת מַרְגָּשׁ קְצָת, וְגַם זֶה לֹא כְּמוֹ בְּהָעֲבוֹדָה בִּבְחִינַת חִיצוֹנִיּוּת הַמֹּחִין שֶׁהוּא בִּבְחִינַת רַעַשׁ וּמַרְגָּשׁ מַמָּשׁ כוּ', וְיֵשׁ לוֹמַר דִּכְמוֹ שֶׁעוֹלָם הַבְּרִיאָה אֵינוֹ בִּבְחִינַת יֵשׁ עֲדַיִן כִּי אִם בְּחִינַת אֶפְשָׁרֵי הַמְּצִיאוּת דְּהַיְנוּ רַק מַה שֶּׁנּוֹתֵן מָקוֹם לְיֵשׁ אֲבָל יְצִירָה הוּא בְּחִינַת יֵשׁ כוּ' וּכְמוֹ שֶׁכָּתוּב בְּמָקוֹם אַחֵר, כְּמוֹ כֵן הוּא הַהֶפְרֵשׁ בְּהַבִּטּוּל שֶׁלָּהֶם דְּהַבִּטּוּל דִּנְשָׁמָה הוּא לֹא בִּבְחִינַת יֵשׁ וּמַרְגָּשׁ רַק שֶׁנּוֹתֵן מָקוֹם לְיֵשׁ בְּזֶה שֶׁאֵינוֹ בִּבְחִינַת בִּטּוּל בִּמְצִיאוּת מַמָּשׁ כְּמוֹ בִּבְחִינַת יִחוּדָא עִילָּאָה, וְהַבִּטּוּל דִּבְחִינַת רוּחַ הוּא בִּבְחִינַת וּמַרְגָּשׁ (וְזֶהוּ עִנְיַן בִּטּוּל הַיֵּשׁ דְּיֵשׁ הַמִּתְבַּטֵּל הוּא בְּרַעַשׁ וְהִתְפַּעֲלוּת

This is not the case with ruach. Even on the high level, ruach produces some feeling in the heart.

v) See footnote of the Rebbe on page 263 ←

וּכְמוֹ עֵצִים הַנִּשְׂרָפִין שֶׁהֵן בְּרַעַשׁ, וְגַם בְּהַבִּטּוּל שֶׁלּוֹ הוּא בִּבְחִינַת יֵשׁ שֶׁזֶּהוּ עִנְיַן הַמֻּרְגָּשׁ כו', וְהַכֹּל עִנְיָן (א'

associated with "supernal/ higher unity" (*yichuda ila'ah*), [when we realize that there is none other than G-d, and therefore all experience of self is lost]. However, the nullification associated with the soul-level of *ruach* involves consciousness of our self and our emotions; this is nullification of the ego [not the self]. When the ego becomes nullified, it is with noise and excitement, as when wood burns, making noise. Even during the process of its own nullification, it experiences itself [becoming nullified], which is the same as feeling oneself.

The purpose of ruach meditation is to arouse the emotions of the heart, but this does not contradict the use of intellect.

(בְּמָקוֹם אַחֵר מְבֹאָר דִּפְסוּקֵי דְזִמְרָה הוּא הַהִלּוּלִים וְתִשְׁבָּחוֹת מֵעִנְיָנִים שֶׁהֵן לְמַעְלָה מֵהַשָּׂגָה וּכְמוֹ הַמְהַלֵּל וּמְשַׁבֵּחַ אֶת הַמֶּלֶךְ בְּעֶצֶם גְּדֻלָּתוֹ שֶׁאֵין לוֹ שׁוּם הַשָּׂגָה בִּגְדֻלַּת וְרוֹמְמוּת הַמֶּלֶךְ כו' וְהוּא הָעוֹשֶׂה בְּחִינַת הַחֲקִיקָה מִבַּחוּץ שֶׁמִּתְרוֹמֵם נַפְשׁוֹ בְּמַדְרֵגָה גְּבוֹהַּ וְעֶלְיוֹנָה יוֹתֵר כו', וְאֵין זֶה סוֹתֵר לְמָה שֶׁנִּתְבָּאֵר לְעֵיל דְּרוּחַ הוּא בְּחִינַת הָאַהֲבָה שֶׁעַל פִּי טַעַם וָדַעַת שֶׁבְּהִתְגַּלּוּת הַלֵּב, כִּי יֵשׁ כַּמָּה מַדְרֵגוֹת בִּבְחִינַת רוּחַ, וְגַם בָּעִנְיָן הַנַּ"ל אֵין הַכַּוָּנָה שֶׁזֶּהוּ בְּלִי הַשָּׂגָה וְהִתְבּוֹנְנוּת כְּלָל, כִּי אִם שֶׁהָעִנְיָנִים הַמְבֹאָרִים בִּפְסוּקֵי דְזִמְרָה דִּכְלָלוּת עִנְיָנָם הוּא עִנְיַן בְּרִיאָה יֵשׁ מֵאַיִן דְּעֶצֶם וְגוּף הָעִנְיָן הַזֶּה הוּא לְמַעְלָה מֵהַשָּׂגַת הַנִּבְרָאִים גַּם לֹא בִּבְחִינַת יְדִיעַת הַמְּצִיאוּת כו', אֲבָל מִכָּל מָקוֹם הֲרֵי יֵשׁ בָּזֶה כַּמָּה הַשָּׂגוֹת וּבִפְרָט בְּהָאוֹר וְחַיּוּת אֱלֹקִי שֶׁבָּא בִּבְחִינַת הִתְלַבְּשׁוּת לְהַחֲיוֹת הָעוֹלָמוֹת דְּבָזֶה הוּא הָעֲבוֹדָה

(Elsewhere, it is explained that the *P'sukei D'zimra*,[17] "Verses of Praise" [appearing in prayer after *Baruch She'amar* and corresponding to the second soul-level, *ruach*], consist of exaltations of matters beyond intellect. This is like the person who praises a king in his majesty, even though this person has no grasp of the king's true greatness. Nevertheless, the sheer act of praying on this level creates an "impression from outside" on the person praying which uplifts and elevates his soul to a higher level. This does not contradict what was explained earlier that *ruach* corresponds to a love of the One Above based upon intellectual meditation revealed in the heart. There are several approaches to the soul-level of *ruach*, and even the approach described above [that *ruach* is based upon meditation on subjects beyond intellect] doesn't imply that the meditation of the *P'sukei D'zimra* is completely beyond intellectual activity. Rather, the general topic of meditation associated with *P'sukei D'zimra* is creation *ex-nihilo* (something "from nothing"), a concept that in essence is beyond the ability of mortal men to grasp.

דְּלְאַהֲבָה אֶת ה' אֱלֹקֶיךָ כִּי הוּא חַיֶּיךָ כו').

Even awareness of the existence of this process is beyond us. Nonetheless, within the process are to be found several ideas, in particular those concerning the G-dly light and energy that en-clothe themselves in creation in order to enliven it. This is the *avoda* of "coming to love the Lord your G-d because He is your life..."[18]

The soul-level of *neshama* is the intermediary level, leading to the *avoda* of the One Above from the essence of the soul, beyond intellect. [This refers to the G-dly core of the soul-level of *neshama*, as is written, "And put in our hearts *bina* to understand." [*Bina* means "understanding," so the implication of the verse is that one must be involved in a process of greater and greater understanding. That is, we request from

וְהִנֵּה בְּחִינַת נְשָׁמָה הוּא מְמֻצָּע לָבוֹא לַעֲבוֹדַת עֶצֶם הַנְּשָׁמָה שֶׁלְּמַעְ' מִטַּעַם וָדַעַת שֶׁזֶּהוּ בְּחִינַת הָאֱלֹקוּת דִּנְשָׁמָה וּכְמוֹ שֶׁאָנוּ אוֹמְרִים וְתֵן בְּלִבֵּנוּ בִּינָה לְהָבִין דְּהַיְנוּ לְהָבִין דָּבָר מִתּוֹךְ דָּבָר, דְּתוֹךְ דָּבָר הוּא בְּחִינַת מְמַלֵּא כָּל עָלְמִין וְדָבָר הוּא בְּחִינַת סוֹבֵב כָּל עָלְמִין.

The soul-level of neshama leads to the essence of the soul, beyond intellect.

the One Above to enable us to undergo a process of understanding one concept from within another. In Hebrew, this is called *lehavin davar, mitoch davar* — "to understand the concept within the concept" — and refers to how we come to understand one idea after having delved deeply into another idea]. The word *mitoch* ("from within") alludes to immanent G-dliness [how He permeates the universe and enlivens it on various spiritual levels], while *davar* — that is, the idea under consideration — alludes to transcendent G-dliness [how He transcends the universe and is essentially beyond it; in other words, when delving deeply into and meditating upon immanent spirituality, we request that the One Above enable us to grasp transcendent G-dliness].

--- **COMMENTARY** ---

4. *CHAYA*

We have thus far examined the soul levels en-clothed in the body, those associated with our actions, emotions, and intellect. We will now take up the levels of the soul which are beyond the body, and beyond the normal perception of the human being. The first of these we'll call "transcendent consciousness," because

Neshama meditation ultimately leads to yediat hashlila and to meditation upon transcendent G-dliness.

וְעַל יְדֵי הַהַשָּׂגָה וְהַהִתְבּוֹנְנוּת דִּבְחִינַת נְשָׁמָה בִּבְחִינַת מְמַלֵּא כָּל עָלְמִין עַל יְדֵי זֶה בָּא לִבְחִינַת סוֹבֵב כָּל עָלְמִין דְּהַיְנוּ הַיְדִיעָה וְהַהַשָּׂגָה בִּבְחִינַת הַפְלָאַת וְרוֹמְמוּת אֵין סוֹף בָּרוּךְ הוּא, אֵיךְ שֶׁהוּא מֻפְלָא וּמְרוֹמָם מֵהָעוֹלָמוֹת, וּבִידִיעַת עֶצֶם הָאוֹר אֵין סוֹף הַמֻּפְלָא, וְהוּא עִנְיַן יְדִיעַת הַשְּׁלִילָה וְהַכָּרַת הַהַפְלָאָה וּבְחִינַת הַהִתְאַמְּתוּת דִּרְאִיַּת עֵין הַשֵּׂכֶל

Meditating on the level of *neshama*, or immanent G-dliness, we ultimately arrive at the level of transcendent G-dliness. This entails understanding of the grandeur of the Infinite One as He transcends creation and knowledge of the essence of His infinite transcendent light. It involves the process of circumscription [literally, negation of knowledge – *yediat hashlila* – in which whatever understanding we gain of G-dliness, we circumscribe and describe G-d as necessarily beyond it]; it also involves recognition of His amazing splendor [*hakarat hahafla*],[19] and confirmation of His existence by way of seeing Him in the mind's eye [*hit'amtut d'reiyat eyn hasechel*].[20]

COMMENTARY

it accesses realms of transcendent spirituality that are beyond the scope of the soul as it is en-clothed in the body.

After we have achieved the third soul-level of "intellect consciousness," in which we have penetrated to the very core of G-dly energy that enlivens the creation, we must continue our intellectual pursuit. Because, the truth is that the G-dly energy enlivening the creation has its own spiritual source beyond the creation. Thus if we achieve "intellect consciousness," we have accessed the spiritual energy within the creation, known in the Chassidic texts as *ohr memalle*, or inner, immanent light.

However, even if we have succeeded in doing this, we still have not arrived at the *source of ohr memalle* — this source is the transcendent light of G-dliness called *ohr makif* which exists beyond the universe, beyond the creation. To get to this point is to realize the soul level of "transcendent consciousness" called in Hebrew *chaya* ("living one"). This demands a special technique within Jewish meditation, called by the Rambam (Maimonides) "circumscription [literally, negation] of knowledge," and by the Chassidim "understanding one thing from within another."

(This knowledge is beyond intellectual grasp. Its true character is only understood by lofty souls of the World of *Atzilut* [the World of Emanation] and *Chabad* of *Atzilut*, which is far beyond the intellect of any created being, as stated in *Tanya*. Within each individual soul, it is the essence of the soul, the G-dliness within it, which is beyond the grasp of the intellect.)

(וִידִיעָה זֹאת הִיא לְמַעְלָה מִבְּחִינַת שֵׂכֶל הַמֻּשָּׂג. וַאֲמִתַּת הַיְדִיעָה הַזֹּאת הִיא רַק בִּנְשָׁמוֹת דַּאֲצִילוּת וְהֵן בְּחִינַת חָכְמָה בִּינָה וְדַעַת דַּאֲצִילוּת שֶׁלְּמַעְלָה מִשֵּׂכֶל הַנִּבְרָאִים וּכְמוֹ שֶׁכָּתוּב בְּסֵפֶר שֶׁל בֵּינוֹנִים שָׁם. וּבְכָל נְשָׁמָה הוּא בְּעֶצֶם הַנְּשָׁמָה שֶׁהוּא בְּחִינַת הָאֱלֹקוּת שֶׁבַּנְּשָׁמָה שֶׁלְּמַעְלָה מִבְּחִינַת שֵׂכֶל מֻשָּׂג כו')

This knowledge is only grasped by lofty souls of the world of Atzilut.

--- **COMMENTARY** ---

Whatever we know about G-d is necessarily deficient. Whatever we can say about Him, and however we understand Him, we cannot know Him as He truly is. Therefore, even the deep awareness and understanding associated with "intellect consciousness" gives us no clue as to how He exists beyond creation. For that, we need to use our understanding of Him (as He is manifest in creation) as a "springboard" to a different realm. We need to circumscribe our knowledge of Him as we know Him from within creation and attempt to reach Him as He exists beyond creation. We do this by negating the spiritual light shining in our minds as a result of *ohr memalle*. This has the effect of giving us a "lift" to the higher level of illumination associated with *ohr makif*, or G-dliness as it transcends creation. It is understood that we don't reject the reality of the initial revelation of immanent light; it is just that we admit it cannot be the whole truth of His existence, and that we, therefore, demand some perception of G-d, as He exists on a transcendent level.

The awareness of "transcendent consciousness" does not come as a clear and precise revelation, as does "intellect consciousness." We are accessing levels that are beyond the senses. Whatever is revealed is amazing and beyond ordinary expression. Nevertheless, some awareness and understanding of transcendent spirituality beyond creation is part of the perception of G-dliness associated with "transcendent consciousness." Such levels are beyond the grasp of most people aside from the most advanced

וּבְכָל זֶה נַעֲשָׂה בְּחִינַת יִחוּד וּדְבֵקוּת נַפְשׁוֹ בְּעַצְמוּת אוֹר אֵין סוֹף בָּרוּךְ הוּא בִּבְחִינַת בָּטוּל בִּמְצִיאוּת מַמָּשׁ, וְהוּא עִנְיַן וְרֹאשׁוֹ מַגִּיעַ הַשָּׁמַיְמָה בְּהִשְׁתַּחֲוָאוֹת דִּשְׁמוֹנֶה

This nullification — which amounts to total abnegation of our very being — brings about a unity of the soul with the essence of the infinite light of G-d (may He be blessed). This then is what is meant by "...and

--- *COMMENTARY* ---

"servants of G-d" (*ovdei HaShem*) — the most accomplished meditators and devotees of the pursuit of truth. However, every Jew can become a "servant of G-d."

"Transcendent consciousness" during prayer is associated with the *Amida*, also known as the *Shmoneh Esreh* ("Eighteen Benedictions"), a prayer which is the pinnacle of the morning service. During the *Amida*, we are totally still and quiet, uttering the blessings under our breath, and asking the One Above to open our mouths since we ourselves are so nullified before Him that we don't have the power even to speak. We take three steps back and then three steps forward, facing the direction of the Temple in Jerusalem, feeling ourselves to be in His Presence as we pray. We bow four times during the *Amida*, and it is then that we are likely, according to the Chassidic literature, to experience "transcendent consciousness" and even unity consciousness (of course, this only occurs if we have meditated through the lower soul levels in prayer).

"Transcendent consciousness" is associated with the World of *Atzilut* ("World of Emanations"). On this level, there is no awareness of self, but only of the Holy One Above. Spiritual awareness of G-d on this level is like a ray coming from the sun; the ray is always connected with its source and ceases to exist the moment the source chooses. ["Transcendent consciousness" is also associated with the first letter, the *yud* of G-d's Name, and with the first of the ten *sephirot* — *chochma* ("wisdom") and with the human species within creation.]

5. YECHIDA

Finally, we come to the highest soul level — *yechida* ("single one") — which we'll describe as "unity consciousness." A few souls come into this world on such a high level that they are constantly in touch with the transcendent light of G-d even

Essay on Service of the Heart - Love Like Fire and Water

its head reached into the heavens" [regarding the ladder in Jacob's dream, mentioned above]. It occurs when we are [absorbed in the most intense moments of prayer, while] bowing during the *Amida* and is accompanied by a state of total nullification of our existence. At such times, our lower three soul-levels (*nefesh*, *ruach*, and *neshama*) are elevated to tremendously exalted heights. Our intellect is empowered to grasp astonishing matters, and we are able to penetrate to the very depths and essence of the concept, in a completely different way than before.

עֲשָׂרָה בִּבְחִינַת בִּטּוּל בַּמְצִיאוּת מַמָּשׁ כו' וְאָז גַּם כְּלָלוּת נֶפֶשׁ רוּחַ וּנְשָׁמָה שֶׁלּוֹ מִתְעַלֶּה שֶׁהֵן בְּמַדְרֵגוֹת נַעֲלוֹת וּמֻפְלָאוֹת בְּיוֹתֵר, כְּמוֹ הַהַשָּׂגָה שֶׁלּוֹ הִיא בְּעִנְיָנִים מֻפְלָאִים יוֹתֵר וְעֶצֶם הַהַשָּׂגָה הִיא עֲמֻקָּה יוֹתֵר וּבְאֹפֶן אַחֵר לְגַמְרֵי (עד נעמט גאר אנדערש א ענין אלוקי)

This is what is meant by "our head reaches the heavens..."

(This is similar to what happens to us when, while operating on the level of *neshama*, we immediately grasp the essence of G-dliness without need of the outer garments which "package" it. It is understood that our grasp of the outer garments is also different than at such a time when we need them in order to grasp the concept. Since we immediately know the

(וּכְמוֹ בְּמַדְרֵגַת הַנְּשָׁמָה הַנַּ"ל כְּשֶׁתּוֹפֵס וּמַשִּׂיג אֶת עֶצֶם הָעִנְיָן הָאֱלֹקִי שֶׁלֹּא עַל יְדֵי לְבוּשֵׁי הַשָּׂגָה מִתְּחִלָּה הֲרֵי מוּבָן שֶׁעַל יְדֵי זֶה גַּם הַשָּׂגָתוֹ בִּבְחִינַת חִיצוֹנִיּוּת הָעִנְיָן הוּא בְּאֹפֶן אַחֵר מִזֶּה שֶׁמַּתְחִיל לִתְפֹּס הָעִנְיָן בְּחִיצוֹנִיּוּתוֹ, דְּמֵאַחַר שֶׁיּוֹדֵעַ אֶת עֶצֶם הָעִנְיָן מִמֵּילָא הַשָּׂגָתוֹ בְּהָעִנְיָן הִיא גְּדוֹלָה וַעֲמֻקָּה בְּיוֹתֵר,

---
COMMENTARY
---

when they are born in a physical body. They are called *tzaddikim*. They have no "evil inclination" hiding or concealing spirituality from them. Therefore, they need not meditate on the greatness of the Creator in order to recognize, feel, and understand His presence at all times.

All Jews possess this aspect in their soul, but very few of us realize it at more than the rarest of moments. It is that part of the soul that is always united with the One Above, which is always receiving "messages" from the One Above (but it depends upon our level of refinement and our commitment to the Torah and its *mitzvot* as to whether we consciously receive these messages). This aspect of the soul comes into full expression if and when it is demanded of us that we give up our life in honor of the One Above. For example, if it were to be demanded

כֵּן וְיוֹתֵר מִכֵּן לְאֵין קֵץ בִּידִיעַת אוֹר אֵין סוֹף בָּרוּךְ הוּא הַמֻּפְלָא וּמְרוֹמָם כוּ', שֶׁגַּם הַהַשָּׂגָה הִיא נַעֲלֵית וְנִפְלָאָה בְּיוֹתֵר כוּ')

essence of the concept, automatically our overall grasp of the topic is deeper and stronger. If this is true [regarding the level of *neshama*, where we meditate on the immanent light of G-d permeating the creation], then it certainly applies to meditation on the infinite light of G-d as it transcends the creation; whatever intellectual grasp is associated with it is very high and astounding.)

וְכֵן הַמִּדּוֹת הַכֹּל הוּא בְּמַדְרֵגָה גְבוֹהָה וְנַעֲלֵית לְאֵין קֵץ כוּ'. וְכָל זֹאת הִיא הָעֲבוֹדָה דִתְפִלָּה בִּבְחִינַת הִתְקַשְּׁרוּת וּדְבֵקוּת נַפְשׁוֹ בֵּאלֹקוּת בִּבְחִינַת נֶפֶשׁ רוּחַ וּנְשָׁמָה שֶׁבְּנַפְשׁוֹ וּבִבְחִינַת נְשָׁמָה לִנְשָׁמָה כוּ').

The above is also true of the emotions. Everything is on an extremely high spiritual level. This is the *avoda* of prayer, which is the uniting of our divine soul (*nefesh, ruach, neshama*, and *nishmeta d'nishmeta*) with G-dliness.

This is what is meant by "pouring out the soul," meaning an elevation and desire for the infinite light above.

וְזֶהוּ גַּם כֵּן מַה שֶּׁהַתְּפִלָּה נִקְרֵאת שְׁפִיכַת הַנֶּפֶשׁ וּכְמוֹ שֶׁכָּתוּב וָאֶשְׁפֹּךְ אֶת נַפְשִׁי לִפְנֵי ה' שֶׁהוּא בְּחִינַת הָעֲלִיָּה וְהָרָצוֹא לָאוֹר אֵין סוֹף בָּרוּךְ הוּא וּכְמוֹ אֵלֶיךָ ה' נַפְשִׁי אֶשָּׂא (וּלְמַעְלָה הוּא מַה שֶּׁהַמַּלְכוּת נִקְרֵאת תְּפִלָּה וּכְמוֹ שֶׁכָּתוּב וַאֲנִי תְפִלָּה וְהוּא בְּחִינַת הָרָצוֹא דְמַלְכוּת דִּלְמַעַן יְזַמֶּרְךָ כָבוֹד כוּ' נְהוֹרָא תַּתָּאָה קָארֵי תָּדִיר לִנְהוֹרָא

This is, as well, what is meant by the description of prayer as "pouring out of the soul," as the verse says [1 Samuel 1:15], "And I'll pour out my soul before G-d..." which indicates an ascent and desire for the infinite light of the One Above. This is also what is indicated by the verse [Psalms 25:1], "To you I will lift up my soul..." (In the abstract, this is why the supernal *sephira* of *malchut* is called "prayer,"

COMMENTARY

that we either bow down before an idol (thereby committing the cardinal sin of idolatry) or be executed, the soul level of "unity consciousness" would dictate that we choose death rather than transgress. That is, our *yechida* would compel us to give up our own life rather than risk spiritual disconnection from the One Above.

However, the subjective experience of "unity consciousness" cannot be achieved by any meditation. That is, unlike the previous soul levels, which we can reach by working on ourselves, the experience of "unity consciousness" is strictly at

Essay on Service of the Heart - Love Like Fire and Water

as it is said [in Psalms 109:4], "I am prayer..." This indicates the longing of *malchut*, the level of "to sing to Your honor..." [The *Zohar* explains that the singing is that of] the "lower illumination" [the soul] crying out to the "higher illumination" [the One Above].) It is also what is referred to as the "fiery flames of desire" and thirst to be included in the essence of the infinite light of the One Above.[21]

עִילָאָה כו׳) וְהוּא בְּחִינַת רִשְׁפֵּי אֵשׁ הַתְּשׁוּקָה וְהַצִּמָּאוֹן לְהִכָּלֵל בְּעַצְמוּת אוֹר אֵין סוֹף בָּרוּךְ הוּא.

The second aspect of prayer is the purification and refinement of the animal soul. It is in this sense that prayer is offered in lieu of the sacrifices, as is written [Leviticus 1:2], "Man, when offering *from you* a sacrifice," indicating that the sacrifice is that of the animal soul within us.[22] It is possible that this is what is meant by "intention" in prayer, as opposed to the "speech" of prayer. Sometimes it is explained that the most important aspect of prayer is the intention within our heart, while the voice (that is, the speech of prayer) is [only] for the sake of arousing us to greater intention during prayer. On the other hand, it is understood from the say-

וְהָעִנְיָן הב׳ בַּתְּפִלָּה הוּא בֵּרוּר וְזִכּוּךְ הַנֶּפֶשׁ הַבַּהֲמִית, שֶׁזֶּהוּ מַה שֶּׁהַתְּפִלָּה הִיא בִּמְקוֹם קָרְבָּן וּכְמוֹ שֶׁכָּתוּב אָדָם כִּי יַקְרִיב מִכֶּם קָרְבָּן כו׳ דְּהַיְנוּ הַקְרָבַת הַנֶּפֶשׁ הַבַּהֲמִית כַּנּוֹדָע. וְיֵשׁ לוֹמַר שֶׁזֶּהוּ עִנְיַן כַּוָּנַת הַתְּפִלָּה וְהַדִּבּוּר דִּתְפִלָּה, דִּלְפְעָמִים מְבֹאָר דְּעִקַּר הַתְּפִלָּה הוּא כַּוָּנַת הַלֵּב וְהַקּוֹל (וְהוּא הַדִּבּוּר דִּתְפִלָּה) הוּא לְעוֹרֵר אֶת הַכַּוָּנָה וּכְמוֹ שֶׁאָמְרוּ רַבּוֹתֵינוּ זִכְרוֹנָם לִבְרָכָה סנד״ל קוֹשֵׁר כְּתָרִים לְקוֹנוֹ מִתְּפִלּוֹתֵיהֶן שֶׁל יִשְׂרָאֵל וּמְבֹאָר בְּמָקוֹם אַחֵר שֶׁזֶּהוּ מֵהָאוֹתִיּוֹת דִּתְפִלָּה, מַשְׁמַע מִזֶּה דְּהָעִקָּר הוּא הַדִּבּוּר דִּתְפִלָּה. וְיֵשׁ לוֹמַר עַל פִּי

The second aspect of prayer is the purification and refinement of the animal soul.

COMMENTARY

the discretion of the One Above. We can refine ourselves, meditating, learning Torah, and fulfilling its *mitzvot*; and if the One Above decides that we are ready, then He may grant us the gift of "unity consciousness."

Yechida is too high to be associated with any world. The Hebrew word for "world" — *olam* — implies hiddenness and concealment. Any world, spiritual or physical, conceals G-dliness to a greater or lesser degree. But, the soul level of "unity consciousness" breaches no hiddenness, and therefore transcends the worlds. Likewise, it is beyond prayer, associated

הַנַ"ל שֶׁהֵן ב' הָעִנְיָנִים הַנַ"ל דְּכַוָּנַת הַתְּפִלָּה הַיְנוּ הָעֲבוֹדָה שֶׁמִּצַּד הַנֶּפֶשׁ הָאֱלֹקִית בְּחִינַת עֲלִיַּת וְהִתְקַשְּׁרוּת נַפְשׁוֹ כוּ', וְהַדִּבּוּר דִּתְפִלָּה זֶהוּ מֵהַבֵּרוּר דְּנֶפֶשׁ הַבַּהֲמִית שֶׁבַּתְּפִלָּה.

ing of the Sages that the angel *Sandal*[23] makes crowns for the Creator from the prayers of the Jewish people, that it is the letters and speech of the prayers which are important (as explained elsewhere).[vi] The conclusion is that our intention is the important aspect of prayer, when considering the G-dly soul and its elevation. But when considering the animal soul within us, which needs refining and purification, it is the speech of prayer which is more important.

vi) See footnote of the Rebbe on page 264

דְּהִנֵּה יָדוּעַ הַהֶפְרֵשׁ בֵּין אוֹתִיּוֹת הַתּוֹרָה וְאוֹתִיּוֹת הַתְּפִלָּה דְאוֹתִיּוֹת הַתּוֹרָה הֵן אוֹתִיּוֹת דְמַ"ה וְאוֹתִיּוֹת הַתְּפִלָּה הֵן אוֹתִיּוֹת דְּבַ"ן.

Now, it is known that there is a difference between the letters of Torah and the letters of prayer. The letters of Torah are the letters of *Ma"h*,[24] [from the already purified World of *Atzilut*], while the letters of prayer are of *Ba"n* [from the lower three worlds which need rectification and elevation].

Ma"h and *Ba"n* are numerical values of the name of G-d. Both are forms of the Tetragrammaton, the four-letter essential name, spelled out to its fullest.	
Ma"h (45)	*Ba"n* (52)
Equals *adam* or "man"	equals *behama*, or "animal"
represents the rectified World of *Tikun* (i.e. *Atzilut*),	corresponds to the not yet rectified realm of *Tohu* (i.e. *Bria, Yetzira, Asiya*)
Yud: Yud-vav-dalet	*Yud*: Yud-vav-dalet
Hai: Hai-alef	*Hai*: Hai-hai
Vav: Vav-alef-vav	*Vav*: Vav-vav
Hai: Hai-alef	*Hai*: Hai-hai

——————— **COMMENTARY** ———————

with the level of prophecy in the scheme of creation. ["Unity consciousness" is associated with the infinite light of G-d, called *keter*, meaning "crown" (referring to the transcendent light, just as the crown transcends the head), which is above even the spiritual World of *Atzilut* ("Emanations"). It manifests itself as a gift from Above for those who have worked hard on

Essay on Service of the Heart - Love Like Fire and Water

The concept here is equivalent to the distinction [mentioned in *Torah Ohr, parshat Mishpatim*] between *avanim* ("stones") and *levanim* ("bricks"). Stones are a creation of G-d, and therefore symbolize the letters that come from above, the letters with which the Torah was given. These letters are appropriate vessels to contain the spirituality of the highest *sephira* — that of *chochma*. Through these letters, the infinite light of G-d is transmitted [and brought into the creation]. Therefore, one who learns Torah must pronounce the words out loud. *Levanim* are man-made, and they symbolize the letters of prayer, which is the speech of man. That is, these are not letters that come from above, but letters that come from below. (Even in the *Amida*[vii] about which it says "there are no words on my tongue," and "Lord, please open my lips," the words are nonetheless words of man. It is just that these are words that flow spontaneously, without any effort on our part when praying. They also emerge without any apparent logical design, since the self-nullification of the prayer is beyond reason, as explained elsewhere.)[viii] The letters of prayer come from the inner recesses and depths of our heart when

וְהוּא עִנְיַן בְּחִינַת אֶבֶן וּלְבֵנָה, דְּאֶבֶן הוּא בְּרִיאָה בִּידֵי שָׁמַיִם וְהֵן אוֹתִיּוֹת הַבָּאוֹת מִלְמַעְלָה שֶׁהַתּוֹרָה נִתְּנָה בְּאוֹתִיּוֹת אֵלּוּ דַּוְקָא שֶׁהֵן כֵּלִים לְגִלּוּי בְּחִינַת חָכְמָה עִילָּאָה וּבָהֶם וְעַל יָדָם קוֹרְאִים וּמַמְשִׁיכִים גִּלּוּי אוֹר אֵין סוֹף בָּרוּךְ הוּא דְּלָכֵן צָרִיךְ לִהְיוֹת עֵסֶק הַתּוֹרָה בְּדִבּוּר דַּוְקָא וּכְמוֹ שֶׁכָּתוּב בַּתּוֹרָה אוֹר דִּבּוּר הַמַּתְחִיל וַיִּרְאוּ אֵת אֱלֹקֵי יִשְׂרָאֵל, וּלְבֵנִים הֵם הַנַּעֲשִׂים בִּידֵי אָדָם וְהֵן אוֹתִיּוֹת הַתְּפִלָּה שֶׁזֶּהוּ דִּבּוּר הָאָדָם, וְהַיְנוּ שֶׁאֵין זֶה אוֹתִיּוֹת הַבָּאִים מִלְמַעְלָה כִּי אִם אוֹתִיּוֹת הַבָּאִים מִלְמַטָּה לְמַעְלָה מֵהָאָדָם הַמִּתְפַּלֵּל (דְּגַם בִּשְׁמוֹנֶה עֶשְׂרֵה שֶׁנֶּאֱמַר עַל זֶה אֵין מִילִין בִּלְשׁוֹנִי רַק אֲדֹנָי שְׂפָתַי תִּפְתָּח, הֵן מִכָּל מָקוֹם דִּבּוּר הָאָדָם רַק שֶׁהוּא דִּבּוּר הַבָּא מִמֵּילָא לֹא בְּכַוָּנָה וּבְסֵדֶר עַל פִּי הַשֵּׂכֶל לְפִי שֶׁהַבִּטּוּל דִּתְפִלָּה הוּא לְמַעְלָה מִטַּעַם וָדַעַת הַמֻּשָּׂג כוּ' וּכְמוֹ שֶׁכָּתוּב בְּמָקוֹם אַחֵר) וְהֵן אוֹתִיּוֹת הַבָּאִים מִקֶּרֶב וְלֵב עָמֹק מֵהַקֵּרוּב שֶׁאַחַר הָרִחוּק, וְהַיְנוּ בְּעָסְקוֹ כָּל הַיּוֹם בְּהַכֹּחוֹת הַטִּבְעִיִּים שֶׁלּוֹ וּמִתְקָרֵב אַחַר כָּךְ בַּתְּפִלָּה גַּם בְּהַכֹּחוֹת הַטִּבְעִיִּים שֶׁלּוֹ דְּלִבִּי וּבְשָׂרִי יְרַנְּנוּ כוּ', הִנֵּה אוֹתִיּוֹת אֵלּוּ נַעֲשִׂים כֶּתֶר לְקוֹנוֹ וּכְמוֹ הָעֲטָרָה

vii) See footnote of the Rebbe on page 264

viii) See footnote of the Rebbe on page 266

--- **COMMENTARY** ---

themselves, but it cannot be expected or predicted. It is associated with the upper tip of the *yud* of G-d's Name and with the *sephira* of *keter* ("crown").]

praying, as we have been far away from the One Above and now we come near. We have been working all day with our natural [physical and mental] abilities, and now we come close to the One Above in prayer, with our natural abilities as well —

שֶׁנַּעֲשֵׂית מֵאֲבָנִים טוֹבוֹת וּמְאִירוֹת (וּכְמוֹ שֶׁכָּתוּב בְּמָקוֹם אַחֵר שֶׁבָּאֲבָנִים טוֹבוֹת יֵשׁ שֶׁמְּאִירוֹת בְּעַצְמָם וְיֵשׁ שֶׁמְּאִירוֹת עַל יְדֵי שֶׁמִּזְדַּכְּכוֹת בִּפְעֻלַּת הַכּוֹכָבִים וְכַנּוֹדָע מֵעִנְיָן שֹׁהַם וְיָשְׁפֵה).

[as it says in Psalms 84:3] "my heart and my flesh sing." Then, the letters of our prayers become "crowns" for the Creator, like a crown that is made of precious shining stones. (Elsewhere, it is written that there are gems which shine of their own accord, and other gems which shine only on account of the polishing they receive from the light of the stars above, as is known regarding the two stones, *shoham* and *yashpe*.)

The letters of prayer are letters that have become purified and refined. (In particular, the letters of prayer represent the words of speech in which we engage all day long. In general, they are our natural abilities that we utilized all day long, for physical purposes.) They become precious and luminescent and thus become crowns for the Creator (which is the topic of the prayer *Yehi Ratzon*,[ix] as explained elsewhere.) Both aspects of prayer mentioned above come about through arousal of our feeling of love, as will be explained, G-d

כָּךְ מֵאוֹתִיּוֹת הַתְּפִלָּה שֶׁהֵן אוֹתִיּוֹת שֶׁנִּתְבָּרְרוּ וְנִזְדַּכְּכוּ (וּבִפְרָטִיּוּת הֵן הַדִּבּוּרִים דְּכָל הַיּוֹם וּבִכְלָלוּת הֵן הַכֹּחוֹת הַטִּבְעִיִּים שֶׁמִּשְׁתַּמֵּשׁ בָּהֶם כָּל הַיּוֹם בְּעִנְיָנָיו הַגּוּפָנִיִּים) וְנַעֲשִׂים טוֹבִים וּמְאִירִים וְנַעֲשִׂים בְּחִינַת כֶּתֶר לְקוֹנוֹ כוּ' (וְהוּא עִנְיָן יְהִי רָצוֹן כוּ' וּכְמוֹ שֶׁכָּתוּב בְּמָקוֹם אַחֵר). וּבְב' הָעִנְיָנִים הַנַּ"ל שֶׁבַּתְּפִלָּה הֵם עַל יְדֵי הִתְעוֹרְרוּת מִדַּת הָאַהֲבָה וּכְמוֹ שֶׁיִּתְבָּאֵר אִי"ה וְלָכֵן כָּל הָעֲבוֹדָה דִתְפִלָּה הוּא לָבוֹא לִבְחִינַת אַהֲבָה:

ix) See footnote of the Rebbe on page 267

willing. Therefore, the entire *avoda* of prayer is in order to attain love [of the One Above].

SYNOPSIS:
All of the labor of prayer is in order to come to love the One Above. As such, prayer includes two aspects: The first is the unity with and the cleaving of our soul to G-dliness, which involves the elevation of our soul by means of strong will and

קִצּוּר. כָּל הַיְגִיעָה דִתְפִלָּה הִיא לָבוֹא לְמִדַּת הָאַהֲבָה כִּי בַּתְּפִלָּה יֵשׁ ב' עִנְיָנִים, הָא' הִתְקַשְּׁרוּת וּדְבֵקוּת נַפְשׁוֹ בֶּאֱלֹקוּת וּלְהַעֲלוֹתָהּ בִּבְחִינַת רָצוֹא כוּ' וְהַב' לְבָרֵר וּלְזַכֵּךְ אֶת הַנֶּפֶשׁ הַבַּהֲמִית, וּשְׁנֵיהֶם

desire. The second is purification and refinement of our animal soul. Both goals are served and motivated by love of G-d. This is the *avoda* of the lower three soul levels — *nefesh*, *ruach* and *neshama* — and their inter-inclusion within their respective higher levels.

נַעֲשִׂים עַל יְדֵי מִדַּת הָאַהֲבָה (וְנִתְ׳ עִנְיַן הָעֲבוֹדָה בִּבְחִינַת נֶפֶשׁ רוּחַ וּנְשָׁמָה וּנְשָׁמָה לִנְשָׁמָה וְהִתְכַּלְלוּת כָּל אַחַת מֵהֶם בְּמַדְרֵגָה שֶׁלְּמַעְלָה הֵימֶנָּה):

CHAPTER 2

פרק ב

Fear is a necessary ingredient, but not of the avoda of prayer.

We must certainly develop the characteristic of fear [of G-d]. In fact, fear is a necessary ingredient of our *avoda* of G-d. It is impossible to serve G-d without fearing Him; indeed, fear [of G-d] is the beginning and foundation [of *avoda*]. However, it is *not* part of the labor of prayer ["the service of the heart"].

וְהִנֵּה זֹאת וַדַּאי אֲשֶׁר צָרִיךְ לִהְיוֹת גַּם יִרְאָה וְאַדְּרַבָּה הַיִּרְאָה הִיא מֻכְרַחַת לִהְיוֹת בְּכָל אֶחָד וְאֶחָד מַמָּשׁ שֶׁאִי אֶפְשָׁר לִהְיוֹת בִּלְעָדֶיהָ וְהִיא גַּם הַתְחָלַת הָעֲבוֹדָה וִיסוֹדָהּ אָמְנָם לֹא זוֹ הִיא הָעֲבוֹדָה וְהַיְגִיעָה דִּתְפִלָּה.

The essential fear is "yirat chait" — fear of transgression. For this, we must guard our senses.

The fear that is essential for everyone to attain is *yirat chait*, [fear of sin, or fear of transgressing His will]. That is, we are afraid to do anything that is against the will of G-d. Fear of sin relates not only to wrongful deeds or transgressions, but also to guarding the senses. We must constantly guard our eyes to prevent them from seeing and block our ears from hearing anything evil. We shouldn't expose our eyesight to all that is in front of us, and of course we shouldn't stare.

דְּהִנֵּה הַיִּרְאָה הַמֻּכְרַחַת לִהְיוֹת בְּכָל אֶחָד וְאֶחָד הוּא עִנְיַן יִרְאַת חֵטְא וְהוּא שֶׁיִּירָא לַעֲשׂוֹת כָּל דָּבָר שֶׁהוּא נֶגֶד הוי' וּרְצוֹנוֹ יִתְבָּרֵךְ וְלָאו דַּוְקָא בִּדְבַר חֵטְא וְעָוֹן בְּפֹעַל מַמָּשׁ כִּי אִם הַהַגְדָּרָה בְּהַחוּשִׁים שֶׁלּוֹ לִהְיוֹת עוֹצֵם עֵינָיו מֵרְאוֹת בְּרַע וְאוֹטֵם אָזְנוֹ מִשְּׁמֹעַ דְּבַר רַע וְהַיְנוּ שֶׁחוּשׁ הָרְאִיָּ' שֶׁלּוֹ אֵינוֹ פָּתוּחַ לִרְאוֹת כָּל מַה שֶּׁלְּפָנָיו וְכָל שֶׁכֵּן בִּרְאִיָּ' וְהִסְתַּכְּלוּת הָאֲמוּרָה

The truth is that seeing — and even more, staring — is the cause of all bad things and can bring us to absolute

(אֲשֶׁר בֶּאֱמֶת הָרְאִיָּ' וְכָל שֶׁכֵּן הַהִסְתַּכְּלוּת הִיא הַסִּבָּה הַגּוֹרֶמֶת לְכָל דָּבָר רַע וְהִיא הַמְּבִיאָה לְרַע

--- COMMENTARY ---

CHAPTER 2: THE FOUNDATION OF MEDITATION

Chapter 1 of *Kuntres Ha'Avoda* is an overview of soul levels that are attainable by steady and concentrated meditation (*hitbonenut*) on G-dly concepts over a period of time. Chapter 2 brings us down to earth. Here, the Rebbe doesn't speak about states of consciousness nor about getting closer to the One Above, but rather about seemingly mundane things like guarding our senses, thought, speech, and action. People who are looking for an immediate "high" in their spiritual work may have a hard time

Essay on Service of the Heart - Love Like Fire and Water

evil, G-d forbid. As is stated [in *Midrash Tanchuma* ch.15], "the eye and the heart are two intermediaries of sin; the eye sees, and the heart desires, and whoever looks ... in the end will transgress." It is known that the main enjoyment which we experience is through eyesight, and the blind person has no enjoyment in anything,[x] as is written elsewhere regarding [the verse in Psalms 90:15] "Make us glad as many days as You have afflicted us." Thus, our sight arouses enjoyment in the soul, and that's why we see that even [seasoned and experienced] "servants of G-d," who are very far from anything bad, are also slightly affected by what they see (aside from those who through their *avoda* have — temporarily at least — removed themselves from anything physical so that at that moment they are not affected by anything). But since they are "servants of G-d," what they see has no permanent effect on them, G-d forbid, but only leaves a fleeting impression which passes away, and immediately they re-connect themselves to what they are [anyway] connected to, and the matter is dismissed from their hearts. However,

גְּמוּר רַחֲמָנָא לִיצְלָן וּכְמַאֲמַר עֵינָא וְלִבָּא תְּרֵין סַרְסוּרִין דַּעֲבֵרָה הָעַיִן רוֹאָה וְהַלֵּב חוֹמֵד וְכָל הַמִּסְתַּכֵּל כו' סוֹף בָּא לִידֵי עֲבֵרָה, וְכַנּוֹדָע דְּעִקַּר הַתַּעֲנוּג הוּא בְּחוּשׁ הָרְאִיָּ' וְהַסּוּמָא אֵין לוֹ תַעֲנוּג בְּשׁוּם דָּבָר וּכְמוֹ שֶׁכָּתוּב בְּמָקוֹם אַחֵר בְּעִנְיַן שַׂמְּחֵנוּ כִּימוֹת עִנִּיתָנוּ, וְעַל כֵּן הָרְאִיָּ' מְעוֹרֵר הַתַּעֲנוּג שֶׁבַּנֶּפֶשׁ, וְלָכֵן אָנוּ רוֹאִים שֶׁגַּם בְּעוֹבְדֵי ה' הָרְחוֹקִים לְגַמְרֵי מִכָּל דָּבָר רַע הִנֵּה עַל יְדֵי הָרְאִיָּ' מִתְעוֹרְרִים וּמִתְפַּעֲלִים קְצָת (לְבַד בְּאוֹתָן שֶׁהָעֲבוֹדָה פּוֹעֵל בָּהֶם שֶׁלְּפִי שָׁעָה עַל כָּל פָּנִים הֵמָּה מִפְשָׁטִים מִן הַגֶּשֶׁם שֶׁבְּעֵת הַהִיא אֵינָם מִתְפַּעֲלִים מִשּׁוּם דָּבָר) רַק לִהְיוֹתָם עוֹבְדֵי ה' אֵין זֶה עוֹשֶׂה בָּהֶם אֵיזֶה חֲקִיקָה חַס וְחָלִילָה כִּי אִם הוּא בְּהַעֲבָרָה בְּעָלְמָא וּמִיָּד יְקַשֵּׁר אֶת עַצְמוֹ אֶל מַה שֶׁהוּא מְקֻשָּׁר וְנִשְׁכָּח הַדָּבָר מִלִּבּוֹ. אֲבָל אוֹתָם שֶׁאֵינָם

Eyesight can be the cause of much negative sensory input.

x) See footnote of the Rebbe on page 267

COMMENTARY

accepting what the Rebbe says in this chapter, and may wonder what this has to do with coming closer to the One Above.

The truth is that we cannot get close to G-d without first establishing a foundation on which to build our spiritual edifice. We cannot create a spiritual environment in our mind unless we have first fulfilled certain conditions of purity and refinement. This involves guarding ourselves from certain sensory inputs and expressions that damage the soul and raise barriers between us and the One Above. Chapter 2 tells us what these inputs

those who are not in the category of "servants of G-d" in the real sense, are caught in this trap [of following their eyes and heart]. This leads them to all kinds of base things, G-d forbid, and pulls them down to the lowest depths. May G-d guard and rescue them.

עוֹבְדֵי ה' כִּדְבָעֵי הֲרֵי הוּא נִלְכָּדִים בַּפַּח הַזֶּה וְהוּא הַמְבִיאָם לְכָל דָּבָר רַע רַחֲמָנָא לִיצְלָן וּמוֹרִיד אוֹתָם לִשְׁאוֹל תַּחְתִּית ה' יִשְׁמְרֵנוּ וְיַצִּילֵנוּ.

Guarding eyesight is vital; if we don't, then all of our avoda is invalid.

Those of us who are concerned about our soul, and who don't wish to bring it to a state of impurity, G-d forbid, should guard our sense of eyesight. And if this is difficult for us, we must overcome our weakness with all of our power. We must know that this matter is vital to our soul, and that if we don't guard ourselves in this regard, then all of our *avoda* of the One Above is invalid. All of our effort will have no effect, and quite the opposite, we will sink lower and lower. Therefore, we should strengthen ourselves and guard ourselves with all of our power, and even if it becomes noticeable [to others], we should pay no attention to what people say. When it comes to matters of physical life and death, no one is concerned about what another person thinks, all the more so with regard to a matter of spiritual life and

וְכָל מִי שֶׁחָשׁ לְנַפְשׁוֹ שֶׁלֹּא לַהֲבִיאָהּ לִידֵי טֻמְאָה רַחֲמָנָא לִיצְלָן יַגְדִּיר אֶת עַצְמוֹ בְּחוּשׁ הָרְאִיָּי. וְאִם הַדָּבָר קָשֶׁה לוֹ יִתְגַּבֵּר עַל עַצְמוֹ בְּכָל תֹּקֶף וָעֹז וְיֵדַע אֲשֶׁר מַמָּשׁ בְּנַפְשׁוֹ הוּא וְאִם לֹא יַגְדִּיר אֶת עַצְמוֹ בָּזֶה כָּל עֲבוֹדָתוֹ כְּאַיִן וּכְאֶפֶס נֶחְשָׁב וְלֹא יִפְעַל דָּבָר בִּיגִיעָתוֹ וַעֲבוֹדָתוֹ וְאַדְּרַבָּא יֵרֵד רַחֲמָנָא לִיצְלָן מַטָּה מַטָּה, וְעַל כֵּן יִתְגַּבֵּר כָּאֲרִי לְהַגְדִּיר אֶת עַצְמוֹ בְּכָל תֹּקֶף וָעֹז וְגַם אִם יְהִי' נִכָּר אַל יָחוּשׁ לְשִׂיחוֹת בנ"א, וַהֲלֹא בְּדָבָר הַנּוֹגֵעַ לְחַיֵּי הַנֶּפֶשׁ בְּגַשְׁמִיּוּת אֵינָם מַבִּיטִים עַל שׁוּם דָּבָר וְכָל שֶׁכֵּן בְּהַנּוֹגֵעַ לְחַיֵּי הַנֶּפֶשׁ הָרוּחָנִי, וְהַכְּבֵדוּת בָּזֶה הִיא רַק בְּעֵת הָרִאשׁוֹנָה שֶׁצָּרִיךְ לְהַכְבִּיד עַל עַצְמוֹ וּלְהִתְגַּבֵּר עַל טִבְעוֹ וּרְצוֹנוֹ וּבְמֶשֶׁךְ הַזְּמַן יִתְרַגֵּל כָּךְ. וּבְהַגְדָּרָה זֹאת יִמְצָא מָנוֹחַ לְנַפְשׁוֹ מִכַּמָּה

―――――― *COMMENTARY* ――――――

and expressions are and how to fend them off.

Chapter 1, detailing many of the higher levels of spiritual consciousness, was a "gift" — it was meant to whet our appetites and let us know what is in store for us if we decide to pursue *hitbonenut*. (And, as it says in Chapter 6 of *Kuntres Ha'Avoda*, "if you're not practicing *hitbonenut*, then what are you doing here?")

Essay on Service of the Heart - Love Like Fire and Water

death. The difficulty in this [exercise in restraint] is only in the beginning, when we have to concentrate in order to overcome our own nature and will.

רָעוֹת וּבִלְבּוּלִים וְאָז יוּכַל לַעֲבֹד עֲבוֹדָתוֹ. וּבִיגִיעָתוֹ יִפְעַל יְשׁוּעוֹת בְּנַפְשׁוֹ בְּעֶזְרָתוֹ יִתְ׳.

The difficulty in guarding our eyesight is only in the beginning.

However, with time, we will become accustomed to doing this, and by guarding ourselves, we will find an escape from much evil and confusion, and then we will be able to serve G-d [in prayer with serenity]. And through our effort we will bring salvation to our soul, with the help of the One Above.

Now, there are people who are far from actually committing any kind of transgression, G-d forbid, but their hearts pull them [nevertheless] to look and to stare. They do so with coldness and detachment, and they feel no excitement at the time they look. But, in truth the underlying reason for their attraction is that the soul is deriving essential enjoyment from bonding with what they are looking at.

וְהִנֵּה יֶשְׁנָם בְּנֵי אָדָם אֲשֶׁר רְחוֹקִים הֵמָּה מֵאֵיזֶה דְּבַר רַע בְּפֹעַל חַס וְחָלִילָה, אֲבָל לִבָּם מוֹשֵׁךְ אוֹתָם לִרְאוֹת וּלְהַבִּיט וְהַהַבָּטָה הִיא כְּמוֹ בְּקֹר רוּחַ וְאֵינוֹ מַרְגִּישׁ בְּעַצְמוֹ בְּעֵת מַעֲשֶׂה אֵיזֶה הִתְפַּעֲלוּת, וּבֶאֱמֶת סִבַּת הַמְשִׁיכָה הוּא מִפְּנֵי שֶׁתַּעֲנוּג נַפְשׁוֹ בְּעֶצֶם הוּא מְקֻשָּׁר בָּזֶה

(This is similar to what is written elsewhere,[xi] regarding [the statement of one of the Sages], "I don't know in which direction I am being led…" [This was said by R'Yohanan ben Zakkai, just before he passed away.

(וְעַל דֶּרֶךְ הַמְבֹאָר בְּעִנְיָן אֵינִי יוֹדֵעַ בְּאֵיזֶה דֶּרֶךְ כו׳, שֶׁיָּכוֹל לִהְיוֹת דְּבַכֹּחוֹת הַגְּלוּיִים הוּא בְּעֵסֶק הַתּוֹרָה וַעֲבוֹדָה וְעֶצֶם נַפְשׁוֹ הִיא בְּתוֹךְ הַקְּלִפָּה וְהַסִּטְרָא אַחֳרָא כו׳

xi) See footnote of the Rebbe on page 268 ⬅

He was a righteous person and could presume that his soul was about to be taken to heaven and not the opposite. Nevertheless, he worried] that it is possible to serve G-d and learn Torah with the conscious faculties, while the essence of the soul is given over to forces opposed to holiness.

--- **COMMENTARY** ---

Here's how it might be possible to relate to Chapter 2 in a personal way. When we realize that there is a path and lifestyle leading to connection with the One Above, we naturally want to "leave behind" everything familiar, in order to cling to the new lifestyle. Some of us do so slowly, making changes step by step, gradually taking on more *mitzvot* of the Torah, while others insist upon "burning all their bridges" in order to get closer to

Kuntres Ha'Avoda - קונטרס העבודה

Even if we observe with detachment, it can bring negative results from the unconscious essence of our animal soul.

כֵּן הוּא בַּדָּבָר הַזֶּה שֶׁגַּם שֶׁהוּא רָחוֹק מֵרַע בְּפֹעַל מַמָּשׁ וְאַדְּרַבָּא הוּא עוֹשֶׂה טוֹב בְּכֹחוֹתָיו הַגְּלוּיִּים. מִכָּל מָקוֹם עֶצֶם תַּעֲנוּג נַפְשׁוֹ הוּא מֻשְׁקָע וּמְקֻשָּׁר בְּעִנְיַן רַע רַחֲמָנָא לִיצְלָן וְזֹאת הִיא סִבַּת הַמְשִׁיכָה אֶל הַהַבָּטָה וְהַהִסְתַּכְּלוּת) וְהַהַבָּטָה עִם הֱיוֹתָהּ בְּקֹר רוּחַ לִכְאוֹרָה הִנֵּה הִיא עוֹשָׂה רֹשֶׁם וַחֲקִיקָה גְּדוֹלָה בַּנֶּפֶשׁ וְלֹא תַּעֲבֹר בְּלִי הִתְעוֹרְרוּת רַע בְּהִתְגַּלּוּת רַחֲמָנָא לִיצְלָן

xii) See footnote of the Rebbe on page 269

(וְעִנְיַן הַקְּרִירוּת בָּזֶה בֶּאֱמֶת הוּא מֵחֲמַת עֹצֶם טִרְדָּתוֹ בַּהַבָּטָה וְהוּא כֹּחַ הַתַּעֲנוּג הַנֶּעֱלָם שֶׁבְּנַפְשׁוֹ שֶׁבָּא בְּהַרְאִיָּ' וְהַהַבָּטָה וְהִיא כְּמוֹ נְקוּדָּה וּמְקוֹר הָרַע רַחֲמָנָא לִיצְלָן. וְכַנּוֹדָע שֶׁבַּנְּקֻדָּה הַמְּקוֹרִית אֵין בָּזֶה הִתְפַּעֲלוּת בְּהִתְגַּלּוּת) וְהִיא מִתְפַּשֶּׁטֶת וּמוֹצִיאָה לְהִתְגַּלּוּת עֹמֶק הָרַע רַחֲמָנָא לִיצְלָן וְהַשֵּׁם יִתְבָּרֵךְ יִשְׁמְרֵנוּ מִכָּל רַע.

So too here. When we look [even with detachment], we may indeed be far from actually committing a sin, and moreover may actually be doing good. Nevertheless, our deepest, subconscious enjoyment is connected to a corrupt matter, G-d forbid, and that's the [real] reason for the temptation to stare. Our staring, even though seemingly performed with detachment, nevertheless makes a strong impression on our soul, [and this impression] will not dissipate[xii] without arousing us to some kind of evil, G-d forbid.

(The truth is that the detachment [with which we stare] is due to an intense [though subconscious] absorption in the matter. It comes from a hidden need in our soul, which is expressed in looking and staring. This [intense absorption] is like the core and origin of bad — G-d save us — where there is no conscious awareness of excitement.) It then expands and brings the depths of evil to the surface, may the One Above save us from all bad things.

COMMENTARY

the One Above as quickly as possible. But, whether slow or quick, we agree that to the extent our previous lifestyle prevented us from connecting to the One Above, it needs to be left behind. There's a precedent for this in the Torah, in the story of the father of the Jewish people, none other than Abraham himself. After he "found G-d" in Mesopotamia (probably present day Iraq), he was told [Genesis 12:1], "Go on your way, from your land, from your birthplace, and from the house of your father." That is, "leave everything behind." The Chassidic commentaries

Essay on Service of the Heart - Love Like Fire and Water

The Sages tell us [in *Esther Rabbah* 7,10]: "What the righteous see, raises them to greatness." This is what is referred to as "looking at the Glory of the King." This takes place with [great] cleaving of the soul to the infinite light of G-d, may He be blessed, and with the deepest and most sublime enjoyment. The opposite is true in regard to the corrupt forces that are opposed to holiness [*Esther Rabbah* continues: "And what the wicked see, lowers them to *gehinom*."]

וְרַבּוֹתֵינוּ זִכְרוֹנָם לִבְרָכָה אָמְרוּ מַרְאוֹת עֵינֵיהֶם שֶׁל הַצַּדִּיקִים מַעֲלִים אוֹתָם לִגְדֻלָּה וְהוּא עִנְיָן לְאִסְתַּכְּלָא בִּיקָרָא דְּמַלְכָּא בִּבְחִינַת דְּבֵקוּת נַפְשׁוֹ בְּעֶצֶם הַתַּעֲנוּג שֶׁבּוֹ בִּבְחִינַת עַצְמוּת אוֹר אֵין סוֹף בָּרוּךְ הוּא וְהַהֶפֶךְ הוּא בִּלְעֻמַּת זֶה כו'.

We are drawn in the direction of what we observe; therefore, we must control our eyesight and this will bring rest and salvation to the soul.

There is an obligation upon all of us to control ourselves and guard our sense of sight. In so doing we will save our soul from evil, and then our *avoda* of the One Above will be accepted, and we will bring salvation to our soul, and will rise higher and higher...

וְהַחוֹבָה הִיא עַל כָּל אָדָם לְהִתְגַּבֵּר עַל עַצְמוֹ וּלְהַגְדִּיר אֶת עַצְמוֹ בְּחוּשׁ הָרְאִיָּה וּבָזֶה יַצִּיל אֶת נַפְשׁוֹ מִן הָרָע וְאָז תִּהְיֶ' עֲבוֹדָתוֹ רְצוּיָ' וְיִפְעַל יְשׁוּעוֹת בְּנַפְשׁוֹ וְיַעֲלֶה מַעְלָה כו'.

The same holds true for the sense of hearing; we must block our ears from hearing forbidden words, such as boasting and scoffing, and anything that isn't appropriate to hear. As the Sages said [in *Ketubot* 5] commenting on the verse [in Deuteron-

וְכֵן בְּחוּשׁ הַשְּׁמִיעָה אוֹטֵם אָזְנוֹ מִשְּׁמֹעַ דִּבּוּרִים הָאֲמוּרִים כְּמוֹ דִּבְרֵי הוֹלֵלוּת וְלֵיצָנוּת וְכָל דָּבָר שֶׁאֵינוֹ הָגוּן וּכְמוֹ שֶׁאָמְרוּ רַבּוֹתֵינוּ זִכְרוֹנָם לִבְרָכָה בִּכְתֻבּוֹת ד"ה סע"א ע"פ וְיָתֵד תִּהְיֶה לְךָ עַל אֲזֵנֶךָ, וְכֵן גַּם

COMMENTARY

explain that the three things that Abraham was told to leave ("land, birthplace, and house of your father") refer to all that is ingrained and habitual in our behavior. "Land" stands for our physical habits and desires; "birthplace" stands for our inborn genetic personality, and the "house of your father" stands for all that we've learned from our family and environment. So, we needn't be embarrassed or feel a need to explain our desire to run away from a spiritually negative past to a future that is filled with connection to the One Above. (We may want, however, to regulate and modify how we go about it in consultation with our personal rabbi or one who knows us well.) As we are

Kuntres Ha'Avoda - קונטרס העבודה

דְּבָרִים בְּטֵלִים שֶׁגַּם הֵמָּה פּוֹעֲלִים פְּעֻלָּה רָעָה בַּנֶּפֶשׁ וּכְמוֹ שֶׁאָמְרוּ רַבּוֹתֵינוּ זִכְרוֹנָם לִבְרָכָה שָׁם אַל יַשְׁמִיעַ אָדָם לְאָזְנָיו דְּבָרִים בְּטֵלִים מִפְּנֵי שֶׁהֵן נִכְוֹות תְּחִלָּה לָאֵבָרִים, הֲרֵי שֶׁגַּם הֵמָּה כו' לַנֶּפֶשׁ כו'.

omy 23:14], "Make for yourselves a peg on your weapon/ear." [That is, we must be able to plug our ears when we hear something we don't need to hear.] This is true as well of idle talk since it also has a negative effect on the soul, as the Sages said there, "One should not let his ears hear idle talk, because his ears are the first of all the limbs to be 'burned' [that is, they are the most sensitive]." Thus, we see that idle talk can also "burn" the soul.

We must guard our hearing and all forms of speech, as well.

וְכֵן הַהַגְדָּרָה בְּדִבּוּר שֶׁלֹּא יְדַבֵּר דִּבּוּרִים הָאֲסוּרִים כְּמוֹ דִּבּוּרִים הַנַּ"ל וְלָשׁוֹן הָרַע וּרְכִילוּת וּכְהַאי גַּוְונָא וְלֹא דְּבָרִים בְּטֵלִים וְלֹא יַרְחִיב פִּיו וּלְשׁוֹנוֹ בְּשׁוּם דָּבָר. וּבְדֶרֶךְ כְּלָל הוּא מְגֻדָּר בְּכָל הַחוּשִׁים וְהַכֹּחוֹת שֶׁלּוֹ מִפְּנֵי פַּחַד אֱלֹקִים שֶׁעָלָיו. וְהוּא עִנְיַן קַבָּלַת עֹל מַלְכוּת שָׁמַיִם, כִּי הַהִפּוּךְ מִזֶּה

In addition, we must be careful with our speech and refrain from speaking that which is forbidden, such as the kinds of speech mentioned above, and *lashon hara* [negative expressions regarding others] and *rechilut* [gossip], and so forth. Included in this category is "idle talk" and speaking unnecessarily at length. In general, we must be circumspect

---- COMMENTARY ----

doing so, we should be aware that we are either consciously or sub-consciously laying the foundation of all of our future connection with the One Above.

In Torah literature, there are instructions for those who want to attain the "way of Torah." One [Avot 6:4] states: "...eat bread with salt, drink water, and sleep on the ground..." In other words, throw away all that is extraneous, do only that which is necessary to maintain your physical well being, and throw yourself into learning Torah until you have reached your goal. It sounds ascetic, but for the one who is fleeing a spiritually empty past and seeking a direct connection with the One Above, there is no greater comfort. At the same time, though, the Torah prescribes such behavior only until we have formed our personal connection and foundation in service of G-d. The way of Torah is not a way of escape from the physical world. We don't detach ourselves entirely from the world. We have to deal with other people, if only to meet our minimal physical needs. More commonly, after

in how we use our senses and abilities and be mindful to fear G-d. This is the result of "accepting the yoke of heaven," which is the opposite of "throwing off the yoke of heaven." The latter is evidenced by the person who [willfully] follows the whims of his heart in order to satisfy his lust; he may not succeed, but even the lapse that allows him to speak whatever arises in his mind (even if forbidden), or to hear and see everything, constitutes a breach which will lead him [down the road] to complete evil. G-d save him. What leads to such openness

הוּא פְּרִיקַת עוֹל. וְהוּא הַהוֹלֵךְ בִּשְׁרִירוּת לִבּוֹ לְמַלֵּא תַאֲוָתוֹ לְכָל אֲשֶׁר יִרְצֶה. וְלָאו דַּוְקָא בִּדְבַר תַּאֲוָה בְּפֹעַל כִּי אִם גַּם הַפְּתִיחָה בַּחוּשִׁים שֶׁלּוֹ לְדַבֵּר כָּל מַה שֶׁעוֹלֶה עַל רוּחוֹ גַּם דִּבּוּר הָאָסוּר וְכֵן לִשְׁמֹעַ וְלִרְאוֹת הַכֹּל שֶׁהֵן הַשְּׁעָרִים וְהַמְּקוֹרִים הַמְּבִיאִים לִידֵי תַאֲוָה וְלִידֵי רַע גָּמוּר רַחֲמָנָא לִיצְּלָן כנ"ל. וְסִבַּת הַפְּתִיחָה הַזֹּאת הוּא מִפְּנֵי פְּרִיקַת עֹל מַלְכוּת שָׁמַיִם שֶׁהוּא כְּמוֹ חָפְשִׁי לְעַצְמוֹ (בִּלְשׁוֹן אַשְׁכְּנַז זייער פריי בײ זיך, ער פילט קיין

Even the lapse that allows us to speak or to hear and see everything is a breach that leads to evil.

--- COMMENTARY ---

having passed the stage of "acquiring Torah," we have to return to function in a world that is neither supportive nor expressive of Torah values. How must we act then? That is the subject of Chapter 2. Because only when you know how to maintain your inner environment and equilibrium can you start building your spiritual edifice through *hitbonenut*.

In general, while Chapter 1 discusses love of G-d, Chapter 2 discusses fear of G-d. Without a certain level of respect which comes from fear, there is no love. If we don't respect G-d, we won't come to love Him either.

Fear of the One Above starts with three different but related mind-states:

#	Mind-state	Sephira	Experience
1.	Kabbalat ol shamayim "Accepting the yoke of heaven"	Malchut "Sovereignty"	Unconscious attitude of subjugation to the will of G-d
2.	Yirat chait "Fear of sin"	Netzach *"Victory"* Hod *"Thanksgiving"* Yesod *"Foundation"*	Avoidance of occasions of sin out of concern not to transgress the will of G-d
3.	Yirat Elokim "Fear of G-d"	Gevura "Strictness/constriction"	Emotion-based fear of G-d

is the [state of] throwing off the "yoke of heaven," whereupon he feels free to do whatever he [that is, his animal soul] wants, and therefore he does whatever his heart desires.

עוֹל אוּף זִיךְ) וּמִשּׁוּם זֶה יַעֲשֶׂה מַה שֶּׁלִּבּוֹ חָפֵץ.

We're different in our own houses than we are with others, especially when they are more important than we are.

We know that our nature is different when we are in our own house alone, than when we are with others. This is all the more true when those with whom we keep company are more important than we are. Under such circumstances, we restrain ourselves in all respects, thinking carefully about how to use each and every faculty: how to stand, how to sit, and how to speak. But, in our own house alone, we don't give these details any consideration and doesn't hesitate to lounge around and talk about whatever we want.

וּכְמוֹ בְּטֶבַע בְּנֵי אָדָם הֲרֵי אֵינוֹ דּוֹמֶה הָאָדָם כְּמוֹ שֶׁהוּא בְּבֵיתוֹ בִּפְנֵי עַצְמוֹ וּכְמוֹ שֶׁיּוֹשֵׁב עִם אֲחֵרִים וְכָל שֶׁכֵּן עִם גְּדוֹלִים וְטוֹבִים מִמֶּנּוּ שֶׁעוֹצֵר אֶת עַצְמוֹ בְּכָל הַכֹּחוֹת שֶׁלּוֹ וְעַל כֻּלָּם בְּחֶשְׁבּוֹן יָבוֹא אֵיךְ לַעֲמוֹד וְלֵישֵׁב וְאֵיךְ לְדַבֵּר אֲבָל בְּבֵיתוֹ כְּשֶׁהוּא לְעַצְמוֹ לֹא יִתְחַשֵּׁב כְּלָל וְיִשָּׁה עַל צִדּוֹ אוֹ יִשְׁכַּב וִידַבֵּר כְּכָל הָעוֹלֶה עַל רוּחוֹ.

This applies as well to *ruchniyut* [spiritual matters]. When our senses are unguarded and totally open, nothing stops us from looking and staring, and this is because we haven't accepted the "yoke of heaven" upon ourselves. We fail to experience (even in a subconscious way) the yoke of

וְכֵן הוּא בְּרוּחָנִיּוּת הַפְּתִיחָה בְּהַחוּשִׁים שֶׁאֵין מַעֲצוֹר לְרוּחוֹ לִרְאוֹת וּלְהַבִּיט וְכוּ' הוּא מִפְּנֵי שֶׁאֵין עָלָיו עוֹל מַלְכוּת שָׁמַיִם כְּלָל שֶׁאֵינוֹ נִרְגָּשׁ בּוֹ כְּלָל (גַּם לֹא בְּהֶעְלֵם) עוֹל הָאָדוֹן אֲדוֹן כָּל הָאָרֶץ בָּרוּךְ הוּא אֲשֶׁר מְיַחֵד מַלְכוּתוֹ

COMMENTARY

1. KABBALAT OL SHAMAYIM

The first is called "accepting the yoke of heaven" (*kaballat ol shamayim*). This is the state of mind that says, "whatever He says to do, that's what I'll take upon myself to do." This is not a conscious attitude. It's not as if we constantly repeat to ourselves that we are under the command of the One Above. Rather, it is an unconscious attitude to life, and it determines our approach to fulfilling the will of the One Above. If we feel that we are subjects of the King, we will at all times want to do what He wants of us and we will constantly worry that we may be doing

Essay on Service of the Heart - Love Like Fire and Water

the Master of the Universe, Who uniquely bestows His kingship on us, and therefore we do whatever we please. Because of this, we absolutely neglect to fear G-d. That is, we are not upset nor at all concerned that this is against the will of G-d, and that this blemishes our soul, destroying it completely. May He save us.

But, when we have accepted the "yoke of heaven" upon ourselves, we are careful in how we use our senses, like a servant[xiii] who is always discreet because the yoke of his master is upon him. He is neither free nor open because he perpetually feels the yoke of the master. Even when he is physically distant from him [the master], he does not escape from this yoke; he feels it always. He gets accustomed to this yoke, and it isn't burdensome to him at all. He doesn't know any other way of being, as written elsewhere.

So it is, as well, with us when we have accepted the "yoke of heaven."

יִתְבָּרֵךְ עָלֵינוּ בִּפְרָט לָכֵן יַעֲשֶׂה כָּל מַה שֶׁיֶּחְפֹּץ וּמִשּׁוּם זֶה לֹא יָשִׂים פַּחַד אֱלֹקִים נֶגֶד עֵינָיו כְּלָל וּכְלָל, וְהַיְנוּ שֶׁלֹּא יִפֹּל לִבּוֹ וְלֹא יָחוּשׁ כְּלָל עַל שֶׁזֶּהוּ נֶגֶד רְצוֹן ה' וַאֲשֶׁר פּוֹגֵם בְּנִשְׁמָתוֹ לְשַׁחֲתָהּ לְגַמְרֵי רַחֲמָנָא לִצְלָן.

אֲבָל כְּשֶׁיֵּשׁ עָלָיו עוֹל מַלְכוּת שָׁמַיִם הֲרֵי הוּא מֻגְדָּר וּמְכֻוָּץ בְּכָל הַחוּשִׁים שֶׁלּוֹ וּכְמוֹ הָעֶבֶד שֶׁהוּא מְכֻוָּץ תָּמִיד מִפְּנֵי עוֹל הָאָדוֹן שֶׁעָלָיו וְאֵין לוֹ שׁוּם חָפְשִׁיּוּת וּפְתִיחָה בְּעַצְמוֹ (ער איז ניט פריי און ניט אפען ביי זיך נאר שטענדיג פארקוועטשט און ווי פארצאמט) מִפְּנֵי שֶׁנִּרְגָּשׁ בּוֹ תָּמִיד עוֹל הָאָדוֹן, וְגַם כְּשֶׁהוּא מְרֻחָק מִן הָאָדוֹן אֵינוֹ יוֹצֵא מִן הָעֹל הַזֶּה הַנִּרְגָּשׁ בּוֹ תָּמִיד וְהוּא מֻרְגָּל בְּעַל הַזֶּה שֶׁאֵינוֹ כָּבֵד עָלָיו כְּלָל וְאֵינוֹ יוֹדֵעַ אַחֶרֶת כְּלָל וּכְמוֹ שֶׁכָּתוּב בְּמָקוֹם אַחֵר,

וּכְמוֹ כֵן הוּא בְּעוֹל מַלְכוּת שָׁמַיִם שֶׁנִּרְגָּשׁ בּוֹ תָּמִיד שֶׁיֵּשׁ לוֹ אָדוֹן

When we accept the "yoke of heaven," we are careful with our senses, and yet we don't find it burdensome.

xiii) See footnote of the Rebbe on page 269

COMMENTARY

that which the King is opposed to. We won't make a move unless we know that this is what the King wants. It sounds clumsy and difficult, but once we become accustomed to this attitude, we don't find it onerous. Quite the opposite, it lends direction and structure to a life that would be otherwise dominated by ego and lust.

Although not explicitly stated by the text, the unconscious mind-state of accepting the "yoke of heaven" corresponds to the lowest of the ten *sephirot*, or G-dly emanations—*malchut*

We're not conscious of the "yoke of heaven" upon us, but it permeates and influences all of our behavior.

עָלָיו, וְהֶרְגֵּשׁ זֶה אֵינוֹ בְּהִתְגַּלּוּת בְּהַכֹּחוֹת כִּי אִם הֶרְגֵּשׁ נֶעֱלָם שֶׁיֵּשׁ עָלָיו עוֹל הַמְכֻוָּץ אוֹתוֹ וּמַגְדִּיר אוֹתוֹ בְּחוּשִׁים שֶׁלּוֹ לִבְלִי לְהִתְפַּשֵּׁט בָּהֶם נֶגֶד רְצוֹן ה' חַס וְחָלִילָה,

וּכְמוֹ כֵן יְהִי' פַּחַד אֱלֹקִים תָּמִיד לְנֶגֶד עֵינָיו שֶׁיִּרָא לִמְרֹד בְּמֶלֶךְ מַלְכֵי הַמְּלָכִים הַקָּדוֹשׁ בָּרוּךְ הוּא כוּ' (דְּעוֹל מַלְכוּת שָׁמַיִם וְיִרְאַת חֵטְא וְיִרְאַת אֱלֹקִים הַכֹּל א' רַק דְּעוֹל מַלְכוּת שָׁמַיִם הוּא בְּהֶעְלֵם וְיִרְאַת חֵטְא וְיִרְאַת אֱלֹקִים הוּא בְּהִתְגַּלּוּת דְּהַיְנוּ הִתְעוֹרְרוּת גְּלוּיִת בְּהַכֹּחוֹת,

We feel at all times that we have a Master. The feeling isn't conscious but is rather a subconscious awareness of a yoke that inhibits us and guards our senses to prevent us from acting freely in a manner that is opposed to the will of the One Above.

Similarly, the fear of G-d must be with us at all times, so that we are afraid to rebel against the King of Kings, the Holy One Blessed be He. (The "yoke of heaven," "fear of sin," and "fear of G-d" are all one [in their inception]. It's just that the "yoke of heaven" is a subconscious trait, while "fear of sin" and "fear of G-d" are conscious traits. That is, they imply a conscious arousal of the soul-powers [so that we become aware of them].

1.	*Kabbalat ol shamayim* "Accepting the yoke of heaven"	Unconscious attitude of subjugation to the will of G-d
2.	*Yirat chait* "Fear of sin"	Avoidance of occasions of sin out of conscious concern not to transgress the will of G-d
3.	*Yirat Elokim* "Fear of G-d"	Conscious emotion-based fear of G-d

---
COMMENTARY

("sovereignty") — which is characterized by awareness of the reign and kingship of the One Above. When we are in this mind-state, we feel that we have nothing of our own, that our ego is nullified, and that all that is important is that which we receive from the levels of holiness that are beyond ourselves. Therefore, we willingly subjugate ourselves to whatever directions we receive that enable us to connect with the One Above, with the King Himself. This attitude is not conscious, but

Essay on Service of the Heart - Love Like Fire and Water

The "yoke of heaven" acts automatically, as when we become instinctively careful in the use of our senses, as if we don't see and don't hear, and likewise don't experience lust or get angry, all of which results from the "yoke of heaven" which is upon us. And fear [of G-d] is [also] necessary when we need reinforcement in order to guard ourselves. That is, [we are able] to control ourselves by power of the fear and awe of G-d before our eyes. Fear of G-d is more outwardly evident than is fear of sin. That is, it [fear of G-d] implies more G-dly awareness, since it is a result of contemplation of G-dliness as will be explained regarding [the verse in Psalms 33:8] "Let all the earth fear G-d."

Just as we must guard our senses, so must we guard our thoughts. We must not think strange thoughts nor negative thoughts, mindful that we fear G-d. At first, we might assume that strange thoughts and negative reflections are the result of the vulgar earthiness of our natural personality

וְלָכֵן עוֹל מַלְכוּת שָׁמַיִם הוּא מַה שֶּׁפּוֹעֵל בְּדֶרֶךְ מִמֵּילָא, הַיְנוּ שֶׁהוּא מַגְדֵּר מִמֵּילָא בְּהַכֹּחוֹת וְהַחוּשִׁים כְּמוֹ שֶׁאֵינוֹ רוֹאֶה וְאֵינוֹ שׁוֹמֵעַ וכו' וּכְמוֹ כֵן אֵינוֹ מִתְאַוֶּה אוֹ אֵינוֹ כּוֹעֵס מִפְּנֵי עוֹל מַלְכוּת שָׁמַיִם שֶׁעָלָיו וְהַיִּרְאָה הִיא בְּמָקוֹם שֶׁצָּרִיךְ הִתְגַּבְּרוּת לִגְדֹּר אֶת עַצְמוֹ וְהַיְנוּ שֶׁמַּגְדִּיר אֶת עַצְמוֹ מִפְּנֵי הַיִּרְאָה וּפַחַד אֱלֹקִים שֶׁנֶּגֶד עֵינָיו, וְיִרְאַת אֱלֹקִים הִיא בְּהִתְגַּלּוּת יוֹתֵר מִיִּרְאַת חֵטְא, וְהַיְנוּ שֶׁיֵּשׁ בָּזֶה יוֹתֵר הֶרְגֵּשׁ אֱלֹקִי הַבָּא עַל יְדֵי אֵיזֶה הִתְבּוֹנְנוּת בֶּאֱלֹקוּת וּכְמוֹ שֶׁיִּתְבָּאֵר בְּעִנְיַן יִרְאוּ מֵה' כָּל הָאָרֶץ כו').

וּכְמוֹ הַהַגְדָּרָה בַּחוּשִׁים הנ"ל כֵּן הוּא הַהַגְדָּרָה בְּחוּשׁ הַמַּחֲשָׁבָה שֶׁלֹּא לַחְשֹׁב מַחֲשָׁבוֹת זָרוֹת וְלֹא יָבִיא אֶת עַצְמוֹ לִידֵי הִרְהוּר מִפְּנֵי פַּחַד אֱלֹקִים כו'. וְהִנֵּה לִכְאוֹרָה סִבַּת הַמַּחֲשָׁבוֹת זָרוֹת וְהַהִרְהוּרִים רָעִים הוּא מֵחֲמַת מִדּוֹת טִבְעִיִּים

The yoke of heaven is instinctive and unconscious, but we also need to develop conscious fear of G-d in order to successfully control ourselves.

COMMENTARY
---

rather the result of a decision to live a lifestyle under the spiritual umbrella of the One Above.

2. *YIRAT CHAIT*

The second mind-state mentioned in Chapter 2 is called "fear of sin" (*yirat chait*), which is an action-oriented fear. When we are in this mind-state, we take care not to make the wrong move and transgress the will of the King. There is little or no emotion involved with fear of sin. Rather, we are simply aware of the

Kuntres Ha'Avoda - קונטרס העבודה

It is also necessary to control our thoughts, which we do in part by refining our physical desires.

דְּמִפְּנֵי שֶׁמִּתְאַוֶּה בְּלִבּוֹ דְּבַר תַּאֲוָה וְחֶמְדָּה הֲרֵי זֶה עוֹלֶה מִן הַלֵּב אֶל הַמֹּחַ לַחְשֹׁב וּלְהַרְהֵר בָּזֶה, וְכַאֲשֶׁר פּוֹעֵל זִכּוּךְ הַמִּדּוֹת הַטִּבְעִיִּים שֶׁלּוֹ שֶׁאֵינוֹ מִתְאַוֶּה לִדְבָרִים חָמְרִיִּים מִמֵּילָא אֵינָם נוֹפְלִים לוֹ מַחְשָׁבוֹת וְהִרְהוּרִים כו'. וּכְמוֹ שֶׁאָנוּ רוֹאִים בְּחוּשׁ דְּכַאֲשֶׁר פּוֹעֲלִים בַּעֲבוֹדָה הַכְנָעַת הַמִּדּוֹת הַטִּבְעִיִּים יַעֲבֹר מֶשֶׁךְ זְמַן שֶׁלֹּא יִפְּלוּ לוֹ מַחְשָׁבוֹת זָרוֹת כְּלָל, וְכַאֲשֶׁר מִתְרַפִּים בַּעֲבוֹדָה וּמִתְגַּבְּרִים הַמִּדּוֹת בְּחָמְרִיּוּת בָּאִים הַמַּחְשָׁבוֹת הַמְבַלְבְּלִים כו'

(וְהִנֵּה בְּחָמְרִיּוּת הַמִּדּוֹת וְתַאֲוָתָם יֵשׁ כַּמָּה פְּרָטִים וְכָל אֶחָד וְאֶחָד יוֹדֵעַ בְּנַפְשׁוֹ אֵיזֶה עִנְיָן פְּרָטִי מַגִּיעַ לְחֶלְקוֹ לְבָרֵר וּלְזַכֵּךְ, אַךְ בְּדֶרֶךְ כְּלָל הַכֹּל תָּלוּי בְּתַאֲוַת אֲכִילָה וּכְמַאֲמָר' אֵין אֲרִי נוֹהֵם מִתּוֹךְ קֻפָּה שֶׁל תֶּבֶן אֶלָּא מִתּוֹךְ קֻפָּה שֶׁל בָּשָׂר וּכְמַאֲמָר' מְלֵי כְּרֵיסֵי זִינָא בִישָׁא וּכְמוֹ שֶׁכָּתוּב וַיִּשְׁמַן יְשֻׁרוּן כו', וְהִיא

traits. The lusts of our heart for objects of physical desire arise from the heart to the mind and cause us to think about them. But when we refine our natural character, we will no longer lust for gross physical things, and then automatically, strange thoughts will not come to mind either. We will see clearly that when, through [self-improvement] work, we subjugate our natural character, for some time no foreign thoughts will arise to disturb us. But, when we weaken in our efforts and our natural characteristics have an opportunity to regroup, negative ruminations come back to plague us.

(There are several details involved in the coarse physical nature and lusts of our character traits, and we all know in our soul which particular trait we must purify and refine. But, in general, all lusts stem from the lust to eat [gluttony], as the sages said [*Berachot* 32,1], "The lion doesn't roar from a trough of straw, but from a trough of meat," and "A full stomach

COMMENTARY

negative ramifications of violating the will of the One Above, and we therefore try our best to guard ourselves from any thought, speech, or action that would lead to a transgression. This causes us to guard our eyesight, to guard our hearing, and to curtail our speech in order to avoid any kind of situation that would lead to sin. The world we live in is so full of sensory stimulation that by simply walking in a public thoroughfare, we may become overwhelmed by negative images and sensations. The problem here is not only that many of these stimuli are

Essay on Service of the Heart - Love Like Fire and Water

is a form of sin" [Also there]. Also, "Yeshurun became fat and kicked..." [Deuteronomy 32:15] The lust for eating is the source of all negative character traits. Regarding Esau, the Torah says [in Genesis 25:34], "And he ate and drank, and got up and left," and the Sages commented that what he left was his "world" [that is, "his world-to-come," which was promised by the birthright he sold to Jacob in return for food]. It is said as well regarding the rebellious son of the Torah that he is judged according to his end [including all the negative character traits he developed after gluttonous eating and drinking]. The refinement of this negative trait promotes the refinement of all character traits, because its weakening — by refraining from eating in response to this lust — weakens all of the negative character traits.)

הַסִבָּה הַגּוֹרֶמֶת לְכָל הַמִדּוֹת רָעוֹת וּכְמוֹ שֶׁכָּתוּב וַיֹּאכַל וַיֵּשְׁתְּ וַיָּקָם וַיֵּלֶךְ שֶׁיָּצָא מֵעוֹלָמוֹ כו', וּכְמוֹ בֵּן סוֹרֵר וּמוֹרֶה שֶׁנִדּוֹן עַל שֵׁם סוֹפוֹ כו' (וְלָאו דַוְקָא בְּלִיסְטוּת אֶלָּא בְּכָל הַמִדּוֹת רָעוֹת). וְזִכּוּךְ הַמִדָּה הָרָעָה הַזֹּאת הוּא הַמְסַיֵּעַ וְהַמֵּקֵל זִכּוּךְ כָּל הַמִדּוֹת כִּי בַּחֲלִישׁוּת הַמִדָּה הַזֹּאת הַיְנוּ שֶׁאֵינוֹ לְמַלֵּא תַאֲווֹת נַפְשׁוֹ נֶחֱלָשִׁים כָּל הַמִּדּוֹת).

The lust for food is the source of all desires.

But the truth is that [negative] thoughts rise spontaneously from the heart to the mind. They are an extension of the emotions, but by effort to purify our emotions, the negative thoughts automatically cease coming to mind, as mentioned above.

אַךְ הָעִנְיָן הוּא דְמַחְשָׁבוֹת אֵלּוּ הֵן הַבָּאִים מִמֵּילָא מִן הַלֵּב אֶל הַמֹּחַ לְהַרְהֵר שֶׁהֵן הִתְפַּשְׁטוּת הַמִדּוֹת וְעַל יְדֵי הָעֲבוֹדָה וְהַיְגִיעָה שֶׁמְזַכֵּךְ אֶת הַמִדּוֹת מִמֵּילָא אֵינָם נוֹפְלִים הַמַּחְשָׁבוֹת כו' כנ"ל.

The *beinoni* [defined in *Tanya*] is one who hasn't transformed the essence of the powers of his animal

וְלִהְיוֹת שֶׁהַבֵּינוֹנִי הוּא שֶׁאֵינוֹ הוֹפֵךְ מַהוּת הַכֹּחוֹת דְנֶפֶשׁ הַבַּהֲמִית רַק הַהִתְפַּשְׁטוּת שֶׁלוֹ וּבִשְׁעַת הַתְפִלָּה

COMMENTARY
---

not acceptable by any spiritual standard, but that the sheer quantity of stimuli overwhelms our senses. Aside from the obvious spiritual benefits that accrue from circumscribing our sensory input, we simply derive a tremendous peace of mind by censoring most of them and focusing on our own spiritual welfare. This is what the Rebbe means in Chapter 2 when he says that if we will focus our attention on our own "four cubits" (our own sensory locale), we will see salvation.

By refining and purifying our emotions, we minimize our lusts, but even if they recur, the "beinoni" pushes them away with both hands.

הֲרֵי הַנֶּפֶשׁ הַבַּהֲמִית הוּא כְּיָשֵׁן שֶׁהוּא כָּפוּף וּבָטֵל וְאֵינוֹ מִתְאַוֶּה תַּאֲוָה כו', וְכַאֲשֶׁר הָעֲבוֹדָה הִיא כִּדְבָעֵי הֲרֵי זֶה נִמְשָׁךְ זְמַן רַב גַּם אַחַר הַתְּפִלָּה שֶׁהַנֶּפֶשׁ הַבַּהֲמִית נִכְנָע וּבָטֵל כו', וּבִפְרָט בִּשְׁקִידַת הַתְּפִלָּה יוֹם יוֹם יִדְרְשׁוּן כו', אֲבָל לִהְיוֹת שֶׁלֹּא נֶהְפַּךְ לְגַמְרֵי הֲרֵי הוּא חוֹזֵר וְנֵעוֹר וְנוֹפְלִים לוֹ מַחֲשָׁבוֹת זָרוֹת וְהִרְהוּרִים כו', רַק שֶׁאֵינוֹ מְקַבֵּל אֶת הַהִרְהוּר הָרַע בְּרָצוֹן חַס וְחָלִילָה וְדוֹחֲהוּ בִּשְׁתֵּי יָדַיִם וּמֵסִיחַ דַּעְתּוֹ מִיָּד שֶׁנִּזְכָּר שֶׁהוּא הִרְהוּר רַע כו', וּכְמוֹ שֶׁכָּתוּב בְּסֵפֶר שֶׁל בֵּינוֹנִים פי"ב ופכ"ז וכ"ח. אֲבָל כְּשֶׁמְּהַרְהֵר בְּרָצוֹן דְּהַיְנוּ גַּם כְּשֶׁנִּזְכָּר שֶׁהוּא הִרְהוּר רַע הֲרֵי הוּא מְהַרְהֵר בּוֹ בְּרָצוֹן שֶׁזֶּהוּ מִפְּנֵי שֶׁאֵין יִרְאַת אֱלֹקִים בְּלִבּוֹ. וְכֵן כַּאֲשֶׁר מַמְשִׁיךְ עָלָיו הִרְהוּרִים רָעִים מִצַּד הַפְרִיקַת עוֹל בְּהִתְפַּשְּׁטוּת הַחוּשִׁים בִּשְׁמִיעַת דִּבְרֵי הוֹלְלוּת וְלֵיצָנוּת וְכָל שֶׁכֵּן בִּרְאִיָּ' וְהַבָּטָה וּמְחַשֵּׁב וּמְהַרְהֵר בָּזֶה וּמְטַמֵּא אֶת נַפְשׁוֹ רַחֲמָנָא לִיצְלָן בְּהִרְהוּרִים רָעִים בְּשַׁאַט נֶפֶשׁ (וּמִמֵּילָא בָּא לִידֵי טֻמְאָה בְּפֹעַל

soul, but only the manifestations thereof [thought, speech and action]. During prayer, his animal soul — which is subjugated and nullified — is as if "sleeping," having no desires [of its own]. When his prayer is as it should be, this condition lasts for a considerable amount of time afterward, since his animal soul remains subdued and nullified, as "day after day they seek Me" [Isaiah 58:2]. However, since his animal soul hasn't been transformed completely, it regroups and revives once more, and the *beinoni* again is subject to strange thoughts and negative reflections. [But] the *beinoni* refuses to willingly give in and pushes these thoughts away with "both hands." He takes his mind off them completely as soon as he recognizes them for what they are — corrupt thoughts — as described in *Tanya*, chapters 12, 27, and 28. But, if he willingly entertains these thoughts [in which he case he is no longer considered a *beinoni*, but a *rasha*] — meaning that even after he recognizes them for what they are, he continues to indulge in them — it is because the fear of G-d has left his

---

COMMENTARY

If accepting the "yoke of heaven" is associated with the lowest *sephira (malchut*, or "sovereignty"*)*, fear of sin is associated with the somewhat higher (but still low in the hierarchy) *sephirot* of *netzach* ("victory"), *hod* ("thanksgiving") and *yesod* ("foundation"). These are the *sephirot* which guide our actions and instincts, though they do not impart conscious emotion or understanding. However, fear of sin is more than an unconscious

Essay on Service of the Heart - Love Like Fire and Water

heart. And if he purposely draws down upon himself such negative thoughts, it is because he has thrown off the "yoke of heaven." He lets himself hear words of frivolity and mockery and even worse, allows himself to see and stare, think and ponder, and in so doing recklessly contaminate his soul, G-d forbid, with impure thoughts (and then automatically he comes to a state of actual uncleanliness, G-d forbid). This [downslide] cannot be attributed to the gross physicality of his character traits alone, but also to his throwing off the "yoke of heaven," and his lack of fear of G-d. Furthermore, [this decline] causes his soul more harm in that afterward he has unclean thoughts even when he doesn't want them, and to a much greater degree than would be expected. He becomes disgusted with himself, but he is unable to free himself from this situation which is known as "the rule of the wicked," where the wicked plague and contaminate him. This is described at length in *Derech Chaim*[xiv] [a tractate from the second Lubavitcher Rebbe], regarding the verse [Psalms 19:14] "also from the wicked may your servants be shaded."

רַחֲמָנָא לִיצְלָן) אֵין זֶה מִצַּד חָמְרִיּוּת הַמִּדּוֹת לְבַד כִּי אִם מִצַּד פְּרִיקַת עוֹל וְהֶעְדֵּר יִרְאַת אֱלֹקִים. וּבָזֶה עוֹד גּוֹרֵם רַע לְנַפְשׁוֹ שֶׁנּוֹפְלִים לוֹ אַחַר כָּךְ מַחֲשָׁבוֹת וְהִרְהוּרִים רָעִים גַּם כְּשֶׁאֵינוֹ חָפֵץ בָּהֶם וְהַרְבֵּה יוֹתֵר מִכְּפִי הַמִּדָּה עַד שֶׁתִּגְעַל נַפְשׁוֹ בָּהֶם וְאֵינוֹ יָכוֹל לְהָסִירָם בְּשׁוּם אֹפֶן וְהוּא עִנְיָן מֶמְשֶׁלֶת זֵדִים דְּחַיָּיבָא מְבַלְבְּלִים לוֹ וּמְטַמְּאִים אוֹתוֹ רַחֲמָנָא לִיצְלָן וּכְמוֹ שֶׁכָּתוּב בַּאֲרִיכוּת בְּדֶרֶךְ חַיִּים בְּעִנְיָן גַּם מִזֵּדִים חֲשׂךְ עַבְדֶּךָ כו'.

If we entertain or encourage such thoughts, it is because we have thrown off the yoke of heaven.

xiv) See footnote of the Rebbe on page 270 ←

And [it is on account of this phenomenon that we seek to develop] cautiousness of thought based upon accepting the "yoke of heaven." We become very careful regarding anything that would bring us to lowly and impure thoughts, and we develop an intense dislike for such impure reflections. Even when such a reflec-

וּבָזֶה הִיא הַהַגְדָּרָה בַּמַּחֲשָׁבָה מִצַּד קַבָּלַת עוֹל מַלְכוּת שָׁמַיִם שֶׁנִּזְהָר מְאֹד לְנַפְשׁוֹ מִכָּל דָּבָר הַמֵּבִיא לִידֵי הִרְהוּר רַע וְאֵינוֹ חָפֵץ מְאֹד בְּהִרְהוּרִים רָעִים, וְגַם כְּשֶׁנּוֹפֵל לוֹ אֵיזֶה הִרְהוּר הִנֵּה מִיָּד שֶׁנִּזְכָּר שֶׁזֶּה הִרְהוּר רַע דּוֹחֵהוּ בִּשְׁתֵּי יָדַיִם וּמֵסִיחַ דַּעְתּוֹ מִזֶּה לְגַמְרֵי מִצַּד יִרְאַת

───── **COMMENTARY** ─────

attitude — it is an awareness-based approach to serving the One Above. It is a result of our taking upon ourselves the "yoke of heaven," and therefore it is informed by our concern not to transgress G-d's will.

Accepting the yoke of G-d and cultivating fear of sin free us completely from negative thoughts.

אֱלֹקִים שֶׁבְּלִבּוֹ. וְעַל יְדֵי הַקַּבָּלַת עוֹל מַלְכוּת שָׁמַיִם הוּא נִצּוֹל מֵהַרְהוּרִים רָעִים שֶׁאֵינָם נוֹפְלִים לוֹ כְּלָל וּכְמוֹ שֶׁכָּתוּב בְּדֶרֶךְ חַיִּים שָׁם פ״ז שֶׁמִּפְּנֵי הֶאָרַת מַלְכוּת שָׁמַיִם הָאֱלֹקִית בּוֹרְחִים הַקְּלִפּוֹת וּכְמוֹ שֶׁכָּתוּב כְּהִמֵּס דּוֹנַג כוּ׳ יֹאבְדוּ רְשָׁעִים מִפְּנֵי הָאֱלֹקִים.

tion occurs to us [spontaneously], as soon as we recognize it for what it is, we push it away with "both hands," and take our mind off it completely. All of this is as a result of fear of sin in our heart. And once we accept upon ourselves the "yoke of heaven," we are freed from negative thoughts completely; it is written in *Derech Chaim*, chapter 7, that as a result of the light of heavenly kingship, the forces opposed to holiness "run away." As it says [Psalms 68:3], "...like wax melts before fire, the wicked are destroyed in front of G-d."

וְעַל כֵּן יִרְאָה זוֹ דִּבְכְלָלָהּ הוּא עִנְיַן קַבָּלַת עוֹל מַלְכוּת שָׁמַיִם הִיא מֻכְרַחַת לִהְיוֹת בְּכָל אֶחָד וְאֶחָד וְאִי אֶפְשָׁר בִּלְעָדֶיהָ כְּלָל כִּי בְּהֶעְדֵּר זֶה הֲרֵי הוּא פּוֹרֵק עוֹל וַהֲרֵי הוּא עָלוּל לְכָל מִינֵי רַע רַחֲמָנָא לִיצְּלָן כנ״ל. וְלָזֹאת עִנְיַן קַבָּלַת עוֹל מַלְכוּת שָׁמַיִם וְיִרְאַת אֱלֹקִים הֲרֵי זֶה מֻכְרָח לִהְיוֹת בְּכָל אֶחָד וְאֶחָד מַמָּשׁ וְעַל יְדֵי זֶה הוּא סָר מֵרָע, וְנִכְלָל בָּזֶה גַּם כֵּן עִנְיַן וַעֲשֵׂה טוֹב, הַיְנוּ לַעֲשׂוֹת כָּל

Therefore, fear of G-d — which in general is a result of accepting upon ourselves the "yoke of heaven" — must exist in each and every one of us. It is perfectly impossible to serve G-d without it, since in its absence, we throw off the "yoke of heaven," and then we are likely to encounter all kinds of negative circumstances, as mentioned above, G-d forbid. And therefore, acceptance of the "yoke of heaven" and fear of G-d are absolutely necessary prerequisites for every one of us in order to avoid anything bad. Included in this is also "doing good," meaning that we are likewise committed to fulfilling everything commanded

---
COMMENTARY

3. YIRAT ELOKIM

The third and final mind-state mentioned in Chapter 2 is *yirat Elokim* ("fear of G-d"). It is a step higher in the hierarchy than *yirat chait* ("fear of sin"). Whereas fear of sin involves no emotional feeling, but caution regarding how to act and curtail the senses, fear of G-d involves fear of the One Above. It is an emotional form of fear. Thus, it corresponds to the higher emotional *sephira* of *gevura* ("strictness/constriction.")

מַה שֶּׁנִּצְטַוָּה וְזֶה שֶׁכָּתוּב סוֹף דָּבָר כו' אֶת הָאֱלֹקִים יְרָא וְאֶת מִצְוֹתָיו שְׁמֹר כִּי זֶה כָּל הָאָדָם,

[by G-d]. This is what is meant by [the verse in Ecclesiastes 12:13] "in the end... fear G-d and fulfill His commandments, since this is the entire duty of a person."

שֶׁהָעִקָּר הוּא בְּחִינַת הַיִּרְאָה שֶׁעַל יְדֵי זֶה דַּוְקָא הוּא סוּר מֵרָע וַעֲשֵׂה טוֹב בְּפֹעַל מַמָּשׁ כו' (דְּאַהֲבָה הוּא בְּעוֹבְדֵי ה', וְגַם אִם אֵינוֹ עוֹבֵד ה' אֵין זֶה שַׁיָּךְ מִכָּל מָקוֹם לְקִיּוּם הַמִּצְוֹת לָסוּר מֵרָע וַעֲשֵׂה טוֹב בְּפֹעַל רַק שֶׁאֵין לוֹ קֵרוּב וּדְבֵקוּת בֶּאֱלֹקוּת (וְהַיְנוּ שֶׁלֹּא קִיֵּם מִצְוַת וְאָהַבְתָּ) וּמִמֵּילָא מִתְגַּבֵּר בּוֹ הַחָמְרִיּוּת וְגַסּוּת הַנֶּפֶשׁ הַבַּהֲמִית וְעִם הֱיוֹתוֹ מְקַיֵּם תּוֹרָה וּמִצְוֹת הֲרֵי הוּא חָמְרִי וְגַס וְנִתְעָב בִּדְבָרִים מְתֹעָבִים בְּתַאֲווֹת הֶתֵּר כו', וּכְמוֹ כֵן אֵין לוֹ שׁוּם חַיּוּת אֱלֹקִי בְּעֵסֶק הַתּוֹרָה וְקִיּוּם הַמִּצְוֹת

Thus, the crux of the matter is [cultivating] fear [of G-d], since only by means of it can we fulfill the positive and negative *mitzvot* in practice. Love of G-d is developed by servants of G-d [those who serve Him in prayer and meditation]. But, even if we do not fall into this category, it need not affect our fulfillment of the *mitzvot*, neither the positive nor the negative *mitzvot*. However, we will lack closeness to the One Above (meaning that we have not fulfilled the *mitzvah* of "you shall love [G-d]"). In such a situation, [it can be assumed that] the coarse nature of our animal soul will come to the fore, and even though we keep the Torah and its *mitzvot*, we will be earthy, vulgar, and crude as a result of [involvement in] gross matters of permitted pleasures. So also, we will totally lack interest in anything G-dly, such as learning Torah or fulfilling *mitzvot*.

The crux of the matter is fear of G-d since only by this means can we fulfill the mitzvoth properly.

(וְיֵשׁ לוֹמַר דְּזֶהוּ מַה שֶּׁכָּתוּב בְּסֵפֶר שֶׁל בֵּינוֹנִים ח"א פ"ד וּבִלְעָדֶיהָ אֵין לָהֶן קִיּוּם אֲמִתִּי כִּי הַמְקַיְּמָן בֶּאֱמֶת כו', הַיְנוּ שֶׁאֵין לָהֶם חַיּוּת וַהֲרֵי הֵן כְּגוּף בְּלֹא נְשָׁמָה, וְדִקְדּוּקֵי מִצְוֹת הֵן וַדַּאי עַל יְדֵי הָעֲבוֹדָה דַּוְקָא

(It is possible that this is what is meant in *Tanya*, Part 1, chapter 4, "and without it [love of G-d] they [the positive *mitzvot*] are not truly fulfilled, because the one who truly fulfills them... [is one who loves G-d]." The meaning here is that [without love of G-d], the *mitzvot* are without life, like a body without a soul. And furthermore, attention to the fine details of the *mitzvot* certainly comes only from *avoda* [that is, working on ourselves to develop attachment to the One Above], as will be explained in chapter 7. Embellishment

וּכְמשי"ת ל פ"ז, וְכֵן הִדּוּר מִצְוָה הוּא עַל יְדֵי הַחַיּוּת שֶׁבַּמִּצְוָה וְהָעִיקָּר שֶׁבָּהּ)

אֲבָל מִכָּל מָקוֹם אֵינוֹ בְּרַע גָּמוּר חַס וְחָלִילָה וְלֹא יַעֲבוֹר חַס וְחָלִילָה עַל שׁוּם דָּבָר, אֲבָל בְּהֶעְדֵּר הַיִּרְאָה הַנַּ"ל הֲרֵי נַפְשׁוֹ בְּרַע הוּא רַחֲמָנָא לִיצְלָן וְכנ"ל, וְעַל כֵּן הַיִּרְאָה הִיא מֻכְרַחַת וְאִי אֶפְשָׁר לִהְיוֹת בִּלְעָדֶיהָ וְזֶהוּ הַנִּקְרָא יִרְאַת שָׁמַיִם שֶׁהוּא עִנְיַן קַבָּלַת עוֹל מַלְכוּת שָׁמַיִם וְיִרְאַת אֱלֹקִים) וְהִיא הַתְחָלַת הָעֲבוֹדָה וִיסוֹדָהּ

of the *mitzvot*, as well, takes place among those who fulfill the *mitzvot* with energy and care.)

Nevertheless, [though crude] we haven't fallen into completely bad ways, G-d forbid, and we won't transgress anything. But if we lack fear [of G-d], we lower our soul into evil, G-d forbid, as described above. Therefore, fear is a necessary ingredient, and it's impossible to be without it. This is called "fear of heaven," which [includes] acceptance of the "yoke of heaven," and "fear of G-d." It is the beginning of the *avoda* of G-d and its foundation.

We must first go through a stage known as "forget your nation and the house of your father," and this enables us to accept the yoke of heaven and the commandments.

וְכַנּוֹדָע דְּקַבָּלַת עוֹל מַלְכוּת שָׁמַיִם קוֹדֶמֶת לְכָל הַמִּצְוֹת וּכְמַאֲמָר' קַבְּלוּ מַלְכוּתִי וְאַחַר כָּךְ קַבְּלוּ גְּזֵרוֹתַי, וּבִפְרָט בַּעֲבוֹדָה הֲרֵי קֹדֶם כָּל דָּבָר צָרִיךְ לִהְיוֹת שִׁכְחִי עַמֵּךְ וּבֵית אָבִיךְ שֶׁהִיא הַיְצִיאָה מֵעִנְיָנָיו שֶׁהוּא מֻרְגָּל בָּהֶם, דְּהִנֵּה עַיִר פֶּרֶא אָדָם יִוָּלֵד בְּכֹחוֹתָיו וְחוּשָׁיו הַטִּבְעִיִּים שֶׁמֵּהַנֶּפֶשׁ הַבַּהֲמִית דְּאַקְדְּמֵי טַעֲנִיתָא הַמּוֹשֵׁךְ אוֹתוֹ לְכָל עִנְיָנִים הַגּוּפָנִיִּים וְהוּא מִתְרַגֵּל בְּעִנְיָנִים אֵלּוּ וְנִשְׁרָשׁ בָּהֶם וְהַיְנוּ שֶׁהַטִּבְעִית עוֹד מִתְגַּבֶּרֶת בְּמֶשֶׁךְ הַזְּמַן,

It is known that accepting the "yoke of heaven" precedes all of the *mitzvot*, as the Sages said [in Mechilta on Exodus 20:3]: "Accept my sovereignty, and afterward accept my decrees…" Certainly, when we begin the *avoda* of G-d [by establishing a relationship with the One Above], we must go through an initial stage called "forget your nation and the house of your father," which means leaving behind all that we have become habituated to. The truth is that "a person is born like a wild donkey" [as is stated in Job 11:12]. When it comes to our natural senses and the abilities of our animal soul, these have a prior claim on us and draw us toward all kinds of bodily attractions. We become accustomed to them and steeped in them, which means that our natural [animal] souls become even stronger with the passage of time.

וְכָל זֶה מַעֲלִים וּמַסְתִּיר עַל הַכֹּחוֹת דְּנֶפֶשׁ הָאֱלֹקִית שֶׁהוּא עִנְיַן חֲלִישׁוּת

All of this serves to conceal the powers of our divine souls, and this

Essay on Service of the Heart - Love Like Fire and Water

concealment [in turn] leads to the weakening of the divine soul, as is stated [Psalms 31:11] "my strength has left me because of my misdeeds." It is known that the word *avon* ["misdeed"] does not imply an actual transgression, but a crookedness and distortion, as evidenced by the person who bends his path and walks in a circuitous fashion. Such is the path of our animal souls, and it causes a weakening and stumbling of the divine soul, as it is written [in Jeremiah 17: 9], "The heart is crooked, it is Enosh," meaning: "It is weak." [Enosh represents the lowest form of humanity, a form that is weak in serving G-d]. The weakness expresses itself in different ways; there may be no revelation of the powers of the divine soul whatsoever.

(And within this there are distinctions. We may be totally unaware of any divine matter or feeling in our souls, meaning that our spiritual powers have become so hidden that we know nothing but the physical world and everything in it. Or, we may feel that the ultimate purpose of man in this world is not to be like a "horse or mule," but rather to strive for a higher purpose. However, the strong pull of the physical doesn't permit us to forsake our physical concerns and draw close to that higher purpose. Sometimes, we [respond to the call of G-dliness], approaching and working hard on it, but we are still unable to receive it — meaning to grasp and experience it — because our [spiritual] faculties are so hidden that the G-dly

הַנֶּפֶשׁ הָאֱלֹקִית וּכְמוֹ שֶׁכָּתוּב כָּשַׁל בַּעֲוֹנִי כֹּחִי. וְיָדוּעַ דַּעֲוֹן אֵין פֵּרוּשׁוֹ חֵטְא וְעָוֹן בְּפֹעַל מַמָּשׁ כִּי אִם לְשׁוֹן עִוּוּת וְעִקּוּם וְהַיְנוּ שֶׁמְּעַקֵּם דַּרְכּוֹ וְהוֹלֵךְ בְּדֶרֶךְ עֲקַלָּתוֹן שֶׁהוּא דַרְכּוֹ שֶׁל הַנֶּפֶשׁ הַבַּהֲמִית עַל יְדֵי זֶה נִכְשָׁל וְנֶחֱלָשׁ כֹּחוֹ (*) הָאֱלֹקִית, וּכְמוֹ שֶׁכָּתוּב עָקֹב הַלֵּב מִכֹּל וְאָנֻשׁ הוּא פִּי' חַלָּשׁ הוּא כו', וְהַחֲלִישׁוּת הוּא בְּכַמָּה אוֹפַנִּים אִם שֶׁלֹּא יֵשׁ הִתְגַּלּוּת הַכֹּחוֹת דְּנֶפֶשׁ הָאֱלֹקִית כְּלָל

(וּבָזֶה גּוּפָא יֵשׁ חִלּוּקִים אִם שֶׁהוּא בְּהֶסַּח הַדַּעַת לְגַמְרֵי מֵאֵיזֶה עִנְיָן וְהֶרְגֵּשׁ אֱלֹקִי בְּנַפְשׁוֹ, וְהַיְנוּ שֶׁכָּל כָּךְ נִתְעַלְּמוּ כֹּחוֹתָיו הָאֱלֹקִיּוֹת עַד שֶׁאֵינוֹ יוֹדֵעַ דָּבָר אַחֵר בְּעוֹלָמוֹ כִּי אִם הָעוֹלָם הַזֶּה וּמְלוֹאוֹ. אוֹ שֶׁמַּרְגִּישׁ שֶׁאֵין זֶה כָּל הָאָדָם לִחְיוֹת בְּעִנְיְנֵי הָעוֹלָם הַזֶּה כְּסוּס וּכְפֶרֶד כו', רַק תַּכְלִיתוֹ הוּא אֵיזֶה עִנְיָן נַעֲלֶה, אֲבָל הִתְגַּבְּרוּת הַטִּבְעִית אֵינוֹ מֵנִיחַ אוֹתוֹ לַעֲזֹב עִנְיָנָיו הַטִּבְעִיִּים וּלְהִתְקָרֵב אֶל הָעִנְיָן הַנַּעֲלֶה, וְיֵשׁ שֶׁמְּקָרֵב אֶת עַצְמוֹ לְאֵיזֶה עִנְיָן אֱלֹקִי וּמַגִּיעַ אֶת עַצְמוֹ בָּזֶה אֲבָל לֹא יוּכַל לְקַבֵּל הַיְנוּ לְהַשִּׂיג וּלְהַרְגִּישׁ הָעִנְיָן מִפְּנֵי הִתְעַלְּמוּת כֹּחוֹתָיו שֶׁאֵינוֹ מֵאִיר בָּהֶם הָאוֹר. דְּהַנֶּפֶשׁ הָאֱלֹקִית הוּא

Otherwise, our animal soul dominates, hiding and concealing the divine soul inside of us.

light does not penetrate to them. The divine soul is like a polished object, which receives light and reflects it. Therefore, everything G-dly is absorbed by the divine soul, and it shines as a result. However, when there is a thick covering that conceals and hides the divine soul, the G-dly light isn't received. This is what is meant by [the verse in Isaiah 59:2] "but your transgressions [came] between yourselves and your G-d." The deviousness of the animal soul conceals the divine soul and acts as a divider between G-dliness and the [divine] soul, which then fails to become illuminated with G-dly light, as written elsewhere.) Or, there may be a minimal revelation of the soul powers of the divine soul, which is [nonetheless] insufficient to overcome the animal soul and its coarseness.

כְּדָבָר מְלֻטָּשׁ הַמְקַבֵּל בְּתוֹכוֹ אוֹר וּמִתְנוֹצֵץ עַל יְדֵי זֶה, וְעַל כֵּן כָּל עִנְיָן אֱלֹקִי הוּא מִתְקַבֵּל בַּנֶּפֶשׁ הָאֱלֹקִית וְהַנֶּפֶשׁ מְאִירָה עַל יָדוֹ, אֲבָל כַּאֲשֶׁר יֵשׁ מִכְסֶה עַב הַמְכַסֶּה וּמַעֲלִים עַל הַנֶּפֶשׁ הָאֱלֹקִית אֵינוֹ מִתְקַבֵּל בְּתוֹכוֹ הָאוֹר הָאֱלֹקִי, וְזֶה שֶׁכָּתוּב כִּי אִם עֲוֹנוֹתֵיכֶם כוּ' בֵּינֵיכֶם וּבֵין אֱלֹקֵיכֶם כוּ' דְּהָעֲוִיּוּת שֶׁמֵּהַנֶּפֶשׁ הַבַּהֲמִית מַעֲלִים וּמַסְתִּיר עַל הַנֶּפֶשׁ הָאֱלֹקִית וּמַפְסִיק בֵּין הַנְּשָׁמָה וְהָאֱלֹקוּת שֶׁאֵינוֹ מֵאִיר בָּהּ אוֹר אֱלֹקִי כוּ' וּכְמוֹ שֶׁכָּתוּב בְּמָקוֹם אַחֵר) אוֹ שֶׁגַּם בְּהִתְגַּלּוּת קְצָת דְּהַכֹּחוֹת דְּנֶפֶשׁ הָאֱלֹקִית אֵין בִּיכָלְתּוֹ לְהִתְגַּבֵּר עַל הַנֶּפֶשׁ הַבַּהֲמִית וְחָמְרִיּוּתוֹ.

If we desire the "life of the soul," we cannot begin with intellect and meditation; we must first lay the spiritual foundation by accepting the yoke of heaven and leaving behind our coarse physical behavior.

וְעַל כֵּן הֶחָפֵץ בְּחַיֵּי נַפְשׁוֹ לְהָאִיר נַפְשׁוֹ הָאֱלֹקִית בְּאוֹר חַיֵּי הַחַיִּים בַּעֲבוֹדָה שֶׁבַּלֵּב וּלְהִתְגַּבֵּר עַל כֹּחוֹתָיו הַטִּבְעִיִּים לְבָרְרָם וּלְזַכְּכָם, אִי אֶפְשָׁר לוֹ לְהַתְחִיל בַּעֲבוֹדָה שֶׁעַל פִּי טַעַם וָדַעַת, הַיְנוּ בְּהַשָּׂגוֹת אֱלֹקוּת וּבְהִתְעוֹרְרוּת בַּלֵּב כוּ' מֵאַחַר שֶׁאֵינוֹ כְּלִי לָזֶה מִפְּנֵי הִתְעַלְּמוּת הַכֹּחוֹת דְּנֶפֶשׁ הָאֱלֹקִית וְהִתְגַּבְּרוּת הַכֹּחוֹת דְּנֶפֶשׁ הַבַּהֲמִית כנ״ל. וְעַל כֵּן רֵאשִׁית כָּל דָּבָר הוּא לְקַבֵּל עָלָיו עוֹל מַלְכוּת שָׁמַיִם לַעֲזוֹב עִנְיָנָיו שֶׁמְּרֻגָּל בָּהֶם מִצַּד הַטִּבְעִית וְלִתֵּן אֶת עַצְמוֹ לֶאֱלֹקוּת,

Thus, if we desire the life of the soul and want to illuminate our divine soul with the light of the "life of the living" through the service of the heart [which is prayer], and if we wish to master our natural [physical] traits and purify and refine them, we cannot start with *avoda* [meditation] based on logic and intellect. We are not a "vessel" for such G-dly understanding and arousal of the heart, because the faculties of our divine soul are so concealed and our animal soul is so strong, as explained above. Therefore, the first thing we must do is accept upon ourselves the "yoke of heaven," leave behind all that we have become accustomed to as a result of our natural, [physical] nature, and give ourselves over to G-dliness. We must serve the One Above just as a [simple] servant [serves his master].

לַעֲבֹד אוֹתוֹ יִתְבָּרֵךְ בְּכָל מִינֵי עֲבוֹדַת עֶבֶד.

(At first glance, we might think that this "leaving behind" could take place by our controlling ourselves, without accepting the "yoke of heaven." However, in truth, the "leaving behind" must be motivated by the fact that we are forsaking behavior that is opposed to the will of G-d. This will last much longer when it is accompanied by a certain light shining into our hearts, as in the story I once told regarding one of the great [early] Chassidim.[xv] After this Chasid had his first personal audience with the Alter Rebbe [first Lubavitcher Rebbe, the Ba'al HaTanya], he succeeded in reaching a state wherein whatever desires arose from his natural, animal soul, he simply wouldn't do. At a minimum, this ["leaving behind"] should be motivated by a subconscious feeling of accepting the "yoke of heaven.")

(וְלִכְאוֹרָה הֲרֵי הָעֲזִיבָה יְכוֹלָה לִהְיוֹת עַל יְדֵי הִתְגַּבְּרוּת עַל עַצְמוֹ גַּם בְּלִי קַבָּלַת עֹל. אַךְ בֶּאֱמֶת צָרִיךְ לִהְיוֹת הָעֲזִיבָה מִצַּד שֶׁזֶּה נֶגֶד רְצוֹן ה'. וְתִתְקַיֵּם בְּיוֹתֵר כַּאֲשֶׁר הִיא מִצַּד הֶרְגֵּשׁ אֵיזֶה אוֹר בְּנַפְשׁוֹ, וְכַאֲשֶׁר כְּבָר סִפַּרְתִּי מֵאֶחָד מֵהַחֲסִידִים הַגְּדוֹלִים אֲשֶׁר בְּהִכָּנְסָהּ הָרִאשׁוֹנָה לְכ"ק אַדְמוּ"ר וְצוּקְלְלְהָ"ה נ"ע זִי"ע פָּעַל בְּעַצְמוֹ שֶׁכָּל מַה שֶּׁרוֹצֶה מִצַּד הַטִּבְעִי לֹא יַעֲשֶׂה (אַז וואס עֶר וויל זאל עֶר ניט טאן). וּלְכָל הַפָּחוֹת יְהִי' זֶה מֵהֶרְגֵּשׁ הַנֶּעֱלָם דְּקַבָּלַת עֹל מַלְכוּת שָׁמַיִם)

The "leaving behind" will be more effective if accompanied by a sense of spiritual illumination shining in our heart.

xv) See footnote of the Rebbe on page 270 ←

By "leaving behind" [our former habits], we remove the coarseness of the animal soul, such that it no longer conceals the divine soul so much. And by the act of giving ourselves over to G-dliness, we prepare ourselves for the service of the heart with meditation upon G-dly concepts. [Then] the G-dly concepts will be retained and well-integrated in our soul. The light of our divine soul will shine and enable us to master our coarse natural tendencies. It has been explained

וּבַעֲזִיבָה זוֹ נִטַּל הַחָמְרִיּוּת דְּנֶפֶשׁ הַבַּהֲמִית שֶׁאֵינוֹ מַעֲלִים וּמַסְתִּיר כָּל כָּךְ עַל הַנֶּפֶשׁ הָאֱלֹקִית, וְהַנְּתִינָה שֶׁנּוֹתֵן עַצְמוֹ לֶאֱלֹקוּת הִיא הַמַּכְשִׁירָתוֹ אֶל הָעֲבוֹדָה שֶׁבַּלֵּב בְּהַשְׂגָּה וְהִתְבּוֹנְנוּת שֶׁיַּשִּׂיג עִנְיָן אֱלֹקִי וְיִתְקַבֵּל בְּנַפְשׁוֹ הֵיטֵב שֶׁיָּאִיר אוֹר נַפְשׁוֹ הָאֱלֹקִית וְיִתְגַּבֵּר עַל הַחָמְרִיּוּת כוּ' וּכְמוֹ שֶׁכָּתוּב בְּמָקוֹם אַחֵר וְנִזְכָּר גַּם כֵּן לְעֵיל דְּהוֹדָאָה הָרִאשׁוֹנָה בְּאָמְרוֹ מוֹדֶה אֲנִי לְפָנֶיךָ

כו׳ הִיא יְסוֹד הָעֲבוֹדָה דְּכָל הַיּוֹם כֵּן וְיוֹתֵר מִכֵּן הוּא בְּקַבָּלַת עוֹל מַלְכוּת שָׁמַיִם שֶׁזֶּהוּ יְסוֹד כָּל הָעֲבוֹדָה, כִּי הַבִּטּוּל וְהַהַנָּחָה הַזֹּאת מַכְשִׁירָתוֹ לִהְיוֹת מֻכְשָׁר וּמְסֻגָּל לְכָל עֲבוֹדָה הֲיְנוּ לַעֲבוֹדָה בְּמֹחַ וְלֵב וְגַם זֶה יְסוֹד מוּסָד לַעֲבוֹדָה בְּמַדְרֵגוֹת הַיּוֹתֵר נַעֲלוֹת כו׳

elsewhere and was also mentioned previously, that the initial *hoda'ah* ["acknowledgment"] when we [rise in the morning and] say *Modeh Ani* ["I acknowledge the One Above"] is the foundation of *avoda* for the entire day. If so, it is certainly true that accepting the "yoke of heaven," is a foundation of all worship of the One Above, since the self-nullification [associated with this acceptance] prepares us for, and renders us capable of, any type of *avoda* of the One Above, including of the mind and of the heart. It is also a suitable foundation for the highest levels [of *avoda* of the One Above].

וְזֶה שֶׁכָּתוּב זֶה הַשַּׁעַר לַה׳ דְּקַבָּלַת עוֹל מַלְכוּת שָׁמַיִם וְהוּא עִנְיַן הַיִּרְאָה הִיא הַשַּׁעַר וְהַפֶּתַח לַעֲלוֹת אֶל ה׳ כו׳ וּכְמוֹ שֶׁכָּתוּב בְּזֹאת יָבוֹא אַהֲרֹן אֶל הַקֹּדֶשׁ, בְּזֹאת דַּוְקָא בְּחִינַת יִרְאָה תַּתָּאָה דָּא תַּרְעָא לְאִעֲלָאָה לָבוֹא אֶל הַקֹּדֶשׁ פְּנִימָה בְּעִלּוּי אַחַר עִלּוּי כו׳ :

This is what is meant by [the verse in Psalms 118:20] "This is the gate to G-d." Acceptance of the "yoke of heaven," which is fear of G-d, is the gateway and opening to [spiritual] elevation toward G-d, as it says (Leviticus 16:3), "With *this* will Aaron come to the *Kodesh* ["Holy of Holies"].[xvi] *This* refers to the lower level of fear, which is the gate by which we enter and ascend into the inner sanctums of holiness, with one elevation after another.[xvii]

xvi) See footnote of the Rebbe on page 271

xvii) See footnote of the Rebbe on page 271

There are two basic levels of fear and two of love:		
1.	*Yirah Tatah* "Lower fear"	Acceptance of the yoke of heaven; fear of sin; fear of G-d
2.	*Ahavat Olam* "Wordly love"	Love focused on G-d as the life-force of the world
3.	*Ahava Rabba* "Great love"	Love focused on the infinite light of G-d
4.	*Yirah Ila'ah* "Higher fear"	Awe

SYNOPSIS:

There certainly must be fear of G-d as well [as the love mentioned in the first chapter], and [though] quite the opposite [of love], fear is vital. The *avoda* of G-d is impossible without it. [By this] we are referring to the "lower level of fear of G-d" and the acceptance of the "yoke of heaven." As a part of taking on the "yoke of heaven" and of developing "fear of G-d," we must guard all of our senses. This applies to our sight and hearing and speech (and it is explained exactly how crucial it is that we guard our eyesight, and that each and every person is obligated to do so) as well as to our thoughts. We shouldn't willingly and recklessly reflect on impure, negative subjects, in deference to the fear of G-d within us (and by so doing, impure reflections will not occur to us). This level of fear is the beginning and foundation of *avoda* of the One Above (as written in *Tanya*, chapter 41, that it is the start of *avoda* and its core and root). It implies that we must leave behind all that we became accustomed to and submit ourselves entirely to G-dliness...

קִצּוּר.

זֹאת וַדַּאי שֶׁצָּרִיךְ לִהְיוֹת גַּם יִרְאָה, וְאַדְרַבָּא הִיא מֻכְרַחַת וְאִי אֶפְשָׁר לִהְיוֹת בִּלְעָדֶיהָ וְהַיְנוּ בְּחִינַת יִרְאָה תַּתָּאָה וְקַבָּלַת עוֹל מַלְכוּת שָׁמַיִם לְהַגְדִּיר עַצְמוֹ בְּכָל הַחוּשִׁים שֶׁלּוֹ מִצַּד קַבָּלַת עוֹל מַלְכוּת שָׁמַיִם וְיִרְאַת אֱלֹקִים שֶׁבּוֹ, וְהַיְנוּ בְּהַחוּשִׁים דִּרְאִיָּ' וּשְׁמִיעָה וְדִבּוּר (וְנִתְ' אֵיךְ שֶׁהַהַגְדָּרָה בִּרְאִיָּ' נוֹגֵעַ מְאֹד וְכָל אֶחָד וְאֶחָד מְחֻיָּב בָּזֶה) וְכֵן הַהַגְדָּרָה בַּמַּחֲשָׁבוֹת שֶׁלֹּא יְהַרְהֵר הִרְהוּר רַע בְּרָצוֹן וְשִׂאָט נֶפֶשׁ מִצַּד יִרְאַת אֱלֹקִים שֶׁבּוֹ (וְעַל יְדֵי זֶה מִמֵּילָא לֹא יִפְּלוּ לוֹ הִרְהוּרִים רָעִים) וְיִרְאָה זוֹ הִיא הַתְחָלַת הָעֲבוֹדָה וִיסוֹדָהּ (וּכְמוֹ שֶׁכָּתוּב בְּסֵפֶר שֶׁל בֵּינוֹנִים פמ"א שֶׁהִיא רֵאשִׁית הָעֲבוֹדָה וְעִקָּרָהּ וְשָׁרְשָׁהּ) וְהוּא לַעֲזֹב הָרְגִילוּת שֶׁלּוֹ וְלִתֵּן עַצְמוֹ לֶאֱלֹקוּת כוּ':

CHAPTER 3

פרק ג

The lower form of fear of G-d is not part of the avoda of prayer.

אָמְנָם כֵּן הוּא אֲשֶׁר הַיִּרְאָה הִיא מֻכְרַחַת לִהְיוֹת בְּכָל אֶחָד וְאֶחָד מַמָּשׁ מַה שֶׁאִי אֶפְשָׁר לִהְיוֹת כְּלָל בִּלְעֲדֵי זֹאת. אַךְ לֹא זוֹ הִיא הָעֲבוֹדָה דִתְפִלָּה, דְּהִנֵּה בִּכְדֵי לָבוֹא לִבְחִינַת יִרְאָה זוֹ אֵין זֶה עַל יְדֵי הִתְבּוֹנְנוּת בִּתְפִלָּה כִּי אִם יֵשׁ לָזֶה עֵצוֹת מְיֻחָדוֹת לְהַמְשִׁיךְ עָלָיו הַיִּרְאָה, וְהֵן בְּכָל הַיּוֹם תָּמִיד

Although we must all possess [the lower level of] fear since nobody can function without it, it is not the *avoda* of prayer. The way we should try to achieve this [lower level of] fear is not through meditation in prayer, but with specific reminders throughout the day that are intended to draw fear down upon us.

		There are two basic levels of fear and two of love:	
1.	*Yirah Tata'ah* "Lower fear"	Fear of G-d as a consequence of sin	Acceptance of the yoke; fear of sin; fear of G-d
2.	*Ahavat Olam* "Wordly love"	Love of G-d as a consequence of His benevolence	Meditation focused on G-d as the life-force of the world
3.	*Ahava Rabba* "Great love"	Love of G-d based on His transcendent greatness	Meditation focused on the infinite light of the G-d transcending the creation
4.	*Yirah Ila'ah* "Higher fear"	Loss of awareness of self before G-d	Awe

(וְכַנּוֹדַע דְּהִתְבּוֹנְנוּת אִי אֶפְשָׁר לִהְיוֹת בִּתְמִידִיּוּת רַק בְּשָׁעָה דִתְפִלָּה שֶׁצְּרִיכִים לְהַאֲרִיךְ

(It is known that meditation cannot be constant. Rather, it should take place during prayer, since it is then

---
COMMENTARY

CHAPTER 3: FEAR AND LOVE

After we've accepted that without control over the stimuli reaching our mind, we don't have the minimum basis for getting closer to the One Above, it's time to start putting things into practice. That means working on the basic, "entry-level" meditations that lead to fear of G-d (described in detail in this chapter) to be followed by the more time-specific meditations before and during prayer that lead to love of G-d (described in Chapters 4 and 5).

that we can meditate at length, each one of us according to our own level and strength. After prayer, the intellectual grasp and [understanding of G-d achieved through] meditation dissipate. Likewise, the love that was born [and revealed] in our heart as a result of the meditation during prayer goes away. Only an impression is left, as is stated in *Tanya*, section 1, chapter 12 and 13. But the [lower] fear described earlier, together with its accompanying stimuli, must be present at all times; it is not connected to the meditative process, but [consists of] concepts that must remain constantly [pervasive] in our memory.)

בְּהִתְבּוֹנְנוּת כָּל חַד וְחַד לְפוּם שִׁיעוּרָא דִילֵיהּ. וְאַחַר הַתְּפִלָּה מִסְתַּלֶּקֶת הַהַשָּׂגָה וְהַהִתְבּוֹנְנוּת, וְכֵן הָאַהֲבָה הַנּוֹלֶדֶת מֵהַהִתְבּוֹנְנוּת בְּהִתְגַּלּוּת בְּלִבּוֹ הִיא רַק בִּשְׁעַת הַתְּפִלָּה וְאַחַר כָּךְ הִיא חוֹלֶפֶת וְעוֹבֶרֶת וְנִשְׁאָר רַק רְשִׁימוּ לְבַד וּכְמוֹ שֶׁכָּתוּב בְּסֵפֶר שֶׁל בֵּינוֹנִים ח"א פי"ב וי"ג, אֲבָל הַיִּרְאָה הנ"ל וְהָעִנְיָנִים הַמְבִיאִים לָזֶה צְרִיכִים לִהְיוֹת תָּמִיד, לְפִי שֶׁאֵין זֶה עִנְיְנֵי הִתְבּוֹנְנוּת כִּי אִם עִנְיָנִים שֶׁצְּרִיכִים לִהְיוֹת תָּמִיד בְּזִכְרוֹן הָאָדָם)

Lower fear is cultivated by constant reminders of G-d's presence and omniscience.

It is stated in *Tanya*, chapter 42:

And moreover, one should remember...[that] the main thing is regularity, as one must get used to focusing his thought constantly, such that it becomes [etched] permanently in his heart and mind as well, that all that he sees with his eyes [are] the heavens and the earth [that is, the outer garments of G-d]...and in this way he will constantly recall their inner core and life-force...and[xviii]

וּכְמוֹ שֶׁכָּתוּב בְּסֵפֶר שֶׁל בֵּינוֹנִים פמ"ב וְעוֹד זֹאת יִזְכֹּר כו' אֶלָּא הָעִקָּר הוּא הַהֶרְגֵּל לְהַרְגִּיל דַּעְתּוֹ וּמַחְשַׁבְתּוֹ תָּמִיד לִהְיוֹת קָבוּעַ בְּלִבּוֹ וּמוֹחוֹ תָּמִיד אֲשֶׁר כָּל מַה שֶּׁרוֹאֶה

xviii) See footnote of the Rebbe on page 272 ←

─────────── COMMENTARY ───────────

There are two levels of fear, and two levels of love. Each divides into various sub-categories and nuances, but all are subsumed by these four basic levels, as follows:

1.	*Yirah Tata'ah* "Lower fear"	Acceptance of the yoke of heaven; fear of sin; fear of G-d	World of *Asiya* "World of Action"
2.	*Ahavat Olam* "Wordly love"	Love focused on G-d as the life-force of the world	World of *Yetzira* "World of Formation"
3.	*Ahava Rabba* "Great love"	Love focused on the infinite light of G-d	World of *Bria* "World of Creation"
4.	*Yirah Ila'ah* "Higher fear"	Awe	World of *Atzilut* "World of Emanation"

בְּעֵינָיו הַשָּׁמַיִם וְהָאָרֶץ כוּ' וְעַל יְדֵי זֶה יִזְכֹּר תָּמִיד פְּנִימִיּוּתָם וְחִיּוּתָם כוּ' וְגַם לִהְיוֹת לְזִכָּרוֹן תָּמִיד לְשׁוֹן חֲזַ"ל קַבָּלַת עוֹל מַלְכוּת שָׁמַיִם כוּ' וּכְמוֹ כֵן יִזְכֹּר תָּמִיד אֵיךְ שֶׁמֶּלֶךְ מַלְכֵי הַמְּלָכִים הַקָּדוֹשׁ בָּרוּךְ הוּא עוֹמֵד עָלָיו וְרוֹאֶה בְּמַעֲשָׂיו וּבוֹחֵן כִּלְיוֹתָיו וְלִבּוֹ כוּ' וְכָל צְעָדָיו יִסְפֹּר כוּ' וְעַל יְדֵי כָּל זֹאת יָבֹא לִידֵי קַבָּלַת עוֹל מַלְכוּת שָׁמַיִם עָלָיו וִיהִי יִרְאַת אֱלֹקִים בְּלִבּוֹ.

Lower fear of G-d underlies the fulfillment of the commandments.

וְהַיְנוּ שֶׁעַל יְדֵי הַזִּכָּרוֹן בַּמֶּלֶךְ הַקָּדוֹשׁ בָּרוּךְ הוּא עַל יְדֵי כָּל מַה שֶּׁרוֹאֶה בְּעֵינָיו כוּ' וְעַל יְדֵי הַזִּכָּרוֹן תָּמִיד שֶׁמְּיַחֵד מַלְכוּתוֹ עָלֵינוּ כוּ' יַמְשִׁיךְ עָלָיו קַבָּלַת עוֹל מַלְכוּת שָׁמַיִם, וּבַזִּכָּרוֹן שֶׁרוֹאֶה וּמַבִּיט בְּכָל מַעֲשָׂיו כוּ' יַמְשִׁיךְ עָלָיו יִרְאַת אֱלֹקִים כוּ' וְהוּא עִנְיָן תְּמִידִי שֶׁצָּרִיךְ לִהְיוֹת כָּל הַיָּמִים לָרֲבּוֹת כוּ'.

וְעוֹד זֹאת שֶׁהֲרֵי יִרְאָה זֹאת הִיא רַק שֶׁלֹּא לִמְרֹד חַס וְחָלִילָה בְּמֶלֶךְ מַלְכֵי הַמְּלָכִים הַקָּדוֹשׁ בָּרוּךְ הוּא לִהְיוֹת סוּר מֵרַע וַעֲשֵׂה טוֹב בְּפֹעַל. וְעִם הֱיוֹת שֶׁזֶּהוּ עִקָּר וִיסוֹד הַכֹּל, מִכָּל מָקוֹם אֵין זֶה עֲדַיִן עִנְיַן הָעֲבוֹדָה

(וּכְמוֹ שֶׁנִּתְבָּאֵר לְעֵיל פ"ב דְּקִיּוּם הַמִּצְוֹת בְּפֹעַל מַמָּשׁ יָכוֹל לִהְיוֹת גַּם בְּלִי עֲבוֹדָה פְּנִימִית דְּעִנְיָנָהּ הוּא) לְקַשֵּׁר וּלְדַבֵּק נַפְשׁוֹ בֶּאֱלֹקוּת

also he must remember at all times the saying of the Sages regarding accepting the "yoke of heaven" ... he also must remember constantly how at all times the King of Kings stands over him and observes his actions and examines his "kidneys and heart," and all of his steps are counted... and in so doing he will come to accept upon himself the "yoke of heaven," and there will be "fear of G-d" in his heart.

This indicates that by remembering the One Above through everything that we see, and by recalling that He uniquely bestows His sovereignty upon us, we will accept upon ourselves the "yoke of heaven." And by remembering that G-d observes everything we do, we will draw down upon ourselves fear of G-d. This is a constant awareness which must be ongoing during all of our days, including [our nights, as well].

In addition, this [lower level of] fear is only that which is required to prevent us from rebelling against the King of Kings, G-d forbid, and to insure that we actually fulfill the *mitzvot*, both positive and negative. Although it is the foundation underlying everything, fear nonetheless is not in the category of *avoda*.

As explained in Chapter 2, actual fulfillment of the *mitzvot* is not dependent upon inner, [meditative] *avoda* whose objective is to unite our

Essay on Service of the Heart - Love Like Fire and Water

[divine] souls with G-dliness and to refine the physicality and natural coarseness of our animal souls. That objective is associated with prayer, "the service of the heart," as explained in Chapter 1. It is achieved through effort, application of intellect, meditation, and through other means (depending upon whether we are dealing with *ruach* or *neshama*, as explained earlier), all of which constitute the process of prayer.

A clear proof is that we see people who are born such that the "yoke of heaven" and "fear of G-d" are "[written] on their faces." They are careful in how they use all of their senses and are unable to do anything against the will of G-d, since "how is it possible to see or look upon something forbidden, and how can one hear, etc., since this is forbidden." They need not work upon themselves at all to become cautious; rather, they instinctively guard themselves because of the "yoke of heaven" which is upon them. They constantly feel the "yoke of the Master, the One Above," and they are always like a "servant before his master."

This is not the case though regarding love [of G-d]. We don't find that love [of G-d] is in our nature from birth. The reason for this is that love of G-d [comes with] proximity and cleaving to G-dliness. It is the outcome of thorough knowledge

וּלְבָרֵר וּלְזַכֵּךְ אֶת חָמְרִיּוּת וְטִבְעִיּוּת דְּנֶפֶשׁ הַבַּהֲמִית. שֶׁזֶּהוּ עִנְיַן הַתְּפִלָּה וַעֲבוֹדָה שֶׁבַּלֵּב וּכְמוֹ שֶׁנִּתְבָּאֵר לְעֵיל פּ"א, לִהְיוֹת שֶׁכָּל זֶה בָּא עַל יְדֵי עֲבוֹדָה וִיגִיעָה בְּהַשָּׂגָה וְהִתְבּוֹנְנוּת וּבְכַמָּה אוֹפַנִּים שׁוֹנִים (כְּפִי הַמַּדְרֵגוֹת דְּרוּחַ וּנְשָׁמָה שֶׁנִּתְבָּאֵר לְעֵיל) שֶׁהִיא הִיא הָעֲבוֹדָה דִּתְפִלָּה.

וּרְאֵיּ מוּחֶשֶׁת לָזֶה שֶׁהֲרֵי אָנוּ רוֹאִין שֶׁיֵּשׁ בְּנֵי אָדָם שֶׁבְּטֶבַע בְּתוֹלַדְתָּם יֵשׁ בָּהֶם קַבָּלַת עוֹל מַלְכוּת שָׁמַיִם וְיִרְאַת אֱלֹקִים עַל פְּנֵיהֶם שֶׁמַּגְדִּירִים הֵמָּה בְּכָל הַחוּשִׁים שֶׁלָּהֶם וְאֵינָם יְכוֹלִים לַעֲשׂוֹת חַס וְחָלִילָה נֶגֶד רְצוֹן ה', כִּי אֵיךְ יִרְאֶה וְיַבִּיט בְּדָבָר הָאָסוּר וְאֵיךְ יִשְׁמַע כוּ' וּכְהַאי גַּוְונָא הֲלֹא זֶה אָסוּר (מען טאר דאך ניט) וְאֵין צָרִיךְ עַל זֶה שׁוּם יְגִיעָה כְּלָל לְהַגְדִּיר אֶת עַצְמוֹ כִּי אִם הוּא מֻגְדָּר מִמֵּילָא מִפְּנֵי קַבָּלַת עוֹל מַלְכוּת שָׁמַיִם שֶׁעָלָיו שֶׁנִּרְגָּשׁ בּוֹ תָּמִיד עוֹל הָאָדוֹן ה' צְבָאוֹת וְהוּא תָּמִיד כְּעַבְדָּא קַמֵּי מָארֵי כוּ',

We find people who are born with innate "fear of heaven," but not with inborn love of G-d.

מַה שֶּׁאֵין כֵּן בְּאַהֲבָה לֹא מָצִינוּ שֶׁיְּהֵא אוֹהֵב ה' בְּטִבְעוֹ וְתוֹלַדְתּוֹ. וְהוּא לִהְיוֹת כִּי הָאַהֲבָה הִיא הַקֵּרוּב וְהַדְּבֵקוּת בֶּאֱלֹקוּת הַבָּאָה עַל יְדֵי יְדִיעָה פְּרָטִית בְּעִנְיָנֵי אֱלֹקוּת בְּהַשָּׂגָה וְהִתְבּוֹנְנוּת טוֹבָה

וּבְהַעֲמָקַת הַדַּעַת וּכְמוֹ שֶׁכָּתוּב וְיָדַעְתָּ הַיּוֹם וַהֲשֵׁבֹתָ אֶל לְבָבֶךָ כו', וְאֵינוֹ שַׁיָּךְ שֶׁיִּהְיֶה כֵּן מִתּוֹלַדְתּוֹ כִּי אִם תָּלוּי בִּיגִיעָה לֵידַע אֶת ה' וּלְהִתְבּוֹנֵן כו', וְעַל יְדֵי הַהִתְעַסְּקוּת וְהַשְּׁקִידָה בָּזֶה הֲרֵי הוּא הוֹלֵךְ מִמַּדְרֵגָה לְמַדְרֵגָה כו'

[and understanding] of specific concepts associated with G-dliness. It demands intellectual acumen and incisive meditation, together with deep insight, as is written [in Deuteronomy 4:39], "And you shall know today and put it in your heart..." Clearly, we are not born this way. [Love of G-d] is dependent upon effort to [get to] know G-d and upon meditation, upon involvement [in spiritual pursuit] and upon persistence; by doing so, we progress from one level to the next.

We may be born with a natural inclination for the avoda of prayer, but not with natural love of G-d.

רַק זֹאת יָכוֹל לִהְיוֹת שֶׁמִּתּוֹלַדְתּוֹ הוּא מְסֻגָּל לַעֲבוֹדָה שֶׁבַּלֵּב דְּהַיְנוּ מִצַּד מַעֲלַת נִשְׁמָתוֹ שֶׁיֵּשׁ לוֹ חוּשִׁים טוֹבִים בְּעִנְיְנֵי אֱלֹקוּת וּמְקַבֵּל אֶת הָאוֹר כִּי טוֹב וְגַם הַנֶּפֶשׁ הַבַּהֲמִית אֵינוֹ מַחְשִׁיךְ וּמַסְתִּיר עָלָיו. וְעַל כֵּן אֵין צָרִיךְ יְגִיעָה כָּל כָּךְ וַעֲבוֹדָתוֹ הִיא אֲמִתִּית בִּבְחִינַת גִּלּוּי אוֹר מַמָּשׁ בְּנַפְשׁוֹ. וְזֶהוּ רַק שֶׁמְּסֻגָּל לַעֲבוֹדָה, אֲבָל צָרִיךְ עֲבוֹדָה וִיגִיעָה לֵידַע וּלְהַשְׂכִּיל וּלְהָבִין כו'

It is possible, however, that we may be more inclined from birth to the "service of the heart." That is, [we may be blessed with a higher soul-level], granting us a certain talent for thinking about G-dliness and receiving illumination from above. At the same time, our animal soul doesn't darken and obscure [as much]. Therefore, we don't need to invest as much effort [in our *avoda*], yet our *avoda* is honest, with actual revelation of [G-dly] light in our soul. This indicates only that we have superb potential for *avoda*. Nevertheless, we still require labor and effort in order to know, to grasp, and to understand.

אֲבָל לֹא יֻלַּד בְּאַהֲבָה בְּטִבְעוֹ בְּתוֹלַדְתּוֹ, מַה שֶּׁאֵין כֵּן עִנְיַן קַבָּלַת עוֹל מַלְכוּת שָׁמַיִם וְיִרְאַת אֱלֹקִים יוּכַל לִהְיוֹת בְּטִבְעוֹ מִתּוֹלַדְתּוֹ כנ"ל, וְהַיְנוּ מִפְּנֵי שֶׁאֵין זֶה תָּלוּי בְּאֵיזֶה יְדִיעָה פְּרָטִית וּבְהַשָּׂגָה וְהִתְבּוֹנְנוּת כִּי אִם בְּהֶרְגֵּשׁ אֱלֹקִי, שֶׁהָאֱלֹקוּת בִּכְלָל נִרְגָּשׁ בְּנַפְשׁוֹ תָּמִיד שֶׁאֵינוֹ נִשְׁכָּח מִמֶּנּוּ אֲפִלּוּ רֶגַע אֶחָד

In any case, we are not born with a natural love. Acceptance of the "yoke of heaven," and fear of G-d on the other hand, may very well be part of our natural birthright, as mentioned earlier, since they are not dependent upon any detailed knowledge, understanding, or on meditation. They are based solely upon a [pervasive] awareness of G-dliness. In general, G-dliness is constantly felt in our soul, such that it is not forgotten for even a minute.

Essay on Service of the Heart - Love Like Fire and Water

And this, in truth, is an experience of the essence of the infinite light of the One Above, beyond any particular [spiritual] level. But it is hidden, [that is, subconscious]. The truth regarding all levels of love and fear of G-d is that fear is [ultimately] spiritually higher than love. While love is [concerned with] illumination and revelation of G-d's infinite light above (and this is so even on the highest levels of love, as explained elsewhere), fear — even the [lowest] level of *yirah tata'ah* — is concerned with the very "essence" of G-d's infinite light. (However, the higher level of fear, [more properly described as "awe"], corresponds to His essence as it is revealed, while the lower fear corresponds to His essence as it is hidden. And within this distinction, there are sub-categories differentiating between "acceptance of the yoke of heaven" [a subconscious process], as opposed to "fear of sin," and "fear of G-d," which are more conscious, meaning that they entail more [awareness and] G-dly feeling, as explained in Chapter 2. And this is what is meant in *Tanya*, chapter 42, that "in order that it [the "fear of sin"] comes to [a state where it influences actual behavior], one must reveal it ...") Therefore, fear is associated with self-nullification and is on a higher spiritual level than is love.

It is thus understood that those of us who don't feel the "yoke of heaven" upon ourselves, nor the fear of G-d in our soul, from birth — on account of the low level of our

(וְהוּא בֶּאֱמֶת הֶרְגֵּשׁ בְּחִינַת עַצְמוּת אוֹר אֵין סוֹף בָּרוּךְ הוּא שֶׁלְּמַעְלָה מִמַּדְרֵגוֹת פְּרָטִיוֹת. רַק שֶׁהוּא בְּהֶעְלֵם כו'. דְּבֶאֱמֶת בְּאַהֲבָה וְיִרְאָה הִנֵּה בְּכָל הַמַּדְרֵגוֹת שֶׁבָּהֶם הַיִּרְאָה הִיא לְמַעְלָה מֵהָאַהֲבָה, דְּאַהֲבָה הִיא בִּבְחִינַת אוֹרוֹת וְגִלּוּיִם דְּאוֹר אֵין סוֹף בָּרוּךְ הוּא. שֶׁכֵּן הוּא גַם בַּמַּדְרֵגוֹת הַיּוֹתֵר גְּבֹהוֹת וְנַעֲלוֹת שֶׁבָּאַהֲבָה וּכְמוֹ שֶׁכָּתוּב בְּמָקוֹם אַחֵר וְהַיִּרְאָה גַם בְּחִינַת יִרְאָה תַּתָּאָה הִיא בִּבְחִינַת עַצְמוּת אוֹר אֵין סוֹף בָּרוּךְ הוּא (רַק שֶׁיִּרְאָה עִילָּאָה הִיא בִּבְחִינַת גִּלּוּי הָעַצְמוּת וְיִרְאָה תַּתָּאָה בִּבְחִינַת הֶעְלֵם כו'. וְיֵשׁ בָּזֶה גּוּפָא הֶפְרֵשׁ בֵּין קַבָּלַת עוֹל מַלְכוּת שָׁמַיִם לְיִרְאַת חֵטְא וְיִרְאַת אֱלֹקִים שֶׁהֵן בְּהִתְגַּלּוּת יוֹתֵר הַיְנוּ יוֹתֵר בִּבְחִינַת הֶרְגֵּשׁ הָאֱלֹקִי וּכְמוֹ שֶׁנִּתְבָּאֵר לְעֵיל פ"ב. וְזֶה שֶׁכָּתוּב בְּסֵפֶר שֶׁל בֵּינוֹנִים פמ"ב שֶׁכְּדֵי שֶׁתָּבוֹא כו' צָרִיךְ לְגַלּוֹתָהּ כו') וְלָכֵן הַיִּרְאָה בִּכְלָל הִיא בְּחִינַת בִּטּוּל וּלְמַעְלָה מִבְּחִינַת אַהֲבָה כו')

וּמִמֵּילָא מוּבָן דְּמִי שֶׁאֵין בּוֹ קַבָּלַת עוֹל מַלְכוּת שָׁמַיִם וְיִרְאַת אֱלֹקִים מִתּוֹלַדְתּוֹ מִצַּד פְּחִיתוּת נַפְשׁוֹ וּבִפְרָט מִצַּד חֲמָרִיּוּת הַנֶּפֶשׁ הַבַּהֲמִית שֶׁמַּמְשִׁיךְ וּמַסְתִּיר וְצָרִיךְ

On all levels, fear of G-d is higher than love of G-d. We fear G-d Himself, while we what we love is spiritual revelation of His light.

[divine] soul, and in particular because of the coarseness of our animal soul that conceals — need [a lot of] עַל זֶה יְגִיעָה וְעֵצוֹת בְּנַפְשׁוֹ כַנַּ"ל אֵין זֶה עֲבוֹדָה שֶׁבַּלֵּב דִתְפִלָּה. work and advice. However, this [work] is not the "service of the heart" of prayer.

We must cultivate the awareness that nothing is hidden or concealed from G-d.

In *Tanya*, chapter 42, the meditation that leads to fear of G-d is explained at length. It says there that we must labor in thought and delve deeply...for a good hour. It [also] says that there is a type of soul, pure in nature, that "as soon as he meditates..." [he achieves "fear of G-d"]. Certainly, we must understand [intellectually] that nothing can hide or conceal anything from G-d, and that no place is devoid of His Presence, and that the universe is full of His honor. G-d stands over us and observes our deeds, for should not the Creator of the eye Himself be able to see, so to speak? Everything is known and revealed before Him.

וְהִנֵּה בְּסֵפֶר שֶׁל בֵּינוֹנִים פמ"ב מְבֹאָר בַּאֲרִיכוּת הַהִתְבּוֹנְנוּת הַמְבִיאָה לִידֵי יִרְאָה וְכוּ' שָׁם לִיגַּע מַחֲשַׁבְתּוֹ לְהַעֲמִיק כוּ' שָׁעָה גְדוֹלָה כוּ', הֲרֵי כ' שָׁם יֵשׁ נֶפֶשׁ זַכָּה בְּטִבְעָהּ שֶׁמִּיָּד שֶׁמִּתְבּוֹנֶנֶת כוּ', וּבְוַדַּאי שֶׁצָּרִיךְ לִהְיוֹת הַשָּׂגַת הָעִנְיָן אֵיךְ שֶׁאֵין שׁוּם דָּבָר מַעֲלִים וּמַסְתִּיר לְפָנָיו יִתְבָּרֵךְ וְלֵית אֲתַר פָּנוּי מִינֵּיהּ וּמְלֹא כָל הָאָרֶץ כְּבוֹדוֹ שֶׁעוֹמֵד עָלָיו וְרוֹאֶה בְּמַעֲשָׂיו דְּהַיּוֹצֵר עַיִן הֲלֹא יַבִּיט בְּעַצְמוֹ כִּבְיָכוֹל וְהַכֹּל גָּלוּי

COMMENTARY

1. YIRAH TATA'AH

The first and lowest level is that of *yirah tata'ah* ("lower fear"). It includes the three sub-levels discussed in Chapter 2—*kabalat ol shamayim* ("acceptance of the yoke of heaven"), *yirat chait* ("fear of sin"), and *yirat Elokim* ("fear of G-d"). It is chiefly brought about by reminders that the One Above is watching us and aware of our every thought, speech, and action. (There are also other levels of *yirah tata'ah* that don't involve awareness of His attention upon us at all times, as we will see.) *Yirah tata'ah* corresponds to the lowest World of *Asiyah* [as well as the final *hey* of the essential four-letter Name of G-d, and to the *sephira* of *malchut*.]

We already learned in Chapter 2 that the lower level of fear includes *kabbalat ol shamayim* ("accepting the yoke of heaven"), as well *yirat chait* ("fear of sin") and *yirat Elokim* ("fear of G-d"). Acceptance of the "yoke of heaven" is an unconscious attitude that permeates our activities, thoughts, and speech, infusing

Essay on Service of the Heart - Love Like Fire and Water

All of the above [constitutes] a profound intellectual concept, requiring us to meditate at length and concentrate intensely, until fear [of G-d] penetrates our heart.

This means that even the naturally pure soul must occasionally meditate at length in order to establish "fear of G-d" in a revealed state in the heart. This is especially true of those of us who have a lowly soul by nature and birth, and even more so if we have become contaminated by the "sins of our youth." Then the natural fear of G-d is absent. And even when we recall the greatness of the One Above, and how His honor permeates the

וְיָדוּעַ לְפָנָיו יִתְבָּרֵךְ דְּכָל זֹאת הִיא הַשָּׂגָה גְּדוֹלָה וְצָרִיךְ לְהַאֲרִיךְ בָּזֶה וּלְהַעֲמִיק דַּעְתּוֹ בְּחֹזֶק עַד שֶׁתִּקָּבַע הַיִּרְאָה בְּלִבּוֹ

(וְהַיְנוּ שֶׁגַּם נֶפֶשׁ זַכָּה בְּטִבְעָהּ צָרִיךְ לְעִתִּים לְהִתְבּוֹנֵן בָּזֶה בַּאֲרִיכוּת הַהִתְבּוֹנְנוּת בִּכְדֵי שֶׁתִּהְיֶה הַיִּרְאָה בְּהִתְגַּלּוּת בְּלִבּוֹ, וּבִפְרָט מִי שֶׁהוּא נֶפֶשׁ שְׁפָלָה בְּטִבְעָהּ וְתוֹלַדְתָּהּ וּבִפְרָט כְּשֶׁנִּטְמְאָה בְּחַטֹּאות נְעוּרִים כו' שֶׁאֵין בּוֹ בְּחִינַת הַיִּרְאָה בְּטִבְעוֹ. וְגַם כְּשֶׁנִּזְכָּר עַל גְּדֻלַּת ה' וְאֵיךְ שֶׁמְּמַלֵּא כָל הָאָרֶץ כְּבוֹדוֹ (שֶׁזֶּהוּ מַה שֶּׁכָּתוּב שֶׁמִּיָּד שֶׁמִּתְבּוֹנֶנֶת כו' כְּשֶׁיִּתְבּוֹנֵן הָאָדָם כו') אֵינוֹ נוֹפֵל

Even the naturally pure soul must occasionally meditate in order to instill fear of G-d into the heart.

--- **COMMENTARY** ---

them with obedience to a Higher Authority. Fear of sin, on the other hand, is a conscious attitude, in which we develop fear of the One Above based on the fact that He is aware of our every move. It differs from the next level up, fear of G-d, in emphasis. The former (fear of sin) places the emphasis on the fear itself and on avoiding occasions of sin, while the latter (fear of G-d) places the emphasis upon its emotional and spiritual dimension. There is more G-dly awareness in fear of G-d than there is in fear of sin, in which we are more aware of our fear of G-d than of G-d Himself. Both lead to proper fulfillment of the commandments of the Torah. But, while fear of sin leads to enhanced adherence to the negative commandments (those things that the Torah forbids) because of fear of transgression, fear of G-d leads to enhanced fulfillment of all the *mitzvot*, both negative and positive, because they are the commandments of the One Above.

Chapter 3 tells us that there are two sub-categories within fear of G-d that lead to more substantial fear of the One Above (though both are still within the category of *yirah tata'ah* "lower fear"): appreciation of and reverence for His power.

עָלָיו הַיִּרְאָה צָרִיךְ לִיגַּע אֶת עַצְמוֹ בִּיגִיעַת בָּשָׂר וִיגִיעַת נֶפֶשׁ הַמְבֹאָר שָׁם וּלְפִי אֹפֶן פְּחִיתוּתוֹ וְשִׁפְלוּתוֹ כָּךְ צָרִיךְ לִיגַּע עַצְמוֹ בַּיְגִיעָה הַנַּ"ל בְּיוֹתֵר עַד שֶׁתִּתְקַבַּע בְּלִבּוֹ הַיִּרְאָה כוּ')

entire universe (which is what is meant by the statement there [in *Tanya* chapter 42] "as soon as he meditates," and "when one meditates..."), no fear of G-d will come over us. Then we must work on our inner self. This includes the "labor of the body," and the "labor of the soul," as described there [in chapter 42]. And we must work hard at this, in proportion to the lowly nature of our soul, until fear of G-d penetrates our heart.

After fear of G-d has penetrated the heart, only a minimal amount of meditation is necessary to maintain it.

עַד שֶׁיַּסְפִּיק לוֹ אַחַר כָּךְ גַּם מְעַט הַהִתְבּוֹנְנוּת הָיְנוּ מַה שֶּׁנִּזְכָּר כוּ' (וְגַם בְּקַבָּלַת עוֹל מַלְכוּת שָׁמַיִם צָרִיךְ לִהְיוֹת הַהִתְבּוֹנְנוּת בִּגְדֻלַּת אוֹר אֵין סוֹף בָּרוּךְ הוּא דְּאִיהוּ מְמַלֵּא כָּל עָלְמִין וְסוֹבֵב כָּל עָלְמִין כוּ' וְהִנִּיחַ הָעֶלְיוֹנִים וְהַתַּחְתּוֹנִים וּמְיַחֵד

After fear of G-d has penetrated our heart, only a minimal amount of meditation is necessary as a reminder. (Acceptance of the "yoke of heaven" also requires meditation. We must consider the greatness of the infinite light of the One Above — that He permeates and transcends all worlds

─────────── COMMENTARY ───────────

After practicing the contemplation leading to fear of sin because He is "standing over us" and watching our every move, we must also meditate upon the wondrous nature of His creation. When we consider G-d's creation and come to the conclusion that He is omnipotent and almighty, our fear is then no longer of punishment alone. It includes another element — appreciation of His power. If we continue to meditate, going into detail about the wondrous and amazing physical nature of creation, we will deepen our fear even more. That is, when we meditate upon the sheer number of creations, how they differ from one another and yet complement each other, and the variety of shapes and sizes, we will arrive at a tremendous reverence and fear of the One Above and His ability to create. This is the kind of appreciation that a scientist, based upon his research and knowledge of the world, might come to even without knowledge of religion; his broad understanding of creation may bring him to a deep belief and reverence for the One Above that transcends mere fear of G-d's ability to reward and punish. However, even this fear is derived from contemplation of the physical

Essay on Service of the Heart - Love Like Fire and Water

[and the entire universe] and, that nevertheless, He "left behind" [so to speak] both the higher and lower [worlds] in order to bestow His sovereignty upon the Jewish people in general and upon each person in particular, as is written in *Tanya*, chapter 41.)

מַלְכוּתוֹ עַל עַמּוֹ יִשְׂרָאֵל בִּכְלָל וְעָלָיו בִּפְרָט כו' כְּמוֹ שֶׁכָּתוּב שָׁם פמ"א).

It is understood that the most propitious time for this meditation, which brings us to fear G-d, is at the time of [morning] prayer, which is a time of *mochin d'gadlut*, [mature intellectual and spiritual mindfulness]. This is a time that is generally appropriate for intellectual grasp of, and meditation upon, G-dly topics. However, this [meditation leading to fear of G-d] can take place at other times as well. For the meditation upon, and grasp of, how G-d truly permeates the upper and lower worlds and how

וּמוּבָן דְּהַזְּמַן הַמְסֻגָּל בְּיוֹתֵר לְהִתְבּוֹנְנוּת הַנַּ"ל הַמְּבִיאָה לִידֵי יִרְאָה הִיא בְּעֵת הַתְּפִלָּה שֶׁהוּא הַזְּמַן דְּמוֹחִין דְּגַדְלוּת וּמֻכְשָׁר בִּכְלָל לְהַשָּׂגָה וְהִתְבּוֹנְנוּת אֱלֹקִי, אֲבָל מִכָּל מָקוֹם הִיא יְכוֹלָה לִהְיוֹת גַּם שֶׁלֹּא בִּזְמַן הַתְּפִלָּה. דְּהִנֵּה הַשָּׂגָה זוֹ אֵיךְ שֶׁהַקָּדוֹשׁ בָּרוּךְ הוּא מָלֵא מַמָּשׁ אֶת הָעֶלְיוֹנִים וְהַתַּחְתּוֹנִים וּמִמֵּילָא הַכֹּל גָּלוּי וְיָדוּעַ לְפָנָיו יִתְבָּרֵךְ זֶה יָכוֹל לִהְיוֹת בְּכָל עֵת וּבְכָל זְמַן. אָמְנָם מַה שֶּׁנּוֹגֵעַ אֶל

The best time to meditate to achieve fear of G-d is before the morning prayers, but it can take place at other times as well.

─────── **COMMENTARY** ───────

creation (G-d's "garments") and not from the spiritual energy enlivening the creation. It is a more mature and developed form of fear of G-d (the more minor form being appreciation of His power), but nevertheless, it remains in the category of *yirah tata'ah*.

In summary:

	Sub-level of *Yirah*	Focus of Meditation	
Yirah Tata'ah "Lower fear"	Acceptance of the yoke of heaven *(Kaballat Ohl Malchut Shamayim)*	Consideration of the infinite light permeating and transcending creation, but that He "gave it all up" in order to be with the Jews	1.
	Fear of sin *(Yirat chait)*	Awareness of G-d's attention upon us at every moment	2.
	Fear of G-d *(Yirat Elokim)*	Appreciation of G-d's power and omnipotence	3.
		Reverence for G-d's ability to create	4.

What is important is to become aware that G-d sees and understands all of our deeds.

הַיִּרְאָה בִּפְרָט הוּא לִהְיוֹת נִרְגָּשׁ בַּנֶּפֶשׁ אֵיךְ שֶׁצּוֹפֶה וּמַבִּיט כוּ' וּמֵבִין כָּל מַעֲשֵׂהוּ כוּ' הִנֵּה הַרְגֵּשׁ זֶה הוּא בְּנָקֵל לְהַרְגִּישׁ בַּנֶּפֶשׁ גַּם לֹא בִּזְמַן הַמֻּכְשָׁר דִּתְפִלָּה דַּוְקָא, מִשּׁוּם דְּהַרְגֵּשׁ זֶה קָרוֹב מְאֹד בְּכָל אֶחָד וְאֶחָד מִיִּשְׂרָאֵל אֵיךְ דְּלֵית אֲתַר פָּנוּי מִינֵיהּ' וְצוֹפֶה וּמַבִּיט וּמַאֲזִין וּמַקְשִׁיב וּמֵבִין כוּ'

everything is therefore [automatically] revealed and known to Him, can take place at any time. But what is particularly necessary, as far as fear is concerned, is that we be conscious that G-d sees and understands all of our deeds. This feeling is easy to generate in the soul, even at times that are not appropriate for prayer, because it is well within the grasp of each and every Jewish person to become aware that no place is devoid of G-d, and that He is looking, listening, paying attention, and understanding...

(וּמִכָּל מָקוֹם בִּכְדֵי שֶׁיִּהְיֶ' בְּקִיּוּם בְּנַפְשׁוֹ זֶהוּ כַּאֲשֶׁר כְּבָר הָיָ' לוֹ אֵיזֶה פְּעָמִים הִתְעוֹרְרוּת זוֹ בִּתְפִלָּה עַל יְדֵי הִתְבּוֹנְנוּת וְהַרְגֵּשׁ הנ"ל שֶׁעַל יְדֵי זֶה נַעֲשָׂה מֻכְשָׁר בִּכְלָל לְהִתְעוֹרְרוּת יִרְאָה. וְיוּכַל

(However, we will not permanently acquire [fear of G-d] in our soul, until we experience this arousal several times during prayer after meditating and [experiencing] the above feeling. By so doing, we become well-prepared overall for the arousal

---
COMMENTARY

Techniques of meditation leading to fear of G-d differ from those leading to love of G-d. Since lower fear — and especially acceptance of the "yoke of heaven" that is a part of it — forms the foundation of all subsequent connection with G-d, it must be with us at all times. We can't get close to the One Above if we forget to fear and respect Him. If we treated someone we claimed to love with disrespect, we could expect that person to distance himself or herself from us. The same is true of G-d. Although in essence, He is close to all of His creations, nevertheless we wouldn't expect Him to make His love felt where He isn't respected.

Understanding the important of maintaining this lower fear, we might well ask: how do we attain it? The Chassidic literature tells us that it's a little like drilling for oil. All the time that the oil is under the earth's surface, it isn't accessible. But, by drilling (i.e. meditating), we open up the oil field and can thereafter return and access it at any time that we want to or need to. The

of fear [of G-d]. And then afterward, we may arouse this feeling at any time. It is also possible that constant practice will lead to the same result, as written in *Tanya* there, "when one will meditate on this for a long hour every day...").

The general point here is that we may consciously experience "fear of G-d" even without meditation, just by recalling the topics which lead to fear, especially if we have a "pure soul." And even those of us who require meditation (and it's good for

לְהִתְעוֹרֵר אַחַר כָּךְ בְּכָל עֵת כו' וְאֶפְשָׁר יוּכַל לִהְיוֹת כֵּן גַּם כֵּן עַל יְדֵי הַשְּׁקִידָה וּכְמוֹ שֶׁכָּתוּב בְּסֵפֶר שֶׁל בֵּינוֹנִים שָׁם כְּשֶׁיִתְבּוֹנֵן בָּזֶה שָׁעָה גְדוֹלָה בְּכָל יוֹם כו').

(וּכְלָלוּת הָעִנְיָן בָּזֶה דְיִרְאַת אֱלֹקִים יְכוֹלָה לִהְיוֹת בְּהִתְגַּלּוּת גַּם בְּלֹא הִתְבּוֹנְנוּת רַק עַל יְדֵי שֶׁיִזְכּוֹר הָעִנְיָנִים הַמְבִיאִים לִידֵי יִרְאָה וּבִפְרָט בְּנֶפֶשׁ זַכָּה. וְגַם מִי שֶׁצָּרִיךְ לָזֶה הִתְבּוֹנְנוּת (וְכֵן בְּכָל אֶחָד וְאֶחָד

COMMENTARY
---

same applies to true of fear of G-d. There is a reservoir of respect and fear of G-d in every Jewish person. It may be covered over — especially in times of transgression and sin, which conceal and obscure the natural fear of G-d that is deep within us. Even so, by constant and applied meditation, it is possible to pierce the layer of obfuscation surrounding this store of natural fear and reveal it. There are those for whom the natural fear is not so hidden and who therefore don't require a lot of meditation to uncover it. But, there are those for whom the reservoir of natural fear requires a lot of work to reveal. That is why the *Tanya* says that if we do not succeed in revealing it immediately, we must continue working at it until we succeed.

Once we have accessed and revealed our hidden store of fear of G-d, we need no longer establish fixed times for meditating upon it. It becomes an integral part of our life and is readily accessible. We need only remind ourselves of it from time to time in order to achieve this lower fear. After we have done so, fear of G-d becomes an integral part of our approach to life, even if we aren't aware of it.

In this respect, fear of G-d differs from love of G-d, which demands constant and regular meditation. Fear differs from love in that it is not associated with a particular level of G-dliness,

Love of G-d cannot possibly develop without meditation, and this takes place only at the time of prayer.

טוֹב לִהְיוֹת לְעִתִּים הַהִתְבּוֹנְנוּת בְּעִנְיָנִים הַמְּבִיאִים לִידֵי יִרְאָה) יְכוֹלָה לִהְיוֹת הַהִתְבּוֹנְנוּת וְהַהֶרְגֵּשׁ פְּנִימִי בְּזֶה שֶׁלֹּא בִּשְׁעַת הַתְּפִלָּה (וּבְוַדַּאי בִּתְפִלָּה הַזְּמַן מֻכְשָׁר יוֹתֵר) אֲבָל הָאַהֲבָה אִי אֶפְשָׁר שֶׁתִּהְיֶה בְּלִי הִתְבּוֹנְנוּת, וְהַהִתְבּוֹנְנוּת הַמְּבִיאָה לִידֵי אַהֲבָה בִּכְדֵי שֶׁיִּנְחוּ וְיִקָּלְטוּ הָעִנְיָנִים בְּמוֹחוֹ וְיֻרְגַּשׁ בְּמוֹחוֹ וְלִבּוֹ לְהִתְפַּעֵל בָּהֶם בְּאַהֲבָה הוּא בִּזְמַן הַמֻּכְשָׁר דִּתְפִלָּה דַּוְקָא

everyone to occasionally contemplate the topics which lead to fear) can meditate and gain an inner experience of fear outside of the regular time of prayer. (But, certainly the time of prayer is more ideally suited). However, love of G-d cannot possibly develop without meditation. The meditation that brings it about — such that the topics [of meditation] become integrated and absorbed in our intellect, as well as felt in our mind and heart, bringing us to an arousal of love [of G-d] — is only [possible] at the appropriate time of prayer.

———— **COMMENTARY** ————

but rather with G-d Himself. If we fear G-d, we fear G-d Himself, in essence, not as He reveals Himself on some spiritual level. Therefore, once we have revealed the hidden store of fear of G-d within ourselves, we need only remind ourselves from time to time that it exists, and "tap into it," rather than make special efforts every day to meditate upon it.

All this does not apply to love of G-d. The meditation techniques that bring us to love the One Above require daily effort. The best time to meditate on the topics that bring us to the love of G-d is at the beginning of the day before morning prayers. The Chabad technique calls for the meditator to first study a Chassidic text and fully understand it, then meditate upon the concepts found within it, and finally to pray. It helps as well to immerse in the *mikveh* ("ritual pool") and to give some *tzedakah* ("charity") before prayers.

This meditation has as its goal to achieve intellectual grasp of particular spiritual levels, which in turn give birth to a thirst for G-d and a desire to draw closer to Him. The actual drawing closer takes place during prayer. But, because we must train our mind to understand very refined and subtle spiritual concepts — of which only an impression remains for the rest of the day — the meditation must take place and be repeated on a daily

All of this is because fear is associated with the essential infinite light of the One Above. And also the meditation [leading to fear] focuses on high and elevated levels of infinite G-dly illumination, as well as upon how G-d Himself sees and observes, so to speak. Love of G-d, on the other hand, is associated with divine

(וְכָל זֶה הוּא מִפְּנֵי שֶׁהַיִּרְאָה הִיא בִּבְחִינַת עַצְמוּת אוֹר אֵין סוֹף בָּרוּךְ הוּא וְגַם הַהִתְבּוֹנְנוּת הִיא בְּמַדְרֵגוֹת גְּבֹהוֹת וְנַעֲלוֹת בְּאוֹר אֵין סוֹף בָּרוּךְ הוּא וְאֵיךְ שֶׁהוּא רוֹאֶה וּמַבִּיט בְּעַצְמוֹ כִּבְיָכוֹל, וְאַהֲבָה הִיא בִּבְחִינַת אוֹרוֹת וְגִלּוּיִים כו׳) וְעוֹד זֹאת שֶׁאַהֲבָה אֵינָהּ בְּהִתְגַּלּוּת כָּל

--- COMMENTARY ---

basis. It's a little like physical exercise — the more you do it, the easier it gets, and the better you become at it. But if you leave it alone, it leaves you.

2. AHAVAT OLAM

Beyond *yirah tata'ah* is the lower level of love of G-d: *ahavat olam* ("wordly love"). It is the level on which we begin to feel closeness to G-dliness. It also is produced by meditation on the outer "garments" of the Creator — that is, on nature and the universe. But, unlike the lower level of fear (in its more mature manifestation of *yirat Elokim*), love of G-d derives from meditation upon the G-dly energy and life-force enlivening each and every aspect of creation. In this respect, the word *olam* in *ahavat olam* means both "world" and "eternal." Although this love of G-d is derived from the world, it is an eternal and integral part of the Jewish soul, inherited from the world's first lover of G-d, our forefather Abraham. It is activated by meditation on creation, but in essence it is present within us from birth. In its natural form, "worldly love," before it has been fanned into flames of fiery love, is associated with the World of *Yetzira* [and with the *vav* of G-d's Name, and with the six emotional *sephirot* (from *chesed* to *yesod*)].

3. AHAVA RABBA

Higher than *ahavat olam* is *ahava rabba* ("great love"). It is derived from meditation on the source of creative energy — the transcendent light and spiritual illumination from Above. That is, while "wordly love" is derived from focusing upon the life-force that enlivens the world, "great love" comes from illumination and revelation [not with divine essence]. Furthermore, love of G-d is not part of our daily consciousness. During the day, only an impression of the spiritual heights of love — the remnant of our [morning] prayers — remains in our consciousness. Fear of G-d, though, must permeate our consciousness at all times (meaning that the latent fear within us must be revealed). This is brought about by cursory meditation, which constitutes the "recalling" [of His Presence] mentioned above. These two factors are dependent upon one another, as explained earlier. [That is, since fear is associated with His essential infinite light, it is always present and pervasive. It doesn't require a lengthy meditation, but just a reminder. But love of G-d flows from awareness of specific levels of spiritual light and illumination, and thus demands lengthy meditation on those levels at specific times.]

הַיּוֹם רַק רְשִׁימוֹ בִּלְבַד וְהַנִּשְׁאָר מֵהַגַּדְלוּת דִּתְפִלָּה, וְיִרְאָה צְרִיכָה לִהְיוֹת בְּהִתְגַּלּוּת כָּל הַיּוֹם (דְּהַיְנוּ הִתְגַּלּוּת דְּיִרְאָה הַמֻּסְתֶּרֶת כו') עַל יְדֵי שֶׁיִּתְבּוֹנֵן בְּהִתְבּוֹנְנוּת קַלָּה כו' שֶׁהוּא עִנְיַן הַזִּכָּרוֹן כו' כנ"ל וְהָא בְּהָא תַּלְיָא וּכְמוֹ שֶׁנִּתְבָּאֵר לְעֵיל.

In the *Zohar*, part 1, in the introduction, it is stated:

Fear is crucial. [What is fear?] That man should venerate his Master; since He is great and governs, He is the foundation and root of all worlds, and everything before Him is as if it doesn't exist.

וּבְזֹהַ"ק בַּהַקְדָּמָה אִיתָא יִרְאָה דְּאִיהוּ עִיקָרָא לְמִדְחַל ב"נ לְמָארֵי' בְּגִין דְּאִיהוּ רַב וְשַׁלִּיט עִקָּרָא וְשָׁרְשָׁא דְּכָלָא עָלְמִין וְכֹלָא קַמֵּי' כְּלָא חֲשִׁיב,

The *Zohar* is speaking here of veneration of G-d's essential great-

וְהַיְנוּ הַיִּרְאָה מֵעֶצֶם גְּדֻלָּתוֹ יִתְבָּרֵךְ (בְּלִי יְצָרֵף לָזֶה אֵיךְ שֶׁעוֹמֵד עָלָיו)

──── **COMMENTARY** ────

meditation upon the transcendent source of that energy, the infinite light of the One Above. If we are able to access this level of love and energy, we totally transform our being into one of G-dliness, in the process destroying our animal nature. *Ahava rabba* is associated with the World of *Bria* [and the first *hey* of G-d's Name, and the *sephira* of *bina*.]

4. YIRAH ILA'AH

Highest of all is *yirah ila'ah* ("higher fear") — awe. After a certain amount of meditation and contemplation on the infinite

ness (leaving out the additional element of G-d standing over us and observing our deeds). Such an experience of His greatness can take place only at the appropriate time of prayer, as "servants of G-d" can testify.

It would seem then that this is a [higher level of] fear of G-d, more aptly described as "awe," which is an inner feeling of self-abashment in front of Him, as explained in *Tanya*, part 1, chapter 4, and in *Reishit Chochmah*, *Sha'ar Hayirah*, chapter 1. It is the "higher fear" (*yirah ila'ah*) described in *Tanya*, chapter 43, where it says: "but the 'higher fear' — awe — is an inner fear which comes from [wonder at] the deep level of G-dliness which is within the worlds…" And in chapter 41: "and *yirah ila'ah* is fear that is akin to abashment…which is a state of total self-nullification, *ma'h* [nothingness] of the *sephira* of *chochmah*; [this self-nullification is the feeling that] 'everything stands before Him as if it were nothing,' like

וְרוֹאֶה בְּמַעֲשָׂיו כִּי אִם מֵעֹצֶם הַגְּדֻלָּה לְבַד) וְהֶרְגֵּשׁ גְּדֻלָּתוֹ יִתְבָּרֵךְ זֶה יָכוֹל לִהְיוֹת בַּזְּמַן הַמֻּכְשָׁר דִתְפִלָּה דַּוְקָא כַּנִּרְגָּשׁ לְעוֹבְדֵי ה'.

וְנִרְאָה דִּירְאָה זוֹ הִיא בְּחִינַת יִרְאָה פְּנִימִית שֶׁמִּתְבּוֹשֵׁשׁ מִגְּדֻלָּתוֹ יִתְבָּרֵךְ הַמְבֹאֶרֶת בְּסֵפֶר שֶׁל בֵּינוֹנִים ח״א פ״ד וּכְמוֹ כֵן בְּרֵאשִׁית חָכְמָה שַׁעַר הַיִּרְאָה פ״א, וְהַיְנוּ בְּחִינַת יִרְאָה עִילָאָה וּכְמוֹ שֶׁכָּתוּב בְּסֵפֶר שֶׁל בֵּינוֹנִים פמ״ג אַךְ הַיִּרְאָה עִילָאָה יְרֵא בֹשֶׁת וְיִרְאָה פְּנִימִית שֶׁהִיא נִמְשֶׁכֶת מִפְּנִימִיּוּת הָאֱלֹקוּת שֶׁבְּתוֹךְ הָעוֹלָמוֹת כו' ובפמ״א כ' וְיִרְאָה עִילָאָה הוּא יְרֵא בֹשֶׁת כו' שֶׁהוּא בְּחִינַת בִּטּוּל מַמָּשׁ בְּחִינַת מַה דְּחָכְמָה דְּכֹלָּא קַמֵּי' כְּלָא חֲשִׁיבֵי כְּבִטּוּל זִיו הַשֶּׁמֶשׁ בַּשֶּׁמֶשׁ כו' וּכְמוֹ שֶׁכָּתוּב שָׁם בפמ״ג, וּמַדְרֵגָה זוֹ הִיא לְמַעְלָה מֵעִנְיַן הַתְּפִלָּה שֶׁנִּתְבָּאֵר לְעֵיל לְקַשֵּׁר וּלְדַבֵּק נַפְשׁוֹ כו'. וְהוּא בִּשְׁמוֹנֶה

Higher fear, or awe, only takes place at the time of prayer, specifically during the "amida."

COMMENTARY

light of the One Above, we reach a state of *devekut* ("cleaving") where we totally forget ourselves. We realize that in essence there is no one other than G-d. We are in awe of Him, unable even to open our own lips without "permission" from Above. Although technically, *yirah ila'ah* is a form of fear, it is not the lower fear of G-d who has the ability to reward or punish us, or fear of G-d's incredible might and wisdom. Neither is it love of Him, that causes us to be attracted to and transfixed by elevated spiritual levels. It is rather the stunning realization that, without Him, nothing exists. That's why it's called awe.

עֲשָׂרָה שֶׁהוּא עִנְיָן בִּטּוּל בִּמְצִיאוּת מַמָּשׁ וּכְמוֹ שֶׁכָּתוּב בפל"ט בְּעִנְיַן הִשְׁתַּחֲוָאוֹת דִשְׁמוֹנֶה עֶשְׂרֵה כו'.

the nullification of the rays of the sun within the sun." The spiritual level of this experience is beyond that of prayer, which has as its goal the "uniting of the soul with G-dliness," as explained already. It is associated with the *Shmoneh Esreh* [within prayer] during which the person is "nullified in existence" [totally lacking awareness of self], as written in chapter 39 of *Tanya* regarding bowing down during *Shmoneh Esreh*.[25]

There is an inner dimension to "lower fear" of G-d, and that is the reverence that we may develop for G-d's creation and creative power.

וּמַה שֶׁכָּתוּב יִרְאוּ מֵה' כָּל הָאָרֶץ כו' כִּי הוּא אָמַר וַיֶּהִי כו' הִנֵּה עַל פִּי פָּשׁוּט הִיא הַיִּרְאָה מִבְּחִינַת יְכָלְתּוֹ יִתְבָּרֵךְ שֶׁהוּא בּוֹרֵא הָעוֹלָם וּמְחַיֵּה אוֹתוֹ וּבִיכָלְתּוֹ יִתְבָּרֵךְ לַעֲשׂוֹת הַכֹּל אַיִן וָאֶפֶס חַס וְחָלִילָה וּבִפְרָט שֶׁמָּא יִגְרֹם הַחֵטְא כו' וּכְעִנְיָן שֶׁכָּתוּב בְּרֵאשִׁית חָכְמָה שַׁעַר הַיִּ"רֵאָה פ"ג בִּבְחִינַת ב' וְג'. אָמְנָם פְּנִימִיּוּת הָעִנְיָן בָּזֶה הוּא הַיִּרְאָה מִגְּדֻלַּת ה' בִּבְרִיאַת וְהִתְהַוּוּת הָעוֹלָמוֹת, דְהִתְהַוּוּת יֵשׁ מֵאַיִן הוּא עִנְיָן נִפְלָא מְאֹד וּכְמוֹ שֶׁכָּתוּב בְּמָקוֹם אַחֵר וּמוֹרֶה עַל עֹצֶם גְּדֻלָּתוֹ יִתְ', וּמִכָּל מָקוֹם יִרְאָה זוֹ הִיא בְּחִינַת יִרְאָה חִיצוֹנִי' שֶׁהֲרֵי אוֹמֵר עַל זֶה יִרְאוּ

And as for the fear mentioned in the verse [from Psalms 33:8-9] — "Let them fear G-d, all the earth...because He spoke and it came to be..." — the simple meaning is that it refers to fear of G-d's omnipotence. Since He created the universe and enlivens it and has within His power to return it to nothingness — and especially because our sins could bring this about, G-d forbid, as is written in *Reishit Chochma, Sha'ar Hayirah*, chapter 3, regarding the second and third levels — [we should fear Him]. However, the inner dimension of this [type of] fear is reverence of His ability to create the universe and worlds. Creation *ex nihilo* (something "from

---

COMMENTARY

Chapter 3 touches briefly on the subject of *yirah ila'ah*, telling us that this level of fear is predicated on the very elevated state of self-nullification known as *bitul b'metziut* ("nullification of existence.") While the lower level of *yirah tata'ah* necessitate only nullification of the ego, but not total negation of self, the higher level of *yirah ila'ah* which leads to awe necessitates that we totally forget our own being. While the lower level lays the foundation and basis for G-dliness as experienced in prayer, the higher level is beyond prayer. It is associated with the *Amida* in which we ask G-d to "open our mouths" because we don't have the ability

Essay on Service of the Heart - Love Like Fire and Water

nothing") is an amazing and wondrous process,[xix] as written elsewhere, and is one indication of the mighty power of the One Above. Nevertheless, this reverence is only external, which is why the literal translation of the [above] verse reads, "let them fear *from* G-d" [in Hebrew, *yiru mei HaShem*]. This is referring to the lower level of fear, as is known[xx] regarding the difference between "fear G-d" [*yiru mei HaShem*] and "fear G-d Himself [*yiru et HaShem*]."[26]

מַה' שֶׁזֶּהוּ יִרְאָה תַּתָּאָה, וְכַנּוֹדָע הַהֶפְרֵשׁ בֵּין יִרְאוּ מַה' לְיִרְאוּ אֶת ה' כו',

xix) See footnote of the Rebbe on page 272

xx) See footnote of the Rebbe on page 274

"Fear of [lit. from] G-d" is considered superficial because it only concerns that which is known and experienced of His greatness in creating the worlds. This is the knowledge that comes about by [meditation upon] His "outer garments," so to speak. Included in this category is meditation on the greatness of G-d in creating such a multitude of creatures in the physical world — that is, the mineral, vegetable, animal, and human kingdoms. [It includes also contemplation on how] He created separate species without limit and measure, and how each one of them draws

וְהַיְנוּ לְפִי שֶׁזֶּהוּ מַה שֶׁנּוֹדַע וְנִרְגָּשׁ גְּדֻלָּתוֹ יִתְבָּרֵךְ מֵהִתְהַוּוּת הָעוֹלָמוֹת דְּהַיְנוּ הַיְדִיעָה עַל יְדֵי לְבוּשִׁים כו'. וּבִכְלָל זֶה גַּם כֵּן הַהִתְבּוֹנְנוּת בִּגְדֻלָּתוֹ יִתְבָּרֵךְ בְּרִבּוּי הַהִתְהַוּוּת לְמַטָּה בְּדוֹמֵם צוֹמֵחַ חַי וּמְדַבֵּר מִינִים מִמִּינִים שׁוֹנִים עַד אֵין קֵץ וְשִׁעוּר וּלְכֻלָּם נִמְשָׁךְ חַיּוּת מְיֻחָד וּפְרָטִי לְפִי מִזְגּוֹ וּתְכוּנָתוֹ, וְכֵן בִּצְבָא מַעֲלָה בְּרִבּוּי יוֹתֵר עַד אֵין שִׁעוּר כו' וּבִגְדוֹלוֹת הַנִּבְרָאִים כו' וּבְרִבּוּי הַהִשְׁתַּלְשְׁלוּת וּבְרִבּוּי עוֹלָמוֹת עַד אֵין מִסְפָּר כו' וְהוּא עִנְיָן מָה רַבּוּ מַעֲשֶׂיךָ וּמָה גָּדְלוּ מַעֲשֶׂיךָ כו'

Reverence is developed by contemplation of the variety, size and number of creatures.

upon a specific spiritual energy that enlivens it, each according to its nature. The same is true concerning the heavenly hosts, of which there are a tremendous variety and number, [literally] "without number." There is also the huge size and mass of the creations. Then there are also the multiple levels of spiritual devolution and innumerable worlds that He created. All of this is implied by the verses [in Psalms 104:24 and Psalms 92:6], "how many are Your works... how great are Your works...[xxi]" ["many' referring to variety, and "great" referring to size]. In general, all of this is [also]

xxi) See footnote of the Rebbe on page 276

COMMENTARY

to speak of our own volition. However, it is not part of the meditative process that is associated with prayer. Rather, it is the result of all of the effort that we invested in prayer, but it is not part of the process itself.

Reverence is still in the category of "lower fear" because it comes from contemplation of the "garments" of creation. It leads to greater fulfillment of the mitzvoth.

וּכְלָלוּת הָעִנְיָן הוּא מַה שֶּׁכָּתוּב גָּדוֹל ה' וּמְהֻלָּל מְאֹד כוּ' וּכְמוֹ שֶׁכָּתוּב בְּמָקוֹם אַחֵר,

וְהַיִּרְאָה הַבָּאָה מִזֶּה עִם הֱיוֹת שֶׁהִיא לְמַעְלָה (בְּעִנְיַן הַהִתְגַּלּוּ') מֵהַיִּרְאָה הַבָּאָה מֵהַהִתְבּוֹנְנוּת דְּהַקָּדוֹשׁ בָּרוּךְ הוּא עוֹמֵד עָלָיו וְרוֹאֶה בְּמַעֲשָׂיו כוּ' מִכָּל מָקוֹם הִיא גַם כֵּן בִּכְלַל יִרְאַת אֱלֹקִים הַנּוֹגֵעַ לַמַּעֲשֶׂה לְבַד, וְהִיא הַיִּרְאָה הַמְבֹאֶרֶת בְּסֵפֶר שֶׁל בֵּינוֹנִים רפמ"ג. וְהִיא בְּחִינַת הַגַּדְלוּת דְּיִרְאַת אֱלֹקִים כוּ', דְּבְדֶרֶךְ כְּלָל עִנְיַן יִרְאַת אֱלֹקִים הוּא שֶׁהַיִּרְאָה הִיא בְּהִתְגַּלּוּת וְלָכֵן יִרְאַת אֱלֹקִים הִיא לְקִיּוּם הַמִּצְוֹת בִּכְלָל, דְּיִרְאַת חֵטְא עִקָּרָהּ הוּא לָסוּר מֵרָע וּכְמוֹ שֶׁכָּתוּב בְּהַקְדָּמַת דֶּרֶךְ חַיִּים וּכְמוֹ שֶׁכָּתוּב בְּסֵפֶר שֶׁל בֵּינוֹנִים תּוֹךְ פמ"ב בִּבְחִינַת יִרְאַת חֵטְא לִהְיוֹת סוּר מֵרָע כוּ' וְיִרְאַת אֱלֹקִים הִיא לְקִיּוּם הַמִּצְוֹת בִּכְלָל הַיְנוּ לִשְׁמֹר מִצְוֹתָיו יִתְבָּרֵךְ מִצַּד יִרְאַת אֱלֹקִים וּכְמוֹ שֶׁכָּתוּב אֶת הָאֱלֹקִים יְרָא וְאֶת מִצְוֹתָיו שְׁמֹר הֵן בְּסוּר מֵרָע וְהֵן בַּעֲשֵׂה טוֹב. וּבֶאֱמֶת הֲרֵי הֶעְדֵּר דְּוַעֲשֵׂה טוֹב חַס וְחָלִילָה הוּא גַם כֵּן חֵטְא וְעָווֹן וְאִם כֵּן הֲרֵי זֶה נִכְלָל גַּם כֵּן בִּכְלַל יִרְאַת חֵטְא (וְהַיְנוּ דְּיִרְאַת חֵטְא מֵאַנְטְ אוֹיף גַּם כֵּן קִיּוּם הַמִּצְוֹת בַּעֲשֵׂה

implied in the verse [in Psalms 48:2, 96:4, 145:3], "Great is G-d and very praiseworthy," as written elsewhere.

While the reverence derived from this meditation is higher (in our conscious awareness) than the fear derived from meditation on how G-d stands over us and observes all our deeds, it is, nevertheless, also in the category of fear leading merely to the fulfillment of the *mitzvot*. This is the fear that is explained in the beginning of chapter 43 of *Tanya*, and it is a more mature and developed dimension of [lower] fear of G-d. In general, fear is a conscious attitude that aids in our overall fulfillment of the *mitzvot*. Fear of sin aids specifically with *sur mei'rah* ["refraining from evil"], as is written in the introduction to *Derech Chaim* and as explained in chapter 42 of *Tanya*: "fear of sin helps one refrain from evil." But fear of G-d leads to overall fulfillment of the *mitzvot*, that is, fulfillment of [all of] His commandments due to fear of G-d, as is written [in Ecclesiastes 12:13]: "Fear G-d and keep His commandments" meaning both negative and positive commandments alike. In truth, failure to fulfill a positive *mitzvah* is also a transgression, and so fulfillment of the positive *mitzvot* is also motivated by fear of sin. The difference is that fulfillment of the

---

COMMENTARY

Yirah ila'ah is associated with the World of *Atzilut* [and with the *yud* of G-d's Name, and with the *sephira* of *chochma*].

Essay on Service of the Heart - Love Like Fire and Water

טוב) רַק הַהֶפְרֵשׁ בָּזֶה דְּיִרְאַת חֵטְא הוּא שֶׁקִּיּוּם הַמִּצְווֹת הוּא מִצַּד יִרְאַת הַחֵטְא וְאֵינוֹ נִרְגָּשׁ בָּזֶה כָּל כָּךְ הָאֱלֹקוּת וְשֶׁהֵן מִצְוֹתָיו יִתְ', וְיִרְאַת אֱלֹקִים הוּא שֶׁקִּיּוּם הַמִּצְווֹת הוּא מִצַּד הַיִּרְאָה שֶׁבּוֹ הַיְנוּ מִצַּד יִרְאַת הָאֱלֹקִי' שֶׁבּוֹ שֶׁנִּרְגָּשׁ בּוֹ יוֹתֵר הָאֱלֹקוּת וְשֶׁהֵן מִצְוֹתָיו יִתְבָּרֵךְ וְעַל כֵּן הוּא שׁוֹמֵר כָּל מִצְוֹתָיו מִצַּד הַיִּרְאָה הָאֱלֹקִית שֶׁבּוֹ. וְזֶהוּ דִּירָא אֱלֹקִים הוּא שֶׁהַיִּרְאָה הִיא בְּהִתְגַּלּוּת יוֹתֵר מִבְּיִרְאַת חֵטְא לִהְיוֹת שֶׁהִיא יִרְאָה אֱלֹקִית.

mitzvot because of fear of sin is equivalent to motivation derived from the fear of transgression alone, and we don't feel so much of the G-dliness of the *mitzvot* — that they are G-d's commandments. But fear of G-d motivates us to fulfill the *mitzvot* because of our own [inner] fear. That is, our fear of G-d induces in us a greater sense of G-dliness, as well as awareness that these are G-d's commandments, and therefore we [are motivated to] fulfill them on account of our fear of G-d. Thus fear of G-d is a more conscious experience than fear of sin, since it implies fear [not only of transgression, but] of the One Above.

(וּמִכָּל מָקוֹם גַּם יִרְאַת חֵטְא הִיא בִּבְחִינַת הִתְגַּלּוּת לְגַבֵּי קַבָּלַת עוֹל מַלְכוּת שָׁמַיִם שֶׁהוּא בְּהֶעְלֵם (וְהִיא, רְצוֹנוֹ לוֹמַר קַבָּלַת עוֹל מַלְכוּת שָׁמַיִם, הִיא גַּם כֵּן לְקִיּוּם הַמִּצְווֹת בִּכְלָל, וְעוֹד זֹאת יְתֵרָה שֶׁפּוֹעֵל עָלָיו בְּכָל תְּנוּעוֹתָיו בִּפְרָט וְהוּא עִנְיַן הַהַגְדָּרָה הנ״ל הַבָּאָה בְּדֶרֶךְ מִמֵּילָא, רַק שֶׁהִיא פְּעֻלָּה נֶעֱלֶמֶת בַּנֶּפֶשׁ) וּבְיִרְאַת חֵטְא הֲרֵי יֵשׁ כָּאן יִרְאָה בְּהִתְגַּלּוּת וּמִכָּל מָקוֹם אֵינוֹ דּוֹמֶה לְהִתְגַּלּוּת שֶׁבְּיִרְאַת

(Nonetheless, even fear of sin is a more conscious experience than accepting the "yoke of heaven," which is a subconscious event and also an aid in keeping *all* of the *mitzvot* [like fear of G-d, as explained above]. Furthermore, it causes us to become careful and guarded in all of our movements. This is the wariness of the senses described earlier that comes about spontaneously, albeit through hidden activity in the soul. There is a conscious experience of fear in fear of sin, and yet it is not the same

--- **COMMENTARY** ---

In summary:

Yirah Tata'ah "Lower fear"	Acceptance of the yoke of heaven; fear of sin; fear of G-d	Nullification of ego; foundation for prayer
Yirah Ila'ah "Higher fear"	Awe	Total negation of self; result of effort invested in prayer

as the conscious revelation of fear of G-d. In fear of sin only the fear is felt, while in fear of G-d, there is revelation and experience of G-dliness [perhaps more aptly described as "spiritual reverence"], wherein the fear itself is G-dly.)

אֱלֹקִים, דְיִרְאַת חֵטְא הוּא רַק הִתְגַּלּוּת הַיִּרְאָה וִירֵא אֱלֹקִים הוּא שֶׁיֵּשׁ כָּאן הִתְגַּלּוּת אֱלֹקֵי שֶׁנִּרְגָּשׁ הָאֱלֹקוּת וְהַיִּרְאָה הִיא יִרְאָה אֱלֹקִית).

The spiritual element in our fear of G-d itself breaks down into two [different] levels: a minor and a mature level. The minor level is the result of constant reminders of G-d's immanence in meditation upon His outer "garments," as described in the end of chapter 42. (The fear coming from awareness that He observes our deeds is more associated with fear of sin.) The mature level of fear of G-d is the product of contemplation of the greatness of G-d as He permeates all the worlds, as explained in *Tanya*, beginning of chapter 43. All of this [meaning, acceptance of the "yoke of

וּבְזֶה גּוּפָא יֵשׁ קַטְנוּת וְגַדְלוּת. וְהַקַּטְנוּת הִיא כְּשֶׁבָּאָה מִזֶּה שֶׁנִּזְכָּר תָּמִיד הַפְּנִימִיּוּת עַל יְדֵי הַלְּבוּשִׁים הַחִיצוֹנִים כוּ' הַמְבֹאָר בסֹפּמ"ב (וְעִנְיַן מַה שֶׁהַקָּדוֹשׁ בָּרוּךְ הוּא רוֹאֶה בְּמַעֲשָׂיו כוּ' שַׁיָּךְ יוֹתֵר לְעִנְיַן יִרְאַת חֵטְא) וְהַגַּדְלוּת הִיא כְּשֶׁבָּאָה הַיִּרְאָה מֵהַהִתְבּוֹנְנוּת בִּגְדֻלַּת ה' דְאִיהוּ מְמַלֵּא כָּל עָלְמִין הַמְבֹאֶרֶת ברפמ"ג. וְהַכֹּל בְּחִינַת יִרְאָה תַּתָּאָה הַשַּׁיָּךְ לְקִיּוּם הַמִּצְוֹת בְּפֹעַל מַמָּשׁ וְהוּא עִנְיַן יִרְאוּ מֵה' כוּ' כִּי הוּא אָמַר וַיֶּהִי כוּ'.

heaven," fear of sin, and the two levels of fear of G-d] falls into the category of *yirah tata'ah* ["lower fear"] associated with actual fulfillment of the *mitzvot*. This is the fear implied in the verse [from Psalms cited earlier], "Let them fear [lit: from] G-d," since "He is the One who spoke, and it came about..."

Higher fear (awe) of G-d flows from experience of His essence.

וְיִרְאָה עִילָּאָה הִיא עֶצֶם בְּחִינַת הַבִּטּוּל בִּבְחִינַת בִּטּוּל בִּמְצִיאוּת הַנִּמְשֶׁכֶת מֵעֶצֶם הָאֱלֹקוּת דְאִיהוּ רַב וְשַׁלִּיט כוּ' וְכוּלָּא קַמֵּיהּ כְּלָא חֲשִׁיב כוּ', וְכֵן מַה שֶׁכָּתוּב בְּמָקוֹם אַחֵר בְּהַהִתְבּוֹנְנוּת שֶׁהָאוֹר אֵין סוֹף נִמְצָא לְמַטָּה כְּמוֹ לְמַעְלָה שֶׁהַיִּרְאָה הַנִּמְשֶׁכֶת מִזֶּה (הַיְנוּ מֵעֶצֶם הָאוֹר אֵין סוֹף בָּרוּךְ הוּא, לֹא מַה שֶּׁעוֹמֵד

Yirah ila'ah ["higher fear" of G-d] is associated with a great measure of self-nullification, known as "nullification of existence" [in which we lose awareness of our very self, as opposed to "nullification of ego," in which our ego is deflated, but our sense of self remains intact]. It flows from experience of the very essence of G-dliness, the awareness that He is great and

Essay on Service of the Heart - Love Like Fire and Water

governs everything, and that everything is as if "non-existent" before Him. It results as well from meditation on how He is present below [in this world] as well as above, as written elsewhere. The fear derived from this awareness (of the essential infinite light of the One Above, not how He is standing over him, watching and observing, but how G-d in His essence is found revealed in the physical world no less than He is in the spiritual worlds above, as written elsewhere) is a very inward awe, equivalent to "nullification of existence."

עָלָיו וְרוֹאֶה וּמַבִּיט כו׳ כִּי אִם מַה שֶׁהָאוֹר אֵין סוֹף כְּמוֹ שֶׁהוּא בְּעֶצֶם הֲרֵי הוּא נִמְצָא לְמַטָּה בִּבְחִינַת גִּלּוּי מַמָּשׁ כְּמוֹ שֶׁהוּא כו׳ וּכְמוֹ שֶׁכָּתוּב בְּמָקוֹם אַחֵר) הִיא בְּחִינַת יִרְאָה פְּנִימִית בִּבְחִינַת בִּטּוּל בִּמְצִיאוּת מַמָּשׁ,

Higher fear (awe) is awareness that all of creation is as "naught" before G-d. It requires a very high level of self-nullification.

Forms of Fear of the One Above		
Yirah Tata'ah (lower fear) *Yiru mei HaShem*	*Kaballat Ohl Malchut Shamayim* acceptance of the "yoke of heaven"	Unconsciousness fear of the One Above
	Yirat Chait fear of sin	Conscious fear of transgression
	Yirat Elokim fear of G-d	Conscious fear of G-d (minor form of *Yirat Elokim* based on reminders of Him)
		Reverence of G-d (mature form of *Yirat Elokim* based upon His almighty power in creation)
Yirah Ila'ah (higher fear) *Yiru et HaShem*)	awareness that all is as if "non-existent" before G-d	Awe predicated upon nullification of one's self before G-d

Fear, in general, is associated with nullification, and correspondingly, it has the effect of nullifying the animal soul (rather than purifying and refining it). [That is,] fear, in general, corresponds to "putting oneself aside." The lesser level of fear (*yirah*

וּבְדֶרֶךְ כְּלָל הַיִּרְאָה הוּא עִנְיָן הַבִּטּוּל וּכְמוֹ כֵן מַה שֶּׁפּוֹעֵל בַּנֶּפֶשׁ הַבַּהֲמִית הוּא גַּם כֵּן עִנְיָן הַבִּטּוּל שֶׁלּוֹ (לֹא עִנְיָן הַזִּכּוּךְ וְהַבֵּרוּר) וּבְדֶרֶךְ כְּלָל הוּא עִנְיָן הֲנָחַת עַצְמוּתוֹ כו׳, רַק דְּיִרְאָה תַּתָּאָה

Lower fear precedes prayer, but higher fear surpasses prayer. Neither involve cleaving to G-d or purifying the animal soul, which take place in love and prayer.

דְּהַיְנוּ קַבָּלַת עוֹל מַלְכוּת שָׁמַיִם וְיִרְאַת חֵטְא וְיִרְאַת אֱלֹקִים הוּא לְמַטָּה בְּמַדְרֵגָה (בְּעִנְיָן הַהִתְגַּלּוּת) מֵעִנְיַן הָעֲבוֹדָה דִתְפִלָּה שֶׁהִיא לְקַשֵּׁר וּלְדַבֵּק נַפְשׁוֹ כוּ׳, וְיִרְאָה עִילָּאָה הִיא לְמַעְלָה הַרְבֵּה מֵהָעֲבוֹדָה דִתְפִלָּה הַנַּ״ל. וְהִתְקַשְּׁרוּת וּדְבֵקוּת נַפְשׁוֹ בֵּאלֹקוּת וְכֵן הַבֵּרוּר וְהַזִּכּוּךְ דְּנֶפֶשׁ הַבַּהֲמִית הוּא עַל יְדֵי מִדַּת הָאַהֲבָה דַּוְקָא. וְלִהְיוֹת שֶׁעִנְיַן הַתְּפִלָּה וַעֲבוֹדָה שֶׁבַּלֵּב הִיא ב׳ עִנְיָנִים הַנַּ״ל כְּמוֹ שֶׁנִּתְבָּאֵר לְעֵיל פ״א, לָזֹאת כָּל הָעֲבוֹדָה וְהַיְגִיעָה דִתְפִלָּה הִיא לָבוֹא לְמִדַּת הָאַהֲבָה:

קָצוּר.

וְהִנֵּה וַדַּאי כֵּן הוּא שֶׁהַיִּרְאָה מֻכְרַחַת לִהְיוֹת בְּכָל אֶחָד וְאֶחָד. אָמְנָם לֹא זוֹ הִיא עִנְיַן עֲבוֹדָה שֶׁבַּלֵּב דִתְפִלָּה, דְהַיִּרְאָה צָרִיךְ לִהְיוֹת בִּתְמִידוּת וּבָאָה רַק עַל יְדֵי הַזִּכָּרוֹן שֶׁיִּזְכּוֹר תָּמִיד בְּמֶלֶךְ מַלְכֵי הַמְּלָכִים הַקָּדוֹשׁ בָּרוּךְ הוּא וְאֵיךְ שֶׁהוּא רוֹאֶה בְּמַעֲשָׂיו וּכְלָלוּת עִנְיָנָהּ הוּא לִהְיוֹת סוּר מֵרָע וַעֲשֵׂה טוֹב בְּפֹעַל מַמָּשׁ, וְיֵשׁ בָּזֶה גַם כֵּן הַתְבּוֹנְנוּת וְהַעֲמָקַת הַדַּעַת אֲבָל הֵן בְּעִנְיָנִים כְּאֵלּוּ שֶׁיְּכוֹלִים לִהְיוֹת וְלִפְעוֹל גַּם שֶׁלֹּא בִּשְׁעַת הַתְּפִלָּה. וְהָעִיקָר בָּזֶה הוּא הַשְּׁקִידָה (וּמִכָּל מָקוֹם מֻכְשָׁר יוֹתֵר הַזְּמַן דִתְפִלָּה) וְקִצּוּר הַהִתְבּוֹנְנוּת (וְהוּא עִנְיַן הַזִּכָּרוֹן הַנַּ״ל) צָרִיךְ לִהְיוֹת תָּמִיד. וְנִתְ׳ עִנְיַן יִרְאָה

tata'ah) — which includes acceptance of the "yoke of heaven," fear of sin, and fear of G-d — is lower (on the scale of revelation) than the *avoda* of prayer, whose purpose it is to unite our soul [to the One Above]. But, the higher level of fear ("awe" or *yirah ila'ah*) is much higher than the *avoda* of prayer. The cleaving of the soul to G-d and also the purification and refinement of the animal soul are a function of love of G-d alone. And since the object of prayer and of the "service of the heart" are precisely these two goals, as mentioned in Chapter 1, the entire effort and labor of prayer is directed toward love of G-d.

SYNOPSIS:

It is certainly true that everyone must develop fear of G-d. However, this is not the content of the "service of the heart" of prayer. Fear must be constant, based upon our memory reminding us at all times of the King of Kings, the One Above, and how He observes all of our deeds. In general, this fear leads us to turning away from bad and doing good, [meaning toward actual fulfillment of the negative and positive *mitzvot*]. Meditation and deep thought are involved in this process, but their focus is on matters that can also be contemplated and effective [at other times, not just] during prayer. The key is regular (with the best time being during prayer) and concise meditation

Essay on Service of the Heart - Love Like Fire and Water

(consisting of the reminders mentioned above) at all times. [In this chapter] were explained the two levels of fear (*yirah tata'ah*, or "lower fear," and *yirah ila'ah*, or "higher fear") as well as the difference between fear of sin (*yirat cheit*) and fear of G-d (*yirat Elokim*), and also the minor and mature levels within fear of G-d. The "service of the heart" of prayer — which involves uniting our soul with G-d as well as purifying and refining our animal soul, and which is described as "and you should know today and put it in your heart..." — is specifically associated with the attribute of love of G-d. And therefore, the entire labor and effort of prayer is aimed at achieving this attribute of love of G-d.

עִילָאָה וְיִרְאָה תַּתָּאָה, וְהַהֶפְרֵשׁ בֵּין יִרְאַת חֵטְא לְיִרְאַת אֱלֹקִים, וְאֵיךְ שֶׁבְּיִרְאַת אֱלֹקִים יֵשׁ בְּחִינַת קַטְנוּת וְגַדְלוּת. וַעֲבוֹדָה שֶׁבַּלֵּב דִּתְפִלָּה שֶׁהוּא עִנְיַן הִתְקַשְּׁרוּת וּדְבֵקוּת נַפְשׁוֹ בֵּאלֹקוּת וּבֵרוּר וְזִכּוּךְ הַנֶּפֶשׁ הַבַּהֲמִית שֶׁהוּא מַה שֶׁכָּתוּב וְיָדַעְתָּ הַיּוֹם וַהֲשֵׁבֹתָ אֶל לְבָבֶךָ כו' זֶהוּ בְּמִדַּת הָאַהֲבָה דַּוְקָא. וְעַל כֵּן כָּל הָעֲבוֹדָה וְהַיְגִיעָה דִּתְפִלָּה הִיא לָבוֹא לְמִדַּת הָאַהֲבָה:

CHAPTER 4 / פרק ד

Two kinds of love; like water, and like fire

xxii) See footnote of the Rebbe on page 277

xxiii) See footnote of the Rebbe on page 278

וְהִנֵּה בָּאַהֲבָה יֵשׁ ב׳ מַדְרֵגוֹת כְּלָלִיּוֹת הָא׳ בְּחִינַת אַהֲבָה כַּמַּיִם וּכְמוֹ שֶׁכָּתוּב זְכֹר אָב נִמְשַׁךְ אַחֲרֶיךָ כַּמַּיִם וְהַב׳ אַהֲבָה בְּרִשְׁפֵּי אֵשׁ וְצִמָּאוֹן (וְהֵן בְּחִינַת חֶסֶד וּגְבוּרָה שֶׁבְּחֶסֶד).xxiii

דְּהָאַהֲבָה כַּמַּיִם הִיא בִּבְחִינַת קֵרוּב וּדְבֵקוּת בֶּאֱלֹקוּת, וְהוּא עַל יְדֵי הַהִתְבּוֹנְנוּת בְּהָאוֹר וְחַיּוּת הָאֱלֹקִי הַמִּתְלַבֵּשׁ בָּעוֹלָמוֹת וּכְמוֹ שֶׁכָּתוּב וְאַתָּה מְחַיֶּ֯ה אֶת כֻּלָּם שֶׁבְּכָל אֶחָד וְאֶחָד הַיְנוּ בְּכָל נִבְרָא וְנִבְרָא בִּפְרָט יֵשׁ אוֹר וְחַיּוּת אֱלֹקִ֯י הַמְחַיֶּ֯ה אוֹתוֹ וּמִבְּשָׂרִי אֶחֱזֶה אֱלֹקָ֯ה שֶׁכָּל אָדָם מַרְגִּישׁ בְּעַצְמוֹ שֶׁיֵּשׁ בּוֹ חַיּוּת הַמְחַיֶּ֯ה אוֹתוֹ וּכְמוֹ כֵן הוּא בָּעוֹלָם שֶׁנִּקְרָא גּוּף גָּדוֹל כַּנּוֹדָע. שֶׁעַל יְדֵי טִיב הַהַשָּׂגָה וְהַהִתְבּוֹנְנוּת בָּזֶה בְּהַעֲמָקַת הַדַּעַת נִרְגָּשׁ וְנִרְאֶה אֶצְלוֹ אֵיךְ שֶׁהָעוֹלָם חַי מֵאוֹר הָאֱלֹקִי. וּכְשֶׁמְקַשֵּׁר וּמַעֲמִיק דַּעְתּוֹ בְּהָאוֹר

When it comes to love of the One Above, there are two general levels.[xxii] One is "love as water," from the verse [in the prayer for rain recited during *musaf* of *Shmini Atzeret*], "Remember the Father, who was drawn after You like water..." The other is described as "love like flames of fire and thirst." (These two levels represent *chesed sheb'chesed* [love within "loving-kindness"] and *gevura sheb'chesed* [strength within loving-kindness]).[27]

"Love like water" is associated with closeness to G-dliness. It results from meditation on the G-dly light and energy en-clothed in the worlds, as is written [in Nechemiah 9:6], "And You enliven them all..." Within each and every specific aspect of creation is to be found a G-dly light and energy which enlivens it. [As it says in Job 19:26,] "From my flesh, I will see G-d"; we all feel within ourselves a life-force enlivening us. And so it is also in the world at large, which is called a macrocosm, as is known. By meditating properly with intellectual understanding, while concentrating deeply, we feel and perceive

―――――― *COMMENTARY* ――――――

CHAPTER 4: LOVE LIKE WATER AND FIRE

Chapter 4 is the heart of *Kuntres Ha'Avoda*. More than any other chapter, it describes the "nuts and bolts" of Jewish meditation.

The previous chapters established the difference between love and fear of G-d. Love of G-d demands attention and meditation at fixed times and intervals (usually before and during

within ourselves how the world gets its life from a G-dly light. When we concentrate and focus our attention on this G-dly light enlivening the universe, we begin to experience the preciousness and spiritual elevation of G-dliness (that is, that G-dliness in itself is very desirable and uplifting). This brings us to unite our soul with G-dliness, such that our entire will and desire is focused on G-d and nothing else. This love grows stronger when we meditate on the fact that G-dliness constitutes the life-force of the universe in general and of our own soul in particular.

הָאֱלֹקִי שֶׁמְּחַיֶּ֗ה אֶת הָעוֹלָם נִרְגָּשׁ אֶצְלוֹ הַיֹּקֶר וְהָעִלּוּי דֶּאֱלֹקוּת (הַיְנוּ מַה שֶּׁאֱלֹקוּת בְּעֶצֶם הוּא עִנְיָן יָקָר וְנַעֲלֶה מְאֹד) וְעַל יְדֵי זֶה מִתְקַשֵּׁר נַפְשׁוֹ וְנִדְבָּק בֶּאֱלֹקוּת אֲשֶׁר כָּל חֶפְצוֹ וּרְצוֹנוֹ הוּא אֱלֹקוּת וְאֵינוֹ חָפֵץ בְּשׁוּם דָּבָר אַחֵר. וְתִגְדַּל הָאַהֲבָה יוֹתֵר כַּאֲשֶׁר מִתְבּוֹנֵן אֵיךְ שֶׁהָאֱלֹקוּת הוּא חַיֵּי הָעוֹלָם בִּכְלָל וְחַיֵּי נַפְשׁוֹ בִּפְרָט

Love like water is an experience of the preciousness of G-dliness, such that we want to be one with it.

(It would seem that here, we are talking about one level of G-dliness—the divine ray of light that is en-clothed in the universe. But, within this level, the first part of the meditation [on the "G-dly light enlivening the world"] focuses on experiencing the G-dliness in the world, while the second part of the meditation [on "our own soul in particular"] results in a feeling and awareness of how divinity is the life-force of the universe in general, and of ourselves in particular.) As it is written [in Isaiah 26:9], "'My soul desires You...,' which is to say, "since You, G-d,

(וְנִרְאֶה שֶׁהַכֹּל הוּא בְּמַדְרֵגָה אַחַת בֶּאֱלֹקוּת הַיְנוּ בְּהֶאָרַת הָאֱלֹקִי הַמִּתְלַבֵּשׁ בָּעוֹלָם, רַק דְּבְהִתְבּוֹנְנוּת הַנַּ"ל הוּא שֶׁמִּתְבּוֹנֵן וּמַרְגִּישׁ אֶת הָאֱלֹקוּת שֶׁבָּעוֹלָם וְהִתְבּוֹנְנוּת זוֹ הִיא שֶׁהַהִתְבּוֹנְנוּת וְהֶרְגֵּשׁ הוּא אֵיךְ שֶׁהָאֱלֹקוּת הוּא חַיּוּת הָעוֹלָם בִּכְלָל וְחַיּוּתוֹ בִּפְרָט) וּכְמוֹ שֶׁכָּתוּב נַפְשִׁי אִוִּיתִיךָ כְּלוֹמַר מִפְּנֵי שֶׁאַתָּה ה' נַפְשִׁי וְחַיֵּי הָאֲמִתִּיִּים לְכָךְ אִוִּיתִיךָ פִּ" שֶׁאֲנִי מִתְאַוֶּה וְתָאֵב לְךָ כְּאָדָם הַמִּתְאַוֶּה לְחַיֵּי נַפְשׁוֹ כו' וְכֵן כְּשֶׁהוּא הוֹלֵךְ כו' כָּךְ אֲנִי מִתְאַוֶּה וְתָאֵב לְאוֹר אֵין סוֹף בָּרוּךְ הוּא חַיֵּי הַחַיִּים

COMMENTARY
---

the morning prayers). Fear, once it has been attained, needs only reminders from time to time. Chapters 2 and 3 explained the details of fear of G-d. Chapter 4 begins to tell us the details of love of G-d.

Just as there are different kinds of love and relationships between people, so it is with the One Above. Most of us have

There is love like water because He is the life-force of the universe, and love like water because He is the life-source of our own soul.

הָאֲמִתִּיִּים לְהַמְשִׁיכוֹ בְּקִרְבִּי עַל יְדֵי עֵסֶק הַתּוֹרָה כו' וּכְמוֹ שֶׁכָּתוּב בְּסֵפֶר שֶׁל בֵּינוֹנִים פמ"ד.

are my soul, and my true life, I desire You; I desire and long for You like one who longs for the life of his own soul..." And so it is when we is go to sleep: "I desire and long for the infinite light, which is true life, to draw it down within myself by learning Torah..." (*Tanya*, chapter 44, from *Zohar*, part. 3, 67a).

There are two "modes" or "rays" of G-dliness in the world. One, the more external, enlivens and maintains the physical creation. It is constant and unchanging. Chassidic literature compares it to speech, since the Torah tells us that G-d created the world with ten utterances. The other mode is the ray of G-dliness that enlivens our souls. It is more personal, intimate, and dependent upon our avoda, or worship of the One Above. Chassidic literature compares it to thought.

We might have assumed that the two meditations mentioned above correspond to the two levels of speech and thought, but the parenthetical note above forewarns us that the two meditations are two dimensions, an inner and an outer, of the same ray of G-dliness enlivening the world, comparable to G-d's speech. The following parantheses indicate that perhaps after all, they correspond to the two different modes of speech and thought.

(וְהַיִּתְרוֹן בְּאַהֲבָה זוֹ שֶׁהִיא בִּבְחִינַת פְּנִימִיּוּת יוֹתֵר, וְהִיא הַמְּבִיאָה אוֹתוֹ לְעֵסֶק הַתּוֹרָה לְהַמְשִׁיךְ אוֹר אֵין סוֹף בָּרוּךְ הוּא בִּפְנִימִיּוּת נַפְשׁוֹ כו' (וְנִרְאֶה דְּהַהַמְשָׁכָה הִיא בְּמַדְרֵגָה גְּבוֹהָה יוֹתֵר הַרְבֵּה מִן הָאַהֲבָה שֶׁנִּתְבָּאֵר לְעֵיל דְּהָאַהֲבָה דְּנַפְשִׁי

(The advantage of this level of love is that it is more internal, and it brings us to learn Torah in order to draw down upon ourselves the infinite light of the One Above into the inner recesses of our soul. And it would seem that this influx [from learning Torah] is on a much higher level than

---

COMMENTARY

experienced love between siblings, such as between brothers and sisters, or love between parents and children. This kind of love is always present, but not always felt. Such, as well, is one kind of love that we feel for the Creator. In the *Song of Songs*, G-d expresses His relationship with the Jewish people as *achoti* ("my sister"), among other appellations. This is a love that is unconscious, but always present. A brother and sister, or parent and child, do not spend a lot of time pining for each other. It

that of the love mentioned earlier. While the love of "You are my soul, I desire You" is brought about by meditation on the ray of G-dliness which enlivens the worlds, the G-dliness brought down by learning the Torah comes from the infinite light of G-d which transcends the worlds, as described in *Tanya*, chapter 23. It is possible that the love of "You are my soul, I desire You" is also above the ray of G-dliness mentioned above [which enlivens creation], as is written elsewhere regarding the injunction [in Deuteronomy 30:20] "to love the Lord your G-d...because He is your life," meaning that He is the life-force of all souls. [If so, then it] is an expression of the four-letter Name of G-d [translated as "Lord" and denoting G-d as He transcends nature] clad in *Elokim* [the name of G-d as He manifests Himself in nature]. It is also transcendent G-dliness enmeshed in immanent spirituality. It is as well the exalted level of the *sephira* of *malchut* [His kingship], as discussed in the Chassidic discourse *Tiku* from the year 5670, starting with the words: *Achat Sha'alti*.[28]

אֲוִיתִיךָ הִיא גַּם כֵּן בַּהֶאָרָה הָאֱלֹקִית שֶׁבָּעוֹלָמוֹת, וְהַהַמְשָׁכָה שֶׁעַל יְדֵי הַתּוֹרָה הֲרֵי הִיא בִּבְחִינַת אוֹר אֵין סוֹף שֶׁלְּמַעְלָה מֵהָעוֹלָמוֹת וּכְמוֹ שֶׁכָּתוּב בְּסֵפֶר שֶׁל בֵּינוֹנִים פכ״ג. וְאֶפְשָׁר דְּהָאַהֲבָה דְנַפְשִׁי אֲוִיתִיךָ הִיא גַּם כֵּן לְמַעְלָה מֵהַהֶאָרָה הנ״ל וּכְמוֹ שֶׁכָּתוּב בְּמָקוֹם אַחֵר בְּעִנְיַן לְאַהֲבָה אֶת ה׳ אֱלֹקֶיךָ כִּי הוּא חַיֶּיךָ דְּהַיְנוּ חַיֵּי הַנְּשָׁמוֹת שֶׁזֶּהוּ מִבְּחִינַת הוי׳ שֶׁבֶּאֱלֹקִים בְּחִינַת סוֹבֵב שֶׁבִּמְמַלֵּא וְהוּא בְּחִינַת הָרוֹמְמוּת שֶׁבַּמַּלְכוּת כו׳ וּכְמוֹ שֶׁכָּתוּב מִזֶּה בִּדְרוּשׁ תִּקְעוּ עת״ר בְּדִבּוּר הַמַּתְחִיל אַחַת שָׁאַלְתִּי.

Love like water because He is our own soul's life-source leads us to learn more Torah.

COMMENTARY
---

is sufficient that they renew the connection from time to time, and their love for each other immediately surfaces. There is no burning desire to be with each other all the time, since in an unconscious sense they are always part of one another. This kind of love of G-d is in our genes; it has been handed down through the generations from the first great lover of G-d, Abraham. It influences our thoughts and permeates our activities, but only subconsciously, without awareness on our part. Nevertheless — just as with the love between siblings or between parents and children — we can raise this love to consciousness and express it. By thinking of His creation and how He maintains it, we can come to conscious awareness and expression of love for the One Above.

A third kind of love like water – because G-d is our "father."

וְהָאַהֲבָה כְּבָרָא דְּאִשְׁתַּדַּל כו' הַמְבֹאֶרֶת שָׁם בפמ״ד הוּא מֵהַהִתְבּוֹנְנוּת שֶׁאַתָּה אָבִינוּ מַמָּשׁ שֶׁזֶּהוּ לְמַעְלָה מַעְלָה מִמַּה שֶׁאַתָּה ה' נַפְשִׁי כו' וְהַהֶרְגֵּשׁ בָּזֶה הוּא בְּאֹפֶן אַחֵר לְגַמְרֵי וְהוּא בְּחִינַת אַהֲבָה פְּנִימִית וְעַצְמִית כו'. וְיֵשׁ לוֹמַר שֶׁזֶּהוּ בְּעֶצֶם הוי' שֶׁלְּמַעְלָה מִשֵּׁ׳ אֱלֹקִים שֶׁהוּא מְקוֹר חַיֵּינוּ (וּכְמוֹ שֶׁכָּתוּב בְּמָקוֹם אַחֵר בְּעִנְיַן הוי' אֱלֹקֵינוּ) וְאָבִינוּ הָאֲמִתִּי בָּרוּךְ הוּא).

Then there is the love of the "son who exerts himself for his father," as explained in *Tanya*, chapter 44, which results from meditation on the concept, "You are our Father" and which, in reality is far beyond the level of "You, G-d, are my soul." The emotion associated with this meditation is completely different—it is an inner and essential love. It might be said that it is associated with the essential [four-letter] Name of G-d, which is above the name *Elokim* and is the source of our lives—as written elsewhere regarding [the verse from Deuteronomy 6:4] *HaShem Elokeinu*, "The Lord is our G-d"—and our true Father, may He be blessed.)

The essential four-letter Name of G-d (which we are forbidden to pronounce and which is known as the Tetragrammaton) corresponds to the various soul-levels and worlds which are the subject of our meditation:

#	Name of G-d	Soul level	Experience	World
5.	Tip of *yud*	*Yechida* "Single one"	Unity consciousness	Infinite light Beyond worlds
4.	*Yud*	*Chaya* "Living one"	Transcendent consciousness	World of *Atzilut* "World of Emanations"
3.	*Hey*	*Neshama* "Soul/breath"	Intellect Consciousness	World of *Bria* "World of "Creation"
2.	*Vav*	*Ruach* "Wind/spirit"	Emotion consciousness	World of *Yetzira* "World of Formation"
1.	*Hey*	*Nefesh* "Enlivening soul"	Action consciousness	World of *Asiya* "World of Action"

——————— **COMMENTARY** ———————

In Chassidic literature, and especially in the *Kuntres Ha'Avoda*, this kind love is known as "love like water." Deep under the surface of the earth are aquifers that we never see, and deep in the Jewish psyche are currents of love of G-d that are part of the collective Jewish consciousness. We don't feel them, but

Essay on Service of the Heart - Love Like Fire and Water

There is, though a certain advantage to meditation on G-dliness as found in the world. In such meditation, our attachment is to the G-dliness within physical things and not to the physical as such. However, although this meditation satisfies our thirst for closeness to G-d, it does not quite bring us to learn Torah. And therein lies the advantage of the love of "You are my soul, I desire You"—it does bring us closer to learning Torah, as mentioned earlier. And since the ultimate purpose of love of G-d is to serve Him with love (as written in *Tanya*, end of chapter 40)—meaning to cleave to Him by fulfilling the *mitzvot* of the Torah—therefore we must develop the above-mentioned love of "You are my soul, I desire You." [There must be] as well the love discussed in chapter 46 of *Tanya*, "as in water, face answers to face" [in which we becomes acutely aware of G-d's love for us, and this arouses, in turn, a tremendous love in our heart for G-d]. So, we must also practice and become constant in the love of the "son who exerts himself for his father," since all of these techniques bring us closer to fulfilling the *mitzvot* of the Torah with love.

וְיֵשׁ יִתְרוֹן גַּם כֵּן בְּהִתְבּוֹנְנוּת הַנַּ"ל בֶּאֱלֹקוּת שֶׁבָּעוֹלָם שֶׁעַל יְדֵי זֶה גַּם בְּהַדְּבָרִים הַגַּשְׁמִיִּים תַּכְלִית רְצוֹנוֹ הוּא בֶּאֱלֹקוּת שֶׁבָּהֶם לֹא בְּהַגַּשְׁמִי מִצַּד עַצְמוֹ, רַק דְּבְהִתְבּוֹנְנוּת זוֹ הֲרֵי הוּא מַרְוֶה נַפְשׁוֹ בְּקֵרוּב לֶאֱלֹקוּת וְאֵינוֹ מֵבִיא כָּל כָּךְ לַעֵסֶק הַתּוֹרָה. וּבְזֶה יִתְרוֹן הָאַהֲבָה דְּנַפְשִׁי אִוִּיתִיךָ הַמְּבִיאָה יוֹתֵר לְעֵסֶק הַתּוֹרָה כַּנַּ"ל. וְלִהְיוֹת דְּתַכְלִית הָאַהֲבָה הִיא הָעֲבוֹדָה מֵאַהֲבָה כְּמוֹ שֶׁכָּתוּב בְּסֵפֶר שֶׁל בֵּינוֹנִים ספ"מ וְהַיְנוּ לִדְבַּק בּוֹ עַל יְדֵי תּוֹרָה וּמִצְוֹות, לָזֹאת בֶּאֱמֶת צָרִיךְ לִהְיוֹת הָאַהֲבָה הַנַּ"ל דְּנַפְשִׁי אִוִּיתִיךָ גַּם הָאַהֲבָה דְּכַמַּיִם הַפָּנִים אֶל הַפָּנִים שֶׁבפמ"ו בְּסֵפֶר שֶׁל בֵּינוֹנִים. וְכֵן לְהַרְגִּיל עַצְמוֹ בְּהָאַהֲבָה כְּבְרָא דְּאִשְׁתַּדַּל כוּ', שֶׁכֻּלָּן הֵן הַמְּבִיאִים לְעֵסֶק הַתּוֹרָה וּמִצְוֹות מֵאַהֲבָה.

A fourth category of love like water – "as in water, face responds to face."

COMMENTARY

---

they influence us. The deep waters of the inner earth might never emerge to the surface, nor even become wells, but because they are there, the earth is fruitful and moist. We may not be aware of our love for the Creator, but it colors and influences our approach to life nonetheless. And if we dig and look for it, it comes to the surface.

Completely different from this is the love between a man and a woman, between husband and wife. In the *Song of Songs*, G-d also refers to the Jewish people as *ra'yati* ("my spouse").

Type of love like water	Aspect of G-dliness	Level of difficulty	Result
"G-dly light enlivening the world"	*Elokim* G-dliness invested in and enlivening the creation (worlds of *Bria, Yetzira, Asiya*)	Easiest meditation, upon ray of G-dliness enlivening creation	Leads to closeness to G-liness in the physical world, weakening of the animal soul
"because He is the life of my soul..." (*Tanya*, ch. 44)	Inner aspect of *Elokim* or perhaps essential four-letter name of G-d illuminating *Elokim* (*malchut* of *Atzilut*)	Intermediate meditation, based on G-dliness in creation or on transcendent G-dliness illuminating creation	Leads to learning Torah and fulfillment of *mitzvot*
"like a son exerting himself for his father" (*Tanya*, ch. 44)	Essential G-dliness, the essential four-letter name of G-d as Creator (*chochma* of *Atzilut*)	More difficult meditation, based upon transcendent G-dliness	Learning Torah and fulfillment of *mitzvot*
"As in water, face answers face..." (*Tanya*, ch. 46)	Essential four-letter name of G-d beyond any connection to creation (above *Atzilut*, *Keter*)	Most difficult meditation, rarely achieved.	Learning Torah and fulfillment of *mitzvot*

רַק שֶׁהִתְבּוֹנְנוּת וְקֵרוּב הנ״ל בְּהָאֱלֹקוּת שֶׁבָּעוֹלָמוֹת הוּא בְּקֵרוּב יוֹתֵר אֶל הַנֶּפֶשׁ וּבְנָקֵל יוֹתֵר לָבוֹא

The meditation and closeness based upon the ray of G-dliness invested in the worlds, as described

─────── **COMMENTARY** ───────

Needless to say, when husband and wife are separated, within a short time, their longing turns into a visceral need and fiery desire to reunite. This is not a simple matter of keeping a memory

Essay on Service of the Heart - Love Like Fire and Water

earlier, is closer to our [divine] soul and easier to achieve. It also has more effect on our animal soul, weakening it and inducing it to love G-dliness, as will be explained soon. Therefore, the *avoda* of the One Above begins with this love and closeness [based upon meditation on the G-dly ray invested in the world], which brings us as well to involvement in Torah and fulfillment of its *mitzvot*, since in general we desire G-dly matters. And in particular, we want to learn Torah and fulfill its *mitzvot*, because they are precious to us, and we derive energy from them, since they are G-dly. As it says in the *Midrash Tanhuma*, "Honor the *mitzvot* since they are My emissaries," and "the emissary of someone is like that very person himself." We then have to continue to strive for the various levels of love of G-d mentioned earlier. By drawing our [divine] soul closer to G-dliness and by weakening our animal soul—due to the love and closeness to the One Above—we prepare ourselves for arrival to the higher levels of love of G-d mentioned earlier.)

לָזֶה, וְגַם זֶה פּוֹעֵל יוֹתֵר עַל הַנֶּפֶשׁ הַבַּהֲמִית לְהַחֲלִישׁוֹ וְשֶׁיִּהְיֶה לוֹ גַּם כֵּן אַהֲבָה לֶאֱלֹקוּת שֶׁיִּתְבָּ' לְקַמָּן בְּסָמוּךְ, וְעַל כֵּן תְּחִלַּת הָעֲבוֹדָה הִיא בְּאַהֲבָה וְקֵרוּב זֶה וְהִיא מְבִיאָה אוֹתוֹ גַּם כֵּן לְעֵסֶק הַתּוֹרָה וְקִיּוּם הַמִּצְוֹת, מִפְּנֵי שֶׁבְּדֶרֶךְ כְּלָל הוּא חָפֵץ בְּעִנְיְנֵי אֱלֹקוּת וּבִפְרָט בְּעֵסֶק הַתּוֹרָה וְקִיּוּם הַמִּצְוֹת מִפְּנֵי הַיֹּקֶר וְהַחַיּוּת שֶׁיֵּשׁ לוֹ בָּהֶן שֶׁהֵן אֱלֹקוּת, וּבְמַאֲמַרַ"ת אִי' כַּבְּדוּ אֶת הַמִּצְוֹת שֶׁהֵן שְׁלוּחַי וּשְׁלוּחוֹ שֶׁל אָדָם כְּמוֹתוֹ כו'. וְאַחַר כָּךְ צָרִיךְ לִהְיוֹת אַהֲבוֹת הַנַּ"ל, אֲשֶׁר בֶּאֱמֶת עַל יְדֵי קֵרוּב נַפְשׁוֹ לֶאֱלֹקוּת וְעַל יְדֵי הַחֲלִישׁוּת דְּנֶפֶשׁ הַבַּהֲמִית הַנַּעֲשֶׂה עַל יְדֵי הָאַהֲבָה וְהַקֵּרוּב הַנַּ"ל הֲרֵי הוּא מֻכְשָׁר לָבוֹא לְמַדְרֵגוֹת אַהֲבוֹת הַנַּ"ל).

The first level of love like water is the easiest to attain and has more effect upon our animal soul.

COMMENTARY
---

alive and re-connecting from time to time. Here, the memory forces itself into their consciousness and won't leave them alone. It is true that separation for a short time can renew and strengthen the bond between them, but within a relatively short period of time the couple feels a burning need to reunite. This kind of love between G-d and man is called "love like fire." It is not a love of familiarity as is "love like water," it is a love of consuming desire and tendency to "lose" oneself out of love for the other. This love is also likened to gold, as opposed to love like water, which is compared to silver.

Afterward, we shift our attention to the spiritual illumination of the higher worlds.

וּבִפְרָט כְּשֶׁמִּתְבּוֹנֵן בַּמַּדְרֵגָה בֶּאֱלֹקוּת שֶׁלְּמַעְלָה מֵהֶהָאָרָה הַמִּתְלַבֶּשֶׁת בָּעוֹלָם הַתַּחְתּוֹן וְהַיְנוּ בָּהָאוֹר הָאֱלֹקִי הַמִּתְלַבֵּשׁ וּמֵאִיר בָּעוֹלָמוֹת הָעֶלְיוֹנִים. וְכַנּוֹדָע דְּבְהָאוֹר דִּמְמַלֵּא כָּל עָלְמִין יֵשׁ בָּזֶה חִלּוּקֵי מַדְרֵגוֹת מַעְלָה וּמַטָּה דְּבְעוֹלָמוֹת עֶלְיוֹנִים מֵאִיר אוֹר עֶלְיוֹן יוֹתֵר וְהַיְנוּ שֶׁהָאוֹר הוּא שָׁם בִּבְחִינַת גִּלּוּי יוֹתֵר בְּלִי צִמְצוּם כָּל כָּךְ וּכְמוֹ שֶׁכָּתוּב בְּסֵפֶר שֶׁל בֵּינוֹנִים פ"מ (כְּמוֹ שֶׁבַּשֵּׂכֶל יֵשׁ כַּמָּה מִינֵי שְׂכָלִים דְּבַשֵּׂכֶל גָּבוֹהַּ וְנַעֲלֶה יוֹתֵר הֲרֵי יֵשׁ בּוֹ גִּלּוּי אוֹר שֵׂכֶל יוֹתֵר, וּבְשֵׂכֶל עָמֹק הַבָּא בִּבְחִינַת הַפְשָׁטָה הָאוֹר וְהַגִּלּוּי בּוֹ בְּיוֹתֵר כוּ׳, וְעַל דֶּרֶךְ זֶה בְּכָל עוֹלָם שֶׁהוּא עֶלְיוֹן בְּמַדְרֵגָה מִתְלַבֵּשׁ בּוֹ אוֹר נִגְלֶה יוֹתֵר שֶׁאֵינוֹ מְצֻמְצָם כָּל כָּךְ שֶׁזֶּהוּ בְּחִינַת הַמַּעְלָה שֶׁבְּהָאוֹר וְכָל שֶׁכֵּן בַּעֲשֶׂר הַסְּפִירוֹת שֶׁבָּעוֹלָם הַהוּא שֶׁהוּא מֵאִיר

Kuntres Ha'Avoda - קונטרס העבודה

This is especially true when we meditate on levels of G-dliness above those invested in the lower world, [raising our attention to] the G-dly light illuminating the upper worlds. As is known, the immanent light that permeates the universe comes on many different levels, higher and lower. In the upper worlds, there shines a "higher" illumination, meaning the light is more revealed there, illuminating with less contraction, as is written in *Tanya*, chapter 40. (The intellect operates on many levels, and on the higher levels there is more revealed intellectual illumination. A deep concept, accompanied by abstraction, contains more light and revelation. So we find in every world, that the higher it is, the more revealed light is shining there, and the less spiritual contraction occurs. This is the special quality of the [G-dly] illumination, and even more of the

---- *COMMENTARY* ----

The goal of meditation, as described in the Chassidic texts, is to move from "love like water" to "love like fire." "Love like fire" has an advantage over "love like water," in the same way as gold has an advantage over silver. (See chapter 50 of the *Tanya*.) "Love like fire" consumes our animal soul, such that we are left with no other desire or interest than G-dliness.

In summary:

"Love like water"	"Love like fire"
Love between siblings, or between children and parents	Love between husband and wife
Familiar connection	Fiery consuming desire
Compared to silver	Compared to gold

Essay on Service of the Heart - Love Like Fire and Water

ten *sephirot* of that particular world, that the G-dly light is shining into them with more revelation.)

There are, as well, variations in each particular level, such as [stated in *Tikunei Zohar* 6, p. 23]: "The supernal mother nests in the throne and the six *sephirot* in *Yetzira*." [This refers to the emphasis on the *sephira* of *bina* in the World of *Bria* and the emphasis on the lower six *sephirot* in the World of *Yetzira*.] The same is true regarding the soul-levels of *nefesh-ruach-neshama*; we all know the advantage of our *ruach* over our *nefesh* and the advantage of our *neshama* over our *ruach*, which is like the advantage of intellect over emotion. So it is with the *nefesh-ruach-neshama* of the Worlds of *Bria-Yetzira-Asiya*. (And, in truth, there is also a distinction as to how the light and G-dly revelation shines. It can be an illumination of an essential inward dimension, or it can shine from an external dimension. The intellect [corresponding to *neshama*] is [generally] the illumination of an inner dimension; the emotions [corresponding to *ruach*] are expressions of a less essential and more external facet; and *nefesh* is the "external of the external" [*nefesh* is an extension of the emotions and is therefore a superficial expression], as written elsewhere.)

בָּהֶם הָאוֹר וְהַגִּלּוּי יוֹתֵר כו')

וְגַם יֵשׁ בָּזֶה חִלּוּקִים בְּמַדְרֵגוֹת פְּרָטִיּוֹת וּכְמוֹ אִמָּא עִילָּאָה מְקַנְּנָא בְּכוּרְסֵי' וְשִׁית סְפִירָן בִּיצִירָה כו', וּכְמוֹ בְּנֶפֶשׁ רוּחַ וּנְשָׁמָה שֶׁבַּנֶּפֶשׁ שֶׁהָאָדָם יוֹדֵעַ בְּעַצְמוֹ מַעֲלַת הָרוּחַ עַל הַנֶּפֶשׁ וּמַעֲלַת הַנְּשָׁמָה עַל הָרוּחַ כְּמַעֲלַת הַשֵּׂכֶל עַל הַמִּדּוֹת כו' וְכֵן הוּא בְּנֶפֶשׁ רוּחַ וּנְשָׁמָה דִּבְרִיאָה יְצִירָה עֲשִׂיָּה כו' (וּבֶאֱמֶת הַהֶפְרֵשׁ בָּזֶה הוּא גַּם כֵּן בְּאוֹפֶן הָאוֹר וְהַגִּלּוּי אִם שֶׁמֵּאִיר בְּחִינַת פְּנִימִיּוּת הָאוֹר אוֹ חִיצוֹנִיּוּת הָאוֹר, דְּמוֹחִין הֵן בְּחִינַת פְּנִימִיּוּת וּמִדּוֹת הֵן חִיצוֹנִיּוּת וְנֶפֶשׁ בְּחִינַת חִיצוֹנִיּוּת דְּחִיצוֹנִיּוּת כו' וּכְמוֹ שֶׁכָּתוּב בְּמָקוֹם אַחֵר)

There are variations in the levels of spiritual illumination of the higher worlds.

COMMENTARY

LOVE LIKE WATER

"Love like water" is the more basic of the two, requiring "entry level" meditation on how the G-dly energy enlivens the universe in general and ourselves in particular. Water possesses the trait of clinging to an object and "bathing" it, and so with the proper meditation we cling to G-dliness and bask in it, developing "love like water." This meditation is a calm, cultivated attempt to develop our positive connection with the One Above using the intellect. It starts with the realization that He

The above paragraph says that the differences in spiritual levels are two-fold: One, they can be in either the macrocosm (here meaning the three worlds of *Bria, Yetzira*, and *Asiya*), or they can be in the microcosm (the soul *neshama, ruach*, and *nefesh*). And within the two, the G-dly light may illuminate either internally (as in the soul-level of *neshama*), or externally (as in the soul-levels of *ruach* and *nefesh*):

World	Sephira emphasis	Kabbalistic description	Soul level	Spiritual "distance"
1. *Asiya*	*Malchut* (submission, acceptance)	"has no qualities it can call its own…"	*Nefesh*	"like through a tiny hole"
2. *Yetzira*	Six *sephirot* from *chesed* to *yesod* (emotions)	*zeir anpin* "six *sephirot* nest in *Yetzira*"	*Ruach*	"like through a window"
3. *Bria*	*Bina* (intellect)	"supernal mother nests in the throne *(Bria)*"	*Neshama*	"far-away"
4. *Atzilut*	*Chochma* (spiritual insight)	"supernal father nests in *Atzilut*"	*Neshama d'neshama*, or *chaya*	"close-by"

וּכְשֶׁמִּתְבּוֹנֵן בְּכָל זֶה בִּבְחִינַת הָאֱלֹקוּת הַמֵּאִיר בְּכָל מַדְרֵגָה וּמַדְרֵגָה וּבְהַעֲמָקַת הַדַּעַת שֶׁיִּקְלֹט הָעִנְיָן הֵיטֵב בְּמוֹחוֹ וְיָאִיר בְּנַפְשׁוֹ וְנַרְגָּשׁ בּוֹ הָעִלּוּי דֶּאֱלֹקוּת (וּבְכָל

When we meditate on all of this, on the different kinds of G-dliness that illuminate every level and delve into the subject deeply, it becomes well embedded in our consciousness. It illuminates our soul, and we feel

──────── **COMMENTARY** ────────

creates and enlivens everything in the world, and that everything in the universe is permeated with His G-dly energy. Within this meditation, Chapter 4 of *Kuntres Ha'Avoda* alludes to three steps, as implied in this statement from near the end of Chapter 4:

"This may be a meditation on the lower world, on the G-dly light and energy infusing each and every aspect of creation and every specific detail. This meditation in itself is enough to bring our soul to an experience of G-dliness and the good and the preciousness associated with it. Or, we may also throw ourselves into this meditation with more

Essay on Service of the Heart - Love Like Fire and Water

the elevation of G-dliness (and at every higher level of illumination, we feel greater elevation). Our soul then gets much closer to G-d and cleaves to G-dliness. This, then, is love of G-d since the nature of water is to cause two things to cling to each other... (So it is on all levels of love of G-d, like that of "You are my soul, I desire You," and the "son who exerts himself for his father." The love is a strong desire to have the infinite light of G-d illuminate our soul and to cleave to Him by fulfilling the *mitzvot* of the Torah. And so it is regarding the love of "as in water, face answers to face," as written in *Tanya*, chapter 49, "to cleave to Him, may He be blessed, with desire..." So it is, as well, regarding the "love like flames of fire," [which causes us to long for G-d], as is written at the end of chapter 38 of *Tanya* regarding love which comes from meditation on His greatness; see what is written in chapter 43 and at the end of chapter 44: "to cleave to Him by fulfilling the *mitzvot* of the Torah"—this is a level of thirst...[as opposed to the level of "love like water"].)

אוֹר עֶלְיוֹן יוֹתֵר נִרְגָּשׁ הָעִלּוּי בְּיוֹתֵר) הֲרֵי מִתְקָרֵב נַפְשׁוֹ מְאֹד בִּבְחִינַת דְּבֵקוּת בֶּאֱלֹקוּת כו' וְזֶהוּ בְּחִינַת אַהֲבָה שֶׁהוּא הַקֵּרוּב וְהַדְּבֵקוּת בֶּאֱלֹקוּת וּכְטֶבַע הַמַּיִם לִדְבֹּק כו' (וְכֵן הוּא בְּכָל מַדְרֵגוֹת אַהֲבָה כְּמוֹ בְּאַהֲבָה דְנַפְשִׁי אִוִּיתִיךָ וְכִבְרָא דְאִשְׁתַּדַּל כו' שֶׁזֶּהוּ מַה שֶׁחָפֵץ מְאֹד שֶׁיָּאִיר אוֹר אֵין סוֹף בְּנַפְשׁוֹ וּלְדָבְקָה בּוֹ עַל יְדֵי הַתּוֹרָה וּמִצְוֹת כו'. וְכֵן בְּאַהֲבָה דְכַמַּיִם הַפָּנִים וּכְמוֹ שֶׁכָּתוּב בְּסֵפֶר שֶׁל בֵּינוֹנִים פמ"ט לִדְבְקָה בּוֹ יִתְבָּרֵךְ בִּדְבִיקָה חֲשִׁיקָה כו'. וְגַם בְּאַהֲבָה כְּרִשְׁפֵּי אֵשׁ הוּא שֶׁחָפֵץ לִדְבְקָה בּוֹ יִתְבָּרֵךְ וּכְמוֹ שֶׁכָּתוּב בסְפל"ח בְּעִנְיַן הָאַהֲבָה הַבָּאָה מֵהִתְבּוֹנְנוּת בִּגְדֻלָּתוֹ יִתְבָּרֵךְ (וְעַיֵּן מַה שֶּׁכָּתוּב בפמ"ג וספמ"ד לִדְבְקָה בּוֹ עַל יְדֵי קִיּוּם הַתּוֹרָה וְהַמִּצְוָה כו' רַק שֶׁהִיא בִּבְחִינַת צִמָּאוֹן כו').

The nature of water is to cause two things to cling together; so love like water "bathes" the soul in G-dliness.

COMMENTARY

energy and focus on how the main point is G-dliness, as in the verse, 'See, I have put before you life and good...' Or, we may focus on how the G-dly light is en-clothed and revealed in the higher worlds, each one of us according to our own level of intellect and level of *avoda*."

Thus we see that the first step in meditation leading to love of the One Above is to focus on the "G-dly light and energy infusing each and every aspect of creation..." This means that we must consider individual creations — whether mineral, vegetable, animal, or human—and think about the G-dly life-force animating

The more that we approach G-dliness, the more we distance ourselves from anything coarse and physical.

וְעַל יְדֵי הַקֵּרוּב וְהַדְּבֵקוּת בֶּאֱלֹקוּת הֲרֵי הוּא מִתְרַחֵק מֵהָעִנְיָנִים הַחָמְרִיִּים הַטִּבְעִיִּים דְּאַהֲבָה הִיא הַעְתָּקָה מִמָּקוֹם לְמָקוֹם וּכְמוֹ שֶׁכָּתוּב הָלוֹךְ וְנָסוֹעַ וּכְמוֹ הַהוֹלֵךְ מִמָּקוֹם לְמָקוֹם כָּל מַה שֶּׁמִּתְקָרֵב אֶל הַמָּקוֹם שֶׁהוֹלֵךְ הֲרֵי הוּא מִתְרַחֵק מֵהַמָּקוֹם שֶׁהָלַךְ מִשָּׁם, וְכָךְ הוּא בָּאַהֲבָה דְּכָל מַה שֶּׁמִּתְקָרֵב יוֹתֵר אֶל אֱלֹקוּת הֲרֵי הוּא מִתְרַחֵק מֵהָעִנְיָנִים הַחָמְרִיִּים וְהוּא עִנְיַן חֲלִישׁוּת הַנֶּפֶשׁ הַבַּהֲמִית שֶׁנֶּחֱלָשׁ טִבְעוֹ הַחָמְרִי עַל יְדֵי הִתְגַּבְּרוּת הָאַהֲבָה, לֶאֱלֹקוּת

By approaching G-d and cleaving to G-dliness, we [simultaneously] distance ourselves from the coarse physicality of the natural world. Love [of G-d] involves moving from one spiritual "place" to another, as indicated in the verse [from Genesis 12:9 about Abraham, a man of kindness and love, who was] "walking and progressing." When we go from one place to another, we simultaneously approach our goal and distance ourselves from our place of origin. So it is with love of G-d; the more that we approach G-dliness, the more we [simultaneously] distance ourselves from anything coarse and physical. This is what is meant by the "weakening of the animal soul"—that is, its physical nature is weakened in proportion to our increased level of love of G-d.

(וּכְמוֹ שֶׁנִּרְגָּשׁ לְכָל עוֹבֵד ה' דְּעַל יְדֵי הַתְּפִלָּה בַּעֲבוֹדָה טוֹבָה בְּהִתְעוֹרְרוּת אַהֲבָה וְקֵרוּב לֶאֱלֹקוּת הִנֵּה גַּם כַּמָּה שָׁעוֹת אַחַר הַתְּפִלָּה הוּא אָדָם אַחֵר (עֶר אִיז גָאר אַ אַנְדֶערֶער) אוֹ גַּם יוֹם שָׁלֵם, וּמוּבָן דְּבִכְדֵי שֶׁתִּהְיֶה הַחֲלִישׁוּת

(When we serve G-d through proper prayer, we experience an arousal of love and desire for closeness to G-dliness, so that we become a different person for several hours thereafter or even for an entire day. Of course, it is understood that in order for this weakening of the ani-

─────────── *COMMENTARY* ───────────

each one. As will be explained in Chapter 6, the meditation must be particular — that is, it must focus not only on the overall concept of creation, but upon specific objects and creations, and the G-dly force enlivening them.

Then, we may "focus on how the main point is G-dliness," meaning not only that there is a force enlivening every aspect of creation, but that it — rather than the physical manifestation of the object — is the true reality of creation. We must be sensitive to the G-dly dimension in our understanding of creation, giving it special attention in our meditation. We must

Essay on the Service of the Heart - Love Like Fire and Water

mal soul to be real, we must meditate not just once or twice but with constant effort every day. The weakened animal soul then becomes, generally speaking, unable to express itself via the limbs of the body [or] through our thought, speech, and action, as written in *Tanya*, chapter 12 and 13.)

It is also true that, through lack of use, our natural physical powers become weaker, as written in *Sha'arei Tshuva* of Rabeinu Yona, z"l, regarding the curbing of lusts—that this happens as a result of actually refraining from the lustful deed. In the course of time, this abstinence brings about a great weakening of physical lusts. In addition, [involvement in spirituality and] getting closer to the One Above awakens us to the vulgarity and grossness of physical things. At the time that we are attracted to them [our physical lusts], we do not

בֶּאֱמֶת הֲרֵי זֶה לֹא בְּפַעַם אַחַת וּשְׁתַּיִם כִּי אִם בִּשְׁקִידַת הָעֲבוֹדָה יוֹם יוֹם וּבְדֶרֶךְ כְּלָל הַחֲלִישׁוּת הִיא שֶׁאֵינוֹ מִתְפַּשֵּׁט לְהִתְלַבֵּשׁ בְּאֶבְרֵי הַגּוּף בְּמַעֲשֶׂה דִּבּוּר וּמַחֲשָׁבָה וּכְמוֹ שֶׁכָּתוּב בְּסֵפֶר שֶׁל בֵּינוֹנִים פי"ב וי"ג).

וְגַם עַל יְדֵי הֶעְדֵּר הַשִּׁמּוּשׁ בַּהַכֹּחוֹת הַטִּבְעִיִּים הֲרֵי הֵם מִתְחַלְּשִׁים וּכְמוֹ שֶׁכָּתוּב בשע"ת לר"י ז"ל בְּעִנְיַן שְׁבִירַת הַתַּאֲוָה שֶׁזֶּהוּ עַל יְדֵי הֶעְדֵּר הָעֲשִׂיָּה בְּפֹעַל וּבְמֶשֶׁךְ זְמַן בְּהֶעְדֵּר הַהִשְׁתַּמְּשׁוּת בָּהֶם הֲרֵי הֵם נֶחֱלָשִׁים הַרְבֵּה. וְעוֹד זֹאת שֶׁעַל יְדֵי הַקֵּרוּב לֶאֱלֹקוּת נִרְגָּשׁ אֶצְלוֹ הַחֲמָרִיּוּת וְהָעֲבִיּוּת שֶׁל הָעִנְיָנִים הַגַּשְׁמִיִּים (די גראבקייט פון דעם) דִּבְעֵת שֶׁהוּא נִמְשָׁךְ אַחֲרֵיהֶם אֵינוֹ מַרְגִּישׁ כְּלָל הָעֲבִיּוּת שֶׁבָּהֶם אֲבָל כַּאֲשֶׁר מִתְקָרֵב לֶאֱלֹקוּת הֲרֵי הוּא מַרְגִּישׁ

We must meditate not just once or twice, but with constant effort, every day.

COMMENTARY

cultivate our awareness of the spiritual dimension that underlies and transcends the physical world.

And, finally, there is the option of including in this meditation a recognition of higher spiritual worlds, as the Rebbe writes: "He may focus on how the G-dly light is clad and revealed in the higher worlds." The G-dly light that we begin to perceive as the true underlying reality manifests itself on higher levels as well. If it gives life to physical creations in the World of *Asiya*, it surely enlivens spiritual creations, such as angels, in the higher Worlds of *Yetzira* and *Bria*. We must develop and cultivate our sense of the spiritual worlds in order to gain some kind of recognition of the "exalted spiritual intellects" (*sichlim nivdalim*) as the Rambam calls them in *Hilchot Yesodei HaTorah*.

There is illumination from the divine soul during prayer, and the powers of the animal soul recede into concealment.

הֵיטֵב אֶת הָעֲבִיּוּת וְהַבַּהֲמִיּוּת אֲשֶׁר בָּהֶם וְאֵינוֹ חָפֵץ בְּשׁוּם אֹפֶן לִהְיוֹת כִּבְהֵמָה

(וְזֶהוּ הַטַּעַם שֶׁבִּכְדֵי לִפְעֹל בְּנַפְשׁוֹ הַכְּפִי' בְּעִנְיָנִים פְּרָטִיִּים הוּא בְּעֵת הַתְּפִלָּה דַּוְקָא מִפְּנֵי שֶׁאָז מֵאִיר בּוֹ הַנֶּפֶשׁ הָאֱלֹקִית וְהַכֹּחוֹת דְּנֶפֶשׁ הַבַּהֲמִית הֵן בְּהֶעְלֵם אָז דְּהוּא עִנְיַן הַחֲלִישׁוּת דְּנֶפֶשׁ הַבַּהֲמִית עַל כֵּן בְּנָקֵל לוֹ אָז לִפְעֹל יוֹתֵר. וְעוֹד מִפְּנֵי שֶׁאָז הוּא רוֹאֶה וּמַרְגִּישׁ הֵיטֵב אֶת הָעֲבִיּוּת בָּזֶה וּבְנָקֵל יִפְעַל בְּעַצְמוֹ לִכְפּוֹת אֶת עַצְמוֹ כו')

וּבִפְרָט כְּשֶׁמִּתְבּוֹנֵן בְּעִנְיַן רְאֵה נָתַתִּי לְפָנֶיךָ אֶת הַחַיִּים וְאֶת הַטּוֹב וְאֶת הַמָּוֶת וְאֶת הָרָע דְּהַגַּשְׁמִי מִצַּד עַצְמוֹ הוּא דְּבַר מָוֶת וּכְמוֹ גּוּף הַמֵּת

think of them as vulgar. But as we become more spiritual, we clearly experience their crudeness and bestiality, and we do not want at all to be like an animal.

(In order to achieve the maximum effect of re-training and restraining our personal tendencies, the best time [for us to meditate] is precisely during prayer. There is illumination emanating from our divine soul at the time of prayer, and the powers of our animal soul recede into concealment—this is what is meant by weakness of the animal soul. Therefore, it is easier to accomplish something at that time. Furthermore, because we are at the time of prayer, and we see and feel the coarseness of physical temptations, it becomes easier for us [to work on ourselves in order] to restrain and re-train [our personal tendencies].)

In particular, when we meditate on the concept [revealed in the verse in Deuteronomy 30:15], "See, I have placed before you life and good,

---

COMMENTARY

It is possible that these three levels of meditation correspond to the lower Worlds of *Asiya*, *Yetzira*, and *Bria*. *Asiya* is the world of individual physical creations, each separate and distinct from the others, each with its own distinct G-dly energy. *Yetzira* is the world of spiritual archetypes (angels), each a general template for many of the specific creations of the world of *Asiya*, about which it would be appropriate to say that the "main point is G-dliness," rather than physicality. And finally, intellect is characteristic of *Bria*, which is so spiritually refined that it allows for only the possibility of created existence. Thus, it is appropriate to allude to *Bria* by saying "each person according to his own level in intellect…"

Essay on Service of the Heart - Love Like Fire and Water

death and evil," [we realize that] the physical by itself is an object of death. Just as a corpse is loathsome, totally devoid of life, decaying and despicable, so anything that is solely physical, bereft of any G-dly intention, offering only physical attraction and lust, is disgusting and loathsome. Meditation at length on this subject will bring us to detest, at least in part, all that is physical and bestial as written in the discourse *Tiku* (5670) mentioned earlier.

הֲרֵי הוּא מָאוּס בְּלִי חַיּוּת וְנִפְסָד וְנִשְׁקָץ בְּיוֹתֵר. כְּמוֹ כֵן כָּל הַדְּבָרִים הַגַּשְׁמִיִּים מִצַּד עַצְמָם בְּלִי הַכַּוָּנָה הָאֱלֹקִית כִּי אִם הַתַּאֲוָה שֶׁבָּהֶם הֲרֵי זֶה דָּבָר מָאוּס וְשֶׁקֶץ, דִּבְאֲרִיכוּת הַהִתְבּוֹנְנוּת בָּזֶה נִמְאָסִים בְּעֵינָיו בְּמִקְצָת עַל כָּל פָּנִים הָעִנְיָנִי׳ הַגַּשְׁמִיִּים הַחָמְרִיִּים וּכְמוֹ שֶׁכָּתוּב מִזֶּה בַּדְּרוּשׁ תִּקְעוּ הנ״ל בַּמַּאֲ׳ הנ״ל.

Another effect of weakening the animal soul is that it prepares us to receive the [G-dly] light. We then come to understand G-dly matters with our natural intellect and also that the main point of existence is G-dliness, while the physical is completely secondary. It doesn't even deserve a name for itself. G-dliness is

וְגַם עַל יְדֵי הַחֲלִישׁוּת דְּנֶפֶשׁ הַבַּהֲמִית נַעֲשֶׂה מֻכְשָׁר לְקַבֵּל אֶת הָאוֹר וְהִיא שֶׁגַּם הַשֵּׂכֶל הַטִּבְעִי יָבִין אֶת הָעִנְיָן הָאֱלֹקִי וְאֵיךְ שֶׁהָעִקָּר הוּא הָאֱלֹקוּת וְהַגַּשְׁמִי הוּא דָּבָר טָפֵל לְגַמְרֵי וְאֵינוֹ עוֹלֶה בְּשֵׁם דָּבָר כְּלָל לְעַצְמוֹ וְאֵיךְ שֶׁאֱלֹקוּת הוּא תַּכְלִית הַטּוֹב מַה שֶּׁאֵין כֵּן הַגַּשְׁמִי

Weakening the animal soul prepares us to receive G-dly light.

--- **COMMENTARY** ---

In summary:

	Meditation of "love like water"		
1.	Focus on: "G-dly light and energy infusing each and every aspect of creation…"	Meditation on how the G-dly life-force enlivens individual creations	World of *Asiya* "World of Action"
2.	Focus on: "how the main point is G-dliness"	Meditation on how G-d's life force is the true reality of creation, in order to cultivate awareness of the spiritual dimension	World of *Yetzira* "World of Formation"
3.	Focus on: "how the G-dly light is en-clothed and revealed in the higher worlds."	Meditation on the various spiritual worlds, in order to gain understanding of the spiritual creations	World of *Bria* "World of Creation"

> *A major principle is to meditate on the level of the natural everyday intellect, so that it can come to terms with G-dly concepts.*

וְהַחְמְרִי אֵינוֹ טוֹב כְּלָל וְאַדְּרַבָּא הוּא רַע וְדָבָר מָאוּס בְּעֶצֶם, וּלְבָבוֹ יָבִין אֵיךְ שֶׁצָּרִיךְ לִרְצוֹת רַק בֶּאֱלֹקוּת וּמִתְעוֹרֵר בֶּאֱמֶת גַּם הוּא בְּרָצוֹן לֶאֱלֹקוּת לְהַנִּיחַ וְלַעֲזֹב כָּל הָעִנְיָנִים הַחָמְרִיִּים וְהַגַּשְׁמִיִּים וְשֶׁיִּהְיֶ' כָּל עֵסְקוֹ בְּרָצוֹן וְחֵפֶץ בְּעִנְיְנֵי אֱלֹקוּת בְּעֵסֶק הַתּוֹרָה וְקִיּוּם הַמִּצְוֹת, וְיִתְ' לְקַמָּן שֶׁזֶּה עִקָּר גָּדוֹל בַּעֲבוֹדָה לְהָבִיא הַהִתְבּוֹנְנוּת לִידֵי הֲבָנַת הַשֵּׂכֶל הַטִּבְעִי שֶׁגַּם הוּא יָבִין הָעִנְיָן הָאֱלֹקִי וְיִתְעוֹרֵר גַּם כֵּן כוּ'

the ultimate good, as opposed to that which is physical and corporeal, which isn't good at all. Quite the opposite, it is totally evil, and absolutely loathsome. Our heart also understands that we should want only G-dliness, and we become truly aroused with a will for spirituality. [This leads us] to leave and forsake all our physical and corporal matters and involve ourselves only with the will and desire for G-dliness, for learning Torah and fulfilling its *mitzvot*. It will be explained later that a major principle of *avoda* is to meditate on the level of the natural intellect [so that] it can come to understand G-dly concepts and get excited about them.

COMMENTARY

BRIDGES

Chapter 4 of *Kuntres Ha'Avoda* describes other meditations leading to love of G-d, based upon the *Zohar* and the *Tanya*. These meditations may be thought of as bridges between "love like water" and "love like fire."

The next progressive step in meditation occurs when we realize that G-d not only enlivens the entire world, but that He also enlivens our very own soul. This, of course, is a much more personal meditation. (In one of the longest Chabad Chassidic discourses, *Be'shaah Sh'hikdimu* 5672, vol. 3, p. 1310, love of G-d "because He is the life of my soul" is described as a realization that we are "the ultimate intention" and that within us is "a higher and more inner light and G-dly energy...") Suddenly, instead of looking outside at the universe to understand G-d, we are looking within, realizing that we are dependent upon, and a "piece of," G-dliness. We realize that in essence, there is no separation between ourselves and G-d (except the barriers that we erect with our transgressions). We then long for G-d almost like a wife pining for her husband. In the words of the *Zohar*: "One should love the Holy One...with a love of the soul and

Essay on Service of the Heart - Love Like Fire and Water

(At first, this starts out as a simple agreement: the animal soul agrees not to prevent the love of G-d or the desire of the divine soul. It doesn't confuse or distract us with its bestial matters. Matters of the divine soul, such as keeping Torah and its *mitzvot*, are not onerous, and the divine soul does not encounter resistance stemming from physicality. By constant

(וּתְחִלָּה הוּא בְּדֶרֶךְ הֶסְכֵּם שֶׁאֵינוֹ מוֹנֵעַ לְהָאַהֲבָה וּלְהָרָצוֹן בְּפֹעַל דְּנֶפֶשׁ הָאֱלֹקִית, וְהַיְנוּ שֶׁאֵינוֹ מְבַלְבְּלוֹ וְאֵינוֹ מַטְרִידוֹ כָּל כָּךְ בְּעִנְיָנָיו הַחָמְרִיִּים וְאֵין לְנֶפֶשׁ הָאֱלֹקִית כֹּבֶד בְּעִנְיָנָיו הָאֱלֹקִיִּים בְּתוֹרָה וּמִצְוֹת וּכְהַאי גַּוְונָא וְאֵינוֹ פּוֹגֵשׁ הִתְנַגְּדוּת לָזֶה מִצַּד הַחָמְרִי, וְעַל יְדֵי שְׁקִידַת הָעֲבוֹדָה נַעֲשָׂה

At first, the animal soul just stays out of the way of the divine soul.

COMMENTARY
---

the spirit, as these are attached to the body, and the body loves them..." We realize that G-d is, in essence, part of our being (which causes us to love Him all the more) and yet we also realize that He doesn't seem to be with us all the time (which causes us anguish). This seeming contradiction motivates us to try to bring G-d into our life more than ever, by learning Torah and fulfilling its *mitzvot*. Therefore, Chapter 4 of *Kuntres Ha'Avoda* tells us that the advantage of this meditation (called "You are the life of my soul") is that it brings us to learn Torah.

Chapter 4 also tells us that there is another, more intense and personal meditation in which we realize not only that G-d is the enlivening force and the life of our souls, but that G-d is our "Father." The natural reaction to Him as the life-force of our souls is to respond as a servant to a master. This love of a servant for a master motivates Torah study and the fulfillment of its *mitzvot*. We want to fulfill the will of our Master so we study His word with great care and attempt to follow His instructions to the most minute detail. However, when we integrate the details of our Master's instructions, we come to realize that He is our "Father." We now want to understand the purpose behind His will for us. In that way, we hope to go beyond the letter of the law and fulfill its spirit. This is described in the *Zohar* as love "like a son who strives for the sake of his father and mother, whom he loves even more than his own body, soul and spirit..." For his father, the son is willing to do anything.

The transformation of the animal soul takes place with love like fire.

הָרָצוֹן גַּם בְּנֶפֶשׁ הַבַּהֲמִית כנ"ל שֶׁגַּם הוּא רוֹצֶה בֶּאֱלֹקוּת וּבְעִנְיְנֵי אֱלֹקוּת וְלֹא זוֹ בִּלְבָד שֶׁאֵין לוֹ כֹּבֶד וְהִתְנַגְּדוּת כִּי אִם שֶׁגַּם מִצַּד הַחָמְרִי הוּא חַי בְּעִנְיְנֵי אֱלֹקוּת וְעוֹשֶׂה כָּל דָּבָר בְּרָצוֹן וְחֵשֶׁק וּבְחַיּוּת גָּדוֹל).

avoda [that is, by constantly attempting to get close to the One Above], the animal soul also comes to desire G-dliness and matters of the spirit. Not only does it not present resistance and opposition, but the corporeal side itself "lives" with G-dly matters and does everything with desire and great enthusiasm.)

אָמְנָם עִקַּר כִּלָּיוֹן וּבִטּוּל הַיֵּשׁוּת דְּנֶפֶשׁ הַבַּהֲמִית הוּא בְּאַהֲבָה כְּרִשְׁפֵּי אֵשׁ דְּנֶפֶשׁ הָאֱלֹקִית לִהְיוֹת כִּי הַנֶּפֶשׁ הַבַּהֲמִית בְּהַדְ' מַדְרֵגוֹת דְּדוֹמֵם צוֹמֵחַ חַי וּמְדַבֵּר הוּא בְּמַדְרֵגַת הַחַי שֶׁזֶּהוּ בְּחִינַת יְסוֹד הָאֵשׁ בְּחִינַת חֲמִימוּת הַתַּאֲוָה,

However, the nullification of the ego of the animal soul is mainly brought about by "love like flames of fire" of the divine soul. This is because the animal soul, on the four levels of "mineral, vegetable, animal, and human," corresponds to the level of "animal," which in turn corresponds to the element of fire, giving rise to the heat of lust [in the soul]. The onslaught of fire in the divine soul, giving rise to flames of desire and thirst for G-dliness, is like "fire which consumes fire." It devours and destroys the power of lust and the fire that [burns in] the animal soul for human pleasures, as written in *Likutei Torah*, in the discourse *Ki Teitzei*, in the first discourse [paragraph 2],[29] and in *L'vaer Inyan Yom HaKippurim*, end of second part.[30] Now, the true "love like flames of fire" (coming

--- **COMMENTARY** ---

The two above-mentioned levels of love of G-d, ("You are the life of my soul," and "like a son striving for his father") correspond to the World of *Yetzira* or to *Bria*, according to the *Tanya*, chapter 44, at different stages. They correspond to *Yetzira* when in a latent state in the person's heart, and to *Bria* when brought to full expression by intellectual meditation. In either case, they are examples of "love like water," as well as *ahavat olam* ("worldly love"), although the *Tanya* goes on to state these two meditations have a component that transcends *ahavat olam*: "...these two distinctions of love...contain a quality of love which is greater and more sublime than the intelligent fear and love, the love termed as *ahavat olam*."

Later, the *Tanya* goes on to describe this greater and more sublime quality as a "blaze of fiery love." So, it would seem that while these

Essay on Service of the Heart - Love Like Fire and Water

וְהִתְגַּבְּרוּת יְסוֹד הָאֵשׁ דְּנֶפֶשׁ הָאֱלֹקִית בְּרִשְׁפֵּי אֵשׁ הַתְּשׁוּקָה וְהַצִּמָּאוֹן לֶאֱלֹקוּת הוּא בְּחִינַת אֵשׁ אוֹכְלָה אֵשׁ לְכַלּוֹת וְלִשְׂרֹף הַכֹּחַ הַמִּתְאַוֶּה וְהָאֵשׁ דְּנֶפֶשׁ הַבַּהֲמִית בְּתַעֲנוּגוֹת בְּנֵי אָדָם כו' וּכְמוֹ שֶׁכָּתוּב בְּלִקּוּטֵי תוֹרָה בְּדִבּוּר הַמַּתְחִיל כִּי תֵצֵא דְּרוּשׁ הָרִאשׁוֹן וּבְדִבּוּר הַמַּתְחִיל לִבְאֵר עִנְיַן יוֹם הַכִּפּוּרִים ספ״ב. וְהִנֵּה אֲמִתִּית הָאַהֲבָה בְּרִשְׁפֵּי אֵשׁ (בְּחִינַת אֵשׁ שֶׁלְּמַטָּה דְּנֶפֶשׁ הָאֱלֹקִית) הִיא הַבָּאָה מֵהִתְבּוֹנְנָה וְהַדַּעַת בִּגְדֻלַּת ה' אֵין סוֹף בָּרוּךְ הוּא (וְעַיֵּן מַה שֶּׁכָּתוּב בְּבֵאוּרֵי הַזֹּהַר פ' תַּזְרִיעַ בְּבֵאוּר מַאֲמַ״ז דמ״ט ע״א ע״פ הֲזֵי עֲלֵיהֶם מֵי חַטָּאת) הַמְמַלֵּא כָּל עָלְמִין וְסוֹבֵב כָּל עָלְמִין וְכוּלָּא קָמֵי' כְּלָא חֲשִׁיב כו',

אֲשֶׁר עַל יְדֵי הִתְבּוֹנְנוּת זוֹ מִמֵּילָא תִּתְפַּשֵּׁט מִדַּת הָאַהֲבָה שֶׁבַּנֶּפֶשׁ מִלְּבוּשֶׁי' דְּהַיְנוּ שֶׁלֹּא תִּתְלַבֵּשׁ בְּשׁוּם דְּבַר הֲנָאָה וְתַעֲנוּג גַּשְׁמִי אוֹ רוּחָנִי לְאַהֲבָה וְלֹא לַחְפֹּץ כְּלָל שׁוּם דָּבָר בָּעוֹלָם בִּלְתִּי ה' לְבַדּוֹ מְקוֹר הַחַיִּים שֶׁל הַתַּעֲנוּגִים כו' כְּמוֹ שֶׁכָּתוּב בְּסֵפֶר שֶׁל בֵּינוֹנִים פמ״ג

True love like fire arises from deep understanding of the heart and recognition of the greatness of G-d.

from below, from the divine soul) arises from deep understanding of the heart and recognition of the greatness of G-d, the Infinite One—which permeates and transcends all the worlds—that everything is as nothing before Him. (See the *Biur HaZohar*, *Parshat Tazriah*, explaining the words of the *Zohar*, p. 49, first side, on the verse, *Hazei aleihem mei chatat*.)

By way of this meditation, the love in our soul will burst out of its "garments," meaning that it will no longer be garbed by any object of physical pleasure. Nor will it be clad in any spiritual pleasure [even the most refined]. We will not love or desire anything whatsoever aside from G-d Himself, the Source of all life, and

---
COMMENTARY
---

two levels of love may initially be described as "love like water," they eventually (through proper meditation) become "love like fire." That is, when our meditation brings us to a complete grasp of the subject, then our love becomes "love like fire."

LOVE LIKE FIRE

In *Be'shaah Sh'hikdimu* 5672, vol. 2, p. 820, it states: "In grasping the subject, one comes to excitement over its inherent G-dliness with flames of fire and desire, but only through complete comprehension..." Thus, an important factor in "love like fire" is complete and total grasp of the subject. Then, the text of Chapter 4 of *Kuntres Ha'Avoda* says in part, "As our meditation

The lust of the animal soul must be transformed into a fiery desire for G-d, corresponding to the sacrifices burning on the altar.

וּסְפּמַ״ד וּבְלִקּוּטֵי תּוֹרָה פ׳ שְׁלַח בְּדִבּוּר הַמַּתְחִיל בְּפ׳ נְסָכִים כְּתִיב וְזֶהוּ עִנְיָן שֶׁהַתְּפִלָּה בִּמְקוֹם קָרְבָּן לְהַקְרִיב אֶת הַנֶּפֶשׁ הַבַּהֲמִית וּלְהַעֲלוֹתוֹ שֶׁיִּתְהַפֵּךְ מִן הַהֶפֶךְ אֶל הַהֶפֶךְ לִהְיוֹת כֹּחַ הַמִּתְאַוֶּה. בְּרִשְׁפֵּי אֵשׁ שַׁלְהֶבֶת לְדָבְקָה בֵּאלֹקִים חַיִּים כוּ׳ כְּמוֹ שֶׁכָּתוּב בְּדִבּוּר הַמַּתְחִיל כִּי תֵצֵא הַנַּ״ל וּבְדִבּוּר הַמַּתְחִיל בְּפ׳ נְסָכִים הַנַּ״ל

of all pleasures..." (as is written in *Tanya*, chapter 43 and end of chapter 44, and in *Likutei Torah*, *Parshat Shlach*, discourse *B'Parshat nesachim ketiv...*). This is what is meant by [the words of the Sages in Talmud *Berachot* 26] "Prayer is in lieu of the sacrifices." We must offer up our animal soul and elevate it so that it turns from one extreme to the other. The [animal soul, which is] "something that lusts" must be transformed into a fiery desire to cleave to the living G-d, as written in the discourse *Ki Teitzei* and in the discourse beginning *B'parshat Nesachim*, as mentioned earlier.

xxiv) See footnote of the Rebbe on page 278 ➤

(וּמַה שֶּׁכָּתוּב בְּדִבּוּר הַמַּתְחִיל כִּי תֵצֵא הַכַּוָּנָה בַּהִתְבּוֹנְנוּת דְּבִרְכוֹת קְרִיאַת שְׁמַע בְּבִטּוּל הַמַּלְאָכִים שֶׁזֶּהוּ בְּחִינַת אֵשׁ שֶׁלְּמַעְלָה דְנֶפֶשׁ הַבַּהֲמִית כוּ׳ וּכְמוֹ שֶׁכָּתוּב מִזֶּה בִּדְרוּשׁ יוֹם טוֹב שֶׁל רֹאשׁ הַשָּׁנָה רס״ו. וּמַה שֶּׁכָּתוּב בְּדִבּוּר הַמַּתְחִיל בְּפ׳ נְסָכִים זֶהוּ בְּחִינַת הָאֵשׁ דְּנֶפֶשׁ הָאֱלֹקִית וְכֵן הוּא בְּדִבּוּר הַמַּתְחִיל וְנִקְדַּשְׁתִּי פ״ה, וּבְנֶפֶשׁ הָאֱלֹקִית

(That which is written in *Ki Teitzei* refers to meditation during the blessings preceding the reciting of *Shema*, regarding the state of nullification of the angels. It is the "fire from above" of the animal soul, as written in the discourse *Yom Tov shel Rosh Hashana*[xxiv], 5666.[31] And that which is written in *B'parshat Nesachim*[32] refers to the fire of the divine soul, and so it is in the discourse, *Venikdashti*, part 5. [33] Within the divine soul, the reference

--- **COMMENTARY** ---

comes to the subject of 'You, G-d, are my very soul,' we will become even more inflamed as we considers our distance..." Consideration of our spiritual distance from the One Above, leading to bitterness, combines with the total grasp mentioned above, to bring about "love like fire." Finally, the *Kuntres Ha'avoda* quotes from *Likutei Torah* regarding "love like fire," saying that it comes about through contemplation of the constant renewal of creation, resulting in fiery love over the "newness" of creation at every instant. This occurs only among those who are able to meditate on a high level on the greatness of G-d. For

is to "fire from below." The "fire from above" of the divine soul is called *ahava rabbah* — "great love" — which transcends all intellect and logic and comes from the attribute of *chochma* within the soul, as taught in the discourse *L'vaer Inyan Yom Hakippurim*, part 2. It corresponds to the fire of the menorah [in the Holy Temple], which is [spiritually] higher than the fire of the altar. [Kabbalistically speaking,] the fire of the altar is associated with *gevura d'imma*, or "power of analytic thinking," while the fire of the menorah is associated with *gevura d'abba*, or the "power of intuitive grasp." The latter was the service of Aaron, [the high priest], when he lit the lights of the menorah, as written there at length in the discourse mentioned earlier. [These Kabbalistic levels refer to two opposite dynamics. *Gevura* in general is strength/restraint, which is required to lift and elevate, but also to draw down levels of spiritual influx. When it is associated with *imma* or *bina* (analytic understanding), it refers to the strength to uplift sparks of holiness from below to above, which is what takes place when sacrifices are burnt on the altar. When it is associated with *abba* (intuitive grasp), it refers to the power to bring down holiness from above to below, which is what Aaron the high priest did when lighting the menorah. To bring holiness down from above to below, such that the physical becomes permeated with the spiritual, is a higher service of G-d than the opposite dynamic, from below to above.])³⁴

הוּא בְּחִינַת אֵשׁ שֶׁלְּמַטָּה (וּבְחִינַת אֵשׁ שֶׁלְּמַעְלָה דְּנֶפֶשׁ הָאֱלֹקִית הוּא בְּחִינַת אַהֲבָה רַבָּה שֶׁלְּמַעְלָה מִטַּעַם וָדַעַת וְהִיא מִבְּחִינַת הַחָכְמָה שֶׁבַּנֶּפֶשׁ כְּמוֹ שֶׁכָּתוּב בְּדִבּוּר הַמַּתְחִיל לְבָאֵר עִנְיַן יוֹם הַכִּפּוּרִים פ״ב, וְהוּא עִנְיַן אֵשׁ הַמְּנוֹרָה שֶׁלְּמַעְלָה מֵאֵשׁ הַמִּזְבֵּחַ, דְּאֵשׁ הַמִּזְבֵּחַ הוּא גְּבוּרוֹת דְּאִימָא וְאֵשׁ הַמְּנוֹרָה בְּחִינַת גְּבוּרוֹת דְּאַבָּא וְזֶה הֲרֵי עֲבוֹדַת אַהֲרֹן בְּהַעֲלָאַת הַנֵּרוֹת וּכְמוֹ שֶׁכָּתוּב מִזֶּה בְּאֹרֶךְ בַּדְּרוּשׁ הנ״ל)

The fire from above of the divine soul corresponds to the light of the Menorah in the Temple.

─────── **COMMENTARY** ───────

the rest of us, complete understanding and bitterness over our distance from the One Above are what bring about "love like fire."

Chapter 4 of *Kuntres Ha'Avoda* refers to the Chassidic series of discourses called *Yom Tov shel Rosh Hashana, 5666* (also from the Rebbe Rashab). There (page 144), "love like fire" is further subdivided into two categories. First, there is love like fire "from below." When we meditate "from below" — contemplating the higher spiritual creations such as angels — we bring what is called

Level of soul	Type of service	Description of service	
Animal soul	Fire from below	Meditation upon the *seraphim* burning with nullification to G-d	1.
	Fire from Above	Revelation of light from Above from the love of G-d of the angels	2.
Divine soul	Fire from below	The sacrifices on the altar, *gevura d'imma*	3.
	Fire from Above	*Ahava Rabba*, Aharon lighting the Menorah, *gevura d'abba*	4.

וְהוּא הַהִתְבּוֹנְנוּת בִּגְדֻלָּתוֹ יִתְבָּרֵךְ בִּפְסוּקֵי דְזִמְרָה וּקְרִיאַת שְׁמַע. וְנִרְאָה דְּבַנֶּפֶשׁ הַבַּהֲמִית פּוֹעֵל רַק בְּחִינַת בִּטּוּל הַיֵּשׁ שֶׁזֶּה שֶׁכָּתוּב בְּסֵפֶר שֶׁל בֵּינוֹנִים שֶׁלֹּא תִתְלַבֵּשׁ בְּשׁוּם דְּבָר הֲנָאָה כו׳ וּבְדִבּוּר הַמַּתְחִיל בְּפ׳ נְסָכִים כ׳ גַּם כֵּן לְהָסִיר הַחֲמִימוּת שֶׁבְּלִבּוֹ כו׳ וּבִכְדֵי לְהָפְכוֹ זֶהוּ עַל יְדֵי בְּחִינַת אֵשׁ שֶׁלְּמַעְלָה הנ״ל

The "fire from below" of the divine soul takes place during meditation on His greatness in *P'sukei D'zimra*, ("Verses of Praise") and in *Kriat Shema*—the reciting of the *Shema* [during prayer]. It would seem that this meditation has the effect on the animal soul of bringing about only *bitul hayesh* ("nullification of the ego"). This is what is meant by *Tanya* [in chapter 43] when it says "[love] shouldn't en-clothe itself in any article of pleasure..." as well as in *B'parshat Nesachim* mentioned earlier, where it says [in chapter 1] "to remove the heat in his heart" [towards worldly pleasures]. In order to [go a step further and] transform it [this heat], we need the "fire from above," already mentioned.

COMMENTARY
---

fire "from below." The angels are aware of the G-dly source that creates them; they are also aware of how that G-dly energy is constantly renewed in its source. This awareness brings them to a state of great excitement and nullification (reflected in the blessings preceding the reciting of the *Shema*). Through this contemplation, our animal soul, which has its own source in these angels, becomes consumed, nullified, and transformed in fiery love for the One Above. This love is called the "fire of the altar," after the animal sacrifices that were brought in the Temple

(It is also possible for this "transformation" to take place by prefacing the "fire from above" of the animal soul during the blessings preceding the *Shema*, [and then the transformation takes place with the "fire from Above" during the reciting of the *Shema* itself], as noted earlier. According to what is written in *V'nikdashti*, it would seem that this is *it'hafcha*, or transforming one's lusts completely into G-dliness, and it takes place on the level of [the angels] called *seraphim*, or those who burn up completely [in their service of the One Above], as written elsewhere. It is also explained in the commentary *V'nikdashti* there, that this is the level of self-nullification associated with the *Shema*. In any case, the topic is not so relevant to what is discussed here.)

(וְאֶפְשָׁר כְּמוֹ כֵן הוּא גַם כֵּן עַל יְדֵי הַקְדָּמַת בְּחִינַת אֵשׁ שֶׁלְּמַעְלָה דְנֶפֶשׁ הַבַּהֲמִית בְּבִרְכַּת קְרִיאַת שְׁמַע כנ"ל) וּמִכָּל מָקוֹם מִמַּה שֶׁכָּתוּב בְּדִבּוּר הַמַּתְחִיל וְנִקְדַּשְׁתִּי נר' שֶׁזֶּהוּ בִּבְחִינַת אִתְהַפְּכָא, וְהוּא בְּמַדְרֵגַת הַשְּׂרָפִים שֶׁנִּשְׂרָף כָּל מַהוּתָם וּכְמוֹ שֶׁכָּתוּב בְּמָקוֹם אַחֵר וְגַם מְבֹאָר שָׁם בְּהַבֵּאוּר שֶׁזֶּה מְסִירַת נֶפֶשׁ דִּקְרִיאַת שְׁמַע. וְאֵין הָעִנְיָן נוֹגֵעַ כָּל כָּךְ לְכָאן).

──────── **COMMENTARY** ────────

in order to draw the person offering the sacrifice closer to the One Above. This is referred to in Kabbalah as the *hey gevurot d' imma* or "five stringencies of analytic thinking" (since *gevura* or "stringency" has the quality of uplifting and elevating).

In response to the fire "from below," wherein our animal soul is consumed, there may be a response from heaven called the fire "from above." If the fire "from below" corresponds to the sacrifices on the altar, then the fire "from above" corresponds to the fire of the menorah, kindled by the Aharon, the high priest. His job was to bring the light of consuming G-dliness down to the Jewish people, to each person according to his own soul-level. This he did by lighting the menorah. The fire "from above" is also described as *ahava rabba* ("great love") by the *Kuntres Ha'Avoda*, since it totally consumes and transfixes the person. In Kabbalah, this is called the *hey gevurot d'abba* (five stringencies of creative thought). In *Yom Tov shel Rosh Hashana, 5666*, the Rebbe mentions that since we don't have the Temple today, we should not be surprised if the "light of the menorah" doesn't shine on us in the form of love like "fire from above." Even so, the Rebbe says, we should do our best to bring the fire "from below," which also consumes the animal soul and draws one to "love like fire."

The love like fire from Above takes place on most elevated levels.

אָמְנָם זֶהוּ בְּמַדְרֵגוֹת גְּבוֹהוֹת וְהַיְנוּ כְּשֶׁיֵּשׁ הִתְגַּלּוּת אוֹר הַנֶּפֶשׁ הָאֱלֹקִית לְהִתְפָּעֵל כָּל כָּךְ בְּהִתְבּוֹנְנוּת גְּדֻלָּתוֹ יִתְבָּרֵךְ לְהַלְהִיב נַפְשׁוֹ כְּרִשְׁפֵּי אֵשׁ וְשַׁלְהֶבֶת עַזָּה וְלַהַב הָעוֹלֶה הַשָּׁמַיְמָה וּלְהִפָּרֵד מִן הַפְּתִילָה כוּ'. וּבְלִקּוּטֵי תוֹרָה דִּבּוּר הַמַּתְחִיל לְבָאֵר עִנְיַן יוֹם הַכִּפּוּרִים מְבֹאָר דְּהִתְלַהֲבוּת בְּרִשְׁפֵּי אֵשׁ תִּהְיֶה מֵהַדָּבָר חִדּוּשׁ בְּהִתְחַדְּשׁוּת הַהִתְהַוּוּת חֲדָשִׁים לַבְּקָרִים, דְּכַאֲשֶׁר יִרְאֶה בְּעֵינָיו (דִּבְזֶה שַׁיָּךְ רְאִיָּ' חוּשִׁית

But this "fire from Above" takes place on most elevated levels, when there is revelation of the light of the divine soul such that the soul becomes so aroused with meditation on His greatness, that the revelation inflames it like a torch of fire. It becomes like a flame rising to the heavens, striving to be separated from its wick. In *Likutei Torah*, in the discourse *L'vaer inyan Yom Hakippurim*,[35] it is explained that the excitement of "love like flames of fire" comes from a sense of newness, a sense of renewal in

---

COMMENTARY

In summary:

Dynamic	Factor leading to "love like fire"	Chassidic Description	Kabbalistic Description	Effect on animal soul
From below	Total grasp of concept combined with bitterness over distance from G-d	Compared to sacrifices offered on the altar	"*gevurot d'ima*," or stringencies of analytic thinking	Shatters the animal soul, but doesn't transform it
From Above (also called *ahava rabba*)	Meditation on His greatness, and awareness of renewal of creation at every instant (rare without the Temple)	Compared to Aharon the High Priest lighting the menorah in the Holy Temple	"*gevurot d'abba*," or stringencies of creative thought	Transforms the animal soul and elevates it to be included in G-dly soul

FACE TO FACE

Finally, one more level of love of G-d is described in Chapter 4 of *Kuntres Ha'Avoda*, based upon a verse in Proverbs 27:19 that reads, "As in water, face responds to face, so the heart of man to man." The *Tanya* describes how G-d "abandoned," so to speak, the higher spiritual worlds and associated Himself with

Essay on Service of the Heart - Love Like Fire and Water

creation at every instant, "new every morning." When we "see" with our own "eyes"—(it is appropriate to speak here of the physical sense of vision, as in the verse [in Isaiah 40:26], "See Who created these...")—and our heart understands, it also catches on fire, as it is written [in Eicha 2:18], "their heart cried out..." This involves revelation of the divine soul, as well.

וּכְמוֹ שֶׁכָּתוּב וּרְאוּ מִי בָרָא אֵלֶּה כו' וְלִבָּבוֹ יָבִין כו' עַל כֵּן יַלְהִיב לִבּוֹ וְיָשִׂים אֵלָיו לִבּוֹ וְנִשְׁמָתוֹ וּכְמוֹ שֶׁכָּתוּב צָעַק לִבָּם כו'. וְגַם זֶה הוּא בְּהִתְגַּלּוּת אוֹר הַנֶּפֶשׁ הָאֱלֹקִית כו'.

But on the average, we who would achieve love "like flames of fire" require meditation on our distance from the One Above. That is, we must think about how far away we are from anything G-dly. We must, first of all, undergo the meditation explained earlier in which we think about the G-dliness inherent in the physical creation, or the nature of the spiritual light and illumination in the upper worlds, and we must feel the preciousness and elevation of G-dliness. We must then combine this with contemplation of our own situation—how far we are from anything G-dly, not only in our soul in general, but even in the garments of our soul: in our thought, speech, and action. This leads us to a state of great bitterness, as a result of which

אַךְ בְּכָל אָדָם בִּכְדֵי שֶׁתִּהְיֶה הָאַהֲבָה בְּרִשְׁפֵּי אֵשׁ הוּא עַל יְדֵי הַהִתְבּוֹנְנוּת בְּרִחוּק שֶׁלּוֹ אֵיךְ שֶׁהוּא מְרֻחָק מֵאֱלֹקוּת, וְהַיְנוּ כַּאֲשֶׁר מִתְבּוֹנֵן בַּהִתְבּוֹנְנוּת הַנַּ"ל בֶּאֱלֹקוּת שֶׁבָּעוֹלָמוֹת הֵן בָּעוֹלָם הַתַּחְתּוֹן אוֹ בְּאֹפֶן הָאוֹר וְהַגִּלּוּי שֶׁבָּעוֹלָמוֹת הָעֶלְיוֹנִים כנ"ל וּמַרְגִּישׁ אֶת הַיְקָר וְאֶת הָעִלּוּי דֶּאֱלֹקוּת, הֲרֵי הוּא מְצָרֵף לָזֶה לְהִתְבּוֹנֵן בְּמַעֲמָדוֹ וּמַצָּבוֹ אֵיךְ שֶׁהוּא מְרֻחָק בְּתַכְלִית מֵאֱלֹקוּת בְּמַחֲשָׁבָה דִּבּוּר וּמַעֲשֶׂה שֶׁלּוֹ וְגַם בִּכְלָלוּת נַפְשׁוֹ הוּא מְרֻחָק לְגַמְרֵי מֵעִנְיַן הָאֱלֹקוּת, הֲרֵי תִּתְמַרְמֵר נַפְשׁוֹ מְאֹד עַל זֶה וְתִתְלַהֵב נַפְשׁוֹ בְּרִשְׁפֵּי אֵשׁ שַׁלְהֶבֶת בְּצִמָּאוֹן וּתְשׁוּקָה לִהְיוֹת מְקֹרָב לֶאֱלֹקוּת, וְהַיְנוּ לָצֵאת מֵהָעִנְיָנִים

But the average meditator must combine total intellectual grasp with bitterness over his distance from G-d in order to attain "love like fire."

COMMENTARY
---

man in this lowest physical world, out of love and devotion to His people. (G-d didn't really "abandon" any part of His creation, but His greatest concern is with His people in this physical universe.) Therefore, we should, in response, cling to Him with the utmost devotion and love. The *Tanya* emphasizes that this clinging gives rise to a "love like fire," though it also contains elements of "love like water."

our soul is motivated to catch on fire, flaming like a torch with thirst and desire to be close to the One Above and to abandon all matters which separate and distance it from G-d. We then become close to G-dliness as well as subjugated to Him in all of our soul powers, and in our thought, speech, and action. And when our meditation centers on the subject of "You, G-d, are my very soul," we will become even more enflamed as we consider our distance [from Him].

הַמַּפְרִידִים וְהַמַּרְחִיקִים אוֹתוֹ וְלִהְיוֹת מְקֹרָב לֶאֱלֹקוּת וְאֵלָיו יִתְבָּרֵךְ יְהִי נָתוּן וּמָסוּר בְּכָל הַכֹּחוֹת שֶׁלּוֹ וּבְמַחֲשָׁבָה דִּבּוּר וּמַעֲשֶׂה שֶׁלּוֹ. וְכַאֲשֶׁר הַהִתְבּוֹנְנוּת הִיא אֵיךְ שֶׁאַתָּה ה' נַפְשִׁי כוּ' עוֹד תַּגְדִּיל הַהִתְלַהֲבוּת בְּיוֹתֵר בְּהִתְבּוֹנְנוּת הָרִחוּק שֶׁלּוֹ כוּ'

The flames of love like fire eradicate and incinerate the animal soul, while love like water only weakens it.

These flames of fire eradicate and nullify the ego of the animal soul, causing it to become totally incinerated and consumed, unlike "love like water" which brings about only a weakening of the animal soul. This is because our involvement [in "love like water"] is only with the G-dly concept, as we strive to understand that G-dly concept and feel G-dliness, and how it is good and elevated. In so doing, we truly come closer to G-d. Through this closeness, our animal soul becomes weakened, but this is only weakening and not nullification. (Nevertheless, it was explained that [through this meditation] we become prepared to understand [and accept] G-dly concepts, and we also become

וְרִשְׁפֵּי אֵשׁ זֶה עוֹשֶׂה כִּלָּיוֹן וּבִטּוּל הַיֵּשׁ דְּנֶפֶשׁ הַבַּהֲמִית שֶׁנִּשְׂרָף וְכָלָה מַמָּשׁ (וְלֹא כְּמוֹ בְּאַהֲבָה כְּמַיִם שֶׁזֶּהוּ בְּחִינַת חֲלִישׁוּת בִּלְבַד לִהְיוֹת שֶׁשָּׁם הַהִתְעַסְּקוּת שֶׁלּוֹ רַק בְּעִנְיָן הָאֱלֹקִי לְבַד, לְהָבִין אֶת הָעִנְיָן הָאֱלֹקִי וּלְהַרְגִּישׁ אֶת הָאֱלֹקוּת וְהַטּוֹב וְהָעִלּוּי בָּזֶה שֶׁעַל יְדֵי זֶה מִתְקָרֵב בֶּאֱמֶת לֶאֱלֹקוּת וְעַל יְדֵי הַקֵּרוּב לֶאֱלֹקוּת מִתְחַלֵּשׁ הַנֶּפֶשׁ הַבַּהֲמִית, אֲבָל הוּא בִּבְחִינַת חֲלִישׁוּת לְבַד לֹא שֶׁמִּתְבַּטֵּל (וּמִכָּל מָקוֹם נִתְבָּאֵר שֶׁנַּעֲשֶׂה מֻכְשָׁר לְהָבִין גַּם כֵּן עִנְיָן אֱלֹקִי וּמִתְעוֹרֵר גַּם הוּא בְּרָצוֹן לֶאֱלֹקוּת וְעַיֵּן מַה שֶּׁכָּתוּב לְקַמָּן בְּסָמוּךְ) אָמְנָם בְּאַהֲבָה דְּכְרִשְׁפֵּי אֵשׁ נִשְׂרָף וְכָלֶה וּמִתְבַּטֵּל הַיֵּשׁוּת

COMMENTARY

This subject is alluded to by the *Kuntres Ha'Avoda* which says that this love contains both *ohr yashar* ("direct light," or illumination from above) and *ohr chozer* ("reflected light," or illumination from below). Two dynamics are described here. One is the love of the One Above for the Jewish people, which induces us to want to cleave to Him, as in "love like water." The other

aroused with a desire for G‑dliness; see what is explained nearby.) However, when it comes to "love like flames of fire," the ego of the animal soul becomes incinerated, consumed, and nullified. This is because our distress over our distance from G‑d brings about the onset of fiery flames and excitement [of love for G‑d], which in turn causes the nullification of the animal soul.

דְּנֶפֶשׁ הַבַּהֲמִית, כִּי מִפְּנֵי שֶׁצַּר לוֹ מֵרִחוּקוֹ מֵאֱלֹקוּת וְזֶהוּ הַגּוֹרֵם לוֹ הָרִשְׁפֵּי אֵשׁ וְהַהִתְלַהֲבוּת הֲרֵי זֶה גּוֹרֵם הַבִּטּוּל בְּנֶפֶשׁ הַבַּהֲמִית,

So it is in general with "love like flames of fire." Its full expression blossoms out of meditation on G‑d's greatness, or at least on the phenomena of constant renewal of creation at all times, as mentioned earlier. Then, the fire of holiness burns and consumes the fire of all that is opposed to holiness. Whenever we amplify the element of G‑dly fire [in our soul], we decrease and cool off the natural element of fire [of the "other side," which isn't holy], as written in the discourse of *B'parshat Nesachim*," end of the first chapter). Furthermore, the power of the natural element of fire becomes elevated and included in love of G‑d "like flames of fire," as explained there.

וְכֵן הוּא בִּבְחִינַת אַהֲבָה כְּרִשְׁפֵּי אֵשׁ בִּכְלָל דַּאֲמִתִּית עִנְיָנָהּ הוּא כְּשֶׁהִיא מִצַּד הַהִתְבּוֹנְנוּת בִּגְדֻלָּתוֹ יִתְבָּרֵךְ אוֹ עַל כָּל פָּנִים מֵחִדּוּשׁ הַהִתְהַוּוּת כוּ' כנ"ל הִנֵּה הָאֵשׁ דִּקְדֻשָּׁה שׂוֹרֵף וּמְכַלֶּה הָאֵשׁ דִּלְעֻמַּת זֶה, דְּבְכָל עֵת שֶׁמַּגְבִּיר כֹּחַ יְסוֹד הָאֵשׁ הָאֱלֹקִי מִתְמַעֵט וּמִתְקָרֵר כֹּחַ יְסוֹד הָאֵשׁ הַטִּבְעִי וּכְמוֹ שֶׁכָּתוּב בְּדִבּוּר הַמַּתְחִיל בפ' נְסָכִים ספ"א). וְעוֹד זֹאת שֶׁגַּם כֹּחַ יְסוֹד הָאֵשׁ הַטִּבְעִי עוֹלֶה וְנִכְלָל לְאַהֲבָה אֶת ה' בְּהִתְלַהֲבוּת וְרִשְׁפֵּי אֵשׁ כוּ' וּכְמוֹ שֶׁכָּתוּב שָׁם.

COMMENTARY
---

is our own striving and awareness of Him from afar, which gives rise to "love like fire." We should be ready to forsake and abandon all of the most important aspects of our physical lives in order to cling to G‑d with love. This will give rise, according to the *Tanya*, to a love "like a burning fire, in the consciousness of the heart and mind..." This is the highest of the levels of love that are mentioned in Chapter 4 of *Kuntres Ha'Avoda*, beyond even the World of *Atzilut*.

Elsewhere in Chassidic literature — specifically in *B'shaah sh'hikdimu* 5672, vol. 2, pp. 972‑4 — is to be found a very deep

Teshuva (tata'ah) shatters the animal soul, but love like fire elevates it.

This, then, is the advantage of "nullification of existence" of the animal soul out of "love like fire," over the process of *teshuva*, ["return" to the One Above]. In *teshuva*, (the lower form, *teshuva tata'ah*), we are consumed with bitterness over our distance from the One Above. We are distressed over our personal matters [the details of our relationship with the One Above] and over our situation and standing in general. (This bitterness must be accompanied by an awareness of G-dliness, since [only] then will the bitterness be charged with G-dly energy, as written elsewhere.) This causes a shattering of the ego and corporeality of the animal soul (also here, it is not a weakening alone), but not such that the animal soul ascends to be included in holiness. (The exception is a case of true *teshuva* in which the essence of the animal soul is transformed [completely]. In order for it to ascend and to be included in holiness, we must do *teshuva ila'ah*. This is the higher form of *teshuva*, in which the light of the soul becomes revealed in a stupendous rush of fiery flames, as is known regarding the power of the energy of *teshuva*.

וְזֶהוּ הַיִּתְרוֹן בְּבִטּוּל הַיֵּשׁוּת דְּנֶפֶשׁ הַבַּהֲמִית בְּאַהֲבָה הנ״ל לְגַבֵּי עִנְיַן הַתְּשׁוּבָה, דְּבִתְשׁוּבָה (הַיְנוּ בִּתְשׁוּבָה תַּתָּאָה) הֲרֵי כָּל הִתְעַסְּקוּתוֹ הוּא בְּהַמְרִירוּת עַל הָרִחוּק שֶׁצַּר לוֹ עַל עִנְיָנָיו הַפְּרָטִיִּים וְעַל מַעֲמָדוֹ וּמַצָּבוֹ בִּכְלָל כו׳ (וְהַהֶרְגֵּשׁ הָאֱלֹקִי שֶׁצָּרִיךְ לִהְיוֹת בָּזֶה הוּא בִּכְדֵי שֶׁתִּהְיֶה הַמְּרִירוּת בִּבְחִינַת חַיּוּת אֱלֹקִי וּכְמוֹ שֶׁכָּתוּב בְּמָקוֹם אַחֵר) וְזֶהוּ שֶׁגּוֹרֵם שְׁבִירַת הַיֵּשׁוּת וְהַחוּמְרִיּוּת דְּנֶפֶשׁ הַבַּהֲמִית (גַּם כֵּן לֹא רַק חֲלִישׁוּת לְבַד) אֲבָל לֹא שֶׁיַּעֲלֶה גַּם הוּא וִיהִי׳ נִכְלָל בִּקְדֻשָּׁה (לְבַד בִּתְשׁוּבָה אֲמִתִּית שֶׁמְּהַפֵּךְ מַהוּת הַנֶּפֶשׁ הַבַּהֲמִית וּבִכְדֵי שֶׁיְהִי׳ עוֹלֶה וְנִכְלָל כו׳ הוּא דַּוְקָא בִּבְחִינַת תְּשׁוּבָה עִילָאָה דְּהַיְנוּ בְּהִתְגַּלּוּת אוֹר הַנְּשָׁמָה בִּבְחִינַת רִשְׁפֵּי אֵשׁ בְּיוֹתֵר כַּנּוֹדָע בְּעִנְיַן תֹּקֶף הָרָצוֹא דִּתְשׁוּבָה),

---

COMMENTARY

explanation of this level of love of G-d. There, it is equated with the level attained by Rabbi Akiva when he entered the *pardes* ("orchard" of Torah secrets) and encountered the "slabs of marble." Upon reaching this level — which is clearly a metaphor for an unspeakably high spiritual revelation—Rabbi Akiva proclaimed, "When you reach the marble slabs, don't cry 'water, water.'" The Chassidic discourse explains that Rabbi Akiva wanted to forewarn the meditator who reaches this level

Essay on Service of the Heart - Love Like Fire and Water

[However], in the above-mentioned love ["like flames of fire"], although bitterness also plays a role, the main experience is an excitement and rush for G-dliness. [In this excitement], the element of natural fire [of the animal soul] also ascends to be included in holiness.)

וּבְאַהֲבָה הַנַ"ל עִם הֱיוֹת שֶׁיֵּשׁ בָּהּ גַּם כֵּן עִנְיַן הַמְּרִירוּת כַּנַ"ל, אֲבָל לִהְיוֹת כִּי הָעִקָּר הוּא הַהִתְלַהֲבוּת וְהָרָצוֹא לֶאֱלֹקוּת עַל כֵּן גַּם הַיְסוֹד הָאֵשׁ הַטִּבְעִי עוֹלֶה וְנִכְלָל בִּקְדֻשָּׁה).

1.	*Teshuva Tata'ah* "Lower repentance"	Distress over our distance from G-d	Shattering of animal soul
2.	"Love like fire"	Excitement over G-dliness, but also remorse over distance from G-d	Transformation of the animal soul and its inclusion in the divine soul
3.	*Teshuva Ila'ah* "Higher repentance"	Revelation of the light of the soul	Transformation of the animal soul

This is the meaning of the *korbanot*, or sacrifices. The fat and blood of the animal correspond to the enjoyment of the animal soul and the hot lust of the blood that are meant to ascend to be included in holiness. (Specifically, the fat offering corresponds to the "love like water," explained earlier. Through it, the animal soul becomes prepared [to accept G-dliness].) When we comprehend a G-dly concept with our natural intellect, and as a result also experience an

וְזֶהוּ עִנְיַן הַקָּרְבָּנוֹת שֶׁהוּא הַקְרָבַת חֵלֶב וָדָם דְּהַיְנוּ בְּחִינַת הַתַּעֲנוּג דְּנֶפֶשׁ הַבַּהֲמִית וּרְתִיחַת הַדָּמִים שֶׁעוֹלֶה וְנִכְלָל בִּקְדֻשָּׁה (וּבִפְרָטִיּוּת הַקְרָבַת הַחֵלֶב הוּא בְּאַהֲבָה הַנִּמְשֶׁכֶת כַּמַּיִם שֶׁנִּתְבָּאֵר לְעֵיל שֶׁעַל יְדֵי זֶה נַעֲשָׂה הַנֶּפֶשׁ הַבַּהֲמִית מֻכְשָׁר כו', הִנֵּה כַּאֲשֶׁר מֵבִין הַשֵּׂכֶל הַטִּבְעִי הֵיטֵב אֶת הָעִנְיָן הָאֱלֹקִי וּמִתְעוֹרֵר גַּם כֵּן בְּרָצוֹן לֶאֱלֹקוּת נוֹטֵל מִמֶּנּוּ הַתַּעֲנוּג (דער געשמאַק) מֵהָעִנְיָנִים הַחָמְרִיִּים (וּבִפְרָט

COMMENTARY

not to think that what he perceives through meditation is "outside" himself; rather, he must recognize that all that stands between himself and the Creator on this level are the blockages that he himself presents (either his sins and transgressions, or his own inability to integrate G-dly revelation). Therefore, just as

בְּהִתְבּוֹנְנוּת דִּרְאֵה נָתַתִּי לְפָנֶיךָ אֶת הַחַיִּים וְאֶת הַטּוֹב כו' שֶׁנִּתְבָּאֵר לְעֵיל) וּמִתְעַנֵּג גַּם כֵּן בְּהַטּוֹב דֶּאֱלֹקוּת וּבְעִנְיְנֵי אֱלֹקוּת. וְהַקְרָבַת רְתִיחַת הַדָּמִים שֶׁהוּא הָאֵשׁ הַטִּבְעִי הוּא בְּהָאַהֲבָה דְּכִרְשָׁפֵּי אֵשׁ בְּחִינַת יְסוֹד הָאֵשׁ דִּקְדֻשָּׁה. אָמְנָם הָאַהֲבָה כַּמַּיִם הִנֵּה מִצַּד עַצְמָהּ פּוֹעֶלֶת הַחֲלִישׁוּת לְבַד כנ"ל וְרַק עַל יְדֵי הַהִשְׁתַּדְּלוּת עִם הַנֶּפֶשׁ הַטִּבְעִית שֶׁיָּבִין גַּם הוּא וְיִתְעוֹרֵר גַּם כֵּן

(אֲשֶׁר כֵּן צָרִיךְ לִהְיוֹת בְּעוֹבְדֵי ה' שֶׁלֹּא לְהִסְתַּפֵּק בְּהַשָּׂגַת הַנֶּפֶשׁ הָאֱלֹקִית לְבַד וּבְהִתְפַּעֲלוּת שֶׁלּוֹ, כִּי אִם לְהִשְׁתַּדֵּל שֶׁיּוּבַן הָעִנְיָן גַּם בַּשֵּׂכֶל הַטִּבְעִי, שֶׁבְּדֶרֶךְ כְּלָל הוּא תָּלוּי בְּהִתְקָרְבוּת וּנְתִינַת הַנֶּפֶשׁ הַטִּבְעִית לָזֶה (דְּעִם הֱיוֹת שֶׁכָּל הַשָּׂגוֹתָיו הֵן בְּהִתְלַבְּשׁוּת בְּהַשֵּׂכֶל הַטִּבְעִי מִכָּל מָקוֹם יֵשׁ בָּזֶה חִלּוּק גָּדוֹל אִם הַהֲכָנָה בַּנֶּפֶשׁ הִיא רַק לְהָבִין הָעִנְיָן בְּשִׂכְלוֹ הָאֱלֹקִי אֵין לָזֶה שַׁיָּכוּת אֶל הַשֵּׂכֶל הַטִּבְעִי וְאֵינוֹ

---

116   Kuntres Ha'Avoda - קונטרס העבודה

awakening for G-dliness, our enjoyment of physical matters is taken away. (This takes place especially during the meditation of, "See, I placed before you life and good," which was explained earlier.) We, too, begin to enjoy the goodness of G-dliness and of G-dly matters. The sacrifice of hot blood, which is the natural fire [within us], corresponds to "love like flames" from the element of fire within holiness. But, "love like water," in and of itself, has only a weakening effect, as mentioned earlier, and only by working with the natural [animal] soul—such that it also understands and becomes aroused— [do we succeed in nullifying the animal soul].

(So should it be among "servants of God."[xxv] They should not be satisfied with intellectual grasp of the divine soul alone and its excitement, but should also strive to have the concept understood by the natural intellect. In general, this is dependent upon the level of the animal soul's closeness to and interest in [the matter]. It is true that all our understanding is en-clothed in the ["external garments" and "packaging" of the] natural intellect. Nevertheless, there is a vast difference. If we use only

xxv) See footnote of the Rebbe on page 279

We should not be satisfied with understanding of the divine soul alone, but should strive for the intellectual grasp of the natural, animal soul as well.

COMMENTARY

when we look into water and see only our own face, so on this level there is nothing between us and G-d except our own ego and the resistance that we present — our own mirrored reflection in the water. (In the discourses of 5666, p. 469, the Rebbe Rashab suggests that the soul is a "garment that clothes the infinite light of G-d, bringing it to en-clothement in the vessels...") If so, this is a meditation associated with the highest levels of perceivable

our G-dly intellect to prepare the animal soul to understand the concept, there will be no connection with the natural intellect and little effect on the animal soul (besides the "weakening" mentioned earlier). But if our preparation is such that the concept is understood and accepted by our animal soul as well, then we will also influence and persuade it with our meditation. Then, in truth, the concept will come to be accepted by our natural intellect, and it, too, [the animal soul] will become aroused [with G-dly love]). Sometimes, additional proofs and demonstrations are necessary in order to persuade the natural intellect to accept the concept.)

פּוֹעֵל כָּל כָּךְ עַל הַנֶּפֶשׁ הַטִּבְעִית (כִּי אִם הַחֲלִישׁוּת הנ"ל), אֲבָל כַּאֲשֶׁר הַהֲכָנָה הִיא שֶׁיִּהְיֶ' מוּבָן וְיוּנַח הָעִנְיָן גַּם בַּשֵּׂכֶל הַטִּבְעִי הֲרֵי הוּא מְקָרֵב וְנוֹתֵן אֶת הַנֶּפֶשׁ הַטִּבְעִית גַּם כֵּן בַּהִתְבּוֹנְנוּת הַהִיא, דְּאָז בֶּאֱמֶת בָּא הַהַנָּחָה גַּם בַּשֵּׂכֶל הַטִּבְעִי וּמִתְעוֹרֵר גַּם הוּא) וְלִפְעָמִים צְרִיכִים לָזֶה רְאָיוֹת וְהוֹכָחוֹת יוֹתֵר בִּכְדֵי שֶׁיּוּנַח הָעִנְיָן בַּשֵּׂכֶל הַטִּבְעִי,

But, on its own without effort, "love like water" won't produce any arousal in the animal soul, while "love like flames of fire" by itself has an [automatic] effect on the animal soul. An element of G-dly fire burns and consumes the natural fire and elevates it to be included in holiness.

אַךְ מֵעַצְמָהּ לֹא תִּפְעַל הָאַהֲבָה כְּמַיִם עַל הִתְפַּעֲלוּת הַנֶּפֶשׁ הַבַּהֲמִית כִּי אִם עַל יְדֵי הִשְׁתַּדְּלוּת, מַה שֶּׁאֵין כֵּן הָאַהֲבָה דְכִרְשִׁפֵּי אֵשׁ שֶׁפּוֹעֶלֶת בְּעַצְמָהּ עַל הַנֶּפֶשׁ הַבַּהֲמִית, דִּיסוֹד הָאֵשׁ הָאֱלֹקִי שׂוֹרֵף וּמְכַלֶּה אֶת הָאֵשׁ הַטִּבְעִי וּמַעֲלֶה אוֹתוֹ לִהְיוֹת נִכְלָל בִּקְדֻשָּׁה.

Now, when love is combined with meditation upon our distance from Him, as mentioned above, it becomes apparent how it has an effect on the animal soul. And so it is when the true "love like fire" [of the divine soul consumes the fire of the animal soul], since fire consumes fire. The truth is that also in this love is to be found a hidden tinge of bitterness, [as in

דְּהִנֵּה כַּאֲשֶׁר הָאַהֲבָה בָּאָה בְּצֵרוּף הַהִתְבּוֹנְנוּת בָּרִחוּק כנ"ל הֲרֵי מוּבָן אֵיךְ שֶׁפּוֹעֵל עַל הַנֶּפֶשׁ הַבַּהֲמִית, אָמְנָם כְּמוֹ כֵן הוּא גַּם בְּאַהֲבָה דְכִרְשִׁפֵּי הָאֵשׁ הָאֲמִתִּית מִשּׁוּם דְּאֵשׁ אוֹכְלָה אֵשׁ. וּבֶאֱמֶת גַּם בְּאַהֲבָה זֹאת יֵשׁ קְצָת תַּעֲרוֹבוֹת מְרִירוּת בְּהֶעְלֵם אוֹ עַל כָּל פָּנִים שֶׁחוֹשֵׁב אוֹדוֹת הָרִחוּק דְּנֶפֶשׁ

COMMENTARY

spirituality attained by only a select few (Rabbi Akiva's colleagues each perceived this spiritual revelation, but only Rabbi Akiva

teshuva described earlier]. At the very least, we think about the distance of our animal soul from G-d. This is necessarily so, since the dynamic of this love is to rise like fiery flames, as in a furious charge and ascent upwards. In such a movement we are aware of anything holding us back (each one of us according to our own level) and preventing us from developing [spiritually] and ascending, and as a result of this, we experience distress. The difference is that in the first version of love of G-d, the love is the result of feeling our distance [from G-d] in combination with meditation on G-dliness. But the true version of this love comes as a result of meditation on His greatness, and only afterward do we experience the bitterness of our distance from G-d. (This is because the light of our divine soul comes into revelation, as mentioned earlier, and the physicality which is holding us back is very subtle, and therefore we are able to get excited about the greatness of G-d.) This is written about in the discourse beginning *B'parshat Nesachim*, end of chapter 2:

> And this is what is meant by *Shema Yisrael—shema—*from a word indicating gathering ["come and listen"]…as in gathering and grouping together all of the soul powers and desires of the element of fire within the natural [animal] soul…by removing his will from them, that is, to regret the past and resolve never to return to folly, because he is an aspect of *Yisrael,* who arose in His thought…

הַבַּהֲמִית (וּמֻכְרָח הָעִנְיָן לִהְיוֹת כֵּן דְּמֵאַחַר שֶׁהוּא בִּבְחִינַת הִתְלַהֲבוּת רִשְׁפֵּי אֵשׁ שֶׁהוּא בְּחִינַת רָצוֹא וְהָעֲלָאָה נִרְגָּשׁ אֶצְלוֹ הַדָּבָר הָאוֹחֵז אוֹתוֹ (בְּכָל חַד וְחַד לְפִי עֶרְכּוֹ) וְאֵינוֹ מַנִּיחוֹ לְהִתְפַּשֵּׁט וְלַעֲלוֹת וְצַר לוֹ מִזֶּה), רַק הַהֶפְרֵשׁ הוּא שֶׁבָּאֹפֶן הָא' הֲרֵי בָּאָה הָאַהֲבָה מֵהֶרְגֵּשׁ הָרִחוּק בְּצֵרוּף הַהִתְבּוֹנְנוּת בֶּאֱלֹקוּת וּבַאֲמִתִּית הָאַהֲבָה הַזֹּאת בָּא הֶרְגֵּשׁ הָרִחוּק לְאַחַר שֶׁמִּתְפַּעֵל בְּאַהֲבָה מֵהַהִתְבּוֹנְנוּת בִּגְדֻלָּתוֹ יִתְבָּרֵךְ וּכְהַאי גַּוְנָא (מִפְּנֵי שֶׁאוֹר נַפְשׁוֹ הָאֱלֹקִית הִיא בְּהִתְגַּלּוּת כַּנַּ"ל וְהַחָמְרִיּוּת הָאוֹחֵז אוֹתוֹ הוּא רַק בְּדַקּוּת וּבִיכָלְתּוֹ לְהִתְפַּעֵל מִגְּדֻלָּתוֹ יִתְבָּרֵךְ) וּכְמוֹ שֶׁכָּתוּב בְּדִבּוּר הַמַּתְחִיל בְּפָ' נְסָכִים סְפּ"ב

לֶאֱסֹף וּלְקַבֵּץ כָּל הַכֹּחוֹת כוּ' עַל יְדֵי עֲקִירַת הָרָצוֹן מֵהֶם דְּהַיְנוּ לְהִתְחָרֵט כוּ' וְהַיְנוּ מִפְּנֵי שֶׁהוּא בְּחִינַת יִשְׂרָאֵל שֶׁעָלָה בְּמַחֲ' כוּ').

Essay on Service of the Heart - Love Like Fire and Water

Thus, the main focus of our effort in the "service of the heart," which is prayer, should be to approach and unite our soul with G-dliness through meditation on the G-dly light en-clothed in the worlds. This may be a meditation on the lower world, on the G-dly light and energy infusing each and every aspect of creation and every specific detail. This meditation in itself is enough to bring our soul to an experience of G-dliness and the good and the preciousness associated with it. Or, we may also throw ourselves into this meditation with more energy and focus on how the main point is G-dliness, as in the verse, "See, I have put before you life and good..." Or, we may focus on how the G-dly light is garbed and revealed in the higher worlds, each one of us according to our own intellectual level and in our level of *avoda*. All of these meditations produce a significant weakening of the animal soul, such that it is not drawn after corporeal matters and doesn't engage our will

וְזֶהוּ עִקַּר הַיְגִיעָה בַּעֲבוֹדָה שֶׁבַּלֵב זוֹ תְּפִלָּה לְקָרֵב וּלְדַבֵּק נַפְשׁוֹ בֶּאֱלֹקוּת עַל יְדֵי הַהִתְבּוֹנְנוּת בָּהָאוֹר הָאֱלֹקִי הַמִּתְלַבֵּשׁ בָּעוֹלָמוֹת אִם בָּעוֹלָם הַתַּחְתוֹן מַה שֶׁיֵּשׁ אוֹר וְחַיּוּת אֱלֹקִי בְּכָל נִבְרָא וְנִבְרָא וּבְכָל דָּבָר בִּפְרָט, דְּעֶצֶם הַהִתְבּוֹנְנוּת הַזֹּאת עַצְמָה מַסְפֶּקֶת גַּם כֵּן לְקָרֵב נַפְשׁוֹ בְּהֶרְגֵּשׁ הָאֱלֹקוּת וְהַטּוֹב וְהַיְקָר שֶׁבֶּאֱלֹקוּת וְיוֹסִיף אֹמֶץ בָּזֶה בְּהִתְבּוֹנְנוּת זֹאת אֵיךְ שֶׁהָעִקָּר הוּא הָאֱלֹקוּת וּבְעִנְיָן רְאֵה כו' אֶת הַחַיִּים וְאֶת הַטּוֹב כו', אוֹ בְּהִתְבּוֹנְנוּת בְּאֹפֶן הָאוֹר וְהַגִּלּוּי הַמִּתְלַבֵּשׁ וּמֵאִיר בָּעוֹלָמוֹת הָעֶלְיוֹנִים כָּל חַד וְחַד לְפוּם שִׁיעוּרָא דִילֵיהּ בְּהַשָּׂגָתוֹ וַעֲבוֹדָתוֹ, שֶׁכָּל זֶה עוֹשֶׂה חֲלִישׁוּת גְּדוֹלָה בְּהַנֶּפֶשׁ הַבַּהֲמִית שֶׁאֵינוֹ נִמְשָׁךְ אַחֲרֵי הָעִנְיָנִים הַחָמְרִיִּים וְאֵינוֹ מִתְפַּשֵּׁט רְצוֹנוֹ בָּהֶם וְיַגִּיעַ לְקָרֵב גַּם אֶת הַנֶּפֶשׁ הַבַּהֲמִית שֶׁגַּם הוּא יָבִין אֶת הָעִנְיָן הָאֱלֹקִי וְיִתְעוֹרֵר גַּם הוּא בִּבְחִינַת קָרוֹב לֶאֱלֹקוּת, וּבְכָל זֶה

The main focus of our effort should be to unite our soul with G-dliness through meditation upon the G-dly light enclothed in the worlds.

COMMENTARY

"returned" to everyday life unharmed by it.)

However, even this level of love doesn't bring satisfaction or total fulfillment. We desire only G-d Himself, and no matter what level we achieve in our meditation, we never grasp G-d Himself, and we are overcome with a spiritual "love-sickness." This condition can only be overcome by the advent of *Mashiach* and the re-building of the Temple, at which point everyone will be able to achieve grasp of the true essence of G-dliness, down here in the physical universe.

יִתְחַזֵּק בְּעֵסֶק הַתּוֹרָה וְקִיּוּם הַמִּצְוֹת לִהְיוֹתָן אֱלֹקוּת כנ״ל,

in physicality. We should strive to bring our animal soul as well to an understanding of G-dly matters, such that it will also be aroused by closeness to G-d. Throughout all this, we will become stronger in our Torah learning and fulfillment of the *mitzvot*, since they are G-dly, as mentioned before.

Even if we are not on a spiritual level to experience these revealed expressions of love of G-d, we should nevertheless get accustomed to thinking about them.

וְהַגְדָּלַת הָאַהֲבָה יוֹתֵר הִיא בִּבְחִינַת נַפְשִׁי אִוִּיתִיךָ כְּשֶׁמִּתְבּוֹנֵן שֶׁאַתָּה ה' נַפְשִׁי כו' (וְיִרְצֶה מְאֹד שֶׁיְּהֵי' גִּלּוּי אֱלֹקוּת בְּקִרְבּוֹ עַל יְדֵי הַתּוֹרָה) וְכֵן בְּאַהֲבָה דִּכְבְרָא דְּאִשְׁתַּדַּל כו' (וְגַם מִי שֶׁאֵינוֹ בְּדַרְגּוֹת אֵלּוּ לִהְיוֹת בּוֹ אַהֲבוֹת הנ״ל בְּהִתְגַּלּוּת יַרְגִּיל עַצְמוֹ בָּזֶה לִהְיוֹת כִּי קָרוֹב הַדָּבָר אֵלָיו כו'). וּבְמַדְרֵגוֹת גְּבֹהוֹת יוֹתֵר וְגַם בִּפְנִימִיּוּת יוֹתֵר הִיא בְּהִתְבּוֹנְנוּת דְּכַמַּיִם הַפָּנִים אֶל הַפָּנִים כו' וְגַם יְלַהֵב לִבּוֹ בִּבְחִינַת הִתְלַהֲבוּת בְּאַהֲבָה כְּרִשְׁפֵּי אֵשׁ (דְּאַהֲבָה זוֹ מִצַּד עַצְמָהּ מֻכְרַחַת לִהְיוֹת מִפְּנֵי שֶׁבָּזֶה דַּוְקָא הִתְגַּלּוּת הָאוֹר דְּנֶפֶשׁ הָאֱלֹקִית יוֹתֵר, וְגַם שֶׁזֶּהוּ עִקַּר בְּחִינַת הָרָצוֹא לֵאלֹקוּת) עַל יְדֵי שֶׁמִּתְבּוֹנֵן בְּמַעֲמָדוֹ וּמַצָּבוֹ אֵיךְ שֶׁהוּא מְרֻחָק כו' וַאֲמִתִּית הָאַהֲבָה הַזֹּאת תִּהְיֶה עַל יְדֵי

A further development of love [of G-d] is that of "You are my soul, I desire you..." which comes about through meditation on the verse, "You, Lord, are my soul" (and results in a strong yearning, brought about by learning Torah, for revelation of G-dliness within us). Then, there is also the contemplation leading to love like that of "a son who exerts himself for his father." (Even if we are not on a spiritual level to experience these revealed expressions of love of G-d, we should nevertheless get accustomed to thinking about them, since [as it says in Deuteronomy 30:14] the "thing is very close to you [to do]..."). On higher levels, and on more inner levels as well, we come to the meditation of "as in water, face answers to face." And then we can also inflame our heart with "love like fire." (We must of necessity come to this level

---

COMMENTARY

All of the levels of "love like fire" described in *Kuntres Ha'Avoda* would seem to be beyond us. *Kuntres Ha'Avoda* acknowledges this, stating that even if we don't think that we can really attain these levels of love of G-d, we should keep trying, because the "thing is very near to you." That is, love of G-d is latent in the heart of every Jew, and we should keep trying to bring it into a state of revelation. *Kuntres Ha'Avoda* further

since only it strongly reveals the light of the divine soul, and also because it is the main expression of the desire and yearning [of the divine soul] for G-dliness.) This we do by meditating on our own status and situation, and how far away we are [from G-d]. But the truest expression of this love comes about through meditation on His greatness. The G-dly fire burns and consumes the alien fire of the animal soul—and elevates it as well to be included in G-dliness—with excitement and flames of fire. About this, the verse says, "And you should know today and put it in your heart," such that the love is revealed in the heart. The word here for "your heart"—*levavcha*—[seems to be plural and] indicates two hearts, corresponding to the closeness and cleaving of the divine soul [to its Source], and to the refinement of the animal soul, such that it, too, becomes nullified and comes to love G-d, which is what is referred to in *Ve'ahavta*, "You should love...with your whole heart," meaning with both inclinations [the good and the bad].

הַהִתְבּוֹנְנוּת בִּגְדֻלָּתוֹ יִתְבָּרֵךְ כו' וְאֵשׁ זֶה הָאֱלֹקִי שׂוֹרֵף וּמְכַלֶּה אֶת הָאֵשׁ זָר דְּנֶפֶשׁ הַבַּהֲמִית וּמַעֲלֶה אוֹתוֹ לִהְיוֹת נִכְלָל גַּם כֵּן בֶּאֱלֹקוּת בִּבְחִי' הִתְלַהֲבוּת וְרִשְׁפֵּי אֵשׁ כו' וְעַל זֶה נֶאֱמַר וְיָדַעְתָּ הַיּוֹם וַהֲשֵׁבֹתָ אֶל לְבָבֶךָ לִהְיוֹת הָאַהֲבָה בְּהִתְגַּלּוּת בַּלֵּב, וְעִנְיַן לְבָבְךָ ב' לְבָבוֹת הַיְנוּ בְּחִינַת הַקֵּרוּב וְהַדְּבֵקוּת דְּנֶפֶשׁ הָאֱלֹקִית, וְהַזִּכּוּךְ דְּנֶפֶשׁ הַבַּהֲמִית שֶׁגַּם הוּא יִתְבַּטֵּל וְיָבוֹא לִבְחִינַת אַהֲבָה שֶׁזֶּהוּ עִנְיַן וְאָהַבְתָּ כו' בְּכָל לְבָבְךָ בִּשְׁנֵי יְצָרֶיךָ כו':

COMMENTARY

emphasizes that only "love like fire" has the ability to consume and incinerate the physical lusts and temptations of the animal soul. While "love like water" has the ability to weaken the animal soul, it cannot eliminate it. The importance of "love like fire" lies in its ability to devour and do away with our animal soul, turning us into different people altogether.

The goal of our meditation should be to fan the spark of G-dly light within us until it becomes a full-blown flame of love for the One Above. We should always keep trying to attain "love like fire," and in the process, at the very least we will develop our love for G-d to the level of "love like water."

SYNOPSIS:

There are two kinds of love [of G-d]. One is "love like water," which comes about by meditation on the G-dliness within the worlds, and which produces closeness and cleaving of our soul to G-dliness such that we seek only the G-dliness within everything. This love also brings us to learn Torah and keep its *mitzvot* and produces in us a weakening and subjugation of the animal soul. The second is "love like fire," and it comes about when, after meditation on G-dliness, we consider how far we are from G-d in both our soul and in our thought, speech, and action. In so doing, we inflame our heart with a fire of desire and thirst, and this fire burns and consumes the natural fire of the animal soul, causing it to be nullified in its very existence. Then, the fire of the animal soul ascends and is included as well in the excitement and flames of fire of love of G-dliness. And this is [really] the goal of the *avoda* of prayer, to come to these two levels of love of the One Above, such that they produce closeness and cleaving to G-d, and the purification and refinement of the physicality and ego of the animal soul, such that it also ascends. In this chapter are also explained higher levels of both types of love of G-d.

קִצוּר.

הִנֵּה יֵשׁ ב' בְּחִינוֹת אַהֲבָה, הָא' אַהֲבָה הַנִּמְשֶׁכֶת כְּמַיִם הַבָּאָה עַל יְדֵי הַהִתְבּוֹנְנוּת בִּבְחִינַת הָאֱלֹקוּת שֶׁבָּעוֹלָמוֹת, שֶׁעַל יְדֵי זֶה נַעֲשֶׂה קֵרוּב וּדְבֵקוּת נַפְשׁוֹ בֶּאֱלֹקוּת וּבְכָל דָּבָר יִרְצֶה רַק הָאֱלֹקוּת שֶׁבּוֹ, וְהִיא הַמְבִיאָה אוֹתוֹ גַּם כֵּן לְעֵסֶק הַתּוֹרָה וְקִיּוּם הַמִּצְוֹת וּבְנֶפֶשׁ הַבַּהֲמִית פּוֹעֶלֶת בּוֹ הַחֲלִישׁוּת וְהַכְנָעָה. וְהַב' הָאַהֲבָה כְּרִשְׁפֵּי אֵשׁ וְהוּא שֶׁלְּאַחַר הַהִתְבּוֹנְנוּת טוֹבָה בֶּאֱלֹקוּת יִתְבּוֹנֵן אֵיךְ שֶׁהוּא מְרֻחָק בִּכְלָלוּת נַפְשׁוֹ וּבְמַחֲשָׁבָה דִּבּוּר וּמַעֲשֶׂה שֶׁלּוֹ, שֶׁעַל יְדֵי זֶה יִתְלַהֵב לִבּוֹ בְּרִשְׁפֵּי אֵשׁ הַתְּשׁוּקָה וְהַצִּמָּאוֹן וְאֵשׁ זֶה שׂוֹרֵף וּמְכַלֶּה אֶת הָאֵשׁ הַטִּבְעִי דְּנֶפֶשׁ הַבַּהֲמִית לִהְיוֹת בִּבְחִינַת בִּטּוּל מַמָּשׁ, וְעוֹלֶה וְנִכְלָל גַּם הוּא בִּבְחִינַת הִתְלַהֲבוּת וְרִשְׁפֵּי אֵשׁ הָאַהֲבָה לֶאֱלֹקוּת. וְזֶהוּ תַּכְלִית הָעֲבוֹדָה דִּתְפִלָּה לָבוֹא לְב' מַדְרֵגוֹת אַהֲבָה הנ"ל שֶׁהֵן בְּחִינַת הַקֵּרוּב וְהַדְּבֵקוּת לֶאֱלֹקוּת. וּבֵרוּר וְזִכּוּךְ הַחָמְרִיּוּת וְהַיֵּשׁוּת דְּנֶפֶשׁ הַבַּהֲמִית לִהְיוֹת גַּם הוּא עוֹלֶה כו'. וְנִתְ' עוֹד מַדְרֵגוֹת גְּבוֹהוֹת יוֹתֵר בְּב' בְּחִינַת אַהֲבָה הנ"ל:

Essay on Service of the Heart - Love Like Fire and Water

CHAPTER 5 / פרק ה

The Hebrew word for "love," *ahava*, comes from the word *ava*, which means "will." The will is the inner dimension of the emotions, and it, as well as the emotions, stems from the intellect. The inner dimension of the emotions rules over and governs them, and it is capable of transforming their very nature. For example, when we detach ourselves from something enjoyable and no longer desire it for some reason, we no longer gain any enjoyment from that experience. The inverse is also true; when we find in front of ourselves a path of pain and suffering, and yet we work on ourselves to accept it, because we know intellectually that it's good for us, we don't feel as much pain and suffering. Quite the opposite, we actually learn to appreciate it. For example, [if we had a bad dream and wish to ameliorate it], we are permitted to fast on the Sabbath day [when fasting is otherwise prohibited], since for us it is beneficial. So, we see that the will can transform the nature of the emotions, since it is [really] the inner dimension of the emotions.

וְהִנֵּה אַהֲבָה הוּא מִלְּשׁוֹן אָבָה שֶׁפֵּרוּשׁוֹ רָצוֹן, וְהַיְנוּ הָרָצוֹן שֶׁהוּא פְּנִימִיּוּת הַמִּדּוֹת וְנִמְשָׁךְ גַּם כֵּן מִן הַשֵּׂכֶל. וְהָעִנְיָן דְּמַה שֶׁהוּא פְּנִימִיּוּת הַמִּדּוֹת הַיְנוּ שֶׁמּוֹשֵׁל וְשׁוֹלֵט עַל הַמִּדּוֹת וְיָכוֹל לְשַׁנּוֹת טֶבַע הַמִּדּוֹת, כְּמוֹ כְּשֶׁמְסַלֵּק רְצוֹנוֹ מֵאֵיזֶה דָּבָר תַּעֲנוּג וְאֵינוֹ רוֹצֶה בּוֹ מִצַּד אֵיזֶה טַעַם וָדַעַת אֵינוֹ מְקַבֵּל נַחַת וְתַעֲנוּג מֵהַדָּבָר הַהוּא, וּלְהֵפֶךְ כְּשֶׁיֵּשׁ לְפָנָיו חַס וְחָלִילָה דְּבַר שֶׁל צַעַר וְיִסּוּרִים אִם הוּא עוֹשֶׂה רְצוֹנוֹ לָזֶה עַל פִּי הַשֵּׂכֶל שֶׁמַּחְיִיב שֶׁהַצַּעַר הַזֶּה טוֹב לוֹ אֵינוֹ מַרְגִּישׁ הַצַּעַר וְהַיִּסּוּרִים כָּל כָּךְ וְאַדְּרַבָּא יְהִי לוֹ תַּעֲנוּג בָּזֶה. וְכַנּוֹדָע בְּעִנְיַן תַּעֲנִית חֲלוֹם בְּשַׁבָּת מִפְּנֵי שֶׁהוּא תַּעֲנוּג לוֹ, הֲרֵי שֶׁהָרָצוֹן מְשַׁנֶּה אֶת טֶבַע הַמִּדּוֹת לִהְיוֹתוֹ פְּנִימִיּוּת הַמִּדּוֹת,

In Hebrew, the word for love (ahava) comes from the word for will (ava).

COMMENTARY
CHAPTER 5: KNOWLEDGE AND UNITY

Now that we know something of the kinds of love of G-d that we can experience, it's time to consider how to get there.

Here in Chapter 5, love of G-d derived from reason and logic is described as "love that is dependent upon something." Most relationships that we form are dependent on something (even if they contain an element of true affection as well). One example is the "love" between Amnon and Tamar (as recounted in 2 Samuel, chapter 13). Amnon was physically attracted to Tamar,

Our will is the inner dimension of our emotions, but our will is also influenced by intellect.

וּמִכָּל מָקוֹם גַּם הָרָצוֹן הוּא עַל פִּי הַשֵּׂכֶל דְּהַיְנוּ מַה שֶׁהַשֵּׂכֶל מְחַיֵּב שֶׁצָּרִיךְ לִרְצוֹת כָּךְ לֹא שֶׁהוּא רוֹצֶה כֵן בְּטִבְעוֹ כִּי אִם מִצַּד חִיּוּב הַשֵּׂכֶל וּכְמוֹ שֶׁכָּתוּב בְּלִקּוּטֵי תּוֹרָה דִּבּוּר הַמַּתְחִיל בְּהַעֲלוֹתְךָ דְּרוּשׁ הָרִאשׁוֹן, וְהוּא בְּחִינַת תִּפְאֶרֶת דְּאִימָא שֶׁנַּעֲשָׂה כֶּתֶר לִזְעֵיר אַנְפִּין כו'. אָמְנָם בִּדְרוּשׁ יָשָׁן מֵרַבֵּינוּ נ"ע אי' דְּאַבָה הוּא בְּחִינַת רָצוֹן שֶׁלְּמַעְלָה מִטַּעַם וָדַעַת. וְהוּא בְּחִינַת הָרָצוֹן הַטִּבְעִי

Nevertheless, the will is also governed by the intellect. Whatever our intellect dictates as the correct path becomes our will. By nature, we may not desire that path, but because logic dictates it, that path becomes our own as written in the first discourse of *Beha'alotcha* in *Likutei Torah*. [In Kabbalistic terms,] this is the process wherein *tiferet d'imma*, the emotions within intellect, become the crown and motivation of the emotions themselves, *na'aseh keter l'za*. However, there is an old Chassidic discourse by the [Alter] Rebbe, [the founder of the Chabad movement], *Nishmato Eden*, which indicates that *ava* ("will") is beyond the intellect; it is our innate will.

וְהַיְנוּ מַה שֶׁבַּטֶּבַע יֵשׁ בַּנְּשָׁמוֹת בְּחִינַת רָצוֹן שֶׁנִּמְשָׁךְ בְּרָצוֹא לְאוֹר אֵין סוֹף בָּרוּךְ הוּא (א צִיא צוּא אוֹר אֵין סוֹף בָּרוּךְ הוּא). וְנוֹדָע דְּרָצוֹן הַטִּבְעִי הוּא בִּבְחִינַת מַקִּיפִים דִּנְשָׁמָה

By nature, there is an aspect of the soul that is drawn [spontaneously] in a spiritual rush toward the infinite light of the One Above. It is known that our natural will coincides with the transcendent levels of our soul.

COMMENTARY

but once he achieved his desire, he was no longer interested in her. This is love that is "dependent upon something," and it dissipates once the real goal has been achieved.

Love of G-d that results from meditation is dependent upon the intellect. When we think deeply into a spiritual topic and then develop love of G-d based on it, our love dissipates when the meditation ceases. Of course, the amount of time the emotion lasts is dependent on the quality of our meditation and on the depth of the emotion generated by it. But, as long as the love is the product of intellectual activity, it is "dependent upon something" — that is, upon our mental process — and it eventually dissipates.

> As explained in Chapter 1, the divine soul has five levels, the lower three of which are en-clothed in the body, and the higher two—the transcendent levels—connect the essence of the soul with its source in the infinite light of G-d. The two highest levels are:

4. *Chaya*	"Living one"	Transcendent consciousness
5. *Yechida*	"Single one"	Unity consciousness

There are two levels of transcendence. The first [highest] level is called the *yechida*, and on this level the will needs no reason or stimulation whatsoever in order to come into expression. The soul is drawn spontaneously to its source in the Creator's essential and infinite light, without any meditation whatsoever being necessary. This is because the Jewish soul is "a part of the One Above" [*Tanya*, chapter 2, from Job 31:2]. Like everything that strives to return to its

וְיֵשׁ בָּזֶה ב' מַדְרֵגוֹת הָא' בְּחִינַת מַקִיף דִּיחִידָה שֶׁהָרָצוֹן הוּא בְּלִי שׁוּם סִבָּה וּבְלִי שׁוּם הִתְעוֹרְרוּת כְּלָל, וְהַיְנוּ שֶׁאֵין צָרִיךְ לְשׁוּם הִתְבּוֹנְנוּת כְּלָל כִּי אִם שֶׁמִּמֵּילָא נִמְשָׁךְ אֶל מְקוֹר חָצְבוֹ בְּחִינַת עַצְמוּת אוֹר אֵין סוֹף בָּרוּךְ הוּא שֶׁהֲרֵי הוּא חֵלֶק אֱלֹקַ' מִמַּעַל וּכְמוֹ טֶבַע כָּל דָּבָר שֶׁנִּמְשָׁךְ לְשָׁרְשׁוֹ וּמְקוֹרוֹ כָּךְ הוּא טֶבַע הַנְּשָׁמָה לִמָּשֵׁךְ וּלְהִכָּלֵל בְּשָׁרְשָׁהּ וּמְקוֹרָהּ בְּחִינַת

Within the will are two transcendent soul-levels; chaya and yechida.

COMMENTARY

Not so, says Chapter 5, when we come to "love that is dependent upon nothing." Two friends, who have true affection for each other, need no reason to help each other, worry about each other, and spend time together. One example is the affection between King David and Jonathan, the son of King Saul (as recounted in 1 Samuel, chatper 18-20). The two were true friends who sought nothing from the bond between them aside from the welfare of one another (this in spite of the fact that King Saul was David's sworn enemy at the time).

In its root, this is the natural love for G-d that is latent within the Jewish soul. It expresses itself on two different levels. First of all, it expresses itself as our desire for real connection with

עַצְמוּת אוֹר אֵין סוֹף בָּרוּךְ הוּא, וְהִיא מְיֻחֶדֶת בֶּאֱמֶת תָּמִיד בִּבְחִינַת עַצְמוּת אוֹר אֵין סוֹף וּכְמַאֲמָר חֲבוּקָה וּדְבוּקָה בָּךְ (וּמַה שֶּׁהוּא בִּבְחִינַת הַמְשָׁכָה וְרָצוֹא, זֶהוּ מִשּׁוּם דְּאֹפֶן מְצִיאוּת הַנְּשָׁמוֹת מִן הָעַצְמוּת הוּא בִּבְחִינַת מַהוּת בִּפְנֵי עַצְמוֹ וּכְמוֹ הַבֵּן מִן הָאָב הֲגַם שֶׁהֵם עֶצֶם א׳ מִכָּל מָקוֹם הַבֵּן הוּא בְּמַהוּת בִּפְנֵי עַצְמוֹ, שֶׁזֶּהוּ הַהֶפְרֵשׁ בֵּין נְשָׁמוֹת לַתּוֹרָה עִם הֱיוֹת שֶׁשְּׁנֵיהֶם מִבְּחִינַת הָעַצְמוּת כו׳ וּכְמוֹ שֶׁכָּתוּב בְּמָקוֹם אַחֵר)

source of origin, so the way of the soul is to be drawn upward and included in its origin — the essential, infinite light of the One Above. The truth is that this level of the soul, the *yechida*, is at all times united with the essential, infinite light of the One Above, as in the phrase [from the *hoshanot* — supplications for rain recited on the third day of *chol hamoed* Succot—describing the soul and G-d]: "embracing and cleaving to You...". (That the *yechida* is drawn to G-d and has a desire for Him is due to the nature of souls in general. The nature of the soul's emergence into existence from G-d's essence is such that the soul has its own identity, or selfhood. This is analogous to a son in relation to his father; although they are of the same essence, nevertheless the son has his own selfhood and identity. This is, as well, the difference between the soul and the Torah,[xxvi] even though both of them are from His essence, as written elsewhere.)

xxvi) See footnote of the Rebbe on page 280

COMMENTARY

the One Above; this is the level of *chaya*, ("transcendental consciousness") mentioned in Chapter 1. Second, it expresses itself as *yechida* ("unity consciousness"). The *yechida* is the essential point of the soul that is never disconnected from the One Above. It is the spark of G-dliness within us which the *Tanya* calls "an integral part of G-d on high."

| Love of G-d based on logic | Love dependent on something | Amnon and Tamar |
| Love of G-d beyond reason | Love dependent on nothing | David and Jonathan |

LOVE DEPENDENT ON SOMETHING

The process leading to "love that is dependent on something" is based upon intellect (*chabad*). This acronym has largely been made famous by the proactive Chassidic group, but its actual

Essay on Service of the Heart - Love Like Fire and Water

The *yechida* comes into expression as *mesirat nefesh* — "giving up one's life" in honor of the One Above. That we may actually give up our own life is due to the fact that it is absolutely impossible for us to be separated from the One Above, G-d forbid. This "stubbornness" comes from the *yechida* of our soul, which is in [constant and] essential connection with the infinite One Above, and it is impossible for it to be any other way, G-d forbid. (This is also expressed in our sincerity and earnestness in the actual fulfillment of the *mitzvot*, both positive and negative. It is as if the very nature of every Jew is to avoid deliberate sin, G-d forbid, as well as not to disregard any *mitzvah*. This is part of the expression of the *yechida* which is the essential connection of

וְהִיא הַמִּתְגַּלָּה בִּמְסִירַת נֶפֶשׁ עַל קִדּוּשׁ הַשֵּׁם דְּזֶה שֶׁמּוֹסֵר נַפְשׁוֹ בְּפֹעַל מַמָּשׁ הוּא מִפְּנֵי שֶׁאִי אֶפְשָׁר לוֹ בְּשׁוּם אֹפֶן לִהְיוֹת נִפְרָד חַס וְחָלִילָה. וְהַיְנוּ מִבְּחִינַת יְחִידָה שֶׁבַּנֶּפֶשׁ שֶׁהִיא בִּבְחִינַת הִתְקַשְּׁרוּת עַצְמִי בְּעַצְמוּת אֵין סוֹף בָּרוּךְ הוּא וְאִי אֶפְשָׁר לִהְיוֹת כְּלָל בְּאֹפֶן אַחֵר חַס וְחָלִילָה (וְכֵן הוּא בִּתְמִימוּת הַמַּעֲשֶׂה בְּסוּר מֵרָע וַעֲשֵׂה טוֹב בְּפֹעַל מַמָּשׁ, שֶׁזֶּהוּ כְּמוֹ טֶבַע בְּכָל אֶחָד וְאֶחָד מִיִּשְׂרָאֵל שֶׁלֹּא יַעֲבֹר בְּמֵזִיד אֵיזֶה עֲבֵרָה חַס וְחָלִילָה וְשֶׁלֹּא יְבַטֵּל אֵיזֶה מִצְוָה חַס וְחָלִילָה, שֶׁזֶּהוּ מִבְּחִינַת יְחִידָה שֶׁבַּנֶּפֶשׁ שֶׁהִיא עֶצֶם הִתְקַשְּׁרוּתוֹ בֶּאֱלֹקוּת כוּ' וּכְמוֹ שֶׁכָּתוּב מִזֶּה בְּדֶרֶךְ חַיִּים ספ"ח. וְכֵן הוּא בְּכָל

Yechida is the innate connection of the soul that needs no arousal.

COMMENTARY
---

meaning is less well known. Chabad stands for three key steps in meditation - *chochma* ("wisdom"); *bina* ("understanding"), and *da'at* ("knowledge"):

We first hear of a concept, or read about it, and we gain an overall grasp of its features. This is called *chochma* (literally "wisdom"), and it corresponds to an initial flash, or inspiration of intellect. Often, this initial inspiration is so ephemeral that — unless we sit down and think about it — it simply dissipates. The process of grasping the concept, analyzing it, and considering all of its details, is called *bina* (intellectual "understanding"). These two processes are so closely related and intertwined that Kabbalah actually refers to the two as "father and mother" and says that they are always together. In this stage of the process, though, the emphasis is on *chochma*, because without the spiritual insight of *chochma*, there can be no analysis on the level of *bina*.

the soul with G-dliness, as written in *Derech Chaim*, at the end of chapter 8. And so it is with each and every test that we face. The *yechida* of our soul empowers us to stand firm against the seduction of the evil inclination which attempts to influence us, may G-d protect us. We refuse to be seduced and stand firm with all of our power. This is what is meant [in *Talmud Niddah* 30] by the phrase:

נִסָּיוֹן וְנִסָּיוֹן שֶׁעוֹמֵד עַל נַפְשׁוֹ נֶגֶד הֲסָתוֹת הַיֵּצֶר הָרָע הַבַּהֲמִית וּמַדִיחַ רַחֲמָנָא לִיצְלָן וַהֲרֵי הוּא מִתְגַּבֵּר עָלָיו בְּכָל תֹּקֶף וְעֹז כוּ׳. שֶׁזֶּהוּ עִנְיָן מַשְׁבִּיעִין אוֹתוֹ שֶׁהוּא לְשׁוֹן שֹׂבַע כַּנּוֹדַע, וְהַיְנוּ שֶׁנּוֹתְנִים לוֹ כֹּחַ וְעֹז מֵעֶצֶם הַנְּשָׁמָה שֶׁקְּשׁוּרָה וּדְבוּקָה בֵּאלֹקִים חַיִּים דְּבְכֹחַ זֶה הוּא עוֹמֵד נֶגֶד כָּל מוֹנֵעַ מִבַּיִת וּמִבַּחוּץ).

"They make him take an oath," [regarding the embryo while still in its mother's womb, that it should take an oath to be a *tzaddik* after it is born]. The Hebrew word for "oath" (*shavuah*) also indicates satisfaction and satiation. This is the condition that results from receiving the power of the essence of the soul, [the *yechida*], which is connected to the living G-d. With this power, we are able to stand up to each and every obstacle, whether originating from within or without ourselves.)

The second transcendent level, chaya, needs arousal to come into expression.

דְּהַמַּדְרֵגָה הַב׳ הִיא בְּחִינַת מַקִּיף דְּחַי׳ דְּעִם הֱיוֹתָהּ גַּם כֵּן בִּכְלָל בְּחִינַת עַצְמוּת הַנְּשָׁמָה מִכָּל מָקוֹם אֵינָהּ בְּחִינַת עַצְמוּת מַמָּשׁ לִהְיוֹת בִּבְחִינַת הִתְקַשְּׁרוּת עַצְמִית כְּמוֹ בְּחִינַת יְחִידָה כִּי אִם שֶׁצְּרִיכִים לְעוֹרֵר הָרָצוֹן וְהַהִתְקַשְּׁרוּת, וְהוּא

The second transcendent level of the soul [below *yechida*] is called *chaya*. While it is true that the *chaya* is also an integral part of the essence of the soul, nevertheless, it is not at one with the essence in the same way as is the *yechida*. While the *yechida* is inherently connected and united, the

--- **COMMENTARY** ---

Once we have grasped the concept well, through the faculty of *bina*, we must then focus on it for the purpose of clarity and feeling. The goal of meditation is to feel the G-dliness within the concept while understanding it deeply, so that we are led to greater levels of love and fear of the One Above. We have truly internalized a concept only when in addition to understanding it, we feel it on a visceral level. The focus and concentration necessary to achieve the visceral feeling is called *da'at* ("knowledge").

Essay on Service of the Heart - Love Like Fire and Water

will and desire for connection of the *chaya* requires arousal in order to come into expression. The arousal takes place through meditation upon the essential infinite light of the One Above, with emphasis on its exalted and elevated status, as written elsewhere.[xxvii] Nevertheless, this will [of the *chaya*] is also both essential and innate, even though it has to be aroused. When aroused and expressed, it is as an essential will that is beyond all thought and logic, and therefore beyond limitation as well.

It is written elsewhere that there is a "love which is dependent upon something," meaning that there is an [external] factor that motivates the love and is the entire reason for its existence. Such a state of love is limited in proportion to the factor that brings the love about. If the factor is eliminated, the love dissipates. Then, there is love that is "not dependent upon anything." It is an essential love,

עַל יְדֵי הַהִתְבּוֹנְנוּת בִּבְחִינַת עַצְמוּת אוֹר אֵין סוֹף בִּבְחִינַת הַפְלָאָתוֹ וְרוֹמְמוּתוֹ כו' כְּמוֹ שֶׁכָּתוּב בְּמָקוֹם אַחֵר. וּמִכָּל מָקוֹם גַּם הָרָצוֹן הַזֶּה הוּא בְּחִינַת רָצוֹן עַצְמִי וְטִבְעִי, הֲגַם שֶׁצְּרִיכִים לְעוֹרֵר הָרָצוֹן, מִכָּל מָקוֹם כְּשֶׁמִּתְעוֹרֵר הוּא בִּבְחִינַת רָצוֹן עַצְמִי שֶׁלְּמַעְלָה מִטַּעַם וָדַעַת וְלָכֵן הוּא בִּבְחִינַת בְּלִי גְּבוּל כו',

וּכְמוֹ שֶׁכָּתוּב בְּמָקוֹם אַחֵר שֶׁיֵּשׁ אַהֲבָה הַתְּלוּיָ' בְּדָבָר דְּהַיְינוּ שֶׁכָּל סִבָּתָהּ הוּא הַדָּבָר הַגּוֹרֵם אֶת הָאַהֲבָה וּמִמֵּילָא הִיא מֻגְבֶּלֶת לְפִי אֹפֶן הַדָּבָר הַגּוֹרֵם וּכְשֶׁמִּתְבַּטֵּל הַדָּבָר מִתְבַּטֵּל גַּם כֵּן הָאַהֲבָה וְיֵשׁ אַהֲבָה שֶׁאֵינָהּ תְּלוּיָ' בְּדָבָר כִּי אִם אַהֲבָה עַצְמִית וּכְמוֹ שְׁנֵי אוֹהֲבִים נֶאֱמָנִים שֶׁאֵין אַהֲבָתָם תְּלוּיָ' בְּשׁוּם דָּבָר דְּאַהֲבָה זוֹ אֵינָהּ מֻגְבֶּלֶת

When it comes into expression, the chaya is beyond all thought and logic, and beyond limitation.

← xxvii) See footnote of the Rebbe on page 281

COMMENTARY

Under normal circumstances, our faculty of *da'at* leads us to appreciation of G-dliness embedded in the creation. Our perception of the physical world remains dominant, but we become more and more aware of the immanent G-dliness enlivening the creation. That is, the creation remains in the foreground even as we become more and more aware of the Creator in the background. This consciousness is called *da'at tachton* ("lower awareness"), and the perception associated with it is called *yichuda tata'ah* ("lower unity"). On this level, we appreciate the essential spiritual unity of the universe but remain aware of, and place emphasis on, the physical reality of creation. When this paradigm is mapped upon the structure of the ten *sephirot*, the *sephira* of *da'at* is "located" below *bina* and above

Love that is not dependent on anything never dissipates.

מֵאַחַר שֶׁאֵינָהּ תְּלוּיָה בַּדָּבָר שֶׁיְּמַדֵּד אוֹתָהּ וְגַם אֵינָהּ מִתְבַּטֶּלֶת לְעוֹלָם וּמִכָּל מָקוֹם יְכוֹלָה לְהִתְעַלֵּם בְּמֶשֶׁךְ זְמַן כְּשֶׁמִּתְרַחֲקִים זֶה מִזֶּה וּמִתְעוֹרֵר עַל יְדֵי אֵיזֶה דָּבָר כְּמוֹ דְּבַר שִׂמְחָה וּכְהַאי גַוְונָא. אָמְנָם כְּשֶׁמִּתְעוֹרֵר הָאַהֲבָה אֵינָהּ מֻגְבֶּלֶת לְפִי אֹפֶן הַדָּבָר הַמְעוֹרֵר מִפְּנֵי שֶׁלֹּא הוּא סִבָּתָהּ בֶּאֱמֶת כִּי הָאַהֲבָה הִיא עַצְמִית בְּלִי שׁוּם סִבָּה רַק שֶׁנִּתְעַלְּמָה וּכְשֶׁמִּתְעוֹרֶרֶת הֲרֵי הִיא בְּעַצְמוּתָהּ כְּמוֹ שֶׁהִיא מִצַּד עַצְמָהּ וַהֲרֵי הִיא בִּלְתִּי מֻגְבֶּלֶת. וּלְמַעְלָה מִזֶּה בְּאֵין עָרוֹךְ אַהֲבָה עַצְמִית מַמָּשׁ כְּמוֹ אַהֲבַת אָב וּבֵן שֶׁאֵינָהּ מִתְעַלֶּמֶת לְעוֹלָם וְאֵין צָרִיךְ

such as that between two loyal friends whose affection for each other is independent of any [external] factors. Their affection is unlimited, since it doesn't depend upon any [outside] factor that limits the love, and so it never completely disappears. It can recede with the passage of time, when the two are geographically far from one another, and then something may cause their love to re-surface — for example, a family *simcha* and the like. But, when their love does re-surface, it is not proportionate to the event that aroused it. The event is not the true reason for their love and affection. Their love for each other is essential, without any reason whatso-

--- **COMMENTARY** ---

the emotional *sephirot* in the structure of the ten *sephirot*. Here, *da'at* functions as the intermediary between the mind and the G-dly emotions, as follows:

Awareness of *Da'at Tachton* and *Yichuda Tata*
Chochma "wisdom"
Bina "understanding"
Da'at **"knowledge"**
Chesed "loving-kindness"
Gevura "strength"
Tiferet "beauty"

Essay on Service of the Heart - Love Like Fire and Water

ever. It can grow faint, but when re-ignited, it returns to its previous, unlimited state. And far beyond this love is true essential love; for example, the love between a father and son, which never grows faint [or disappears] at all. It needs no factor whatsoever to arouse it, and it is constantly present.

לְשׁוּם דָּבָר הַמְעוֹרֵר וְהִיא בִּתְמִידוּת מַמָּשׁ.

And so it is with the soul. There is a love of G-d in the soul that is "dependent upon something" — such as logic and reason. The entire basis and foundation of this love is comprehension of, and meditation upon, G-dly concepts. Since in this meditation, the essential love of the soul is not shining, and it is only the conscious faculties of the soul that provide G-dly illumination, the love that develops is of the emotions of the heart [alone]. It is the result of meditation, and it is limited in relation to the meditation. It disappears after the meditation is over—this is [generally] after prayer, the time of service of the mind and heart. This is true as well of those emotions that arise spontaneously from the mind — see Chapter

וְכָךְ הוּא בַּנֶּפֶשׁ דְּאַהֲבָה הַתְּלוּיָה בְּדָבָר בַּנֶּפֶשׁ הִיא הָאַהֲבָה שֶׁעַל פִּי טַעַם וְדַעַת שֶׁכָּל סִבָּתָהּ הִיא הַהַשָּׂגָה וְהַהִתְבּוֹנְנוּת בֶּאֱלֹקוּת, לְפִי שֶׁאֵינוֹ מֵאִיר בָּזֶה בְּחִינַת הָאַהֲבָה הָעַצְמִית שֶׁבַּנֶּפֶשׁ רַק בְּחִינַת הַכֹּחוֹת הַגְּלוּיִּים לְבַד וְהִיא בְּחִינַת הָאַהֲבָה דְּמִדּוֹת שֶׁבַּלֵּב שֶׁסִּבָּתָהּ הִיא הַהִתְבּוֹנְנוּת וְהִיא מֻגְבֶּלֶת לְפִי אוֹפֶן הַהִתְבּוֹנְנוּת וּמִתְעַלֶּמֶת לְאַחַר הִתְחַלְּקוּת הַהַשָּׂגָה וְהַהִתְבּוֹנְנוּת (הַיְנוּ לְאַחַר הַתְּפִלָּה שֶׁהוּא זְמַן הָעֲבוֹדָה בְּמֹחַ וְלֵב. וְדָבָר זֶה הוּא גַּם כֵּן בַּמִּדּוֹת שֶׁבָּאִים בְּדֶרֶךְ מִמֵּילָא מֵהַמֹּחִין, עַל פִּי מַה שֶּׁנִּתְבָּאֵר לְעֵיל בפ״א בְּפִי׳ רְעוּתָא דְּלִבָּא (רַק שֶׁבַּאֲמִתִּית בְּחִינַת פְּנִימִיּוּת הַמֹּחִין שֶׁנִּתְבָּאֵר לְעֵיל

In the soul, there is love dependent upon something – on reason and logic.

COMMENTARY

LOVE DEPENDENT ON NOTHING

However, there are times when we undergo a paradigm shift and experience a different level of consciousness. (Here, we are not referring to prophecy, about which the Rambam says in *Hilchot Yesodei HaTorah* 7:1, "Among the principles that one must know is that G-d visits prophecy upon man and he becomes a different person." Prophecy is an actual experience of G-dly revelation, while here we are speaking only of intellectual grasp of spirituality.). We come to the conclusion that G-d is the true reality and the creation is temporal. G-d creates the physical

1, the explanation of *re'uta d'liba*. (But regarding the true "inward mindfulness" described earlier, "disappearance" of the love does not really occur...). Even though the emotions [that rise spontaneously from the mind] are internal [and closer to the essence], they are still emotions based upon reason and logic. And as written elsewhere, even service [of G-d] based upon intellect may give rise to either internal or superficial emotions. It is known that love can grow to surpass even the intellect that gave rise to it. This is because the emotions have a source [of their own] that is beyond the intellect, which is [what the Kabbalists mean when they say], *z'a b'atika achid v'talia*, "the G-dly emotions are united with, and dependent upon, His essence and enjoyment."[xxviii] And in truth, when the emotions achieve the pinnacle of growth, they don't disappear even after the time of prayer.

אֵינוֹ שַׁיָּךְ בָּזֶה הַתְעַלְּמוּת כָּל כָּךְ כו׳) דְּעִם הֱיוֹת שֶׁזֶּהוּ בְּחִינַת פְּנִימִיּוּת מִכָּל מָקוֹם הֲרֵי הֵן מִדּוֹת שֶׁעַל פִּי טַעַם וָדַעַת וּכְמוֹ שֶׁכָּתוּב בְּמָקוֹם אַחֵר שֶׁגַּם בַּעֲבוֹדָה שֶׁעַל פִּי טַעַם וָדַעַת יֵשׁ בְּחִינַת פְּנִימִיּוּת הַלֵּב וְחִיצוֹנִיּוּת הַלֵּב) (וְהִנֵּה נוֹדָע שֶׁיָּכוֹל לִהְיוֹת הַגְדָּלַת הָאַהֲבָה יוֹתֵר מֵהַמֹּחִין הַמּוֹלִידָהּ וְזֶהוּ מִבְּחִינַת שֹׁרֶשׁ הַמִּדּוֹת שֶׁלְּמַעְלָה מֵהַמֹּחִין שֶׁזֶּהוּ עִנְיַן דִּזְעֵיר אַנְפִּין בְּעַתִּיקָא אָחִיד וְתַלְיָא כְּמוֹ שֶׁכָּתוּב בְּמָקוֹם אַחֵר, וְהַגְדָּלָה זוֹ כָּאָמוּר אֵינָהּ מִתְעַלֶּמֶת גַּם לְאַחַר הַתְּפִלָּה כו׳)

xxviii) See footnote of the Rebbe on page 282

COMMENTARY

universe and He can cease creating it at any instant. Therefore, G-d is real and the creation is questionable.

It is this paradigm shift which gives rise to "love that is dependent upon nothing." This is the awareness that is associated with the level of *chaya*, or transcendent consciousness. It is granted as a gift from Above to those of us who have sufficiently meditated and refined our consciousness. Since it is a gift and not directly dependent on any effort we have invested, we can't predict when it will be bestowed. We can prepare ourselves for it, but there is nothing that we can do to guarantee that it will come. Thus, the love of G-d associated with it (also called *ahava rabba*) is dependent upon nothing.

This consciousness is also brought about through the faculty of *da'at*, but this time *da'at* is on a different level completely. It is called *da'at elyon* (higher knowledge), and the perception associated with it is called *yichuda ila'ah* (higher unity). On this

Essay on Service of the Heart - Love Like Fire and Water

Now, the love in the soul that is "not dependent upon anything" is love of G-d that is [totally] beyond reason and logic. It is an essential love of G-d, within which we find two levels [*chaya* and *yechida*]. The first level is the transcendent level of love and will for connection known as *chaya*, which requires arousal (since it is not the true essence of the soul that is in absolute proximity to the infinite One Above) by meditation on the amazing exaltedness of His infinite light (this, too, is beyond anything that is graspable by human intellect). But once ultimately aroused, this love expresses the very essence of the soul. This is because in truth, it is not the meditation that gives rise to this love [of the One Above]. Rather, within the essence of the soul is a love and intense will for the infinite light of G-d [that is aroused through meditation]. But the *yechida* within the soul does not

וְאַהֲבָה שֶׁאֵינָהּ תְּלוּיָ' בַּדָּבָר הִיא הָאַהֲבָה שֶׁלְּמַעְלָה מִטַּעַם וְדַעַת דְּהַיְינוּ שֶׁהִיא בְּחִינַת אַהֲבָה עַצְמִית וּבָזֶה יֵשׁ בּ' מַדְרֵגוֹת, הָא' בְּחִינַת אַהֲבָה דְּהַיְינוּ הָרָצוֹן דְּמַדְרֵגַת מַקִּיף דְּחַיִּ' שֶׁצְּרִיכָה מִכָּל מָקוֹם הִתְעוֹרְרוּת (לְפִי שֶׁאֵינוֹ בְּחִינַת עַצְמוּת הַנְּשָׁמָה מַמָּשׁ שֶׁהִיא בִּבְחִינַת קֵרוּב מַמָּשׁ בְּעַצְמוּת אֵין סוֹף בָּרוּךְ הוּא וְלָזֹאת צְרִיכָה הִתְעוֹרְרוּת) עַל יְדֵי הִתְבּוֹנְנוּת הַהַפְלָאָה דְּאוֹר אֵין סוֹף (שֶׁזֶּהוּ גַּם כֵּן לְמַעְלָה מִבְּחִינַת טַעַם וְדַעַת הַמּוּשָּׂג מַמָּשׁ) אָמְנָם כַּאֲשֶׁר מִתְעוֹרֵר הוּא בִּבְחִינַת רָצוֹן עַצְמִי, כִּי בֶּאֱמֶת לֹא הַהִתְבּוֹנְנוּת הִיא סִבַּת הָאַהֲבָה כִּי אִם מַה שֶׁבְּעֶצֶם יֵשׁ בַּנְּשָׁמָה בְּחִינַת אַהֲבָה וְרָצוֹא לְאוֹר אֵין סוֹף בָּרוּךְ הוּא. וּבְחִינַת יְחִידָה שֶׁבַּנֶּפֶשׁ אֵין צָרִיךְ לְשׁוּם הִתְעוֹרְרוּת כְּלָל לְפִי שֶׁהוּא בִּבְחִינַת קֵרוּב עִם הָעַצְמוּת וְאֵינוֹ

And there is love dependent upon nothing – beyond reason and logic. It requires meditation on the infinite light of G-d.

COMMENTARY
---

level, our awareness is of G-d, with creation secondary. G-d is in the foreground, occupying our attention, and His creation is in the background. In this paradigm, the *sephira* of *da'at* is situated above *chochma* and *bina* in the structure of the ten *sephirot*, as opposed to below them. It functions as an intermediary drawing the infinite light of G-d into our mind and emotions together. On this level, *da'at* is the vehicle for bringing down the infinite light of G-d and causing the intellect and the emotions to function as one, in an organic unity. This is the essence of an elevated spiritual experience — we surpass our own ego and are able to view ourselves and the world from a higher, G-dly plane.

Love dependent on nothing is associated with chaya and yechida.

שַׁיָּךְ בָּזֶה שׁוּם הִתְעַלְּמוּת כְּלָל, וּכְמוֹ אַהֲבַת אָב וּבֵן דְּעִם הֱיוֹת שֶׁאֵינָהּ בְּהִתְגַּלּוּת אֵינָהּ מִתְעַלֶּמֶת לְעוֹלָם וְהִיא בִּבְחִינַת הִתְקַשְּׁרוּת עַצְמִית וּתְמִידִית כוּ' וּכְמוֹ שֶׁכָּתוּב בְּמָקוֹם אַחֵר.

וְהִנֵּה בְּחִינַת רָצוֹן הַנַּ"ל הֲגַם שֶׁזֶּהוּ מַדְרֵגָה גְּבוֹהָה מְאֹד בַּעֲבוֹדָה מִכָּל מָקוֹם אֵין זֶה פּוֹעֵל כָּל כָּךְ עַל הַחָמְרִיּוּת דְּנֶפֶשׁ הַבַּהֲמִית מִפְּנֵי שֶׁהוּא לְמַעְלָה מִבְּחִינַת הִתְלַבְּשׁוּת

require an arousal at all. It is in such close proximity to the essence [of G-d] that it never [loses its connection nor] becomes hidden at all. It is analogous to the love between father and son—although it is not always expressed, it never disappears. This is an essential, constant bond, as written elsewhere.

Now the will for connection mentioned earlier [the *chaya*], despite being an exceedingly high level of "service of the One Above," nevertheless does not have a noticeable effect on the gross earthiness of the animal

---

COMMENTARY

Also in the paradigm of *da'at elyon*, the ten *sephirot* are arranged differently. Instead of being arranged in a linear fashion, as in *da'at tachton* (lower knowledge) the *sephirot* are arranged in a series of triplets. *Da'at* is located above the intellectual *sephirot* of *chochma* and *bina*, followed by the emotional triplet of *chesed*, *gevura*, and *tiferet*, and finally the action triplet of *netzach*, *hod*, and *yesod*, followed by *malchut*:

Awareness of *Da'at Elyon* and *Yichuda Ila'ah*	
Da'at "knowledge"	
Bina "understanding"	Chochma "wisdom"
Gevura "strength"	Chesed "loving-indness"
Tiferet "beauty"	
Hod "thanksgiving"	Netzach "victory"
Yesod "foundation"	
Malchut "sovereignty"	

Essay on Service of the Heart - Love Like Fire and Water

soul. That is because it is above being clad in the animal soul. (Although love which is beyond logic and reason is generally "love like fire"—aside from *ahava beta'anugim* [love with delight] or cleaving to the One Above, within which there are two levels: *ohr yashar*, ["direct light" from above to below] and *ohr chozer* ["reflected light" from below to above],^xxix as explained elsewhere—nevertheless since the soul-level that gives rise to this love is above being garbed in the animal soul, it doesn't have much effect upon it.36)

בְּנֶפֶשׁ הַבַּהֲמִית (עִם הֱיוֹת דְּהָאַהֲבָה שֶׁלְּמַעְלָה מִטַּעַם וָדַעַת בְּדֶרֶךְ כְּלָל הִיא בִּבְחִינַת אַהֲבָה כְּרִשְׁפֵּי אֵשׁ (לְבַד בְּחִינַת אַהֲבָה בְּתַעֲנוּגִים שֶׁהִיא בִּבְחִינַת דְּבֵקוּת וְגַם בָּזֶה יֵשׁ בְּחִינַת אוֹר יָשָׁר וְאוֹר חוֹזֵר וּכְמוֹ שֶׁכָּתוּב בְּמָקוֹם אַחֵר) וּמִכָּל מָקוֹם לְפִי שֶׁמַּדְרֵגָה זוֹ דִּנְשָׁמָה הִיא לְמַעְלָה מֵהִתְלַבְּשׁוּת בְּנֶפֶשׁ הַבַּהֲמִית אֵינָהּ פּוֹעֶלֶת כָּל כָּךְ עַל הַנֶּפֶשׁ הַבַּהֲמִית.

xxix) See footnote of the Rebbe on page 283 ←

It's true that this level [love from the *chaya*] is also subject to concealment and obfuscation by the animal soul, (as is written in the *Tanya*, chapter 19, and in *Igeret HaKodesh*, chapter 4). Still, [the animal soul may escape], when the arousal of transcendent love of G-d comes from our animal soul itself, from its predicament of exile [where it was consigned] when the inner sanctum of our heart

הֲגַם שֶׁעַל מַדְרֵגָה זוֹ יֵשׁ גַּם כֵּן הֶעְלֵם וְהֶסְתֵּר הַנֶּפֶשׁ הַבַּהֲמִית וּכְמוֹ שֶׁכָּתוּב בְּסֵפֶר שֶׁל בֵּינוֹנִים פִּי"ט וּבְאִגֶּרֶת הַקֹּדֶשׁ סִי' ד' דִּבּוּר הַמַּתְחִיל אֵין יִשְׂרָאֵל נִגְאָלִין אֶלָּא בִּצְדָקָה, הִנֵּה בֶּאֱמֶת כַּאֲשֶׁר הִתְעוֹרְרוּת הַמַּקִּיף דִּנְשָׁמָה הִיא מִצַּד הַנֶּפֶשׁ הַבַּהֲמִית דְּהַיְנוּ מִן הַמֵּצַר דְּגָלוּת הַנְּשָׁמָה דְּהַיְנוּ מַה שֶׁהִלְבִּישׁ בְּחִינַת פְּנִימִית נְקֻדַּת לְבָבוֹ בָּזֶה לְעֻמַּת זֶה כו' וְעוֹד

Love on the level of chaya has no effect on the animal soul, but sometimes the animal soul breaks out of its own bounds and transforms itself.

--- COMMENTARY ---

HITAMTUT

What leads to the paradigm shift described above? The answer is: focus and concentration (see *Yom tov shel Rosh Hashana 5666*, page 151, and *B'sha'ah shehikdimu 5672*, vol. 2, page 1180). Focus and concentration lead us to three more meditative events; *hakara* (recognition), *hitamtut* (validation), and *re'iya b'eyn hasechel* (seeing in the mind's eye).

After delving deeply into a concept, abstracting and removing as much of the "packaging" and "garments" as possible — a process known as *p'nimiyut bina* ("inner dimensions of understanding") — we come to recognize and feel the essence

יוֹתֵר מִזֶּה כַּאֲשֶׁר צַר לוֹ מְאֹד מֵחָמְרִיּוּת הַנֶּפֶשׁ הַבַּהֲמִית וְגַסּוּתוֹ בְּרִבּוּי תַּאֲוֹתָיו עַד שֶׁהִלְבִּישׁ גַּם פְּנִימִית נְקֻדַּת לְבָבוֹ בָּזֶה, וּמִזֶּה נַעֲשָׂה הַיְצִיאָה בִּבְחִינַת תֹּקֶף הָרָצוֹא שֶׁלְּמַעְלָה מִטַּעַם וָדַעַת, הֲרֵי זֶה פּוֹעֵל עַל הַנֶּפֶשׁ הַבַּהֲמִית לְהָסִיר הַהֶעְלֵמוֹת וְהַהֶסְתֵּרִים וְגַם לְהָפְכָם לֶאֱלֹקוּת (כִּי יֵשׁ בָּזֶה כַּמָּה מַדְרֵגוֹת בְּאֹפֶן הָרָצוֹא וְתָלוּי בְּהַמֵּצַר הַקּוֹדֵם כו'), אֲבָל כַּאֲשֶׁר הַהִתְעוֹרְרוּת הוּא מִצַּד הַנְּשָׁמָה (דְהַיְנוּ מֵהִתְבּוֹנְנוּת הַהַפְלָאָה דְּאוֹר אֵין סוֹף בָּרוּךְ הוּא) אֵין זֶה פּוֹעֵל כָּל כָּךְ עַל הַחָמְרִיּוּת דְנֶפֶשׁ הַבַּהֲמִית. וּמַה שֶּׁכָּתוּב בְּסֵפֶר שֶׁל בֵּינוֹנִים פמ"ג בְּהָאַהֲבָה הַבָּאָה מֵהִתְבּוֹנְנוּת גְּדֻלָּתוֹ יִתְבָּרֵךְ וּכְמוֹ שֶׁנִּתְבָּאֵר לְעֵיל פ"ד, זֶהוּ הַכֹּל בְּמַדְרֵגַת הַנְּשָׁמָה שֶׁמִּתְלַבֶּשֶׁת בַּנֶּפֶשׁ הַבַּהֲמִית וּכְמוֹ שֶׁכָּתוּב בְּאִגַּה"ק סִי' הַנַּ"ל שֶׁזֶּהוּ בְּחִינַת חִיצוֹנִיּוּת הַלֵּב וְכֵן הוּא בְּסֵפֶר שֶׁל בֵּינוֹנִים בְּהַקְדָּמַת ח"ב הַנִּקְרָא חִנּוּךְ קָטָן).

became en-clothed in the "opposing forces" [that is, forces opposed to holiness]. And even more, [the animal soul may find a way out] when we suffer terribly from its coarse physicality with its multiple lusts which even en-clothe the innermost spiritual point of the heart. It is this that produces the [motivation and strength for the soul] to exit all limitations and leave them behind with a rush to G-d, beyond all reason and logic. When this happens, it has an effect on the animal soul, freeing it of all constraints and concealments and even turning them into G-dliness. (There are several levels of ascent to the One Above, depending upon the previous limitations [of the soul].) But, when the arousal comes from the divine soul [alone] (that is, through meditation on the exalted infinite light of G-d), it does not have much of an effect on the physical coarseness of the animal soul. As for that which is written in the *Tanya*, chapter 43, concerning the love of G-d which comes from meditation on His greatness, and which was explained earlier in Chapter 4 [that the love has an effect on the animal soul], this is speaking of the divine soul as en-clothed in the animal soul, as written in *Igeret HaKodesh*, chapter 4, mentioned earlier, where it is stated that this takes place in the outer, external levels of the heart, and so is also stated in the *Tanya*, introduction to part 2, *Chinuch Katan*.

COMMENTARY

of the concept through *da'at*. As noted earlier, we not only understand but internalize it to the point of experiencing the concept on a gut level. This is *hakara* and it is the inner soul experience of *da'at*.

But, one cannot say about the *yechida* of the [divine] soul that it has no effect on the coarseness of the animal soul. Certainly, upon revelation of the *yechida*, there is a complete metamorphosis of the animal soul, which is transformed from one extreme to the other. For example, if we were ready to actually die in order to sanctify the Name of G-d, and for whatever reason were saved by Him, there would be no doubt, nor even shadow of a doubt, that our animal soul would be transformed completely, from one extreme to the other. We would become a totally different person. The experience of revelation of the essence of our soul would certainly bring about a change in our animal soul as well, which would become transformed completely. This is not unlike the effect of giving up our life for G-d, [knowing that we must die in order to sanctify the Name of the One Above], when the animal soul wants only to live.

אָמְנָם בִּבְחִינַת יְחִידָה שֶׁבְּנֶפֶשׁ אִי אֶפְשָׁר לוֹמַר שֶׁאֵינוֹ פּוֹעֵל עַל חָמְרִיּוּת הַנֶּפֶשׁ הַבַּהֲמִית, דְּוַדַּאי בְּהִתְגַּלּוּת בְּחִינַת יְחִידָה שֶׁבַּנֶּפֶשׁ הֲרֵי זֶה פּוֹעֵל בַּנֶּפֶשׁ הַבַּהֲמִית לַהֲפוֹךְ עֶצֶם מַהוּתוֹ מֵהֶפֶךְ אֶל הַהֶפֶךְ, וּכְמוֹ כְּשֶׁבָּא לִידֵי מְסִירַת נֶפֶשׁ בְּפֹעַל מַמָּשׁ עַל קִדּוּשׁ הַשֵּׁם וּמֵאֵיזֶה סִבָּה מֵהַשֵּׁם יִתְבָּרֵךְ נִצַּל מִזֶּה הִנֵּה בְּלִי שׁוּם סָפֵק וּסְפֵק סְפֵיקָא שֶׁנִּשְׁתַּנָּה נַפְשׁוֹ הַטִּבְעִית וְנִתְהַפֵּךְ מִן הַקָּצֶה אֶל הַקָּצֶה שֶׁנַּעֲשָׂה אָדָם אַחֵר מַמָּשׁ, שֶׁהֲרֵי הֲרֵי אֶצְלוֹ הִתְגַּלּוּת עֶצֶם הַנְּשָׁמָה מַמָּשׁ וְזֶה בְּוַדַּאי פּוֹעֵל עַל נַפְשׁוֹ הַבַּהֲמִית הַטִּבְעִית לְשַׁנּוֹתָהּ וּלְהַפְכָהּ לְגַמְרֵי וּכְמוֹ שֶׁפּוֹעֵל בּוֹ עֶצֶם הַמְּסִירוּת נֶפֶשׁ שֶׁיֵּהָרֵג עַל קִדּוּשׁ הַשֵּׁם שֶׁהַנֶּפֶשׁ הַטִּבְעִית מִצַּד עַצְמָהּ רוֹצָה רַק לִחְיוֹת

Upon revelation of the yechida, there is a complete metamorphosis of the animal soul.

COMMENTARY

If we don't stop there but continue to concentrate, we will experience a validation or corroboration of our meditation, called *hitamtut* (from the word for *emet*, meaning truth); this validation is accompanied by seeing the concept in our mind's eye, called *re'iya b'eyn hasechel*. *Hitamtut* is a unifying "moment of truth," an epiphany that confirms our meditation. It is a revelation of the overall picture occuring after we have focused properly on the details of G-dliness in the creation (see ch. 4 of the Mittler Rebbe's *Sha'ar HaYichud*).

In part, *hitamut* is intellectual — after concentrating on the details for a long time, we are suddenly able to synthesize them into a coherent whole. However, there is also a spiritual

(An investigation is needed in order to ascertain whether there is a hidden power within the animal soul enabling it to surrender and die in sanctification of G-d's Name. This power of giving ourselves up comes from an essential bond that simply does not permit us to become separated from G-dliness. Such a level of commitment is only appropriate to the divine soul, and not to the natural soul which comes from *klipat nogah*, [the level of concealment of G-dliness within which there is mixed good and bad]. The ability of the animal soul to "surrender," as well as the thirst of the animal soul for G-dliness[xxx]— accompanied with extra power beyond the thirst of the divine soul itself, as is known—is all a result of the divine soul having a [positive] effect upon the animal soul. The same is true of

(וְצָרִיךְ עִיּוּן אִם יֵשׁ בְּהַנֶּפֶשׁ הַטִּבְעִית גַּם בִּבְחִינַת כֹּחַ נֶעְלָם לִמְסֹר נַפְשׁוֹ בְּפֹעַל מַמָּשׁ עַל קִדּוּשׁ הַשֵּׁם, שֶׁהֲרֵי הַכֹּחַ דִּמְסִירוּת נֶפֶשׁ הוּא מִצַּד הַהִתְקַשְּׁרוּת עַצְמִית שֶׁאִי אֶפְשָׁר לוֹ לִהְיוֹת נִפְרָד מֵאֱלֹקוּת, וְזֶה שַׁיָּךְ רַק בַּנֶּפֶשׁ הָאֱלֹקִית לֹא בַּנֶּפֶשׁ הַטִּבְעִית שֶׁהִיא מִקְּלִפַּת נֹגַהּ, וְהַמְסִירוּת נֶפֶשׁ דְּנֶפֶשׁ הַטִּבְעִית וְכֵן בְּחִינַת תֹּקֶף הָרָצוֹא דְּנֶפֶשׁ הַטִּבְעִית שֶׁהוּא בְּתִגְבֹּרֶת יְתֵרָה מֵהָרָצוֹא דְּנֶפֶשׁ הָאֱלֹקִית מִצַּד עַצְמָהּ כַּנּוֹדָע, הַכֹּל מֵהַנֶּפֶשׁ הָאֱלֹקִית שֶׁפּוֹעֵל עַל הַנֶּפֶשׁ הַטִּבְעִית, וְכֵן הַהַעֲלָאָה דְּנֶפֶשׁ הַבַּהֲמִית מִצַּד עַצְמָהּ וְכַנּוֹדָע בְּעִנְיַן הַהַעֲלָאָה מִלְּמַטָּה לְמַעְלָה שֶׁזֶּהוּ מַה שֶּׁהַתַּחְתּוֹנִים מִצַּד עַצְמָם עוֹלִים כוּ' שֶׁזֶּהוּ עִנְיַן מַיִם תַּחְתּוֹנִים בּוֹכִין כוּ' וּכְמוֹ שֶׁכָּתוּב בְּמָקוֹם אַחֵר. כָּל זֶה הוּא מַה שֶּׁהַנֶּפֶשׁ הָאֱלֹקִית פּוֹעֵל

xxx) See footnote of the Rebbe on page 286

COMMENTARY

component in *hitamtut* because the "whole" that emerges from the revelation is greater than the sum of all the details. We are lifted to a new level of G-dly understanding and perception, which transfixes our attention and mesmerizes us. It therefore leads immediately to *re'iya b'eyn hasechel*, or grasping the concept so clearly that it is as if one sees it in his mind's eye (but not with the naked eye).

In prayer, *hitamtut* corresponds to the sentences that we say immediately after the first three paragraphs of the *Shema*. At that point in morning prayers, we recite several phrases beginning with the word *emet*. This is the time during prayer that our divine soul "takes over," so to speak. With the revelation of *hitamtut* from above, it breaks free of the bonds of our animal soul. It then leads us into the highest point of the prayer, the

Essay on Service of the Heart - Love Like Fire and Water

בַּנֶּפֶשׁ הַבַּהֲמִית וְיֵשׁ בָּזֶה יִתְרוֹן מִצַּד שֹׁרֶשׁ וּמָקוֹר דְּהַהֶעְלֵמוֹת וְהַהֶסְתֵּרִים שֶׁלְּמַעְלָה מִבְּחִינַת הַגִּלּוּי כַּנּוֹדָע, אֲבָל לֹא שֶׁהַנֶּפֶשׁ הַבַּהֲמִית בְּעַצְמוֹ בְּטִבְעוֹ יִרְצֶה בֶּאֱלֹקוּת. וְאֵין זֶה סוֹתֵר לְמַה שֶּׁכָּתוּב בְּכַמָּה דּוּכְתֵי שֶׁהַכֹּחַ הַמִּתְאַוֶּה בְּעַצֶם אֵינוֹ רַע וּכְמוֹ שֶׁכָּתוּב בְּלִקּוּטֵי תּוֹרָה דִּבּוּר הַמַּתְחִיל זֹאת חֻקַּת הַתּוֹרָה זֶהוּ רַק שֶׁאֵין בּוֹ צִיּוּר רַע בְּעֶצֶם אֲבָל מִכָּל מָקוֹם אֵינוֹ טוֹב וְאַדְּרַבָּא בְּטִבְעוֹ הוּא נִמְשָׁךְ לְעִנְיָנִים חָמְרִיִּים וְאִם כֵּן עִנְיַן הַמְּסִירוּת נֶפֶשׁ עַל קִדּוּשׁ הַשֵּׁם הוּא הֵפֶךְ טִבְעוֹ לְגַמְרֵי)

the ascent and elevation of the animal soul of its own volition, as is known regarding the spiritual elevation of anything in the lower worlds which takes place through the power and incentive of the creations themselves. [This is known in Kabbalah as] "the lower waters cry out [to G-d]..." as written elsewhere. Yet, all of this is [part of] the effect that the divine soul produces within the animal soul. It is true that there is a certain superiority in this [love of the animal soul over the love of the divine soul]. [Its love] transforms the source of the animal soul—which comes from a place of hidden [essential] G-dliness that transcends spiritual revelation, as is known. But, this isn't to say that the animal soul, of its own volition and by its own nature, now desires G-dliness. Nor does this contradict what is written elsewhere in several places that the power of lust and desire isn't bad in of itself, as written in *Likutei Torah*, in the discourse beginning with *Zot chukat HaTorah*. What this does mean is that the animal soul, in and of itself, does not adopt any specific evil form. However, it [certainly] isn't good, and in fact quite the opposite, its nature is to be drawn toward the vulgar and the physical. And if so, the whole matter of surrendering ourselves in order to sanctify His Name is really opposed to the nature of the animal soul.)

COMMENTARY

Amida, which is recited silently in the presence of the One Above.

It must be noted that *Hitamtut* and *re'iya b'eyn hasechel* do not necessarily lead us to the soul-experience of *chaya* and to *da'at elyon*. This depends on the content of our meditation. If the meditation is focused upon "immanent G-dliness" (*memalle kol olamin*) - concepts of G-dliness en-clothed in the creation, whether in physical creation or in the higher spiritual worlds, -

Revelation of the divine soul transforms the animal soul, as does teshuva.

The divine soul has an effect upon the animal soul, such that it has no objection and presents no obstacle to our surrendering ourselves. Quite the opposite, it as well wants to give itself up for the sake of G-d. We understand that the deep-seated coarseness of the animal soul becomes transformed totally from one extreme to the other. This is similar to true *teshuva*, ("return" to the One Above), in which the expression and revelation of the essence of the soul transforms the basic nature of the animal soul, especially when the [primal] scream [for G-d] is coming from the animal soul itself. When we find ourselves in such dire straits that we lose our [sense of constructive existence], this is an indication that our suffering and feeling of being stifled come from our animal soul. It is the animal soul that feels that things are not good, and it

וְהַנֶּפֶשׁ הָאֱלֹקִית פּוֹעֵל עָלָיו שֶׁאֵין שׁוּם מְנִיעָה מִצִּדּוֹ לִמְסֹר נַפְשׁוֹ וְאַדְּרַבָּא גַּם הוּא רוֹצֶה לִמְסֹר נַפְשׁוֹ בְּפֹעַל מַמָּשׁ, מִמֵּילָא מוּבָן שֶׁגַּם עֶצֶם הַחֻמְרִיּוּת שֶׁלּוֹ מִתְהַפֵּךְ לְגַמְרֵי מִן הַקָּצֶה אֶל הַקָּצֶה, וּכְמוֹ בִּתְשׁוּבָה אֲמִתִּית בִּיצִיאַת וְהִתְגַּלּוּת עֶצֶם הַנְּשָׁמָה הֲרֵי מִתְהַפֵּךְ מַהוּת עֶצֶם הַנֶּפֶשׁ הַבַּהֲמִית וּבִפְרָט כַּאֲשֶׁר הַצְּעָקָה הִיא גַּם מִן הַנֶּפֶשׁ הַבַּהֲמִית, וְהַיְנוּ כַּאֲשֶׁר הַמֵּצַר הוּא בְּעֹמֶק בְּיוֹתֵר שֶׁאֵין לוֹ שׁוּם מָקוֹם בְּעַצְמוֹ (אַז די ניט גוטסקייט איז זייער טיף און זייער שטארק אז ער האט ניט קיין שום צופרידענקייט און קיין שום נחת בעצמו און האט בײַ זיך קיין שום ארט בפועל ממש) שֶׁזֶּהוּ הוֹרָאָה שֶׁהַצַּעַר וְהַמֵּצַר הוּא מֵהַנֶּפֶשׁ הַבַּהֲמִית שֶׁהַנֶּפֶשׁ הַבַּהֲמִית לֹא טוֹב לוֹ וּמִצְטַעֵר עַל רִחוּקוֹ (וְהַיְנוּ מַה שֶּׁהַנֶּפֶשׁ הָאֱלֹקִית פּוֹעֵל עָלָיו כַּנַּ"ל)

COMMENTARY

then the corroborating experience of *hitamtut* will be also be of G-dliness en-clothed in and enlivening the world; it will then be on the level of *neshama* rather than *chaya*). We will experience deeper insight into the very essence and G-dly nature of creation (as described in chapters 1 and 4), and we will be granted total grasp and recognition of the essence of G-dliness within creation (see *Yom Tov shel Rosh Hashana*, 5666, page 150). It is when the meditation leading up to *hitamtut* includes concepts of transcendent G-dliness (*sovev kol olamim*), that the resultant revelation includes recognition of the amazing, exalted nature of G-dliness as He surpasses creation. This is the experience of *chaya*, as described below.

Essay on Service of the Heart - Love Like Fire and Water

experiences distress over its distance [from G-d] (as a result of the influence of the divine soul, as mentioned above). The suffering of the animal soul is immense. (This is for two reasons: One, because the animal soul itself has brought about this distance; indeed, it is because of the animal soul that this [distance] is natural; and two, because the animal soul is not an inherently G-dly power.) We understand that there is a sense of G-dliness within this experience of suffering. It comes from the experience of distance, as written elsewhere regarding remorse — that through it, the suffering is magnified. And in the [primal] scream with which we cry out from the bitterness of our soul—with the strength of abandoning our limitations and with a rush to the One Above (as if we were running away from death to

שֶׁהַצַּעַר שֶׁלוֹ הוּא גָּדוֹל בְּיוֹתֵר (וְזֶהוּ מִב׳ סִבּוֹת א׳ מִפְּנֵי שֶׁהָרִחוּק הוּא מֵאִתּוֹ וּבִסִבָּתוֹ וְזֶה אֶצְלוֹ עִנְיָן טִבְעִי, וְהַב׳ מִפְּנֵי שֶׁאֵינוֹ כֹּחַ אֱלוֹקִי בְּעַצְמָם) (וּמוּבָן דִּבְהַצַּעַר יֵשׁ בּוֹ הֶרְגֵּשׁ הָאֱלֹקִי מִמַּה שֶׁנִּתְרַחֵק כְּמוֹ שֶׁכָּתוּב בְּמָקוֹם אַחֵר בְּעִנְיַן הַמְּרִירוּת דְּעַל יְדֵי זֶה הַצַּעַר גָּדוֹל בְּיוֹתֵר כו׳) הִנֵּה בְּהַצְּעָקָה שֶׁצּוֹעֵק בְּמַר נַפְשׁוֹ בִּבְחִינַת תֹּקֶף הַיְצִיאָה וְהָרָצוֹא (כְּבוֹרֵחַ מִן הַמָּוֶת אֶל הַחַיִּים כו׳) הֲרֵי מִשְׁתַּנֶּה מַהוּתוֹ לְגַמְרֵי מִכֹּל וָכֹל כו׳. וּמוּבָן מִכָּל הַנ"ל דִּבְחִינַת הַתְגַלּוּת יְחִידָה שֶׁבַּנֶפֶשׁ פּוֹעֵל גַּם עַל הַחֲמָרִיּוּת וְהוֹפֵךְ מַהוּתוֹ לְגַמְרֵי (וְהַיְנוּ מִפְּנֵי שֶׁבְּחִינַת יְחִידָה שֶׁבַּנֶפֶשׁ מִפְשֶׁטֶת לְגַמְרֵי וְאֵין לָהּ שׁוּם אֲחִיזָה כְּלָל בְּהַכֹּחוֹת פְּנִימִיִּים הֲרֵי הִיא פּוֹעֶלֶת בְּכָל מָקוֹם מִצַּד הַהַגְדָּרָה שֶׁעֶצֶם

COMMENTARY

ANOTHER WAY

The path to the soul-level of *chaya* requires a new technique. After using our *da'at* to focus on a concept, we bypass *hakara*, *hitamtut* and *re'iya b'eyn hasechel*, and instead we perform what the Rambam calls "circumscription of knowledge" (*yediat hashlila*, already described in the commentary to chapter one). That is, recognizing that G-d is beyond whatever positive description or human comprehension we may apply to Him, we may decide to override our intellectual grasp by describing it in negative terms. Negation here means that we use our understanding as a springboard to arrive at a higher understanding. By circumscribing our understanding, and couching it in negative terms, we actually extend our grasp of G-dliness by a quantum

הַנֶּפֶשׁ מְגֻדֶּרֶת עַל כָּל פָּנִים בְּגוּף כְּמוֹ שֶׁכָּתוּב בְּמָקוֹם אַחֵר, וְהָרְאָיָ' שֶׁהֲרֵי בְּחִינַת יְחִידָה נִמְצָא בֶּאֱמֶת בְּכָל הַכֹּחוֹת עַד גַּם בְּסוֹף מַעֲשֶׂה וּכְמוֹ שֶׁכָּתוּב בְּמָקוֹם אַחֵר).

life...)—we completely transform our essence. From all of this, we understand that a revelation of the *yechida* of the soul has an effect on the coarse earthiness [of the animal soul] and transforms it completely. (This is because the *yechida* of the soul is totally abstract and has no connection with any of the inner soul powers. Therefore, it has an overall effect on the totality of the soul, since the essence of the soul is defined as[xxxi] being en-clothed in the body, as written elsewhere. The proof of this is that the *yechida* is found in all of the powers of the soul, including the lowest level of the power of action, as written elsewhere.)

xxxi) See footnote of the Rebbe on page 288

The *yechida*, being totally abstract, is not limited by any of the ten soul powers, which are the inner manifestations of the ten *sephirot* within the soul of a person. However, even though it is not enclothed in the body, the *yechida* is nonetheless associated with it, and may influence any or all of the ten soul powers all of which exist on the five levels of the soul (both the animal and the divine soul).

Sephira	External Manifestation	Soul Power
Keter: *Atik Yomin* *Arich Anpin*	Unattainable transcendence Attainable transcendence	Enjoyment Will
10. *Chochma*	Spiritual Insight	Self-nullification
9. *Bina*	Intellectual Analysis	Happiness
8. *Da'at*	Visceral knowledge	Recognition
7. *Chesed*	Kindness	Love of G-d
6. *Gevura*	Strictness/Strength	Fear of G-d
5. *Tiferet*	Beauty	Mercy
4. *Netzach*	Pro-activity	Security
3. *Hod*	Re-activity	Integrity
2. *Yesod*	Perseverance	Truth
1. *Malchut*	Sovereignty	Humility

———————— **COMMENTARY** ————————

level. We project ourselves to a whole new plane of G-dliness that allows room for both our previous limited grasp and for

Essay on Service of the Heart - Love Like Fire and Water

The hidden love of G-d in each of us as Jews—such that each and every one of us naturally craves G-dliness—is a desire that has no effect on our physical nature. We see clearly that even though each and every Jew truly wants G-dliness, and that this is our nature, nevertheless on a conscious level we are attracted to worldly matters. This is because our "hidden love" is transcendent and unconscious. This is the case as well regarding revelation of the transcendent desire [or soul level] of *chaya*, which comes about through the arousal of meditation, as described earlier. Although it is a very high level, expressing a true reality within our [divine] soul, nevertheless it has no effect on the corporeality of the animal soul. This is because as a

אַךְ בְּחִינַת הָאַהֲבָה מְסֻתֶּרֶת שֶׁבְּכָל אֶחָד וְאֶחָד מִיִּשְׂרָאֵל שֶׁכָּל אֶחָד וְאֶחָד רוֹצֶה בְּטִבְעוֹ בֶּאֱלֹקוּת, הֲרֵי הָרָצוֹן הַזֶּה אֵינוֹ פּוֹעֵל בַּחָמְרִיּוּת, וּכְמוֹ שֶׁאָנוּ רוֹאִין בְּחוּשׁ דְּעִם הֱיוֹת דְּכָל אֶחָד וְאֶחָד מִיִּשְׂרָאֵל רוֹצֶה בֶּאֱמֶת בֶּאֱלֹקוּת שֶׁזֶּהוּ בְּטֶבַע בְּנַפְשׁוֹ, וּמִכָּל מָקוֹם בְּהַכֹּחוֹת הַגְּלוּיִּים הֲרֵי הוּא נִמְשָׁךְ אַחֲרֵי עִנְיְנֵי הָעוֹלָם. וְזֶהוּ מִפְּנֵי שֶׁהָאַהֲבָה הִיא בִּבְחִינַת מַקִּיף וּבְהֶעְלֵם הִנֵּה כְּמוֹ כֵן הוּא גַּם בְּהִתְגַּלּוּת בְּחִינַת הָרָצוֹן דִּבְחִינַת מַקִּיף דְּחַיָּ' הַבָּא עַל יְדֵי הִתְעוֹרְרוּת הַהִתְבּוֹנְנוּת הַנַּ"ל, הֲגַם שֶׁהִיא מַדְרֵגָה גְּבוֹהָה מְאֹד וְהִיא אֲמִתִּית בַּנֶּפֶשׁ מִכָּל מָקוֹם אֵין זֶה פּוֹעֵל עַל הַחָמְרִ' דְּנֶפֶשׁ הַבַּהֲמִית מִפְּנֵי שֶׁהָרָצוֹא הוּא בִּבְחִינַת מַקִּיף

Even though we crave spirituality, we are tempted by physical attractions.

COMMENTARY

a new spiritual awareness. (For example, while we cannot describe G-d as "merciful" in the same sense as man is merciful, we can say about Him that He is *not* the opposite of merciful. His mercy is not limited by our definitions, but is infinitely greater. Thus, we negate our own understanding of what "merciful" means in order to gain some kind of idea of what G-dly mercy may be.)

This is what the Chassidic teachings mean by "understanding one thing from another." By taking our understanding of G-dliness as en-clothed in the creation and negating it, we arrive at a glimpse of G-dliness as it surpasses and transcends the creation. This technique ultimately brings us to "knowledge of that which is amazing" (*yediat hahafla'ah*), which is also called "gazing upon the glory of the King" (*istaclut b'yikara d'malka*). We now are able to soar to the infinite light of the One Above, an experience which is equivalent to the love of "fire from

The chaya is a transcendent desire for G-dliness that does not affect our physical nature.

דְּנֶפֶשׁ שֶׁאֵינוֹ מְלֻבָּשׁ בְּהַכֹּחוֹת פְּנִימִיִּים וּבַכֹּחוֹת הַטִּבְעִיִּים. וַהֲרֵי זֶה כְּמוֹ עִנְיַן הָאֱמוּנָה שֶׁהִיא גַּם כֵּן בִּבְחִינַת מַקִּיף (רַק שֶׁזֶּהוּ כְּמוֹ שֶׁבָּא בִּבְחִינַת מַלְכוּת וְהוּא בְּחִינַת כֶּתֶר מַלְכוּת כו') שֶׁאָמְרוּ רַבּוֹתֵינוּ זִכְרוֹנָם לִבְרָכָה עַל זֶה גַּנָּבָא אַפּוּם מַחְתַּרְתָּא רַחֲמָנָא קָרֵי' שֶׁהוּא מַאֲמִין בֵּהּ' וּבְהַשְׁגָּחָתוֹ וִיכָלְתּוֹ יִתְבָּרֵךְ וּמִכָּל מָקוֹם אֵין זֶה פּוֹעֵל עָלָיו שֶׁלֹּא לַעֲבוֹר עַל רְצוֹנוֹ יִת', דְּעִם הֱיוֹת שֶׁמִּצַּד הַנֶּפֶשׁ הוּא מַאֲמִין בֶּאֱמֶת מִכָּל מָקוֹם מִצַּד הַחֻמְרִיּוּת הֲרֵי הוּא עוֹשֶׂה הֵפֶךְ רְצוֹנוֹ יִתְבָּרֵךְ וְהַיְנוּ מִפְּנֵי שֶׁזֶּהוּ בִּבְחִינַת מַקִּיף לְבַד שֶׁאֵינוֹ נִרְגָּשׁ בִּפְנִימִיּוּת, וּכְמוֹ כֵן הוּא בְּחִינַת הָאַהֲבָה שֶׁבִּבְחִינַת מַקִּיף שֶׁבַּנֶּפֶשׁ שֶׁאֵינוֹ פּוֹעֵל כָּל כָּךְ

transcendent desire for G-dliness, it is not en-clothed within the natural inner soul powers. It is like faith, which is also [unconscious and] transcendent (although faith expresses the transcendent powers of the soul as en-clothed in the lowest of the ten *sephirot—malchut—* where it is called *keter malchut*). About this, the Sages said [in *Eyn Yaakov*, tractate *Berachot*, p. 63], "The thief, at the mouth of the tunnel [which he is digging in order to break in] prays to G-d." The thief believes in G-d and in His Divine Providence and His omnipotence, and yet nevertheless, this doesn't impress him enough to refrain from transgressing [and opposing] G-d's will. In his divine soul, he truly believes, but his crass physical nature

---
COMMENTARY
---

above" mentioned in Chapter 4 of *Kuntres Ha'Avoda*. It is the illumination of the menorah of Aharon the high priest, and it may be experienced either as "great love" (*ahava rabba*) or "love with deep enjoyment" (*ahava b'tanugim*). Because it is not based on intellect alone, but upon recognizing and seeing (in the mind's eye) the infinite light of the One Above, it is "love that is dependent upon nothing." In this case of meditation upon matters that transcend creation, *hitamatut* leads to *hakarat ha'haflah* (recognition of exalted matters beyond creation) and to experience of *reiah d'chochma* (vision of insight/wisdom).

Whether pursuing meditation upon G-dliness as revealed in creation (on the level of *neshama*), or upon transcendent G-dliness surpassing creation (*chaya*), we must first go through the process of stripping away our perception of reality, in order to become aware of G-dliness within creation. In so doing, we reach what is called "inner dimensions of understanding" (*pnimiyut bina*). As noted above, it is on this level that we can penetrate to the

leads him to behave in violation of what G-d wants. This is because his faith is only transcendent and is not felt inside. So it is, as well, regarding the love that is transcendent in his soul. It doesn't affect his physical nature so much. Even though the transcendent aspect of his love of G-d brings him close to G-d, and he truly desires G-dliness, when it comes to his natural inner soul powers, he acts in a deviant manner altogether.

עַל הַחֲמָרִיּוּת, דְּעִם הֱיוֹת שֶׁמִּצַּד הַמַּקִּיף הוּא בִּבְחִינַת קֵרוּב וְרוֹצֶה בֶּאֱמֶת בֶּאֱלֹקוּת הִנֵּה כְּשֶׁבָּא בִּבְחִינַת כֹּחוֹת פְּנִימִיִּים וְכֹחוֹת טִבְעִיִּים הוּא בְּאֹפֶן אַחֵר לְגַמְרֵי.

--- **COMMENTARY** ---

very soul of creation, the G-dliness that is enlivening it (*neshama*). This is the beginning of meditation, in which there is no *bina* without *chochma*.

However, in the latter stages of meditation, the opposite is true. After stripping away perceived layers of reality to arrive at *pnimiyut bina*, we achieve *hakara*,. Then, the processes that lead to *hitamtut* and *re'iyah* take us in the "opposite" direction, from below to above. The validation of *hitamtut* and the mental vision of *re'iya* are associated with *chochma*. So, although the initial process (known as *Chabad*) proceeds from *chochma* through *bina* to *da'at*, the subsequent revelation of G-dly understanding brings us in the opposite direction, from *da'at* to *chochma*. Only after experiencing true G-dly reality through *hakara* (deep recognition) of *da'at*, are we able to apprehend truth with the faculty of *chochma*. (See *Yom tov shel Rosh Hashana 5666*, page 150 and also page 373).

The process of circumscription of knowledge (*yediat hashlila*) leads to *yichuda ila'ah* and the soul level of *chaya*. However, the true experience of *yichuda ila'ah* is not based upon meditation. It is an experience of the highest level of the soul - the *yechida* - which is so intimately connected with the One Above that no amount of meditation will reveal it. Even meditation upon matters surpassing creation and based upon *yediat hashlila* will not bring us to the soul level of *yechida*. This is because the *yechida* is the essence of the soul that is connected to G-d. It therefore recognizes and experiences G-dliness without any meditation whatsoever (See *B'sha'ah shehikdimu 5672*, v.2, p.1180).

Many people undergo a spiritual arousal during Rosh Hashana and Yom Kippur, but is has no effect upon them the rest of the year.

(וְדָבָר זֶה נִרְאֶה בְּחוּשׁ בְּכַמָּה בְּנֵי אָדָם בְּרֹאשׁ הַשָּׁנָה וְיוֹם הַכִּפּוּרִים שֶׁמִּתְפַּעֲלִים מְאֹד בְּנַפְשָׁם וְאֵין זֶה פּוֹעֵל לְשַׁנּוֹת בֶּאֱמֶת דַּרְכָּם וַהֲלִיכָם בְּכָל הַשָּׁנָה בִּבְחִינַת וְיַעֲקֹב הָלַךְ לְדַרְכּוֹ כו', וּבָזֶה יֵשׁ כַּמָּה אוֹפַנִּים שֶׁהֲרֵי גַּם הַקַּלִּים וְגַם עוֹבְרֵי עֲבֵרָה רַחֲמָנָא לִיצְלָן מִתְעוֹרְרִים בְּיוֹם כִּפּוּר וּבִפְרָט בְּעִתִּים מְיֻחָדִים כְּמוֹ בִּתְקִיעַת שׁוֹפָר וּבִנְעִילָה דְיוֹם כִּפּוּר וּמִכָּל מָקוֹם אַחַר כָּךְ הֲרֵי הֵם כְּמוֹ שֶׁהָיוּ מִקֹּדֶם בְּלִי שִׁנּוּי, וְיֵשׁ מֵהֶם אֲשֶׁר בְּרֹאשׁ הַשָּׁנָה וְיוֹם כִּפּוּר בּוֹכִים מֵעֹמֶק לִבָּם עַל מַצָּבָם הַחָמְרִי וּמִתְפַּלְלִים וּמְבַקְּשִׁים עַל הַפַּרְנָסָה וּכְהַאי גַּוְונָא אִישׁ אִישׁ כְּפִי הִצְטָרְכוּתוֹ וְאֵינָם שָׂמִים עַל לִבָּם לְתַקֵּן מַצָּבָם הָרוּחָנִי וְלִהְיוֹת סוּר מֵרַע וַעֲשֵׂה טוֹב בְּפֹעַל מַמָּשׁ עַל כָּל פָּנִים. אָמְנָם גַּם בִּירֵאֵי אֱלֹקִים וַאֲשֶׁר בִּכְלָל עוֹבְדִים יֵחָשְׁבוּ שֶׁמִּתְעוֹרְרִים בֶּאֱמֶת בְּרֹאשׁ הַשָּׁנָה וְיוֹם כִּפּוּר בְּעַצְמָם נַפְשָׁם בִּתְשׁוּבָה וּבְקַבָּלַת עוֹל מַלְכוּת שָׁמַיִם,

(It is seen clearly that many people become aroused [to serve G-d] from their very souls on Rosh Hashana and Yom Kippur. Nevertheless, the arousal does nothing to change their courses and paths during the remainder of the year; about this it is written [in Genesis 32:1], "Yaakov went on his way," [indicating the way of Torah and *mitzvot*]. There are various degrees and styles, but even the least observant Jews "wake up" during the High Holidays, and particularly during the special times of blowing the *shofar*, and during *Ne'ila* [the closing prayer of Yom Kippur]. Still, they afterward return to their previous lifestyles, without any variation. Then, there are those who cry from the depths of their hearts over their economic situations during Rosh Hashana and Yom Kippur. They pray and request income for the year, each one according to his needs. It doesn't occur to them to do anything to rectify their spiritual situations, at least to turn away from evil and

---

COMMENTARY

As pointed out in Chapter 4, even *re'iah d'chochma* and *hitamtut* do not ultimately lead to spiritual satisfaction. We will not be satisfied with visions and revelations, but we want G-d Himself. Therefore, even though these phenomena are described as "gazing upon the glory of the King," they only lead to "love-sickeness" (*cholat ahava*). Love-sickness is the result of seeing something desirable that is as yet unattainable — at least not until the advent of the Messianic Age, when we will be able to grasp G-dliness with the naked eye (see *Besha'ah shehikdimu 5672*, vol. 2, page 1200-1203).

turn toward that which is good. There are also those who fear G-d, who are included in the category of "servants [of G-d]," and who are truly stimulated on Rosh Hashana and Yom Kippur from the very essence of their souls, with repentance and acceptance of the "yoke of heaven." And at that particular hour, their distance from the One Above truly bothers them to a great extent, and they cry honestly from bitterness of the soul. At that time, they accept the kingship of the One Above and resolve to be subordinated to G-d during the entire year, to learn Torah, and to keep the commandments. They resolve not to get involved in other matters, but in general to submit themselves only to G-d. With the passage of this auspicious time, however, even these people return to their physicality and nature, each one according to his own traits and character, whether to lusts of the heart, or pride and arrogance, or anger, etc. And it is truly amazing how their natures do not change at all, and how after such an arousal and resolution they can return to their previous spiritual condition. The reason for this is their failure to serve G-d during the entire remainder of the year.

שֶׁבִּאוֹתָהּ שָׁעָה בֶּאֱמֶת צַר לוֹ מְאֹד עַל רִחוּקוֹ מֵה' וּבוֹכֶה עַל זֶה בֶּאֱמֶת בְּמַר נַפְשׁוֹ וּמְקַבֵּל עָלָיו בְּאוֹתָהּ שָׁעָה עוֹל מַלְכוּתוֹ יִתְבָּרֵךְ לִהְיוֹת מָסוּר וְנָתוּן לֶאֱלֹקוּת כָּל הַשָּׁנָה בְּעֵסֶק הַתּוֹרָה וְקִיּוּם הַמִּצְוֹת וְלֹא יִתֵּן נַפְשׁוֹ לְעִנְיָנִים אֲחֵרִים וּבְדֶרֶךְ כְּלָל לִהְיוֹת מְשֻׁעְבָּד לַה' לְבַדּוֹ, וּבַעֲבוֹר הַזְּמַן הַנַּ"ל חוֹזֵר לְחָמְרִיּוּתוֹ וְטִבְעוֹ אִישׁ אִישׁ כְּפִי מִדּוֹתָיו הַטִּבְעִיִּים אִם בְּתַאֲוָה וְחֶמְדַּת הַלֵּב אוֹ בְּהִתְגַּבְּהָהּ וְהִתְנַשְּׂאוּת אוֹ בְּכַעַס וּכְהַאי גַּוְונָא, וְנִפְלָא הַדָּבָר מַמָּשׁ אֵיךְ שֶׁאֵינוֹ מִשְׁתַּנֶּה הַטֶּבַע כְּלָל וְאֵיךְ לְאַחַר הִתְעוֹרְרוּת וְהֶסְכֵּם כָּזֶה יַחְזֹר לִהְיוֹת כְּמִקֹּדֶם אַךְ סִבַּת הַדָּבָר הוּא הֶעְדֵּר הָעֲבוֹדָה כָּל הַשָּׁנָה,

It is truly amazing how their nature is not changed after such an arousal.

COMMENTARY

PITFALLS

Chapter 5, points out a potential pitfall of utilizing the above techniques. If we get so involved with the elevated levels of holiness that we forget the all-important task of purifying and elevating our animal soul, then we are neglecting our duty. If only our divine soul is serving G-d, then we are neglecting our obligation to also refine and elevate our animal soul. This is the

There are those who work on themselves all year long, and they operate on a higher spiritual rung.

דְּמִי שֶׁעוֹבֵד עֲבוֹדָתוֹ כָּל הַשָּׁנָה בְּהַכְנָעַת הַחֹמֶר בִּכְלָלוּת, וְהָעִקָּר בְּהַכְנָעַת הַכֹּחוֹת וְהַמִּדּוֹת פְּרָטִיּוֹת עַל יְדֵי הָעֲבוֹדָה פְּנִימִית בְּמֹחַ וְלֵב אִם בְּאַהֲבָה כְּמַיִם אוֹ בְּאַהֲבָה דְּכְרִשְׁפֵּי אֵשׁ וּכְמוֹ שֶׁנִּתְבָּאֵר לְעֵיל פ"ד. וַדַּאי הַהִתְעוֹרְרוּת דְּעֶצֶם הַנְּשָׁמָה דְּרֹאשׁ הַשָּׁנָה וְיוֹם כִּפּוּר פּוֹעֵל הַרְבֵּה עַל הַחָמְרִיּוּת שֶׁלּוֹ, וַעֲבוֹדָתוֹ אַחַר כָּךְ בְּכָל הַשָּׁנָה הִיא בְּמַדְרֵגָה נַעֲלֵית יוֹתֵר הֵן מִצַּד הַנְּשָׁמָה וְהֵן בְּהַזִּכּוּךְ דְּנֶפֶשׁ הַבַּהֲמִית שֶׁהַכֹּל הוּא בְּעִנְיָנִים גְּבוֹהִים וְנַעֲלִים יוֹתֵר כִּי בִּכְלָלוּתוֹ הוּא נַעֲשֶׂה בְּדַרְגָּא עֶלְיוֹנָה יוֹתֵר

But there are those who continue to serve the One Above all year long, by subjugating their physical natures in general, but mainly by subduing specific traits through inner service of the mind and heart, whether with "love like water" or "love like fire" (as described in Chapter 4). Certainly [in their case] the arousal of the essence of the soul on Rosh Hashana and Yom Kippur has a powerful effect on their physical nature, and their service of the One Above during the entire rest of the year is on a higher level. [This applies to] both the service of the G-dly soul itself, as well as the refinement of the animal soul. In either case, all of their spiritual efforts are on a more elevated plane, because in general they [are operating] on a higher spiritual rung.

COMMENTARY
---

danger of "transcendent consciousness" (the level called *chaya*); meditation on this level may lead us to be so involved with the spiritual that we forget that our soul was put down in a physical body in order to refine and uplift it. The way to avoid this pitfall is to begin our meditation on the simple, down-to-earth level of appreciating the G-dliness en-clothed in creation, as in the entry-level meditation leading to "love like water." This is an understanding that the natural, physically-oriented animal soul can also grasp, and therefore it can become involved and transformed through the meditation process. If, at each step along the way we make sure that we understand the concept — not only on a transcendent spiritual level but also in a way that the animal soul understands — we will then continue to transform and elevate the animal soul. If, though, we neglect the lower, simple levels of understanding and go straight to the transcendent levels of "love like fire," we run the risk of leaving our animal soul behind. Only by nurturing the animal soul with

(The animal soul also contains various different levels, including the three levels of ox, sheep, and goat, as known.[xxxii] For those whose animal soul is not so coarse, there are many things on which they will not have to work, while others may need to expend tremendous energy and labor on them. But through the above-mentioned arousal during the *"avoda"* [of prayer] of the entire year, the animal soul also abandons its coarseness. It rises to new and higher levels, and then the work that they must do to refine their physical nature becomes an entirely different kind of labor.)

(שֶׁהֲרֵי גַּם בְּהַנֶּפֶשׁ הַבַּהֲמִית יֵשׁ כַּמָּה חִלּוּקֵי מַדְרֵגוֹת, וְכַנּוֹדָע מִכְּלָלוּת הַג' מַדְרֵגוֹת דְּשׁוֹר כֶּשֶׂב וְעֵז, וּמִי שֶׁהַנֶּפֶשׁ הַבַּהֲמִית שֶׁלּוֹ אֵינוֹ גַּס כָּל כָּךְ יֵשׁ כַּמָּה דְּבָרִים שֶׁאֵין צָרִיךְ עַל זֶה יְגִיעָה כְּלָל מַה שֶּׁזּוּלָתוֹ צָרִיךְ עַל זֶה יְגִיעָה רַבָּה, וְעַל יְדֵי הִתְעוֹרְרוּת הַנַּ"ל אַחֲרֵי הָעֲבוֹדָה דְּכָל הַשָּׁנָה, הִנֵּה גַּם הַנֶּפֶשׁ הַבַּהֲמִית יוֹצֵא מִגַּסּוּתוֹ וְהוּא בְּדַרְגָּא עֶלְיוֹנָה יוֹתֵר וּמִמֵּילָא הָעֲבוֹדָה שֶׁלּוֹ בְּזִכּוּךְ הַחָמְרִיּוּת הוּא בְּאֹפֶן אַחֵר).

By appropriate arousal during prayer all year long, the animal soul becomes refined.

⬅

xxxii) See footnote of the Rebbe on page 288

(It is true that the situation of the animal soul during Rosh Hashana and Yom Kippur is not comparable to its position during the year, and there are times when it is far from G-d—as is written [in Proverbs 24:16]: "A *tzaddik* falls seven times...[and rises each time]" — nevertheless, it is on a higher level.)

(וְאִם כִּי וַדַּאי אֵינוֹ דּוֹמֶה מַעֲמַד וּמַצָּב הַנֶּפֶשׁ הַבַּהֲמִית בְּכָל הַשָּׁנָה לִכְמוֹ שֶׁהוּא בְּרֹאשׁ הַשָּׁנָה וְיוֹם כִּפּוּר וְגַם יֵשׁ רְחוּקִים לְעִתִּים (עַל דֶּרֶךְ שֶׁבַע יִפּוֹל כו') מִכָּל מָקוֹם הוּא בְּדַרְגָּא עֶלְיוֹנָה כו').

--- **COMMENTARY** ---

"love like water" will we later be able to consume and transform it with "love like fire." "Love like water" weakens the animal soul, and then "love like fire" performs the *coup de grace*, finishing it off.

That also is the reason why so many people come to the synagogue on the High Holidays of Rosh Hashana and Yom Kippur and yet do not seem to be affected by their experience during the entire rest of the year. They experience a spiritual high on Rosh Hashana and Yom Kippur, that is honest and real at the time. However, they fail to live up to the decisions and resolutions that they themselves made at that time. The reason that they fail, says the Rebbe Rashab, is because they do not work upon themselves the rest of the year, meditating on

Without work all year long, our physical nature asserts itself and remains strong.

But, lacking the service [prayer] all year long, our physical nature remains intact, at full strength. Then our spiritual arousal of Rosh Hashana and Yom Kippur — even though honest, as previously mentioned, since we are not really far from G-d in the sense of being a sinner or transgressor, G-d forbid, and outwardly we learn and pray—has no effect on our corporeal nature and does not truly transform it. The arousal itself, even though honest within our soul, is nevertheless transcendent and does not permeate our inner soul powers to become felt and experienced in actual deed. That is, the suffering and bitterness of the soul aren't experienced as deep distress and discomfort over specific negative details that bother us, but rather as a general condition of "I am not the way I should be." The same is true concerning our acceptance of the

אֲבָל בְּהֶעְדֵּר הָעֲבוֹדָה כָּל הַשָּׁנָה וְהַחָמְרִיּוּת הִיא בְּתָקְפָּהּ וּגְבוּרָתָהּ הִנֵּה הַהִתְעוֹרְרוּת דְּרֹאשׁ הַשָּׁנָה וְיוֹם כִּפּוּר הֲגַם שֶׁמִּתְעוֹרֵר בֶּאֱמֶת כנ"ל (מִפְּנֵי שֶׁאֵינוֹ בִּבְחִינַת רָחוֹק מַמָּשׁ לִהְיוֹת אֶת פּוֹשְׁעִים נִמְנָה חַס וְחָלִילָה, וְאַדְּרַבָּא בַּחִיצוֹנִיּוּת הֲרֵי הוּא בְּעֵסֶק הַתּוֹרָה וַעֲבוֹדָה) אֵין זֶה פּוֹעֵל עַל הַחָמְרִיּוּת לְשַׁנּוֹתָהּ בֶּאֱמֶת, וְגַם עֶצֶם הַהִתְעוֹרְרוּת הֲגַם שֶׁהִיא אֲמִתִּית בַּנֶּפֶשׁ הֲרֵי הִיא בִּבְחִינַת מַקִּיף לְבַד שֶׁאֵינָהּ נִרְגֶּשֶׁת בְּהַכֹּחוֹת פְּנִימִיִּים לִהְיוֹת שַׁיָּךְ לַפֹּעַל מַמָּשׁ, וְהַיְנוּ שֶׁגַּם הַצַּעַר וּמְרִירוּת נַפְשׁוֹ אֵינוֹ בִּבְחִינַת הֶרְגֵּשׁ הַצַּעַר וּמְרִירוּת עֲמֻקָּה מִפְּרָטֵי הָעִנְיָנִים הַלֹּא טוֹבִים שֶׁלּוֹ כִּי אִם מִכְּלָלוּת הַלֹּא טוֹב שֶׁלּוֹ, וְכֵן הַקַּבָּלַת עוֹל שֶׁמְּקַבֵּל עָלָיו עוֹל מַלְכוּתוֹ יִתְבָּרֵךְ בְּרֹאשׁ הַשָּׁנָה לִהְיוֹת מָסוּר וְנָתוּן אֵלָיו יִתְבָּרֵךְ וְכֵן

COMMENTARY

G-dliness and finding their own inner deficiencies that they need to rectify. Therefore, the spiritual arousal that they experience on Rosh Hashana and Yom Kippur goes to waste. Only when they "plow the ground," so to speak, preparing ourselves for the high revelations of the transcendental levels of the soul, can these revelations have a long-term effect on their animal soul.

Of course, we cannot say of the *yechida*, the highest transcendent level of the soul, that it has no effect upon the animal soul. Even though it is not en-clothed in the body, it nevertheless has an effect upon the animal soul. Since it is the level of the soul that is always united with G-d, it needs no stimulation or arousal to come into expression. It is always

Essay on Service of the Heart - Love Like Fire and Water

"yoke of heaven" during Rosh Hashana, [when we] submit ourselves to G-d, and concerning our arousal to do *teshuva* on Yom Kippur, [when we] resolve to become a different person altogether than we were before. These commitments don't seep into us and permeate our personality. They don't [change us or] cause us to conduct ourselves differently, and even more, they don't affect our specific behavior in turning away from evil and toward good.

בְּהִתְעוֹרְרוּת תְּשׁוּבָה דְּיוֹם כִּפּוּר שֶׁמְּקַבֵּל עָלָיו לִהְיוֹת בְּאֹפֶן אַחֵר מִכְּמוֹ שֶׁהָיָ' אֵין זֶה בָּא בּוֹ בִּבְחִינַת פְּנִימִיּוּת לִהְיוֹת בֶּאֱמֶת בְּהַנְהָגָה אַחֶרֶת לְפֹעַל וּמִכָּל שֶׁכֵּן שֶׁאֵינוֹ בָּא בְּעִנְיָנִים פְּרָטִיִּים הֵן בְּסוּר מֵרַע וְהֵן בְּוַעֲשֵׂה טוֹב

(This means that even our decision to be involved only in Torah and *mitzvot* and not to throw ourselves into worldly matters does not apply to specifics, that is, the very things in which we are lacking and deficient [and which need work]. From the outset, we did not make it our goal to become aware of our specific deficiencies and to honestly regret them. So, our seeming commitment and

(דְּהַיְנוּ גַּם מַה שֶּׁמְּקַבֵּל עָלָיו לַעֲסֹק בְּתוֹרָה וּמִצְוֹת וְשֶׁלֹּא יִתֵּן נַפְשׁוֹ לְעִנְיְנֵי הָעוֹלָם אֵין זֶה בִּדְבָרִים פְּרָטִים שֶׁהֵן הֵן אוֹתָם הַדְּבָרִים שֶׁבָּהֶם הוּא הַגֵּרָעוֹן וְהַחִסָּרוֹן שֶׁלּוֹ, כִּי מִתְּחִלָּה אֵינוֹ נוֹתֵן נַפְשׁוֹ לְהַרְגִּישׁ פְּרָטֵי הַחֶסְרוֹנוֹת שֶׁלּוֹ וּלְהִצְטַעֵר עֲלֵיהֶם בֶּאֱמֶת וְכֵן הַקַּבָּלָה וְהַתִּקּוּן הַמְדֻמֶּה אֵינוֹ בִּפְרָטֵי הַדְּבָרִים הָאֵלּוּ. וְזֹאת לָדַעַת שֶׁגַּם אִם הֻרְגַּשׁ

--- *COMMENTARY* ---

"there," united with G-d, even without meditation on His greatness. At the same time, it is not governed by the limitations of existence; it is at once transcendent and permeating the body.

That is why it is the *yechida* that enables us to give up our life "in honor of G-d," if necessary. If faced with a choice — either to commit one of the three cardinal sins or to give up our life — we, as Jews, will give up our life without thinking, in order to avoid disconnection with the One Above.

This is a function of the *yechida*, that level of the soul that cannot and will not be separated in any way from G-d. Just as it is totally connected with the One Above, it also has complete control over the physical body and its functions. Therefore, when the *yechida* comes into revelation, it overrides and transforms the animal soul.

Without deep inner awareness of our deficiencies, it is impossible to rectify them.

רectification [of our deficiencies] are not geared to specifics. It should be known that even if we experience pain and remorse over the appropriate details, our commitment may not lead to their rectification. It is possible that our resolution may apply only to our general situation. If so, it will not have an effect when it comes to our specific problems. It is also possible that the commitment itself is not coupled with real action, and then, even if we experience the appropriate remorse, our commitment will not necessarily be appropriate [and effective in changing the specifics of our behavior]. So, the correct intention and effort must be devoted to both of these factors, in order that they be appropriate. What is certain is that without deep inner awareness of our own specific deficiencies, it is impossible for us to truly commit ourselves to any rectification.) [Our awareness] will only affect us in general, so that we won't be "bad" and we'll be "good", and therefore [the effect] is only temporary, and it will fade away and disappear afterward.

הַצַּעַר וְהַמְּרִירוּת הִיא עַל הָעִנְיָנִים הַפְּרָטִיִּים, מִכָּל מָקוֹם אֵינוֹ מֻכְרָח שֶׁהַקַּבָּלָה תִּהְיֶה גַּם כֵּן בְּתִקּוּן הַפְּרָטִים דְּיָכוֹל לִהְיוֹת שֶׁהַקַּבָּלָה תִּהְיֶ' רַק עַל הַכְּלָל, וּמִמֵּילָא לֹא יָבוֹא לִידֵי פֹּעַל כְּשֶׁבָּא לְיָדוֹ הָעִנְיָנִים הַפְּרָטִים וְגַם עֶצֶם הַקַּבָּלָה יָכוֹל לִהְיוֹת בְּאֹפֶן כָּזֶה שֶׁאֵינָה שַׁיֶּכֶת לַפֹּעַל מַמָּשׁ, וְנִמְצָא דְּגַם אִם תִּהְיֶה הַמְּרִירוּת כִּדְבָעֵי אֵינוֹ מֻכְרָח עֲדַיִן שֶׁתִּהְיֶה הַקַּבָּלָה כִּדְבָעֵי. וְצָרִיךְ לִהְיוֹת כַּוָּנַת הַמְכֻוָּן וִיגִיעָתוֹ עַל שְׁנֵי הַדְּבָרִים שֶׁיִּהְיוּ רְצוּיִים אָמְנָם זֹאת וַדַּאי שֶׁבִּבְלִי הֶרְגֵּשׁ פְּנִימִי וְעֹמֶק מִפְּרָטֵי הַחֶסְרוֹנוֹת שֶׁלּוֹ אִי אֶפְשָׁר שֶׁתִּהְיֶה הַקַּבָּלָה כִּדְבָעֵי לְמֶהֱוֵי) רַק בִּכְלָלוּת שֶׁלֹּא יִהְיֶ' רַע וְיִהְיֶ' טוֹב וּמִמֵּילָא זֶה רַק לְפִי שָׁעָה וְיַחֲלֹף וְיַעֲבֹר אַחַר כָּךְ.

The reason for this is also a deficiency in our service [of G-d] all year long. When we work on ourselves all year long, rectifying and refining our character traits, we become well aware of exactly what we need to fix, each one of us according to the "portion" of natural attributes entrusted us to fix and refine. We strive with "labor of the soul" and "labor of the flesh" all year long to purify these

דְּסִבַּת הַדָּבָר הוּא גַּם כֵּן בְּהֶעְדֵּר הָעֲבוֹדָה דְּכָל הַשָּׁנָה, דְּכַאֲשֶׁר כָּל הַשָּׁנָה הוּא עוֹבֵד וּמְיַגֵּעַ אֶת עַצְמוֹ בְּתִקּוּן וְזִכּוּךְ מִדּוֹתָיו שֶׁיּוֹדֵעַ הוּא אֶת עִנְיָנָיו מַה שֶּׁהוּא צָרִיךְ לְתַקֵּן, אִישׁ אִישׁ כְּפִי מַה שֶּׁנִּתַּן לוֹ לְתַקֵּן וּלְזַכֵּךְ מֵהַמִּדּוֹת הַטִּבְעִיִּים וּמִתְיַגֵּעַ בִּיגִיעַת נֶפֶשׁ וִיגִיעַת בָּשָׂר כָּל הַשָּׁנָה לְבָרֵר וּלְזַכֵּךְ הַמִּדּוֹת הָאֵלּוּ, הִנֵּה בְּרֹאשׁ הַשָּׁנָה וְיוֹם כִּפּוּר שֶׁהוּא עֵת

Essay on Service of the Heart - Love Like Fire and Water

traits. Then, on Rosh Hashana and Yom Kippur, which are a time of favorable will from above, when G-d "unsheathes His holy arm," [the right arm represents revelation and kindness] and "the Source of light draws near to the spark," the essence of our soul becomes aroused and revealed. The general service at that time is one[xxxiii] of inner awareness and [happens at the level of] essence of the soul, as is known. It focuses on those things that we worked on all year long. [During the period of the High Holidays], we are in a state of distress and deep bitterness, touching the very essence of our soul. Our acceptance of the "yoke of heaven" and our commitment to do *teshuva* also come from the essence of our soul, but in such a way that they [the acceptance and the commitment] affect our actions and involve those things on which we have worked. And this is because in essence we are *p'nimi* [dedicated to truly working on ourselves, finding and rectifying our inner deficiencies] in our service all year long. Therefore, during Rosh Hashana and Yom Kippur, when the service comes from the essence of the soul, we perform it with inner feeling and consciousness. We are supported in this service by the revelation from above [that is characteristic of the Ten Days of *Teshuva*] as well as the revelation of the essence of our own soul (which

Without prayer all year long, the high holidays will provide soul stimulation only at the time they occur.

xxxiii) See footnote of the Rebbe on page 289

רָצוֹן לְמַעְלָה וְחָשַׂף ה' אֶת זְרוֹעַ קָדְשׁוֹ בִּבְחִינַת קָרוֹב הַמָּאוֹר אֶל הַנִּצוֹץ הַמְעוֹרֵר בְּנֶפֶשׁ הָאָדָם הִתְגַּלּוּת עֶצֶם נַפְשׁוֹ, וּכְלָלוּת הָעֲבוֹדָה בַּזְּמַן הַהוּא הִיא בְּחִינַת פְּנִימִיּוּת וְעַצְמוּת הַנֶּפֶשׁ כַּנּוֹדָע, הִנֵּה כָּל זֶה בָּא בְּעִנְיָנִים אֵלּוּ שֶׁעוֹסֵק בָּהֶם כָּל הַשָּׁנָה רַק שֶׁהוּא בִּבְחִינַת מֵצַר וּמְרִירוּת עֲמֻקָּה הַנּוֹגֵעַ לוֹ בְּעַצְמוּת וּפְנִימִיּוּת נַפְשׁוֹ וְכֵן הַקַּבָּלַת עוֹל מַלְכוּת שָׁמַיִם וְקַבָּלַת הַתְּשׁוּבָה הִיא בְּעַצְמִיּוּת נַפְשׁוֹ אֲבָל הוּא בְּאֹפֶן שֶׁיִּהְיֶה נוֹגֵעַ לְפֹעַל מַמָּשׁ, וּבְאֵלּוּ הָעִנְיָנִים שֶׁעוֹסֵק בָּהֶם. וְהַיְנוּ מִפְּנֵי שֶׁבְּעֶצֶם הוּא פְּנִימִי בַּעֲבוֹדָתוֹ בְּכָל הַשָּׁנָה וּכְמוֹ כֵן הוּא בַּעֲבוֹדָה דְרֹאשׁ הַשָּׁנָה וְיוֹם כִּפּוּר שֶׁהִיא בִּבְחִינַת עֶצֶם הַנֶּפֶשׁ הֲרֵי זֶה בִּבְחִינַת הֶרְגֵּשׁ פְּנִימִי, וְגַם מְסַיֵּעַ לוֹ הַגִּלּוּי מִלְמַעְלָה וְהִתְגַּלּוּת עַצְמוּת נַפְשׁוֹ (הַנִּרְגָּשׁ בִּפְנִימִיּוּת) לְהָסִיר מֵאִתּוֹ חֲמָרִיּוּת הַמִּדּוֹת הַטִּבְעִיִּים שֶׁהוּא עוֹסֵק בְּבֵרוּר וְזִכּוּךְ שֶׁלָּהֶם (וּכְמוֹ שֶׁנִּתְבָּאֵר לְעֵיל שֶׁנַּעֲשָׂה בְּדַרְגָּא עֶלְיוֹנָה יוֹתֵר). אֲבָל בְּהֶעְדֵּר הָעֲבוֹדָה כָּל הַשָּׁנָה, הִנֵּה בְּרֹאשׁ הַשָּׁנָה וְיוֹם כִּפּוּר הֲגַם שֶׁמִּתְעוֹרֵר בְּנַפְשׁוֹ הֲרֵי זֶה רַק כְּמוֹ דָּבָר בְּעִתּוֹ, שֶׁהַשָּׁעָה הוּא לְהִתְפַּעֵל וּלְהִתְעוֹרֵר (מִצַּד הַגִּלּוּי מִלְמַעְלָה כַּנַּ"ל שֶׁמֵּאִיר עַל כָּל אֶחָד וְאֶחָד מִיִּשְׂרָאֵל (יוֹתֵר מֵהַכְּרוּזִים שֶׁבְּכָל יוֹם שֶׁגַּם הֵם נִרְגָּשִׁים בְּכָל אֶחָד

we experience with inner feeling and consciousness). This helps us shrug off the physical facade of those natural attributes that we are engaged in refining (and as explained earlier, this takes place [during the High Holidays] on a higher level). However, without the service [of prayer] all year long, Rosh Hashana and Yom Kippur will provide stimulation for our soul only at the time they occur, since it is a time of spiritual excitement and arousal (on account of the aforementioned revelation from above, that illuminates every Jewish person, even more so than the "spiritual messages" which come down everyday and are experienced by everyone,[xxxiv] as is known). This is particularly true of those who are in the category of "servants of G-d," meaning those who are close to the service we're discussing here. But [for the rest], the arousal is only from transcendence, rather than from inner feeling and truth. Therefore, it is not effective in truly changing the person. The arousal may be real on the level of transcendence, but it has no effect on the physicality of the person and will not truly change it.

וְאֶחָד כַּנּוֹדָע, וּבִפְרָט בְּאוֹתָן שֶׁבִּכְלָל עוֹבְדִים יֵחָשְׁבוּ דְּהַיְנוּ הַקְּרוֹבִים לְעִנְיַן הָעֲבוֹדָה שֶׁבָּזֶה מְדַבְּרִים כָּאן), אֲבָל הוּא בִּבְחִינַת מַקִּיף לְבַד בְּלִי הֶרְגֵּשׁ בִּפְנִימִיּוּת וַאֲמִתִּית הַנַּ"ל, וְלָכֵן אֵין זֶה שַׁיָּךְ לִפְעַל וְעַל כֵּן הֲגַם שֶׁהִתְעוֹרְרוּת הִיא אֲמִתִּית בִּבְחִינַת הַמַּקִּיף דְּנֶפֶשׁ אֵין זֶה נוֹגֵעַ אֶל הַחָמְרִיּוּת לְשַׁנּוֹתָהּ בֶּאֱמֶת).

xxxiv) See footnote of the Rebbe on page 290

xxxv) See footnote of the Rebbe on page 291

Only the ardent love of ahava rabba, beyond reason, can transform the animal soul.

וּמַה שֶּׁכָּתוּב בְּמָקוֹם אַחֵר דְּדַוְקָא בְּחִינַת אַהֲבָה רַבָּה שֶׁלְּמַעְלָה מִטַּעַם וָדַעַת מְהַפֵּךְ מַהוּת הַנֶּפֶשׁ הַבַּהֲמִית, זֶהוּ דַּוְקָא לְאַחַר הָעֲבוֹדָה תְּחִלָּה בִּבְחִינַת טַעַם וָדַעַת בְּמֹחַ וְלֵב, וְנוֹדָע דְּהָעֲבוֹדָה שֶׁעַל פִּי טַעַם וָדַעַת הִיא רַק בִּבְחִינַת בִּטּוּל הַיֵּשׁ לְבַד, וּבִכְדֵי שֶׁיִּהְיֶ' הַבִּטּוּל בִּמְצִיאוּת הוּא בְּאַהֲבָה רַבָּה שֶׁלְּמַעְלָה מִטַּעַם וָדַעַת שֶׁעַל יְדֵי זֶה שֶׁתִּתְבַּטֵּל מַהוּת הַנֶּפֶשׁ הַבַּהֲמִית וּמִתְהַפֵּךְ לְטוֹב, וּבָזֶה יֵשׁ גַּם כֵּן מַדְרֵגוֹת וְאֵין כָּאן מְקוֹמוֹ לְבָאֵר

It is written elsewhere[xxxv] that only *ahava rabbah* ("transcendent love"), which is love beyond reason and logic, is capable of transforming the essence of the animal soul. This occurs only after a previous service of logic and reason within the mind and heart. As is known, the service which corresponds to reason and intellect produces only nullification of the ego (*bitul hayesh*). In order to achieve full nullification of the self (*bitul b'metziut*), we need first to achieve *ahava rabbah* beyond reason and intellect. By way of this love,

Essay on Service of the Heart - Love Like Fire and Water

the very essence of the animal soul becomes nullified and transformed into a positive entity. There are various levels within this process, and this isn't the place to discuss them. The main point is that all of this can only be achieved if preceded by an inner service [of reason and logic] in the mind and heart, and while purifying and refining the natural attributes. If we engage in the "labors before Shabbat" in the exercise of intellect—which correspond to bending the will of the animal soul (*itkafia*)—we "eat on Shabbat." That is, we succeed in actualizing the desire and "transcendent love" of the soul beyond logic and reason, which corresponds to the complete transformation (*it'hafcha*) of the animal soul. All this is as written in *Torah Ohr*, in the discourses beginning with *Vayakhel*, and *Kechu ma'itchem truma*, and as explained in *Likutei Torah*, in the discourse beginning with *Levaer inyan Yom HaKippurim* regarding the "fire coming down from above" and the "fire from below..."

אֲבָל כָּל זֶה דַּוְקָא בְּהַקְדָּמַת הָעֲבוֹדָה פְּנִימִית בְּמֹחַ וְלֵב לְבָרֵר וּלְזַכֵּךְ אֶת הַמִּדּוֹת טִבְעִיִּים, וּמִי שֶׁטָּרַח בְּעֶרֶב שַׁבָּת בַּעֲבוֹדָה שֶׁעַל פִּי טַעַם וְדַעַת בִּבְחִינַת אִתְכַּפְיָא יֹאכַל בְּשַׁבָּת בִּבְחִינַת הָרָצוֹן וְאַהֲבָה רַבָּה שֶׁלְּמַעְלָה מִטַּעַם וְדַעַת לִהְיוֹת בִּבְחִינַת אִתְהַפְּכָא כוּ׳ וּכְמוֹ שֶׁכָּתוּב בְּתוֹרָה אוֹר דִּבּוּר הַמַּתְחִיל וַיַּקְהֵל וְדִבּוּר הַמַּתְחִיל קְחוּ מֵאִתְּכֶם תְּרוּמָה, וּכְמוֹ שֶׁכָּתוּב בְּלִקּוּטֵי תוֹרָה דִּבּוּר הַמַּתְחִיל לְבָאֵר עִנְיָן יוֹם הַכִּפּוּרִים בְּעִנְיָן אֵשׁ שֶׁל מַעְלָה וְאֵשׁ שֶׁל מַטָּה כוּ׳.

All this can only be achieved if preceded by detailed meditation based on logic and reason.

SYNOPSIS:

Ahava, meaning "love,"comes from the Hebrew word *ava*, meaning "will." It is explained elsewhere that this is a will beyond logic and reason, and that it is a [very] high level of serving G-d, although it doesn't affect the physicality of the animal soul. This is because it happens on a transcendent level of the soul which is too high to become en-clothed in the animal soul. Therefore even when it becomes truly aroused with an [abstract] will for connection with the One Above (like in every Jew on Rosh Hashana and Yom Kippur), it is not experienced inside, and doesn't change our nature, unless it is preceded by an inner service of logic and reason in the mind and heart. (But the revelation of the true transcendent level of *yechida* has the effect of transforming and turning over the earthy nature of the animal soul completely.)

קִצוּר.

הִנֵּה אַהֲבָה לְשׁוֹן אָבָה רָצוֹן. וּמְבֹאָר בְּמָקוֹם אַחֵר שֶׁהוּא בְּחִינַת הָרָצוֹן שֶׁלְּמַעְלָה מִטַּעַם וָדַעַת. וְעִם הֱיוֹת שֶׁזֶּהוּ מַדְרֵגָה גְּבוֹהָה בָּעֲבוֹדָה, אֵין זֶה פּוֹעֵל עַל הַחָמְרִיּוֹת דְּנֶפֶשׁ הַבַּהֲמִית מִפְּנֵי שֶׁזֶּהוּ בִּבְחִינַת מַקִּיף דְּנֶפֶשׁ שֶׁלְּמַעְלָה מֵהִתְלַבְּשׁוּת וְעַל כֵּן גַּם שֶׁמִּתְעוֹרֵר בֶּאֱמֶת בִּבְחִינַת הָרָצוֹן הנ"ל (וּכְמוֹ בְּכָל אֶחָד וְאֶחָד בְּרֹאשׁ הַשָּׁנָה וְיוֹם הַכִּפּוּרִים) אֵין זֶה נִרְגָּשׁ בִּפְנִימִיּוּת וְאֵינוֹ מְשַׁתֶּנֶּה הַטֶּבַע עַל יְדֵי זֶה וְנִתְבָּאֵר דְּהִתְגַּלּוּת אֲמִתִּית בְּחִינַת הַמַּקִּיף דִּיחִידָה פּוֹעֵל לְשַׁנּוֹת וּלְהֲפֹךְ הַטִּבְעִיּוּת לְגַמְרֵי) כִּי אִם בְּהַקְדִּים תְּחִלָּה הָעֲבוֹדָה פְּנִימִית שֶׁעַל פִּי טַעַם וָדַעַת בְּמֹחַ וְלֵב כו':

CHAPTER 6

Avoda [of prayer] based upon reason and logic may be only superficial and external. In such a case, it is not really *avoda* [at all] and doesn't have any effect on the gross nature of our animal soul, failing to subjugate and nullify it. This [type of *avoda*] results from meditation that is only general; that is, when we meditate on a G-dly concept and fail to do so with true intellectual grasp. We fail to get an accurate understanding of the subject, which would lead to knowledge and true internalization of the concept as it is, nor do we delve into the depths of the subject. Instead, we are satisfied with a meditation on, for example, the overall concept of creation *ex nihilo* (something "from nothing").

(We may also sense the general wonder of the subject, but we don't direct our attention toward becoming aware of the G-dly power that creates something from nothing. That is, we don't think about the specific level of G-dliness that is doing the creating,

פרק ו

וְהִנֵּה בַּעֲבוֹדָה שֶׁעַל פִּי טַעַם וְדַעַת יֵשׁ גַּם כֵּן שֶׁהָעֲבוֹדָה הִיא בִּבְחִינַת מַקִּיף לְבַד, שֶׁאֵין זֶה עֲבוֹדָה וְאֵינוֹ פּוֹעֵל עַל חָמְרִיּוּת הַנֶּפֶשׁ הַבַּהֲמִית לְהַכְנִיעוֹ וּלְבַטְּלוֹ, וְהוּא כַּאֲשֶׁר הַהִתְבּוֹנְנוּת הִיא בִּבְחִינַת כְּלָלוֹת לְבַד, וְהַיְנוּ דִּבְאֵיזֶה עִנְיָן אֱלֹקִי שֶׁמִּתְבּוֹנֵן בּוֹ אֵינוֹ מִשְׁתַּדֵּל לְהִתְבּוֹנֵן בּוֹ בִּבְחִינַת הַשָּׂגָה מַמָּשׁ לֵידַע וּלְהַשִּׂיג אֶת הָעִנְיָן בֶּאֱמֶת כְּמוֹ שֶׁהוּא וּלְהַעֲמִיק דַּעְתּוֹ בָּזֶה, כִּי אִם מִסְתַּפֵּק בְּהִתְבּוֹנְנוּת בִּכְלָלוּת הָעִנְיָן הַהוּא, וּכְמוֹ בִּכְלָלוּת עִנְיַן בְּרִיאָה יֵשׁ מֵאַיִן

(וְנִרְגָּשׁ אֶצְלוֹ גַּם כֵּן כְּלָלוּת עִנְיַן הַהַפְלָאָה שֶׁבָּזֶה מִבְּלִי שֶׁמֵּשִׂים לִבּוֹ לֵידַע אֶת הַכֹּחַ הָאֱלֹקִי הַמְהַוֶּה מֵאַיִן לְיֵשׁ דְּהַיְנוּ אֵיזֶה מַדְרֵגָה פְּרָטִית בֶּאֱלֹקוּת הוּא וְאֵיךְ הוּא אֹפֶן הַהִתְהַוּוּת מֵאַיִן לְיֵשׁ וּפְרָטֵי

> *Superficial avoda based upon general meditation is not really avoda at all.*

COMMENTARY

CHAPTER 6: ENGRAVING FROM WITHIN AND WITHOUT

Chapter 6 of *Kuntres Ha'Avoda* is devoted to the difference between proper, detailed meditation, and shallow, superficial meditation.

It starts by telling us what we should avoid. It says, first of all, that shallow and superficial meditation is like someone trying to grasp a complex topic at first glance — there's no depth to our understanding of the subject, and we only get the main points of it, without any true and lasting grasp. This may be good enough to maintain our fear of G-d, which is anyway

Creation from nothing is a truly amazing process.

הַהַפְלָאָה בָּזֶה, וְכַנּוֹדָע דְּעִנְיַן בְּרִיאָה יֵשׁ מֵאַיִן הוּא עִנְיָן נִפְלָא מְאֹד שֶׁאֵינוֹ מֻשָּׂג בֶּאֱמֶת בְּשֵׂכֶל אֱנוֹשִׁי אֵיךְ וּמַה הוּא שֶׁזֶּהוּ עִנְיַן מַה שֶּׁזֶּהוּ רַק בְּחֵיק הַבּוֹרֵא וַאֲמִתִּית כֹּחַ הַהִתְהַוּוּת הוּא מִבְּחִינַת עַצְמוּת אֵין סוֹף בָּרוּךְ הוּא שֶׁהוּא לְבַדּוֹ בְּכֹחוֹ וִיכָלְתּוֹ לְהַוּוֹת יֵשׁ מֵאַיִן כוּ' וּכְמוֹ שֶׁכָּתוּב בְּמָקוֹם אַחֵר)

nor do we think about how this creation *ex nihilo* takes place. We don't make ourselves aware of the details and how wondrous this process is. Creation *ex nihilo* is a truly amazing process, the "how and what" of which are not really understood by human intellect, since that is a secret which is only in the possession of the Creator. The real power of creation comes from the essence of the Infinite Light of the One Above, "with Whom alone rests the power and ability to create something from absolute nothing," as written elsewhere [*Tanya, Igeret Hakodesh 20*].) xxxvi

xxxvi) See footnote of the Rebbe on page 292 ➤

אוֹ בִּכְלָלוּת עִנְיַן גְּדֻלַּת ה' בְּעִנְיַן הַהִתְהַוּוּת. וְכֵן בְּדֶרֶךְ כְּלָל אֵיךְ דְּאִיהוּ מְמַלֵּא כָּל עָלְמִין וְאִיהוּ סוֹבֵב כָּל עָלְמִין כוּ' וְעִם הֱיוֹת שֶׁמִּתְפָּעֵל בְּנַפְשׁוֹ וּמִתְלַהֵב עַל הָעִנְיָנִים הָאֱלֹקִי (ער ווערט צעקאכט אויף אֱלֹקוּת מִיט א הִתְפַּעֲלוּת הָרָצוֹא כוּ'), הֲרֵי זֶה בִּבְחִינַת מַקִּיף לְבַד וְאֵין זֶה הִתְפַּעֲלוּת אֲמִתִּי כִּי אִם דִּמְיוֹן כּוֹזֵב (וּכְמוֹ שֶׁכָּתוּב בַּאֲרִיכוּת בְּקֻנְטְרֵס הַתְּפִלָּה).

Or, we may briefly contemplate the greatness of G-d in the creation of the universe. In passing, we may consider how "He permeates all the worlds and He transcends all the worlds." But, if we become intrigued and stimulated by this G-dly subject, the excitement is only superficial. It implies no true intensity of interest, but only an illusory facade (as is written about at length in *Kuntres HaTefila*).

COMMENTARY
---

innate in the Jewish soul and needs only gentle reminders in order to surface. But love of G-d requires determined work and attention, and that can only come about through detailed meditation.

Detailed meditation has two stages: "engraving from without" and "engraving from within."

"Engraving from without" is necessary in order to stimulate our heart and produce interest in spiritual matters. This involves detailed meditation on topics such as creation *ex-nihilo* (something "from nothing"). Or we may choose to meditate

Essay on Service of the Heart - Love Like Fire and Water

[Thus we see that] general meditation is somewhat akin to a reminder, by which we recall G-dliness. This is not sufficient to arouse love of G-d, for which we need solid knowledge and intellectual grasp, as this is the only way to achieve real love of G-d.

(Regarding "fear of G-d," simple recall is sufficient. We must remind ourselves of the aspects of G-dliness that bring us to the fear of the One Above, as explained in Chapter 3, where it is also explained that we must first understand the concept [which leads to "fear of G-d"], and afterward a reminder is sufficient.)

But, a reminder alone is not sufficient to arouse love of G-d. Even if we know the topic [well] and have already meditated upon it many times, we must return and actually meditate upon it anew every time that we want to achieve true love of the Creator. Possibly, this is because *bitul* (self-nullification) is in the nature of every Jewish soul, as written elsewhere regarding the verse [in Malachi 3:10] *Ki tihyu atem eretz cheifetz*,[xxxvii]

וְהָעִנְיָן הוּא כִּי הַהִתְבּוֹנְנוּת בְּדֶרֶךְ כְּלָלוּת, הִיא רַק כְּמוֹ זִכָּרוֹן שֶׁנִּזְכָּר עַל אֱלֹקוּת. וְזֶה אֵינוֹ מַסְפִּיק לְעוֹרֵר אֶת הָאַהֲבָה כִּי אִם צָרִיךְ לִהְיוֹת יְדִיעָה וְהַשָּׂגָה מַמָּשׁ, וְעַל יְדֵי זֶה דַּוְקָא מִתְעוֹרֵר הָאַהֲבָה,

(וּבְיִרְאָה מַסְפִּיק הַזִּכָּרוֹן שֶׁזּוֹכֵר אֶת הָעִנְיְנֵי אֱלֹקוּת הַמְּבִיאִים אֶת הַיִּרְאָה וּכְמוֹ שֶׁנִּתְבָּאֵר לְעֵיל פ"ג (וְנִת' שָׁם דְּמִכָּל מָקוֹם צָרִיךְ לִהְיוֹת בִּתְחִלָּה הַשָּׂגַת הָעִנְיָן וְאַחַר כָּךְ מַסְפִּיק הַזִּכָּרוֹן)

מַה שֶּׁאֵין כֵּן בְּאַהֲבָה אֵינוֹ מַסְפִּיק הַזִּכָּרוֹן לְבַד וְגַם שֶׁיּוֹדֵעַ אֶת הָעִנְיָן וּכְבָר הִתְבּוֹנֵן בּוֹ כַּמָּה פְּעָמִים הִנֵּה בְּכָל פַּעַם וּפַעַם בִּכְדֵי שֶׁתִּהְיֶה הָאַהֲבָה אֲמִתִּית צָרִיךְ לִהְיוֹת הִתְבּוֹנְנוּת מַמָּשׁ דַּוְקָא. וְיֵשׁ לוֹמַר מִפְּנֵי שֶׁעִנְיַן הַבִּטּוּל יֵשׁ בְּטֶבַע בְּנִשְׁמוֹת יִשְׂרָאֵל וּכְמוֹ שֶׁכָּתוּב בְּמָקוֹם אַחֵר בְּעִנְיָן כִּי תִהְיוּ אַתֶּם אֶרֶץ חֵפֶץ דְּנִשְׁמוֹת יִשְׂרָאֵל הֵן

> *General meditation is like a reminder, sufficient to recall fear of G-d, but not enough to arouse love.*

> *Self-nullification is so ingrained in the Jewish psyche that it is sufficient for us to simply recall G-d.*

xxxvii) See footnote of the Rebbe on page 292

--- COMMENTARY ---

on the greatness of the Creator based upon the incredible variety, harmony, and number of creations. We may delve deeper and meditate on how each particular aspect of creation receives the G-dly light and energy that is necessary for its own maintenance and growth. Chassidic literature is replete with guided meditations on the above topics, and if we are able to delve into Chassidic discourses on our own, we can extract from them the necessary ingredients to begin meditating alone or with the help of a *mashpiah* ("spiritual guide").

meaning that Jewish souls "are like land which is ready for sowing," and the Torah and its *mitzvot* are the seeds; this is due to the *bitul* which is latent in the essence of the Jewish soul. [Also as the verse in Deut. 7:7] states, *Ki atem hame'at mikol ha'amim*, meaning that "you, the Jews, are constantly minimizing yourselves"; this corresponds to the Jewish calendar that follows the moon, because "you," a small people (the Jews) count the smaller luminary (the moon), just as Yaakov was the smaller (younger) son and David as well was the smallest and youngest. The ingredient of self-abnegation is so ingrained in the Jewish psyche that it is sufficient for us to simply recall G-d in order to achieve full subjugation to Him and His will. However, love of G-d is different. Although it also comes to us as an inheritance from our forefathers, nevertheless love is not as natural as *bitul*, which

הָאָרֶץ הָרְאוּיָה לִזְרִיעָה עַל יְדֵי תּוֹרָה וּמִצְוֹת מֵחֲמַת כֹּחַ הַבִּטּוּל שֶׁבָּהֶם בְּעֶצֶם וּכְמוֹ שֶׁכָּתוּב כִּי אַתֶּם הַמְעַט מִכָּל הָעַמִּים שֶׁמְּמַעֲטִים אֶת עַצְמָם כו׳, וְהוּא עִנְיָן יִשְׂרָאֵל מוֹנִין לִלְבָנָה דָא׳ קָטָן מוֹנֶה לִקְטַנָּה יַעֲקֹב בְּנָהּ הַקָּטָן וְכֵן וְדָוִד הוּא הַקָּטָן כו׳, וּמִפְּנֵי שֶׁיֵּשׁ בָּהֶם עִנְיַן הַבִּטּוּל בְּטֶבַע לָכֵן מַסְפִּיק עַל זֶה גַּם הַזִּכָּרוֹן דֶּאֱלֹקוּת שֶׁמִּתְבַּטֵּל עַל יְדֵי זֶה וּמֵנִיחַ אֶת עַצְמוֹ לְגַבֵּי אֱלֹקוּת וּרְצוֹנוֹ יִת׳. אֲבָל עִנְיַן הָאַהֲבָה הֲגַם שֶׁהִיא גַּם כֵּן בִּירֻשָּׁה לָנוּ מֵאֲבוֹתֵינוּ מִכָּל מָקוֹם אֵין זֶה כְּמוֹ טֶבַע הַבִּטּוּל וְהַנָּחַת עַצְמוּתוֹ שֶׁבְּכָל אֶחָד וְאֶחָד מִיִּשְׂרָאֵל (וַאֲמִתִּית עִנְיַן הָאַהֲבָה מְסֻתֶּרֶת שֶׁבְּכָל אֶחָד וְאֶחָד בִּירֻשָּׁה מֵהָאָבוֹת מְבֹאָר בְּסֵפֶר שֶׁל בֵּינוֹנִים פי״ח שֶׁזֶּהוּ הַכֹּחַ וּמְסִירוּת נֶפֶשׁ שֶׁבְּכָל אֶחָד וְאֶחָד מִיִּשְׂרָאֵל מִשּׁוּם שֶׁאִי אֶפְשָׁר לוֹ לִהְיוֹת נִפְרָד חַס וְחָלִילָה מֵאַחְדוּתוֹ יִת׳), וּבִפְרָט

COMMENTARY

For an example of such a Chassidic discourse, see end of commentary to this chapter.

But in order to achieve the kind of spiritual love that transforms our life — rectifying our animal soul and establishing G-dliness as our main concern—we must strive for the "engraving from within" that accompanies meditation on the G-dly energy within creation. Here, our main concern is not with creation per se, but with the G-dly light that energizes all aspects of creation. "Just as the soul fills the body, so G-d fills and permeates the universe"—and this is true regarding both the higher spiritual creations and also the lower, physical

Essay on Service of the Heart - Love Like Fire and Water

is the ability to nullify and put ourselves aside that is inherent in every Jew. (The true nature of the love hidden in every Jewish soul as an inheritance from our forefathers is explained in the *Tanya*, chapter 18 as the power of *mesirat nefesh*, or "giving up the soul" that is within every Jew. It is impossible for us as Jews to separate ourselves, G-d forbid, from G-d's unity and oneness.) Because love of G-d involves the revelation of something [that is, it requires effort to unveil something inside of ourselves], therefore, it cannot take place without solid intellectual understanding and without meditation.

שֶׁהָאַהֲבָה הִיא הִתְגַּלּוּת דָּבָר עַל כֵּן אִי אֶפְשָׁר לִהְיוֹת כִּי אִם עַל יְדֵי הַשָּׂגָה וְהִתְבּוֹנְנוּת מַמָּשׁ.

Love of G-d is not as natural as fear. Love develops only through deep meditation.

As a general rule, light meditation alone brings us bitterness and a worried heart. This is because we feel the core of the concept, on which we are meditating, to be distant. (That is, the concept is not integrated in our mind since we don't grasp all the details with which it is understood. Also, with our overall knowledge, we grasp only the general nature of G-dliness, which is beyond true en-clothement and integration in our mind. This is similar to the difference^xxxviii between the point of *chochma* which is like a lightning flash of insight — called *pele* (wondrous) — and the [down-to-earth analytic] understanding of *bina*, as is known. [*Chochma* is ethereal, beyond understanding, while *bina* brings the fleeting insight of *chochma* into clear

וְעַל פִּי הָרַב הַהִתְבּוֹנְנוּת בִּבְחִינַת כְּלָלוּת לְבַד הִיא הַמְּבִיאָה לִידֵי מְרִירוּת וְלֵב דּוֹאֵג, דִּלְהְיוֹת שֶׁעֶצֶם הָעִנְיָן מֻפְלָא מִמֶּנּוּ (דְּהַיְנוּ שֶׁאֵינוֹ בִּבְחִינַת הִתְיַשְּׁבוּת בְּמוֹחוֹ מֵאַחַר שֶׁאֵינוֹ מַשִּׂיג הַפְּרָטִים שֶׁבָּהֶם נִתְפָּס וּמִתְיַשֵּׁב הָעִנְיָן, וְגַם דְּבִידִיעָה כְּלָלִית הֲרֵי הוּא תּוֹפֵס אֶת הַכְּלָל דֶּאֱלֹקוּת שֶׁהוּא לְמַעְלָה מִבְּחִינַת הִתְלַבְּשׁוּת וְהִתְיַשְּׁבוּת מַמָּשׁ, וְעַל דֶּרֶךְ הַהֶפְרֵשׁ בֵּין נְקֻדַּת הַחָכְמָה. שֶׁבִּבְחִינַת בָּרָק הַמַּבְרִיק וְנִקְרֵאת פֶּלֶא לְהַשָּׂגַת דְּבִינָה כַּנּוֹדָע) הֲרֵי זֶה עוֹשֶׂה הַכִּוּוּץ בְּמוֹחוֹ וּבְנַפְשׁוֹ. וְגַם בִּידִיעָה וְהֶרְגֵּשׁ גַּם בְּמִקְצָת הַהַפְלָאָה דֶּאֱלֹקוּת (הַיְנוּ מַה שֶּׁמֻּפְלָא אֶצְלוֹ מֵחֲמַת הֶעְדֵּר הַהַשָּׂגָה. וְגַם שֶׁתּוֹפֵס הָעִנְיָן כְּבָר

xxxviii) See footnote of the Rebbe on page 293 ←

COMMENTARY
---

creations. "Therefore," says the *Kuntres Ha'Avoda*, "the beginning of our detailed meditation must be upon the influx of G-dly energy drawn down from [above] in order to enliven the lower, physical creations." This meditation must be undertaken with much labor and concentration, so that we can "come alive with love of G-d."

Light meditation alone brings us to bitterness and worry over our distance from the One Above.

שֶׁהוּא בִּבְחִינַת פֶּלֶא עֲדַיִן כנ"ל) נִרְגָּשׁ פְּחִיתוּת וְשִׁפְלוּת עַצְמוֹ אֵיךְ שֶׁהוּא מְרֻחָק מֵאֱלֹקוּת (וְעַל דֶּרֶךְ שֶׁנִּתְבָּאֵר לְעֵיל פ"ר בְּעִנְיַן הָאַהֲבָה דְּכִרְשְׁפֵּי אֵשׁ שֶׁבְּהָרָצוֹא וְהָעֲלִיָּ' הוּא מַרְגִּישׁ אֶת הַחָמְרִיּוּת שֶׁנֶּאֱחָז בָּה כו' וְעַל כֵּן בָּא לוֹ הָעֲבוֹדָה דִּתְפִלָּה בִּמְרִירוּת וּבְלֵב דּוֹאֵג. וּבְיוֹתֵר הוּא בְּמִי שֶׁיֵּשׁ לוֹ חוּשׁ בְּעִנְיָן אֱלֹקִי שֶׁבְּעֶצֶם יֵשׁ לוֹ קֵרוּב לִידִיעָה וְהֶרְגֵּשׁ עִנְיָן אֱלֹקִי, וְכַאֲשֶׁר הַהִתְבּוֹנְנוּת הִיא רַק בִּבְחִינַת כְּלָלוּת וּבִבְחִינַת זִכְרוֹן הָאֱלֹקִי בִּלְבַד, הַתְּפִלָּה שֶׁלּוֹ הִיא בִּמְרִירוּת עֲצוּמָה וּבִבְכִיָּ' וּבְלֵב דּוֹאֵג בְּיוֹתֵר

intellectual focus].) Therefore, a general meditation produces [worry and] contraction in our mind and soul. This is true as well of our awareness and experience (even if only on a minor scale) of the amazing loftiness of G-dliness. (It is lofty to us because of our lack of intellectual understanding, and also because we grasp the concept only as it transcends us, as mentioned earlier.) We become conscious of our own lowliness and inferior standing, insomuch as we are distant from G-dliness. (This is similar to what was explained in Chapter 4 regarding "love like fire" in the rush and ascent to G-dliness, during which we experience our own corporeal nature holding us back.) Therefore, we approach the *avoda* of prayer with bitterness and a worried heart. This is especially true of those of us who have a natural talent for detecting and experiencing anything G-dly. Since in essence we are close to knowledge and perception of G-dly concepts, when our meditation is shallow and based on simple reminders of G-d alone, we will pray with a feeling of tremendous bitterness and [our] crying is accompanied by a very worried heart.

COMMENTARY

Below in this commentary is a translation of a *sicha*, or discussion delivered by the Lubavitcher Rebbe, *ztz'l*, on the subject of meditation. In order to augment the discourse and also to get us started, here is a possible "game plan" for how to do *hitbonenut* according to *Kuntres Ha'avoda*.

1. First of all, the building blocks of creation are the four categories of mineral, vegetable, animal, and human. Take a few examples of each, for which you know the Hebrew names.
2. Contemplate each of the creations that you have chosen, each one individually, in each of the categories of mineral,

(It is known that a worried heart is a vessel for receiving the secrets of the Torah and experiencing G-dliness in the inner recesses of our soul, as is written in *Sha'ar HaYichud* [of the Mitteler Rebbe], chapter 6. This experience must take place before prayer, the main time for this being *tikun chatzot*, [the prayers at midnight]. In this way [by praying *tikun chatzot*], we transform ourselves into vessels to receive G-dly awareness during prayer, as is written there. But, if our prayers are preceded by only a general meditation without the benefit of *tikun chatzot*, then we only become empty vessels, devoid of any inner [G-dly] light. There are variations in this phenomenon, and the more *p'nimi* [dedicated to G-dliness] we are, the more our heart is troubled by the immense gulf between ourselves and G-dliness. And those of us who are less *p'nimi* are disturbed by our own perceived distance from the One Above. In any case, in terms of action and behavior, this is not important.)

וְנוֹדָע שֶׁלֵּב דּוֹאֵג הוּא כְּלִי לְקַבָּלַת רָזִין דְּאוֹרַיְתָא לְהַרְגִּישׁ עִנְיָן אֱלֹקִי בִּפְנִימִיּוּת נַפְשׁוֹ וּכְמוֹ שֶׁכָּתוּב בְּשַׁעַר הַיִּחוּד פ"ו. וְזֶה צָרִיךְ לִהְיוֹת קֹדֶם הַתְּפִלָּה וְהָעִקָּר בְּתִקּוּן חֲצוֹת שֶׁעַל יְדֵי זֶה נַעֲשֶׂה כְּלִי לֶאֱלֹקוּת בִּתְפִלָּה כְּמוֹ שֶׁכָּתוּב שָׁם, וּבְאֹפֶן הַנַ"ל בִּתְפִלָּה הוּא רַק שֶׁנַּעֲשָׂה כְּלִי אֲבָל אוֹר פְּנִימִי אֵין בּוֹ) וּבָזֶה יֵשׁ חִלּוּקֵי' דְּמִי שֶׁהוּא פְּנִימִי יוֹתֵר הַלֵּב דּוֹאֵג נַעֲשֶׂה בְּיוֹתֵר מֵהַפְלָאָה דֶּאֱלֹקוּת, וּמִי שֶׁאֵינוֹ פְּנִימִי כָּל כָּךְ לִבּוֹ דּוֹאֵג בְּיוֹתֵר עַל רְחוּקוֹ מֵהָאֱלֹקוּת. וּמִכָּל מָקוֹם לַפֹּעַל אֵין זֶה נוֹגֵעַ

Mere general meditation before prayer turns us into vessels without content.

COMMENTARY
---

vegetable, and animal. (Human is more difficult since there aren't a variety of species that we can name in Hebrew.) Take time to visualize each of them, and then consider its Hebrew name, visualizing the Hebrew letters as well. This is the "engraving from outside" mentioned by the *Kuntres Ha'avoda*.

3. Remember that your goal is to not only visualize the physical creation, but to capture a feeling and understanding of the spiritual life-force enlivening it. That life-force is conveyed by the Hebrew letters that form its name.

4. Go through this process with each of the creations that you choose within the mineral, vegetable and animal realms. Don't worry about the time that this will take — it's laborious at first but becomes easier with practice.

Shallow, general meditation will not bring happiness in learning Torah.

We are also unable to open up our mind to learning Torah. It is known that true bitterness [over our distance from G-d] leads afterward to happiness in prayer and Torah study as a result of the meditation which is explained in *Tanya*, chapters 31 and 26. If we practice only a shallow, general meditation, we do not find happiness in learning Torah either. In most cases, we will also learn Torah with a worried heart and sad spirit. However, when we engage in a detailed [and honest] meditation, in order to understand a G-dly concept with our minds, we achieve happiness of the soul, as is written [in Psalms 113:9], *aim habanim smaicha*, "the mother of

וְאֵינוֹ מְפַקֵּחַ דַּעְתּוֹ גַּם בְּעֵסֶק הַתּוֹרָה. אֲשֶׁר בִּמְרִירוּת אֲמִתִּי יָדוּעַ שֶׁבָּאָה הַשִּׂמְחָה אַחַר כָּךְ בַּתְּפִלָּה וּבְעֵסֶק הַתּוֹרָה עַל יְדֵי הַהִתְבּוֹנְנוּת הַמְבֹאָר בְּסֵפֶר שֶׁל בֵּינוֹנִים פל״א וְעַיֵּין מַה שֶׁכָּתוּב בפכ״ו. וּבָזֶה אֵין בּוֹ הַשִּׂמְחָה גַּם בְּעֵסֶק הַתּוֹרָה. וְעַל פִּי הָרֹב עֵסֶק הַתּוֹרָה שֶׁלּוֹ הוּא גַּם כֵּן בְּלֵב דּוֹאֵג וְרוּחַ עָצֵב, מַה שֶׁאֵין כֵּן בְּהִתְבּוֹנְנוּת בְּדֶרֶךְ פְּרַט שֶׁיּוֹדֵעַ וּמַשִּׂיג אֶת הָעִנְיָן אֱלֹקִי שֶׁנִּתְפָּס בְּמוֹחוֹ הֲרֵי הוּא בִּבְחִינַת שִׂמְחַת הַנֶּפֶשׁ וּכְמוֹ שֶׁכָּתוּב אֵם הַבָּנִים שְׂמֵחָה, וְגַם שֶׁעַל יְדֵי זֶה נַעֲשֶׂה בִּבְחִינַת קֵרוּב לֶאֱלֹקוּת שֶׁבָּזֶה תִּהְיֶה שִׂמְחַת נַפְשׁוֹ בְּיוֹתֵר (עַד

COMMENTARY
---

5. When you feel that you have internalized that the real creation is the specific spiritual energy that enlivens it, visualize the creation together with its spiritual energy, and prepare to project your impression to a higher plane — a spiritual plane.

6. The next higher spiritual plane is that of the world of *yetzira*, or general templates of creation. Try to abstract the physical qualities of each category of creation described above; and visualize them from a spiritual perspective. Hardness, for example, may mean spiritual impermeability, while color may represent a kind of spiritual mood. Even though the species you have chosen within each category may have different and even opposite characteristics, they should all be included within the spiritual category which you are striving to imagine — that of the world of general templates of creation, or angels in *yetzira*. They are general because they transcend the specific qualities of the physical world of *asiya*. This should produce an inner *bitul* or feeling of nullification, as well as elevation.

the children is happy"—[where there is *aim habonim*, (*bina* or understanding), there is *simcha* (happiness)]. Through detailed meditation, we also come close to G-dliness, from which we derive the greatest amount of happiness in our soul. (This can occur to such an extent that we may need advice on how to maintain a balance between happiness and a sense of *bitul*, "self-nullification." This balance is the concept of "fear of G-d" within "love of G-d," as written in *Torat Chaim*, it seems to me, in the discourse *Vateled Ada*, regarding various types of song, and see there as well the discourse *V'aleh toldot Yitzhak* regarding the wells...)

שֶׁצְּרִיכִים עֵצוֹת לָזֶה שֶׁתִּהְיֶה הַשִּׂמְחָה בִּבְחִינַת בִּטּוּל שֶׁהוּא עִנְיַן הִתְכַּלְלוּת הַיִּרְאָה בָּאַהֲבָה וּכְמוֹ שֶׁכָּתוּב בְּתוֹרַת חַיִּים כִּמְדֻמֶּה בִּדְרוּשׁ וַתֵּלֶד עָדָה בְּעִנְיַן שִׁיר פָּשׁוּט וְכָפוּל כו' וְעַיֵּן מַה שֶּׁכָּתוּב שָׁם בְּדִבּוּר הַמַּתְחִיל וְאֵלֶּה תּוֹלְדוֹת יִצְחָק בְּעִנְיַן וְכָל הַבְּאֵרוֹת כו')

Through detailed meditation, we come close to G-dliness, from which we derive great happiness.

About this [detailed meditation], it is written [in Psalms 100:2], "Serve the One Above with happiness..." This is the key to making real changes in our life. [As a result of the detailed meditation,] an impression of the light is left on our soul all day, and all of our focus is on G-dly matters

וְעַל זֶה נֶאֱמַר עִבְדוּ אֶת ה' בְּשִׂמְחָה, וְהִיא דַּוְקָא הַשַּׁיֶּכֶת לַפֹּעַל, וְהַיְנוּ שֶׁנִּשְׁאָר רֹשֶׁם הָאוֹר בְּנַפְשׁוֹ כָּל הַיּוֹם וְכָל עִנְיָנוֹ הוּא בְּעִנְיְנֵי אֱלֹקוּת לְבַד, וְעַל יְדֵי זֶה נַעֲשָׂה חֲלִישׁוּת הַנֶּפֶשׁ הַבַּהֲמִית הַטִּבְעִית כְּמוֹ שֶׁנִּתְבָּאֵר לְעֵיל פ"ה. וּמַה גַּם בִּכְדֵי שֶׁגַּם הַנֶּפֶשׁ

COMMENTARY

7. After considering these spiritual creations and engraving them upon your consciousness, prepare to extrapolate to the next higher level — the world of *bria*. Consider each of the spiritual entities of *yetzira* that we imagined above - the general templates — and contemplate how they would exist as "potentialities." If the general template and archetype for trees, for example, existed only in potential, consider how it would exist. That which is in potential, not yet formed, carries with it far more possibilities than that which is formed already, even if formed spiritually. Considering the creations of the world of *bria* as "possibilities of creation," should give us another spiritual elevation and should produce even more *bitul*, or nullification to the One Above.

Detailed meditation enables the animal soul to understand and absorb G-dly concepts.

הַבַּהֲמִית יָבִין הָעִנְיָן הָאֱלֹקִי כְּמוֹ שֶׁנִּתְבָּאֵר לְעֵיל פ"ה, הֲרֵי בְּהִתְבּוֹנְנוּת בְּדֶרֶךְ כְּלָלוּת אֵין זֶה שַׁיָּךְ כְּלָל לְהַשָּׂגַת הַנֶּפֶשׁ הַבַּהֲמִית, וְרַק כְּשֶׁבָּא הָעִנְיָן בִּבְחִינָה פְּרָטִית בְּהַשָּׂגָה טוֹבָה יְכוֹלָה לִהְיוֹת הַהַשָּׂגָה גַּם בְּהַשָּׂגַת הַנֶּפֶשׁ הַבַּהֲמִית שֶׁגַּם הוּא יָבִין כו').

וְעַל כֵּן עִקַּר הָעֲבוֹדָה בַּתְּפִלָּה הִיא בְּהִתְבּוֹנְנוּת בְּדֶרֶךְ פְּרָט דַּוְקָא בְּאֵיזֶה עִנְיָן אֱלֹקִי שֶׁמִּתְבּוֹנֵן אִם בְּעִנְיַן בְּרִיאָה יֵשׁ מֵאַיִן בִּפְרָטִיּוּת הָעִנְיָנִים בָּזֶה כנ"ל, אוֹ בִּגְדֻלַּת ה' בְּעִנְיַן הִתְהַוּוּת בְּרִבּוּי הַנִּבְרָאִים וּגְדוֹלֵי הַנִּבְרָאִים וּלְכָל אֶחָד וְאֶחָד נִמְשָׁךְ חַיּוּת מְיֻחָד לְפִי מִזְגוֹ וְתִכוּנָתוֹ וּכְמוֹ שֶׁכָּתוּב הַמּוֹצִיא בְּמִסְפָּר צְבָאָם כו' מוֹנֶה מִסְפָּר כו' לְכֻלָּם

alone. In this way, we weaken the animal soul, as explained in Chapter 4. This [detailed meditation] helps the animal soul as well to understand the G-dly concept as explained in Chapter 5. While a general meditation has no effect upon the intellectual comprehension of the animal soul, a detailed meditation leading to a solid grasp of the concept, helps bring about the intellectual understanding of the animal soul as well.

Therefore, the main *avoda* of prayer is in detailed meditation, no matter what the subject of the meditation may be. It may be in the details of creation *ex nihilo* (from nothing). Or, it may be a meditation on the greatness of G-d as expressed in the tremendous variety of creations and their size. Or, it may be on how each individual creation receives its own spiritual energy according to its char-

---

COMMENTARY

8. Finally, we should strive for the "engraving from within" — the spiritual energy imparted by the Hebrew letters alone. Chassidic literature tells us that the letters are associated with *malchut*, or the final *sephira* of the world of *atzilut*.

To reach this level, our meditation must divest itself of all form, even the refined and subtle archetypes of creation (or angels of *yetzira*) and of potential creation (angels of *bria*). Our meditation must be able to access the spiritual energy of the letters of the Hebrew alphabet alone. Thus, we concentrate on the Hebrew letters alone of each creation that we originally chose, divesting them of any form. This is a tall order, but even if we can't achieve it right away, we should at least know what it is and how to strive for it with the above set of preparations.

acter and nature, as is written [in Isaiah 40:26], "He who takes out by number the heavenly hosts," and as written there also, "He counts each one [star]...and to each He calls its own name." About this it is written there as well, "Great is our Lord, and tremendously powerful..." in the creation and bringing into existence of the creations. Regarding this verse, the Sages said that the "measure of height" of the "creative power is... [236 parsaot]."³⁷ This is also the topic of the verse [in Isaiah above], "Raise your eyes to the heights...from immense strength and with great power, no individual is missing..." This refers to the G-dly power inherent in the very act of creation itself. It also indicates that creations were made to endure, both as species [men, animals, plants] and as individuals [the heavenly bodies], as written elsewhere^xxxix at length, and in this [too] is revealed the infinite power of G-d in the world. We should meditate as well on

שֵׁמוֹת יִקְרָא וְעַל זֶה אָמְרוּ גָּדוֹל אֲדוֹנֵינוּ וְרַב כֹּחַ בִּבְרִיאַת וְהִתְהַוּוּת הַנִּבְרָאִים וּכְמַאֲמָרָם ז"ל ע"פ זֶה שֵׁעוּר קוֹמָה שֶׁל יוֹצֵר בְּרֵאשִׁית כו', וְזֶהוּ גַּם כֵּן מַה שֶּׁכָּתוּב שְׂאוּ מָרוֹם עֵינֵיכֶם כו' מֵרֹב אוֹנִים וְאַמִּיץ כֹּחַ אִישׁ לֹא נֶעְדָּר וְהוּא עִנְיַן הַכֹּחַ הָאֱלֹקִי בְּעֶצֶם עִנְיַן הַבְּרִיאָה וְהַהִתְהַוּוּת. וְגַם שֶׁנִּתְהַוּוּ בְּאֹפֶן כָּזֶה שֶׁהֵן קַיָּמִין בַּמִּין וּבָאִישׁ כו', כְּמוֹ שֶׁכָּתוּב הָעִנְיָן בְּמָקוֹם אַחֵר בָּאֹרֶךְ, וְאֵיךְ שֶׁבָּזֶה נִרְאֶה וְנִגְלֶה כֹּחַ הָאֵין סוֹף שֶׁבָּעוֹלָם כו'. וְגַם יִתְבּוֹנֵן אֵיךְ שֶׁכֻּלָּם מְהַלְלִים וּמְשַׁבְּחִים לְהַקָּדוֹשׁ בָּרוּךְ הוּא (וּכְמוֹ שֶׁכָּתַב הרמב"ם בְּהִלְכוֹת יסה"ת שֶׁיּוֹדְעִים וּמַכִּירִים אֶת עַצְמָם וְאֶת עֶלָּתָם וּמַכִּירִים אֶת מִי שֶׁאָמַר וְהָיָ' הָעוֹלָם כו', וּכְמוֹ שֶׁכָּתוּב מִזֶּה בְּמָקוֹם אַחֵר), וְיֵשׁ בָּזֶה כַּמָּה חִלּוּקֵי מַדְרֵגוֹת בְּאֹפֶן הַהִלּוּל וְהַשֶּׁבַח שֶׁלָּהֶם בַּנִּבְרָאִים הָעֶלְיוֹנִים לְפִי אֹפֶן הַהַשָּׂגָה שֶׁלָּהֶם, עַל יְדֵי הָאוֹר וְהַחַיּוּת הָאֱלֹקִי הַמִּתְלַבֵּשׁ

The main "avoda" of prayer is in detailed meditation. The subject may be creation from nothing, or the variety and number of creations, or the harmony of creation, etc...

xxxix) See footnote of the Rebbe on page 294 ←

COMMENTARY
---

9. The meditator will want to continue by contemplating all of the ten *sephirot* of the world of *Atzilut*, with their corresponding soul-powers and names of the One Above, and even higher. This is a meditation that transfixes and mesmerizes, as described by the *Kuntres Avoda*, but if we don't undertake it, then **"what are we doing here?"**

Chapter 6 of *Kuntres Ha'Avoda* tells us that many people stumble in thinking that they will receive G-dly illumination as soon as they begin the meditative process. When this doesn't happen, they become disillusioned and end their effort almost

This narrative of praise of G-d lifts us to a higher level, and makes an "impression from the outside" upon us.

בְּתוֹכָם לְהַחֲיוֹתָם וּכְמָה שֶׁכָּתוּב הַלְלוּ אֶת ה׳ מִן הַשָּׁמַיִם הַלְלוּהוּ בַּמְּרוֹמִים וְכוּ׳ שֶׁהֵן ד׳ עוֹלָמוֹת אֲצִילוּת בְּרִיאָה יְצִירָה וַעֲשִׂיָּה כוּ׳ שֶׁמִּתְחַלְּקִים בְּהָאוֹר וְהַגִּלּוּי וּבַהִלּוּל וְהַשֶּׁבַח שֶׁלָּהֶם כוּ׳, וְכָל זֶה הוּא עִנְיַן סִפּוּר שְׁבָחָיו שֶׁל מָקוֹם שֶׁעַל יְדֵי הַהִתְבּוֹנְנוּת וְהִתְפַּעֲלוּת נַפְשׁוֹ בְּעִנְיָנִים אֵלוּ נַעֲשֶׂה הַחֲקִיקָה מִבַּחוּץ, שֶׁיּוֹצֵא מִמַּעֲמָדוֹ וּמַצָּבוֹ וּמִתְעַלֶּה נַפְשׁוֹ בְּדַרְגָּא עֶלְיוֹנָה יוֹתֵר וּמִתְקָרֵב לֶאֱלֹקוּת כוּ׳.

how all the creations praise and extol the One Above (as the Rambam wrote in *Hilchot Yesodei HaTorah* — that they [the higher creations] know and recognize themselves and where they came from, and they recognize "He who 'spoke' and the world came into existence," as written elsewhere on the subject.) Within this meditation are to be found many levels and varieties of praise of the higher creations, each according to its perception and understanding, and each according to the G-dly light and energy invested in it in order to enliven it, as is written [in Psalms 148], "Praise G-d from the heavens, praise Him in the heights," referring to the four worlds[xl] of *Atzilut*, *Bria*, *Yetzira*, and *Asiya*, that differ from each other in levels of illumination and revelation, and in how they praise the One Above. All of this constitutes a narrative of praise of the One Above. By meditation and excitement over these topics, an "impression is made from the outside," causing us to relinquish our previous station in order to come to a higher and more elevated [spiritual] status, approaching the One Above.

xl) See footnote of the Rebbe on page 294

COMMENTARY

---

as soon as it began. Meditation upon G-dliness and spirituality demands persistence and determination. The soul would not have descended from the spiritual worlds above to be en-clothed in a physical body if it was not necessary, and if it was not possible for us to serve G-d in meditation, prayer, and *mitzvot*. Therefore, we should not get discouraged, but rather stay focused on the G-dly energy of the subject of meditation. We should also be consistent, never failing to take a few minutes before prayer for this contemplation. This is the whole purpose of the soul descending to this world, or as the *Kuntres Ha'Avoda* says, "otherwise, what is it doing here in this world?"

Together with the meditation described above, we must also locate and identify which of our character traits are in need of

Essay on Service of the Heart - Love Like Fire and Water

However, [we must strive, in addition, to experience] the "impression from the inside" that actually brings us closer to G-dliness, while also training our animal soul to love G-dliness. This results from the meditation described in Chapter 4, in which we concentrate upon the G-dly light and energy shining into the worlds. Here, we are referring to G-dliness that is en-clothed in creation. This is not the second level that is referred to in *Sha'ar HaYichud*, chapter 5,[38] [in which two levels of G-dly illumination are described]. There, the second [higher] level is meditation upon what is called the *aiyn HaEloki*, or "G-dly nothingness," which is a far higher spiritual level than that which we are referring to here. Of the two levels

אָמְנָם בְּחִינַת הַחֲקִיקָה מִבִּפְנִים לִהְיוֹת בִּבְחִינַת קֵרוּב מַמָּשׁ לֶאֱלֹקוּת וְגַם הַנֶּפֶשׁ הַבַּהֲמִית יְהִי לוֹ אַהֲבָה לֶאֱלֹקוּת, הוּא עַל יְדֵי הַהִתְבּוֹנְנוּת שֶׁנִּתְבָּאֵר לְעֵיל פ"ד בִּבְחִינַת הָאוֹר וְהַחַיּוּת אֱלֹקִי שֶׁמֵּאִיר בָּעוֹלָמוֹת (הַיְנוּ מַה שֶׁבָּא בִּבְחִינַת הִתְלַבְּשׁוּת בָּעוֹלָמוֹת, וְאֵין זֶה מַה שֶׁכָּתוּב בְּשַׁעַר הַיִּחוּד פ"ד בַּמַּדְרֵגָה הַב' דְּהַיְנוּ הַהִתְבּוֹנְנוּת בְּהָאַיִן הָאֱלֹקִי כו', שֶׁזֶּהוּ מַדְרֵגָה גְּבוֹהָה יוֹתֵר בְּאֵין עֲרֹךְ, דְּמַה שֶׁכָּתוּב שָׁם ב' הָעִנְיָנִים הָא' הִתְהַוּוּת הַנִּבְרָאִים וְהַנֶּאֱצָלִים וְהַב', הָאַיִן הַמְהַוֶּה כו', הַכַּוָּנָה בַּמַּדְרֵגָה הָא' בִּבְחִינַת הָאוֹר וְהַחַיּוּת הַמִּתְלַבֵּשׁ בַּנִּבְרָאִים וְנֶאֱצָלִים, וּכְמוֹ נֶפֶשׁ הַגַּלְגַּלִּים וְכֵן נֶפֶשׁ

But, we must also strive to attain the "impression from the inside" that comes from meditation on the G-dly energy en-clothed in the world.

COMMENTARY
---

rectification. This can take place only through detailed introspection. Last, but not least, we must resolve to create a fixed schedule for this detailed meditative effort, in order that it become a permanent part of our routine. Then we will merit to achieve love of the One Above and succeed in rectifying our own animal soul.

CHASSIDIC DISCOURSE

In order to bring the above advice into perspective and make it accessible to everyone, including those who do not have access to Chassidic literature, included below is a translation of a discourse of the Lubavitcher Rebbe, *z'l* (the *sicha* is printed in Yiddish in *Likutei Sichot*, vol 6, *parshat Yitro*). This discourse may be used as a starting point for meditation. This discourse begins by comparing the giving of the Torah at Mt. Sinai to a wedding. Both, it points out, are accompanied by "five voices," or harmonious components. It continues:

הַמַּלְאָכִים הָעֶלְיוֹנִים שֶׁהוּא בְּחִינַת הָאוֹר וְהַחַיּוּת שֶׁלָּהֶם וְכֵן בַּנֶּאֱצָלִים הָאוֹר הַמִּתְלַבֵּשׁ בְּעֶשֶׂר סְפִירוֹת דַּאֲצִילוּת בְּכָל סְפִירָה וּסְפִירָה בִּפְרָט כוּ', וְהַמַּדְרֵגָה הַב' הוּא בְּחִינַת עַצְמוּת הָאַיִן הָאֱלֹקִי וְהַיְנוּ בְּחִינַת אוֹר עַצְמוּת הַמַּאֲצִיל שֶׁלְּמַעְלָה מִבְּחִינַת הִתְלַבְּשׁוּת בַּנִּבְרָאִים וְנֶאֱצָלִים

described there [in *Sha'ar HaYichud*], the first is "creation of creatures and emanations [*sephirot*]," while the second is the "[G-dly] nothingness that creates." The first level refers to the [spiritual] light and energy that is invested in the creations and *sephirot*. It includes the "soul" of the planets and of the higher angels, which is their [spiritual] light and energy, and the "soul" of the *sephirot*, which is the [spiritual] light en-clothed in the ten *sephirot* of the World of *Atzilut*, each and every one individually. The second [higher] level is that of the essence of the "divine nothingness" (*aiyn HaEloki*) which is the light of the essence of the Emanator Himself, above and beyond investment in the creations and emanations.

COMMENTARY

A "voice" (*kol*) in Chasidic nomenclature is a drawing down and revelation of something that was previously hidden. This we see exemplified by the human voice, which reveals and expresses one's intellect and emotions. One's voice corresponds to what he wants to express (when one issues a command, for example, he speaks in an imperative voice, while when he explains an intellectural concept he will speak softly and persuasively). So the spiritual voices from above correspond to the various G-dly revelations that they come to express. The five voices that accompanied the giving of the Torah, then, correspond to five different themes, each higher than the previous one. Each theme is brought down and expressed by one of the five "voices."

The exalted spirituality of Torah is expressed in the fact that it is accompanied by five voices, while the creation of the universe is associated with the number "four." There are four spiritual "worlds" leading ultimately to the creation of our physical world, and each (including the spiritual) contains the four categories of creation — mineral, vegetable, animal, and human. "Four" is associated not only with the creation, but with the Creator as well. He performed the act of creation with His four-letter

Essay on Service of the Heart - Love Like Fire and Water

(All of this refers to the "nothingness" which has a connection to "something" [the "something of creation"—*yesh hanivrah*]. There are two levels to this "nothingness"; one is merely a ray that is en-clothed in the "something" [in order to create it], and the second is the essence of the "nothingness" itself, above its investment in creation. This [second level] is referred to there [in *Sha'ar HaYichud*] as *chochma* [which in general lowers itself to become invested in the creation]. However, what is written there refers to *chochma* in the sense of *koach mah*, ["the power of nullification"], which turns the "something" of [creation] into "nothing" [spirituality]. It completely nullifies creation, in a manner of the [absolute] *bitul* of *chochma*—for elaboration turn to *Imrei Bina*, chapter 58,[39] on the subject of *yoreh*. This is not as might appear there [in *Sha'ar Hayichud*] at first glance, that the first [lower] level refers to [meditation upon] the creation of existence and substance, while the second [higher] level refers to [meditation upon the] G-dly light and energy. Instead, it is as described above. And what is described here [as the subject for meditation] is equivalent to the first [lower] level over there [in *Sha'ar HaYichud*]—the [spiritual] light and energy en-clothed in creation, which is the soul and life-force of the creations and what they are able to grasp intellectually.)

(וְהַכֹּל בִּבְחִינַת הָאַיִן שֶׁל הַיֵּשׁ, שֶׁיֵּשׁ בָּזֶה ב' מַדְרֵגוֹת בְּחִינַת הֶאָרַת הָאַיִן הַמִּתְלַבֵּשׁ בְּהַיֵּשׁ, וּבְחִינַת עֶצֶם הָאַיִן שֶׁלְּמַעְלָה מֵהִתְלַבְּשׁוּת כו'. וּמַה שֶּׁכָּתוּב שָׁם שֶׁזֶּהוּ בְּחִינַת חָכְמָה, הַיְנוּ כְּמוֹ שֶׁחָכְמָה הִיא בְּחִינַת כ"ח מ"ה שֶׁעוֹשֶׂה לַיֵּשׁ אַיִן (רְצוֹנוֹ לוֹמַר בִּבְחִינַת בִּטּוּל מַמָּשׁ בְּאֹפֶן הַבִּטּוּל דְּחָכְמָה) וְעַיֵּן מַה שֶּׁכָּתוּב בְּאִמְרֵי בִּינָה פנ"ח בְּעִנְיָן בְּחִינַת יוֹרֶה כו'), וְלֹא כְּמוֹ שֶׁנִּרְ' שָׁם בִּתְחִלַּת הָעִיּוּן דְּמַדְרֵגָה הָא' הִיא בְּהִתְהַוּוּת הַיֵּשׁ וְהַחֹמֶר וְהַמַּדְרֵגָה הַב' הִיא בִּבְחִינַת הָאוֹר וְהַחַיּוּת הָאֱלֹקִי כו', אֶלָּא הַכַּוָּנָה כנ"ל. וּמַה שֶּׁנִּתְבָּאֵר כָּאן הִיא מַדְרֵגָה הָא' דְּשָׁם דְּהַיְנוּ בְּחִינַת הָאוֹר וְהַחַיּוּת הַמִּתְלַבֵּשׁ שֶׁזֶּהוּ בְּחִינַת נֶפֶשׁ הַנִּבְרָאִים וְהַשָּׂגָתָם כו').

COMMENTARY

essential name (also known as the "Tetragrammaton"). Each of the four letters is the source of one of the four worlds, and within the four worlds, each letter of His name is the source of each of the four categories of creation — mineral, vegetable, animal, and human. Since, as the *Zohar* tells us, G-d "looked into the Torah

	Description	Text Source	Spiritual Level
1. *Yesh ha'nivrah* "created reality"	Force (*Koach*); creative power within creation	Mentioned here, but not subject of meditation	*Malchut* the direct source of creation *ex nihilo*
2. *Ayn shel hayesh ha'nivrah* "the existential nothingness"	Energy (*Chayut*); G-dly light interfacing with creation	The first level in *Sha'ar Hayichud*, mentioned here as **the subject of meditation**	*Chochma* or *koach mah* nullifies "something of creation into spiritual nothing"
3. *Ayn HaEloki* "the divine nothingness"	Light (*Ohr*) the infinite light which illuminates the Essence, above creation	The second level in *Sha'ar Hayichud* of the Mittler Rebbe, chapter 5, not for meditation here	*Keter* creates from "nothing into something"
4. *Yesh Ha'amiti* "true G-dly reality"	Essence Cannot be described even as "light" or as "infinite"	Not mentioned here	Before the *tzimtzum* ("great contraction")

וְהַיְנוּ אֵיךְ דְּאִיהוּ מְמַלֵּא כּוּלְהוּ עָלְמִין דִּכְשֵׁם שֶׁהַנְּשָׁמָה מְמַלֵּא אֶת הַגּוּף כָּךְ הַקָּדוֹשׁ בָּרוּךְ הוּא מְמַלֵּא אֶת הָעוֹלָם, הֵן בָּעוֹלָם הַתַּחְתּוֹן בְּכָל נִבְרָא וְנִבְרָא בִּפְרָט שֶׁיֵּשׁ בּוֹ אוֹר אֱלוֹקִי. הַמְחַיֶּ"י אוֹתוֹ וְהֵן בְּעוֹלָמוֹת עֶלְיוֹנִים בְּאוֹפַנֵּי הָאוֹרוֹת וְהַגִּלּוּיִים בְּכָל עוֹלָם וְעוֹלָם בְּעֵשֶׂר הַסְּפִירוֹת שֶׁבָּעוֹלָמוֹת וּבַנִּבְרָאִים

[The meditation here in Chapter 6 of *Kuntres Ha'Avoda*], therefore, is on how He permeates all the worlds. Just as the soul fills the body, so G-d permeates the universe. This is true regarding the lower world, in which each and every specific creation contains the G-dly light that enlivens it. It is true as well regarding the upper [spiritual] worlds, each according to

─────────── **COMMENTARY** ───────────

and created the universe," everything found in the creation comes from and is also found in the Torah. Therefore, we must be able to find the four levels of the essential name of G-d within the Torah itself.

its own level of illumination and revelation, and each containing its own ten *sephirot* and creations, as explained earlier in Chapter 4. In general, the [G-dly] light and energy [of the creation] emanates from the *sephira* of *malchut* ["sovereignty," the tenth and lowest of the ten *sephirot* of the World of *Atzilut*], which creates and enlivens the [lower three] worlds of *BY'A* (*Bria, Yetzira,* and *Asiya*). About this, the verse [in Nehemia 9:6] says, "And You enliven them all..." [The letters of "You," *aleph-tav*] allude to the letters of the supernal speech of *malchut* of *Atzilut* and to the [G-dly] light en-clothed within these letters. (It is possible that this allusion refers to the vessels of the ten *sephirot* within *malchut* of *Atzilut*, which become the "soul" of

שֶׁבָּהֶם כו׳ וּכְמוֹ שֶׁנִּתְבָּאֵר לְעֵיל פ״ד, וּכְלָלוּת הָאוֹר וְהַחַיּוּת הוּא מִבְּחִינַת מַלְכוּת דַּאֲצִילוּת הַמְהַוֶּה וּמְחַיֵּי כְּלָלוּת עוֹלְמוֹת בְּרִיאָה יְצִירָה עֲשִׂיָּה, וְעַל זֶה נֶאֱמַר וְאַתָּה מְחַיֶּה אֶת כֻּלָּם שֶׁהֵן אוֹתִיּוֹת דִּבּוּר הָעֶלְיוֹן דִּבְחִינַת מַלְכוּת דַּאֲצִילוּת וּבְחִינַת הָאוֹר הַמִּתְלַבֵּשׁ בָּאוֹתִיּוֹת כו׳ (וְיֵשׁ לוֹמַר דְּזֶהוּ בְּחִינַת הַכֵּלִים דְּעֶשֶׂר סְפִירוֹת דְּמַלְכוּת דַּאֲצִילוּת שֶׁנַּעֲשִׂים בִּבְחִינַת נְשָׁמָה לְעֶשֶׂר סְפִירוֹת דִּבְרִיאָה יְצִירָה עֲשִׂיָּה וּבְחִינַת הֶאָרַת הַקַּו הַמֵּאִיר בַּכֵּלִים דְּעֶשֶׂר סְפִירוֹת דְּמַלְכוּת שֶׁבַּקַּע הַפַּרְסָא עִמָּהֶם כו׳ כְּמוֹ שֶׁכָּתוּב בָּאגה״ק סי׳ כ׳ דִּבּוּר הַמַּתְחִיל אִיהוּ וְחַיּוֹהִי חַד, וּבִפְרָטִיּוּת בַּנִּבְרָאִים דִּבְרִיאָה יְצִירָה עֲשִׂיָּה יֵשׁ לוֹמַר

There must be detailed meditation on the G-dly light enlivening creation.

COMMENTARY

Now we can begin to grasp the exalted loftiness of the Torah, as expressed in the phrase that it was given "accompanied by 'five voices.'" In addition to the four levels and categories associated with creation and the essential name of G-d, Torah includes a higher level that transcends the Holy Name itself. This is obvious from the first words of the Ten Commandments, with which the Torah was given to us from above to below: "*I* (Whomever I am, beyond grasp or even hint by any letter whatsoever), *the Lord*, (and nevertheless) *your G-d*, (your strength and life-energy)." All five dimensions of Torah, including that which transcends the Name of G-d, were given to us here in the physical world, and this is what is meant by "given with five voices."

We have no way of directly grasping the nature of a spiritual creation. We can only begin to get a handle on it by extrapolating from physical objects in our environment that come from

שֶׁזֶּהוּ ב' מִינֵי חַיּוּת דִּבְחִינַת כֹּחַ וְאוֹר דִּבְחִינַת כֹּחַ זֶהוּ מִבְּחִינַת הַכֵּלִים דִּבְרִיאָה יְצִירָה עֲשִׂיָּה, וּבְחִינַת אוֹר הוּא מִבְּחִינַת אוֹר הַנְּשָׁמָה וְגַם לְמַעְלָה מִזֶּה כו' שֶׁעַל זֶה נֶאֱמַר אֵין קָדוֹשׁ כַּהוי' כַּמָּה קַדִּישִׁין אִינוּן וְלֵית קָדוֹשׁ כַּהוי' שֶׁהוּא קָדוֹשׁ וּמֻבְדָּל וּמִכָּל מָקוֹם מִתְלַבֵּשׁ כו' וּכְמוֹ שֶׁכָּתוּב בְּמָקוֹם אַחֵר,

the ten *sephirot* of the lower worlds of *Bria*, *Yetzira*, and *Asiya*.) It could be alluding as well to a reflection of the ray of G-dly light that radiates into the vessels of the ten *sephirot* of *malchut*. In the process of creation, this ray descends with the *sephira* of *malchut* and together they "break through" the "curtain" [separating the World of *Atzilut* from that of creation *BY'A*]. This is written about in *Igeret Hakodesh*, chapter 20, beginning with *ihu...chad*. In greater detail, we can say that there are two kinds of G-dly energy invested in the creations of the lower worlds of *BY'A*: *Koach*, (power) and *Ohr*, (light). *Koach* is the G-dly light that comes from the vessels of *BY'A*, and *ohr* comes from the [spiritual] lights of the soul [of the ten *sephirot* of *BY'A*], and above and beyond this as well. About them, the verse [in 1 Samuel 2:2] states, "There is no holiness like that of *HaShem* (the four-letter essential Name of G-d)...[xli]" [The interpretation of the *Zohar* on this verse is that] "there are many levels of holiness, but none of them are as holy as the four-letter Name of G-d," which is holy and exalted. Nevertheless, He is involved and invested [in creation], as written elsewhere.

xli) See footnote of the Rebbe on page 296

COMMENTARY
---

spiritual sources. By analyzing a physical object, we can estimate and gain some kind of insight into its spiritual source. So, the best way to understand the four letters of His Name (and in this way to gain an appreciation of Torah, which was given with five voices, higher than the essential name of G-d), is by analyzing the four categories of creation (mineral, vegetable, animal, and human) in this physical world. They correspond to the four letters of the Name of G-d, from which they are created and spiritually influenced.

The distinction between the mineral and vegetable worlds is the following: in an inanimate object, one sees only its physical substance and body. One can detect no movement or sign of life, even though the mineral object has an inanimate soul, which is spiritual and brings it into being. An object of the vegetable

Malchut, the lowest of the ten *sephirot*, is the direct source of creation. This is because it:
1) Absorbs G-dly influx from the upper nine *sephirot* of *Atzilut*, and
2) Conducts it to the "lower worlds" of *Bria*, *Yetzira*, and *Asiya*.

This it does by lowering itself through the *parsa* ("curtain") separating *Atzilut* and the lower worlds. The purpose of the *parsa* is to produce apparent distance from G-d in which the creation appears to be separate from Him, much as a physical curtain blocks most, but not all light. What spiritual influx does pass through may take on the following forms:

1. Letters of Hebrew alphabet	Correspond to the *sephira* of *malchut*.	Create the physical world with power (*koach*)
2. Vessels of *malchut*	Contain the light of the upper nine *sephirot* of the World of *Atzilut*	Impart the spiritual element of energy (*chayut*) to the physical world
3. Light of the *kav*, the ray of G-dliness that extends from above *Atzilut*	Conveys the quality of the infinite G-dly light (*ohr*) from above *Atzilut*	Imparts an illumination (*ohr*) that transcends the duality of physical vs. spiritual

Light of holiness in general is brought down into the world via the name of G-d. Just as when we want to attract someone's attention, we call his or her name, so the way to draw holiness down into the creation is to pray and meditate using His divine name. Thus, the *Kuntres Ha'Avoda* tells us that the above paths and techniques bringing down holy light from Above are accessed by using His essential four-letter name, known as the Tetragrammaton.

Therefore, the beginning of our detailed meditation must be upon the influx of G-dly energy drawn down from the spiritual constellations above in order to enliven the physical creations below. This corresponds to

וְעַל כֵּן הַהִתְבּוֹנְנוּת בְּדֶרֶךְ פְּרָט הִיא תְּחִלָּה בְּשֶׁפַע הַחַיּוּת דְּנִבְרָאִים הַתַּחְתּוֹנִים מֵהַמַּזָּלוֹת הָרוּחָנִיִּי וּכְמַאֲמָר אֵין לְךָ עֵשֶׂב מִלְמַטָּה כו' וּכְמוֹ שֶׁכָּתוּב אֲנִי אֶעֱנֶה אֶת הַשָּׁמַיִם וְהֵם יַעֲנוּ כו' וְלָכֵן הַגַּשְׁמִי בָּטֵל אֶל

———————— *COMMENTARY* ————————

world, however, contains spiritual energy that may be detected with one's five senses. In this respect, there is a much greater gulf between the mineral and vegetable kingdoms than between the vegetable, animal, and human kingdoms. The latter three worlds all have something in common — the spiritual energy

The beginning of detailed meditation should be on the G-dly energy in creation. Everything in the physical world has a spiritual counterpart above.

הָרוּחָנִי כו' וְהַמַּזָּלוֹת מְקַבְּלֵי מִשְׁמְרֵי הָאוֹפַנִּים וְהָאוֹפַנִּים מֵהַחַיּוֹת כו' עַד בְּחִינַת הַמַּלְכוּת כו' וּכְמוֹ שֶׁכָּתוּב מִזֶּה בִּדְרוּשׁ תִּקְעוּ עַ"ר בַּדִּבּוּר הַמַּתְחִיל אַחַת שָׁאַלְתִּי, וְהוּא בְּחִינַת הַחַיּוּת דִּבְחִינַת כֹּחַ. וְכֵן הוּא בִּבְחִינַת הַחַיּוּת דִּבְחִינַת אוֹר מִמַּדְרֵגָה לְמַדְרֵגָה וּבְאֹפֶן בְּחִינַת הָאוֹר שֶׁבְּכָל מַדְרֵגָה וּמַדְרֵגָה כו').

the saying of the sages [in *Breishit Rabba* 10,6], "There is no blade of grass below...[which doesn't have a spiritual counterpart above that makes it grow]." And [in Hosea 2:23], "I will answer the heavens, and they will answer...[the earth...]" Therefore, the physical creation is nullified to the spiritual. The [spiritual] constellations themselves receive their influx from the "remainders" of the *ofanim* [lower angels of *Asiya*], and the *ofanim* from the *chayot* [angels of *Yetzira*, who are higher on the spiritual hierarchy than *ofanim*], and so forth, all the way up to *malchut* of *Atzilut*. This is written about in the Chassidic discourse *Achat Sha'alti* in the book of discourses of the year 5670. It [the G-dliness invested in the creation] is the *chayut*, or enlivening energy of the level of *koach*, "power." This is also true concerning the *chayut* or enlivening energy of *ohr*, "light," as it descends from one level to the next, each level of light with its own characteristics.

In each of the three lower worlds there exists a class of angels, messengers of G-d whose mission is to manifest His presence and rule over the created entities of the lower worlds:	
1. *Asiya* "World of Action"	*Ofanim* "Wheels of the chariot"
2. *Yetzira* "World of Formation"	*Chayot* "Living creatures"
3. *Bria* "World of Creation"	*Seraphim* "Fiery angels"
4. *Atzilut* "World of Emanation"	Beyond all but the most refined angels

——————— **COMMENTARY** ———————

enlivening them may be detected and experienced — and the only difference between them lies in exactly how the energy becomes revealed (as we will see). In the mineral world, however, there is no possibility of finding any spiritual revelation.

Essay on Service of the Heart - Love Like Fire and Water

The nullification of each spiritual level to the level above it continues up to the initial revelation of the ray of the infinite light of the One Above. The ray [which is the first revelation of G-dly light after the great contraction] is the [source of] immanent, permeating light, which illuminates the worlds. The essence of the ray [is the infinite spiritual light that] illuminates the worlds of infinity above the World of *Atzilut*, while a reflection of the ray shines into the World of *Atzilut* and concludes there. Nevertheless, some light of this reflection breaks through the spiritual barrier separating *Atzilut* from the lower worlds of *BY'A* and is then described as "holy," as mentioned earlier.

וּמַגִּיעַ הָעִנְיָן עַד כְּלָלוּת בְּחִינַת גִּלּוּי הַקַּו מֵאוֹר אֵין סוֹף בָּרוּךְ הוּא שֶׁהוּא בְּחִינַת הָאוֹר פְּנִימִי שֶׁמֵּאִיר בְּתוֹךְ הָעוֹלָמוֹת כו' דִּבְחִינַת עַצְמִיּוּת הַקַּו מֵאִיר בְּעוֹלָמוֹת הָאֵין סוֹף שֶׁלִּפְנֵי הָאֲצִילוּת וְהֶאָרַת הַקַּו מֵאִיר בְּעוֹלָם הָאֲצִילוּת וּמִסְתַּיֵּים שָׁם וּמִכָּל מָקוֹם בָּקַע הַפַּרְסָא עִמָּהֶם כו' כנ"ל, וְהוּא בְּחִינַת קָדוֹשׁ כנ"ל (וְהַהִתְבּוֹנְנוּת בִּבְחִינַת גִּלּוּי הַקַּו שֶׁבַּאֲצִילוּת הוּא בְּחִינַת יִחוּדָא עִילָאָה בִּכְלָל, וְהַהִתְבּוֹנְנוּת בְּמַדְרֵגוֹת דִּבְרִיאָה יְצִירָה עֲשִׂיָּה הוּא בְּחִינַת יִחוּדָא תַּתָּאָה. וּמִכָּל מָקוֹם בְּחִינַת אוֹר הנ"ל יֵשׁ לוֹמַר שֶׁזֶּהוּ לְמַעְלָה מִבְּחִינַת יִחוּדָא תַּתָּאָה כו'). וְעַיֵּין מַה שֶּׁכָּתוּב בְּשַׁעַר

Every spiritual level is nullified to the level above it.

COMMENTARY

In general, the vegetable kingdom is closer to the mineral than it is to the animal and human realms. So much so, that when one divides the four categories into "soul" and "body," the vegetable world is included with the mineral under the heading of "body" rather than "soul," which includes the animal and human kingdoms. Just as their names suggest, that which falls into the category of vegetation doesn't fit in the category of animal. The gulf between the two categories becomes clearer when we remember that until the great flood in the time of Noah, only vegetation was allowed as food, and only after the flood did it become permissible to eat animals.

The explanation is the following: The quality of spiritual energy invested in the animal kingdom is a "soul" type of energy, which explains why the animal has a will of its own (in which its soul is expressed). The animal's body is directed and guided by the will of the soul, which is so much a part of the animal that the animal's very essence is not physical substance, but

הַיִּחוּד פ"ד (וְשָׁם הַהִתְבּוֹנְנוּת בִּפְרָטִיּוּת בְּכָל סְפִירוֹת פְּרָטִיּוּת מֵרֵישׁ כָּל דַּרְגִּין עַד סוֹף כָּל דַּרְגִּין שֶׁהוּא יִחוּד פְּרָטִי כְּפִי מַהוּת וּמַדְרֵגַת הַסְּפִירָה הַהִיא כו׳).

(Meditation on the revelation of the ray within *Atzilut* leads to the state known as *yichuda ila'ah*, [wherein we experience G-d as the true reality while His creation seems ephemeral]. Meditation on the ray within the worlds of *BY'A* leads to the experience of *yichuda tata'ah*, or lower unity, [in which one experiences the creation as reality, while maintaining some awareness of the oneness of the Creator within the creation]. Still, the light mentioned earlier [that breaks through the separation] would seem to be higher than *yichuda tata'ah*. See *Sha'ar HaYichud*, chapter 4,[40] [which describes] meditation in detail of each particular *sephira*, from the highest levels to the lowest, as a particular *yichud*, [deep grasp of the nullification of each level to the level above it] according to the essence and level of each particular *sephira*.)

Detailed meditation demands intense effort.

וּבְכָל הָעִנְיָנִים הָאֵלּוּ תִּהְיֶה הַהִתְבּוֹנְנוּת בִּיגִיעַת נֶפֶשׁ כְּמוֹ שֶׁכָּתוּב בְּסֵפֶר שֶׁל בֵּינוֹנִים פמ"ב שֶׁלֹּא תִּכְבַּד עָלָיו הָעֲבוֹדָה (וְכַאֲשֶׁר יִקְרֶה לְעִתִּים קְרוֹבוֹת שֶׁיִּכְבַּד עָלָיו עִנְיַן הַהִתְבּוֹנְנוּת וּמִתְרַשֵּׁל בַּזֶּה וְאֵין לוֹ שׁוּם חִיּוּת בִּתְפִלָּה וּמִמֵּילָא נַעֲשֶׂה הַכְּבֵדוּת בְּכָל הָעִנְיָנִים

In respect to all of the above-mentioned concepts, the meditation must take place with great effort of the soul, as mentioned in *Tanya*, chapter 42: "the labor should not be onerous to it [the soul]." (It is not uncommon for us not to feel like meditating. We may become negligent, having no energy for

---

COMMENTARY

"soul." This is not true of the vegetable kingdom — not only does the enlivening energy of a plant have no effect upon its physical characteristics, but the energy itself is a "bodily" energy, because its entire purpose is only to grow and enlarge the plant.

The distinction between the vegetable and animal kingdoms is expressed in the following (among other things): The life-energy (growth) of a plant is dependent on its being planted in a specific place (and when we uproot the plant from its place, it loses its ability to grow). An animal, however is not limited to a particular place, although it has other limitations. The reason is the following: a physical object is delimited by "space." Since the life quality of a plant is a "bodily" quality, the plant is limited to a particular place. But since the energy enlivening an animal

prayer, and as a result our lethargy extends itself to all of our spiritual matters. We may become like a stone. But if our [spiritual] life is dear to us, we must overcome this lethargy and enter into meditation with *kabalat ohl*, [acceptance of an obligation, even though we may not feel like it]. When we do so, putting ourselves into a meditative state, the energy and enjoyment will come to us. [We should return to the advice of the *Tanya*, chapter 42]: "...to labor within thought" and meditate upon it at great depth, bringing the concept close to ourselves and strongly focusing our attention upon it until the G-dly concept illuminates our soul, and our soul becomes united with G-dliness. Then, our only desire all day long will be for G-dliness, and nothing else will

וְנַעֲשָׂה כְּאֶבֶן מַמָּשׁ (אז עס נעמט זיך ניט צו קיין זעך). וְכָל הֶחָפֵץ בְּחַיָּיו צָרִיךְ לְהִתְגַּבֵּר עַל עַצְמוֹ לִכְנוֹס אֶל הַהִתְבּוֹנְנוּת בְּדֶרֶךְ קַבָּלַת עוֹל, וְכַאֲשֶׁר יִכְנוֹס בְּהִתְבּוֹנְנוּת יִתְעוֹרֵר אֶצְלוֹ הַחַיּוּת וְהַתַּעֲנוּג בָּעִנְיָן, (עס ווערט איהם די זאך געשמאק און דער ענין לעבט ביי איהם) לִיגַּע מַחֲשַׁבְתּוֹ וְיִתְבּוֹנֵן בָּזֶה בְּהַעֲמָקָה טוֹבָה וּלְקָרֵב הָעִנְיָן לְעַצְמוֹ וְיִתְקַע דַּעְתּוֹ בָּזֶה בְּחֹזֶק עַד שֶׁהָעִנְיָן הָאֱלֹקִי מֵאִיר בְּנַפְשׁוֹ וְנַפְשׁוֹ מִתְקָרֶבֶת וּמִתְקַשֶּׁרֶת בְּהָאֱלֹקוּת, וְכָל רְצוֹנוֹתָיו כָּל הַיּוֹם הוּא רַק בֶּאֱלֹקוּת וְאֵינוֹ שַׁיָּךְ לְשׁוּם עִנְיָן אַחֵר כו' וְיִשְׁתַּדֵּל לְהָבִיא אֶת הָעִנְיָן לִידֵי הַהַשָּׂגָה דְּשֵׂכֶל הַטִּבְעִי (כמו שנתבאר לעיל פ"ד) שֶׁגַּם הוּא

By overcoming our lethargy, we'll experience spiritual energy and enjoyment.

COMMENTARY

---

is spiritual ("soul") energy, it is not so limited in space (it can move).

Although both are of a "bodily" nature, there is a huge gulf between the mineral and vegetable kingdoms (in a certain sense, more so than between the vegetable and animal). The same is true of the "soul" categories of animal and human; there is a tremendous chasm between them. The human world is infinitely removed from the animal kingdom, since man is the "chosen" of creation, for whom the rest of creation was brought into existence. Just as the point that separates the mineral from the vegetable kingdom is that "mineral" existence is expressed in an inanimate body, so it is from the opposite direction. That which separates the human realm from every other category is the ability to speak, which is the ultimate expression of the soul and spirit, as will be explained.

Then, nothing else will matter to us, and the animal soul will also be aroused to love of G-d.

be of importance to us. We should [also] strive to make the subject understood in the intellectual framework of our animal soul (as explained in Chapter 4), such that it, too, will comprehend the G-dly concept. When the divine soul is aroused to love, the animal soul will also be stirred to love G-d. This applies as well to the love of "You are my soul, I desire You..." which is "to love G-d, because He is your life," referring to the life of all [G-dly] souls in particular, as explained there. This applies as well to the love of "as in water, face responds to face," as is written in the *Tanya*, chapters 46 through 50. (The introduction to the second section of the *Tanya*, called *Chinuch Katan*, it is written that [meditation

יָבִין אֶת הָעִנְיָן הָאֱלֹקִי וּבְהִתְעוֹרְרוּת הָאַהֲבָה דְנֶפֶשׁ הָאֱלֹקִית יִתְעוֹרֵר גַּם הוּא בְּאַהֲבָה לֶאֱלֹקוּת כו'. וְכֵן הַהִתְבּוֹנְנוּת בְּעִנְיָן נַפְשִׁי אִוִּיתִיךָ כו' שֶׁהוּא עִנְיָן לְאַהֲבָה אֶת הוי' אֱלֹקֶיךָ כִּי הוּא חַיֶּיךָ חַיֵּי הַנְּשָׁמוֹת בִּפְרָט כְּמוֹ שֶׁנִּתְבָּאֵר לְעֵיל שָׁם, וְגַם בְּהִתְבּוֹנְנוּת דְּכַמַּיִם הַפָּנִים אֶל הַפָּנִים כו' כְּמוֹ שֶׁכָּתוּב בְּסֵפֶר שֶׁל בֵּינוֹנִים מפמ"ו עַד פ"נ (ובח"ב בַּהַקְדָּמָה הַנִּקְרָאת חִנּוּךְ קָטָן כ' הֵן דֶּרֶךְ כְּלָל כִּי הוּא חַיֵּינוּ מַמָּשׁ כו' וְהֵן דֶּרֶךְ פְּרָט שֶׁכְּשֶׁיָּבִין וְיַשְׂכִּיל בִּגְדֻלָּתוֹ כו' וְאַחַר כָּךְ יִתְבּוֹנֵן בְּאַהֲבַת ה' הַגְּדוֹלָה וְהַנִּפְלָאָה כו' אֲזַי כַּמַּיִם הַפָּנִים כו').

arouses love], "both a general meditation on the fact that He is our life absolutely, and also a detailed meditation with which we understand G-d's greatness... and then meditate on G-d's great and wonderful love for us [leading then to love of Him], "as in water, face responds to face...")

COMMENTARY

The true definition of "spirit" is removal from any category or description through which the spiritual entity might otherwise be grasped or defined. This is true even of descriptions and categories that transcend the five senses that apprehend a physical object. For even though a spiritual entity may belong to a category that delimits its existence and distinguishes between it and any other spiritual object, nevertheless its very spirituality bespeaks a refinement and simplicity that transcends description. The simplicity to be found in a spiritual object expresses itself in several ways, among them:

1. A spiritual entity does not contradict the existence of any other object or entity. Just as we see in the most abstract and refined ideas: The more abstract and refined they are,

Casual meditation may cause a state of superficial excitement over G-dliness, from which we may quickly cool off.

Even when we meditate in a peremptory manner, our soul becomes excited. (For this no effort is necessary, neither for the meditation itself—since it is only superficial, akin to a reminder with which we recall G-dliness—nor for the excitement [of the meditation], which comes about spontaneously. For in a transcendent way everyone gets excited over G-dliness, and yet the excitement has no bearing on anything practical. It does not bring about any closeness to G-dliness or the fulfillment of His will. Even the bitterness described above [resulting from a haphazard contemplation of G-dliness] is very easily achieved by considering the lofty level of G-dliness from which we are distant. This is particularly true of those of us who have a talent for meditating on G-dly matters, as explained earlier.) And when afterward we begin to meditate on a concept in a [serious and] detailed way, our previous [condition of] excitement will "cool off" completely. (This will be the case as well when we begin to pray with a certain amount of energy after we have learned Chassidut before prayers. When we then start to pray with some detailed meditation, we will become [indifferent and] cold.)

וְהִנֵּה כַּאֲשֶׁר מִתְבּוֹנֵן בִּבְחִינַת כְּלָלוּת בִּלְבַד וּמִתְפַּעֵל בְּנַפְשׁוֹ (דְּעַל זֶה אֵין צָרִיךְ יְגִיעָה הֵן בְּהִתְבּוֹנְנוּת מֵאַחַר שֶׁהִיא בִּבְחִינַת כְּלָלוּת לְבַד וַהֲרֵי הוּא רַק כְּמוֹ זִכָּרוֹן שֶׁנִּזְכָּר עַל אֱלֹקוּת כנ"ל, וְהֵן הַהִתְפַּעֲלוּת בָּאָה בְּלִי שׁוּם יְגִיעָה כְּלָל, כִּי בִּבְחִינַת מַקִּיף כָּל אֶחָד מִתְפַּעֵל עַל אֱלֹקוּת, וְאֵין זֶה *) לְשׁוּם פֹּעַל כְּלָל, הַיְנוּ שֶׁאֵין בָּזֶה שׁוּם קֵרוּב לֶאֱלֹקוּת וְאֵינָה מְבִיאָה לִידֵי קִיּוּם רְצוֹנוֹ ית', וְגַם הַמְּרִירוּת שֶׁנִּתְבָּאֵר לְעֵיל הִיא בְּנָקֵל מְאֹד עַל יְדֵי הַהַפְלָאָה דֶאֱלֹקוּת כנ"ל וּבִפְרָט בְּמִי שֶׁיֵּשׁ לוֹ חוּשׁ בְּעִנְיָן אֱלֹקִי כוּ' וּכְמוֹ שֶׁנִּתְבָּאֵר לְעֵיל) וּכְשֶׁמַּתְחִיל אַחַר כָּךְ לְהִתְבּוֹנֵן בְּאֵיזֶה עִנְיָן בְּדֶרֶךְ פְּרָט יִתְקָרֵר לְגַמְרֵי מֵהַהִתְפַּעֲלוּת הַקּוֹדֶמֶת (וְכֵן הוּא כַּאֲשֶׁר מַתְחִיל לְהִתְפַּלֵּל בְּאֵיזֶה חַיּוּת עַל יְדֵי עֵסֶק הַדְּבָרֵי אֱלֹקִים חַיִּים שֶׁקֹּדֶם הַתְּפִלָּה כְּשֶׁמַּתְחִיל אַחַר כָּךְ בַּתְּפִלָּה בְּאֵיזֶה הִתְבּוֹנְנוּת פְּרָטִית מִתְקָרֵר כוּ'),

---
COMMENTARY

the more room they leave for other ideas and concepts.

2. Because of its spiritual nature, a non-corporeal object tends toward that which is above and beyond it (as is found even in "spirituality within physicality," such as fire, which is the most refined of the physical elements. Because of its spiritual nature, it strives "upwards"). This is because the true nature

The previous excitement did not imply any real closeness to G-dliness.

הִנֵּה עַל קֵרוּר הִתְפַּעֲלוּת הַקּוֹדֶמֶת אַל יָחוּשׁ וְאַל יִדְאַג כְּלָל, כִּי אֵינָהּ הִתְפַּעֲלוּת אֲמִתִּי, וְאֵינָהּ עִנְיָן וּדְבָר מַה הֵן מִצַּד עַצְמָהּ כִּי אֵין בָּזֶה קֵרוּב לֶאֱלֹקוּת (וְגַם הַחַיּוּת הַנַּעֲשֶׂה עַל יְדֵי לִמּוּד דִּבְרֵי אֱלֹקִים חַיִּים קֹדֶם הַתְּפִלָּה הִיא רַק הַקְדָּמָה וּכְמוֹ כְּלִי לְקָרוּב לֶאֱלֹקוּת כַּאֲשֶׁר יַעֲבֹד עֲבוֹדָתוֹ בִּתְפִלָּה כִּדְבָעֵי לְמֶהֱוֵי) וְהֵן מִצַּד שֶׁאֵינָהּ שַׁיֶּכֶת לִפְעֹל בְּעֵסֶק הַתּוֹרָה וְקִיּוּם הַמִּצְוֹת בְּסוּר מֵרַע וַעֲשֵׂה טוֹב וּבְזִכּוּךְ הַמִּדּוֹת טִבְעִיּוֹת וְהַיְנוּ דְּבִשְׁעַת מַעֲשֶׂה הוּא רַק הִתְפַּעֲלוּת דְּמִיּוֹנִי, וְלֹא נִשְׁאַר מִזֶּה

Now, regarding the "cooling off" of the excitement, we should not worry at all. The previous excitement was not real; nor was it something to be concerned about, for two reasons. One: It contained no feeling of closeness to G-dliness. (Also, the energy generated by learning Chassidut before prayers [in the morning] is merely a prelude [to proper prayer], like a vehicle enabling us to come close to G-d through proper *avoda* during prayer.) Two: It had no practical effect on our learning of Torah nor on our fulfillment of *mitzvot*, neither by doing good (positive

---
COMMENTARY
---

of a spiritual object is not to remain within the limits of its own existence, but to strive to leave its own existence and be included in its source above.

This is why the human realm contains the true essence of spiritual "soul." The distinction between man and the animal world lies in the intellect that the human possesses, which gives rise to the two benefits listed above:

1. Intellect is not limited or categorized by the world of emotions. Since man has intellect, he needn't remain under the sway of the emotions to which he has a natural tendency from birth. (Other creations are limited by the nature of their natural emotions.) He has free choice to choose the nature of his own emotions. That's the reason that man includes within himself all the categories of existence found in the creation (which is why he's called a "small world") — he's not limited by categories.

2. The striving and inclination of the intellect is to leave its own existence and be included in a higher level. In this as well is to be found the major distinction between man (who is characterized by intellect), and animals (characterized by emotions). As the Torah says, "The spirit of man is to be

Essay on Service of the Heart - Love Like Fire and Water

mitzvot) nor by turning away from bad (negative *mitzvot*). The previous excitement also did nothing to help us refine our natural characteristics. [Clearly] the excitement was only imaginary and therefore left no impression on us for the rest of the day. If so, we never really became [indifferent and] cold, because in truth we were never really excited with a true inner arousal, which only results from meditation and solid grasp of G-dly concepts. The superficial excitement that we did felt would have faded anyway after a short time, without leaving any impression.

(What is preferable to the above is praying with attention to the simple meaning of the words and feeling spiritual energy in doing so. Even though this [prayer] is devoid of the excitement of love of G-d, or of the refinement of our naturally coarse character traits, still, there is a certain inner feeling there. We are able to latch on to something—namely the G-dly energy in the words of our

שׁוּם רֹשֶׁם עַל כָּל הַיּוֹם, וְאִם כֵּן אֵין זֶה שֶׁנִּתְקָרֵר כִּי לֹא נִתְחַמֵּם וְלֹא נִתְפַּעֵל עֲדַיִן בִּבְחִינַת הִתְפַּעֲלוּת פְּנִימִי וַאֲמִתִּי, הַבָּאָה דַּוְקָא עַל יְדֵי הִתְבּוֹנְנוּת וְהַשָּׂגָה טוֹבָה בֶּאֱלֹקוּת, וְהִתְפַּעֲלוּת הַנַ"ל מִמֵּילָא יַחֲלֹף וְיַעֲבֹר בְּמוּעָט זְמַן מִבְּלִי שֶׁנִּשְׁאַר אַחֲרֵי' שׁוּם רֹשֶׁם כו'

(וְיוֹתֵר טוֹב מִזֶּה הַמִּתְפַּלֵּל בְּכַוָּנָה בְּפִי' הַמִּלִּים וְיֵשׁ לוֹ חַיּוּת בַּתֵּבוֹת, דְּעִם הֱיוֹת שֶׁלֹּא יֵשׁ בָּזֶה הִתְפַּעֲלוּת אַהֲבָה וְגַם לֹא זִכּוּךְ חָמְרִיּוּת הַמִּדּוֹת טִבְעִיִּים מִכָּל מָקוֹם יֵשׁ בָּזֶה אֵיזֶה רֶגֶשׁ פְּנִימִי וַהֲרֵי הוּא נֶאֱחָז בְּאֵיזֶה דָּבָר הַיְנוּ בַּחֲיוּת הָאֱלֹקִי שֶׁבַּתֵּבוֹת הַתְּפִלָּה הָאוֹחֵז אוֹתוֹ בְּמִקְצָת עַל כָּל פָּנִים גַּם בְּמֶשֶׁךְ הַיּוֹם, מַה שֶׁאֵין כֵּן בַּהִתְפַּעֲלוּת מֵהַזִּכָּרוֹן הַכְּלָלִי

The excitement was only imaginary; it would have been better to pray with the simple meaning of the words alone.

COMMENTARY

drawn upward, while the spirit of the animal is to descend"; animals are attracted by the physical world ("down"), while man is drawn to that which is above himself.

Since man is a microcosm ("small world") of the larger universe, all of the four kingdoms in the macrocosm (universe) are to be found in man himself, in a clear and revealed fashion. This is true not only of man's body, but his soul as well. As explained in Chassidic literature, letters (of the alphabet) constitute the "mineral" in man, emotions correspond to the vegetable, the intellect corresponds to the animal, and the source of speech corresponds to the human realm.

prayer. This grips us a little bit at least and also remains with us throughout the day. This is not the case though, in the excitement resulting from the superficial reminder of G-dliness mentioned earlier. In that case, there is nothing that holds us, since the excitement dissipates and dissolves immediately.) What difference is there whether the excitement disappears as a result of beginning a [true and] detailed meditation (although in truth if we persist in our meditation we will in the end come to G-dly excitement), or whether we cool off [and become indifferent], because there is no revelation of G-dly light in our soul?

הנ"ל שֶׁאֵין כָּאן דָּבָר הָאוֹחֵז אוֹתוֹ כִּי חוֹלֵף וְעוֹבֵר מִיָּד) וּמַה לוֹ אִם נִתְקָרֵר עַל יְדֵי הַתְחָלַת הַהִתְבּוֹנְנוּת בְּעִנְיָן פְּרָטִי (אֲשֶׁר בֶּאֱמֶת אִם יַעֲמֹד עַל דָּרְשׁוֹ וְיִתְחַזֵּק בַּהִתְבּוֹנְנוּת יָבוֹא כָּל סוֹף לִידֵי הִתְפַּעֲלוּת אֱלֹקִי) אוֹ שֶׁנִּתְקָרֵר מִמֵּילָא מִפְּנֵי שֶׁלֹּא יֵשׁ גִּלּוּי אוֹר אֱלֹקִי בְּנַפְשׁוֹ

Many beginners expect to receive G-dly illumination as soon as they begin to meditate.

Many beginners in the "service of the heart" stumble in that they don't know and recognize the nature of *avoda*. They expect to immediately receive G-dly [illumination and spiritual] light in their souls and to become truly excited with love of G-d. Then, when the excitement goes away at the very beginning of their efforts to meditate (and we will soon explain the reason), they lose heart. They then say to themselves, "Why should

(וְרַבִּים מֵהַמַּתְחִילִים בַּעֲבוֹדָה שֶׁבַּלֵּב יִכָּשְׁלוּ בָּזֶה שֶׁאֵינָם מַכִּירִים וְיוֹדְעִים עִנְיַן הָעֲבוֹדָה וְרוֹצִים שֶׁמִּיָּד יָאִיר הָאוֹר בְּנַפְשָׁם וְיִתְפַּעֲלוּ בְּהִתְפַּעֲלוּת אַהֲבָה אֲמִתִּית, וְכַאֲשֶׁר מַרְגִּישִׁים בְּנַפְשָׁם שֶׁאַדְּרַבָּא נִתְקָרְרוּ בִּתְחִלַּת הַהִתְבּוֹנְנוּת (וְסִבַּת הַדָּבָר יִתְבָּאֵר בְּסָמוּךְ) נוֹפֵל לִבָּם בְּקִרְבָּם (זייי פאלין בייַ זיך אַראָפּ) וְאוֹמְרִים

COMMENTARY

The explanation is the following: The purpose of letters is to supply influx and revelation (the Aramaic word for letter, *ata*, indicates illumination, as in the verse, [Isaiah 21:12] *ata boker*, "the morning comes"). Letters, said to be from the soul's essence, are as deeply embedded in the soul as they are distinct from its other components. The other levels of the soul involve the person himself (emotions, for example, describe the person, whether he is a kind person or a strict person, etc.). Letters, though, are only a tool that reveals one's abilities and talents. They do not involve the person himself.

Essay on Service of the Heart - Love Like Fire and Water

we get involved in meditation? We're not suited for this!" Thus, their own false illusions lead them to give up, and it would have been better for them to pray with the simple meaning of the words alone. The positive side of this is that they do begin to pray according to the simple meaning, but what usually happens is that they eventually fall away even from that. The truth is that this is a huge error, and there is no small amount of manipulation of the *yetzer hara* ("evil inclination") involved in it. The evil inclination tries hard to entice us away from true *avoda* with all kinds of tricks, so that we won't feel love for G-d, won't come closer to Him and won't refine our naturally earthy character. It is totally incorrect to say that we are "unsuited" for *avoda* (in reality, there can be no such situation, since all souls descended into the world [in physical bodies] in order to purify and refine the animal soul, as it is written [Psalms 139:16],[xlii] "The days in which they were to be formed,

לְעַצְמָן לָמָה לָהֶן לַעֲסֹק בְּהִתְבּוֹנְנוּת שֶׁאֵינָם מְסֻגָּלִים לָזֶה לְפִי דִּמְיוֹנָם וּמִתְיָאֲשִׁים מִזֶּה, וְטוֹב לָהֶם יוֹתֵר לְהִתְפַּלֵּל עַל פִּי פְּשׁוּט וְהַטּוֹב הוּא שֶׁמִּתְפַּלְּלִים אַחַר כָּךְ בְּכַוָּנַת פֵּרוּשׁ הַמִּלִּים, וְעַל פִּי הָרֹב נוֹפְלִים גַּם מִזֶּה, וּבֶאֱמֶת זֶה טָעוּת גָּדוֹל וְיֵשׁ בָּזֶה הַרְבֵּה מִתְעָרוֹבוֹת תַּחְבּוּלוֹת הַיֵּצֶר שֶׁמִּתְאַמֵּץ לְהַדִּיחַ חַס וְחָלִילָה מֵהָעֲבוֹדָה הָאֲמִתִּית בְּכָל מִינֵי תַּחְבּוּלוֹת שֶׁלֹּא לָבוֹא לִידֵי הִתְעוֹרְרוּת אַהֲבָה לִהְיוֹת בִּבְחִינַת קָרוֹב וְשֶׁלֹּא לְזַכֵּךְ הַחָמְרִיּוּת שֶׁלּוֹ. וּבְשׁוּם אֹפֶן אֵין הַדָּבָר כֵּן שֶׁאֵינוֹ מְסֻגָּל בֶּאֱמֶת לַעֲבוֹדָה (דְּבֶאֱמֶת אֵין זֶה בִּמְצִיאוּת כְּלָל, כִּי כָּל הַנְּשָׁמוֹת בָּאוּ וְיָרְדוּ לְמַטָּה לְבָרֵר וּלְזַכֵּךְ אֶת הַנֶּפֶשׁ הַבַּהֲמִית וּכְמוֹ שֶׁכָּתוּב יָמִים יֻצָּרוּ וְלוֹ אֶחָד בָּהֶם, דְּיוּצָרוּ הוּא מִלְּשׁוֹן וַיִּיצֶר בַּחֶרֶט וְהוּא עִנְיַן קִשּׁוּר הַנֶּפֶשׁ עִם הַגּוּף בִּכְדֵי לַעֲשׂוֹת הַכֹּל בִּבְחִינַת אֶחָד, וְעַל זֶה נִתְּנוּ לוֹ יָמִים וְשָׁנִים כְּפִי הַבֵּרוּרִים שֶׁצָּרִיךְ לְבָרֵר,

Their false illusions lead them to give up quickly. This is the work of the evil inclination.

xlii) See footnote of the Rebbe on page 296 ←

COMMENTARY

Since letters are a relatively superficial component of the soul, the soul-energy en-clothed in them is very contracted. It is accompanied by such great concealment that the letters themselves reveal no life force whatsoever. They don't even express the life-force corresponding to the vegetable kingdom, which is growth. That's why they are described as "mineral." In this respect, the distinction between letters and the other components of the soul is much greater than the differences between the other components themselves. Since the other powers of the soul

Everyone has their individual avoda and portion to refine in life.

וְאִם לֹא הָיִ' צָרִיךְ לְבָרֵר בֵּרוּרִים לְחֶלְקוֹ לֹא הָיָה בָּא לְמַטָּה כו' וּכְמוֹ שֶׁכָּתוּב יְמֵי שְׁנוֹתֵינוּ בָּהֶם כו' וְכַנּוֹדָע, וּמִמֵּילָא הֲלֹא נִתַּן לוֹ הַכֹּחַ לַעֲבֹד עֲבוֹדָתוֹ לְבָרֵר כו' וְזֹאת וַדַּאי שֶׁהַנְּשָׁמָה יֵשׁ בָּהּ כֹּחַ הָאַהֲבָה לֶאֱלֹקוּת)

for it too was one of them…" The word for "formed" (*yutzorue*) is similar to the Biblical phrase *vayotzar bacheret*, meaning "welding," and it indicates unity of the soul with the body and making them one. For this purpose, we were given "days and years" [on earth], according to the task of purification that we must achieve in our lifetime, and if we would not need to purify our particular portion, our soul would not have descended into this world, as it is written [in Psalms 90:10], "the days [years] of his life are seventy or eighty…" as known. Thus, it is understood that we were given the potential to perform our [particular] *avoda* and purify [our portion]. [This is regarding the *avoda* of refining the animal soul. As to the *avoda* of arousing love in the divine soul], there is no doubt whatsoever that our soul has the potential for love of G-d [which only needs to be revealed].

We must persist in detailed meditation without worrying about how much time and effort it takes.

רַק שֶׁצָּרִיךְ לְהִתְגַּבֵּר וּלְהוֹסִיף אֹמֶץ בְּהִתְבּוֹנְנוּת טוֹבָה לְהָבִין וּלְהַשִּׂיג אֶת הָעִנְיָן וְלֹא יָחוּשׁ עַל הַזְּמַן וְעַל יְגִיעַת נַפְשׁוֹ בָּזֶה בְּהַעֲמָקָה טוֹבָה שֶׁיּוּנַח אֶצְלוֹ הָעִנְיָן. וּבִלְתִּי סָפֵק וּסְפֵק סְפֵיקָא. אֲשֶׁר יָבוֹא לִידֵי הִתְעוֹרְרוּת אַהֲבָה וְעַל יְדֵי שְׁקִידַת הָעֲבוֹדָה יִהְיֶ' לוֹ בְּנָקֵל מִזְּמַן לִזְמַן עֶצֶם דְּבַר הָעֲבוֹדָה וְתִהְיֶה אֲמִתִּית יוֹתֵר).

We must persist and persevere in proper meditation in order to understand the subject without worrying about the time and the soul-effort that we are expending on this. We should delve deeply into the concept, until it becomes clear to us. There is no doubt, nor shadow of a doubt, that we will achieve love of G-d. By constant and consistent *avoda*, the process will gradually become easier and the *avoda* itself will become truer.

COMMENTARY

involve and express the person himself, his soul-energy resides within them in a revealed and clear fashion (and the differences between them are only in the amount and nature of the revelation, as will be explained). Letters, whose only purpose is to draw down influx and provide revelation, are a virtually separate entity from the soul. (It is the same in the macrocosm, that is, in the universe itself. The mineral kingdom expresses no

Essay on Service of the Heart - Love Like Fire and Water

The reason for our indifference at the beginning of meditation is that it feels like a burden.

The reason [we may experience indifference and] "coldness" at the beginning of meditation is mainly because we feel that the *avoda* of prayer is burdensome. We don't want to take upon ourselves the burden of meditative worship with real effort of the mind and heart. This is particularly true of those of us who have gotten somewhat used to the "easy bread" of imaginary excitement which is generated by shallow meditation. In such circumstances, the "yoke" of *avoda* [of detailed meditation] is particularly onerous. This is the main reason that when we begin to meditate—and this is the beginning of true *avoda*—we "cool off" completely; the meditation is difficult for us. (If we experience a general arousal to pray after studying Chassidut before [morning] prayers, as mentioned earlier, and experience no difficulty in the *avoda*, but, quite the opposite, are willing to put in the effort, we

וְסִבַּת הַקְּרִירוּת בְּהַתְחָלַת הַהִתְבּוֹנְנוּת הָעִקָּר הוּא מִפְּנֵי שֶׁתִּתְכַּבֵּד עָלָיו עִנְיַן הָעֲבוֹדָה שֶׁאֵינוֹ רוֹצֶה לְקַבֵּל עָלָיו עוֹל הָעֲבוֹדָה בִּיגִיעָה מַמָּשׁ בְּמֹחַ וְלֵב, וּבִפְרָט מִי שֶׁהֻרְגַּל בְּמִקְצָת בַּלֶּחֶם הַקַּל בְּהִתְפַּעֲלוּת הַדִּמְיוֹנִי מֵהַהִתְבּוֹנְנוּת בִּבְחִינַת כְּלָלוּת, כָּבֵד עָלָיו בְּיוֹתֵר עוֹל הָעֲבוֹדָה וְזֹאת הִיא הַסִּבָּה הָעִקָּרִית שֶׁכַּאֲשֶׁר מַתְחִיל לְהִתְבּוֹנֵן שֶׁזֶּהוּ הַתְחָלַת הָעֲבוֹדָה הָאֲמִתִּית מִתְקָרֵר מְאֹד מִפְּנֵי שֶׁהַדָּבָר כָּבֵד עָלָיו (וְגַם מִי שֶׁיֵּשׁ לוֹ הִתְעוֹרְרוּת כְּלָלִי לִתְפִלָּה עַל יְדֵי לִמּוּד הַדִּבְרֵי אֱלֹקִים חַיִּים קֹדֶם הַתְּפִלָּה כנ"ל הִנֵּה אִם הָעֲבוֹדָה בְּעַצְמָם אֵינָהּ כְּבֵדָה עָלָיו וְאַדְרַבָּא חָפֵץ הוּא לַעֲבֹד עֲבוֹדָתוֹ לֹא יִתְקָרֵר כְּלָל, וְהַהִתְעוֹרְרוּת הַכְּלָלִי הנ"ל מְסַיֵּעַ לוֹ הַרְבֵּה בַּעֲבוֹדָתוֹ לְהַרְגִּישׁ אֶת הָעִנְיָן אֱלֹקִי הֵיטֵב וּלְהִתְעוֹרֵר בֶּאֱמֶת וּלְהִתְקָרֵב בֶּאֱמֶת כו'. אֲבָל

COMMENTARY

life whatsoever, it is much further removed from the other three realms than they are separate from each other. In all of them is to be found at least some life and soul-energy.)

The second category, the vegetable kingdom, corresponds to the emotions. The emotions involve and "touch" the soul, and are not considered "mineral objects," as letters are. The emotions may undergo great turmoil and excitement. Nevertheless the soul-energy invested in the emotions is unequal (and out of range) to that in the intellect. The very fact that the emotions become aroused (in Hebrew, the word for excitement is related by its root to the word for action or activity) and cause the person to

With regular meditation, we come to feel the spiritual energy of the concept immediately.

כַּאֲשֶׁר הָעֲבוֹדָה בְּעֶצֶם כְּבֵדָה עָלָיו, הִנֵּה בְּהַתְחָלַת הָעֲבוֹדָה הָאֲמִתִּית יִתְקָרֵר גַּם מֵהַהִתְעוֹרְרוּת הַקּוֹדֶמֶת) וְגַם סִבָּה לָזֶה הֶעְדֵּר הָרְגִילוּת דְּמִי שֶׁמֻּרְגָּל בְּהִתְבּוֹנְנוּת יוֹדֵעַ אֵיךְ לִתְפֹּס עִנְיָן אֱלֹקִי, וְהַיְנוּ שֶׁמִּיָּד מַגִּיעַ אֶל הָעִנְיָן עַצְמוֹ וְנִכְנָס תֵּכֶף בְּהַשָּׂגַת הָעִנְיָן, וּמַתְחִיל אֶצְלוֹ מִיָּד חַיּוּת הַהַשָּׂגָה (וְלֹא חַיּוּת הָעִנְיָן שֶׁמַּשִּׂיג, שֶׁזֶּה אִי אֶפְשָׁר לִהְיוֹת וְאֵין צָרִיךְ לִהְיוֹת בְּהַתְחָלַת הַהִתְבּוֹנְנוּת (כִּי יְהִי' מֻטְעֶה בְּהִתְפַּעֲלוּת מִכְּלָלוּת הָעִנְיָן לְבַד) עַד שֶׁיִּתְבּוֹנֵן וְיַשִּׂיג הָעִנְיָן הֵיטֵב) אֲבָל בְּהֶעְדֵּר הָרְגִילוּת הִנֵּה בְּהַתְחָלַת הַהִתְבּוֹנְנוּת הֲרֵי הוּא תּוֹפֵס רַק בְּזֹהֲרוּרִית הָעִנְיָן לֹא בְּעִנְיָן עַצְמוֹ, וּמִמֵּילָא אֵין לוֹ עֲדַיִן חַיּוּת בָּזֶה, וְגַם נוֹדַע בְּעִנְיַן הַהִתְבּוֹנְנוּת הֲגַם שֶׁהִיא הַשָּׂגָה שִׂכְלִית הֲרֵי אֵינָהּ כְּמוֹ הַלִּמּוּד בְּאֵיזֶה עִנְיָן שֶׁהַהִתְעַסְּקוּת הִיא בְּשִׂכְלִי לְבַד, אֲבָל בְּהִתְבּוֹנְנוּת הֲרֵי צָרִיךְ לִהְיוֹת הַהֶרְגֵּשׁ שֶׁהַהִתְעַסְּקוּת שֶׁלּוֹ הוּא בְּעִנְיָן אֱלֹקִי וּכְמוֹ

won't "cool off" at all. The above general arousal [after learning] helps us immensely in our *avoda* and enables us to profoundly feel the G-dly concept and to become truly aroused and come truly close to G-d. But, when the *avoda* itself is difficult for us, then in the beginning of true detailed meditation, our previous [general] excitement will wane.) Another reason [for this coldness] is lack of consistency. When we meditate regularly, we know how to grasp a G-dly concept. We immediately go straight to the subject itself, feeling right away the [G-dly] energy inherent in the understanding. (Here, we're not referring to the energy of the concept that we grasp, because that cannot occur and also need not occur at the beginning of our meditation. If it did, the excitement would be false, being that it is based on general impressions alone. The energy comes only after we have meditated and come to solid understanding of the concept.) However, with lack of consistency, what we grasp at the begin-

---
COMMENTARY

"leave" his present status and position, indicates their distinction from intellect. However much the person thinks and uses his mind, it never brings him to change his emotional status and leave his previous (personal) position behind. He remains calm. This is an indication that the emotions fail to reach the person himself [his inner core]. They involve the person only insofar as he has to do with "another" — be it another person, idea, object, etc. Only regarding the "other" do the emotions find expression

Essay on Service of the Heart - Love Like Fire and Water

ning of our meditation is only an aura of the concept, and not the concept itself. Therefore, we feel no real energy from the subject. Also, it is known that even though meditation is a mental process, it is not similar to approaching an academic subject in which the study is strictly intellectual. During meditation, we must [also] feel that we are involved with a G-dly concept, as explained in Chapter 1. This, too, is dependent upon regularity. Those who are regular and consistent in their *avoda* acquire this awareness in their souls. They feel that along with the immense effort they put into knowledge and intellectual grasp of the depth of the concept, they also develop an awareness of, and involvement with, a G-dly concept. This awareness powerfully enlivens the meditation. Those who are just beginning their *avoda*, however, have not yet acquired this awareness in their souls, and it minimizes the energy that they experience at the beginning of their meditation.

שֶׁנִּתְבָּאֵר לְעֵיל פ"א, וְזֶה גַּם כֵּן תָּלוּי בָּרְגִילוּת שֶׁהַמֻּרְגָּלִים וְשׁוֹקְדִים בָּעֲבוֹדָה נִקְנֶה זֹאת בְּנַפְשָׁם, שֶׁעִם הִשְׁתַּדְּלוּתָם הָעֲצוּמָה בִּידִיעַת וְהַשָּׂגַת עֹמֶק הָעִנְיָן יֵשׁ בָּהֶם גַּם כֵּן הַרְגָּשָׁה זוֹ שֶׁכָּל הַהִתְעַסְּקוּת הִיא בְּעִנְיָן אֱלֹקִי שֶׁזֶּה נוֹתֵן חַיּוּת רַב בַּהִתְבּוֹנְנוּת, וּבַמַּתְחִילִים בָּעֲבוֹדָה לֹא יֵשׁ עֲדַיִן הַקִּנְיָן הַזֶּה בְּנַפְשָׁם, שֶׁכָּל זֶה מְמַעֵט אֶת הַחַיּוּת בְּהַתְחָלַת הַהִתְבּוֹנְנוּת.

But when we realize that the entire purpose of our descent into this world is in order to serve the One Above down here in a body with an animal soul, and to purify and refine our natural traits. **And without *avoda*, what are we doing here in the world?** Was it for this that we were created—to eat and drink like an animal? To be involved in all the matters of the world which are lower in level

אֲבָל כַּאֲשֶׁר יָשִׂים הָאָדָם אֶל לִבּוֹ שֶׁכָּל יְרִידָתוֹ בָּעוֹלָם הוּא בִּכְדֵי לַעֲבֹד אֶת ה' לְמַטָּה בְּגוּף וְנֶפֶשׁ הַבַּהֲמִית וְהִינוּ לְבָרֵר וּלְזַכֵּךְ אֶת הַמִּדּוֹת טִבְעִיִּים שֶׁלּוֹ. וּבְהֶעְדֵּר הָעֲבוֹדָה מַהוּ עִנְיָנֵנוּ בָּעוֹלָם, וְהָכִי בִּשְׁבִיל זֶה נִבְרָא לִהְיוֹת כְּמוֹ בַּעֲלֵי הַחַיִּים לַעֲסֹק בַּאֲכִילָה וּשְׁתִיָּ', וְכֵן בִּכְלָל לַעֲסֹק בְּעִנְיְנֵי הָעוֹלָם שֶׁהֵן לְמַטָּה בְּמַדְרֵגָה מִמֶּנּוּ (וּכְמוֹ שֶׁאָמְרוּ

But, if we are not involved in the avoda of meditation, then what are we doing here in the world?

--- **COMMENTARY** ---

and arousal. The matters of others, whether it be their good or bad qualities, affect our emotions. He becomes either attracted to the other with love and affection or wishes to escape and run away from them out of fear.

Man's purpose is to reach beyond the creation altogether.

xliii) See footnote of the Rebbe on page 298

הַחוֹקְרִים שֶׁכָּל דָּבָר נִבְרָא בִּשְׁבִיל אֵיזֶה תַּכְלִית דְּהַיְנוּ לְהַגִּיעַ לְמַה שֶּׁלְמַעְלָה מִמֶּנּוּ. וְתַכְלִית הַדּוֹמֵם הוּא בִּשְׁבִיל הַצּוֹמֵחַ וְתַכְלִית הַצּוֹמֵחַ לִכָּלֵל בְּמַדְרֵגַת הַחַי, וְתַכְלִית הַחַי לִכָּלֵל בְּמַדְרֵגַת הַמְדַבֵּר, וְתַכְלִית הַמְדַבֵּר הוּא לְהַגִּיעַ לְמַה שֶּׁלְמַעְלָה מֵהָעוֹלָם כוּ'), וּבְהֶעְדֵּר הָעֲבוֹדָה הֲרֵי הוּא נִמְשָׁךְ אַחֲרֵי תַּאֲווֹת הַיֵּצֶר הָרַע שֶׁיָּכוֹל גַּם כֵּן לְהִתְאַוּוֹת לִדְבָרִים הָאֲסוּרִים כוּ' שֶׁבָּזֶה הוּא גָּרוּעַ כוּ' גַּם מִבַּעֲלֵי חַיִּים הַטְּמֵאִים כוּ' וּכְמוֹ שֶׁכָּתוּב בְּסֵפֶר שֶׁל בֵּינוֹנִים פכ"ט וְגַם מִלּוּי תַּאֲוָותָיו בְּתַאֲווֹת הֶתֵּר הֲרֵי זֶה חֵטְא וְעָווֹן, שֶׁהֲרֵי צָרִיךְ לִהְיוֹת קַדֵּשׁ עַצְמְךָ בַּמֻּתָּר לָךְ שֶׁהִיא מִצְוַת עֲשֵׂה דְּאוֹ' כְּמוֹ שֶׁכָּתוּב בְּסֵפֶר שֶׁל בֵּינוֹנִים מפכ"ז וספ"ל, וּלְבַד זֹאת הֲרֵי אֵינוֹ מַשְׁלִים הַכַּוָּנָה שֶׁבִּשְׁבִיל זֶה נִבְרָא דַּאֲמִיתִית כַּוָּנַת יְרִידָתוֹ וּבְרִיאָתוֹ לְמַטָּה הוּא בִּכְדֵי לְהַעֲלוֹת אֶת הַנֶּפֶשׁ הַבַּהֲמִית וְכָל עִנְיְנֵי הָעוֹלָם וּכְמוֹ שֶׁכָּתוּב בְּתוֹרָה אוֹר דִּבּוּר הַמַּתְחִיל לְהָבִין הַטַּעַם

than we ourselves? (As the philosophers said,[xliii] everything in the universe was created for a purpose, and the purpose [of all creation] is to arrive at a level above its own. The purpose of the mineral world is to be included in the vegetable, and the purpose of the vegetable world is to be included in the animal world. The purpose of the animal world is to be included in the human, and the purpose of the human is to reach that which is over and beyond creation altogether.) Lacking in *avoda* [of meditation and prayer], we are attracted by the lusts of the *yetzer hara*, which can lead us to be attracted to forbidden matters. At that point, we become lower than even the "impure animals," as written in *Tanya*, chapter 29. Even satisfying ourselves with [the physical] lusts that are permitted by the Torah is a [sort of] transgression, since the Torah commands us to "make ourselves holy in permitted matters," which is a positive Biblical commandment, as mentioned in *Tanya*, end of chapter 27 and end of chapter 30. Aside from

───────── *COMMENTARY* ─────────

In this particular detail — that emotions have more to do with the aspect of the soul which relates to the "other," (unlike intellect which deals with the soul itself) — the emotions are more like letters than intellect. Neither letters nor emotions are connected with the soul itself, so inevitably they relate to the "other." (Letters are vehicles of expression of the soul, while emotions are illuminations of the soul, as it emerges into revelation).

Essay on Service of the Heart - Love Like Fire and Water

that, we are not fulfilling the intention for which we were created. For the true intention behind our creation and descent down here is in order to elevate our animal soul and all of the worldly matters, as written in *Torah Ohr* in the discourse *Lehavin ha ta'am shenishtaneh yetzirat guf ha'adam*. This is indicated [as well] in the verse, [in Isaiah 45:12], "It was I who made the earth and I created man upon it,"

שֶׁנִּשְׁתַּנָּה יְצִירַת גּוּף הָאָדָם כו', וּכְמוֹ שֶׁכָּתוּב אָנֹכִי עָשִׂיתִי אֶרֶץ וְאָדָם עָלֶיהָ בָרָאתִי, דְּזֶה שֶׁאָנֹכִי מִי שֶׁאָנֹכִי עָשִׂיתִי אֶרֶץ הוּא בִּשְׁבִיל הָאָדָם וְהָאָדָם עָלֶיהָ בָרָאתִי בְּגִימַטְרִיָּה תרי"ג לְקַיֵּם תרי"ג מִצְוֹת לְתַקֵּן בָּהֶם וְעַל יָדָם אֶת הָעוֹלָם כו'.

The true intention behind our creation is the elevation of our animal soul and our portion in worldly matters.

wherein the word for "I" in Hebrew is *Anochi*, which refers to the essence of G-d, as in "I am who I am." [See commentaries to Genesis 27:19.] He created the earth for man, and the numerical value here for "created" (*barati*) is 613, indicating the 613 *mitzvot*, which Jews are to fulfill, thereby rectifying the universe.

When we take all of this to heart, we will accept the obligation of *avoda* upon ourselves without any difficulty whatsoever. We won't feel any [indifference or] coldness whatsoever, G-d forbid. Quite the opposite, we will experience [much] stimulation and motivation in our *avoda* and will overcome our natural resistance and engage in true [and detailed] meditation. Regularity and persistence in our *avoda* will aid us as well, as

וְכַאֲשֶׁר יָשִׂים אֶל לִבּוֹ אֶת כָּל הנ"ל יְקַבֵּל עָלָיו הָעֲבוֹדָה וְלֹא תִכְבַּד עָלָיו הַדָּבָר כָּל כָּךְ, וְאָז לֹא יַרְגִּישׁ שׁוּם קְרִירוּת חַס וְחָלִילָה, אַדְּרַבָּא יְהִי' לוֹ חַיּוּת בַּעֲבוֹדָה וְיִתְגַּבֵּר לְהִתְבּוֹנֵן בְּהִתְבּוֹנְנוּת אֲמִתִּית וְגַם הַרְגִּילוּת וְהַשְׁקִידָה בַּעֲבוֹדָה יְסַיֵּעַ לוֹ כנ"ל, וְהָעוֹלָה עַל כֻּלָּנָה הוּא הַסִּיּוּעַ מִלְמַעְלָה לָזֶה שֶׁחָפֵץ בַּעֲבוֹדָה אֲמִתִּית וּכְמַאֲמָר הַבָּא

COMMENTARY

All of this exemplifies the four fundamental categories of creation of the macrocosm, the created universe. The vegetable category is enlivened by a "body-energy," which places it closer to the mineral kingdom, while the animal kingdom is enlivened by a life-force which amounts to a "soul" energy, placing it closer to the category of the "speaking" or human world. And just as the distinction between the vegetable and animal kingdoms is that plants are limited to a particular place while animals can move about, so is the distinction between emotions and intellect

mentioned before. And most important of all is the assistance and support accruing from above when we desire true *avoda* of the One Above. As the Sages said, "One who comes to purify himself is assisted from above" in all aspects of *avoda*. Meditation should be done properly; be experienced in the soul and provide arousal in the heart. It should enable the divine soul to overpower the animal soul. (In *Kuntres Ha'Tefila*, it is explained that there are various preparations that can make our *avoda* true and proper.[41])

לְטַהֵר מְסַיְּעִין לוֹ בְּכָל פְּרָטֵי הָעֲבוֹדָה הֵן בַּהִתְבּוֹנְנוּת שֶׁתִּהְיֶה בְּטוֹב וְשֶׁיִּרְגַּשׁ הָעִנְיָן בְּנַפְשׁוֹ וְשֶׁיִּתְעוֹרֵר בְּלִבּוֹ, וְהֵן בְּהִתְגַּבְּרוּת הַנֶּפֶשׁ הָאֱלֹקִית עַל הַנֶּפֶשׁ הַבַּהֲמִית כו' (וּבְקוּנְטְרֵס הַתְּפִלָּה נִתְבָּאֲרוּ כַּמָּה עִנְיְנֵי הֲכָנוֹת בִּכְדֵי שֶׁתִּהְיֶה הָעֲבוֹדָה אֲמִתִּית כִּדְבָעֵי לְמִיהֱוֵי).

The ultimate avoda is detailed meditation leading to love of G-d in the heart.

What emerges from the above treatise is that the ultimate purpose of *avoda* of the One Above is detailed meditation leading to arousal of the trait of love of G-d in our heart. This leads as well to purification and refinement of our animal soul. This is not true of cursory meditation, which leads only to an illusory excitement, and which fails to alter the animal soul. It remains at full strength. Even so, it is impossible to say that this [general meditation] has no effect whatsoever upon the animal soul,

הָעוֹלֶה מִכָּל הַנַּ"ל דְּתַכְלִית הָעֲבוֹדָה הִיא בְּהִתְבּוֹנְנוּת בְּדֶרֶךְ פְּרָט שֶׁעַל יְדֵי זֶה מִתְעוֹרֵר בְּמִדַּת הָאַהֲבָה בַּלֵּב, וְעַל יְדֵי זֶה נַעֲשֶׂה בֵּרוּר וְזִכּוּךְ הַנֶּפֶשׁ הַבַּהֲמִית, מַה שֶּׁאֵין כֵּן בְּהִתְבּוֹנְנוּת בְּדֶרֶךְ כְּלָל שֶׁהִתְפַּעֲלוּת הִיא בְּדֶרֶךְ דִּמְיוֹן, וְאֵינוֹ פּוֹעֵל עַל הַנֶּפֶשׁ הַבַּהֲמִית שֶׁנִּשְׁאָר בְּתָקְפּוֹ כְּמוֹ שֶׁהוּא, וְהֲגַם שֶׁאִי אֶפְשָׁר לוֹמַר שֶׁאֵינוֹ פּוֹעֵל כְּלָל עַל הַנֶּפֶשׁ הַבַּהֲמִית דְּוַדַּאי אֵינוֹ דּוֹמֶה כְּמוֹ שֶׁלֹּא הָיְ' עוֹבֵד כְּלָל,

---

COMMENTARY

(as they exist in the microcosm, in man himself). Emotions themselves (including the intellect leading to emotions) are subsumed in a particular category and description, from which they cannot emerge. The man of kindness is restricted by his natural tendency to perform deeds and acts of kindness toward others; however, within his emotional limitations he may grow from immaturity to full maturity. The minor fondness that he feels early in life may blossom later in life to a great love. And the same is true of the man of strength and judgment...

> *The souls of our generation are not "new" souls that never came down to this world before.*

דְּגַם עַל יְדֵי הָעֲבוֹדָה בְּאֹפֶן הַנַּ"ל נִרְאֶה בּוֹ אֵיזֶה זִכּוּךְ וְדַקּוּת (א אײדעלקײט), הָעִנְיָן הוּא דְּהִנֵּה כָּל אֶחָד וְאֶחָד יֵשׁ לוֹ מִדָּה פְּרָטִית מֵהַמִּדּוֹת הַטִּבְעִיּוֹת שֶׁעָלָיו לְבָרֵר וּלְזַכֵּךְ אוֹתָהּ, כִּי נוֹדָע דְּנִשְׁמוֹת דְּעַכְשָׁו אֵינָם נְשָׁמוֹת חֲדָשׁוֹת שֶׁלֹּא הָיוּ עוֹד לְעוֹלָמִים כְּלָל, כִּי אִם נְשָׁמוֹת יְשָׁנוֹת שֶׁכְּבָר הָיוּ בָּעוֹלָם וּבָאוּ עוֹד הַפַּעַם בָּעוֹלָם לְבָרֵר מַה שֶּׁלֹּא בֵּרְרוּ בַּפַּעַם הַקּוֹדֵם, וְלִהְיוֹת דְּהַנֶּפֶשׁ הַבַּהֲמִית הֲרֵי בָּא בְּצִיּוּר קוֹמָה שְׁלֵמָה יֵשׁ בּוֹ הַכֹּל גַּם אוֹתָן שֶׁכְּבָר נִתְבָּרְרוּ רַק שֶׁהֵן בּוֹ בִּבְחִינַת חֲלִישׁוּת מֵאַחַר וְהִתְבָּרְרוּ כְּבָר, וְהַמִּדָּה שֶׁלֹּא נִתְבָּרְרָה הִיא בּוֹ בְּתֹקֶף וְעַל כֵּן עַל אוֹתָן הַמִּדּוֹת שֶׁנִּתְבָּרְרוּ מִכְּבָר פּוֹעֵל עֲלֵיהֶם גַּם הַהִתְבּוֹנְנוּת בִּבְחִינַת כְּלָלוּת, דְּהַיְנוּ שֶׁאֵיזֶה הִתְעוֹרְרוּת אֱלֹקִי שֶׁבְּנַפְשׁוֹ פּוֹעֵל עַל הַמִּדּוֹת הַנַּ"ל לְזַכּוֹתָם מֵאַחַר שֶׁכְּבָר הָיוּ זַכִּים

since certainly the animal soul does not remain as if there were no *avoda* at all. Even a haphazard meditation will produce some sort of refinement. Nevertheless, the point is the following: Each and every one of us has a particular trait among our natural characteristics that we must purify and refine. It is known that the souls of our generation are not "new" souls which never came down to this world at all; they are "old" souls that were already in this world and have come down an additional time in order to refine that which they failed to purify in the previous descent. Now since the animal soul is a complete structure, it has all of its soul powers, including those that were already purified. However, those that were already purified are present in a weak form, since they've already been refined, while the trait(s) which have yet to be purified remain at full strength. Therefore, a light meditation will have an effect only on those traits that have already been refined. Any type of G-dly arousal of our [divine] soul will have an effect upon these [already purified] traits and refine them [a bit more], since they've been refined already.

--- **COMMENTARY** ---

The intellect, though is different. Not only is the intellect not so limited by a particular tendency or description, (as we see, that one can understand even those things to which he is utterly and viscerally opposed), but pure intellect (unadulterated by emotional tendencies) can even bring about change in our natural emotional make-up. Among intellectuals, there are individuals who are insightful, analytic and deep thinkers. Emotions tend

We have "old" souls that have undergone refinement in previous generations, yet we all have character traits that remain in need of work.

(וְדַאי בְּבוֹאָם בְּהַצִּיּוּר קוֹמָה דְהַנֶּפֶשׁ הַבַּהֲמִית מֵחָדָשׁ אֵינָם זַכִּים כָּל כָּךְ כְּמוֹ שֶׁהָיוּ כְּשֶׁנִּתְבָּרְרוּ בַּפַּעַם הַקּוֹדֵם וְאִם לֹא יְהִי עוֹבֵד בַּפַּעַם הַזֶּה יִתְגַּבְּרוּ וְיִתְעַבּוּ בְּיוֹתֵר, וְהַיְנוּ שֶׁמְּקֻלְקָל חַס וְחָלִילָה גַּם מַה שֶּׁתֻּקַּן מִכְּבָר, אַךְ בַּעֲבוֹדָה קַלָּה כְּמוֹ בְּהִתְעוֹרְרוּת כְּלָלִי הנ"ל מִזְדַּכְּכִים כו'),

(Certainly upon entering anew the complete structure of the animal soul, these traits do not remain as refined as they were when purified the previous time around. Without *avoda* upon them now [as well], they will become much stronger and coarser. Then, even that which was previously rectified will now become damaged, G-d forbid. But, [even] with a casual *avoda* such as the general arousal [and meditation] mentioned above, they become polished and refined.)

אֲבָל בִּכְדֵי לְבָרֵר וּלְתַקֵּן אוֹתָהּ הַמִּדָּה שֶׁלֹּא נִתְבָּרְרָה עֲדַיִן שֶׁהִיא אֶצְלוֹ בְּתֹקֶף וְשָׁוֶה הָעִקָּר שֶׁמַּגִּיעַ לְחֶלְקוֹ לְבָרֵר, אִי אֶפְשָׁר לְבָרְרָהּ בַּעֲבוֹדָה קַלָּה כִּי אִם עַל יְדֵי עֲבוֹדָה וִיגִיעָה בִּיגִיעַת בָּשָׂר וִיגִיעַת נֶפֶשׁ הַמְבֹאָר בְּסֵפֶר שֶׁל בֵּינוֹנִים פמ"ב, וּבְמִדָּה זֹאת בֶּאֱמֶת הָעֲבוֹדָה בִּבְחִינַת כְּלָלוּת אֵינוֹ פּוֹעֵל מְאוּמָה וַהֲרֵי הִיא בְּתָקְפָּהּ כְּמוֹ שֶׁאֵינוֹ עוֹבֵד כְּלָל.

However, in order to purify and rectify whatever character trait that did not yet become purified and that remains at full strength—and is the main component of our task to purify in the world—we must not be satisfied with casual *avoda*. We must work hard and strive with labor of the flesh and labor of the soul, as explained in *Tanya*, chapter 42. When it comes to this trait [that has fallen to us and is our specific duty to purify and rectify], a shallow *avoda* [based upon simple reminders of G-dliness] won't have any effect whatsoever. The trait will remain at full strength as if there were no *avoda* at all.

וְכַנִּרְאֶה בְּחוּשׁ בְּטֶבַע בְּנֵי אָדָם בְּאֵיזֶה מִדָּה פְּרָטִית שֶׁנִּרְאֶה בָּהֶם בְּתֹקֶף הִנֵּה כַּאֲשֶׁר עוֹבֵד עֲבוֹדָתוֹ בַּעֲבוֹדָה אֲמִתִּית בְּמוֹחַ וְלֵב בְּהִתְבּוֹנְנוּת פְּרָטִית בְּהַשָּׂגָה גְּמוּרָה

We see clearly in human nature that when we work on a particular personality trait that stands out and when we perform our *avoda* truly and properly in our mind and heart, [it

---

COMMENTARY

to be one-dimensional (either kind and outgoing, or strict and introverted, etc). (However, when our intellect gets involved with our emotions, the emotions become more varied.)

Essay on Service of the Heart - Love Like Fire and Water

has an effect]. Through detailed meditation involving full understanding and clear perception—such that we feel the concept and our heart is aroused with love of G-d ["like water"], or with "love like fire"—the personality trait gradually becomes purified and refined. It becomes weakened and, at the same time, closer [to the One Above], losing its arrogance and independence, as described in Chapter 4.

וּבַהֲנָחָה טוֹבָה וְנִרְגָּשׁ אֶצְלוֹ הָעִנְיָן וּמִתְעוֹרֵר בְּלִבּוֹ בְּאַהֲבָה בִּבְחִינַת קֵרוּב וּדְבֵקוּת אוֹ בִּבְחִינַת רִשְׁפֵּי אֵשׁ כוּ׳ מִתְבָּרֵר וּמִזְדַּכֵּךְ מְעַט מְעַט הַמִּדָּה הַהִיא בִּבְחִינַת חֲלִישׁוּת וּבִבְחִינַת קֵרוּב וּבִבְחִינַת כִּלָּיוֹן הַיֵּשׁוּת כוּ׳ כְּמוֹ שֶׁנִּתְבָּאֵר לְעֵיל פ״ד

Within our *avoda*, we must identify the particular character trait that has fallen to our lot to rectify—this trait is bound to be stronger—and apply all of our powers in our *avoda* to correct this particular trait, as is known. However, when the *avoda* is only superficial [based upon "reminders of G-dliness" alone], the trait remains at full strength exactly as it was before and shows no positive change whatsoever. [For example], there are those who are lighthearted (with "white bile"), possessing a tendency toward lust and [physical] enjoyment, frivolity, scoffing, and the like. And

(וּבַעֲבוֹדָתוֹ צָרִיךְ לֵידַע הַמִּדָּה הַפְּרָטִית שֶׁמַּגִּיעַ לְחֶלְקוֹ לְתַקֵּן הַיְנוּ אֵיזֶה מִדָּה שֶׁהִיא בּוֹ בְּתֹקֶף יוֹתֵר וְיִתֵּן כָּל כֹּחוֹתָיו בַּעֲבוֹדָתוֹ עַל הַמִּדָּה הַזּוֹ הַפְּרָטִית כַּנּוֹדָע). אֲבָל כַּאֲשֶׁר הָעֲבוֹדָה הִיא בִּבְחִי׳ כְּלָלוּת לְבַד נִשְׁאֲרָה הַמִּדָּה הַהִיא בְּתָקְפָּהּ מַמָּשׁ כְּמוֹ קֹדֶם הָעֲבוֹדָה וְאֵינוֹ נִרְאֶה בָּהּ שׁוּם שִׁנּוּי לְטוֹב, כְּמוֹ מִי שֶׁיֵּשׁ מִי שֶׁהוּא בְּטֶבַע מָרָה לְבָנָה בְּתַאֲווֹת וְתַעֲנוּגִים וְהוֹלְלוּת וְלֵיצָנוּת וּכְהַאי גַוְונָא וְיֵשׁ שֶׁהוּא בְּטֶבַע הַמָּרָה שְׁחוֹרָה כְּמוֹ בְּכַעַס וּמִדּוֹת אַכְזָרִיּוּת וְכֵן בַּעֲצָלוּת וַעֲצָבוּת כוּ׳

Within avoda, we must identify the traits that have fallen to our portion to rectify.

there are those with a darker nature (with "black bile"), possessing a tendency toward anger and cruelty, as well as those who tend toward laziness

---
COMMENTARY

After all is said and done, our intellect is no more than the "animal" world within his soul. The main advantage of the human species (which is completely removed from the animal world) expresses itself in the origin of the power of speech. Which is why man is called a "speaker" (*medaber*) rather than a "thinker" (*maskil*).

The explanation is the following: the spirituality and abstract refinement that accrues to man because of his intellect, which

and depression. (Specifically, these tendencies correspond to the four [physical] elements [fire, air, water, and earth] mentioned in *Tanya*, section 1, chapter 1.) There is "blue bile and green bile," etc.

(וּבִפְרָטִיּוּת הֵן בְּהַד' יְסוֹדוֹת הַמְבֹאָרִים בְּסֵפֶר שֶׁל בֵּינוֹנִים ח"א פ"א וְכֵן יֵשׁ מָרָה אוֹכְמָא וּמָרָה יְרוֹקָא כו':

In discussing the make-up of the natural soul of man, the *Tanya* (first section, end of ch. 1) says that it consists of four types of character traits, corresponding to the four physical [Aristotelian] elements: air, water, earth, and fire, which give rise to:	
Fire	Anger, arrogance
Earth	Laziness, lethargy, and depression
Water	Lusts bringing physical enjoyment
Air	Scoffing, idle talk, wastefulness

―――――――― *COMMENTARY* ――――――――

gives him the power to forsake all categories and choose whatever path he wishes (including that which isn't according to his own natural tendencies, and even to transform his natural leanings), is nonetheless still associated with his own existence. Even when man chooses, by dint of his intellect, to take a path that is the opposite of his own natural character, it is because so his own existence and understanding dictates. The same is true of the other aspect of man's spirituality — that which his "spirit tends upward." Even though he is drawn to that which is beyond him, and indeed he leaves behind his own nature and character, he does so because his own intellect grasps the benefit in so doing — in achieving a spiritual level beyond his own. (With his own understanding, he comes to the conclusion that he is limited and that there are things that are beyond his intellect). It's understood then that even his striving to supersede himself is based upon his own existence.

The power of speech, though, is different: Speech allows us to transcend our own existence and communicate with another person. This implies a lack of "self." (That is, our ability to communicate with another is not based on our existence, since nothing in ourselves requires that we communicate with

Essay on Service of the Heart - Love Like Fire and Water

Light, general meditation will not produce refinement and rectification of bad character traits.

Now, when our meditation is only casual—even though we may become excited and [even] inflamed in our soul or achieve bitterness and a worried heart as mentioned earlier—no change whatsoever takes place in our natural character traits. They appear as strong as ever. That is, after prayer, we will continue with our frivolity and scoffing exactly as before prayer. Or we will indulge our lusts and hedonistic pleasures just as before. Quite the contrary, our natural character traits may be even stronger than before.

הִנֵּה בָּעֲבוֹדָה הַנַ"ל שֶׁהַהִתְבּוֹנְנוּת הִיא רַק בִּבְחִינַת כְּלָלוּת הֲגַם שֶׁמִּתְפַּעֵל וּמִתְלַהֵב נַפְשׁוֹ מִזֶּה וְגַם בִּבְחִינַת מְרִירוּת וְלֵב דּוֹאֵג כַּנַ"ל, אֵין שׁוּם שִׁנּוּי כְּלָל בְּהַמִּדּוֹת הַטִּבְעִיִּים, וְנִרְאִים בְּתָקְפָּם כְּמוֹ מִקֹּדֶם, וְהוּא שֶׁלְּאַחַר הַתְּפִלָּה יְהִי בְּהוֹלְלוּת וְלֵיצָנוּת בְּשָׁוֶה מַמָּשׁ כְּמוֹ קֹדֶם הַתְּפִלָּה, אוֹ בְּתַאֲווֹת וְתַעֲנוּגִים כְּמוֹ מִקֹּדֶם, וְאַדְּרַבָּא יָכוֹל לִהְיוֹת בְּתֹקֶף יוֹתֵר

There are two reasons for this. The first reason is the joy that we feel in our soul over our excitement and agitation. (This is an experience of *yeshut*, or ego, that usually coexists with *avoda* based upon reason and logic. However, in true *avoda*, the process of meditation should coincide with *bitul*, or "self-nullification." This is similar to what was explained earlier, that *avoda* done with happiness must be accompanied by *bitul*, so that the happiness should not be selfish or egotistical. However, in the casual

(די) מִפְּנֵי שִׂמְחַת נַפְשׁוֹ צוּפְרִידֶענְקֵייט) מֵהַהִתְפָּעֲלוּת וְהִתְלַהֲבוּת שֶׁלּוֹ (דְּהַיְנוּ הַרְגָּשַׁת הַיֵּשׁוּת, שֶׁבְּדֶרֶךְ כְּלָל יֶשְׁנָהּ בַּעֲבוֹדָה שֶׁעַל פִּי טַעַם וָדַעַת, רַק שֶׁבַּעֲבוֹדָה אֲמִתִּית יֵשׁ בָּזֶה הַבִּטּוּל, וּכְמוֹ שֶׁנִּתְבָּאֵר לְעֵיל שֶׁצָּרִיךְ לִהְיוֹת בִּטּוּל בַּעֲבוֹדָה בְּשִׂמְחָה שֶׁלֹּא תִּהְיֶה בִּבְחִינַת יֵשׁוּת כוּ', מַה שֶּׁאֵין כֵּן בַּעֲבוֹדָה הַנַ"ל לֹא יֵשׁ בָּזֶה הַבִּטּוּל כִּי אִם הַרְגָּשַׁת עַצְמוֹ) אוֹ שֶׁמִּפְקַח דַּעְתּוֹ בָּזֶה מֵהַמְּרִירוּת לֵב דּוֹאֵג (וּמוּבָן שֶׁבָּזֶה מְאַבֵּד גַּם הַמְעַט טוֹב

COMMENTARY

someone else. Rather, the origin of speech is so high that it completely defies any description or category whatsoever, even that which "lumps" us together with another person). Therefore, the power of speech expresses the true and essential spirituality and abstract refinement of the soul.

Based upon the above explanation of the nature and distinctions between the four categories of created existence (mineral, vegetable, animal and human, in the macrocosm and in the

avoda described earlier, there is no nullification of the ego, but rather experience and feeling of the self.) The second reason is that our bitterness and our worried heart lead us to [excessive] openness of mind [leaving us open to frivolity, scoffing, lust and pleasure even more then before we prayed]. (It is understood that if this happens, we lose whatever bit of good there was in our *avoda* since there was at least some positive [G-dly] feeling in it, and in this [excessive] openness [even to topics and stimuli opposed to holiness], we lose this feeling completely).

שֶׁיֵּשׁ בַּעֲבוֹדָה זוֹ דַּהֲלֹא מִכָּל מָקוֹם הָיָ׳ בּוֹ אֵיזֶה הֶרְגֵּשׁ טוֹב, וּבְהַפִּקּוּחַ הַנַּ״ל נֶאֱבַד הַהֶרְגֵּשׁ הַזֶּה לְגַמְרֵי).

Similarly, if we are hot-tempered and cruel, we will remain the same after this perfunctory *avoda*. We will become angry, have no mercy on our fellow man, and act toward others in a very hardened manner. These traits may become even stronger [than before we prayed], either because of our arrogance [as in the first reason given earlier], or as a result of our bitterness [as in the second reason], which by nature leads to anger. (Those of us who by nature are not so expansive may experience the general overall effect of this light meditation for some time, without it leading to the expansion of our natural character traits. This is especially true when the bitterness is very strong, which in truth is depression; in this case the overall effect [of the general meditation] lasts quite a bit of time.)

וְכֵן מִי שֶׁהוּא בְּמִדַּת הַכַּעַס וּמִדּוֹת אַכְזָרִיּוּת יְהִי׳ כֵּן לְאַחַר הָעֲבוֹדָה כְּמוֹ קֹדֶם הָעֲבוֹדָה לְהִתְכַּעֵס וְלִבְלִי לְרַחֵם עַל זוּלָתוֹ וּלְהִתְנַהֵג אִתּוֹ בְּמִדּוֹת תַּקִּיפוֹת, וְיָכוֹל לִהְיוֹת גַּם כֵּן עוֹד הִתְגַּבְּרוּת בָּזֶה מִצַּד הַיֵּשׁוּת שֶׁלּוֹ, אוֹ מִצַּד הַמְּרִירוּת שֶׁבְּטֶבַע מֵבִיא לִידֵי כַּעַס כו׳ (רַק מִי שֶׁבְּטִבְעוֹ אֵינוֹ בְּהִתְפַּשְּׁטוּת כָּל כָּךְ יָכֹל לִהְיוֹת שֶׁיַּחֲזִיק הַמַּקִּיף מֵהָעֲבוֹדָה בַּדֶּרֶךְ הַנַּ״ל אֵיזֶה מֶשֶׁךְ זְמַן בְּהֶעְדֵּר הִתְפַּשְּׁטוּת הַמִּדָּה הַטִּבְעִית, וּבְיוֹתֵר הוּא בְּהִתְגַּבְּרוּת הַמְּרִירוּת (שֶׁבֶּאֱמֶת זֶהוּ עַצְבוּת) שֶׁמַּחֲזִיק אֶצְלוֹ זְמַן רַב).

COMMENTARY

microcosm), we can gain a certain understanding of the differences between the four worlds: *Asiya*, *Yetzira*, *Bria*, and *Atzilut*.

The beginning of created existence (in which the creation has a distinct awareness of itself) is in the World of *Bria*. But, since *ayn*, or "spiritual nonexistence," still illuminates this level, it is clear in *Bria* that created existence is not true and real.

Essay on Service of the Heart - Love Like Fire and Water

Those of us who do not fool ourselves and are not too mistaken about ourselves understand well the truth of the matter. [We understand] how our principal negative character traits (those which we have not yet rectified, as mentioned earlier) remain inside of us at full strength without any change. We acknowledge that our *avoda* has not had any effect upon us. And in order to fulfill the supernal intention, for which our soul descended into this world—that being to purify our natural character traits, as described earlier regarding the imperative of doing *avoda* in this world (and all the more so, not to destroy our mission, G-d forbid, by making our natural traits even stronger)—we must agree in our heart to dedicate a fixed hour and proper amount of time to the exercise of prayer. We must resolve to do this *avoda* with effort, meditating on one of the G-dly concepts mentioned earlier or similar ones. Our meditation must be specific and detailed. (It is understood that we must

וּמִי שֶׁאֵינוֹ מַטְעֶה וּמְרַמֶּה כָּל כָּךְ יֵדַע הֵיטֵב אֲמִתִּית הַדָּבָר אֵיךְ שֶׁעִקְרֵי הַמִּדּוֹת הָרָעוֹת שֶׁלּוֹ (הַיְנוּ אוֹתָן שֶׁלֹּא נִתְבָּרְרוּ עֲדַיִן כנ"ל) הֵן אֶצְלוֹ בְּתָקְפָּם בְּלִי שׁוּם שִׁנּוּי וְלֹא פָּעַל שׁוּם דָּבָר בַּעֲבוֹדָתוֹ הנ"ל, וּבִכְדֵי לְהַשְׁלִים הַכַּוָּנָה הָעֶלְיוֹנָה שֶׁבִּשְׁבִיל זֶה יָרְדָה נִשְׁמָתוֹ לְמַטָּה, דְּהַיְנוּ לְבָרֵר הַמִּדּוֹת טִבְעִיִּים הַמַּגִּיעִים לְחֶלְקוֹ, כְּמוֹ שֶׁנִּתְבָּאֵר לְעֵיל בְּעִנְיַן הֶכְרֵחַ עֲבוֹדַת הָאָדָם לְמַטָּה (וּמִכָּל שֶׁכֵּן שֶׁלֹּא לִשְׁחִיתָהּ חַס וְחָלִילָה בְּהִתְגַּבְּרוּת הַמִּדּוֹת טִבְעִיּוֹת), יְנַדְּבוּ לִבּוֹ לִתֵּן עֵת וּזְמַן נָכוֹן לַעֲסֹק הַתְּפִלָּה, וְיִתְגַּבֵּר עַל עַצְמוֹ לַעֲבֹד בַּעֲבוֹדָה וִיגִיעָה בְּהִתְבּוֹנְנוּת בְּאֵיזֶה עִנְיָן אֱלֹקִי בָּעִנְיָנִים שֶׁנִּתְבָּאֲרוּ לְעֵיל וְכַיּוֹצֵא בָּהֶם בְּהִתְבּוֹנְנוּת פְּרָטִית דַּוְקָא (וְכַמּוּבָן שֶׁצָּרִיךְ לֵידַע אֶת הָעִנְיָנִים הֵיטֵב וּבְהִתְבּוֹנְנוּת מִתְקָרְבִים אֵלָיו יוֹתֵר) וּבְכַמָּה פְּעָמִים שֶׁמִּתְבּוֹנֵן בְּאֵיזֶה עִנְיָן מִתְבָּרֵר אֶצְלוֹ הָעִנְיָן יוֹתֵר (עס ווערט אִיהם אַלְץ

In order to avoid fooling ourselves, we need to dedicate a fixed hour and appropriate amount of time to prayer and detailed meditation.

COMMENTARY

Rather, the spiritual nonexistence that creates the World of *Bria* is the true and real existence. The very awareness of this brings the creations of the world of *Briah* to nullification [as, for example, the category of animal, whose body is subjugated to its soul, to the extent that its existence is its soul, or like intellect, which strives upward toward that which is beyond it and in so doing transcends its own existence]. The creations of the World of *Bria* are comparable to simple substance, which has no form (shape, character or color). The creations of the World

As we meditate, spiritual concepts will become clearer to us and permeate us — we will become aroused with true love for G-d in our hearts.

קלערער דער עִנְיָן) וּמִתְעַצֵּם אֶצְלוֹ (עס ווערט פאראייניגט מיט איהם) וְיִתְעוֹרֵר בְּהִתְעוֹרְרוּת אַהֲבָה בֶּאֱמֶת (וּכְבָר נִתְ' בְּקוּנְטְרֵס עֵץ הַחַיִּים אֵיךְ שֶׁקָּרוֹב הַדָּבָר מְאֹד לְכָל אֶחָד וְאֶחָד) וּבָזֶה יְקַיֵּם מִצְוַת הָאַהֲבָה וְיַשְׁלִים הַכַּוָּנָה הָעֶלְיוֹנָה בְּבֵרוּר וְזִכּוּךְ הַמִּדּוֹת טִבְעִיִּים (בָּאוֹפַנִּים שֶׁנִּתְבָּאֲרוּ לְעֵיל פ"ד) וּבָזֶה יִחְיֶ' חַיֵּי עוֹלָם בְּעֵסֶק הַתּוֹרָה וּמִצְוֹת כו':

know the subjects well, and then in meditation they [the subjects] will become closer to us.) Then every time we meditate on a particular topic, it will become clearer to us and permeate us. We will become aroused with a true love. (It was already explained in *Kuntres Eitz Chaim* how this *avoda* is truly close to everyone.) In so doing, we will fulfill the *mitzvah* of love of G-d and also fulfill the supreme intention of purifying and refining our own natural character traits (in the ways described in Chapter 4). At the same time, we will gain *chayei olam* ("everlasting life of the spirit") with involvement in Torah and *mitzvot*.

COMMENTARY

of *Yetzira*, possess a general [archetypal, non-specific] form, and those of *Asiya* take on a specific, particular form. [For example, in the vegetable and mineral kingdoms is felt the "bodily" character of the creation, as mentioned above. The nature of the vegetable body is not to be nullified to its bodily life-force. This is true of letters and emotions, which indicate and respond to the "other" — meaning that their existence is felt in relation to the "other"]. Even the "simple substance" of the World of *Bria* takes on "existence" and its simplicity is only that of "existence" — "simple substance." In this, it is similar to the intellect, which, as refined and abstract as it may be, remains the intellect.

Diametrically opposed to this, is the World of *Atzilut*, which is totally G-dly and spiritual, completely transcending the realm of created existence. It is the world of *ayn*, or spiritual nonexistence.

Corresponding to the four worlds of *Atzilut*, *Bria*, *Yetzira*, and *Asiya* (including the spiritual dimension of *Asiya*), which are spiritual and nevertheless bear similarities to the four categories of created existence (mineral, vegetable, animal, and human), are the four letters of the Holy Name of the One Above. The four

Essay on Service of the Heart - Love Like Fire and Water

SYNOPSIS:

Even *avoda* [of the One Above) based upon logic and reason may be superficial. This happens when we are satisfied with a general meditation [without attention to details]. Even though we may become excited and worked up (usually with bitterness and sadness), the excitement is only imaginary. It leaves no impression and does not affect our natural character traits whatsoever. They remain at full strength, [even though] our

קִצוּר

וְהִנֵּה הָעֲבוֹדָה שֶׁעַל פִּי טַעַם וְדַעַת יֵשׁ גַּם כֵּן שֶׁהָעֲבוֹדָה הִיא בִּבְחִינַת מַקִּיף לְבַד, וְהוּא כְּשֶׁהַהִתְבּוֹנְנוּת הִיא רַק בִּכְלָלוּת הָעִנְיָן דְּעִם הֱיוֹת שֶׁמִּתְפַּעֵל וּמִתְלַהֵב (וְעַל פִּי הָרֹב הוּא בִּבְחִינַת מְרִירוּת וְעַצְבוּת) הוּא רַק הִתְפַּעֲלוּת דִּמְיוֹנִי, וְאֵינוֹ מִזֶּה שׁוּם רֹשֶׁם וְאֵינוֹ פּוֹעֵל כְּלָל עַל הַמִּדוֹת טִבְעִיִּים שֶׁהֵן אֶצְלוֹ בְּחֹזֶק שֶׁזֶּה חֶלְקוֹ וְעִנְיָנוֹ בָּעוֹלָם לְבָרְרָם

COMMENTARY
---

letters of His Name are the transcendent source and origin of all of creation. They are comparable (on a far higher, "out of range" plane) to the four categories of creation which are indeed influenced by them after a tremendous amount of contraction and descent of His holy, infinite light. From this, it is understood that the four letters of G-d's Name (including the *yud*) do not yet constitute the highest expression of infinite abstract spirituality, because they have some relationship to the lower categories of physical creation.

Now we can begin to understand the special nature of Torah, which was given in "five voices." This tells us that with Torah there is a fifth level, beyond the four "possible" levels discussed above. It is the true abstract and spiritual infinity which is the essence of the Torah, as it is united with the infinite light of the One Above, may He be blessed. That is, as well, the explanation of the connection between a bridegroom and Torah, such that both are connected with the same number of "five voices." A bridegroom also expresses a fifth power — the power of giving birth (the commandment of "be fruitful and multiply" is the purpose of marriage) — connected with a higher and more abstract level than the "existence" of the four categories of creation mentioned above.

life's mission is to purify and refine them. If we desire life of the soul and to fulfill the supernal intention from above, we must perform *avoda* of prayer with detailed meditation, as explained in detail. The meditation must take place with deep concentration, through which we will become aroused to true love of G-d. In so doing, we will fulfill the supernal intention, which is (1) purification and refinement of the animal soul, and (2) the fulfillment of the *mitzvot* of the Torah.

וּלְזַכְּכָם, וְהֶחָפֵץ בְּחַיֵּי נַפְשׁוֹ וּלְהַשְׁלִים הַכַּוָּנָה הָעֶלְיוֹנָה בְּהֶכְרַח לַעֲבֹד בַּעֲבוֹדָה וִיגִיעָה בַּתְּפִלָּה בְּהִתְבּוֹנְנוּת בִּבְחִינַת פְּרָטִיּוּת דַּוְקָא (וְנִתְ' אֵיזֶה עִנְיְנֵי הִתְבּוֹנְנוּת בִּבְחִינַת פְּרָטִיּוּת) וּבְהַעֲמָקַת הַדַּעַת שֶׁעַל יְדֵי זֶה דַּוְקָא יִתְעוֹרֵר בְּאַהֲבָה בֶּאֱמֶת וְעַל יְדֵי זֶה יַשְׁלִים הַכַּוָּנָה הָעֶלְיוֹנָה בְּבֵרוּר וְזִכּוּךְ הַנֶּפֶשׁ הַבַּהֲמִית וּבְקִיּוּם הַתּוֹרָה וְהַמִּצְוֹת כוּ'.

COMMENTARY

Despite the tremendous elevation, essence, and abstract simplicity of Torah, which transcends the four letters of G-d's Name, it was nonetheless, given with five voices. That means that the Torah was given with the four aspects of His Divine Name, and with a fifth highest aspect that accompanied the four. That is the meaning of the Torah being given with five general levels. The reason is the following: The four levels of the Torah associated with His exalted and Holy Name correspond to and arouse the four spiritual levels in man: *Nefesh* (enlivening soul), *ruach* (emotional dimension), *neshama* (intellect), and *chaya* (will). Simultaneously, the essence of the Torah has the power to arouse the *yechida* of the soul — the level in man that is connected to the *Yachid*, the One Above. That's why all five voices of the Torah were given together; He wanted all four "lower levels" of the soul to be illuminated and permeated with the highest level, the *yechida*. He wanted the very existence of man to be permeated with the power to turn the world (which consists of mineral, vegetable, animal, and human) into a dwelling place for the One Above, in all of His holy essence.

Essay on Service of the Heart - Love Like Fire and Water

CHAPTER 7 — פרק ז

There is another phenomenon (resulting from superficial *avoda*), and it occurs when we adopt refined and elevated behavior when, in truth, we have not refined [or elevated] any detail [of our personality] at all. We demand of ourselves all that is admirable and lofty, desiring, for example, to be on high spiritual rungs of *avoda*. We want to take on new levels of carefulness and stringency and to fulfill the *mitzvot* with added elaboration. (In this particular detail, we will indeed embellish the *mitzvot* in any number of ways, because embellishment of the positive *mitzvot* is far easier than being careful not to transgress the negative *mitzvot*.) However, we are unable to control ourselves when it comes to actual situations, and in particular, when our natural character traits are involved. This is because our animal soul [still dominates, though it] does not completely hide and conceal our divine soul, and our divine soul is a little bit revealed.

וְהִנֵּה יֵשׁ עוֹד צִיּוּר בָּזֶה (שֶׁהוּא גַּם כֵּן תּוֹלֶדֶת הָעֲבוֹדָה בִּבְחִינַת כְּלָלוּת) וְהוּא שֶׁנִּרְאֶה בּוֹ דַקּוּת וְעִנְיָנִים נַעֲלִים. וּבֶאֱמֶת אֵינוֹ מְזֻכָּךְ בְּשׁוּם פְּרָט וַהֲיִנוּ שֶׁרוֹצֶה וְתוֹבֵעַ מֵעַצְמוֹ כָּל דָּבָר טוֹב וְנַעֲלֶה וּכְמוֹ שֶׁרוֹצֶה לִהְיוֹת דַּוְקָא בְּמַדְרֵגוֹת גְּבוֹהוֹת בָּעֲבוֹדָה, וּלְדַקְדֵּק בְּכַמָּה זְהִירוּת וְחֻמְרוֹת וּלְהַדֵּר בְּכַמָּה הִדּוּרֵי מִצְוָה (וּבִפְרָט זֶה יַעֲשֶׂה כֵּן בֶּאֱמֶת וִיהַדֵּר בְּכַמָּה עִנְיָנִים, כִּי הַהִדּוּר בַּעֲשֵׂה טוֹב בְּנָקֵל בְּאֵין עֲרוֹךְ מֵהַזְּהִירוּת בְּסוּר מֵרָע) וּלְהֵפֶךְ לֹא יוּכַל לַעֲמוֹד עַל נַפְשׁוֹ כְּלָל בְּאֵיזֶה עִנְיָן לַפֹּעַל, וּבִפְרָט בְּעִקְּרֵי הַמִּדּוֹת טִבְעִיִּים שֶׁלּוֹ, וְזֶהוּ מִפְּנֵי שֶׁהַנֶּפֶשׁ הַבַּהֲמִית אֵינוֹ מַעֲלִים וּמַסְתִּיר אֶצְלוֹ כָּל כָּךְ עַל הַנֶּפֶשׁ הָאֱלֹקִית וְעוֹמֵד הַנֶּפֶשׁ הָאֱלֹקִית בִּקְצָת הִתְגַּלּוּת.

Another result of superficial meditation; we may adopt refined behavior that is out of touch with our real spiritual level.

COMMENTARY

CHAPTER 7: SPIRITUAL HONESTY

Chapter 7 of *Kuntres Ha'Avoda* describes one more phenomenon that may occur to us when we meditate in only a perfunctory, superficial fashion, contemplating G-dly topics only enough to barely awaken and reveal our divine soul. By doing so, we catch a glimpse of the highest spiritual rungs and naturally want to ascend there. But we haven't done any work on our animal soul to refine and purify it, and therefore any behavior that reflects a high spiritual level on our part isn't real. We may adopt embellishments of the *mitzvot* and stringencies in *halacha*,

This may be from birth or we may have slightly revealed our G-dly soul through loud prayer.

(אִם שֶׁזֶּהוּ אֶצְלוֹ כָּךְ מִתּוֹלַדְתּוֹ אוֹ שֶׁהֵבִיא אֶת הַנֶּפֶשׁ הָאֱלֹקִית לִידֵי הִתְגַּלּוּת עַל יְדֵי כַּמָּה פְּעָמִים בַּעֲבוֹדָה בְּהִתְגַּלּוּת נַפְשׁוֹ בְּהִתְפַּעֲלוּת וָרַעַשׁ, דְּעִם הֱיוֹת שֶׁהִיא הִתְפַּעֲלוּת חִיצוֹנִית (וְהַסִּימָן עַל זֶה שֶׁבָּאָה בִּצְעָקוֹת וְגַם בִּתְנוּעוֹת חִיצוֹנִיּוֹת כוּ') מִכָּל מָקוֹם הֲרֵי זֶה פּוֹעֵל קְצָת הִתְגַּלּוּת הַנֶּפֶשׁ הָאֱלֹקִית (רְצוֹנוֹ לוֹמַר כְּמוֹ שֶׁאָמַרְנוּ קְצָת הִתְגַּלּוּת שֶׁהִיא הִתְגַּלּוּת הֶאָרָה חִיצוֹנִית לְבַד מֵהַנֶּפֶשׁ הָאֱלֹקִית לֹא הִתְגַּלּוּת הַכֹּחוֹת פְּנִימִיִּים שֶׁלּוֹ שֶׁהֵן שֵׂכֶל וּמִדּוֹת) וְגַם בִּטּוּל כְּלָלִי בְּהַנֶּפֶשׁ הַבַּהֲמִית שֶׁאֵינוֹ מַעֲלִים וּמְכַסֶּה כָּל כָּךְ

This may be the case from birth or we may have caused our divine soul to be revealed on several occasions with loud praying in a state of high excitement, which brought us in touch with the divine manifestation of our soul. Although it is true that this is a superficial excitement (the proof of which is the accompaniment of shouting and exaggerated movements), nevertheless such behavior does produce some revelation of our divine soul, even if only a little. ("Some revelation" means here a lone ray of the divine soul, as opposed to full disclosure of the inner powers of the soul, [including] its intellect and emotions.) It [such behavior] also produces an overall nullification of the animal soul, such that it doesn't conceal [the divine soul] so much.

(שֶׁזֶּהוּ עַל יְדֵי הִתְגַּלּוּת הַהֶאָרָה חִיצוֹנִית דְּנֶפֶשׁ הָאֱלֹקִית וְגַם עַל יְדֵי הַבִּטּוּל חִיצוֹנִי בְּחָמְרִיּוּת הַגּוּף וְנֶפֶשׁ הַבַּהֲמִית בְּהַצְּעָקוֹת וּתְנוּעוֹת חִיצוֹנִיּוֹת שֶׁמְּבַטֵּל עַצְמוֹ וְכָל מַה שֶּׁסְּבִיבוֹ, שֶׁכָּל זֶה פּוֹעֵל עַל הַבִּטּוּל

This is a result of the revelation of the ray of our divine soul—and also of the superficial nullification of the natural earthiness of our body and of our animal soul—which takes place with shouts and exaggerated movements, nullifying our ego and all that

--- **COMMENTARY** ---

but when we are tested from above, we are unable to withstand the temptations of our animal soul and our physical inclinations.

In such a situation, our problem is twofold, says the *Kuntres Ha'Avoda*. Number one: There is no connection between our barely awakened divine soul and our animal soul. The result is that, although we might find ourselves spiritually higher, there is no effect upon our animal soul, and therefore we have not changed fundamentally. Number two: We are striving for a level far beyond what is realistic and honest for ourselves, and therefore

is in our environment. All of this produces an overall nullification of our animal soul, [but this] is only external. It is not comparable to the nullification of earthiness in general, which is produced by bitterness [of the soul over our distance from G-d], involving an actual shattering of the physicality that causes its complete nullification.

כְּלָלֵי דְּנֶפֶשׁ הַבַּהֲמִית שֶׁזֶּהוּ גַּם כֵּן רַק בִּטּוּל חִיצוֹנִי. וְאֵין זֶה כְּמוֹ בִּטּוּל הַחָמְרִיּוּת בִּכְלָל הַנַּעֲשֶׂה עַל יְדֵי הַמְּרִירוּת שֶׁהוּא עִנְיַן שְׁבִירַת הַחָמְרִיּוּת שֶׁהַחֹמֶר מִתְבַּטֵּל בָּזֶה,

The external nullification described here does not produce a state in which the physical dimension is shattered and eradicated in and of itself. Rather, this is similar to what is described in the *Tanya*, chapter 13, regarding the level of the *beinoni* ("intermediate person") in which the animal soul is "sleeping," so to speak, but can awaken and be roused from its sleep. It is similarly possible to describe the external nullification of the animal soul, mentioned earlier. Since the divine soul is somewhat revealed, in response to it, we desire everything G-dly and demand of ourselves all that is positive and elevated. However, our animal soul has not achieved any elevation whatsoever, and when it comes to a test of our negative character traits, we are unable to control ourselves.

אֲבָל בְּעִנְיָן הַנַּ"ל אֵין זֶה שֶׁנִּשְׁבָּר וּמִתְבַּטֵּל בְּעַצְמוֹ, וַהֲרֵי זֶה בְּדֻגְמַת מַה שֶׁכָּתוּב בְּסֵפֶר שֶׁל בֵּינוֹנִים פי"ג בְּמַדְרֵגַת הַבֵּינוֹנִים שֶׁהַנֶּפֶשׁ הַבַּהֲמִית הוּא כְּיָשֵׁן שֶׁיָּכֹל לַחֲזֹר וּלְהִתְעוֹרֵר מִשְּׁנָתוֹ כֵּן הוּא בְּעִנְיָן הַנַּ"ל בִּכְלָלוּת הַחָמְרִיּוּת דְּנֶפֶשׁ הַבַּהֲמִית) וְלִהְיוֹת דְּהַנֶּפֶשׁ הָאֱלֹקִית הוּא בְּהִתְגַּלּוּת קְצָת) לָכֵן מִצַּד הַנֶּפֶשׁ הָאֱלֹקִית הוּא רוֹצֶה הַכֹּל וְתוֹבֵעַ מֵעַצְמוֹ כָּל דָּבָר טוֹב וְנַעֲלֶה, וּמִצַּד הַנֶּפֶשׁ הַבַּהֲמִית אֵינוֹ שַׁיָּךְ עֲדַיִן לְשׁוּם דָּבָר, וּכְשֶׁבָּא לְאֵיזֶה דָּבָר מֵהַמִּדּוֹת רָעוֹת דְּנֶפֶשׁ הַבַּהֲמִית אֵינוֹ יָכֹל לַעֲמֹד עַל נַפְשׁוֹ כוּ'.

Since our divine soul is slightly revealed, we desire everything that is G-dly, positive and elevated.

COMMENTARY
---

we have no orderly personal approach to spiritual growth.

The solution is that we must look deeply and honestly within ourselves, in order to find the level of approach that is real. We must be honest about what spiritual rung we are holding onto, and where we want to — and can — go. Only then will we make our spiritual effort part of our basic behavior.

There's another crucial piece of advice for anyone who would undertake to approach the One Above in *avoda*: Find a *mashpia*.

In the state described above, there are two drawbacks. One is that there is no link between our divine soul and our animal soul. The excitement of our divine soul has no effect whatsoever upon our animal soul. The second drawback is that we want everything. We go beyond our own spiritual level, [to a level] that is not real for us and there is no order at all in our *avoda*, as will be explained soon. The reason for both of these drawbacks is that our *avoda* is only superficial. It is based solely upon a casual, overall grasp of G-dliness. (Without even the general meditation mentioned in Chapter 6, wherein we at least contemplate a concept in a passing way; here, the whole approach lacks meditation, and involves only superficial knowledge of the general concept of G-dliness.)

וְהִנֵּה בְּאֹפֶן הַזֶּה יֵשׁ ב' מִינֵי גֵּרָעוֹן, הָא' שֶׁאֵין הִתְחַבְּרוּת דְּנֶפֶשׁ הָאֱלֹקִית עִם הַנֶּפֶשׁ הַבַּהֲמִית דְּהַהִתְפַּעֲלוּת דְּנֶפֶשׁ הָאֱלֹקִית אֵינוֹ פּוֹעֵל מְאוּמָה עַל הַנֶּפֶשׁ הַבַּהֲמִית. וְהַב' מַה שֶּׁרוֹצֶה הַכֹּל וְהוֹלֵךְ לְעֵילָא מִדַּרְגֵּי' שֶׁאֵין זֶה אֱמֶת, וְאֵין שׁוּם סֵדֶר בַּעֲבוֹדָתוֹ וּכְמוֹ שֶׁיִּתְבָּאֵר בְּסָמוּךְ, וְסִבַּת שְׁנֵיהֶם הוּא הָעֲבוֹדָה בִּבְחִינַת מַקִּיף לְבַד הַבָּאָה מִצַּד הַיְדִיעָה כְּלָלִית דֶּאֱלֹקוּת (גַּם לֹא בִּבְחִינַת הִתְבּוֹנְנוּת כְּלָלִית שֶׁנִּתְבָּאֵר לְעֵיל פ"ו דְּעַל כָּל פָּנִים הוּא חוֹשֵׁב וּמִתְבּוֹנֵן בְּאֵיזֶה עִנְיָן בִּכְלָלִיּוּתוֹ, וְכַאן אֵינוֹ בְּדֶרֶךְ הִתְבּוֹנְנוּת כְּלָל כִּי אִם רַק בְּדֶרֶךְ יְדִיעָה בִּבְחִינַת מַקִּיף בִּכְלָלוּת עִנְיָן הָאֱלֹקוּת).

However, our animal soul has not been elevated at all, and when it comes to a test, we are unable to control ourselves.

Therefore, whatever excitement is generated has no connection whatsoever with our animal soul and is unable to produce any nullification of it (as explained in Chapter 6 and even more so here, since the *avoda* is

וְעַל כֵּן אֵין לְהִתְפַּעֲלוּת שַׁיָּכוּת כְּלָל לְנֶפֶשׁ הַבַּהֲמִית לִפְעֹל בּוֹ הַבִּטּוּל (וּכְמוֹ שֶׁנִּתְבָּאֵר לְעֵיל פ"ו וְכַאן הוּא בְּיוֹתֵר לְפִי שֶׁהוּא יוֹתֵר בִּבְחִינַת מַקִּיף עַצְמוֹ. וְעִם הֱיוֹת שֶׁאֵין זֶה

─────────── COMMENTARY ───────────

A *mashpia* is a Chassidic mentor who has already been or knows how to go to the spiritual places that we want to go. He is acquainted with the nuances and subtleties of the spiritual search, and can help others get to where they want to go. However, that means hard work: One, to take on the guidance of the *mashpia*, and two, to devote time and effort to meditation. A *mashpia* is hard to come by these days; the true *ovdim* of yesteryear were decimated by the Holocaust and our orphan generation has

Essay on Service of the Heart - Love Like Fire and Water

even more superficial; although here we are not dealing with the actual transcendent levels of the soul [that are not en-clothed in the body], nevertheless the state described above is more transcendent than that produced by a general meditation). Those of us who practice this *avoda* detach our divine soul from our animal soul and demonstrate our excitement with a lot of noise. [But] this isn't the tumult of the animal soul being nullified, as when the *ofanim* [lower angels, corresponding to the animal soul], "make a great [spiritual] noise." (See *Likutei Torah*, in the third discourse of *Parshat Ha'azinu*, and in *Ani Hashem Elokeichem* in the first discourse.) Neither is it the noise of involvement in *avoda*[xliv] according to logic and reason, which is [accompanied by] feeling of the self, as hinted at in the verse [from 1 Kings 19:11]: "...and after the wind, there was noise...", as explained elsewhere.[42] Rather, this is detachment of the divine soul, exiting [the animal soul] with superficial noise and excitement,

בִּבְחִינַת מַקִּיפִים מַמָּשׁ שֶׁבַּנֶּפֶשׁ, מִכָּל מָקוֹם הֲרֵי זֶה בִּבְחִינַת הַמַּקִּיף עַצְמוֹ יוֹתֵר מֵהַהִתְבּוֹנְנוּת בִּבְחִינַת כְּלָלוּת) וּבִפְרָט שֶׁבָּאֹפֶן עֲבוֹדָה הַזֹּאת הוּא מוֹצִיא אֶת הַנֶּפֶשׁ הָאֱלֹקִית מִן הַנֶּפֶשׁ הַבַּהֲמִית (עֶר רייסט אויס דעם נֶפֶשׁ הָאֱלֹקִית וּכְמוֹ בּוֹרֵחַ כו') וּמִתְפַּעֵל בְּרַעַשׁ גָּדוֹל (וְאֵין זֶה הָרַעַשׁ דְּבִטּוּל הַנֶּפֶשׁ הַבַּהֲמִית, וּכְמוֹ וְהָאוֹפַנִּים כו' בְּרַעַשׁ גָּדוֹל דְּבִדוּגְמָא בְּנֶפֶשׁ הָאָדָם הוּא הָרַעַשׁ דְּנֶפֶשׁ הַבַּהֲמִית כְּמוֹ שֶׁכָּתוּב בְּלִקּוּטֵי תּוֹרָה דִּבּוּר הַמַּתְחִיל הַאֲזִינוּ דְּרוּשׁ הַגָּדוֹל וּבְדִבּוּר הַמַּתְחִיל אֲנִי ה' אֱלֹקֵיכֶם דְּרוּשׁ הָרִאשׁוֹן, וְלֹא הָרַעַשׁ בְּמַרְגָּשׁ שֶׁבַּעֲבוֹדָה שֶׁעַל פִּי טַעַם וְדַעַת שֶׁהוּא עִנְיַן וְאַחֲרֵי הָרוּחַ רַעַשׁ כו. כְּמוֹ שֶׁכָּתוּב בְּמָקוֹם אַחֵר, רַק הוּא הַיְצִיאָה דְּנֶפֶשׁ הָאֱלֹקִית הַנַּ"ל שֶׁיּוֹצֵא בְּרַעַשׁ וְהִתְפַּעֲלוּת חִיצוֹנִי כו') וַהֲרֵי הוּא מִסְתַּפֵּק לְגַמְרֵי בִּיצִיאָה וְהִתְפַּעֲלוּת זֹאת, וַהֲרֵי הֵן מֵאֹפֶן הַהִתְפַּעֲלוּת מִצַּד עַצְמָהּ וְהֵן

Our divine soul is detached from our animal soul, and we demonstrate this with much noise and superficial excitement.

xliv) See footnote of the Rebbe on page 301 ←

COMMENTARY

yet to replace them with true mentors. However, like everything else in Torah, "If you search for it like silver and gold..."

Finally, the *Kuntres Ha'Avoda* tells us that the beginning of our *avoda* — our "service of the heart" — should not be focused on the highest levels of spirituality, as manifested by transcendent G-dliness. Rather, we should concentrate on G-dliness that is en-clothed in the creation enlivening it — that is, on immanent G-dliness. When we contemplate G-dliness as en-clothed in

as described earlier. And we are satisfied completely with this detachment [of the divine soul] and [its accompanying] excitement. Whether regarding the nature of the excitement itself or regarding the nature of the *avoda* [that produced it], there is no connection whatsoever with the animal soul. Whatever overall nullification of the animal soul takes place is because there is a revelation of a ray from the divine soul, which in turn produces an overall nullification of the animal soul, as mentioned earlier. Even an external nullification has an effect upon the animal soul, as mentioned, but the nullification is surface-deep (in addition, it only repels the animal soul, but doesn't shatter it). This transcendent soul excitement is what motivates us to demand everything of ourselves [that is, all that is admirable and lofty, and as a result], we go beyond our [own real] level. In general, [this means] there is no order in our *avoda* of the One Above.

מֵאֹפֶן הָעֲבוֹדָה, אֵין לָזֶה שׁוּם שַׁיָּכוּת אֶל הַנֶּפֶשׁ הַבַּהֲמִית, וְהַבִּטּוּל הַכְּלָלִי שֶׁנַּעֲשָׂה עַל כָּל פָּנִים בַּנֶּפֶשׁ הַבַּהֲמִית כנ"ל, הוּא מִפְּנֵי שֶׁמִּכָּל מָקוֹם הִתְגַּלּוּת הֶהָאָרָה דְּנֶפֶשׁ הָאֱלֹקִית פּוֹעֵל עַל הַבִּטּוּל כְּלָלִי דְּנֶפֶשׁ הַבַּהֲמִית. וְגַם הַבִּטּוּל חִיצוֹנִי פּוֹעֵל עָלָיו כנ"ל, אֲבָל הוּא בִּטּוּל כְּלָלִי לְבַד (וְגַם זֹאת לֹא בְּדֶרֶךְ שְׁבִירָה רַק בְּדֶרֶךְ דְּחִיָּ' לְבַד וכנ"ל) וְהַהִתְפַּעֲלוּת בִּבְחִינַת מַקִּיף עַצְמוֹ הִיא גַּם כֵּן הַסִּבָּה מַה שֶּׁרוֹצֶה וְתוֹבֵעַ מֵעַצְמוֹ כָּל דָּבָר וְהוֹלֵךְ לְעֵילָא מִדַּרְגֵּי' וּבְדֶרֶךְ כְּלָל שֶׁאֵין שׁוּם סֵדֶר בַּעֲבוֹדָתוֹ.

We must know our true level of avoda and what to demand from ourselves.

In truth, we must know within ourselves our level of *avoda* of the One Above; we should know what it is that we should demand of ourselves. (It is understood that here, we're not referring to the basic requirements of "doing good" [positive *mitzvot*] and "avoiding bad" [neg-

דְּהִנֵּה לְפִי הָאֱמֶת צָרִיךְ הָאָדָם לֵידַע בְּעַצְמוֹ לְפִי מַדְרֵגָתוֹ בַּעֲבוֹדָה בַּמֶּה יִרְצֶה וּמַה יִּתְבַּע מֵעַצְמוֹ (וּמוּבָן שֶׁאֵין הַכַּוָּנָה בְּעִנְיָנִים עִקָּרִיִּים דְּסוּר מֵרָע וַעֲשֵׂה טוֹב וּכְמוֹ שֶׁכָּתוּב בְּמָקוֹם אַחֵר דִּבְקִיּוּם הַמִּצְוֹת שָׁוִים כָּל יִשְׂרָאֵל בְּלִי שׁוּם חִלּוּק וְהֶפְרֵשׁ

———————— **COMMENTARY** ————————

the worlds and enlivening them, we can proceed in an orderly, step-by-step fashion in understanding G-dly concepts and spiritual growth. We should apply ourselves with concentration, persistence, and diligence, and we will surely succeed in revealing the storehouse of spirituality inside ourselves that leads to love of G-d.

ative *mitzvot*]. As written elsewhere, in regard to observing the commandments, all Jews are equal, without any distinction or differentiation whatsoever. Here, the intent is that those who are beginning *avoda* must be strict with themselves—this, in truth is obligatory for each and every Jew, because, as is explained in Chapter 6, the purpose of the descent to this world is to serve G-d. We must make ourselves "holy" [proceed beyond the "letter of the law"], whether in matters of "avoiding bad" or of "doing good." (Included within this are various rabbinical enactments that serve as "fences" [to prevent transgression of Biblical commandments]. Here we say "various" [and not "all"], because while many such enactments apply equally to all Jews, others are pertinent only to "servants of G-d"—to those who have chosen to be especially diligent in their *avoda* of the One Above. And among the enactments that pertain to "servants of G-d," there are variations, as stated [Psalms 50:3, regarding G-d]: "There is a mighty tempest around Him" [which suggests that the higher our level, the more precise and careful we must become]. Included within this are also admonitions regarding ethical behavior within the *Agada* of the Talmud and "Ethics of the Fathers," and various ways of "beautifying" the *mitzvot*.) This is because all of the above constitutes the main path to refinement and rectification, which is the ultimate purpose of *avoda*.

Then there is also the reason explained in *Likutei Torah*, in the discourse *V'shama aviha et nidra*. In these matters, we must know what to demand from ourselves. We shouldn't demand everything from ourselves.

Those who are just beginning in avoda should be strict with themselves.

If nothing about avoda concerns us, we're in a bad spiritual state, and so if everything concerns us, it is also not good.

ourselves. Those of us who care about nothing are in a very worrisome situation. (Regarding positive *mitzvot*, we evince no appreciation of the preciousness and spiritual value of any *mitzvah*, but rather we fulfill the *mitzvah* perfunctorily, "Like a man who does things by rote" [Isaiah 29:13], that is, in a cold manner. There is no energy in our performance, and we certainly don't seek to embellish and "beautify" the *mitzvah*. Regarding the negative commandments, we don't care and it doesn't concern us to look closely—for example, to see if something is definitely kosher. We prefer to rely upon assumptions. It doesn't bother us, and we don't care, so we won't trouble ourselves to get to the truth. Worse, we are not overly strict in the various matters mentioned above, with which a "servant [of G-d]"—the one who truly wants to get close to G-d—should be strict.) Likewise, it isn't good when everything matters to us, as will be explained.

דְאַרְף אַרִין,) כְּשֵׁם שֶׁגָּרוּעַ מְאֹד כַּאֲשֶׁר שׁוּם דָּבָר לֹא אִכְפַּת לוֹ (בְּוַעֲשֵׂה טוֹב הוּא שֶׁאֵין לוֹ שׁוּם יֹקֶר וַחֲבִיבוּת בְּאֵיזֶה דָּבָר (אַז עֶס זָאל אַרִין אוּן מֶעֶנֶען דִי זַאךְ) וְעוֹשֶׂה רַק כְּמִצְוַת אֲנָשִׁים מְלֻמָּדָה בִּקְרִירוּת בְּלִי שׁוּם חַיּוּת בַּדָּבָר וּמִכָּל שֶׁכֵּן שֶׁאֵינוֹ מְהַדֵּר בָּהּ, וּבְסוּר מֵרַע הוּא שֶׁלֹּא אִכְפַּת לוֹ לְעַיֵּן וּלְדַיֵּק בְּאֵיזֶה דָּבָר אִם הוּא בֶּאֱמֶת בְּתַכְלִית הַכַּשְׁרוּת עַל דֶּרֶךְ מָשָׁל רַק סוֹמֵךְ עַל הַסְּתָם, (עֶס רִירְט אִיהֶם נִיט אָן דִי זַאךְ אוּן עֶס אַרְט אִיהֶם נִיט עֶר זָאל נאכזוכן דֶעם אֲמִתִּית הַדָּבָר) וּמִכָּל שֶׁכֵּן שֶׁאֵינוֹ מַחְמִיר עַל עַצְמוֹ בְּאֵיזֶה עִנְיָנִים כנ״ל שֶׁהָעוֹבֵד צָרִיךְ לְהַחְמִיר עַל עַצְמוֹ כו'), כְּמוֹ כֵן לֹא טוֹב כַּאֲשֶׁר כָּל דָּבָר אִכְפַּת לוֹ (אַז אַלְץ אַרְט) וּכְמוֹ שֶׁיִּתְבָּאֵר.

In the beginning, we must be concerned about that which is especially important (within the framework of extra stringency and caution [not actual sins], as noted above). When we have accepted the new level of stringency, then we may take on other items of strictness. So it is with true *avoda*. When we pray with proper diligence and intention of the mind and heart and attain a spiritual level, then matters of strictness in fulfilling the *mitzvot* truly make a difference

דְּהִנֵּה בַּתְּחִלָּה דְאַרְף אַרִין דָּבָר שֶׁהוּא חָמוּר יוֹתֵר (הַכֹּל בְּחֻמְרוֹת וְדִקְדּוּקִים כנ״ל) וְכַאֲשֶׁר פּוֹעֵל בְּעַצְמוֹ הַדָּבָר הַזֶּה הֲרֵי הוּא בָּא אַחַר כָּךְ לְעוֹד עִנְיָן שֶׁהוּא דָּבָר דְּקְדּוּק וְחֻמְרָא יוֹתֵר, וְכֵן הוּא בַּעֲבוֹדָה אֲמִתִּית כַּאֲשֶׁר עוֹבֵד עֲבוֹדָתוֹ בַּעֲבוֹדָה הָרְצוּיָ' וּמְכֻוֶּנֶת בְּמֹחַ וְלֵב, שֶׁהוּא עוֹמֵד בְּאֵיזֶה דַרְגָּא (עֶר הַאלְט עֶפֶּעס בַּיי אַ עִנְיָן), אָז אִכְפַּת לוֹ בֶּאֱמֶת עִנְיְנֵי הַחֻמְרוֹת

Essay on Service of the Heart - Love Like Fire and Water

to us. We then strive to be very precise and to make ourselves holy. We decide what is appropriate, according to our spiritual level, such that we take on those matters that truly concern us. When our diligence in *avoda* is honest, we will not be concerned with a level of strictness or "beautification" of a *mitzvah* that is, as of now, beyond us. But what is on our level will be truly important to us, and this will empower us to go on to a yet higher spiritual level. Besides ascending in the *avoda* itself, we will advance in the level of strictness and "beautification" of *mitzvot*, and all of it will be honest. We will continue with unceasing persistence and will not discontinue at any time. The newfound level of strictness will become very important to us, and we will not deviate from it, G-d forbid, no matter the situations in which we find ourselves. With this *avoda*, we will truly rectify and refine our soul and rise to a very high spiritual level.

But, if everything is important to us, including those things that are far beyond our own spiritual level, then our approach is not honest. Although temporarily we may desire this [particular level of strictness] as a result of our superficial arousal, it isn't real; [there is no real] inner feeling. That is why the arousal is only momentary. As soon as it ends, our desire ceases as well. True *avoda* is like this: although the inner arousal doesn't last

וְהַדִקְדוּקִים וְרוֹצֶה לְדַקְדֵּק בְּעַצְמוֹ וּלְקַדֵּשׁ עַצְמוֹ, וְאָז הוּא מְדַקְדֵּק בְּעַצְמוֹ מַה שֶׁרָאוּי לוֹ לְפִי מַדְרֵגָתוֹ שֶׁהַדָּבָר הַזֶּה אִכְפַּת לוֹ בֶּאֱמֶת (ד"י זא"ך ארט עס טאקע מיט א אמת), וְכַאֲשֶׁר הָעִנְיָן הוּא אֶצְלוֹ בָּאֲמִתִּית לֹא אִכְפַּת לוֹ דָּבָר דְּקִדּוּק וְחֻמְרָה אוֹ הִדּוּר שֶׁלְּעֵילָא מִמַּדְרֵגָתוֹ עֲדַיִן, אֲבָל מַה שֶׁהוּא בְּמַדְרֵגָתוֹ אִכְפַּת לוֹ בֶּאֱמֶת, וַאֲמִתַּת הַדָּבָר הַזֶּה מַכְשִׁירָה אוֹתוֹ לָבוֹא לְעִנְיָן נַעֲלֶה יוֹתֵר, כִּי מִתְעַלֶּה גַּם בְּעֶצֶם עֲבוֹדָתוֹ וּמִתְעַלֶּה בְּעִנְיְנֵי הַדִקְדוּקִים עַל עַצְמוֹ וּבְהִדּוּרִים יוֹתֵר, וְהַכֹּל הוּא בֶּאֱמֶת בְּנַפְשׁוֹ וּבְקִיּוּם שֶׁאֵינוֹ נִפְסָק וְאֵינוֹ מִתְבַּטֵּל בִּזְמַן מֵהַזְּמַנִּים וְהֵמָּה אֶצְלוֹ כְּעִנְיָנִים עִקָּרִיִּים שֶׁלֹּא יַעֲבֹר עֲלֵיהֶם חַס וְחָלִילָה בְּאֵיזֶה מַעֲמָד וּמַצָּב שֶׁיִּהְיֶה, וּבְכָל זֶה מְתַקֵּן וּמְזַדֵּךְ נַפְשׁוֹ בֶּאֱמֶת, וּמִתְעַלֶּה עַל יְדֵי זֶה בְּמַדְרֵגָה גְּבוֹהָה וְנַעֲלֵית כו'.

אֲבָל כַּאֲשֶׁר כָּל דָּבָר אִכְפַּת לוֹ גַּם מַה שֶּׁלְּמַעְלָה מִמַּדְרֵגָתוֹ הֲרֵי זֶה אֵינוֹ אֱמֶת (הֲגַם שֶׁלְּפִי שָׁעָה הוּא רוֹצֶה בָּזֶה מִצַּד הַהִתְעוֹרְרוּת שֶׁלּוֹ בִּבְחִינַת הַמַּקִּיף שֶׁלּוֹ, אֲבָל אֵין זֶה בֶּאֱמֶת בִּבְחִינַת הֶרְגֵּשׁ פְּנִימִי (אָז דאס ארט איהם טאקע באמת) וְעַל כֵּן הוּא רַק לְפִי שָׁעָה בִּלְבַד, דִּכְשֶׁנִּפְסָק הַהִתְעוֹרְרוּת נִפְסָק גַּם הָרָצוֹן הַנַּ"ל, דְּלֹא כֵן הוּא בַּעֲבוֹדָה אֲמִתִּית שֶׁהֲגַם שֶׁהַהִתְעוֹרְרוּת פְּנִימִי

We must decide what is appropriate to our spiritual level, and adopt whatever is real for us.

If everything is important to us, including things far beyond our spiritual level, that our approach lacks honesty.

הֲרֵי לֹא יֵשׁ כָּל הַיּוֹם, מִכָּל מָקוֹם הַפְּעֻלָּה מִזֶּה אֵינוֹ נִפְסָק לְעוֹלָם מִפְּנֵי שֶׁאִכְפַּת לוֹ בֶּאֱמֶת (ווייל איהם ארט טאקע באמת). וִיסוֹד הַדָּבָר הוּא מִפְּנֵי שֶׁהוּא אֱמֶת בְּעֵת הָעֲבוֹדָה (הַיְנוּ שֶׁהַהִתְעוֹרְרוּת הִיא אֲמִתִּית) עַל כֵּן גַּם הַפְּעֻלָּה הִיא אֲמִתִּית (וְעַל כֵּן גַּם כֵּן רֹשֶׁם מֵהַהִתְעוֹרְרוּת נִשְׁאָר עַל כָּל הַיּוֹם, וְהַכֹּל עִנְיָן אֶחָד), אֲבָל כַּאֲשֶׁר הַהִתְעוֹרְרוּת אֵינָהּ אֲמִתִּית (דְּעַל כֵּן לֹא נִשְׁאָר מִמֶּנָּה שׁוּם רֹשֶׁם וּכְמוֹ שֶׁנִּתְבָּאֵר לְעֵיל פ"ו) גַּם הַפְּעֻלָּה הִיא רַק לְפִי שָׁעָה וְנִפְסֶקֶת מִיָּד,

וְזֹאת הִיא הַנִּסְבָּה מַה שֶּׁאָנוּ רוֹאִין בִּבְנֵי אָדָם שֶׁלִּפְעָמִים מְדַקְדְּקִים וּמַחְמִירִים וְלִפְעָמִים לֹא (הַיְנוּ דְּעִנְיָן אֶחָד גּוּפָא לִפְעָמִים כָּךְ וְלִפְעָמִים כָּךְ) וּמִתְחַלְּפִים וּמִשְׁתַּנִּים בְּעִנְיְנֵיהֶם מִיּוֹם לְיוֹם וּמִשָּׁעָה לְשָׁעָה, וּמִכָּל שֶׁכֵּן כַּאֲשֶׁר בָּאִים בְּאֵיזֶה מֵצַר וְדֹחַק (אַז עֶס ווערט איינג פָּאר דעם אנדערען) הֲרֵי הֵם מִתְדַּמִּים לְכָל אָדָם וּבְדֶרֶךְ כְּלָל מִשְׁתַּדְּלִים לְהַצְנִיעַ וּלְהַעֲלִים הַדְּבָרִים וְכָל זֶה הוּא מִפְּנֵי שֶׁאֵינוֹ אֱמֶת, דְּמִי שֶׁהוּא אֶצְלוֹ בַּאֲמִתִּית לֹא יִשְׁתַּנֶּה וְלֹא יֵצַר לוֹ מֵהַזּוּלַת (וּלְהֵפֶךְ אֵינוֹ עוֹשֶׂה הַדָּבָר בְּדֶרֶךְ בְּלִיטָה). וְסִבַּת הַדָּבָר הוּא הֶעְדֵּר הָעֲבוֹדָה הָאֲמִתִּית דְּמִשּׁוּם זֶה לֹא אִכְפַּת לוֹ בֶּאֱמֶת שׁוּם דָּבָר, וְיָכֹל לִרְצוֹת הַכֹּל גַּם מַה שֶּׁלְּמַעְלָה מִמַּדְרֵגָתוֹ וְהוּא רַק לְפִי

the entire day, the effect it has upon us never ceases, since it truly matters to us. This is because it is real at the time of our *avoda* (the arousal itself is real), and therefore the effect is also real. (As a result, an impression of the arousal lasts the entire day, and the two things [the arousal and the impression] are one). But, when the arousal isn't honest (and therefore makes no impression upon us at all, as explained in Chapter 6), then also the effect is merely temporary and doesn't last at all.

This is the reason that we see people who are sometimes careful to take on stringencies, and at other times they are not careful (within one *mitzvah* or custom, they will only sometimes take on extra cautiousness). Such people change and vary their behavior regarding *mitzvot* from day to day and even from hour to hour. This is even more true when they are in difficult circumstances. Then, they try to appear like any other person, and generally try to hide and conceal things. This is because their conduct [in taking on extra strictness] is not real. Those of us for whom [the acceptance of stringencies and "beautifications" of the *mitzvot*] are real won't vary or be affected by anyone else. (Just the opposite — we won't act in an obvious way that stands out.) [In any case], the reason

Essay on Service of the Heart - Love Like Fire and Water

for this is lack of honest *avoda*, on account of which we are not truly concerned with anything. We may want everything, including that which is above our spiritual level, but this desire is only temporary, for as long as the arousal lasts. Being transcendent, [this desire] can occur at any time, but it soon fades and goes away (because it [results from] an easy and unreal *avoda*). Therefore, we become frequently aroused with a desire [to be extra cautious in *mitzvot*], and then [our desire] dissipates immediately. This is particularly true of the style described here, in which the *avoda* reveals a ray of our divine soul, bringing us to care about and want everything [every strictness]. However, [this desire] is not real and true. The truth comes step by step, in which each step is true and real on its own. According to the level that we achieved in our own *avoda*, we take on new stringencies and extra caution. But when we demand of ourselves to go beyond our [spiritual] level, this is not real. And then, also those behaviors that are on our spiritual level—that is, which every "servant of G-d" must be strict about—also are not honest for us. That we should truly care is still beyond us.

שָׁעָה הַיְנוּ בְּעֵת הַהִתְעוֹרְרוּת, וְלִהְיוֹת שֶׁהִתְעוֹרְרוּת הַמַּקִּיף יָכוֹל לִהְיוֹת בְּכָל שָׁעָה, וּמִיָּד חוֹלֵף וְעוֹבֵר (שֶׁהִיא עֲבוֹדָה קַלָּה וּבִלְתִּי אֲמִתִּית) עַל כֵּן מִתְעוֹרֵר גַּם הָרָצוֹן הַנַּ"ל לְעִתִּים קְרוֹבוֹת וְנִפְסָק מִיָּד, וּבִפְרָט בְּאֹפֶן שֶׁמִּתְבָּאֵר כָּאן דְּהַיְנוּ שֶׁבַּעֲבוֹדָתוֹ הוֹצִיא הִתְגַּלּוּת הֶאָרָה דְּנֶפֶשׁ הָאֱלֹקִית, הֲרֵי הוּא רוֹצֶה וְאִכְפַּת לוֹ הַכֹּל, אֲבָל אֵין זֶה אֱמֶת, כִּי הָאֱמֶת בָּא בְּהַדְרָגָה דַּוְקָא, וְכָל דַּרְגָּא הִיא אֲמִתִּית בְּעַצְמָהּ, דִּלְפִי עֵרֶךְ מַדְרֵגָתוֹ בָּעֲבוֹדָה הוּא מַחְמִיר וּמְדַקְדֵּק בְּעַצְמוֹ כַּנַּ"ל, אֲבָל כַּאֲשֶׁר רוֹצֶה וְתוֹבֵעַ מֵעַצְמוֹ לְמַעְלָה מִמַּדְרֵגָתוֹ אֵין זֶה אֱמֶת) הִנֵּה גַּם מַה שֶׁהוּא לְפִי מַדְרֵגָתוֹ, רְצוֹנוֹ לוֹמַר מַה שֶׁכָּל אֶחָד וְאֶחָד מֵעוֹבְדֵי אֱלֹקֵי' צָרִיךְ לְהַחְמִיר עַל עַצְמוֹ גַּם זֶה אֵינוֹ בֶּאֱמֶת אֶצְלוֹ, דְּזֶה שֶׁיִּהְיֶ' דָּבָר נוֹגֵעַ לוֹ בֶּאֱמֶת (אַ אמת'ער אַרִין) לֹא יֵשׁ עֲדַיִן.

The truth emerges step by step, in which each step is honest and real on its own.

This is similar to learning [Torah]. To start with, we must learn the simpler topics, and then move on to more sophisticated and elevated topics. We must progress from the "light" to the "heavy." But, when we start with the "heavy" topics, we won't come to understand them properly,

וַהֲרֵי זֶה בְּדֻגְמָא כְּמוֹ בְּלִמּוּד הֲרֵי מִתְּחִלָּה צְרִיכִים לִלְמֹד עִנְיָנִים פְּשׁוּטִים וְאַחַר כָּךְ יוּכַל לִלְמֹד עִנְיָנִים גְּבוֹהִים וְנַעֲלִים, וּמִן הַקַּל יָבוֹא אֶל הַכָּבֵד, אֲבָל כַּאֲשֶׁר יַתְחִיל מִן הַכָּבֵד הֲרֵי לֹא יֵדַע אוֹתוֹ לַאֲמִתּוֹ מֵאַחַר שֶׁלֹּא לָמַד אֶת

since we didn't learn the lighter topics first. Moreover, we don't know the lighter and easier subjects, and we are left "empty on both sides" [*Bava Kamma* 60:1]. Those of us who strive for a spiritual level that is beyond our own achieve an elevated level that isn't real, and even the matters that are on our level are not real.

הַקַּל תְּחִלָּה, וְגַם אֶת הַקַּל אֵינוֹ יוֹדֵעַ, וְנִשְׁאָר קֵרֵחַ מִכָּאן וְקֵרֵחַ מִכָּאן, וּכְמוֹ כֵן בְּמִי שֶׁהוֹלֵךְ לְעֵילָא מִדַּרְגֵּיהּ הֲרֵי מַה שֶּׁלְּמַעְלָה מִמַּדְרֵגָתוֹ אֵינוֹ אֱמֶת, וְגַם מַה שֶּׁבְּמַדְרֵגָתוֹ גַּם כֵּן אֵינוֹ אֱמֶת.

So it is for those of us who meditate in the shallow manner described in Chapter 6. We fail to truly achieve any spiritual level. There is no order in our *avoda*, so that we can hold on to one level and climb to the next. Such a description is appropriate only for those of us who perform our *avoda* honestly. We understand truly, and with inner feeling. When we experience spiritual arousal, it is genuine. We honestly desire to reach the goal of our meditation, whether it be closeness and cleaving to the One Above ["like water"], or yearning and thirst for Him ["like fire"]. We stand on a definitive spiritual rung, and what we demand of ourselves and our behavior is in proportion to that rung. We act honestly according to our level. All this is genuine, meaning that it truly matters to us, and we are firmly committed to it, without wavering. So, we progress from one level to the next. But, if we don't hold onto any particular matter [in our *avoda*]—because we don't grasp the subject at all, and have no inner feeling or true arousal, as mentioned in

In honest avoda, we stand on a definitive spiritual rung, and our behavior is appropriate to that rung. What we comprehend, we truly comprehend, with inner feeling.

(וְכֵן הוּא בַּעֲבוֹדָה בְּהָעוֹבֵד בְּהִתְבּוֹנְנוּת בִּבְחִינַת כְּלָלוּת שֶׁנִּתְבָּאֵר לְעֵיל פ"ו שֶׁהֲרֵי גַּם הוּא אֵינוֹ מַחֲזִיק בְּאֵיזֶה עִנְיָן בֶּאֱמֶת וּמִכָּל שֶׁכֵּן שֶׁאֵין סֵדֶר בַּעֲבוֹדָתוֹ דְּהַיְנוּ שֶׁנֹּאמַר שֶׁעוֹמֵד בְּדַרְגָּא זוֹ וְהוֹלֵךְ מִדַּרְגָּא לְדַרְגָּא, דְּזֶה שַׁיָּךְ רַק בַּעֲבוֹדָה אֲמִתִּית דְּמַה שֶׁהוּא מַשִּׂיג הוּא מַשִּׂיג בֶּאֱמֶת וּבְהֶרְגֵּשׁ פְּנִימִי וּבְמַה שֶּׁמִּתְעוֹרֵר הֲרֵי הוּא מִתְעוֹרֵר בֶּאֱמֶת וְרוֹצֶה בֶּאֱמֶת בָּעִנְיָן הַהוּא אִם בִּבְחִינַת קֵרוּב וּדְבֵיקוּת אוֹ בִּבְחִינַת רָצוֹא וְצָמָאוֹן כוּ' וַהֲרֵי הוּא עוֹמֵד בְּאֵיזֶה דַּרְגָּא בֶּאֱמֶת, וּלְפִי עֵרֶךְ זֶה הוּא תּוֹבֵעַ מֵעַצְמוֹ בְּהַנְהָגָתוֹ בְּפֹעַל, אוֹ שֶׁבֶּאֱמֶת מִתְנַהֵג כֵּן בְּפֹעַל, וְכָל זֶה הוּא בֶּאֱמֶת שֶׁאִכְפַּת לוֹ הַדָּבָר בֶּאֱמֶת וְהוּא אֶצְלוֹ בְּתֹקֶף וְחֹזֶק וְאֵינָהּ מִשְׁתַּנָּה, וְכֵן הוּא הוֹלֵךְ מִדַּרְגָּא לְדַרְגָּא כוּ', אֲבָל זֶה שֶׁאֵינוֹ מַחֲזִיק בְּאֵיזֶה עִנְיָן (עֶר הַאלְט נִיט בַּיי עֶפֶּעס אַ זַאךְ) כִּי אֵינוֹ מַשִּׂיג הָעִנְיָן כְּלָל, וּמִכָּל שֶׁכֵּן שֶׁאֵין בּוֹ הֶרְגֵּשׁ פְּנִימִי וְלֹא הִתְעוֹרְרוּת אֲמִתִּי וּכְמוֹ שֶׁנִּתְבָּאֵר לְעֵיל פ"ו, הֲרֵי אֵינוֹ עוֹמֵד בְּאֵיזֶה דַּרְגָּא, וּמִמֵּילָא אֵינוֹ

Chapter 6—we don't stand on any rung of spiritual ascent whatsoever. As a result, we have no real desire to hold onto any particular spiritual level. But, since we are, at least, involved with *avoda*, our soul demands that we be in the worthy situation and circumstances of "sanctifying ourselves." However, in the absence of organization and gradual ascent [in our *avoda*] and with our expectations not absolutely honest, because the matter [our spiritual level] is not really that important to us—we strive for goals that are too lofty. It is easier for us to want (and sometimes to really achieve) things that are exceedingly high, even though for us they aren't real, than to grasp and incorporate a lower level [of *avoda*] that is real. In the beginning of our *avoda*, we are likely to reach for ends that are too high, only to stop immediately thereafter and remain in a state of vacillation.

All of the above regards the divine soul. Since it is somewhat revealed, as mentioned earlier — and this is true as well of the imaginary excitement described in Chapter 6 in which there is a bit of spiritual arousal—it brings us to desire all that is [spiritually] commendable. However, this isn't a true aspiration, as mentioned earlier, and therefore we start and stop. (The arousal [for all the worthy aspects of spirituality] also starts and stops, and

רוֹצֶה בְּאֵיזֶה דָּבָר בֶּאֱמֶת שֶׁיַּחֲזִיק בָּהּ, וּמִכָּל מָקוֹם לִהְיוֹתוֹ מִתְעַסֵּק בַּעֲבוֹדָה עַל כָּל פָּנִים, הֲרֵי נַפְשׁוֹ תּוֹבַעַת לִהְיוֹת בְּמַעֲמָד וּמַצָּב טוֹב לְקַדֵּשׁ עַצְמוֹ כו', אַךְ מִצַּד הֶעְדֵּר הַסֵּדֶר וְהַהַדְרָגָה וּמִצַּד שֶׁהַתְּבִיעָה בְּעֶצֶם אֵינָהּ בֶּאֱמֶת לַאֲמִתָּהּ שֶׁנּוֹגֵעַ לוֹ הַדָּבָר בֶּאֱמֶת, תּוֹפְסִים (חאפט מען זיך אן) בִּדְבָרִים גְּבוֹהִים וְנַעֲלִים דַּוְקָא, כִּי בְּנָקֵל יוֹתֵר לִרְצוֹת (וְגַם לְקַיֵּם לְעִתִּים) דְּבָרִים גְּבוֹהִים שֶׁלֹּא בֶּאֱמֶת מִלְּהַחֲזִיק בְּדָבָר נָמוּךְ בַּמַּדְרֵגָה אֲבָל בֶּאֱמֶת וְעַל כֵּן מַתְחִילִים כַּמָּה עִנְיָנִים שֶׁהֵן טוֹבִים וְנַעֲלִים וְנִפְסָק מִיָּד וְעוֹמְדִים תָּמִיד בְּשִׁנּוּיִים כו').

וְכָל זֶה הוּא מִצַּד הַנֶּפֶשׁ הָאֱלֹקִית, דִּלִהְיוֹת שֶׁהַנֶּפֶשׁ הָאֱלֹקִית אֶצְלוֹ בְּהִתְגַּלּוּת קְצָת כַּנַּ"ל (וּכְמוֹ כֵן בְּהִתְפַּעֲלוּת הַדִּמְיוֹנִי שֶׁנִּתְבָּאֵר לְעֵיל פ"ו הֲרֵי יֵשׁ בּוֹ אֵיזֶה הִתְעוֹרְרוּת) עַל כֵּן הוּא רוֹצֶה בְּכָל הָעִנְיָנִים הַטּוֹבִים רַק שֶׁאֵינוֹ רָצוֹן אֲמִתִּי כַּנַּ"ל עַל כֵּן הוּא מַתְחִיל וּמַפְסִיק כו' (שֶׁכֵּן גַּם הַהִתְעוֹרְרוּת נִפְסֶקֶת וּמִתְעוֹרֶרֶת וְחוֹזֵר וְנִפְסָק וְגַם הַהֶאָרָה גּוּפָא מִתְגַּלֵּית וּמִתְעַלֶּמֶת

But, in the absence of order and gradual ascent in our approach, we strive for lofty matters that are beyond us.

> *In the meantime, the animal soul has no aspirations, because the arousal of the divine soul has had no effect on the animal soul.*

וּמִתְגַּלֶּה וְחוֹזֵר כו'), אֲבָל מִצַּד הַנֶּפֶשׁ הַבַּהֲמִית אֵינוֹ רוֹצֶה בְּשׁוּם דָּבָר עֲדַיִן כִּי לֹא פָּעַל עֲדַיִן עַל הַנֶּפֶשׁ הַבַּהֲמִית מְאוּמָה, רַק הַבִּטּוּל חִיצוֹנִי הַכְּלָלִי הנ"ל, וְגַם אִם פּוֹעֵל אֵיזֶה דָּבָר עַל הַנֶּפֶשׁ הַבַּהֲמִית הוּא רַק בְּכֹחַ וְחַיִל (בִּלְשׁוֹן אַשְׁכְּנַז אפגעריסען עפעס פון איהם) לֹא בְּדֶרֶךְ בֵּרוּר, וְלָכֵן כַּאֲשֶׁר בָּא לְאֵיזֶה דָּבָר הַנּוֹגֵעַ לַנֶּפֶשׁ הַבַּהֲמִית, אֵינֶנּוּ עוֹמֵד עַל נַפְשׁוֹ כִּי הַנֶּפֶשׁ הַבַּהֲמִית עוֹדֶנּוּ בְּתָקְפוֹ (בְּיוֹתֵר בְּהַמִּדָּה הַטִּבְעִית הַמַּגִּיעַ עַתָּה לְחֶלְקוֹ כְּמוֹ שֶׁנִּתְבָּאֵר לְעֵיל פ"ו) וְלֹא נִזְדַּכֵּךְ כְּלָל בְּאֹפֶן הָעֲבוֹדָה הנ"ל, וּכְמוֹ שֶׁנִּתְבָּאֵר לְעֵיל פ"ו שֶׁהַזִּכּוּךְ דְּנֶפֶשׁ הַבַּהֲמִית הוּא דַּוְקָא בַּעֲבוֹדָה הָאֲמִתִּית, שֶׁנֶּחְלַשׁ הַטִּבְעִית שֶׁלּוֹ עַל יְדֵי קֵרוּב נַפְשׁוֹ לֶאֱלֹקוּת, וּבְיוֹתֵר שֶׁבְּאֹפֶן הָעֲבוֹדָה יוּכַל גַּם הַנֶּפֶשׁ הַבַּהֲמִית לְהָבִין אֶת הָעִנְיָן הָאֱלֹקִי (וְנִת' שֶׁכֵּן צְרִיכִים לְהִשְׁתַּדֵּל בְּאֹפֶן הַהִתְבּוֹנְנוּת) וְעַל יְדֵי זֶה הוּא בָּא גַּם כֵּן לִידֵי אַהֲבָה לֶאֱלֹקוּת, וּבְאַהֲבָה בְּרִשְׁפֵּי אֵשׁ נַעֲשָׂה כִּלָּיוֹן וּבִטּוּל הַיֵּשׁ דְּנֶפֶשׁ הַבַּהֲמִית כו' כְּמוֹ שֶׁנִּתְבָּאֵר לְעֵיל בְּאֹרֶךְ:

then is aroused and once more ceases. The ray [of the divine soul] bursts into revelation and disappears, and then reveals itself and again disappears.) But, in the meantime, the animal soul aspires to nothing, because the entire arousal and revelation [of the divine soul] had no effect on the animal soul, aside from a superficial, general neutralization, as mentioned earlier. If any changes do take place in the animal soul, they are only the product of power and coercion and not of persuasion. Therefore, when it comes to something that tempts our animal soul, we are unable to control ourselves. The animal soul is still at full strength ([this is] all the more so true regarding whatever natural trait has fallen to us to purify now, as mentioned in Chapter 6). It hasn't been refined at all by the *avoda* mentioned earlier [in Chapter 6 and in Chapter 4]. As explained earlier in Chapter 4, only true *avoda* [with detailed meditation] leads to refinement of the animal soul, weakening its natural components by exposing it to G-dliness. In this way of serving G-d, the animal soul is also enabled to understand G-dly matters. (And there it is explained that this is what we must strive for within meditation.)

Through this process, the animal soul comes to love G-d, and in "love like fire," the ego and natural components of the animal soul dissolve and disintegrate, as explained there at length.

Essay on Service of the Heart - Love Like Fire and Water

Those of us who are concerned about our soul should exert ourselves in detailed meditation.

And therefore, in accordance with all that has been explained, those of us who are concerned about our soul should exert ourselves to serve the One Above with a proper "service of the heart"—prayer—in detailed meditation. We should not seek to go beyond our level by meditating upon lofty heights of G-dliness. Rather, we should focus upon those levels that are close to us (aside from those of us who have already gotten accustomed to *avoda* and have the ability to grasp the higher levels, each according to his own spiritual rung). In general, this refers to meditation on levels of immanent G-dliness, in which we focus upon the Divine light and energy en-clothed in the worlds.

Through honest [and detailed] meditation and deep concentration, we will achieve true familiarity with, and cleaving of, the soul to G-dliness (that is "real" according to our level). In so doing, we will fulfill the commandment to love G-d, which will bring us to learn Torah and fulfill its *mitzvot*. This love will also purify and refine our animal soul. We should strive to understand everything with our natural intellect, which is the major factor that leads to refinement of our animal soul, turning it to love G-d. As we were commanded [in Deut. 6:5], "And you should love the Lord, your G-d," which refers to love resulting from intellectual grasp and meditation. [The meditation itself] is

וְעַל כֵּן עַל כָּל הַדְּבָרִים הַנַּ"ל כָּל מִי שֶׁחָס לְנַפְשׁוֹ יִתְגַּבֵּר עַל עַצְמוֹ לַעֲבֹד אֶת ה' בָּעֲבוֹדָה הָרְצוּיָה בָּעֲבוֹדָה שֶׁבַּלֵּב זוֹ תְּפִלָּה בְּהִתְבּוֹנְנוּת בְּדֶרֶךְ פְּרָט דַּוְקָא, וְלֹא יֵלֵךְ בִּגְדוֹלוֹת לְהִתְבּוֹנֵן אֶל מַדְרֵגוֹת גְּבוֹהוֹת בֶּאֱלֹקוּת רַק בְּמַדְרֵגוֹת הַקְּרוֹבִים אֵלָיו (כִּי אִם מִי שֶׁכְּבָר מֻרְגָּל בָּעֲבוֹדָה שֶׁבִּיכָלְתּוֹ לָבוֹא לְמַדְרֵגוֹת גְּבוֹהוֹת בָּעֲבוֹדָה כָּל אֶחָד וְאֶחָד לְפוּם שִׁיעוּרָא דִילֵיהּ כוּ') וּבְדֶרֶךְ כְּלָל בִּבְחִינַת מְמַלֵּא כָּל עָלְמִין דְּהַיְנוּ בַּהֶאָרָה הָאֱלֹקִית שֶׁבָּאָה בִּבְחִינַת הִתְלַבְּשׁוּת בָּעוֹלָמוֹת,

שֶׁעַל יְדֵי הִתְבּוֹנְנוּת אֲמִתִּי וּבְהַעֲמָקַת הַדַּעַת יְהִי' קָרוֹב וּדְבִיקוּת נַפְשׁוֹ לֶאֱלֹקוּת בֶּאֱמֶת (רְצוֹנוֹ לוֹמַר בֶּאֱמֶת שֶׁלּוֹ לְפִי מַדְרֵגָתוֹ) וּמְקַיֵּם בָּזֶה מִצְוַת אַהֲבַת ה' וְהִיא הַמְּבִיאָה אוֹתוֹ לְעֵסֶק הַתּוֹרָה וְקִיּוּם הַמִּצְוֹת וּבָהּ וְעַל יָדָהּ מְבָרֵר וּמְזַכֵּךְ אֶת הַנֶּפֶשׁ הַבַּהֲמִית, וְיִשְׁתַּדֵּל לְהָבִיא הַדְּבָרִים לִידֵי הֲבָנַת הַשֵּׂכֶל הַטִּבְעִי, שֶׁעַל יְדֵי זֶה עִקָּר וְזִכּוּךְ הַנֶּפֶשׁ הַבַּהֲמִית שֶׁיָּשׁוּב גַּם כֵּן לְאַהֲבַת ה' כוּ' וְעַל זֶה נִצְטַוִּינוּ כְּמוֹ שֶׁכָּתוּב וְאָהַבְתָּ אֶת ה' אֱלֹקֶיךָ כוּ' שֶׁהִיא הָאַהֲבָה הַבָּאָה עַל יְדֵי הַשָּׂגָה וְהִתְבּוֹנְנוּת שֶׁזֶּהוּ עִנְיַן שְׁמַע יִשְׂרָאֵל שֶׁהוּא עִנְיַן שְׁמִיעָה וְהַשָּׂגָה כוּ' וּבְכָל לְבָבְךָ בִּשְׁנֵי יְצָרֶיךָ שֶׁהוּא

Through honest meditation and deep concentration, we will achieve cleaving and devotion of our soul to G-dliness.

בְּחִינַת קֵרוּב וּדְבֵיקוּת הַנֶּפֶשׁ הָאֱלֹקִית בֶּאֱלֹקוּת וְשֶׁגַּם הַיֵּצֶר הָרָע יָשׁוּב לְאַהֲבַת ה' כו', וְזֶהוּ הָעֲבוֹדָה שֶׁבַּלֵּב לְהִתְעוֹרֵר בְּלִבּוֹ בְּאַהֲבָה לַה' וְלִהְיוֹת לִבִּי וּבְשָׂרִי יְרַנְּנוּ כו'

commanded in the verse, *Shema Yisrael...* ("Hear O Israel..."), where "hearing" refers to intellectual understanding. [Then, we come to love] "with all of your heart" referring to both inclinations—the divine soul seeks proximity to G-d, wanting to cleave to Him, and the evil tendency changes to love G-dliness. This constitutes "service of the heart," triggering within our hearts a love of G-d such that our heart and flesh rejoice.

שֶׁכָּל זֹאת הוּא עַל יְדֵי הַשָּׂגָה וְהִתְבּוֹנְנוּת שֶׁעַל זֶה נֶאֱמַר וְיָדַעְתָּ הַיּוֹם וַהֲשֵׁבֹתָ אֶל לְבָבֶךָ ב' לְבָבוֹת כו'. וְזֶהוּ שֶׁלֹּא נֶאֱמַר צִוּוּי עַל אַהֲבָה כִּי אִם בְּמִשְׁנֵה תוֹרָה, דְּהִנֵּה דּוֹר הַמִּדְבָּר הָיָ' לָהֶם גִּלּוּי אֱלֹקוּת מִלְמַעְלָה בִּבְחִינַת רְאִיָּ' מַמָּשׁ מִצַּד הַחִבָּה הָעֶלְיוֹנָה וּכְמוֹ שֶׁכָּתוּב כְּבִכּוּרָה בִתְאֵנָה בְּרֵאשִׁיתָהּ רָאִיתִי אֲבוֹתֵיכֶם כוּ' וְהָיָ' בָּהֶם הָאַהֲבָה מִמֵּילָא וּבִבְחִינַת דְּבֵיקוּת מַמָּשׁ בְּחִינַת אַהֲבָה בְּתַעֲנוּגִים כוּ' וּכְמוֹ שֶׁכָּתוּב וַיֶּחֱזוּ אֶת הָאֱלֹקִים וַיֹּאכְלוּ כוּ' וְתִרְגֵּם אוּנְקְלוּס וַהֲווֹ חֲדָאן כוּ' (וְיֵשׁ לוֹמַר דְּהָעִקָּר הָיָ' בָּהֶם בְּחִינַת הַיִּרְאָה וּבִטּוּל שֶׁעַל יְדֵי רְאִיַּת הַמַּהוּת בְּחִינַת יִרְאָה עִילָאָה וּכְמוֹ שֶׁכָּתוּב וַיִּירְאוּ מִגֶּשֶׁת כוּ'). אֲבָל

All of this is the product of intellectual acumen and meditation, about which the verse says, "And you should know today and put in your heart..." referring to both hearts [the G-dly inclination which resides in the right ventricle and the evil tendency in the left ventricle]. This is the reason the commandment to love G-d didn't appear in the Torah until the fifth book (Deuteronomy). The generation that left Egypt and journeyed in the desert merited the revelation of G-dliness from above. They could literally "see" spirituality as a result of the great love that was expressed for them from above, as it says [in Hoshea 9:10], "Like a new fig in its beginning, so I saw your forefathers..." They spontaneously experienced *ahava b'taanugim* ("love of delights") for the One Above, cleaving to Him completely. It is written [in Exodus 24:11], "They saw G-d and they ate..." and Onkelos [the Aramaic translation there] says "and they were happy" (though it is possible to say that their main experience was one of awe of G-d and self-nullification as a result of perceiving the essence of G-dliness, *yirah ila'ah*, as it says there, "they were afraid to approach"). It was the following generation which received the command to love G-d; that is, they were commanded to undertake an *avoda* leading to love, that being meditation.

And that brings us to the ultimate purpose in the labor of "service of the heart" (prayer): it is to strive within ourselves in true meditation with depth of concentration in order to arouse love of G-d, such that it will bring us to fulfillment of the *mitzvot* of the Torah and also to purification and refinement of our animal soul. And it was already explained that it is absolutely necessary that there be acceptance of the "yoke of heaven" and the lower fear of G-d (guarding our senses), because they are indispensable and unceasing. But, the *avoda* and effort of prayer is to arrive to the love of G-d, and also in so doing to fulfill the true intention of the One Above.

SYNOPSIS:

There is another way [of serving G-d], and that is with superficial, noisy excitement, the result of general knowledge of G-liness alone, which gives rise to a revelation of a reflection of the divine soul. On account of this revelation, we desire and demand of ourselves spiritual goals beyond our [true] spiritual level. However, this isn't honest, because true "service of the heart" progresses from step to step, and each step along the way is

הַדּוֹר שֶׁאַחַר כָּךְ נִצְטַוּוּ עַל הָאַהֲבָה דְּהַיְנוּ שֶׁעַל יְדֵי עֲבוֹדָתָם יָבוֹאוּ לִבְחִינַת אַהֲבָה וְהַיְנוּ עַל יְדֵי הִתְבּוֹנְנוּת כו'.

וְזֶהוּ תַּכְלִית הָעֲבוֹדָה וְהַיְגִיעָה בָּעֲבוֹדָה שֶׁבַּלֵּב זוּ תְּפִלָּה לִיגַע אֶת עַצְמוֹ בְּהִתְבּוֹנְנוּת הָאֲמִתִּי בְּהַעֲמָקַת הַדַּעַת לְהִתְעוֹרֵר בְּאַהֲבָה לַה' שֶׁעַל יְדֵי זֶה הוּא קִיּוּם הַתּוֹרָה וּמִצְווֹת וְעַל יְדֵי זֶה הוּא בֵּרוּר וְזִכּוּךְ הַנֶּפֶשׁ הַבַּהֲמִית כו'. וּכְבָר נִתְבָּאֵר דִּבְהֶכְרֵחַ שֶׁיִּהְיֶ קַבָּלַת עֹל מַלְכוּת שָׁמַיִם וְיִרְאָה תַּתָּאָה שֶׁאִי אֶפְשָׁר לִהְיוֹת בִּלְעָדֶיהָ וְהוּא עִנְיָן תְּמִידִי אָמְנָם הָעֲבוֹדָה וִיגִיעָה דִתְפִלָּה הִיא לָבוֹא לִבְחִינַת אַהֲבָה זֹאת כנ"ל דִּבְכָל זֶה מַשְׁלִימִים אֲמִתַּת הַכַּוָּנָה הָעֶלְיוֹנָה כו':

קִצּוּר.

יֵשׁ עוֹד אֹפֶן וְהוּא עִנְיַן הִתְפַּעֲלוּת חִיצוֹנִי בְּרַעַשׁ עַל יְדֵי הַיְדִיעָה כְּלָלִית דֶּאֱלֹקוּת שֶׁעַל יְדֵי זֶה מוֹצִיא הֶאָרַת הַנֶּפֶשׁ הָאֱלֹקִית לִידֵי הִתְגַּלּוּת וּמִשׁוּם זֶה הוּא רוֹצֶה וְתוֹבֵעַ מֵעַצְמוֹ כַּמָּה עִנְיָנִים טוֹבִים וְנַעֲלִים שֶׁהֵן לְמַעְלָה מִמַּדְרֵגָתוֹ אֲבָל אֵין זֶה אֱמֶת כִּי הָאֱמֶת בָּא בְּהַדְרָגָה דַּוְקָא וְכָל דַּרְגָּא הִיא אֲמִתִּית לְפִי מַדְרֵגָתוֹ וְעַל יְדֵי זֶה הוֹלֵךְ מִדַּרְגָּא לְדַרְגָּא אֲבָל בָּאֹפֶן הנ"ל אֵין זֶה

true on its own level in such a way that we progress from one step to the next. When we reach too high, our progress is not real. Therefore it changes and vacillates all the time. And although it produces a general external nullification of the animal soul, nevertheless it produces no essential nullification whatsoever, such that the animal soul would desire anything spiritual. Therefore, when it comes to some sort of [spiritual] test [from above], we are unable to control ourselves and pass the test. So, those of us who are concerned about our soul must push ourselves to serve G-d with proper *avoda*, meaning a detailed meditation, each one of us according to our level. In so doing we will arouse a love of G-d [in himself], leading to fulfillment of *mitzvot* of the Torah, as well as purification of our animal soul. And this is the ultimate purpose of all our *avoda* of prayer (and of course there must be constant "fear of G-d" as well, as explained), and in this way we will fulfill the supernal intention from above.

בֶּאֱמֶת. וְעַל כֵּן מִשְׁתַּנֶּה וּמִתְחַלֵּף בְּכָל עֵת, וּמִצַּד הַנֶּפֶשׁ הַבַּהֲמִית הֲגַם שֶׁפּוֹעֵל בּוֹ בִּטּוּל כְּלָלִי חִיצוֹנִי אֲבָל בְּעֶצֶם אֵין בּוֹ בִּטּוּל כְּלָל עֲדַיִן וְאֵינוֹ רוֹצֶה בְּשׁוּם דָּבָר טוֹב וְלָכֵן כְּשֶׁבָּא לְיָדוֹ אֵיזֶה נִסָּיוֹן לֹא יוּכַל לַעֲמֹד. וְעַל כֵּן כָּל מִי שֶׁחָס לְנַפְשׁוֹ יִתְגַּבֵּר עַל נַפְשׁוֹ לַעֲבֹד אֶת ה' בַּעֲבוֹדָה הָרְצוּיָ' בְּהִתְבּוֹנְנוּת פְּרָטִית כָּל אֶחָד וְאֶחָד לְפִי מַדְרֵגָתוֹ וּלְהִתְעוֹרֵר בְּאַהֲבָה שֶׁעַל יְדֵי זֶה הוּא קִיּוּם הַתּוֹרָה וּמִצְוֹת וְעַל יְדֵי זֶה הוּא בֵּרוּר הַנֶּפֶשׁ הַבַּהֲמִית וְזֶהוּ תַּכְלִית הָעֲבוֹדָה וְהַיְגִיעָה דִתְפִלָּה (וּבְהֶכְרֵחַ שֶׁתִּהְיֶה גַּם כֵּן הַיִּרְאָה בִּתְמִידוּת כְּמוֹ שֶׁנִּתְבָּאֵר לְעֵיל פ״ב וְג׳) וּבָזֶה מַשְׁלִים הַכַּוָּנָה הָעֶלְיוֹנָה כוּ':

NOTES

1. *Nishmata d'nishmata* is a technical term for *chaya*, the fourth level of the soul. While the *Zohar* mentions only four levels — *nefesh, ruach, neshama* and *nishmata d'nishmata* — Midrashic, later Kabbalah and Chassidic literature refers to the five levels of the soul listed in the text: *nefesh, ruach, neshama, chaya* and *yechida*.

2. *Yichuda ila'ah* literally means "higher unity." It refers to a state of mind in which our primary awareness is of G-d and His oneness in the universe, and if we have any awareness of the physical creation, it is as something very secondary. Another term for the same awareness is *da'at elyon*. Similarly, *yichuda tata'ah* means "lower unity," and refers to the state of mind in which our primary awareness is of the physical world and creation. G-d is in the background and we are not directly aware of Him. Also known as *da'at tachton*. For more explanation of both *yichuda ila'ah* and *yichuda tata'ah*, see Ch. 5 and the accompanying commentary.

3. *Hitamtut* is confirmation or corroboration of our meditative understanding. It comes as a "moment of truth" or realization from Above, hence the root word *emet*. In Chassidic literature it is usually also associated with *re'iya de eyn hasechel*, or seeing in the mind's eye. It follows a deep process of meditation on G-dly topics, wherein we penetrate to the G-dly core of the subject, stripping it of its outer layers of explanation and arriving to the very essence of the matter. Then, we may be granted a "moment of truth" in which we see the G-dly subject in our mind's eye, which accompanies *hitamtut*. For more explanation, see ch. 5 and accompanying commentary.

4. *Pnimiyut Bina* is the stage of understanding in which we strip away the external "trappings" of the G-dly concept in order to arrive to the G-dly kernel of thought. Human intellect is incapable of grasping a G-dly concept without some sort of description, example, or external "handle." However, by focus, concentration and persistence, we can break through the shrouds of intellectual "packaging" and discover the spiritual kernel. *Pnimiyut Bina*, or core understanding, is the tool to achieve this end.

5. Supernal Bride (*Kalah Ila'ah*) is a way of describing the *sephira* of *bina*, with its corresponding soul-power of analytic understanding. Since *bina* receives the raw materials of G-dly understanding from *chochma*, and then processes and analyzes them, it is on the receiving end and is therefore referred to as the *kalah*, or bride. On the other end, the analytic process of *pnimiyut bina* "consumes" the shrouds of externality and brings us to the spiritual core of the concept. Thus, it is called *kalah* for a second reason —

because it "consumes" (in Hebrew, also *kalah* from *lechalot* meaning "to consume") the external trappings of the physical world.

6. The following table should clarify the meaning of the paragraph:

Ch. 16 of *Tanya*: "and also his *nefesh* and *ruach*..."	*Ruach* combines with *nefesh* to become one (*Nehy* within *nefesh*)	In *avoda*, a slightly elevated general acknowledgment (acquiescence)
Described earlier in *Kuntres Ha'Avoda*: "our *nefesh* also rises..."	*Nefesh* rises to *ruach*	Specific acknowledgment on the level of *ruach* (natural love and fear)
Described later in this chapter: "the heart responds spontaneously..."	*Ruach* rises to *neshama* (cleaving of the emotions to intellect)	Intellectual love and fear (unity with the G-dly light)

7. Page 156-157

8. *Mochin* is the Kabbalistic term for spiritual influx. Literally meaning "brains," *mochin* is the spirituality that we bring into the world with our *avodat HaShem*. Without our service of the One Above, the universe runs according to the laws of nature. Service of the One Above insures that G-dly energy will permeate the laws of nature, elevating the universe in order to reveal the presence and oneness of G-d. *Mochin* in general has a component which is emotional, but subservient to the intellect. *P'nimiyut hamochin*, or pure intellect, though, completely transcends the emotions of the heart.

9. Inter-inclusion (described above) leads to *tikun* (rectification). It takes place in the following three steps, which are implicit in the rest of this chapter:

Ha'ara (Illumination)	The higher level illuminates the lower level	The lower becomes aware and strives for the higher level
Hamshacha (Drawing down)	The higher level interacts with the lower level	The lower level takes on characteristics of the higher but retains its own identity
Hashra'ah, or *Hitcalelut* (Permeation or Inter-inclusion)	The higher level elevates the lower level and they become one	The lower level becomes subsumed by the higher

10. *Reuta d'liba* is one of the goals of meditation. Latent in the heart are emotions of G-dly fear and love that may be awakened and fanned into flames by the active meditation described in *Kuntres Haavoda*, ch. 4 and 5. When performed properly, the heart ignites into love "like fire." The point of ignition is called *reuta d'liba*, or the "will of the heart." As described in *Sefer Ma'amorim 5670, Parshat Trumah*, "the *makif* of *chaya* is in essence *reuta d'liba*, the will that transcends reason. It is also the natural desire for G-dliness in the soul, which wants to be included in its source..." It may come either as the result of active meditation, as mentioned, or come from Above as a result of previous *avoda*.

11. *Rayayoti* — the verse in Song of Songs (4:1) reads, "Behold, you are beautiful, my love, behold, your eyes are dove's eyes..." In the Chassidic discourse (in *Likutei Torah*) on the verse, the following interpretation is offered: "Like by way of example, a pair of doves, male and female; the female receives from the male, so Above, the Blessed One is compared to a bridegroom, and the Jews to a bride. And the Jews are described as 'receiving from Him,' and just as doves peer intently at each other, so from everything, one can learn to observe intently and see that there is none other than Him, and that He is one, and to nullify ourselves completely...and just as doves peer at each other constantly and enjoy seeing each other, so the Jews are in a state of constantly "seeing the glory of the King" from everything they perceive..."

12. *Zeir Anpin* — The biggest contribution of the Ari to the study of Kabbalah was the concept of *partzufim*. A *partzuf* is a structure of *sephirot*, and while the earlier Kabbalists spoke of individual *sephirot*, it was the Ari who introduced the concept that groups of *sephirot* interact together.

Among the ten *sephirot* of *Atzilut*, there are five such major structures, or *partzufim*, and other less important groupings. The five major *partzufim* are *Arich Anpin* (in *Keter*), *Chochma, Bina, Zeir Anpin* (the seven *sephirot* from *chesed* through *malchut*), and *Nukva* (*malchut* itself). Each *partzuf* is composed of its own structure of ten *sephirot*. Since all *partzufim* posess the same set of ten *sephirot*, each on their own level, they are able to interact as groups, as opposed to individual *sephirot*.

The importance of *Zeir Anpin* (or *za'a,* as it is called for short) is its influence on the creation, through *malchut*. *Za'a* imparts the qualities of kindness, constriction, mercy, etc. in the creation. It is a "male," influence-imparting structure that is dependent upon our *avodat HaShem*. When we pray and perform mitzvot, and learn Torah, G-dly influx is drawn down from the infinite light of G-d into the *partzuf* of *za'a*, and through *malchut*, into the creation. When we do the opposite, influx is withheld, with the consequences being negative for the creation. Since *za'a* is therefore in a constant state of flux, and since like the emotions, it relates to the "other," namely, the universe, the *partzuf* of *za'a* is associated with our *"emotions."*

13. Not only *za'a*, but also the *sephirot* of *chochma* and *bina* are each blessed with full *partzufim* of ten *sephirot*. When referred to as full-fledged *partzufim*, *chochma* and *bina* are called *abba* and *imma* in Kabbalistic literature. Their importance lies in their transcendent connection with creation. Like wisdom and understanding in the person, their presence is helpful but not crucial. Just like the person can exist without being overly wise, so the universe can exist without added doses of *chochma* and *bina*. However, the universe is better off with more *chochma* and *bina*. When we serve the One Above properly, the influence of *chochma* and *bina* is revealed in the creation through increased nullification of the creation to G-d and through intellect. When we don't serve Him properly, the law of entropy predominates. Since *chochma* and *bina* transcend the creation and yet the creation is better off with them, *chochma* and *bina* are associated with intellect and understanding.

14. *Memalle kol olamim* (literally, "filling or permeating" creation). This is the term used to refer to immanent spirituality, or the level of G-dliness which is enclothed in the creation in order to create and eniven it. Its two main characteristics are that it is graspable — the person can achieve a firm intellectual understanding of this level of G-dliness — and it exists on various spiritual levels. The creation is divided into four categories — mineral, vegetable, animal and human — and the quality of G-dly energy necessary to enliven each level differs from category to category, as well as among specific species within each category. Similarly, the body is composed of different levels and systems — the head, the heart, the kidneys, etc. The soul is enlothed in each level in a different way and provides a different life-energy for each level, and yet on every level, its life-energy is evident. Therefore, "as the soul fills the body" is an apt simile to describe the phenomenon of immanent spirituality (*memalle kol olamim*) that enlivens the creation.

15. *Sovev kol olamim* (literally "transcending" creation). This is the G-dly light that transcends the creation, affecting it from afar. Unlike *memalle kol olamim*, this spiritual phenomena is not readily graspable and does not readily express itself on identifiable levels. Since it is beyond our grasp, we can only achieve a vague awareness of its presence, but we cannot grasp and understand it. Therefore, it is comparable to human will, or general knowledge. When we will or want something, we know that it won't necessarily come to fruition. And sometimes we will or know something in general, without being cognizant of all of its details, becoming aware of

them only later. So, will and general knowledge are both apt metaphors for *sovev kol olamim*, or transcendent G-dliness.

16. *Yediat Hashlila* (literally "negated, or circumscribed knowledge") is, according to the Rambam, the highest form of intellectual service of G-d. Human descriptions of G-d necessarily fall short of the mark, since He far transcends our puny ability to grasp and understand Him. But, if so, what does the Torah mean when it describes G-d with such adjectives as "almighty," "merciful," "vengeful," "wise," and the like? The Rambam suggests that these adjectives, while not precisely describing G-d in the same way as they do human beings, implies that G-d is not *not* that. That is, the adjectives of the Torah are meant to imply that G-d is not the opposite of the description. He is, of course, that which is described by the adjective, be it wise, almighty, vengeful, etc., but not in a way that is describable and graspable by human intellect. Rather, He is far Above any adjective we might apply, but He is not the opposite of it. The performance of this intellectual exercise of negating or circumscribing our knowledge of Him is, according to the Rambam, the highest form of *avodat HaShem*. But, here in the *Kuntres Ha'Avoda*, the process of stripping the intellectual concept of its external trappings and arriving to the essential spiritual core is not to be equated with *yediat hashlila*. That comes at a later stage of *avoda*, as we will soon see. For more on this subject, see commentary to Chapter 5.

17. *P'sukei D'Zimra* (literally "verses of praise"). This is the section of prayer in the morning extending from *Baruch She'amar* up to *Yistabach* (before saying *Barchu*). It is characterized by verses from *Psalms* and other parts of the *Tanach*, which praise the One Above for His wisdom and omnipotence in creating the universe. Psychologically, this section of the prayers has the effect of making an "impression from the outside" on the person who is praying. While the word *zimra* literally means "song," it also comes from the phrase, *lezamer aritzim*, or "to cut away thorns." When we approach prayer in the morning, there are many "thorns" — obstacles that could affect our mindset, distracting and disturbing us. When we give ourselves over to reciting the prayers during the stage of *P'sukei D'Zimra*, they have the effect of clearing our heads of all these "thorns" and allowing us to concentrate on getting close to the One Above.

18. See Chapter 4 and accompanying *pirush* for explanations of this level.

19. *Hakarat hahaflah* (literally, "recognition of wonderful elevation") — Chabad meditation follows a process of stripping away the external trappings of thought (the "garments" of the concept) in order to arrive at the spiritual essence of the idea. This process of *p'nimiyut bina* may be followed by an experience of *da'at*. That is, once we have arrived at the essential kernel of the concept, we may be "rewarded" with a vision of its G-dly

essence. We will experience this as a deep recognition (*hacara*, the inner dimension of *da'at*). Depending upon the subject and style of the meditation, the revelation from Above may be wonderful and astonishing (*niflah*), far transcending worldly matters. This happens when the process utilized is *yediat hashlila* (circumscribing or negation of knowledge, also known in the text as *lehavin davar mitoch davar*). Since the person is striving to penetrate matters that are beyond intellect, he is "rewarded" with revelation that is beyond intellect, with *hacarat hahafla'ah*. For more explanation, see commentary to Chapter 5.

20. *Re'iya b'eyn hasechel* (literally "seeing in the mind's eye") — Meditation undertaken on our own initiative is in the category of "hearing." That is, all that we grasp, analyze, and understand is based on our intellect, rather than upon what we directly experience of G-dliness. This happens because while we cannot directly apprehend G-d, we can be aware of Him and understand Him to some extent by studying the effect He has upon the universe in creating and maintaining it. This is called hearing. Moses, though, wanted to instill in the Jews the power to directly see G-dliness. If he would have entered the land of Israel, he would have succeeded, but G-d permitted him only to look at the land of Israel from afar, from the mountains of Moab (*M'av* — from *Av* — from *chochma*, associated with seeing). In so doing, he instilled in the Jewish soul the power to "see in the mind's eye." That is, we may meditate so deeply and accurately, that our power of imagination "sees" what our naked eye is not allowed to see (until the coming of *Meshiach*). Therefore, after the deep experience of *hacara*, we may be granted vision in our mind's eye — a visual experience in his imagination that transcends the hearing and understanding that he experienced up to now. For more on these terms see commentary to Chapter 5.

21. For more on this subject, see commentary to Chapter 4.

22. For more on this subject, see commentary to Chapter 4.

23. *Sandal* is the name of the angel who elevates the prayers of the Jewish people to the One Above. The Talmud (*Chagiga* 13) says that he "ties crowns for his Creator from the prayers of the Jews." His job is two fold; he must "shield" the Jews from excessive revelation from Above, and yet be able to capture their longing for G-d in their prayers and elevate them Above. That's why he is called *Sandal* — just as a sandal covers the foot, shielding it from dirt and ground, so the angel *Sandal* is associated with the covering — the *parsa* — that separates between the worlds of *Yetzira* and *Asiya*. He effectively cuts the illumination from *Yetzira* into *Asiya* to a minimum, and then "catches" the prayers of the Jewish people and carries them upward to their ultimate destination — our Father in Heaven (*Derech Mitzvotecha, mitzvat mila*, page 7).

24. *Ma"h* and *Ba"n*, as indicated in the chart, are numerical values of the name of G-d spelled out to its fullest in various ways, also as indicated in the chart. It remains only to elucidate what is meant by a "rectified" world as opposed to non-rectified. The world of *Atzilut* is "rectified" (and therefore also called *Tikun*) because all of its ten *sephirot* are composed of ten *sephirot* of their own. Therefore, the *sephirot* of *Tikun* are able to undergo inter-inclusion with each other, and are *butel*, or nullified, and work together for the benefit of all of them. This is called *Tikun*, or rectification, and is associated with the name *Ma"h* (*gematria* 45, or *adam* meaning "man"). The not-yet-rectified world of *Tohu* is characterized by ten *sephirot* which do not undergo inter-inclusion, do no "cooperate," and are involved only with their own individual "welfare." This situation is called *Tohu*, or chaos, and is associated with the name *Ba"n* (*gematria* 52, or *behama* meaning "animal").

25. In Chapter 1, we learn that the elevation of the lower soul-levels (*nefesh, ruach* and *neshama*) to be included in *nishmata d'nishmata* is associated with the *Shmoneh Esreh (Amida)* even though the elevation there is the result of love. And yet here in Chapter 3, it seems that the even higher level of *yirah ila'ah*, or awe, supposedly surpassing prayer, is nonetheless associated with the *Shmoneh Esreh* as well! It would seem that the elevation of the lower soul levels to be included in their source takes place during the *Shmoneh Esreh* in general, while the self-nullification and awe associated with *yirah ila'ah* take place specifically during the four occasions of bowing down during *Shmoneh Esreh*.

26. This distinction is drawn in *Likutei Torah, Parshat Bamidbar* (in the discourse *Besha'ah shehikdimu*, paragraph 3). There, *yiru mei HaShem* is equivalent to *yirah tata'ah* or lower fear of G-d, while *yiru et HaShem* is equivalent to *yirah ila'ah*, or awe.

27. As mentioned in Chapter 1, the *sephirot* go through a process of inter-inclusion, in which each of them takes on some of the qualities of all of the others. Hence, each *sephira* includes all of the other ten *sephirot*. Here, since we are interested in developing the overall quality of love of G-d (associated with the *sephira* of *chesed*), and there are two specific categories of love of G-d (like "fire," and like "water") they both are included within the overall quality. Thus, love like water is *chesed* within *chesed*, while love like fire is *gevura* within *chesed*.

28. While the influx brought down to the world by learning Torah is from the infinite, transcendent light of G-d (*ohr*), the meditation focusing upon G-dliness enclothed in the creation is transcendent light enlcothed in the immanent enlivening force of the creation (*chayut*). Thus, it is an

"intermediate" level, lower than the transcendent light of G-d, but higher than the immanent spirituality enclothed in the creation (*koach*).

29. The third paragraph of the discourse reads as follows, "And in order to bring down the fire from Above, it's a *mitzvah* to bring [fire] from below, as an arousal via meditation upon the source from whence the [animal soul] was taken in the supernal "chariot," the source of the lust of the animal soul…[the meditation consists of] how the [angels] of the "chariot" are nullified to the "image of man" [the ten *sephirot* of the world of *Atzilut*]…and are enflamed and panting with desire…to be nullified and included in the illumination of G-dliness that is shining down upon them. And automatically, this illumination of love [from Above] will illuminate as well the power of lust of the animal soul that comes from there, and arouse the person's heart to detach itself from physical pleasures…"

30. The end of the second paragraph of the discourse reads, "…like an animal sacrifice consumed by fire on the altar, so should one arouse his love in prayer with flames of fire igniting from his heart, because the source and foundation of fire is in the heart, and it will consume and burn the animal soul within him…"

31. In the discourse beginning, "*Vayigash alav*…", p. 125, "[the fire on the altar]…is the service of prayer with love, with flames and flames of fire, since this holy fire burns and consumes the foreign fire of the 'other side'…" And on page 142, in the discourse beginning, "*Vayeileich*…" is to be found a detailed explanation of the two levels of fire of the animal soul (fire from below and fire from above).

32. The summary at the end of the discourse reads, "the *seraphim* [angels which are consumed by fiery desire for G-d] are from the element of G-dly fire, and there is a corresponding element in the G-dly soul of man, but it is composed of all four physical elements [earth, wind, fire and water]. And it is written, 'G-d will illuminate my darkness' — this takes place by meditation on the subject of '*HaShem* is our *Elokim*' [essential name of G-d as He transcends the creation is our G-d within creation], through which [meditation] we come to love [Him]. This is what is meant by the 'consuming fire'…"

33. The discourse (paragraph 5) reads, "And also the G-dly soul includes and is compounded of four spiritual elements that are G-dly. The element of water is in the brain and that of fire is in the heart. And the relative composition of the four elements isn't the same in every person. There are those for whom the element of water predominates, and there are those for whom the element of fire is predominant. This is like coals, by way of example, that burst into flames, as opposed to coals that smolder quietly without burning, containing a spark of fire that remains hidden. Nonetheless, since they contain a hidden spark, when one blows hard upon the spark, it then ignites the entire coal

into flames of fire. So, also is the situation of the G-dly soul within man. It may contain an element of G-dly fire in the heart that is revealed and intense, like burning coals. Or, it may contain an element of G-dly fire that is hidden, like smoldering coals with only a spark of fire among them. But, a spark there is, inside each and every Jewish person. One has only to blow upon it hard for it to ignite and enflame and encompass the entire set of coals in a revealed way, and so the G-dly soul in man needs ignition in the heart so that it will become revealed...and this is the entire process of prayer up until *kriat she'ma*, as the person meditates on the greatness of G-d, how He uttered and the world came into existence..."

34. A discussion of this topic is to be found in the series of discourses, *Yom Tov shel Rosh Hashana* 5666, p. 142, and in the second volume of the series of discourses, *Be'sha'ah Shehikdimu, 5672*, pp. 840 and 974.

35. Here, the motivation for achieving "love like fire" is different than in footnote 3. The third paragraph of the discourse reads, "...it's a *mitzvah* to bring from [below], fire from below via meditation on the greatness of G-d, each according to his individual abilities and to excite his heart and soul to serve G-d and then his meditation gives birth to a bold love that's like flames of fire. That happens when he meditates on "something new," as when we see clearly that one who sees something new gets quite excited, and so our Sages said, 'Every day should be like new...' And this takes place when we meditate how in truth every morning brings something new [a new influx of G-dliness from Above]..."

36. See the discourses of the Rebbe Rashab of the year 5660, beginning *Samchuni b'ashishot:* "We know that there are two kinds of enjoyment, corresponding to *chesed* and *gevura*, about which it is said '*ahava beta'anugim* — love of abundant enjoyments' (plural), and they are the love of *ohr yashar* [direct illumination] and of *ohr chozer* [reflected illumination]. The enjoyment of *ohr yashar* is in the drawing down [of G-dly illumination] from Above to below, and the enjoyment of *ohr chozer* is in elevating from below to Above. The latter [is a love of] desire and yearning, as is known that such desire and yearning contains tremendous enjoyment, leading [even] to expiration of the soul..."

By way of possible explanation, *ahava beta'anugim* is composed of two elements; number one, it is aroused by meditation (*ohr chozer*, initiative of the person below), and number two, it is an essential love that is implanted in the Jewish soul from Above (*ohr yashar*). See *Besha'ah shehikdimu 5672*, vol. 2, p. 754. See also vol. 3 of *Besha'ah shekikdimu*, pp. 1246-7 in parentheses: "It's possible to say that this love [of desire and yearning from below] is on the same level as *ahava teta'anugim*, in terms of enjoyment..."

Alternatively, the reference may be to chapter 9 of the *Tanya*, in which it is written, "That is to say, that the person shall steadily rise to attain to the degree of 'abundant love,' a supreme affection surpassing that of 'ardent love' that is comparable to burning coals. This is what is called in Scripture 'love of delights' [*ahava beta'anugim*] which is the experience of delight in G-dliness, of the nature of the world to come. This delight is in the wisdom, in the intellectual pleasure of comprehending and knowing G-d, to the extent that one's intellect and wisdom can grasp [Him]. This is the element of 'water,' and 'seed,' i.e., light that is sown in the holiness of the divine soul that converts to good the element of 'water' in the animal soul, from which the lust for mundane pleasures had been previously derived."

It is possible that the intellectual pleasure of "abundant love" (*ahava beta'anugim*) is what is meant by "direct illumination" (*ohr yashar*) while the conversion of the element of water in the animal soul to pleasure in G-dliness is what is meant by "reflected illumination" (*ohr chozer*), as when one engages in *teshuva*, or return to the One Above.

37. The verse reads in translation, "Great is our lord, and tremendously powerful." The two words translated as 'tremendously powerful' - *verav koach* - carry the numerical value of 236. *Koach* has the numerical value of 28, which is the same as the number of letters of the first verse of Genesis, referring to the creation of the universe. *Verav*, meaning 'and tremendously' carries the numerical value of 208, which is also the *gematria*, or numerical value of *ohr* (light), with the *collel* (added value of one for the totality of letters together – a common kabalistic technique). *Ohr* is the transcendent spiritual source of *koach*, and together, they represent *orot* and *calim* (light and vessels) - the building blocks of creation and hence its spiritual "size" – 236.

38. This reference in the original is clearly a typographical mistake and should read *Sha'ar HaYichud* of the Mittler Rebbe, chapter 5, rather than chapter 4.

39. *Imrei Bina* of the Mittler Rebbe (son of the Alter Rebbe) is considered the deepest and most cerebral of Chabad Chassidic discourses. It was written for the Mittler Rebbe's chassid, Reb Yekutiel Lepleker, who through persistence and determination (and not through natural abilities alone) became an *oved HaShem*. The discourse is devoted to explaining the words of the *Shema* in Chassidic terms. In chapter 58 of the discourse, two words from the first paragraph of the *Shema* — *yoreh* and *malkosh* — are discussed. According to the Talmud (Tractate *Ta'anit 5A*), *yoreh* is the rain that falls in the fall, while *malkosh* is the rain that falls in the spring. The discourse ties the two kinds of precipitation to the two aspects of *ayn*, or spiritual nothingness, mentioned in chapter 6 of *Kuntres Ha'Avoda* and chapter 5 of *Sha'ar HaYichud*. *Yoreh*, the autumn rainfall, softens the earth and causes the seeds to rot away,

thereby causing them to germinate into plants later on. It thus corresponds to the power of nullification of creation to its spiritual source. *Malkosh*, on the other hand is the rain that causes the germinated seed to develop to its fullest. It thus corresponds to the power of creation from nothing into something. It is upon the former level (*yoreh*) that the *Kuntres Ha'Avoda* in chapter 6 recommends that we meditate. This level of *ayn shel hayesh ha'nivrah* corresponds to the *koach mah*, or power of seeing of *chochma* that descends to creative existence in order to nullify it to its source.

40. Chapter 4 of the Mittler Rebbe's *Sha'ar Hayichud* discusses the relative merits of meditation on a general topic, such as "the light of the World of *Atzilut* and how it is out of range of the infinite light of G-d," versus meditation upon particulars, such as each *sephira* in each world and how it is nullified to the particular level above it. The conclusion is that while a general meditation may lead us to quick conclusions and errors in our understanding, meditation on particulars tend to remain accurate. While the feeling of G-dly excitement and interest may be minimized in a meditation upon details, still, we ultimately arrive at a truer general picture after focusing upon the details in meditation.

41. Chapter 11 of *Kuntres Ha'Tefila* describes five preparations for prayer:
    - Removing all thoughts of worldly concerns and remaining stationery.
    - Meditating on G-dly concepts as presented in the Chassidic discourses of the Sages.
    - Nullifying ourselves through bitterness over our distance from the One Above.
    - Arousing compassion upon our souls which came from a high spiritual place to be enclothed in a physical body.
    - Awareness and meditation on the fact that we are standing before G-d Himself and not just a manifestation Him.

42. See *BeSha'ah shehikdimu* 5672, vol 2, p. 822-825 (sections 399-400)

APPENDIX I
Letter from the Previous Rebbe

Translator's Note:

The following is a letter from the previous Lubavitcher Rebbe, Harav Yoseph Yitzhak Schneerson, *ztz'l* (1880-1950). He was the director of *Tomchei T'mimim*, Lubavitch Yeshiva, until he took over the helm as the Rebbe of Chabad/Lubavitch when his father, the Rebbe Rashab *(nishmato eden)* passed away in 1920. He remained in this capacity until he himself passed away in 1950. In 1927, he was briefly jailed in Bolshevik Russia for disseminating Judaism, and then expelled from Russia, whereupon he moved Poland, and subsequently (in 1940), to New York. Upon his passing, he was succeeded by his son-in-law, HaRav Menachem Mendel Schneerson, *ztz'l*. This letter was written by the previous Rebbe in Riga, in response to questions asked by the Chassidim of the city of Bilgoria, in 1931. It was added as an appendix to the original edition of *Kuntres Ha'avoda*, printed in 1963 by Kehos Publication Society. The subject matter – love of G-d – is common to both the *Kuntres Ha'avoda*, and to this letter. However, while the *Kuntres Ha'avoda* describes "love like fire" and "love like water," the letter speaks of a different (but overlapping) duality – love derived from creation *(ahavat olam)*, and "great love" *(ahava rabba)*.

4 Shvat, 5691 (1931)
Riga

TO:
Our close friends and chassidim of the city of Bilgoria
May the One Above live with you
Peace and blessings

RE:
In answer to your questions as to what is written in *Torah Ohr* (of the Ba'al HaTanya on *Breishit*) in the discourse entitled *Osri Legefen*, and in the *Tanya*, chapter 43, concerning the levels of *tzadikim* ("holy ones") and the service of *ba'alei teshuva* ("those who return to G-d"),

concerning the levels of [G-dliness] drawn down into the garments of the soul in *Gan Eden,* and the levels of *ahava rabba* ("great love") and *ahava beta'anugim* ("love accompanied by immense enjoyment")

There are three kinds of love [of G-d]. They are:
- *ahavat olam* ("love based in the world"),
- *ahava rabba* ("great love"), and
- *ahava beta'anugim* ("love accompanied by immense enjoyment").

Each kind of love includes myriad levels and aspects that vary one from the other and have numerous offshoots. Because of their incredible subtlety, there are inner similarities between the categories, even though overall they are quite distinct from each other.

Ahavat olam

The word *olam* [which means "world"] indicates concealment *(he'elam)* and also eternity, as is written (in Exodus 21:6), "and he will serve him forever" *(veavado leolam).* Although in this passage the Torah is talking about a servant who will serve his master only until the Jubilee, which is the fiftieth year, nonetheless in relation to man – whose lifespan is seventy years and if he has strength eighty, and once upon a time one hundred and twenty – the number fifty is large. The word *olam* therefore connotes eternity. And also regarding the higher/supernal world, it is written (Isaiah 45:17) *l'ulmei ad,* meaning "forever and for all eternity" (from the nusach of Kaddish - *leolam u'lmay olmaya*). Now, these two definitions of *olam* – [concealment and eternity] – are diametrically opposed to each other. *Olam* in the sense of concealment implies limitation and restriction, since the very existence of concealment implies limitation and restriction. And *olam* in the sense of eternity connotes infinity. And the two – limitation and infinity – have nothing in common. They are two aspects of love, distinguished by their very essence. Yet, despite this, they are both called by one name: *ahavat olam.*

Ahavat olam [when implying concealment] means love derived from the world or from creation. Within this love are to be found many distinct sub-levels. Every level sub-divides into thousands and tens of thousands of sub-levels, since this kind of love is subordinate to the quality of our [soul levels] *neshama, ruach* and *nefesh,* our intellect, and to the composition of our personality. These sub-divisions apply not only to *ahavat olam*, but also to every category and level of love, as well as to fear of G-d. But it is especially applicable to *ahavat olam* since it is the lowest level [of love]. Overall, it is called *ahavat olam* since it derives from aspects of the world/creation, as is written (Deut. 30:20): "love G-d your Lord since He is your life." That is, just as we love the life of our soul, so we love G-d since G-d is our life. And so, it is called *ahavat olam* since the life-force of the world is G-dliness. But within it is implied another general aspect-opposite of the first – that all the life-force of the creation comes only from a ray of light and reflection [of G-dliness] that is insignificant in relation to the infinite light of the One Above, may He be blessed.

We see, then, that this one general level has two specific branches. Unique to each branch is a specific concept and a meditation associated with it. And yet, both of them are hewn from one source, and that is the limitation and restriction associated with the word *olam*, as it is describes concealment. Both are as one, even though they are distinct in their very essence, since the first level of [life-force] implies closeness and proximity, while the second level of [ray and reflection] implies tremendous distance. Nevertheless, both of these levels derive from our intellectual pursuit, meaning that they develop in proportion to our intellect and grasp.

Ahavat olam [when implying eternity] means eternal love and suggests that [the love] is natural and essential, without variation, replacement, or exchange, and it is independent of both time and place. Within it are several aspects and levels, describing its very essence. As above, in the first level [of concealment], it expresses itself differently according to our individual *neshama*, *ruach* and *nefesh* and according to our level of intellect and composition of personality. And so it is on all levels of this love, with the major difference – between the first *ahavat olam* [concealment] and the second [eternity]. In the first kind of *ahavat olam* [concealment], the essence of the love itself depends upon our level of *nefesh*, *ruach* and *neshama*. However, in the second kind, only the overall expression of love and the way it becomes revealed are determined by our *nefesh*, *ruach* and *neshama*. But the love is equally present in everyone's soul. Why this is so is simple – the first love [derived from meditation on the world] results from a reason, meaning that it is automatically derived [as a result of a specific meditation]. If so, then, love comes about as a result of a reason.

This is not true of the second kind of love – the eternal love – wherein the reason and result are one and the same. Nevertheless, there is an advantage to the first kind of love [based in concealment and limitation]: since it emerges as a result, it brings with it action that produces effects. There are consequences to this kind of love, and they magnify the love. For example, a person who loves the life of his soul will act upon it – he will eat, drink and rest. And he will engage in other activities – all of them the consequence of one factor: his love for life. The overall result of what he does will be an increased connection of the life-force with the limbs of his body, as well as elevation of the limbs of his body and their refinement in order that they receive more subtle and elevated energy of the soul (as explained elsewhere concerning the nature of connection of the life-force with the limbs).

Thus, by way of this example, we may also understand the first kind of love [associated with concealment and limitation]. Since it emerges as a result, it has consequences, and the consequences themselves bring about certain effects. And these are fulfillment of the Torah's mitzvot with desire and motivation. As the Alter Rebbe said (in the *Tanya*, chapter 4), "the one who truly fulfills the mitzvot is one who loves G-d." But, the second love [associated with eternity] is not a result of anything, and therefore doesn't have any [immediate] effects or consequences. Since it is natural and essential, it acts at all times according to its essential nature, which is not in accordance with the categories of action associated with a ray of light or reflection.

To make this clearer, we can refer to elsewhere (perhaps in *Likutei Torah* on *Shir HaShirim*, "Shishim haima malachot," p. 39A) where it is explained that the deep sources of water flowing in the core of the earth never become revealed. Those which do become revealed for some reason, or are dug up, are actually from the upper, accessible layers of the earth's surface, while the deepest waters are so subterranean that they never become revealed. However, they do exist, and even though they have no visible effect and bear no apparent relationship to anything tangible, their very existence is its own justification within the bowels of the earth. And because of them, the earth is moist. And even though there is no discernible relationship between the subterranean fountains and the moisture of the earth, nevertheless since within the earth are to be found these fountains and this water, for reasons known to the Master of All Reasons, the earth's surface is moist. And since it is precisely the land that is moist, it is land that gives rise to germination and vegetation. Even though it is water that causes the growth of vegetation, this takes place only when the water irrigates land. The proof is that as long as the water is in the clouds, it doesn't produce vegetation, and only upon its descent to the earth does it benefit humanity with vegetation. But, the very reason that growth of vegetation takes place only upon land is because the moisture is present there. And the fact that moisture is present on the land is the result of the deep fountains within the bowels of the earth. Even though there is no apparent relationship, nevertheless their presence – the presence of the deep waters within the earth – has a natural effect. Like two people who are dwelling in one apartment without any apparent connection between each other whatsoever, nevertheless the very fact that the two of them are in the same place causes them to have an effect upon one another. The effect that they have on one another takes place naturally [inadvertently]. That is, it doesn't take place as an "action and its effect." In "action and effect" the action en-clothes itself in the effect, since it takes place in proximity and can enmesh itself. But, this is not the case here, where the subterranean fountains are found deep in the bowels of the earth. Nevertheless, the very fact of their existence means that the surface of the earth will be moist.

From this example, we may understand the love of *ahavat olam*, wherein *olam* means eternal. From the very fact of its existence in the world, [this love] has an ongoing effect. Just as the very existence of the fountains deep in the bowels of the earth makes something happen, so too this love. However, this love is even more essential, since the deep waters are only essential within the framework of natural, physical elements, while this love is essential within the realm of the soul. Therefore, while we may speak of an "action" in relation to it, in this context the nature of the "action" is to be swallowed up within the nature and essence [of the love itself]. So, we discern here one level that gives rise to two aspects, divergent from each other and even opposite: 1) natural and 2) essential. Even though each exists in its own category, they come together to produce one effect.

In general, then, there is:

- *Ahavat olam* (concealment) with its two components:
    - proximity [like one's life-force] and
    - distance [as a ray and reflection from Above].
- *Ahavat olam* (eternity) with its two sub-categories:
    - natural [having an inadvertent effect on "another"] and
    - essential [existing for its own sake].

And yet they all have the same name: *ahavat olam*.

Ahava rabba

Ahava rabba ("great love") comes as a gift from Above [to the one] who has prefaced it with the first level of *ahavat olam* (concealment), in its second component [distance, based upon meditation on how entire creation is but a ray/reflection of the Creator]. It is an intellectually based love, emerging and derived from contemplation and meditation. It is certainly not necessary to explain that this love is dependent upon all of the above. That much can be deduced from the second form of *ahavat olam* (eternal). If eternal *ahavat olam* is unchanging, irreplaceable and independent of time and space, and its revelation is dependent upon all of the above, then all the more so is *ahava rabba* dependent upon all of the above factors, coming as it does after the *avoda* of *ahavat olam* (concealment).

It then becomes clear that this love has the same benefits that we mentioned earlier regarding the first level of *ahavat olam* (concealment) versus the second; that is, it produces results and has consequences, as mentioned above. The difference is that in the first *ahavat olam* (concealment), the love is in the heart alone. It has an effect and motivates us to fulfill the Torah's mitzvot, since the one who truly fulfills them is the one who loves G-d, as mentioned above.

However, this applies to the mitzvot alone. Every mitzvah that we fulfill, we fulfill with motivation and energy. *Ahava rabba*, though, is recognizable on all levels of our being and faculties, and not only in the heart, which is the seat of emotions. [For example], the person who runs to do a mitzvah; his running contains energy, enjoyment and motivation together. And at every opportunity and place, he is surrounded and motivated by this love, and he forgets about himself completely. He doesn't feel himself, because the project gets done and is completed as if it took place on its own – automatically. The aura that surrounds him from Above envelopes him from every side and angle, and enlivens him with an inner energy.

This is understood by way of learning Torah in public, to which there are two approaches. The public learning itself fulfills the commandment to learn Torah. There are those who fulfill it by rote, like learned people following a fixed routine and custom wherever Jews are found. When the learning takes place with energy – whether the learning itself occurs with desire or whether there is effort expended to gain more members to join the learning – this is an indication that there is motivation in the public learning. This is the first level.

But, when we merit an arousal of *ahava rabba*, then love permeates all of our faculties. That is, aside from the learning itself, which takes place in a completely different fashion – whether regarding the subject or in his understanding of it – we now learn in a way that we can apply to all of our actions. In addition, love surrounds us at all times. Whether we are in motion or standing, in our head and heart is always the same matter: learning Torah in public. We are so dedicated and devoted to the matter that the environment has no influence upon us whatsoever. It also makes no difference to us whether the subject is the oral or the written Torah, whether the revealed or concealed/inner dimensions of Torah, whether the participants are learned or simple folk, or whether the location is a place of Torah or not. That is, since we are so totally devoted to and overcome by this great love and concern for learning Torah in public, in every place that we find ourselves, whether in a fixed or in a temporary location, we think, consider and discuss the matter of learning Torah in public.

The truth is that Jews are not subject to "coincidence," since it is written (Psalms 37:23), "by G-d are the steps of man established." Every place that a Jew passes, even if [seemingly] by happenstance, is the result of Divine Providence that for one reason or another arose in His *machshava keduma* ("supernal thought"). When a Jew journeys and finds himself in a place where he had no plans to be and he prays there – whether the morning, afternoon or evening prayers – or recites one of the songs of David, king of Israel, or a verse of Torah, that turns out to be the very reason that he found himself in that place. For each and every movement is by Divine Providence. He may think that it was a coincidence, but in truth it was directed by the light of Torah and *avodat habirurim* – the service of elevation of the universe.

Ahava beta'anugim

This general category of love – a*hava beta'anugim* ("love accompanied by immense enjoyment") – transcends all of the others. It is associated with those whose service of G-d is on the level of *ovdei Hashem benishmatam*, "those who serve G-d with their soul." This is an overall service involving the soul [and not the purification of the body, which has already occurred on lower levels of *avoda*]. The enjoyment is of the *makifim* ("transcendent" levels of the soul) that far surpass the level of *p'nimim* ("immanent" or permeating levels of revelation of the soul). Nevertheless, there are variations and divisions to be found among these levels as well, in general and in particular.

Enjoyment, while also one of the faculties of the soul and not the soul itself, is nonetheless the highest of the soul faculties in general, and the closest to the essence of the soul. Similarly, the faculty of will is not one of the particular faculties of the soul, as [for example] the intellect is a particular soul power. Rather, the will is a general faculty consisting only of the inclination of the soul toward that which the soul wants in a particular matter. And all the more so is this true, then, of enjoyment, which is close to the soul and unites with it in total unity. Nevertheless, enjoyment also includes several aspects and levels, such as "compound" enjoyment of a particular matter versus "simple" enjoyment that is not compounded with anything else. And simple enjoyment can include "conscious" experience, or [a "subconscious" experience and] can take place devoid of any conscious feeling whatsoever. The highest of all is simple enjoyment which is not compounded with any other feeling whatsoever.

The three types of love

The three types of love described here constitute general categories, and even though each one is defined and limited by its category, nonetheless any intelligent person understands that spiritual categories are not like stone or iron dividers or like colored reflectors of red and black or green, or like taste which may be sweet or sour or sharp. All of these are merely categories of the physical and its substance. Here, though we are speaking of spiritual levels and their hierarchy, as the Rambam explained (in *Hilchot Yesodei HaTorah* 2:6-7) regarding angels. If so, then, within all three categories of love are to be found offshoots that are similar and comparable to one another. Like, for example, the first type of love [*ahavat olam*] within the first category [concealment], wherein we develop love for G-d as we love the life-force of our own body. Within this love are to be found desire and will that are also the basis and categories of *ahava rabba* and *ahava beta'anugim*. For the foundation of *ahava rabba* is will accompanied by desire (as mentioned above), and the foundation of *ahava beta'anugim* is enjoyment. This is even more true regarding the second type of *ahavat olam* [eternal], which contains elements of the first, plus an unconscious will that never ceases, that is similar in concept to *ahava rabba*, except that *ahava rabba* is conscious. And as any conscious will, [it acts] with forceful and tremendous power. But the natural will, even if essential, is unconscious. Since it is essential, it contains something of the *ahava beta'anugim* that is united with the soul, as mentioned above. And in this respect, *ahava rabba* and *ahava beta'anugim* also have something in common with each other [both are closely connected with the essence of the soul].

In this way, we can understand what [the Alter Rebbe] means in *Tanya*, chapter 43, [when he equates] *ahava rabba* with *ahava beta'anugim*. Each has within it dimensions that are similar to levels beneath them. The reason for this is that the lower levels – in *ahavat olam* – are also spiritual. And this is also true of the opposite: the highest sub-level of *ahava beta'anugim* (such as simple enjoyment that is neither experienced nor felt) is also only a power of the soul and not the soul itself. And so we see that all spiritual levels relate to one another. And therefore all of them are called by one name: love.

Servants of G-d

Now, regarding servants of G-d, there are several levels and categories. But, in general they may be divided into two: *tzadikim* and *ba'alei teshuva*. Although it's possible to sub-divide each of them into several aspects and sub-categories, the main subdivisions are also two [in each case]:

- among *tzadikim*, there are:
    - those who serve G-d with their bodies and
    - those who serve G-d with their soul
- among *ba'alei teshuva*, there are:
    - those who return to G-d upon having transgressed, and
    - those who serve G-d at all times like those who are "returning" to Him, because they constantly feel deficient in their service of G-d

Those who are considered "servants of G-d [because they serve G-d] with their bodies" are those who do the *avoda* of the mind and of the heart. Here, the intention is *avoda* with labor: labor of the flesh and labor of the soul. The physical substance of the body conceals G-dliness and hides the light of the soul, and the entire *avoda* is for the purpose of removing the concealment and obscurity. Within this are found various levels and not all are equal.

Those who would serve G-d with their souls are those whose physical substance and body does not hide or obscure their souls at all. Even though they are en-clothed in a body, all of their limbs are holy and do not obscure any of the illumination of the soul at all. As written (in Exodus 2:2) regarding Moses, "And she [his mother] saw that he was good," meaning (according to Rashi) that the house was filled with light. This was because the physical substance of his body was itself "good," and there was no necessity for *avoda* or labor [to improve it] at all. Even though such people need some sort of real *avoda*, it does not involve the same labor as those who serve G-d with their bodies.

The *avoda* of a *ba'al teshuva* involves shattering his entire being and essence, and transforming himself from one extreme to the other. In place of the transgression, during which he turned away from the "straight and narrow path," and the fear of G-d was not "in front of his eyes," and, "he said to G-d [that] ...he doesn't desire His path" [Job 21:14], and "the wicked praises himself for the lusts of his soul" [Psalms 10:3], he now, at the time of his *teshuva* ("return"), transforms all his ways-from the inner recesses of his soul and the depths of his heart. He maintains the path of life while fulfilling the Torah's mitzvot; he develops fear of G-d and is worried and concerned over every detail, including over subtle nuances of the sages' [decrees]. His whole purpose is to eviscerate his own desires until he has no will for anything physical, and he minimizes his eating and drinking and sleeping, and [even] has enjoyment in bringing about his own suffering [for the sake of getting closer to G-d].

Now, it is known that *teshuva* does not refer merely to the simple matter of return to G-d after transgression or sin. *Teshuva* involves, as the verse (in Ecclesiastes 12:7) proclaims, "And the spirit returned to G-d who granted it." The point is: "to G-d who granted it," meaning that we elevate ourselves to a higher stage and level, about which it is said (in Morning Prayers) "the soul that You put within me." The verse (in Ecclesiastes 12:7) says, "to G-d who granted it [the soul]," because all of our *avoda* should be in order to elevate our [soul levels of] *nefesh*, *ruach* and *neshama* to a place that transcends [the level from which] "you gave." This is an *avoda* in which we are very strict with ourselves. On every level of this *avoda*, including the highest, we finds fault with ourselves, and all that we do "is considered as a sin." All we want is to raise and elevate ourselves to a higher level. This is similar in concept to the *avoda* of the High Priest in the Holy Temple on Yom Kippur, during which it was necessary for him to immerse several times in the mikveh. In general, there are two types of immersion; one that takes the person from impurity to purity, and another that takes the person from one level of purity to a yet higher level of purity. And these are the elevations of Yom Kippur.

Now, both types of servants of G-d, *tzadikim* and *ba'alei teshuva*-as distant as they may be from one another in form and essence-nevertheless bear some kind of relationship to each other. [This is because] according to the true Torah (mentioned above), that which is spiritual is not measurable within the categories and definitions of limited physical substance. [This applies] to the first type of *tzadik* and the first type of *ba'al teshuva*, as well as the second type of *tzadik* and the second type of *ba'al teshuva* in particular.

For, the first type of *tzadik*, whose every aspect is involved with cleansing and refining his physical nature, [shares a common element] with the first *ba'al teshuva*, whose entire mission is shattering his physical nature. And the second type of *tzadik*, whose entire *avoda* involves the light of his soul, [shares a common element] with the second type of *ba'al teshuva*, whose entire *avoda* surrounds the elevation of his soul.

What emerges from all this leads us to understand the two kinds of servants of G-d: *tzadikim* and *ba'alei teshuva*. Their corresponding four types of service are included in two general categories: the *avoda* of the body and the *avoda* of the soul. The first level of *tzadikim* [*ovdei HaShem* with their bodies] and the first level of *ba'alei teshuva* [those who return from sin and transgression] are considered *avoda* of the body. And the second level among *tzadikim* [*ovdei HaShem* with their souls] and the second level of *ba'alei teshuva* [those who return to elevate their souls to a higher level] are entirely involved with the *avoda* of illumination of the soul. The difference between them is only regarding the direction and path of their *avoda*. For the direction of *avoda* of the *tzadikim* involves drawing G-dliness down from above to below, while the direction of *ba'alei teshuva* is to elevate from below to above. *Tzadikim*, even of the first type [involving the refinement of the body] draw down from above to below. This is because the refinement and cleansing of their bodies takes place through the illumination of Torah, mitzvot and prayer. They have no connection with evil, whatsoever. And *ba'alei teshuva*, also of the second category [who seek to return only to approach closer to G-d, not to expiate sins], serve G-d from below to above, since all of their concern is to ascend in elevation after elevation with devotion of their soul.

The descent of the soul into the body is for the purpose of elevating it through one elevation after another by fulfilling the Torah's mitzvot down here in this world, as is known. However, how is it possible for the soul to receive such high revelation of G-dliness? This is only possible through the fulfillment of physical mitzvot in this world, as the mitzvot are garments for the *neshama* [when it ascends] to the levels of *Gan Eden*.

And in this we find the two categories of *tzadikim* and *ba'alei teshuva*. The general *avoda* of *tzadikim* is drawing down [G-dliness] from above to below and in cleansing and purifying the physical substance in order to remove the dust and dirt that has gathered there. That is what is meant by the phrase [in Genesis 49:11], "and he laundered his garments in wine." For this purpose, they draw down supernal enjoyment.

And what was suggested [in your letter] regarding *ahava beta'anugim* is inaccurate. Rather, [*ahava beta'anugim*] is a drawing down of supernal enjoyment, meaning that it is neither a drawing down of His supernal will nor of His *chochma* ("wisdom") and *bina* ("understanding"). Since here we are speaking of the *avoda* of *tzadikim* and *tzadikim* personify "fulfilling the will of G-d," therefore their path of service includes knowledge and intellectual grasp. Conceivably, they may draw down "only" His will or "only" His intellect (*chochma* and *bina*), but for this very reason, the Alter Rebbe wrote that their *avoda* draws down the element of "supernal enjoyment."

However, the *avoda* of *ba'alei teshuva* involves self-sacrifice because of the evil that is in their souls. The intention here is not to evil in the sense of transgression, but to the second kind, wherein the *ba'al teshuva* seeks to leave behind an insufficient past [and return to G-d for the purpose of elevating his soul, not for expiation of sin]. In comparison to that which exists above, however, this lower level is called "evil." Therefore, they draw down an "expensive" [refined] garment that is meant for the head. As is known, there are two categories of garments: 1) of the body, and 2) of the head. The garment of the head is called a veil and it is more refined than the garments of the body. (See the Chasidic discourse in *Torah Ohr*, starting with the words *Asri Legefen*, regarding the two aspects of white wine and red wine and two garments and the *makifim* that are over these garments.) This is the service of *ba'alei teshuva*, and it constitutes "washing his robe [*suso*-from the word *masveh*, or veil] in the blood of grapes..." [Breishit 49:11]

Now, the second kind of *ba'al teshuva* surpasses even the level of *tzadikim*. His category is explained elsewhere, regarding the *Mashiach*, who "comes to persuade the *tzadikim* to do *teshuva*".

And what [was written in your letter] regarding chapter 43 of *Tanya*, seeking to equate the *teshuva* of Rabbi Eliezer ben Durdaya and *ahavat olam*, is correct. But, in seeking to prove that this level surpasses *ahava rabba*, it is incorrect. Rabbi Eliezer ben Durdaya achieved his huge elevation because of his level of *teshuva*. The love that was revealed in his heart, the Alter Rebbe explains, was a "temporary injunction" by Divine Providence from Above for the purposes of that particular moment. As written elsewhere regarding the verse (in Shmuel 2, 14:14), "those who are repelled from you will [no longer] be repelled." [This refers to those who didn't approach G-d and the Torah before the advent of the Messianic Age for reasons that were beyond them will in the future be enabled to see the light and approach G-d.]

This can take place in one of two ways: either by G-dly proximity, [bringing about] tremendous positive influx of physical benefits, or by distance (G-d forbid) bringing about great suffering. All [physical and spiritual] paths are dangerous, and [sometimes], through various and sundry means, a soul strays off the straight path (G-d forbid) and falls into the depths of *klipot* [forces opposed to holiness]. [It then] stands ready and waiting at a crossroads and may become destroyed completely (G-d forbid), [but] G-d brings about all kinds of circumstances, [since] He-the cause of all causes and reason of all reasons-desires the *teshuva* of the wicked and not their death. Therefore, he brings about opportunities for *teshuva*. This is what occurred in the case of Rabbi Eliezer ben Durdaya; because of the simple and coarse things that were said to him, his heart was broken inside of him over his tremendous detachment [from G-d], and in his excitement and love for G-d, his soul expired. But, this took place as a private arousal at that specific moment.

In closing

According to all that is explained above, regarding the connections of the offshoots of one level [of love] to another, it shouldn't be difficult at all [to understand] how the natural love of the G-dly soul (*ahavat olam*, second type, relating to eternity) is similar to *ahava beta'anugim*, and also how "gazing at the glory of the King" on the second level is similar to the second level of *ba'alei teshuva* on the second level [those who return for purposes of elevating the soul], on which there is elevation with enjoyment.

He who desires their peace and blesses them... (R' Yoseph Yitzhak Schneerson)

Appendix II

Footnotes of the Lubavitcher Rebbe, R' Menachem Mendel Schneerson to the Kuntres Ha'avoda of the Rebbe Rashab

i) Page 4 (Page 4 in the translation as well)

Note: "Effort on all of its levels..." See *Torat Shalom, Sefer Hasichot, Sichat Simchat Torah 5666* (1905), sections 3-5. See also *Derech Chayim* (part 3 of the *Sha'ar Hatshuva* of the Mitteler Rebbe), section 12 and onward. [See also] *Kuntres Hitpa'alut* of the Mittler Rebbe, and elsewhere

From *Torah Shalom* of the Rebbe Rashab, *Sichat Simchat Torah 5666* (1905-6), Sections 3-5, Page 61 (apparently notes from the Rebbe Rayatz, *ztz'l*):

"There are four stages to prayer, corresponding to the four levels of the soul; *nefesh-ruach-neshama* and *neshama d'neshama*, which corresponds to the two *makifim* ("transcendent levels") of *chaya* and *yechida*. Our prayers begin on the level of *nefesh*, meaning "acknowledgment," as written, *Hodu L'HaShem* ("Acknowledge/give thanks to the Lord..."). Now, it is known that acknowledgment is not mere agreement (a "nod of the head"), but rather implies surrendering ourselves (while giving ourselves over). While in this state, we "relinquish ourselves" to G-dliness. For example, one who concedes to his friend, even though he may not understand why, nevertheless admits that his friend is correct. In this sense, he "relinquishes himself" to his friend. And so it is in serving G-d: We deliver ourselves to G-dliness. This means that in the beginning [when we arise in the morning] as we say *modeh ani lefanecha* ("I acknowledge/give thanks to You"), we cede ourselves to G-d in our entirety, even though we do not yet know the details that are involved in this "concession." And afterward [when we start to pray], we say *Hodu LaShem* ("Give thanks/acknowledge the Lord") and we do know the details involved, as known regarding the phrase *Hodu LaShem vekiru b'shmo* ("Give thanks/acknowledge...proclaim His name")...this is the level of *nefesh*.

And afterward, during the *pesukei dezimra* ("verses of song"), we experience the level of *ruach*, during which we recite praises of the One above; how He enlivens and creates the universe, as we say, *Baruch sheamar vehaya haolam* ("Blessed be He Who uttered and the universe came into existence..."). Or, as we also say, "He Who covers the heavens with clouds, Who prepares rain for the land, Who causes the mountains to sprout fodder, Who gives sustenance to the animals and to the offspring of ravens who call..." In this manner, we arouse within ourselves excitement that goes beyond our mere intellectual grasp. Rather, it develops in proportion to our recital of His praises, [as we consider] how He enlivens the universe and the manner in which [creations] are able to accept Him. And even though it is not understood how all of creation is able to accept Him and His energy, nevertheless they do accept Him. And about this, the psalms say, "He Who covers the heavens with clouds, Who prepares rain for the land, Who causes the mountains to germinate..." [All of these phrases] allude to the hiding and concealment [of G-dliness] that enable us to accept [His divine influx] – for from the perspective of G-dly influence it was not necessary to create the world in this manner. Yet, nevertheless He hides and conceals Himself so that we will be able to accept His [goodness]...and from this we become emotionally stimulated. And this is the level of *ruach*, which is devoid of [intellectually infused] love derived from meditation. For, [regarding meditation], the emphasis is upon what we understand of the good and the benefit of G-dliness, which is what induces us to desire and cling to G-dliness. But, this is not the case regarding the *pesukei dezmira*, which are associated with [pure] emotional stimulation.

For, there is such a thing as excitement of the emotions. While the intellect does not become excited in any more than a refined manner, the emotions are receptive to stimulation. This is what occurs during the *pesukei dezimra*, as we recite praises and our emotions are aroused. This is not the love and fear with which we "love the Lord" and fear Him, but this is rather the excitement of the very essence of the emotions themselves. This is a necessary stage of divine service, for it is impossible to achieve the characteristics of [intellectually infused] love and fear without prior stimulation of the emotions during the *peshukei dezimra*. This is a necessary pre-requisite, (which is demanded of us). Without it, it is impossible to fulfill the service of reciting the *kriat shema*, since the order of prayer requires that we first achieve the level of *ruach* during *pesukei dezimra*, only after which we recite the blessings prior to the *kriat shema*, and finally the *kriat shema* [itself], with intellectual grasp.

Now, the blessings preceding *kriat shema* require [that we activate] intellect, in order to grasp the nullification of the angels [to G-d]. [We need to understand] how they say *kadosh*, and how [they grasp] that the infinite light of G-d is holy and removed. [They grasp] that what shines down here to the worlds is a mere ray [of G-dliness], which is why the angels are nullified. The point is that this should be meaningful for us as we pray, for if not, why would the service of the angels be important to us – what have they to do with us? But, what is significant here is what [their service] means to us [which is that we as well should be nullified to G-d]. And then afterward during the phrase *baruch kavod* ["Blessed be His Honor..." – here the angels beseech G-d for divine revelation] we may attain some greater level of feeling within ourselves. That is, we may notice that we have a stronger desire for revelation of G-dliness within our soul and within the universe. For, the angels say *baruch* [indicating a desire for G-dliness that is beyond them]...because they are unable to grasp [the G-dly levels that are beyond them]. And we know that we are higher than these angels (the *ofanim*, angels of *asiya*), but nevertheless, there is still no essential divine light shining within us. And even though as we develop understanding, that is as we say the phrase *kadosh*, conscious light shines within, nevertheless this is not revelation of G-d's essential light. For, there are many different varieties of spiritual levels prior to revelation of the essential light of the Infinite One Above, as known regarding the explanation of *baruch kevod Hashem mimkomo* – "Blessed be the Lord from His place" – referring to descent of the essential infinite light below. And the difference is that with this [level of essential revelation], we become like a "*tzadik* who eats to satisfaction."

For, when the essential light does not shine [within us], extraneous aspects may remain [in our soul]. It is written that during prayer, we experience divine illumination. However, that may cause us to feel good for a short time after the prayers, but soon afterward we find ourselves attracted to the physical realm. That is why it is important to "guard" the feeling for G-dliness that we experience during our prayers, for if not, we are tempted by the physical (unless one is naturally spiritual, meaning that he prays for an extended period of time, and after many consecutive days and many prayers, he experiences the divine light and for a long duration).

That is, after much devotion during prayer, the G-dly feeling remains with us. Not that this leads us to experience anything new in our feeling for G-dliness (like one who thinks for a long time, and when he stops for a bit, new ideas arise in his mind), but just that we take much time to experience G-dliness (repeatedly, like one who is standing for awhile in the air of *gan eden*). That is why one of the explanations of the word *atzeret* [as in the festival of *Shemini Atzeret*] is that it comes from the term *atzara*, meaning "stopping," "absorbing." And so is stated in books (*Bina le'itim*), that when someone is aroused with a good trait, he must remain with it for some time and become immersed in it. But, we cannot really say "immersed," because we do not fully understand [the arousal] to such a great extent. Rather, we are "involved with it," "taken with it." And, as a result, we are less involved with the physical world.

All of this applies when our feeling for G-dliness is based upon the divine light that permeates the worlds. But, when our meditation and feeling is for the essential infinite light that transcends the worlds, then we lose our connection to anything physical whatsoever. This is the condition of a "*tzadik* who eats to the satisfaction of his soul." While meditating upon G-dliness enclothed in the worlds, it is impossible to come to a state of *bitul bemetziut* ("total nullification of the self"). Since this level of G-dliness is enclothed in the world, it is to be expected that it possesses the trait of "existence." Only from meditation upon G-dliness that transcends the worlds is it possible to attain the level of nullification of existence associated with "the *tzadik* who eats to the satisfaction of his soul."

However, it is necessary to understand that all this takes place within the "inner dimensions" of *bina* (*pnimiyut bina*), and not within the external manifestations of intellect. The external intellect is the ability to understand and grasp the concept and feel it in our soul…but [the spiritual levels described above] are associated with *pnimiyut bina*. This occurs as we meditate on G-dliness that is enclothed in the worlds and experience the G-dly illumination in our soul, and then we subsequently proceed to meditate upon the lofty and amazing nature of the essence of the infinite light which is above our grasp – for the essence of the infinite light is beyond whatever our thoughts are capable of grasping – from this, we automatically understand that whatever we do grasp is not the essence of the infinite One…

And then we meditate upon the nature of this lofty light. For this purpose, we must first return to the original meditation, but with more internal focus and with stronger concentration. And we understand that this is not yet the essence [of G-dliness], and that the essence is yet more lofty and elevated, and thus this is not the essence. And then, we focus upon the nature of that elevation, which means that [whatever we grasp in the spiritual realm] above, [we postulate that] "this is not" the essence. We must somehow develop a feeling for this – it is not enough [for us] down here to say, "this is not it" – for that goes without saying. Rather, in order to appreciate what is meant above when we say that essence is "not this" – we need to develop a sense of recognition of the nature of "lofty elevation." For example, we may recognize the nature of a great person. We may be able to pinpoint a certain characteristic of his that is lofty and elevated, because his loftiness does not mean that he is removed from all other men. It only means that he is, of his own nature, elevated and lofty. And therefore, he automatically possesses certain character traits that lend him his lofty character…[and so the person meditating] must first grasp that the essence of the infinite light is elevated and lofty. [At first], he accepts the existence of loftiness with blind faith, without any intellectual proof that this is indeed the case. And thereafter, he continues to meditate and comes to recognize the nature of the loftiness and elevation. This process is associated with *pnimiyut bina*, which is [also] the technique known as *yediat hashlila* ("negation of knowledge"). With it, one is able to shine revealed essential G-dly light below. And then, as he experiences the essential infinite light, he is becomes completely detached from anything physical whatsoever. He can "eat a bagel" without relating to it whatsoever.

And then, this is followed by meditation on the [essential] name *Havaya* in two different modes. Either everything is nullified in existence, or everything is G-dliness, and then there is no connection whatsoever to anything physical. And as is known regarding one who ate a bagel [the intention may be to the *Malach*, son of the Mezritcher Magid. He was oblivious in meditation to the extent that his soul was ready to leave his body, but the Alter Rebbe, who was his study partner, inserted a bagel into the *Malach's* mouth, thereby bringing him "back down to earth." The *Malach* later said that the Alter Rebbe "saved his life," for his soul was about to leave his body], who was on the level of, "everything is G-dly."...

And after this stage, we arrive afterward to *reiyah* – "vision" of the very essence of G-dliness, which occurs during the *shmonah esreh*. This occurs on the soul level of *yechida*, on which the *neshama* is an intermediary between the soul enclothed in the body and the very essence of the soul. And it is impossible to begin the *shmonah esreh* without first prefacing it with the order of prayer to begin with –

Except during *mincha*, when we begin our prayers with the *shemonah esreh*. For, the prayer of *mincha* is the *shemonah esreh*; one, because it follows the *shacharit* prayer, and moreover because it is an *et ratzon* – an "auspicious time." ...and therefore, we are able to begin with *shemonah esreh*, but otherwise, we are unable to begin with *shemonah resreh* without first reciting the prayers before hand...but the order of prayer is such that we must preface with the soul levels of *nefesh ruach* and *neshama* and then afterward we may arrive to the *yechida*. It comes out, then, the *neshama* is the intermediary.

From *Derech Chaim* of the Mitteler Rebbe, Ch. 12, Page 30:

"Now, the details of *tshuva* correspond to the soul levels of *nefesh-ruach-neshama-chaya*, which consist of four levels. The first is *tshuva* of the *nefesh*, as written, "The *nefesh* that sins, and it will return." The second corresponds with *ruach*, as written, "And the *ruach* will return to *Elokim*." The third level corresponds with *neshama*, as written, "If man devotes his heart, his spirit and *neshama*, to G-d he will be gathered." And the fourth level is *tshuva* corresponding to *chaya* (also called *mazla*), as written, "And man was [created as] a living (*chaya*) soul."

Now, [the level of *tshuva* associated with *chaya*] corresponds to the letters *lamed-mem* of the word *tzelem adam* ("image of man" – spelled *tzadi-lamed-mem*). The first letter *tzadi* of *tzelem* corresponds to the soul [as en-clothed in the body], including the three levels of *nefesh-ruach-neshama*. And the second letter *lamed* corresponds to *chaya* and the *mem* to the *yechida* of the soul. And the rectification of *tshuva* must affect the blemish that inflicts all of the *tzelem* [the "image" in which man was created]. For, whoever sins, blemishes the entire "image of G-d" that is within him. . . And, it is written, "But, in the image, man walks," referring to the *tzelem* ("image") of G-d alone, as known. And even if he already rectified his *nefesh-ruach-neshama* by doing *tshuva*, he will still need to rectify his *mazal*, which is blemished until he fixes the *lamed-mem* of *tzelem* (such as occurred during the *tshuva* of the *yechida* that was performed by R' Eliezer ben Durdaya and Natan Detzutzita, and the like)...

[The rest of Ch. 12 and subsequent chapters of *Derech Chayim* delve into the details of *tshuva* on the various levels of the soul].

From *Kuntres Hitpa'alut* of the Mitteler Rebbe, Page 77 (in the Kehot edition, *Maamorei Admor Haemtzai – Kuntresim*, pub. 1991)

[Here, the Mitteler Rebbe describes five levels of meditation as they occur within the natural, "intellectual" soul. Later, he goes on to describe the same five levels as they occur in the Divine soul...]

"It would appear that there are five levels, one above the other, and each one of them will be explained so that no mistake will be made. The first level, the lowest of all of them, occurs when the meditator desires only to attain some sort of excitement – from which he derives energy – and nothing more. This is just about the lowest level of them all, so low that it is near the level of external excitement of the heart explained above, in which the meditator experiences only himself. This is not G-dly excitement at all. For, he has no desire or intention regarding G-dliness at all. His goal is not that G-dliness should dwell in his soul, or that he should develop a connection to G-dliness. His only desire is to experience some of the energy of G-liness, so that he can consider himself "successful."

Nevertheless, there is some good mixed in here, concealed within his hidden love for G-d. That is, [the good] is masked as a "foreign" garment, as if he desires G-dliness. In any case, his main desire is to experience G-dly excitement, but if it weren't for G-d, he would have no desire at all for [even the excitement]. Although, this is not his conscious aim – he would never consciously entertain the notion that his real desire is to experience G-dliness in his soul (not for his own enjoyment, but out of desire for G-dliness). About this [state of consciousness], we say, "G-dliness is good for me"…

And the second level above this, is likened to "hearing from afar," wherein the meditator heard of G-dliness and meditates on G-dliness alone, understanding the concepts well until he accepts and confirms them in his mind at least, which is a true and real process. Nevertheless, the concepts remain far from him, and he asks, 'what benefit' to the soul will come from this. [He asks] because the activity of meditation on G-dliness is very important in his eyes and acceptable to him as a way of acknowledging G-d. And in his mind, the importance of G-dliness become greater and more exalted, until it occupies the ultimate pinnacle of importance in his mind and in his heart as well. But, he desires that G-dliness should become fixed in his soul and heart in a conscious and revealed manner, not quietly and "from afar." Now, this is a higher level, since it is closer to real G-dly excitement…for at least the matter of meditation on G-dliness is important to him and he greatly desires it. His main goal and will is to approach G-dliness. But, however much he labors, he fails to achieve any G-dly excitement at all in his heart and mind. He labors not for himself, but for the sake of G-dliness alone, for it is only closeness to G-d that he seeks, so that it becomes fixed in his soul. This is the main "entry level" approach to meditation for those who truly search for and demand G-dliness with integrity, with positive intention, for G-dliness alone.

Now, the third level above this is called a "positive thought that combines with action." That means, that it produces emotions of love and fear of G-d that are associated with action alone. The explanation is the following; although in the second level described above, the person has a positive attitude toward G-dliness, meaning that he desires only to be close to G-d and not far from Him. And this is because of the preciousness of G-dliness that he experiences in his mind. But, this does not mean that he becomes at all excited in his mind, for G-dly matters remain completely beyond him. He would like for these matters to be closer to him, but that has not yet happened yet. Thus, G-dliness remains a matter of acknowledgment in his mind, and nothing more. And therefore, it is not called a "good thought," but merely a "thought."

This may be understood by way of illustration regarding worldly matters. We see that there are two trains of thought. One occurs as man thinks about something [positive]; how it is good and praiseworthy until it becomes very important in his eyes. For example, a treasure of wealth that is in the possession of someone else, or upon the great honor and glory of the king or his minister or the like. This is called objective or "cold" thought, which is not at all associated with the thinker in a personal way whatsoever. He will never achieve this status - neither the wealth nor the greatness – he merely thinks about it because of its significance and importance in his eyes. He would very much like for something so positive and praiseworthy to come his direction.

And the second train of thought occurs as he considers something good for himself, such as the profit that he may gain from a good business transaction, or the honor and greatness or attainment of great wealth that he may achieve for himself. Such thoughts elicit great excitement from him, as well as interest and a bit of attraction within his soul, which is called "progress from his place." We clearly observe that upon the arrival of a good business deal that is important, he labors with all of his power of thought and becomes very attached to the proposition, with excitement that we call "cleaving" within thought…and this is what we call "hearing" within thought. The sign of this occurring is when he is so involved that it "moves him" a bit.

And so it is regarding meditation upon G-dly concepts. This type of thought, wherein he cleaves heartily to a matter that is important to him, is called a "good thought that combines with action." At the very least, from this thought will be born love and fear of G-d that spurs him to action. The "cold" and objective thought mentioned above, even when he truly desires to approach and become excited, will not stimulate him to experience "hearing" within thought. He meditates "from afar", merely acknowledging G-dliness as mentioned…and nothing emerges from this ["frigid"] thought other than a resolution to "refrain from evil." That is to say, since the meditation is real and honest, it is appropriate and [will aid him] in refraining from evil and doing good – but this is merely the lowest level…

But, the "good thought" mentioned above, also applies to reciting the *shema Yisrael* ("Hear Oh Israel…")…followed by *veahavta* ("You shall love…"), since the main point [of the *Shema*] is only the excitement of "hearing" within thought, mentioned above. And from it develops love, but nevertheless, no excitement of the heart develops as of yet, but merely excitement within thought. So, this level of love is only for the purpose of action and not for anything internal, such as excitement of the heart, at all…All this is called *dechilu verechimu* ("fear and love" in the language of the Zohar). Even though they are associated with action alone, nonetheless they lend much light and energy to his thought processes. This is similar, for example to a thought that is very personal to someone regarding worldly matters. Within this thought, he develops love and excitement at the very least, and he comes to fear the opposite, as if from damage and destruction…

The fourth level above this occurs as, upon meditating on G-dliness, we attain proper excitement as described above, and immediately experience stimulation of the heart, including illumination and great energy. This is a much more internal experience than the stimulation of the "good thought" mentioned above (and yet, it is not the real G-dly excitement of experiencing G-dliness in the heart as well, which is an experience of the G-dly soul as it expands through the body. That level is far above even the fifth level that we will presently explain). And about this fourth level, we say, "You shall love…with all your heart" – with emphasis on the heart. This is the main point of *avoda shebeleiv* – prayers – to belabor ourselves so much in meditation that our heart becomes excited…[which occurs] after much effort. For regarding matters of the world, as soon as a good idea occurs to us, and we are mentally stimulated, the excitement immediately translates into love like fire of desire or the opposite - with bitterness in response to anything negative or hateful within the thought. But, in service of G-d, it is not easy to produce excitement of the heart through stimulation of the mind, because the G-dliness that we do experience during this meditation is not drawn consciously down to the heart. Rather it remains transcendent and inspirational in the mind. Now, there are many levels to this regarding the nature of excitement of the heart; there are those who are excited in the heart more than in the mind and there are those who become excited more by joy…

The fifth level, above the previous one, is the inner intention within the heart, that transcends even excitement within the heart. The explanation of this is that, as known, even when we experience total excitement in the heart, with desire and joy or bitterness on account of our meditation, within the moment of excitement in the heart is condensed the entire "length" of the G-dly concept about which we were excited, leaving nothing but what is relevant to the excitement in the heart alone. That is, what arises from a synopsis of the intention of the meditation regarding *memalle* ("immanent spirituality") and *sovev* ("transcendent G-dliness") and the like, is the main point and origin of the intention...for everything stands before Him as naught, etc...

As a result of this concise synopsis [of the meditation], the heart becomes even more excited. However, this [experience] is actually a minor revelation compared to the essence of the intention in his heart [that develops as a result] of the full length of [meditation upon] the G-dly concept on which he focused in his mind and heart. There, [the full] length and breadth is beyond our ability to experience in the heart. By way of example from matters of the world; when man devotes attention from the very depths of his mind to the greatness of some good business deal, and his whole soul is attached to it, nevertheless he may not be able yet to direct his heart to the matter and get excited about it because he is totally involved with his whole mind and heart in the essential quality of the deal itself. This is called *mochin degadlut* ("mature mindfullness") within our intellectual faculties (*chabad*)....

...and although there are also emotions of love and fear concealed [within this level of consciousness], they are called "intellectual love and fear" alone. They are beyond natural love and fear of the heart...intellectual love and fear are inseparable from the [intellectual] essence of the meditation itself. Rather, [they emerge] spontaneously and automatically, of necessity without our choice or will at all. And within the heart, they also emerge spontaneously, just as one who spontaneously claps his hands out of happiness. And the sign of this is that the excitement is constant while he is under the influence of this meditation, and it does not interrupt at all, unlike natural love and fear [during meditation on the third and fourth levels], which dissipate only to return again. And therefore, the concept of "labor" does not apply to this intellectual love and fear so much...and beyond this there is also the simple will which far transcends any meditation whatsoever, but is rather an essential and simple will from which and because of which the intellect emerges, as known...

[Starting on page 139, the Mitteler Rebbe describes the five levels of *nefesh-ruach-neshama-chaya-yechida* in the Divine G-dly soul]:

"Above are explained five general levels of the natural soul alone, aside from the level on which there is nothing G-dly whatsoever. [That level] relates only to one who seeks excitement devoid of any conscious G-dly intention – only unconscious motivation. Now, there is a similar level as well within the Divine soul, when it is a state of ultimate lack of consciousness, or concealed awareness....When it comes to performance of mitzvoth alone, which is the lowest level of the soul, in action alone...then if it weren't for the natural essence of every Jewish spark within the soul, to refrain from evil and to do good, then their own *avoda* and fear of G-d called *frumkeit* ("religiosity"), would not suffice [to continue fulfilling Torah and mitzvoth]. But, with the motivation of *avoda* and fear within each and every one according to his abilities, the natural essential power of the G-dly soul on each and every detail of refraining from evil and doing good is strengthened and the person clings to his level without varying or becoming lenient or transgressing to err or allowing himself become permissive. And in this there are great differences from one person another, from a complete *tzadik* to one who is totally evil person in his deeds.

Now, certainly this involvement in action and avoidance of evil together with commitment to good coming from the essence of the G-dly soul is first initiated in thought. [Specifically], this is the will for G-dliness within thought, to fulfill His will in action at the very least, and not to transgress His will in deed. And this thought is devoid of any internal illumination or energy whatsoever. It is cold, like the "cold thought" of the natural soul regarding G-dly meditation.

Now, the second level, somewhat above this is more internal, for it is beyond simple positive action in merely fulfilling the mitzvoth, which is the level of *nefesh* mentioned above. It is the level of *ruach* which transcends *nefesh*, corresponding to the second level of the natural soul, called excitement of the "good thought." This is understood by way of example of the Jews who exited from Egypt, all of the nation, children and women, on account of the simple faith within their soul, since they believed in G-d. Even though to begin with, out of "lack of spirit," they did not listen to Moshe, when their spirit returned to them, they believed with a G-dly spirit that was essential and rooted in their souls from the G-dly soul, with internal light and energy. And all of them went out of Egypt, which was an act of total excitement in their thought and inner will, called "progress from their place." This is comparable to the "good thought" spoken of earlier regarding something that is close to the person. And as a result of this, even though it may not be so applicable to the person in action alone – that is, leaving Egypt - but it produces light and energy in the soul that is much more internal than the "cold thought" above, which is concealed within action of refraining from evil and doing good, without energy whatsoever…

This is further understood from the example of the ingathering of the sparks of holiness that fell through the "shattering of the vessels," whether of the idol worshippers [where the "sparks" dwelt for several hundred and thousands of years, and now they totally awaken and return], or of converts who convert, which is an amazing and wonderful phenomenon. That someone should experience a desire to convert, is due to nothing other than a G-dly spirit blowing through him, even without him being aware of it. This is comparable to the converts in the time of Abraham, such as Aner, Eshkol and Mamre, and similar [events occur] in every generation…

This is further understood by the example of *ba'alei tshuva* [Jews who strayed from the path of Torah and mitzvoth, who seek their way back]. Although formerly sunken in many kinds of evil lusts and serious transgression, nevertheless, their spirit arouses to return in *tshuva*. And there are those who return from the very depths of their heart, to the extent of crying out their soul, such as R' Elazar ben Durdaya, who expired while crying. Rebi was envious of him, saying the he "acquired his world to come in one moment."…This corresponds to what was explained above regarding the "good thought that combines with action" of love and fear in the mind, including excitement, at least…Now, from all this, we may grasp the general topic of essential excitement of the G-dly soul, in an internal manner, which is the level of *ruach*, above the level of *nefesh* which is nothing more than the action itself, as explained above.

Now, the third level above this is the essential excitement of the level of *neshama*, as written, *kol haneshama tehalel* ("the entire soul praises…"). And also as written, "If he will devote his heart and his spirit to Him, then his soul will be gathered to Him…" This level corresponds to what was previously mentioned regarding the "detached excitement" of the natural soul; as it attains the stimulation known as a "good thought" within the physical heart, with excitement that he experiences like fiery flames of desire…in the G-dly soul. This is essential excitement of the physical heart, resulting from true grasp of G-dliness within the divine soul as it is enclothed within the intellectual grasp of the natural soul. This is what is meant by, "My heart and my flesh sing to the living G-d" – the physical flesh of the heart itself sings to G-d. This is like the excitement associated with a melody that resonates in the physical heart, which emerges spontaneously, by itself and automatically, without any choice or labor whatsoever, but just because of the essential excitement of the G-dly soul…And this is the main difference between the conscious excitement within the heart coming from the natural soul – when he himself knows and is aware and feels his excitement. And therefore, without a doubt the G-dliness is distant and concealed in this state, for there is "one who is excited" and therefore he is an "entity" [implying lack of nullification to G-d] in and of himself. This is true to the extent that he turns his excitement, rather than G-dliness, into the main goal, as mentioned above regarding the excitement of the heart that is not for G-d at all but for his own enjoyment revealed in his soul. But, the essential excitement of the G-dly soul, although it is felt in the heart, is not conscious at all. And it is not a conscious experience at all, to the extent that he does not know of it at the time that it occurs and neither does it "feel" itself. This is comparable to the excitement and desire that a son has for his father in his heart. Since it is natural and essential excitement, he doesn't experience it himself as excitement and is unaware of it, for the most part, and so regarding the excitement of the father for the son….this level exists among most people who have not yet sullied their G-dly soul, nor damaged themselves with the impurity of the body and foreign lusts so much…

 And the fourth level is a [concentrated point] of intention within the mind, that is above any excitement that may still be experienced within the heart. For example, this is comparable to the fourth level within the natural soul, when one is totally absorbed to the depths of his mind and heart, in the amazing nature of something positive. His soul is attracted to it, preventing him from experiencing any excitement in his heart. Now, this is called "intellectual fear and love," as when the intellect itself is excited. This is not the excitement that comes from a concise synopsis of the concept [under meditation]. Now, the essential excitement of the heart mentioned above, of which he is unconscious, emerges suddenly without any preparation. It is like, for example excitement that appears suddenly, causing one to clap his hands. So as well, this "song" within the physical heart emerges spontaneously of its own accord, just as any essential excitement, and this is the main sign of its appearance. And this level also contains a more internal element, when the meditator is drawn after a concise synopsis [of the concept] in his mind. This is the depth of essential intention within the concept…

 Nevertheless, it is not within range of the essential excitement within the inner intention of the mind, when the intellectual point of the concept itself is aroused. This is called *kavana*…this *kavana* refers to the essence of the essential G-dly light in and of itself, and not as the result of his intellectual grasp and understanding. It is above the length and breadth of grasp of *bina*, although it subsequently expresses itself in intellectual grasp…and this *kavana* contains essential, unmitigated enjoyment of the essence and simplicity of the G-dly soul. It is the source of Shabbat prayers… which are above the weekday prayers… Similarly, every day of the week during the *kriat shema*, a reflection and ray shines from Shabbat…And for that reason, the excitement of the *kriat shema*, with love, is different from that of the *pesukei dezimra*. During the *pesukei dezimra*, the excitement is felt, from the mind to the heart, just as during the excitement of the angels, with a noise and commotion…and during the *kriat shema* as we say *shema Yisrael* to the soul, so that it surrenders itself as we say *echad*, up to *veahavta* – the result is that we produce love within the natural soul as well… But, during the essential excitement within the point of *kavana* in the mind, the excitement of the heart with conscious love becomes included within it…and since this is more internal and essential, it comes as something that is not felt, and does not even experience itself…in general this is the level of *chaya* – *koach mah* – of *chochma* within the G-dly soul. There is where illuminates the *mazla* and *tzelem* ("image"), which is the *makif* of *chaya*, within which dwells the *neshama yeteira* of Shabbat which is the *makif* of *yechida*, the highest of all…and it does not illuminate in a revealed manner at all, but rather shines from afar, hidden, and this is the inner fifth level to be explained…

And the fifth level is the essential *yechida* itself, which is also called the "simple song," indicating that it comes from the essence and ascends with song, and is therefore called a simple song...for the "double song" mentioned above is essential enjoyment that comes as a private revelation, particular to every person according to his grasp of G-dliness, just as souls "enjoy the ray from the *ziva ila'ah*" of *atik* within *malchut* of *Atzilut*. Each person according to the extent of his own point of grasp, enjoys G-dly intellect, and not all souls are equal in this. But, the "simple" song is accompanied by abstract enjoyment that is the source of all kinds of specific enjoyments of this [spiritual] nature. Therefore, it comes as enjoyment that is all-inclusive of all essential [kinds of] enjoyment...This is like by way of example, one who is immersed in escaping and saving himself from certain death – his entire point of will within the essence of his soul is aroused. It touches his very essence, and thus all of his other desires, such as love for money or for his wife and children, fall by the wayside. All of a sudden, they are unimportant to him, since they are included in the very essence of this will that touches his very essence. He is then fully involved and nothing remains [of his other desires], and he feels nothing whatsoever of himself. This is the love of *bekol meodecha* ("with all of your might"), without limit and above his *nefesh-ruach-neshama*, and also above the *koach mah* within his soul, that comes enclothed in the *kavana* of the mind. But, this is beyond intellect and logic completely, for there is no logic at all behind the inner, simple, abstract desire and enjoyment – not even a "concealed" will that sometimes exists in the origins of abstract intellect. And since this level is not common at all among the vast majority of people, therefore to speak of it at length is extraneous. But, nevertheless, it is present in a concealed manner in every Jewish spark [soul] on Shabbat, in their souls, and it is called the *neshama yeteira*, which is the *makif* of *yechida*...

[For more elucidation of the topic of *hitbonenut* and the soul levels of *naranchai*, see the series *Besha'ah shehikdimu 5672* (1912) of the Rebbe Rashab, vol. 2, page 803-831 (chapters 391-404)]

ii) Page 4 (Page 4 in the translation as well)

Note: "the self-nullification of acknowledgment..." See *Sha'ar lag b'omer* in the *Siddur*. See the discourse *Kol dodi* of the year *5668* (1908). And the discourse *Vayahas Caleb* of the year *5614* (1914).

From the Siddur with Chasidut of the Alter Rebbe, *Sha'ar Lag B'omer*, page 606

"...and this is why we say *modim anachnu lach sheatah Elokeinu* ("We acknowledge/thank You that You are our G-d...") – because You are our G-d. [This alludes] to the supernal thought, wherein the collective Jewish nation arose in its source, the origin from which they were hewn. And therefore, automatically, we acknowledge [Him] with this concession, without need of any sign or proof at all... but this acknowledgment takes place in the G-dly soul alone as it exists in its source and origin above in "thought." However, as the soul descends and becomes en-clad in the physical substance of the body, which obscures it, it is not capable of achieving this level of acknowledgment, of "You are Our Lord our G-d," Who constantly renews [the universe] from nothing to something, since the corporeality of the body conceals this level of acknowledgment.

For that reason, the sages established *modim derabanen* – "rabbinic acknowledgment," [the phrase that we recite during the *shemoneh esreh*, beginning with the word *modim*], which is *hoda'ah lehoda'ah* - "conceding that we must acknowledge." That is, we concede that the appropriate response to You is to acknowledge/thank You.

Now, the explanation is that there are two levels to acknowledgment. The first is acknowledgment that results from awareness and knowledge, as one who grasps [for example] and recognizes the mighty greatness and majesty of a king. And therefore, he concedes and acknowledges that so it is, since he recognizes and understands. The same is true of a sage – we concede his amazing wisdom since we recognize and grasp his greatness. However, there is a level of acknowledgment below this, which takes place when we lack knowledge. This occurs when it is not within our power to grasp or to recognize at all, any of the might, majesty or wisdom as it really exists. All that we can do is know and recognize that [the king or the sage] is lofty in his wisdom and therefore we must concede to him with admission and great praise, just as a poor person admits the greatness of the king, even though he has no concept of the king's essential greatness as it really exists. Nevertheless, he admits that he must concede and praise this greatness, even though he does not grasp it. And this takes place as a result of the great distance of the one who concedes [from the object of his praise]. For, the greater the gulf, the less he will be capable of admitting out of knowledge. Rather, we are forced to simply admit because we must do so. And this is what the sages meant when they said, "Most acknowledgments, [because] He is a G-d of acknowledgments," indicating that there are a myriad levels of acknowledgment/giving thanks.

The more that we contemplate the greatness of the infinite light above, which is exalted and beyond intellectual grasp, [the more we realize that] we do not know how to acknowledge it out of knowledge and grasp. We are only capable of admitting that we must acknowledge. And in this manner, we succeed in conceding up to the highest levels, with many acknowledgments of concession and admission, in proportion to the distance of the intellectual grasp…and this in general is the reason that the sages established *modim derabanen*, to express the general concept of admission of acknowledgment.

From the discourse *Kol dodi* of the year *5668* (1908), of the Rebbe Rashab, Page 152:

"…and the soul faculty of *hod* [is what motivates us] to bow and acknowledge G-d, Who enlivens and creates everything, as if naught before Him. And although we do not grasp this, we acknowledge, as written in Tanya, *Igeret Hakodesh, siman* 15, (entitled *lehavin mashal u'melitza*). This concept corresponds to what is written in *Likutei Torah*, in the discourse *Bayom Hashmini Atzeret*, [regarding] the distinction between prostrating oneself and bowing from the waist. We prostrate ourselves when we undersatand and grasp the truth about the greatness of G-d and His unity, and we focus our concentraion strongly upon this. Then, the concept penetrates and illuminates us in a revealed manner, and automatically we become nullfied in an internal manner. We are truly nullified within, and whatever is the opposite, meaning not nullified to G-d truly concerns us to the very inner point of our heart. [This is so] until we subdue the *sitra achra* and transform all the evil within it and it possesses no other will at all.

However, bowing (from the waist) occurs when we do not understand or grasp at all, how it is that the entire creation is as if naught before Him, and the concept does not shine in our soul, yet nevertheless we labor ourselves in prayer, meditating upon how all levels of revelation, even of the higher spiritual worlds, are nothing but a mere ray that has no significance whatsoever. And everything is before Him as truly naught, and the creations themselves are as nothing in their own estimation and experience as well. And even though we do not grasp the essence of the matter in and of itself, how and what it is, nevertheless we know that is the truth (and we also grasp how this is true, but our grasp is without true understanding that illuminates the matter, enabling us to feel and experience it inside)…

(Page 159)…Now, just as the faculty of *netzach* ("security and determination") never changes nor varies at all, so the faculty of *hod* ("acknowledgment and gratitude") does not vary or change. The faculty of *hoda'ah* is found in each and everyone, at all times, even though it may be in a state of intellectual immaturity and grasp, nevertheless *hoda'ah* still occurs. We are always capable of admitting the truth. And all the moreso that everyone possesses the attribute of admission within acknowledgment, which is permanent.

For, as known, there are two types of *hoda'ah*: One is acknowledgment that results from logic and intellect. That is, we understand, at the very least, that we must concede. For example, we concede to a friend that his perspective is correct, even though our own reasoning may not necessarily agree. Nevertheless we may grasp that the truth corresponds with the point of view of our friend, and because of that we concede to him. Or, we may acknowledge a great sage or king; even though we have no idea or grasp of his wisdom because we have no ability of intellect to plumb the depth of his wisdom. And the same may be true of the majesty and greatness of a king, of which we have no idea or grasp of even how to go about achieving knowledge of his loftiness and greatness. Nevertheless we understand that he is majestic and lofty and that he is a great king or sage.

And the second category occurs when we know nothing, meaning that we, with our intellect and grasp know nothing and totally fail to grasp that he is lofty and majestic or that the sage is very wise. All we know is the truth of the matter that he is wise, and to this we admit, and concede and acknowledge even though we in ourselves know nothing of this at all. Now, in general, the power of acknowledgment - and in particular of the second category of acknowledgment – such that even when we do not grasp anything we concede and nullify ourselves – comes from the very essence and core of the soul…

From the discourse, *Vayahas Caleb 5674* (1914), in the series *Besha'ah shehikdimu*, vol. 2, page 516:

"In general, there are three stages of development; *ibur* ("pregnancy"), *yenikah* ("nursing"), and *mochin* ("intellect," or "maturity"). *Ibur* is the ultimate immaturity, when all of the faculties are concealed and there is no indication of intellect as of yet. For example, the embryo when in the womb of its mother, is doubled over, with its head between its knees, indicating that all that is revealed of his faculties are the instinctual faculties of *nehi* (*netzach*, *hod* and *yesod*) alone. The intellectual faculties of *chabad* (*chochma*, *bina* and *da'at*) as well as the emotional faculties of *chagat* (*chesed*, *gevura* and *tiferet*) are concealed…

…Now, *nehi* within *nehi* corresponds to the attribute of *hoda'ah*, or "acknowledgment." This occurs when we do not grasp the matter at hand, for if we grasped it then it would not be appropriate to concede or admit it, for after all, we grasp the matter. Only when we do not grasp the matter does it become necessary to concede the matter. And yet there is still some amount of intellectual influence present, since we reason that we must acknowledge. That is, we reason that the matter is as stated [or described to us]. Even though the matter is not settled in our mind so that we know how and what it is, nevertheless we do know that it is so. Just as, for example regarding a very wise man, who speaks of deep and elevated concepts - even one who does not know and is not familiar with his thinking, and therefore does not grasp at all the nature of his wisdom and its loftiness, is nevertheless aware that this man possesses very lofty wisdom. He has at least that much connection to intellect, that at least he recognizes the amazing nature [of wisdom] even though he may not know the nature of [the sage's] ideas since he cannot grasp the concepts.

And so in the realm of spirituality, we say *modim anachnu lach she atah HaShem Elokeinu* – "we acknowledge You, that You are the Lord our G-d." In general, He creates the words from nothing to something, and in particular Jewish souls are aware of this, since the Jews "arose within His thought." Now, even though we may have no idea or grasp of the matter of creation from nothing to something, nor how it occurs, and in particular we have no idea of the amazing details, nevertheless we know that G-dliness creates and brings into existence from nothing to something. And when it comes to speaking of these matters, as during the *pesukei dezimra*, we experience a little bit of feeling and we become excited within, which in turn produces nullification to G-d. And although there is not a lot of intellect in this, and there is no more than a bit of knowledge alone, nevertheless we know and we have some kind of connection to the matter.

Now, this is true of most people who are not involved in attempting to grasp inner concepts of G-dliness. Still, they know of the matter of creation from nothing to something in general, and they are stimulated by it. For, acknowledgment of admission occurs as we say *modim anachnu lach, al sheanu modim lach* – "we acknowledge that we must concede to You." That is, we have no connection to this knowledge and we experience no knowledge or feeling at all, and yet we are nullified to G-dliness. Acknowledgment [alone] occurs when we have some form of knowledge and feeling…"

iii) Page 5 (Page 9 in the translation)

Note: "*Bina* – the supernal bride…" See *Likutei Torah* on "Song of Songs" at the very beginning, as well as the discourse *Beyom HaShmini, 5693* (1933), [from the Rebbe Rayatz, *ztz"l*], published in *Kuntresim aleph, Kuntres* 21.

From *Likutei Torah* of the Alter Rebbe, *Shir haShirim* ("Song of songs") in the very beginning: (Page *aleph*).

"As known, G-d is called a *chatan* ("bridegroom"). And the Jewish people are called a *callah* ("bride"). And this is as a result of the descent and influence of Torah on the Jewish nation. As the sages said, the verse, "On the day of His wedding" refers to *matan Torah* – the giving of the Torah. And that is why one who makes the *chatan* happy merits to the Torah which was given with five "voices," as mentioned in the first chapter of Talmud *Berachot*. For, *chatan* is *chut darga* ("lowered level"). That is, *chatan* alludes to the descent and drawing down of the infinite light from Above, in order to enclothe in the Torah. And the Jewish nation is the source of Jewish souls, and every individual spark of the Jews is an aspect of *callah* – the bride.

Now, the word *callah* has two definitions. One, is from the Hebrew word *claiyon* ("destruction"), as in something that consumes and swallows up everything. For, the name *callah* is a noun that is indicative of action, such as *rachah* ("soft"), *zachah* ("meritorious") or *dakah* ("thin"). And here, *callah* indicates destruction and consumption…

The second meaning of *callah* comes from the phrase, *caltah naphshi* ("my soul expires"), referring to the desire of the soul to cling and be included in His G-dly illumination…And the matter is as follows; in the *kriat shema* there are found two kinds of *mesirat nefesh*, or self sacrifice. The first is when we "deliver" our souls as we say the word *echad*. And the second occurs as we say *bekol napshecha* – "with all of your soul," even if he takes your soul…

From the discourse, *Bayom Hashemini 5693* (1933) of the Rebbe Rayatz *ztz'l*, in *Kuntres Maamorim Aleph, kuntres 21*, Page 511 (*resh-nun-vov*):

"...and they are the two kinds of self-sacrifice of the *kriat shema*, to deliver the soul while reciting the words *echad*, as well as during the phrase *bekol nafshecha* ("with all of your soul") – "even if he takes away your soul." For the *avoda* required to arrive at this level of *mesirat nefesh* of *echad* takes place when we meditate on the first verse of the *kriat shema - Shema Yisrael Havaya* is our G-d, *Havaya* is one. For the seven heavens and the earth and the four directions of the universe are nullified and united in ultimate unity. "just as You were before the world was created, so You are after the world was created" - with total equality. And so it is concerning creation – after it was created the creatures are just as before creation, for the infinite light shines in a revealed manner after the *tzimtzum* ("contraction" of G-dly light) just as before. And if so, just like before the *tzimtzum* there was no existence whatsoever, so after the *tzimtzum* there is also no existence whatsoever. All is totally nullified in existence, as written elsewhere regarding meditation on this topic. During true meditation, delving deeply using our faculty of *da'at*, we become truly nullified and united with Him.

This is called *callah*, from the phrase *caltah she'ari* ("my self is consumed") – interpreted by Onkelos to mean "destruction of my physicality" – complete destruction of the sense of "existence." And then, not only are the lusts and foreign desires nullified, but they do not exist at all...for since the nullfication is of the nature of "all stands before Him as naught" - with a nullification and unity before Him, they are totally lacking existence."

iv) Page 7 (Page 18 in the translation)

Note: "And the heart also becomes excited..." See *Kuntres Hatefila*, chpt. 4-6

From the synopses of the chapters of *Kuntres Hatefila*, appearing on Pages 15, 17 and 18 of *Kuntres Hatefila* of the Rebbe Rashab.

Ch. 4: "True *avoda* involves labor of the mind with intense concentration, automatically producing excitement of the heart – this is what draws in the heart."

Ch. 5: "*Da'at* ("knowledge" which becomes deeply ingrained and integrated with the emotions) is an independent intellectual faculty (apart from the ability to focus and concentrate). It implies the ability to feel, and to experience the concept under consideration. The nerves (organs) responding to this feeling are mostly in the mind. And then, the excitement that develops in the heart is true and real."

Ch. 6: "Here, it is explained that there is excitement of the heart that occurs merely as the result of a *bachein* ("residual emotional impression" coming from contemplation of a topic). It is not deep and it dissipates quickly. The main goal is that the essence of G-dly light should illuminate in our mind, and this comes only as the result of laborious meditation. The advice [to aid in achieving this goal] is to accustom ourself to learning with great devotion and depth."

v) Page 9 (Page 25 in the translation)

Note: "…the world of *Briah* does not…" See the Chassidic discourse *Ain omdim lehitpalel* in the series of discourses of the year *5666* (1905-6) (*Yom-tov shel Rosh Hashana*…) of the Rebbe Rashab. See also the letter of the Rebbe R'Yoseph Yitzhak from the 15 of Mar Cheshvan, *5698* (1938) at length.

From the discourse, *Ain Omdim*, in the series *Yomtov shel Rosh Hashana 5666* (1906) of the Rebbe Rashab, page 484: "…the quality of the world of *Briah* is that it is the first entity that the G-dly void carries within itself…and therefore the world of Briah, while implying new creation, is nonetheless not a full-fledged entity… but rather possibility of creation, meaning that it 'allows room' for created existence. That is, the G-dly void [from which all creation devolves] implies lack of existence and its absence, while Briah allows room for existence."

From the letter of the Rebbe Rayatz *ztz'l*, dated 15th of Cheshvan, *5698* (1938) at length [the writer requests from the Rebbe a clarification of the concept of 'worlds,' and the Rebbe answers at length – 11 pages. Regarding the world of *Briah*, the Rebbe says], "the world of *Briah* is the second of the four worlds. It is called *Briah* since it is the first entity after *Atzilut*, and since it exists. Even though it is a spiritual world and called a "hidden world," and the spiritual light of *Atzilut* illuminates there, especially the *sphera* of *bina*, [intellectual analysis] of *Atzilut* (in the world of *Atzilut* itself the light of the *sephira* of *chochma* [spiritual insight] is dominant) – and therefore *Briah* is called the world of intellectual grasp, nevertheless, it is called *Briah* for two reasons:

Among the distinctions between the worlds of *Atzilut* and *Briah* – even though they are many – is that *Atzilut* is called *ayn* since it is not grasped by the intellect, while *Briah* is called *yesh* since it is understood. [It is graspable] since it has existence, and its existence is called *Briah*, as the Ramban said, that in the holy tongue of Hebrew, no word indicates emergence from nothing into something aside from the word *barah* (creation). That is to say, that the difference between *Briah* and *Atzilut* is that everything in *Atzilut*, whether *heichalot*, *spherot*, *orot*, or *kelim* etc. exists as well in *Briah*.' However, while *Atzilut* is a revelation of the hidden [infinite light Above] rather than an expression of anything new, *Briah* is a creation from nothing into something. And since it takes on [the qualities of] existence, even though a very refined existence, as the Ramban wrote – a refined existence devoid of substance, whose only quality is that it is prepared to take on form - nevertheless, it does exist, which is why it is called *Briah*.

The word *briah* denotes something that exists in a state of revelation, as we see in *halacha* regarding the status of an animal that has a thorn lodged in its windpipe – 'we don't suspect that [the thorn] *hivrih'* – dislodged outside of the windpipe. The Aramaic translation of *chutz* (outside in Hebrew) is '*bara*.' That is, since the object exists outwardly in a revealed manner, it is called a *briah*.

vi) Page 10 (Page 34 in the translation)

Note: "and explained elsewhere…" See *Likutei Torah* in the explanation to the discourse, *Eileh Pikudei*, section 4 and onward.

From *Likutei Torah* of the Alter Rebbe, *parshat Pekudei*, Page *zayin* (between 12 and 14), left column: "Now, just as a crown is made of precious stones, which are in essence minerals, but which have been refined so that they are translucent and shining – in this manner is created the crown of the king. Similarly, the sages said the the angel "*Sanda'l* creates crowns for his Creator from the prayers of the Jews." This is because the letters of prayers, called "stones," when refined by the self sacrifice of the Jews as they utter the word *echad* (during the *kriat shema*), become like a crown. And so regarding the fulfillment of mitzvoth, which include the mitzvoth from the Torah and the seven rabbinic commandments, are the 620 pillars of light of which comprise the *sephira* of *keter*. This occurs because when the light is forced to descend all the way to physical world of *asiya*, for example into the parchment of the *tefilin* and the wool of *tzitzit*, which is similar to mineral, the highest light becomes "wedged" in the lowest place. And that is what attracts the light from above the entire spiritual chain of creation, which is associated with the *sephira* of *keter*. And that is why the sages said that, "in the future, the righteous will sit with their crowns on their head…" For the revelation of G-dliness in *gan eden* is not merely from the "river that emerges from the *gan*" which is *chochma* and *bina* which provide revelation for the soul alone. Rather, in the future, upon the resurrection of the dead, there will occur illumination of the body as well…and this takes place via revelation of G-dly light from above the spiritual chain of creation, that is able to descend to the lowest of levels.

vii) Page 10 (Page 35 in the translation)

Note: "Even in the *amida*…" See in the *siddur* accompanied by Chassidut of the Alter Rebbe, in the discourse *Adni sfosay*… ("G-d please open my lips" - in the prayers of Rosh Hashana). See also *Torat Chaim*, parshat *Noah*, chpt. 28. See as well the end of the discourse, *VeHaish mishtaeh*, in *Torat Chaim, parshat Chayei Sarah* (chpt 17)

From the Alter Rebbe's *siddur* on Rosh Hashana, Page 474: "And this is what is meant by *Adni sfatai tiftach* ("*Adni*, open up my lips…"); as we proceed from *geula* (the end of kriat shema) to *tefila* (the *amida*), we bring the G-dly spark within our soul closer, making it into a vessel capable of receiving the light of *Z'a d'Atzilut* (the lower seven *sephirot* of Atzilut). Our G-dly soul becomes absorbed in the name *Adni*, which is also the *sephira* of *malchut* as known, and is also called *dina demalchuta* ("the law of the kingdom"). But, the *aleph* (first letter of *Adni* sweetens [the *din*]…and that is why we say *Adni sfatai tiftach*; that is to say, 'You open my lips with the five enunciators of the mouth (the "five stringencies" which break up the voice into words), which are the five divisions [of speech] in any way that You want. This is not dependent upon speech itself at all, but rather upon the *aleph*…

…the speech of prayer is silent since the person is nullified to the very essence of G-dliness. By way of example, one who is deeply involved in his own thought processes and does not consciously choose his words…rather his words are expressed and emerge spontaneously according to the nature of his intellect…so in prayer we say 'G-d please open up my lips.' There is no choice expressed in this speech, as written regarding Chana, that "her lips were moving but her voice was not heard," indicating the nullification of speech, for at that point the speech is guided only by the *aleph* that sweetens…

…and afterwards, we say *upi yagid tehilatecha* – "my mouth will tell Your praises" – as the simple voice that divides into the five enunciations of the mouth, draws G-dliness down to the lowest levels…"

From *Torat Chaim* of the Mitteler Rebbe, parshat *Noah*, chpt. 28: "…and therefore, we say *Adni sfatai tiftach*…for there are no words on my tongue at all, not even a silent word. There is only, "You open my lips," since I am totally nullified in the very essence of my soul (for silent speech in and of itself, such as one who is preoccupied and mutters words with his lips while absorbed in thought, is one who has ascended to his own source within his *koach hamaskil*, the source of intellect, called "*adam*." However, during the *amida*, all aspects of human speech are totally nullified to G-d's essence. Our silent speech emerges spontaneously without aid from ourselves. We can only say, "You open my lips," as did Chana, whose lips moved automatically because of the *makif* of *yechida* within the inner point of her heart. This is like the verse, "And they screamed from the heart," with an inner scream, since then we are like one who is completely paralyzed. As it says in the Zohar, "the still small voice – this is the silent prayer – that is where the King is found"…)

And this is a result of tremendous lowliness and bitterness of the soul, to the extent that the person cannot "go out" of himself at all, and becomes like a "point" as he exists within the essence of his soul beyond intellect and also beyond Divine will and delight, like one who prostrates himself to the ground before the king. He is totally nullified in every sense, from within and without (and that is why our prayer then has the ability to arouse the infinite light that is beyond Torah and mitzvoth, as above).

From *Torat Chaim* of the Mitteler Rebbe, *parshat Chayei Sarah* (chpt 17):

"…this is the difference between two different kinds of nullification of the self; nullification of the ego occurs during the silent *amida*. This is described by the verse, "What did you seek?" It alludes to the path of arrival to nullification of our intellect to the ultimate degree. To begin with, we grasped [to understand the concept], which is why we can now say, "What did you seek?" This is said after one has arrived to the depth of the concept, the *ayn*, or Divine void of the *yesh* of intellect grasp – this is what is expressed by the verse, "What did you seek?" This is similar to one who arrives to the depth of a concept which is above intellectual grasp, but is not (yet) concrete (in his mind). At that point, he mutters very quietly with his lips, as one who is preoccupied delving to the depths of some intellectual concept. He does not intend to speak, but his words emerge spontaneously, very silently as known (and that is why during the *amida*, since we are in such a state of nullification of the ego, that we are unable to speak with any real intention. All we can say is, "Lord, open up my lips"…and nonetheless there is some speech present.

But, the origin of *nefilat apayim* ("putting our head down" during *tachanun*, when we ask for forgiveness for transgressions) is the very essence of the Divine void (*ayn*), corresponding to the phrase, "No thought can grasp Him whatsoever." It is not appropriate to describe this state as "What did you seek…" And therefore there is no speech whatsoever, but only total silence. And that is the vessel to receive *reiya* – "vision" of G-dliness, face to face as when one prostrates himself to the ground. For, there is no vessel that is capable of accepting the very essence of His infinite light. There is no mental intention or level of nullification of the ego [that can serve as a vessel for His infinite light], but rather only this complete and total silence like a stone.

viii) Page 11 (Page 35 in the translation)

Note: "As written elsewhere regarding *avanim* (stones)" – See *Likutei Torah* in the discourse *Vesamti Cadcad...* (the second), section 3. See also the discourse, *Velakachta es shtey...* in the series of discourses of the year *5668* (1908) of the fifth Lubavitcher Rebbe, the Rebbe Rashab).

From *Likutei Torah* of the Alter Rebbe, parshat *Re'eh*, Page *Caf-zein* (27) – Section 3

"Now we may understrand the topic of precious stones: they are of the mineral category, and nevertheless they shine. And from where do they have this ability to shine? In the main, their development is from the stars – and not from the stars that we can see, for those stars are countable – there are roughly one thousand of them. Rather, it comes from the stars that are invisible to us, for they are truly unlimited in number at all. And they are not revealed and evident to us, but they have the power to illuminate within precious stones. Because they are of the mineral category, which is the lowest level, therefore they receive a ray of light from the stars, which are without number at all, which are the invisible stars that are beyond the stars that we are able to see.

Now, since there are a huge, unlimited number of stars, so there are muliple rays of light shining within precious stones, imparting multiple different appearances, and descriptions. For there are many shades of transparency – there is transparency that is completely pure, and there is transparency that is not so clear. And so are the appearances, for stones divide into a myriad different varieties, but in general there are twelve stones corresponding to the twelve tribes of Israel...

...Now, also in general, their appearance falls into two categories. There are those that shine with "direct illumination," meaning that they illuminate and with their light it is possible to see others. That is, when we bring such stones into darkness, they shine, since their light radiates from within outward. And, there are other stones that shine and throw off their light like a bolt of lightening in the eye of the observer. Their beautiful ray flashes in the eye of the observer – this is the light of "reflected illumination."

Now, these represent two kinds of *tzadikim*, the *tzadik elyon* ("upper *tzadik*"), [whose *avoda* is] from above to below, and the *tzadik tachton* ("lower *tzadik*"), [whose *avoda* is] from below to above. These are Yoseph the *tzadik* and Binyamin the *tzadik*. Binyamin shone from below to above, with "reflected illumination," representing the yearning and desire of lower creation to connect with their spiritual source...for they do not wish to remain below...

And Yoseph the *tzadik* represents "direct illumination," from above to below, to draw down influence to the lower worlds of *BY"A*...

From the discourse *Velakachta et shtey* in *Sefer Maamorim 5668* (1908) of the Rebbe Rashab), Page 109.

"In general, it is known that there are two types of precious stones. One is the kind of gem that from the beginning of its existence was essentially pure, and the light shone within it from "birth." And there is another kind of gem which was not so essentially pure, but is refined and purified during its period of development within the earth. And even after removing it from the earth, it needs some kind of action of man to draw out the light that was hidden within it.

Regarding stones and bricks in general; stones are a creation from the heavens, while bricks are made by man. And so, among precious gems, both of these categories also exist. Moreover, their illumination is also dissimilar. For the stones in which the light exists from their "birth" shine with "direct illumination," with rays of light that descent and expand. They emit rays of light of one color, according to the color of the stone. And from the stones which need polishing and refinement, the light does not descend and shine from them, but rather flashes, creating sparks of light, which are not of only one color, but of several colors.

And so we observe regarding stars as well. There are stars that shine with direct illumination such as a straight ray of light that descends from above to below, without moving. And it descends in one color. And there are stars which flash and emit sparks of light, while also moving, and appearing in several colors.

And it is known that the precious stones come from the influence of the stars, which is why we find both of these categories among precious stones as well."

ix) Page 11 (Page 36 in the translation)

Note: "And this is what is meant by 'May it be His will…'" See *Likutei Torah, Shir HaShirim*, in the discourse *Ma yafo peamayich…*

From *Likutei Torah* of the Alter Rebbe, *Shir haShirim*, Page 86, in the discourse *Ma yafo peamayich…* "…all of the requests within the *shemoneh esreh*…are requests for a change in the Supernal Will that transcends the Torah, which comes from the supernal *sephira* of *chochma*. Whereas the conduct of the creation is according to Torah…similarly the long exile is according to the Torah and therefore we request that there should be a variation in His will, from above the will that is expressed in the Torah that comes from *chochma*; that is, we make our request from the *Ba'al Haratzon*, the 'Master of the Will' Himself…"

Chapter 2

x) Page 11 (Page 39 in the translation)

Note: "And the blind person has no enjoyment…" – see *Yoma* 74B

[There the gemora discusses the nature of "affliction" on Yom Kippur, when the Jews are commanded to "afflict" themselves. The Gemora mentions a verse from the Torah, "He afflicted you and let you go hungry, He fed you the *manna*…" (*Devarim* 8:3) in order to suggest that "affliction" means "not eating" proper food. The Gemora then goes on to suggest that, "one who sees what he eats cannot be compared to one who does not see what he eats." R' Yoseph suggests that this is a reference to blind people who get no satisfaction from their food. And Abaye adds, "One who has a meal, should eat it only during the daytime."

xi) Page 12 (Page 41 in the translation)

Note: "This is similar to what is written elsewhere…" See *Likutei Torah* in the summaries of the discourse *Lo Tashbit* ("There should never cease to be salt…") that appears at the end of the section on *Vayikra*. See also the discourse beginning with the words, *Ashreinu* ("Happy are we…") in *Sefer maamorim 5696* (1936, of the Rebbe Rayatz, *ztz'l*), printed in *Kuntres 32* (found in *Sefer Maamorim Kuntresim* vol. 2).

[The reference is to the statement of R' Yochanan ben Zacai, as he lay on his sick-bed, "I do not know in which direction I am being led" - whether to Heaven or G-d forbid in the other direction (*Berachot* 28B). His students were confounded by his statement, because they knew him to be completely righteous and just, and therefore there was no reason for him to go anywhere but to "heaven." In *Likutei Torah*, it is explained, "Even though he was involved in Torah his entire life, out of tremendous modesty he found room to doubt about himself regarding the [unconscious] aspects of his soul that transcend intellect. These are faculties of the soul associated with *Keter*, and his doubt was whether he had constantly drawn down these aspects from a state of concealment to a state of revelation. This is similar to R' Akiva who said, "Whether I served G-d with all my soul, I haven't ascertained." And nevertheless by uniting the *chochma* in our soul with the *chochma* of the One above as it is manifest in the Torah, in this manner, spontaneously, the very essence of our soul becomes included in the infinite light above, the transcendent illumination of *sovev kol olamim*."

The *maamor, Ashreinu* cites the reference from *Likutei Torah* above, but gives a somewhat different explanation: (Page 732) "And now we can understand R' Yohanan ben Zakai's statement and his doubts, for although R' Yohanan was constantly involved in Torah, and was very wise sage in knowledge of G-d's Torah and also involved in serving G-d, nevertheless he was afraid of the day of judgment regarding the world to come. For, if it is necessary to rectify something in this world, then it is possible to do *tshuva*, but in the world to come, *tshuva* is not applicable. And therefore, R' Yochanan was afraid of the day of judgment. Moreover, R' Yohanan had doubts regarding "which direction he would be led," meaning that he was doubtful whether the essence of his soul had been involved in *avodat Hashem*, and whether in any case his *avoda* had been as complete as it should be when coming from the essence of the soul. And it is impossible to know the true situation regarding the essence of the soul and its level of perfection. For example, there are high souls whose intellect and emotions are stuck in the *sitra achra* ("other side," opposed to holiness) but because they are high souls residing in a high world, they can easily do *tshuva*. And there are souls of whom the intellect and emotions are involved in *avodat HaShem*, while the essence of the soul is low, coming from the *sitra achra* and they can easily be drawn back there, G-d forbid. And therefore, "I don't know my own soul," where it is, and what it is…"

All this indicates that even the spiritually "accomplished" person who peers indifferently at something indecent (as mentioned in *Kuntres Avoda*) will not remain unaffected by it. Although he may not consciously experience the effects immediately, something in the very essence of his soul may be influenced, and then the results could appear much later.

xii) Page 12 (Page 42 in the translation)

"And it will not dissipate..." See the mishna in *Zavim*, Ch.2, Mishna 2, "He saw before he thought..."

[The Mishna deals with the subject of one who experienced a seminal flow that may or may not make him impure as a *zav* (which is a particular impurity from the Torah requiring him to wait several days and then go through a purification process). With the first experience of discharge, he is not considered impure, and the mishna informs us that after the first experience, the sages would question him regarding seven factors; what he ate, what he drank, what he carried, if he jumped, if he was ill, if he saw a woman or if he thought about a woman. Certain foods, for example, such as meat and oil, or milk, cheese, eggs, wine and oil, may lead to an experience of impurity, as may drinking. Also, carrying a heavy object may strain the person to the point of experiencing a seminal flow, as may jumping or illness. Finally, if one "saw a woman, even without thinking about her" – this may lead to seminal emission, as may thinking about her without actually seeing her. If any of these events occurred, then the sages declared that the person was not a *zav* (because it was then possible to say that the experience of seminal flow was caused by one of the seven events, rather than by an unclean bodily condition). However, it was still necessary for the person to go to the *mikveh* and wait until the next evening in order to be considered 'pure.'

For the purposes of *Kuntres Avoda*, what we need to know is that "if a man saw, even without thinking about" a woman, this may also lead to an experience of seminal emission – and this proves the point that even looking upon something indecent in a "indifferent fashion" without thinking about it can lead to impurity.

xiii) Page 13 (Page 47 in the translation)

Note: "like a servant..." – See the series of discourses entitled *mikneh rav* – "Much cattle..." that begins on page 308 of *Yom Tov shel Rosh Hashana 5666* (1906) of the Rebbe Rashab

This series of *maamorim* discusses at length the difference between a *ben* ("son") and an *eved* ("servant") in service of G-d. A *ben* is of course close to his father (the corollary is a Jew in relation to G-d, our "Father in heaven"), and therefore he has some concept of what his father wants and how to achieve it. The father passes on his plans and aspirations to his son, who then sets about helping his father to put them into effect. But of course the son also has his own ideas and is affected by the moods, attitudes and level of success of his father. Therefore, the level of work and effort put out by the son may vary, depending upon whether he likes what he is doing, or thinks it is a good idea, or finds success. In other words, the *ben* is in it for his father and for himself, and he uses his mind and energy to the utmost to further his father's agenda and by extension, his own. The corollary in service of G-d is the Jew who is learned and G-d fearing, and who uses his own faculties and intelligence to "figure out" what G-d wants from him. Since he puts as much emphasis on his own understanding as upon what the Torah tells him, his service of G-d may vary, depending upon if he "agrees" or how he "feels." He will never deviate from the Torah, but he may apply its commandments in different ways, to different degrees, at different times.

The *eved* ("servant"), by contrast has no agenda of his own; his agenda is the agenda of his master. His master tells him what to do, and the effort that he pours into fulfilling his master's instructions is not dependent upon either understanding them or agreeing with the instructions. His task is to simply fulfill the will of his master, and to that he is totally dedicated. Therefore, his own intellect and emotions do not play a role in his performance of the task. He throws himself into fulfilling his master's will with all of his being because his entire purpose is to fulfill his master's will – that is why we say that his master's will is his own will. And because his entire purpose is the fulfillment of his master's will, he does not waver; he remains focused and consistent. The corollary in serving G-d is the person who fulfills the mitzvoth and learns Torah not because he wants more understanding or appreciation, but because he was told to do so. He will not look for the "why's" of the instructions that he received, but will simply set about fulfilling them to the utmost of his ability – simply because "his Master said."

Here in *Kuntres Avoda*, this approach applies to the person who "fences" and guards his senses in order to remain focused on Torah and G-dliness. Although there is a strong emotional and intellectual temptation to allow some other influences to affect him, he conducts himself like a "servant," concentrating only on the job at hand.

xiv) Page 15 (Page 53 in the translation)

Note: "In *Derech Chaim* (of the Mitteler Rebbe), Ch. 4"

[The *Derech Chaim* of the Mitteler Rebbe (son of the Alter Rebbe) was written as a book of Chassidic "*musar*" to be read during the days of Ellul, preceding Rosh Hashana, when the "King is in the field." That is, during the month of Ellul, it is relatively easy to approach G-d and to do *tshuva* and return to the ways of Torah and mitzvoth. However, when one throws off the "yoke of Heaven" in order to do whatever he wants, then he finds himself under the influence of negative forces over which he has no control.

As explained in Ch. 4 (page 14), "And the explanation is as mentioned regarding "throwing off the yoke of Heaven" – when a person conducts himself according to the dictates of his heart [evil inclination], which is the source of all his [physical] desires, the origin of his willful conduct is his own insistence upon throwing off the will of G-d. That means that he has removed his own desire to accept the will of G-d, and he lacks even the will to want [G-dliness]. From this emerges automatically the "will of his heart" which feels "good" in its "freedom," to serve "strange masters." And this is because the source of his soul, the *yechida*, which is beyond intellect and logic is cut off and excised. This condition is called *omek rah* ("the depths of evil") and it is the concealed source of the origin of all evil desires. If so, from this flows the power of the *klipot* [negative forces, which conceal G-dliness] called *kitrin demasabuta* ("crowns of impurity"), which are various stages of impurity that sully his soul with strange and foreign thoughts, without any desire or knowledge or choice on his part…"

Thus, the one who has insisted upon taking himself out of the realm of serving G-d and being subservient to Him, will find himself subservient to evil powers that are beyond him, and he rapidly finds himself out of his own control.]

xv) Page 16 (Page 59 in the translation)

Note: "The reference is to the Alter Rebbe. For the details of the story, see the *sichot* of 13th of *Tammuz 5691* (1931) in *Kuntres* 15, as well as *Kuntres Chai Ellul 5703* (1943), *sicha* 6."

[In both cases, the reference is to the well-known story of R' Shmuel Munkus, chasid of the Alter Rebbe, who while attending a *simcha* of one of the Chasidim, grabbed a plate of meat and threw it in the "garbage." The initial reaction of the Chassidim who were present at the *simcha* was to punish R' Shmuel because Jewish law does not permit Jews to waste food or other valuables. And so they did, but soon after R' Shmuel received his punishment, the local *shochet* (who was not aware that the meat had already been thrown out) entered the room with a great commotion and instructed all who were present not to eat the meat. His wife had accidentally mixed up the kosher meat with some non-kosher meat and it was the non-kosher meat that had made its way to the *simcha*. Whereupon the Chasidim grabbed R' Shmuel and asked him, "why are you getting involved in miracles and *ruach hakodesh* ("holy spirit")?" (It was considered uncouth for the Chasidim, however spiritually accomplished, to reveal knowledge of anything that they could not have known in a natural manner. That was considered to be the realm of the Rebbe, not of the chassidim). They demanded to know how R' Shmuel had known that the meat was not kosher. R' Shmuel replied, "I did not know anything. When I first met the Rebbe, I made a resolution that no physical temptations would attract me. When I brought the food, I had a tremendous desire for it, and I saw that all the others also had a strong desire for the food. I decided that this meat must be forbidden, since no permitted food causes such a strong desire. This corresponds to the Rebbe's statement, regarding the verse, "There is much grain [to be produced] from the power of the oxe" – the power of attraction of the animal soul is stronger than the power of attraction of the G-dly soul within man, and that is why I threw the meat into the 'garbage."

This is the story to which the Rebbe Rashab refers with the words, "…he succeeded in reaching a state wherein whatever desires arose from his natural, animal soul, he simply would not do."]

xvi). Page 17 (Page 60 in the translation)

Note: "From the Zohar, section 3, page 108A"

[The reference is to a verse regarding the vestments of the High Priest as he approached the Holy of Holies on Yom Kippur; "With this will Aharon approach the holy place…" (Lev. 16:3) The Zohar further explains that "this" also refers to natural, ingrained fear of G-d (that is expressed by guarding our senses, the content of Ch. 2 of *Kuntres Avoda*)– only if a person possesses this trait will he be able to approach G-d.]

xvii). Page 17 (Page 60 in the translation)

Note: From the Zohar, section 1, page 5A

Here, the Zohar calls the lower fear described in Ch. 2 of *Kuntres Avoda* the "Gate of Ascent." It is the key that unlocks all other spiritual levels, and once we possess this level, we may ascend one spiritual level after another…

Chapter 3

xviii) Page 17 (Page 63 in the translation)

Note: "In Tanya, the text reads *tamid al pnimiyutam vechiyutam* – "In this way, he will be focused **constantly on their inner core and life force**…" And perhaps it should also read that way here…"

[The text here in *Kuntres Avoda*, when quoting Tanya, Ch. 42 omits the word "on" and reads simply, "He will constantly recall their inner core and life force." This footnote corrects the omission and points out that the original text of Tanya contains the word "on."]

xix) Page 20 (Page 79 in the translation)

Note: "An amazing and wondrous process…" See the discourse beginning with the words, *Yehuda atah* (in the series, *Yom Tov shel Rosh Hashana 5666* of the Rebbe Rashab). See *Torat Shalom*, the book of *sichot* of the Rebbe Rashab, in the *sicha* of *Simchat Torah* of the year *5676* (1916), sections 5-7. See also the discourse *Veacharei uri* of the year *5702* (1942), printed in the Yiddish *maamorim* of the Fredike Rebbe (the Rebbe *Rayatz, ztz"l*).

[In the *maamor, Yehuda atah* (page 135),

"…although at first glance we might ask, what is so amazing about G-d being removed and above the worlds? The worlds in general exist on a relatively low level, so what is wonderful and amazing about Him being aloof from them? But, in truth it is known that the creation of the lower worlds is in itself an extremely amazing matter, since creation from nothing to something is in the power of the Creator and not in the realm of creation. That is, there is nothing among creatures that even hints at the process [of creation] whatsoever. He is completely removed from creation and no creature has any concept whatsoever of how it is created from nothing to something. Similarly, the [process] of creation is amazing, [since] it consists of enclothement of His creative power within creation while it [simultaneously] remains completely hidden and concealed from creation, as written elsewhere. And the general matter of creation of the worlds is a function of His greatness, as in the saying, "*Gedula* – this is the act of creation," and as written, "Great is the Lord…' That a multitude of worlds and creations and the greatness of the creations and in particular the process that takes place from nothing to something – this is a great and wonderful matter…"

From *Torat Shalom* (*Sichot* of the Rebbe Rashab), page 224-5,

"The meditation that leads to [love like fire] takes place upon the greatness of *Havaya* in the creation of the words, as written, "How great are your deeds, *Havaya*…" For, a tremendous multitude of creations without number were created, as evidenced in the four categories of mineral, vegetable, animal and man. And within each category in particular are to be found an infinite number of variations. For example, in the mineral world, there are simple stones and then there are precious stones, and so is the case throughout the four categories of creation. And each and every creation has a particular divine light and energy enclothed within it according to its level and according to the essential nature of its creation. And similarly among the supernal angels, there are a tremendous number without limit, as the sages said, "One thousand thousands serve Me, and a myriad myriads stand before Me." The quantity of angels within one "troop" is a myriad (ten thousand), and there are an unlimited myriad number of troops. And similarly regarding the meditation associated with the verse, "He Who counts the number of stars, and calls each of them by name" – try going out and counting the stars – see if you are able to count them – and yet He counts the stars and likewise calls each of them by name – it is He Himself Who calls them by name. And this is the divine providence by which He watches over each and every creation in particular, and this entire [meditation] has the affect of producing great excitement in our soul.

Nevertheless, sometimes it may occur to us that from a G-dly perspective, this is not remarkable at all. All of this is amazing from the point of view of man – the multitudinous numbers of creation and how there is a finite number of stars and how He calls each of them by name – but from a G-dly point of view, this is not remarkable at all, and if so, what is there to get excited about? Now, this is nothing more than an example of "coldness", as in the verse regarding Amalek, "who cooled you off" – this [throwing doubt into the picture] is the *klipah* associated with Amalek, as written elsewhere (in the *maamor* entitled *Zachor* of the year *5665*). For the excitement that man experiences is only regarding what is amazing to him, and this has nothing whatsoever to do with anyone else – it does not matter at all if another is not aroused that much. Only when he himself finds the matter amazing should he become quite excited. And so it is regarding the tremendous number of creations and how He counts all of them; since this to him is amazing, he should become aroused from the idea, and it need not concern him whatsoever if someone else is not excited. Since he finds the matter amazing, he should be excited, and it matters not that from a divine perspective it is not at all remarkable. For, since from his perspective, the creation is amazing, from this he should be excited. By way of example, a very wise man will become excited only by matters that arouse him – and what excites a normal person will not excite the wise person. But, it should excite the normal person, and he should not be concerned; once he himself finds the matter stimulating, he should be excited by it. And so it is regarding meditation upon G-dly matters; since all of this takes place within the person who is meditating, and from his perspective he finds it amazing, therefore he should be excited and it should not matter whatsoever that from a divine perspective the topic is unremarkable. This is nothing more than *klipat Amalek,* (a level of concealment of G-dliness that "cools us off" and throws doubt into our intellectual pursuit, without reason]) for regarding simple physical matters such an idea would not occur to him at all (that because another person is not moved, therefore he himself should not become excited). Rather, because from his perspective this is an amazing matter, he himself should be excited by it.

And so it is regarding meditation on the tremendous number of creations and how G-d counts the stars and calls all of them by name. All this should produce great excitement within the soul, as should meditation on how all is created from nothing to something, and the fact that creation from nothing to something takes place from "out of range." Now, this creation from "out of range" is associated with a command, for a command is precisely what is necessary for that which is amazing and out of range. All sovereign matters take place by way of command, since [the king and his subjects] are so out of range of one another. Regarding matters that are within range of each other, there is no need for [a king and his] subjects. How could it be any other way – but matters that are out of range necessitate a command. As, for example, the king said, "Uproot the mountain," so is the matter of creation from nothing to something. It takes place by way of command, as written, "He said and it took place, He commanded…" – this meditation, regarding how He commanded and within this [command] is felt the matter of sovereignty – implies a process that takes place precisely when the process takes place from out of range. For something that proceeds according to logic and intellect, must proceed [in a predictable fashion], and the matter of kingship does not apply. Only a process that takes place from "out of range," necessitates a command. And automatically, the meditation on this process produces a feeling for His Kingship, and therefore it elicits from within us a feeling of *bitul*, or self nullification. And so it is regarding meditation on how everything is included in its source before it is created, and how likewise after they are created they remain in their source – this is not comparable to *koach* and *poel* ("cause and effect"). For as in the case of physical movement, the movement was not "part of him" before he moved, and also after he moved there was nothing remaining of the initial power that caused the person to move. This is not true though of creation from nothing to something, for the "something" was first including in the "nothing" even before it was created, and also after it was created it remains included in its source. This is because the nature of creation is *hitchadshut* – "renewal" – just as the light and ray of the sun undergoes renewal, so the world was included in its source even before it became revealed. And also after it is "revealed" it remains included in its source. And so it is with the creations of all creatures – since they undergo the process of "renewal" from nothing to something, they are included in their source even before they are created."

From *Sefer Maamorim Yiddish* of the Fredike Rebbe, R' Yoseph Yitzhak *ztz"l*, page 71

The *maamor* is long and very nuanced, and a full translation would be difficult. Here is the summary of the second section which the Fredike Rebbe gives us on page 71: "The creation from nothing to something is not comparable to the process by which a craftsman makes a vessel. The energy [that creates and enlivens creation] is very concealed from the creation. It is not similar to "cause and effect," such as intellect and emotions or thought and speech. [In such cases], the cause is close to the effect, and the effect is aware of and grasps the cause. Creations know nothing more than the existence of existence of G-dly energy."]

xx) Page 20 (Page 79 in the translation)

Note: "As known regarding the difference between…" See *Likutei Torah* (in the discourse *Besha'ah shehikdimu*, third section). See also the discourse *Amar R' Y', Lo barah*, from the *maamorim* of the Fredike Rebbe of the year 5694 (1934) in *Kuntres 24*. See also the discourse *Amar Rabah…Kol adam* from the year 5702 (1942) in the *Sefer Maamorim Yiddish* of the Fredike Rebbe *ztz"l*.

[From *Likutei Torah, Parshat Bamidbar, Besha'ah shehikdimu*…in the third section of the discourse (page 13, column 2):

"The purpose of Torah and mitzvoth in drawing down His Will to be revealed below is in order to fulfill the verse, "And the Lord commanded us to observe all of the these laws in order to fear G-d Himself *(leyireh et HaShem)*," as it says, "All of His holy ones fear G-d Himself" *(yiru et HaShem)*. Yet, we must understand – why does the verse specify, "His holy ones"? For, elsewhere there is another verse that says, "All of the earth should be afraid of G-d" *(yiru m'HaShem)*...

...The difference is that the verse, "All the earth should be afraid of G-d" refers to the lower fear of G-d, from our perspective in which the lower physical world seems to be the true existence. But in the interpretation of the verse, "All of His holy ones fear G-d Himself," there is a word *(et)* which [serves no obvious purpose, and] is nullified to His Name *Havaya*, with a true and real nullification. [From this perspective], what is above possesses true existence while what is below is truly as if nonexistent...and we facilitate this level of nullification by learning Torah, about which is said, "If there is no *chochma*, there is no fear,"...And this is what is meant by *yiru et HaShem* ("All of His holy ones fear G-d Himself") – this level of fear is brought down as we say blessings *(asher kideshanu bemitzvothav* – "He Who has sanctified us with His commandments") – for this we were commanded to fear G-d Himself]

From the discourse, *Amar R'Yehuda, Lo Bara* in *Sefer Maamorim Kuntresim Beit*, of the Rebbe Rayatz *ztz'l*, page 535 (283 in Hebrew)

"There are two types of meditation. One leads to the lower form of fear

of G-d, *yirah tatah*, and the other leads to development of the higher form of fear of G-d; *yirah ilah*. For, it is written, *Kel deyot Havaya* - "*Havaya* is a G-d of Divine perspectives" – a lower perspective *(da'at tachton)* and a higher perspective *(da'at elyon)*. The lower perspective is that our physical world truly exists and what is above is as if non-existent, since the creation occurs from nothing to something. And the truth is that "out of His goodness, He constantly renews the creation every day," and this takes place from nothing to something. . And when we meditate upon this, we develop fear of G-d. However, the fear that we achieve is "lower fear," as written, "All the world is afraid from G-d," and it is written, "For He said and it happened," which also refers to the meditation mentioned above. For all of creation took place from a superficial ray of His G-dliness.

More in particular, the fear of G-d associated with this verse ("All the

world is afraid from G-d") stems from the fear that evolves when we delve deeply into the concept of Divine providence. But in general, both of these "fears" are in the category of "lower fear," which is why the verse employs the word "from G-d," indicating a mere reflection of something that is concealed.

But, the higher fear corresponds to the perspective that what is Above is

real, and what is below is as if "nothing," since the infinite light of G-d is the most real existence, while all that is below is like nothing, since "everything stands before Him as naught." And by meditating upon this and integrating it within, that the infinite light of G-d is the true existence, we produce total nullification of the self within. And this is the *yirah ilah* ("upper fear"), to which the Torah serves as an introduction. As we say, "And G-d commanded us in all these laws to fear Him..." and it says, "All of His holy ones fear G-d Himself." The verse utilizes the word *et*, although it is extraneous and totally nullified to the name *Havaya*. This is the level called *yirah ilah*, and it occurs only among His holy ones. [He] has "sanctified us with His commandments," and it is Torah and mitzvoth that bring us to this fear of G-d."]

From the discourse *Amar Havaya Rabah*, Page 45 in *Sefer Maamorim Yiddish*

["The verse states, "*Havaya* is a G-d of Divine perspectives," implying two perspectives;

one from below and the other from above. The lower perspective is based upon the understanding of man in creation, that the lower world exists and that creation occurs from nothing to something. The explanation is that when man does not know what something is, he calls it *ayn*, or "nothing." And the fear of G-d that man attains as a result [of this perspective] corresponds to the verse, "All the world is afraid from G-d." This very same fear comes from meditation that all that is created comes from a mere reflection [of G-dliness], and this kind of fear is called "lower fear" and it serves as an introduction and entry to Torah.

The higher perspective corresponds to a higher knowledge, that what is above is the true *yesh* ("existence") and that which is below is *ayn*, or "nothing." What is above truly "exists" – it is the real existence while what is below may be described as "everything stands before Him as naught." From this meditation results an appreciation of the concept of the infinite light of G-d – how it is the true *yesh* and existence. Upon reflecting on this [perspective], the person becomes totally nullified in his own existence. This is the level called "upper fear" and Torah is the entry [and pathway] to this level of fear.

These are the two levels of fear: *yira tatah* ("lower fear") and *yirah ilah* ("higher fear"). The lower fear stems from meditation on creation in the lower world and it serves as an introduction to learning Torah. The higher fear (*yirah ilah*) comes from meditation on matters concerned with the higher perspective (*da'at elyon*), and to this level, Torah serves as an introduction and a vessel to attain this fear.

xxi) Page 20 (Page 79 in the translation)

Note: "All of this is implied in the verses, 'How many are Your works…how great…'" See *Torah Ohr* in the discourse *Vayedaber* in *parshat Vaera* (the second). See also the discourse *Se'u marom eineichem* of the *Tzemach Tzedek* (in the introduction to his *Sefer HaChakira*). See also the discourse *ein aroch lecha 5694* (1934), from the Rebbe Rayatz *ztz'l*

Torah Ohr on *parshat Vaera*, Page 111 (*nun-vov*), column 2:

"It is written, 'How many are Your works…' and it is written 'How great are Your works…' 'How many are Your works…' refers to the lower physical realms and all of the creations of this world, which are divided into various species in various different ways. There are myriad levels of creation within the mineral, vegetable, animal and human worlds – some within the mineral category and some within the vegetable category. And each and every species, such as apples, nuts and almonds, possesses its own taste. The same is true of the vegetable category; each species has its own taste, and each is distinct from the other. And so regarding different kinds of herbs; each of which has its own taste. The [origin of the] taste is spiritual, coming from the *mazal* that influences it from above. For, "There is no herb below that is without a *mazal* above [that influences it]…"

"…But the verse, 'How great are Your works…' refers to the higher worlds, including angels and souls who derive enjoyment from G-dliness. And no one form of enjoyment is similar to any other. As the sages said, 'In the future, G-d will bequeath 310 worlds to each and every *tzadik*…' And at first glance it is not understood – why does every *tzadik* need so many worlds? Does *tzadikim* have a need for property?

Rather, the matter is as follows; the reward for a mitzvah is the mitzvah itself. That is, the reward for the mitzvah is the descent of supernal enjoyment from Above, which enables souls to bask in the ray of the *shechina*. And each and every mitzvah draws down its own variety of enjoyment. Furthermore, each *tzadik* is different from his fellow in regard to his *avoda* and the quality of love and fear of G-d that he experiences. For, there are those who are aroused [with love of G-d] and there are those who are aroused [with fear…]. It is for this reason that in the future G-d will bequeath to each *tzadik* what he needs [according to his individual approach]. For, every *tzadik* resides in his own "dwelling," by himself, in regard to the reflection and the nature of intellectual grasp that he achieves, and he derives enjoyment and basks in G-dly illumination in a way that is disctinct from the enjoyment and intellectual grasp of his fellow *tzadik* – each according to his unique talents and abilities.

And this ray of the *shechina* includes an uncountable myriad number of levels and kinds of souls-enjoyment, for it stems from the infinite One above.

From Intro to *Sefer HaChakira* of the *Tzemach Tzedek*, from the discourse *Se'u Marom Eineichem*, Page 206

Similar to "He Who uttered and the universe came into existence"…the unique One of the universe, the primordial One Whose existence is obligatory – He is able to grant durability and powerful energy even to limited creatures – which is not according to the nature of such limited beings. And about this is said, "How great are Your works, Lord…"

And this is what [the Alter Rebbe] meant in his explanation of the verse, "Raise your eyes and see Who created these…" – the prophet [who uttered these words] showed us how a mere ray of the infinite light of the Unlimited One, [illuminates] even down here in this physical world of *asiya* which is certainly limited…

From *Sefer Maamorim 5694* (1934) of the Rebbe Rayatz *ztz'l* – Not found

Ch. 4

xxii) Page 22 (Page 86 in the translation)

Note: "When it comes to love of the One above, there are two general levels…" See the note in *Kuntres Eitz Hayim*, Ch. 2 (Page18)

["There are several sub-levels within these two levels. Therefore, there is no contradiction between what appears here and what appears elsewhere regarding other distinctions between kinds of love, as well as regarding the essence of meditation that is associated with them – for explanation of several of these levels of love, see further on in Ch. 16 [of *Kuntres Eitz Hayim*]. See also Ch. 4 of *Kuntres Avoda*, and the *sichot* of *Simchat Torah 5668* (1908) and *5676* (1916), both of which appear in *Torah Shalom* of the Rebbe Rashab. Furthermore regarding different kinds of love, see *Torah Ohr* (of the Alter Rebbe) and *Torat Chayim* (of the Mitteler Rebbe) in the discourses entitled *chachlili einayim*. And see the letter that my father-in-law (the Rebbe Rayatz) wrote to the Chasidim of Bilgoria in the year *5691* (1931), which is printed at the end of *Kuntres Avoda* – etc…]

xxiii) Page 22 (Page 86 in the translation)

Note: "with flames of fire – "An investigation is needed in order to determine why sometimes – in the handwritten text of the Rebbeim – the phrase *rishpei aish* ("flames of fire") is preceded by a *beit* (*b'rishpei aish*, meaning "with flames of fire"). While, elsewhere, including here in *Kuntres Avoda*, it sometimes appears written with a *caf* (*c'rishpei aish*, meaning "like flames of fire.")

As for example, within Tanya, in Chapters 3, 9 16, 17, 43, 50 and in *Igerot Hakodesh siman* 4, it is written in the second manner, with a *caf*. And in Ch. 44, both versions appear. However, it is possible to distinguish between the two, as anyone who examines the text will be able to discern."

xxiv) Page 26 (Page 106 in the translation)

Note: "And as written in the drosh *Yom Tov shel Rosh Hashana 5666*…"
[In the two discourses, *Yehuda atah* and *Vayeileich Ish*…

From the discourse *Yehuda atah*, in *Yom Tov shel Rosh Hashana 5666*, of the Rebbe Rashab, Page 134; "And this is the *avoda* of the Divine soul, six days of the week, to refine and rectify the animal soul, about which it is said, "Six days you shall work," referring to the service and labor of the Divine soul to refine the animal soul. And the main *avoda* takes place during prayer, as known that prayer was established in place of the sacrifices, and just as during the sacrifices an animal was offered on the altar and was subsumed in the fire from Above, [which descended] in the shape of a lion consuming the sacrifices - for, the animal itself is from the element of fire, since the animal category corresponds to fire among the [four] elements - and for that reason it is included and burnt within the fire from Above, as "fire consumes fire." And it was also necessary that fire be brought from "below," as the sages said, that "even though fire descends from above [to consume the sacrifices], it is a mitzvah to bring from the common [profane], as well. A similar process takes place now during prayer as we sacrifice our animal soul so that the two become included – fire from above and fire from below…

…(Page 136) and this [meditation on creation from nothing to something, and how all creation is constantly renewed at every instant] is the fire from below, after which must follow fire from above, associated with the animal soul in particular. This takes place during the blessings preceding the *kriat shema* and then during the *kriat shema* itself, the fire of the Divine soul descends from above in flames of fire and incinerates and consumes the animal soul completely…and yet later during the *shemoneh esreh* it receives its reward of *ahavah raba* from above, in response to the *avoda* and labor of the Divine soul working within on the mind and the heart to refine and rectify the animal soul…and then love illuminates from Above…

From the discourse *Vayeleich Ish*, from *Yom Tov shel Rosh Hashana* of the Rebbe Rashab, Page 137

[Now, the fire from above of the animal soul comes from meditation upon the nullification of the angels, and how they become ignited and excited with flames of fire to become included and nullified in the Divine light of *Havaya* that flows down upon them. For, as this occurs,

Divine light of love illuminates them, and also illuminates the power of lust and temptation that is innate within our animal soul. The light arouses our heart to become detached from the physical pleasures into which we have sunk, and to draw us after its source to be nullified and included in the light of *Havaya*. Regarding this, the sages of the Great Assembly decreed that we should say the blessings of the *kriat shema*, two of them preceding the *shema*, wherein we repeat and recite the *avoda* of the angels, and how they are nullified to *Havaya*].

xxv) Page 27 (Page 116 in the translation)

Note: "So it should be among servants of G-d"

See the discourse *Tiku* of the year 5667 (within the series, *Yom Tov shel Rosh Hashana 5666*) of the Rebbe Rashab, as well as *Torat Shalom* of the Rebbe Rashab, *sicha* of *Simchat Torah 5669*, letter *yud* and on. She also *sichot* of the year Rebbe *Rayatz 5693* (1933) in *Kuntres 23*

[From the discourse *Tiku 5667* of the Rebbe Rashab, in *Yom Tov shel Rosh Hashana 5666* page 349-50]

"…When the meditation is upon lofty concepts such as the exalted and amazing nature of the infinite light, at such times the light of the Divine soul illuminates greatly, since these are matters that are close to it. The soul grasps them and intellectualizes upon them and understand them well…And throughout this [process], much light of the Divine soul illuminates, and so occurs during the excitement and rush of the G-dly soul (as it exists on its own among those who serve G-d with their souls with *ahavah rabba* and *ahava betaanugim*) – there is a large amount of illumination and revelation of the G-dly soul as its faculties shine (and this takes place totally out of range of the animal soul…). [However], the light of the Divine soul should shine within range of the animal soul. In so doing, the G-dly soul descends to become hidden and concealed so that its illumination and power does not shine in a revealed fashion as it does on its own. But in this manner, it achieves refinement of the animal soul.

However, when the Divine soul shines with a tremendous amount of revealed light that is completely out of range of the animal soul, then although the animal soul may become rectified, this is similar to the process of *tshuva* that takes place when the Divine soul is aroused with tremendous desire just because it is tormented over its distance [from G-d]. This sort of arousal affects a transformation of the animal soul, which becomes changed in its very essence, as known and explained elsewhere. Nonetheless, this is not called "refinement" of the animal soul since the animal soul itself is not aroused to participate. Rather it becomes nullified automatically as a result of the strength of revelation and arousal of the Divine soul.

But, regarding the bitterness of those who are called *marei dechushbana* ("masters of accounting" – those who look within themselves and examine themselves closely) and also those whose arousal to do *tshuva* comes from their animal soul (this occurs because of the suffering of the animal itself), which is tormented and extremely troubled over its distance…and the scream [for freedom] emerges from the animal soul…as written [when the Jews screamed to G-d during the Egyptian slavery], "and they groaned on account of the work and they screamed" –this was the cry of the body over the difficult labor…and similarly in the spiritual realm there may occur a cry from the animal soul itself…"

Torat Shalom of the Rebbe Rashab, page 129-131

For example, regarding the *avoda* of prayer; during prayer we must also be involved with the body and the animal soul. We must meditate regarding all of our bodily matters, and we must correctly know what is the situation and status of our body regarding all of its natural matters, whether they exist as cold [temptations], or boiling [lusts], and whether we are in essence a coarse person in nature, who is focused mainly upon matters of this world, or whether our essence is not so coarse, but rather [our animal nature] is nothing more than an extension of ourselves. That is, there may be side reasons that cause us to be more coarse while eating and drinking. And so, we must also make a true accounting of our situation and the status of our animal soul, with its bad emotions that we find within, to know exactly what they are...

(page 131); And this is the explanation of what is meant by "a connection with the body and the animal soul." All kinds of intellectual meditation, whatever the meditation is from the Divine soul, which arouses all (spiritual) matters... must have a connection to the body and the animal soul as well (see what is written about this in the discourse *matzah zu* of the year *5655*). And then automatically, if there is a connection with the body and the animal soul, then it will leave an impression, at least, for the entire day.

From the *sichot* of the Rebbe *Rayatz* of the year *5693* (1933) – Not found

Ch. 5

xxvi) Page 30 (Page 126 in the translation)

Note: "This is as well the difference...See the discourse, V*ayedaber...bemidbar Sinai* (in the series *Yom Tov shel Rosh Hashana 5666*) and the discourse *Haoseh Succato 5699* (1939)

[From *Vayedaber...bemidbar Sinai*, in the series *Yom Tov shel Rosh Hashana 5666* of the Rebbe Rashab, page 235:

"Although it was explained earlier that the source of souls is higher than *Atik* which precedes the *gulgulta* of *A"K*, and although it was also explained that the source of souls is beyond the Torah, we could resolve the issue by saying that...the source of souls is the very essence of the Divine enjoyment of G-d while the source of the Torah is from *chochma* (Divine wisdom), within which is embedded the essence of *Atik*, or the very essence of Divine enjoyment (see what was explained in the discourse *Ki Yedativ* at the end). And this is the advantage that Jewish souls have even over the inner dimensions of the Torah, since Jewish souls are enrooted in the very innermost aspects [of Divine enjoyment], while the Torah comes from the inner dimension of *Atik* as it is enclothed in the *chochma* of *A"K* – see what is written in the discourse *Vayishlach Yaakov*.

In any case, the descent of illumination of the essence of *Atik* into Jewish souls takes place through [the "intermediary" of] Torah. As known, the difference between Torah and Jewish souls is that regarding Torah, it is said the Torah and G-d are entirely one, while Jewish souls were created as independent entities, with their own "self" and identity. A son, for example, although coming from the same essence and self as the father, nevertheless possesses his own self and identity, analogous to Jewish souls…"

From the discourse, *Haoseh Succato 5699* from the Rebbe Rayatz, Page 48-9

"This we do know; G-d desires a dwelling place in the lower worlds, and as is known, this means that He desires that His infinite essence should be revealed down here…Now, this desire is fulfilled by Jewish souls. For, since Jewish souls are enrooted in the very essence of the infinite light, from where they descend via the ten *sephirot*, therefore they are the only ones by whom it is possible to fulfill the Divine intention to make a dwelling place so to speak, for His very essence. Although it is true that the Torah is also enrooted in His essence, nevertheless the Torah does not by itself facilitate the fulfillment of His Divine intention. For, the unity of Torah is that it and the One above are one, since the Torah comes from the very essence, and is united with His essence. However, in order to bring that down to be revealed in the world, there needs to be one who can receive from above and draw down to "who" or "what" is below. All that is revealed in the world comes through a *mashpia-mekabel* ("benefactor and beneficiary") relationship. To begin with, we receive, and then we give, as the sages said about the Jordan river, that it "takes from here and gives to there." The matter of taking and giving exists whether in spiritual ascent or in descent. For, every ascent and descent takes place as a process of "give and take."

…Now, a descent of this nature, meaning by way of "give and take" takes place only among Jewish souls. For although Jewish souls are enrooted in His essence, nevertheless the nature of their creation from His essence is that they emerge as "independent agents," with their own identity. As for example, a son who comes from the essence of the father that is beyond anything conscious and revealed, yet the nature of his creation from the father's essence is that the son becomes an independent entity. And that is the reason that Jewish souls fulfill the Divine intention to make for Him a dwelling place in the lower worlds."

xxvii) From page 30 (Page 129 in the translation)

Note: "And as written elsewhere…" See the discourse *Vezot Haterumah* (from the series, *Tiku* of the year *5670*)

"And the explanation is as follows; the *makif* known as *chaya* is not the very essence of the soul, and for that reason it is not connected as essentially with the infinite light above as is the *makif* known as *yechida*, which is essentially included [within the infinite light above]. For, since [the *yechida*] is the very essence and self of the soul, it is near to its source and origin in the infinite light, which is experienced within. And that is why it is essentially connected without any arousal, meaning that the connection is of the essence [of the soul] with the essence [of the infinite light above]. However, the *makif* of *chaya* is not the essence of the soul, and it does not experience its own source and origin. And therefore, the arousal to become included [in the infinite light above] needs to come about via a reason and stimulus, and in that manner it is aroused. Still, the desire to be included [in the infinite light above] does not come from the intellect alone, as it does during *avoda* according to logic and reason. Rather, the desire emerges on its own, of its own nature, but nonetheless it needs a reason to arouse it.

By way of explanation; there are two types of love; one that is dependent upon something, and one that is not dependent upon anything. Regarding love that is dependent on something, its entire existence is dependent upon whatever causes the love, and when that dissipates, the love itself dissipates. But, love that is not dependent upon anything is essential love, which is not dependent upon any reason. Nevertheless, this love could weaken and disappear in the course of time, until it is re-aroused, as in two loving friends who trust each other and whose love is not dependent upon anything. Nevertheless, in the course of time, they may forget their love and it will disappear. This is unlike the love between father and son, which is never forgotten or weakened even after many years and days, since the bond between them is essential, totally within the essence of their souls. And therefore they are bound to one another with a tie that neither weakens nor disappears forever. For, even when the bond is not apparent, it is not because it has disappeared in essence. And for that reason when it is revealed, it does not occur with great excitement, since it is a bond of the very essence.

However, love between two friends does not occur with such essential bonding and for that reason there may occur some amount of weakness and concealment, whereupon something is needed to arouse it, such as a happy occasion for one of them, for the love to re-ignite. But, when it does re-ignite, it is unlimited, beyond the range of the occasion that arouses it. Moreover, the love is not limited to the reason that aroused it, such as the happy occasion that one of them experienced. Rather, the love and happiness is far greater since their love is an essential love that is not dependent upon anything – it just needs something to catalyze it."]

xxviii) From Page 31 (Page 132 in the translation)

Note: "This is the concept of *z'a b'atika talia…*" ("The G-dly emotions are united with and dependent upon His essence and enjoyment."). See *Torat Chaim* of the Mitteler Rebbe (the second discourse beginning with the word *Breishit*, in section 15 and on. See also the explanation to the discourse *Leviatan zeh* in *Likutei Torah* of the Alter Rebbe).

[From *Torat Chaim* of the Mitteler Rebbe, *parshat Bereishit*, second *drosh*, section 16]

"Although it is explained and understood from all of the above [previous sections in *Torat Chaim*] that the intellect within the mind governs and rules at the very least over the emotions of the heart [and] our natural feelings are subjugated to the intellect within the mind. Nevertheless, as they exist in their natural state, the essential power of the natural emotions is much stronger than the power of intellect. And this is because the true source of their creation as they exist in essence is far above the source of the power of intellect within the mind…And that [source] is the *yechida* within the soul itself, which is beyond the origin of intellect within the soul, which is called the "intellectual soul." And therefore the intellect has no ability to master the emotions of the heart except as the emotions "pass through the mind." And then, only their expansion and expression alone are influenced by the instructions of the intellect. But, there is no power whatsoever within the intellect to transform the very nature of the emotions. For, the nature of the emotions as they exist in the essence of the soul is very strong and powerful, far moreso than even the power of the intellect within the essence of the soul. (As will be explained, this is because as it says in kaballah, "*z'a* [the emotions] is united with *atika*," higher than *mocha stima* which is the source of intellect – which is nothing other than *chochma* within *keter* of *arich*…)

And for that reason, we see the exact opposite of what was mentioned above regarding the control of the mind over the heart. Even after the intellect within the mind instructs the natural emotions to expand and act according to the dictates of the logic of the mind alone, nevertheless when there occurs an overwhelming arousal of emotions within the heart, the excitement is far greater than the stimulation that occurs within the mind. That is, the emotions become excited without any reason or logic whatsoever. The excitement is emotional in essence, as the emotions exist in their natural state within the heart, to the extent that the intellect is unable to stop or extinguish the excitement of the heart at all. And this is because the emotions totally overwhelm the intellect in the mind because they are strong and powerful in their essence, moreso than the intellect [itself] as mentioned above."

From *Likutei Torah* of the Alter Rebbe, *parshat Shemini*, page *yud-tet* (19A, or 37), column 2

"In the *Idra Zuta*, page 292... 'Z'a [the lower six *sephirot* corresponding to the emotions] is dependent upon *atika kadisha* [the super-conscious faculties of the soul, of which we are general unaware, but which influence us in any case] and united with it,' for *z'a*, which is the *midot* ("emotions") of *Atzilut* is, in its source, above the source of *ava* [*chochma* and *bina* – the intellect], but it descends below. Like, by way of example, the emotions of man; even though they emerge and become revealed via the intellect...nevertheless in the main, the emotions originate from above the intellect. And therefore, within the emotions, it is possible to find overwhelming energy, beyond what is present in the intellect that gives rise to them."

xxix) Page 31 (Page 135 in the translation)

Note: "Within which we find two levels, *ohr yashar* and *ohr chozer*..." See *Torat Chaim* in the discourse *Vayitain lecha*, section 2. See also the discourse *Samchuni B'ashishut* of the year 5660 (1900)

From *Torat Chaim* of the Mitteler Rebbe, in the discourse *Vayitain lecha*, section 2, Page 149, column 4:

"But, we must explain what is meant by *ahavah beta'anugim* ("love with enjoyment"), which applies to a kind of love that includes two categories of enjoyment. One is enjoyment that comes as *ohr pnimi* ("immanent G-dliness") that is clad in a vessel [illumination that shines into our mind and heart; we feel and understand it]. The second enjoyment comes down to us as *ohr makif* ("transcendent G-dliness"), which is beyond the limitations of a vessel [this enjoyment comes from awareness of something that is beyond us, but we do not feel it emotionally or grasp it intellectually].

Now, within *ohr makif* ("transcendent illumination") there are also two kinds of enjoyment. There is transcendent enjoyment that we experience as *ohr yashar* ("direct illumination"). And the second transcendent enjoyment comes to us as *ohr chozer*, or "reflected light." But, in general, they are two kinds of enjoyment, one associated with *chesed* ("kindness" which descends from above), and the other with *gevurah* ("stringency" which enables spiritual ascent), both within *taanug* ("enjoyment"). For, [the enjoyment] of "direct illumination" is associated with *chasadim* that descend and are drawn down like water, from above to below. And the illumination of "reflected light" comes from *gevurot*, which ascend from below to above, as known.

We may understand all of the above according to simple physical human enjoyments that we may observe among our fellow men. Among them are those that that we may integrate and experience with our own faculties, such as the enjoyment of taste; there is the taste of sweetness on the palate, and so forth regarding all the foods that we eat and swallow. Similarly regarding love between man and his fellow, as when the heart is attracted with interest and devotion within. And so, all of the enjoyments that attract the heart of man, such as wealth and riches and every thing positive that our heart considers – they all come from the *chasadim* that descend like water in accordance with the limitations of the vessel that contains them.

Then, there are enjoyments that come as transcendent experiences, such as the enjoyment of a journey or of a nice painting or of clothes and nice houses and the like. And similarly, there is enjoyment that accompanies honor and recognition of one's status, which provide essential enjoyment for the soul, without entering into the heart in a manner that is felt and limited. And so as well, there is the enjoyment of a pleasant aroma such as the scent of good perfume that the soul – and not the body - enjoys. And similarly, there is enjoyment associated with victory and glory, and the like.

But, the enjoyment associated with intellect and love, or with *chesed* or *gevura* – this comes to us as *ohr pnimi*, felt in a limited and conscious vessel. This is the enjoyment of one whose nature is to express kindness, etc. Like, for example the love that man experiences for his wife, is associated with the *chasadim* of "direct illumination." And there are also enjoyments that are expressed as the *gevurot* of "reflected illumination,' such as the desire of a woman for her husband, which comes with yearning and expiry of the soul…which is equivalent to "enjoyment" with flames of fire of excitement – enjoyment to the point of expiry of the soul. And so regarding any lust and desire for anything attractive, as well as the lust of the soul such as for food and for physical intimacy.

However, there is a difference between *chasadim* and *gevurot*. [The difference is] like the distinction between the flow of *chesed* and the enjoyment associated with the flow of *gevurah*, or between man and woman. Or, between mentor and student. Among all these, there are many details and fine distinctions in the way that they occur. In general, though, they are two levels; *chesed* and *gevura*, *makif* ("transcendent") and *pnimi* ("immanent").

Regarding the enjoyment associated with the *chasadim* of direct illumination (*ohr yashar*), the transcendent illumination associated with it results from the tremendous amount of enjoyment, that just does not "fit" into our mind and heart to begin with. Take, for example, the enjoyment that one might experience from a positive announcement arriving in a manner beyond comprehension. And so regarding the flow of enjoyment associated with a deep concept. Or the love that Rebbe Akiva experienced, which was so great that he could not contain himself upon hearing the deep secrets of the Torah. The illumination was so tremendous that the influx from his intellect was beyond what his faculties could contain. And so regarding a sweet taste or a journey or a very nice picture or garments of majesty and beautiful houses, about which the Torah says, "And you will multiply possession of nice houses and silver and gold and your heart will be elevated…" and as it says, "You got fat and thick…and you kicked [rebelled]." Such as occurred with the ten tribes…

Now, the enjoyment associated with the *makif* of "reflected illumination" - *gevurot* - occurs when one is unable to contain the amazing and wonderful enjoyment in his mind and heart, and [the enjoyment] then ascends as "reflected light," totally unfitted to the person's faculties ("vessel"). This is like, for example, when all of a sudden one hears a positive announcement that arrives unexpectedly. This pressures him in mind and heart, and his spirit ceases to function and may even leave his body, as when Sarah heard the announcement that her son Yitzhak was [almost] sacrificed, and as when Yakov heard that his son Yoseph was still alive. This is what happens any time that expiry of the soul is accompanied by very deep intellectual enjoyment, which is sweet to the soul, to the extent that the soul [wants to] leave the body. This was the case regarding R' Akiva, whose eyes filled with tears [as he heard secrets of the Torah]. Or in the story of the passing of the three sages of the Idra Raba. So it is regarding all kinds of enjoyment associated with "reflected illumination" – such experiences take place with great strength and power of ascent - accompanied by nullification of the "student" to his mentor and benefactor…to the point that he may become "love-sick…."

…But, the enjoyment of "direct illumination" occurs as immanent light that settles within the mind and heart, like water settling into a container. And the person then becomes sated with this kind of enjoyment…similar to [spiritual] enjoyment in the world to come. This is similar, as well, to the enjoyment of Shabbat meals, as well as to the enjoyment of souls in *gan eden*, as they bask in the rays of the *shechina*…this is the *makif* of hidden enjoyment of "direct illumination" that settles within and expands. [Finally], this is comparable to one who is capable of accepting greatness and wealth without limit.

And in general, *ahava be'taanugim* ("love with delights") is the love of a mentor for his student and the inter-inclusion of the two *makifim* ("transcendent levels") of *chesed* and *gevura*. It is the enjoyment of "direct illumination" and "reflected illumination" together. As in the word *sha'ashuim* ("delights")…and as when the *chatan* ("bridegroom") enjoys his *callah* ("bride")…

From the discourse *Samchuni B'ashishut* of the year 5660 (1900), from the Rebbe Rashab, page 77-78.

"…It is known that there are two categories of *taanug* ("enjoyment"), which correspond to *chesed* and *gevura*, about which is said, *ahava beta'anugim* – in the plural. And these are the enjoyment of *ohr yashar* ("direct illumination") and of *ohr chozer* ("reflected illumination"). The enjoyment associated with "direct illumination" comes to us from above to below, and the enjoyment of "reflected illumination" involves ascent from below to above. It involves desire and yearning, as known that desire and yearning are part of a will that includes tremendous enjoyment. And this yearning and desire produce expiry of the soul, as written, "My soul yearned and expired," as a result of this great enjoyment. Now this "expiry" transpires among the faculties of the soul that are enclothed within the limbs of the body, in a settled manner (*ohr b'cli*), as they "move" from their place to ascend and become included within the essence of the soul which is above the entire category of "faculties." This is what constitutes the expiry and ascent of the faculties of the soul, whereupon automatically the whole essence of the soul elevates and ascends above. For, the attachment of the essence of the soul to the body is only by way of the faculties. In essence, the soul is not at all within the category of the body. Although it is explained elsewhere that in general, the connection of the soul with the body occurs only on account of G-d's power "to achieve amazing accomplishments," such as uniting the spiritual with the physical, nevertheless this takes place via the faculties of the soul which are enclothed in the limbs of the body in a settled manner. For, they are contracted and limited according to the nature of the limbs, as written elsewhere. And within them is grasped the essence of the soul…

…Now, the enjoyment that is associated with "reflected illumination" is expressed as ascent from below to above. It is mainly expressed precisely as "lack of grasp" of something. That is, when one yearns for and desires something, as a result of the power of enjoyment in his soul for that particular object, and yet for the time being he is unable to attain that object, then all of his abilities and powers ascend in desire for unity with the object, to the extent that he may experience expiry of the soul. Since this enjoyment comes from the very essence of his soul, called the *yechida*, it involves every aspect of his soul. That is, all of his faculties are attracted to the object of his enjoyment. But in the absence of attaining his objective, all the faculties of his soul unite in the essence of his power of enjoyment which is the essence of his soul – the *yechida* – to the extent of expiry...But, when he does attain his goal and achieve enjoyment, then there is no ascent of the soul. Rather there occurs an amazing unity and clasping [of the soul] with the object of his enjoyment, which enlivens and "returns" his soul to him, with enjoyment from above to below.

Now, within the enjoyment of "direct illumination" as well, it is possible to find the phenomena of "expiry of the soul." This occurs when the revelation of enjoyment is so strong, that the powers of the soul are unable to contain such great "goodness." This is as explained above; enjoyment is a function of the very essence of the soul – the *yechida* of the soul. Yet, here as well, we find both "immanent light" and "transcendent light." The immanent light comes to us as limited, contracted enjoyment that is enclothed within the faculties of the soul, integrated within, such as the faculty of *chochma*, within which is clad a reflection and ray of enjoyment. We are able to observe this when, as we receive a new insight or idea, we are filled with enjoyment...The same is true with eating, when we eat a sweet food and enjoy it, the joy settles within and permeates our faculties and causing them to become stabilized. That means, that the revelation and unity of enjoyment within the limbs of the body occurs in an established and settled fashion, as it should...

...All this takes place as *ohr pnimi*, which is a contracted form of enjoyment. But, sometimes, a ray of enjoyment may illuminate from above without any contractions whatsoever. And this ray is incapable of becoming "established" within the powers of the soul and the limbs of the body. An example occurred in the Talmud when R' Akiva's eyes brimmed with tears as a result of the many secrets of the Torah that were revealed to him. And it is known that tears come as the result of the limitations of the vessel of the mind to contain illumination. The illumination of the soul is so great that the intellect and the faculties of the mind are no longer able to contain or tolerate it. And as a result, tears emerge – this is why R' Akiva's eyes teared over; his mind was incapable of accepting this level of revealed illumination. And this is as well the explanation of the three sages who passed away in the Idra, on account of the great revelation of light that was impossible for them to accept. Similar events will occur in the future, about which is written, "In tears they will come," as a result of the great level of enjoyment that will occur at that time. For, when a very high revelation of enjoyment comes down to us, it is impossible to accept it with our faculties. This may even cause total expiry of the soul, as may occur during the enjoyment of song and music.... But, all this is not because the soul and its faculties ascend above, but rather just the opposite – the soul remains below and draws down revelation from above to below, so that a strong revelation of enjoyment descends. A strong attraction of the soul occurs, [accompanied by] cleaving and unity to the pleasant melody and song. [But], since the soul-faculties are limited and contracted, when the revelation of enjoyment occurs, it completely nullifies [the faculties] and causes them to become included in the essential light of the soul that shines upon them [from above].

xxx). Page 32 (Page 138 in the translation)

Note: "the thirst of the animal soul..." See the discourse, *Vekol ha'am roim* of the year *5662* (1902) from the Rebbe Rashab. And also of the year *5678* (1918)

From *Sefer Maamorim 5662* (1902) of the Rebbe Rashab, Page 266:

"...when the animal soul hides and conceals the Divine soul and establishes obstacles and obstructions in all of its paths of worship, this causes an intense response from the Divine soul, with much ardor of *ahavah rabba* ("Great love") that is unlimited, and beyond logic and intellect.

In general, this [love] comes from beyond the source and origin of the Divine soul, for the origin [of the Divine soul] is the "form" (*tzura*) of Adam the primordial man (*A"K*). And as known, any "form" of man includes both intellect and emotions. And if so, "Great love" that is beyond logic and intellect is from beyond the source and origin of the Divine soul.

Now, true elevation of the Divine soul is a result of the thirst of the animal soul itself, meaning that when the animal soul on its own is "troubled" by its great distance and experiences a great thirst for G-dliness, this in turn creates an elevation of the Divine soul as well...

(Page 267)...regarding the thirst of the animal soul; there are times that it suffers tremendously on account of its distance from G-d, and becomes aroused with a desire [for G-dliness]. [At such times], the animal soul in essence has no connection to G-dliness so it does not feel the goodness of G-lliness. And its distance [from G-dliness] is intrinsic, meaning that it is far because of the presence of evil within it. And as it becomes tormented over the gap [between itself and G-d], it feels no additional positive element of proximity [to spirituality], but only a desire to escape from death, G-d forbid. There is no feeling of good and life within it. Rather, there is only a feeling of torment as a result of the tremendous distance, and this totally shatters the very fabric of the animal soul. And [from there], its [outward] form becomes eradicated as well.

And this then produces a tremendous desire in the Divine soul as well, as a result. That is, the soul experiences an arousal of true *tshuva* as the distance from G-d touches the soul to its very depths and inner recesses. This takes place to the extent that it forgets completely about any proximity [to G-d that it might have experienced], because of the intensity of the torment and bitterness in his soul over distance from G-d...

"And also from the year *5678* (1918)" –

This would appear to be a mistake, as there is no discourse by the name *Vekol ha'am roim* in the *Sefer maamorim 5678*. Perhaps the intention was to the year *5675* (1915 - in the series *Besha'ah shehikdimu 5672*, vol. 2, page 1007-8) in which appears a discourse entitled *Vekol ha'am roim*.

"And so it is in the spiritual realm, as in learning Torah, which necessitates great labor, as the phrase says, 'If one says, I labored and I found it, believe him.' Furthermore, the Torah remains only with the person who "kills himself" over it...and success in learning takes place only after much great labor, dedication and devotion, during which the person throws himself entirely into learning the Torah. And sometimes he will experience great sorrow and suffering, G-d forbid from his lack of knowledge. And it becomes very difficult for him, to the extent that he is ready to give up his own life and his heart and spirit are totally broken within him. And then precisely at that point, a great spiritual light shines upon him and he grasps the concept. On the contrary, it comes to him with great illumination. And so occurs regarding the labor of prayer, in which it is impossible to achieve understanding and proper meditation in order to grasp G-dly concepts in such a way that they are established and integrated in his mind and heart and he is aroused with love and fear of G-d unless he first experiences the lowliness and bitterness of a contrite mind...and the two are dependent upon one another; for according to the range that the person is broken in his heart and crushed, feeling low and heavy-headed, with a broken heart and tremendous embarrassment, over his self-induced distance from G-d, etc...to precisely that extent the divine light shines and illuminates his soul afterward with intellectual grasp and arousal of love of G-d..."

xxxi) Page 33 (Page 142 in the translation) – "the essence of the soul is defined…"

Note: See the discourse *Az yashir* of the year 5700 (1940), from the Rebbe Rayatz, *z'l*, page 62

"That the soul may become en-clothed in the body [is a phenomenon that] occurs only as a result of the power the "Infinite One," Who causes amazing events to occur. At any rate, this applies only to the *nara'n* (*nefesh-ruach-neshama*, the lower three soul-levels) of the soul, but the essence of the soul is not in the category of en-clothement within the body. In truth, the essence of the soul is also connected with the body, and that is why it is impossible for one soul to be en-clothed in two bodies. (As in the story in the *Idra Rabba*: Once Eliyahu failed to come to the *Idra*, and when R' Shimon ben Gamliel inquired as to his where-abouts, he was answered that Eliyahu had to rescue Rav Hamnuna Saba and his friends. And out of respect for R' Hamnuna Saba, Eliyahu came enclothed in a body. And if he had come to the *Idra*, he would also have had to come as a soul in a body, out of respect for R' Shimon bar Yochai. But, it is impossible for one soul to come en-clothed in two bodies. For, this is one of the distinctions between a soul and the sun; the sun is not defined by the "light" that emerges from it, [even though] the light of the sun illuminates everywhere that the sun is to be found. But, the soul, though far surpassing the spiritual level of the sun, it is not capable of entering two bodies because the essence of the soul is designated by and united with its light and illumination.

Now, as to the reason for this, we must say that it is because the [level of the] soul en-clothed in a body, although a mere ray and reflection of the soul, is also essential. That means that although it is only a ray and not the very essence of the soul, nevertheless there is a difference between the soul as it remains above and the soul as it descends to be enclothed in the body. The soul that remains above is the essence and the soul within the body is only a ray. Nevertheless since it is a ray of the essence of the soul, it contains an element of the essence of the soul itself. The light of the sun is only light – it does not reflect the essence [of the sun] at all, but the soul - although also light - is essential. And within the particular level of the soul that is enclothed in the body, is to be found the light and overall energy that enlivens the body in general. From it come the soul powers that become enclothed in the limbs…"

xxxii) Page 34 (Page 149 in the translation)

Note: "As known, including the three…" See the *sichot* of the Rebbe Rashab of *Simchat Torah 5661* (1901 – in the *sefer Torah Shalom*, *sefer hasichot*). See also the discourse *mashachni* (the second one) of the year 1940 of the Rebbe Rayatz *z'l*

"From *Torat Shalom* of the Rebbe Rashab, *5661*: *sichat Simchat Torah*, Page 10 (section 4): "One of the Chasidim asked, 'what should we do if we meditate but it has no effect on our emotions?

Someone else who was present began to scream at the chasid who asked the question, but the Rebbe Rashab said, "Let him ask, I specifically want people to ask questions…"

And then he answered; "this is a result of the coarseness of the physical. For that reason, there must be introductions and preparations – a little bit of denying oneself – and we must ask about that, within are found three levels – the oxe, sheep and goat. The oxe is one who gores, who gores when someone bothers him – like Binyamin Shines."

The Rebbe's brother, R' M. asked him, "why do you single him out, he is here?" and the Rashab answered him, "That is what my job is, as I have several times said, I am a 'shul-klopper.' Believe me that I mean myself as well, so that if anyone thinks that I do not mean myself, they cannot say that."

And then he said a second time, "An oxe that gores is like Binyamin Shines, who asks now what do we achieve with this happiness, why are we dancing? Why are we crawling over the vent, we have not learned any Chasidut, and we understand nothing about the simcha of Torah and mitzvoth…"

From the discourse, *Mashachni* of the year 5700 (1940)…Not found

xxxiii) Page 35 (Page 153 in the translation)

"The general service at that time…" See the discourse *Shir hama'a lot mimaamakim*…" of the year 5703 (1943) of the Rebbe Rayatz *ztz'l*.

From the discourse, *Shir hama'alot* of the year 5703 (1943) from the Rebbe Rayatz *ztz'l*, page 19:

"We first begin to say the psalm *shir hama'alot* during the morning services of the first day of Rosh Hashana, which follows the introduction of worship during the night time prayers on the first night of Rosh Hashana. Now, it is known that in general the *avoda* of Rosh Hashana takes place within our concealed and unconscious soul powers, and all of the worship of Rosh Hashana and Yom Kippur invokes the essence of the soul… We know, from books and from the sages, that on the eve of Rosh Hashana as darkness falls, the inner delight and inner will [of HaShem] within the *sephira* of *malchut* ascends and departs above, far beyond to its very source, to its ultimate elevation within *malchut* of the infinite light above…this knowledge should make us quake in the essence of our soul, and should shake all of our soul faculties; not only the revealed and conscious ones, but also the unconscious faculties. And in particular, the knowledge that we, and every other Jewish individual has the power to arouse [the Divine] delight and will within *malchut*, and that this takes place when we accept upon ourselves the yoke of His reign – [should cause us to quake].

And when we meditate upon all that we experienced during the course of the year and we recall matters that were not positive, [such reflections] take away our power and strength to stand in front of G-d and request that He accept us as His servant, even before we have done any *tshuva* or expressed regret for our past deeds. Like by way of example in the physical world, a servant who has escaped from his master or rebelled out of negligence and sinned against his him, who now desires to return and to accept the yoke of his master, would not have the nerve to stand in front of him and say to him, "Now I have come and it is my will to serve my master," without first conceding his transgressions and asking for mercy from his master, that he should forgive and pardon him. And he would cry from the depths of his heart and accept upon himself the yoke of his master in anything that he says to him.

So it is regarding our *avoda*; first we must express regret from the very depths of our heart over the past, and then arouse great mercy on our soul, with requests for leniency and crying from the depths of our heart and from the inner recesses of all of our faculties. We should beg for our lives, that our Master should accept us as His servant. This, in general is the *avoda* of prayer during the nighttime of Rosh Hashana. And afterward during the morning prayers, we recite *mima'akim keraticha*, for by accepting the yoke of heaven, we call upon and draw down the delight and will of His reign upon us from the depths that exist above.

xxxiv) Page 36 (Page 154 in the translation)

Note: "Are experienced by everyone..." See *Likutei Torah* in the explanation of the discourse, *Ki Teitzei* (the second one). See also the discourse *Az yashir* in the *Sefer maamorim 5700* (1940) of the Rebbe Rayatz *ztz'l*

From *Likutei Torah* of the Alter Rebbe, *parshat Ki Teitzei*, Page 72:

"Now, similarly within the soul of man, the Torah says, "And *Elokim* created man in His image, in the image (*tzelem*, or *tzadik-lamed-memsofit*) of *Elokim*..." ...The most important function of this "image" is to serve as an intermediary between G-dliness and the soul. For, the soul is a creation from nothing to something via the Divine light that is en-clad in [the *sephira* of] *malchut* of *Asiya*, in the *kelim*, or "vessels." Nevertheless, it is still G-dly, since it is created from the "image of G-d." And it is divided into two facets. One comes from the letter *tzadi* of the word *tzelem* ("image"). It is the G-dliness within the soul. And the other facet comes from the letter *lamed* (the second letter of *tzelem*, or "image"). It is the *makif* ("transcendent level"), also known as *mazla*. As the sages said, *mazleh hazi* – "their *mazal* saw." From there, the *tzadi* descends to become clad in the soul, as known regarding the saying of the Ba'al Shem Tov regarding the *bat kol* ("voice") that announces, "return, wayward children..." This is strange, for who is there to hear [the announcement]? And if so, what effect does it have? But, the *mazal* "sees" the announcement, and the result is the spiritual arousal of the soul that we experience within the body when something descends to it from above, from this *mazal*. And that is why it is called a *mazal* since it draws down flow (*nozel*) and influence. And the *mazal* is G-dliness that does not become enclothed in the soul at all, for it is above the level even of an angel. As R' Chaim Vital said in his *Shaar Hakedusha*, "And the prophecy on the highest level of them all is revelation of the soul itself, since it is above any revelation of *gilui Eliyahu*, since the soul is beyond the body which is influenced by the letters *lamed* of the *tzelem*..."

From the discourse *Az yashir* from the *Sefer Maamorim 5700* (1940) of the Rebbe Rayatz *ztz'l*, page 64 (section 5):

"...the purpose of the *cruz* ("announcement" from Above) is to awaken people so that they pay attention, return to G-d and get involved in Torah. But, since people do not hear these "announcements," what purpose do they serve? And so it is regarding *tshuva*; there occur "announcements" from above, such as the *cruz*, "Return, wayward children." Here, the word "wayward" implies wildness, or behavior that does not follow any kind of order or organized conduct. And in *avoda*, "wayward" occurs when we forget the true intention from above, which is for the soul to descend into the body…the purpose of the announcement is to arouse people to do *tshuva*, but since they do not hear the announcement, so what is the purpose in making them?…

…But the matter is as follows: People do not hear the "announcements" from above because of the opaqueness and concealment of the body and natural soul. Since they are concerned with bodily matters and heavily involved in physical lusts and enjoyment…even of permitted matters, so aside from the fact that they are "sunken" in these matters, as time goes by, things that were previously merely "permitted" become "necessary." …and then they do not even permit the person to "hear" spiritual matters…"

xxxv) Page 36 (Page 154 in the translation)

Note: "It is written elsewhere…" See the discourse *Veki tomru mah nochal* of the year *5678* (1918)

From *Sefer maamorim 5678* (1918) of the Rebbe Rashab, Page 307:

"The matter is as follows; love that is motivated by intellect and logic is limited by the intellect, and therefore it corresponds to the vessel of the heart and to the faculties that are able to contain it. And for that reason, the love includes elements of the person's own existence, since it is delineated by the powers of his soul. And that is why as much he polishes his deeds so that they are very refined, nevertheless, he remains a person unto himself, and he is not rectified to the extent of not experiencing himself at all.

But, the love that is transcendent in the soul is unlimited, and the vessel of the heart and faculties of the soul are unable to contain it. With this love, he is totally unable to remain within the [boundaries of] his own existence. And it is precisely with this [ove] that he may succeed in achieving full rectification of his deeds, so that his physical actions are also for G-d alone.

And as we see when the soul shines as a result of the transcendent levels of his soul, such as during Rosh Hashana and Yom Kippur - at such times our actions take place in a different manner altogether, in such a way that we do not experience the temptations of our soul. On a yet higher level, this is similar to what occurs on Shabbat – since according to true reality, physical enjoyment is really enjoyment of G-dliness, and it is a mitzvah to enjoy the Shabbat with eating and drinking – [therefore] the enjoyment is G-dly enjoyment…"

Ch. 6

xxxvi) Page 36 (Page 158 in the translation)

Note: "That He alone…" "*Igeret Hakodesh siman* 20"

In Tanya, fourth section (*Igerot Hakodesh*), *Igeret* 20:

"The light [of the *kav*] is similar to the Illuminator, which is the very self and essence of the Emanator, may He be blessed, Whose existence is from He Himself and is not the effect of another cause that preceded Him, G-d forbid. And therefore, He alone possesses the power and ability to create something from nothing, from absolutely zero, without any prior reason or causation…"

xxxvii) Page 37 (Page 159 in translation)

Note: "Regarding the verse *Ki Tihiyu* – see the discourse *Habaim yishrash* in *Torah Ohr*

"Now, the hundred blessings [that a Jew must say every day] occur in the mode of speech, but what brings the influx from a state of concealment into revelation? This takes place when we fulfill the mitzvoth. Take, for example, sowing seeds: Most garden variety seeds are inedible, since they are only seeds without any taste. But when the seeds are planted in the ground and the power of germination that is within the ground permeates them, the seeds produce edible food, even though the seeds themselves are totally inedible. And even though seeds of grain are edible, nevertheless when they are planted they produce much more food, similar in nature to the seeds themselves.

This is similar, then to performance of mitzvoth. Mitzvoth descend to the world and become enclothed in physical objects such as the parchment of *tefilin*, and the threads of wool that go on *tzitzit*, and the like among other mitzvoth. And when a Jew places them on his head, they produce revelation of G-dliness; first of all of *chochma* (associated with the first parchment - *kodesh*) and then of *bina* (associated with the second parsha – *vehaya ki*)…And this takes place only when a Jewish person dons them on his head, unlike if they are placed on a table, when no revelation occurs whatsoever. And although man's forehead is physical like the table, and moreover when a non-Jew places *tefilin* on his head, there is also no revelation…nevertheless the example of the power of germination within the earth is still valid. For, just as fruit will not grow just anywhere on the earth – for example, in the desert virtually nothing grows at all - similarly the Torah says about Jews, "When you will be like a desirable land for Me…"

xxxviii) Page 37 (Page 161 in the translation)

Note: "This is similar to the difference…" See *Torat Chaim* in the discourse *eleh toldot Noach*, Ch. 6. *Likutei Torah* in the discourse *Alei Be'er*, first section. The discourse *VeAvraham Zaken* 5702

From *Torah Chaim* of the Mitteler Rebbe, in the discourse *Eleh Toldot Noach*, Chapter 6

"The explanation is that *chochma* is the "mentor", meaning that it is like a new flash of intellect that shines like lightening. It is called *hitchachamot* (the ability to produce *chochma*), and it [employs] the power of *havana* to bring out all kinds of new intellect. It also has the potential to develop ideas from nothing to something, from the hidden intellect called *maskil*, from which flows much new intellect, in accordance with the person's power of *chochma*, whether small or large. Now, the outer manifestation of this is a lightening flash of intellect that emerges as a new revelation of *chochma*, but it is short and concise, a hidden synopsis as in one point. And it comes to expression in the grasp and explanation of *bina*…

…but the inner manifestation of *chochma* is beyond being a source or "mentor" to *bina* as in the category of intellect mentioned above. Rather, it is as if a new idea "fell" into the mind, into the power of *chochma* within, without having yet come into revelation, even to the person himself. Rather it is like a flash of lightening that passes through the brain, "from one side to the other," without yet settling into the mind…and therefore the person is unable to express it in a conscious fashion and to bring it into manifest intellect grasp, even to himself, and all the moreso to others. This is the *ayn* ("void") of *chochma* that is concealed as if in one point, still lacking expression, although it is the very essence of the inner illumination and influx of *chochma* as it exists in its source.

From *Likutei Torah* of the Alter Rebbe, *parshat Chukat*, page *samech-beit* (or 124)

"…all the days of man's life, when his soul is enclad in his body in this world, are only in order [for the soul] to become like a 'well' that flows beneath the surface – specifically beneath the surface, since water flowing through the soil of the earth becomes purified and refined – so that the soul becomes refined by fulfillment of physical Torah and mitzvoth, as well as when the G-dly soul overwhelms and subdues the animal soul…

…however, in order to produce this "well"-like revelation, two types of digging must occur – *chafira* and *criah*. Both are needed in order to remove the soil of the earth that blocks the opening of the well. However, *chafira* involves moving the large clods of earth, while *criah* is necessary to move the smaller more refined pebbles and dirt. And we as well need to remove all of the blockages that conceal the hidden love inside of ourselves, as well as to subdue the "other side" that is opposed to holiness, whether by reinforcing ourselves by restraining from evil, or by restraining ourselves in those activities that are permitted to us [but in which we need not get overly involved]. Additionally we may need to reinforce our performance of positive mitzvoth and to learn more Torah than we were accustomed and to give more *tzedaka* than was previously our nature. All these items and similar are in the category of "digging" in order to remove the coarse physical obstacles and to nullify them, revealing our inner love…

…(next page) Now, from this 'well,' as a result of this digging, emerges "living water" that is more enduring than the "love like fire" with flames of excitement that occurs during prayers with meditation. That love dissipates after prayers and passes, but the "living waters"… are an expression of love without end…"

From the discourse, *VeAvraham Zaken*…in the *Sefer Maamorim 5702* (1942) of the Rebbe Rayatz, *ztz'l*, Page 64-65

"Now, the order of man's *avoda* as described in the *Zohar* (*Bamidbar* 120A)…must correspond to what took place on the altar, as explained in the Mishna in tractate *Zevachim*, "the priest ascended the ramp of the altar and turned, revolving to arrive at the southeast corner" – wherein south corresponds to *chesed* or love. And that is followed by the east, as is known that the east represents *chochma* ("wisdom"). The sun (which is *yesod aba* - the "foundation of *chochma*") shines from the east…and [the word] "east" (*mizrach*) is related to the word *ezrach* ("citizen") - which corresponds to *chochma* (as in the verse *maskil le'eitan ha'ezrachi* - "Instruction from Eitan the Ezrahi" – Psalm 89:1). That is, following the stimulating experience of love and cleaving to G-d, we must become nullified (self-nullification is the inner dimension of *chochma*) to G-d in a manner that surpasses our love. And this [nullification is associated with] *chochma ila'ah*. *Chochma* and *bina* are called *ayn veyesh* ("nothing and something"). *Chochma* is above intellect – it [expresses] only the essential content of intellect that flashes and shines within the mind. But, we are still unable to grasp it. And this is merely the level of *chochma* that stands in proximity to *bina*, meaning the aspect of *chochma* that is called *yesod aba*. The true nature of *chochma* transcends even the flash of inspiration. It is, rather the *hitamtut* ("confirmation" and "affirmation") that is associated with *reiyah* ("vision") of *chochma*.

Bina, however is the grasp and understanding of the intellect, as it expands and extends itself. And therefore, real excitement and arousal occur only in *bina*, where meditation takes place, rather than in *chochma*. This is because [the process] of meditation (*hitbonenut*) can only take place regarding something that has emerged from a state of intellectual grasp to become something that "exists." That is why emotional excitement, such as love and desire like fire, results from meditation, for [such love and desire] is also an "entity" that "exists," something substantial…"

xxxix) Page 38 (Page 167 in the translation)

Note: "As written elsewhere - See the previous note in Ch. 3 and in the citations there."
From Ch. 3 See note xix on page 272

xl) Page 39 (Page 168 in the translation)

Note: "Referring to the four worlds of *Atzilut, bria, yetzira and asiya*: *Siddur* of the *Ariz'l*. For an explanation according to Chassidut, see the *siddur* (of the Alter Rebbe) regarding these verses. See also the discourse *Amar R'Y yhai chelki*… of the year *5701* (1941).

Essay on Service of the Heart - Love Like Fire and Water

From the *Siddur* of the Alter Rebbe, on Psalm 148 in the *Psukei dezimra*, Page *Samech-Hey* (65 in the Hebrew letters):

[The first two verses say, "Praise the Lord, praise the Lord from the heavens, praise Him from the heights. All of His angels praise Him, all of His hosts praise Him." In the *siddur*, the Rebbe explains (based on the *Ariz'l*) that the four terms, "heavens," "heights," "angels," and "hosts" refer to the four worlds of *Atzilut, bria, yetzira* and *asiya*:]

"Now, the explanation of "heavens" (*shamayim*), is that it refers to *z'a* (the lower six or seven *sephirot*) of *Atzilut*....The reason is that *z'a*, which is the "emotions" of *Atzilut*, are the mainstay of the *mashpia* ("mentor" or "benefactor") to the lower separate worlds of *BY"A*, as known. And all influx must come through *chesed* ("kindness"), as it is written, *olam chesed yibaneh* ("the world is built upon kindness"...).

...Now, the explanation of *meromim* ("heights") is that it refers to *malchut* of *Atzilut* as it is concealed within *bria*. At that point, it is called *marom*, as written *se'u marom eineichem* – "Raise your eyes to the heights" – for as known, the difference between "heavens" and "heights" is that "heavens" refers to the very essence of the sky...while "heights" refers to what we are able to see. It is what is evident to the one who stands below, to whom the essence of the sky is not visible at all. He is able to detect only what descends as a ray of light, visible to the eye. And since the heavens are extremely elevated...therefore what we are able to see is called *marom*, for His [true] heights are not fathomable or graspable. But, the term *marom* indicates loftiness and elevation alone, meaning to say that He is high, above what we may see – which is why we say "raise your eyes to the heights..."

...the explanation of "His angels" is that it refers to the world of *yetzira*, as written in the *siddur* [of the *Ariz'l*] that the four worlds of *ABY"A* are hinted to in the four praises mentioned here: *shamayim, meromim,* angels and hosts...now, the reason that angels are associated with *yetzira* is because an angel – *malach* – is an emissary (*shaliach*), and the entire world of *yetzira* functions as an "emissary" to deliver something...it possesses no qualities of its own – so the world of *yetzira* merely enables revelation of what was previously concealed. And therefore, "His angels" are in *yetzira*. And in truth, there is an advantage to *yetizra* over *asiya*, in that the angels [of *yetzira*] are totally nullified within, just as a proper messenger. Similarly, the angels of are nothing more than emissaries who reveal the divine influx from its state of concealment in *bria*...unlike the angels of *asiya* who possess an existence and identity of their own....

So, "All of His angels praise Him" appears first, after which we say, "All of His hosts..." in reference to the world of *asiya*. This is because a "host" is nothing more than a foot soldier of the king. He is not one who stands before the king, ready to do his bidding, but rather one who stands ready to go out to war. And this is similar to the seventy "ministers" of *asiya* and all of the planets and constellations and the nine orbits which accept their influx from *malchut* of *malchut* of *asiya*, as known..."

From the discourse, *Amar R' Yosi*, in *Sefer Maamorim 5701* (1941) of the Rebbe Rayatz, *ztz'l*, Page 10

"...the psalm, "Praise the Lord from the heavens," alludes to all of the creations of the heavens and the earth, and the inter-inclusion of the worlds *ABY"A*, as written in the *siddur* of the *Ariz'l*, "Praise be the Lord from the heavens" refers to *Atzilut*, "Praise be the Lord from the heights" refers to *bria*, "His angels" to *yetzira* and "His hosts" to *asiya*. "Praise be the sun and the moon" refers to the inclusion of *asiya* within *yetzira*, "stars of light" to inclusion of *yetzira* in *bria*, "the heaven's heavens" of *bria* in *Atzilut* and "the waters that are over the waters" refers to the elevation of *Atzilut* to the very essence of the Emanator…

(page 12)…And thisis what is meant by "Praise the Lord from the heavens," indicating descent of illumination and revelation from the light of the world of Atzilut, from where it is drawn in order to become "Praise be He in the heights," in the "angels" and the "hosts," which are the three worlds of *BY"A*. That is, by way of meditation during the *pesukei dezimra*, we arrive to the *avoda* of *kriat shema* with nullification and unity of the worlds…"

xli) Page 39 (Page 174 in the translation)

Note: "About them, the verse (Samuel 2:2) states, 'There is no holiness like that of *Havaya*'…" – See *Likutei Torah*, in *Shir haShirim* in the discourse *Tzeana u'reana* (the first one), in the beginning.

From *Likutei Torah* of the Alter Rebbe, *Shir haShirim* ("Song of songs"), in the discourse *Tzeana u'reana* (the first one), on Page *kaf-aleph* (21 in Hebrew letters):

"…And this is what is meant by *Ayn kadosh k'Havaya* ("There is no holiness like that of the Name *Havaya*…") – the Zohar (in *parshat Tazriah* 43A) explains that there are several levels of *kadosh* ("holiness"), but none of them are holy like *Havaya*…" The matter is as follows; the name *Havaya* indicates that He creates everything, and even though He creates everything, He is nevertheless holy and removed from them. He is *sovev kol olamim* – "transcendent illumination of the worlds" – unlike the soul [that fills the body, which is *memalle kol olamim* – "immanent illumination"]. And for that reason, this category of holiness is not to be found among all the other expressions of holiness that exist above. Regarding all of the other levels of *seder hishtalshelut* ("spiritual chain of creation"), whatever is called "holy" - meaning that it is somehow "removed" - does not imply the following two opposites: On one hand, it permeates and penetrates, and on the other, it is holy and removed. Above, though, the infinite light of *sovev kol olamim*, which is holy and removed nevertheless descends to create all of the worlds. The main impetus for creation comes from the *makif* ("transcendent light"), as written in Tanya at the end of Ch. 23 and the end of Chapter 48…And that is why "there is no holiness like that of *Havaya*." And this is what is meant by "He grasps all worlds" – via *sovev kol olamim,* He creates and energizes all worlds from nothing to something - and despite all this, "there is none who grasp Him and He is holy and removed."

xlii) Page 42 (Page 185 in the translation)

"as it is written (Psalms 139:16), "The days in which they were to be formed…")

Note: "See *Likutei Torah* in the discourse, *Al ken yomru*, section 3, and in the discourse *Ki tihiyena le'ish*…"

From *Likutei Torah* of the Alter Rebbe, *parshat Chukat*, discourse *Al ken yomru*, section 3, Page 130

"And this is what is meant by *al ken yomru hamoshlim, bo'u Cheshbon* – "And therefore the poets would say, Come to [the city called] *Cheshbon*..." – here the word for "poets" (*moshlim*) also means "those who govern," and alludes to those who have control over their physical nature and temptations. And the verse is precise, referring to a city called *Cheshbon*, which also means "accounting." That is, "Come and make an accounting of the world." The word for "world" is *olam*, from the word *he'elam*, meaning concealment, and those who "govern over their natures" alludes to souls that have descended to this world. They must "make an accounting" of why they came into a physical body in this dark world. It is the ultimate descent, but it is for the purpose of ascent. That is, [they have come down] in order to subdue the "other side" that is opposed to holiness, and in the process the glory of G-d becomes publicized in the world...

And another explanation – in fact, the main one – of "accounting of the world" is that most of the hiding and concealment of this world takes place right here in the lowest of all worlds, which is why the darkness here is thick and doubled-over. And therefore, in order to illuminate this opaque darkness, we need to draw down a far greater light and illumination, so that the darkness will have no effect, and will in fact shine like light. Minimal illumination is incapable of illuminating the thick darkness. In a normal house, a conventional candle is sufficient, but deep in the cellar, where the atmosphere is thick and dark (since it is within the deepest most physical part of the earth), a huge light is necessary in order to illuminate the thick atmoshpere. A thin candle will not suffice, and may even be extinguished by the physical nature of the atmosphere.

And so it is regarding the process of illuminating the darkness of the world of physical *asiya*; it demands the highest illumination. And that is why souls descend to this world, so that by the "candle of G-d – the soul of man" [may illuminate]. Also, a candle is compared to a mitzvah and the Torah is compared to light – so that in this manner the soul is able to illuminate and subdue the darkness, [transforming it] to light. That is what is meant by "accounting of the world" – according to the amount of concealment, so we must maximize the light of Torah and mitzvoth.

From *Likutei Torah* of the Alter Rebbe, *parshat Ki Teitzei*, discourse *Ki Tihiyena le'ish*... on Page 74

"Now, the purpose of the descent of the Divine soul to this world is in order to en-clad it in the natural animal soul and do battle with it, with the goal of refining it and separating the good within it from the bad. [The purpose is to] elevate it to G-d, and in so doing transform darkness to light. That is why we are called "Yisrael," as written that "You struggled (*sarit*) with *Elokim* (in this context, "angels") and overcame," meaning that the G-dly soul will overcome the enlivening animal soul, transforming its thoughts and emotions that are not devoted to G-d, from evil to good...

...And this is what is meant by the verse, "The days of our years in them are seventy years..." The phrase "in them" is quite precise, because the verse is referring to two souls, between which there is a new war every day. And therefore, their level of energy is not equal – one has more vitality than the other. It all depends upon the level of war that is necessary to do battle with the animal soul. For, according to the portion of evil within it are the number of years that it are necessary to struggle with it until it is transformed to good.

That is what is meant by the verse, "And now, Israel, what does G-d ask from you..." where-in "now" refers to the present era, when good and evil are mixed. The soul is called "Yisrael" because it must rule over and overwhelm the animal soul, transforming it from bad to good. But, regarding the future it is said, "And I will wipe away the spirit of impurity from the land," and there will be no more evil at all. It will not be necessary to fight any more and at that time, our names will no longer be Yisrael...."

xliii) Page 43 (Page 190 in the translation)

Note: "And as the philosophers said…" – See *Sefer Ikarim, Maamor* 3, first chapter. See *Kuntres Umayan, Maamor* 1. *Sichat* 19 *Kislev* of the year 5680 (!920), section 6 (in *Torat Shalom, sefer Hasichot*). The discourse *lema'an da'at* of the year 5690 (1930) (*Kuntres vov*)

From *Sefer HaIkarim* of R' Yoseph Albo, *maamor* 3, Ch. 1 (Page 197 in the Warsaw edition, reprinted in Jerusalem in 1960)

"This that man…grasps in thought and understanding more than other animals, is because he is a higher form of creation, and more complete than them…and it is not appropriate to think that because the other animals live without need of shade from draught or of shelter from rain, and they do not need to "fix" or do anything in order to obtain their sustenance, but rather all of their sustenance is available…and even moreso, some of them have certain skills, such as predators and carnivorous birds that have the ability to hunt and thus to find their sustenance – that therefore they are a more complete form of creation than man. This was suggested by some of the earlier thinkers, who expressed this opinion, and they would said that man is incomplete in comparison to the other animals, since the other animals do not need anything to "ride" in order to travel from one place to another since they themselves travel easily, moving more than the human species. Similarly, they do not need to prepare themselves for war with their enemies, since all of the tools of war are already found with them naturally, such as the horns of an oxe and the tusks of the pig and the thorns of the porcupine and shield of the turtle…and moreover animals do not need clothes because their "garments" are created with them naturally. And they need no preparation of food since their food is ready for them at all times. But, man is missing all of this; he needs clothes for the outside of his body and buildings to live within for shelter and to protect himself from rain and water. And he needs to do much preparation of his food so that he will be able to sustain himself, and similar other activities.

But, when we look closely at this opinion, we see that it is totally lacking in basis. When we look into the creations that exist…and all of the low entities that are created, we find that all of them pursue perfection, each in its own way. That is, each creation that comes later [higher in the chain] is more admirable than the previous one, as if to say that the physical substance of creation flows always from a less perfected to a more perfected and complete form. For, first the substance of creation takes on the form of the elements [wind, water, fire and earth], and afterward it ascends to the level of the mineral world, of which the elements are the more primitive origins. And then it ascends to the vegetable category, of which the mineral world is the more primitive source, and from there it ascends to the animal kingdom, of which vegetation is a more primitive source. And then it ascends to the level of man, and the animals are the primitive form of man. And there stands the creation. It is as if each segment [of creation] prepares for the segment that follows it; so it would appear among lower creations that each one serves the purpose of the segment that follows it…ascending from one segment to the next we reach the highest segment, which is the human form – and there the creation stands because it is the ultimate purpose of all the lower creations.

As evidence that the physical substance moves always from a state of lesser being to a higher state of existence…is that we find the species known as a "sponge" as an intermediary between the mineral and the vegetable categories. And we find the sea sponge that possesses nothing more than the sense of "feeling" as an intermediary between the vegetable and the animal categories. And there is the monkey that serves as an intermediary between animals and man, and man is the pinnacle of existence.

If so, [the creation] is impossible without the existence of man, who is the ultimate goal of the lower creations; he is the most important and complete of all of them, emerging as the sum total of all of the previous forms which are more abstract than him. And therefore, he is the greatest of all of them, and conquers the animals beneath him and rules over them since his abilities are of a general nature, while the abilities of the animals are particular - they are unable to grasp general matters. And that is why they possess particular "tools" and specific skills, according to their individual abilities. There are those with particular abilities to fight in specific ways, such as the tusks of the pig and the horns of the oxe and the thorns in the skin of the porcupine and the shield on the turtle to protect it. But, since man is the ultimate being among the lower creations, he gathers together all of the perfection and particular abilities that are found among all the other animals. His abilities are general and his intellect is also general, meaning that he grasps all of the skills of the animal in general; he grasps the general drift of things, not merely particular details. And therefore, all of his skills are general, such as the hands with which he can fight any kind of war that the animals fight, and to defeat the animal bemeath him. He may grab a spear in place of horns that are on the animal, and a sword in place of the tusks on the pig, and a shield in his hand, or he may don armor to protect himself as does the turtle. And the tools of war weren't [created] as part of his form as they were among the animals, so that they shouldn't be an extra burden for him to carry constantly. And for this reason, the Creator gave him general tools and skills, whether for the purpose of war…and he gave him the power of general intellect in order to achieve the general goals and not merely particular ones and the ability to grasp the general outline of all particular ideas that all of the animals might use and use their skills when needed and to set them aside when not needed…and so regarding clothes which are separate from his body so that he need only don them when necessary during the winter and not during the summer…and gave him wisdom and understanding to build houses that are strong to fend off those who would damage him…

From *Kuntres Umayan* of the Rebbe Rashab, *Maamor* 1, Ch. 3 (page 64)

"Now, everything is the world was created for a purpose. And the purpose of everything is to ascend to a higher level than where it stands presently. The purpose of the vegetable world is to become included in the animal world, the purpose of the animal world is to become included in the human world, and the purpose of the human world is fulfilled when our spirit ascends to be included in the spiritual world above us. This takes place as we learn Torah, which is the wisdom and will of the One above, and the Torah and Holy One Blessed be He are One.

And when man is involved in Torah and delves into it carefully in order to truly understand its concepts, he becomes united with the wisdom and will of G-d, with an incredible unity (as written in the first book of Tanya, Ch. 5). And in this manner his soul ascends to become united and included in His wisdom may He be blessed, whether the person is involved in the *nigleh* ("revealed aspects" of the Torah, such as Talmud and *halacha*) of Torah, which is the essence of His wisdom and will (for thus He concluded in His wisdom that a particular object is kosher or unfit)…or whether he is involved in the inner dimensions of Torah (*nistar* – "concealed" wisdom), which are the knowledge and grasp of G-dliness. For what the rabbis revealed to us of this subject is the inner dimension of His wisdom, and when man is involved in this, it unites him with the inner wisdom of G-d, far above the outer manifestations (*nigleh*) of Torah…"

From *Torat Shalom* of the Rebbe Rashab, *sichat* 19 *Kislev*, *5680* (1920), section 6, Page 243

(At the end of the meal, a rabbi came from Tshernigov and someone from Petrograd and yet another came from a general meeting, and the Rebbe Rashab said to them), "You missed the (delivery of) Chasidut, but I will say a few words: In the *Sefer Ikarim* it states that the purpose of the mineral, vegetable, animal and human worlds is to ascend to that which is above them. For, the major purpose of all creation is to ascend to what is above it: The purpose of the mineral world is to ascend to the vegetable, meaning that the vegetable world should emerge from it. The purpose of the vegetable world is to elevate to the animal world, meaning that the animals eat from it and are nourished as it becomes a part of them. The purpose of the animal world is to ascend to the human world, meaning that humans must eat [animals] and be nourished as they become part of man. And the purpose of the human is to ascend to that which is above him. Now, the advantage of the human being is that he possesses intelligence, and this is his advantage over the mineral, vegetable and animal. And the purpose of the human being is to ascend to what is beyond intellect, meaning that he must ascend to G-dliness, since that is the level of the intellect in essence.

And so it is written in the *Ikarim*. [But], we say (that is, Chasidut says) that the purpose of the human being is to become like an animal (*chai* - but also meaning "life-energy," or "vitality"). For, the animal lives without intellect. So, from what does he live – from *chai* ("life-energy"), which is G-dliness. For without G-dliness, no life exists, and *chayut* comes only from G-dliness, as written, "And *Havaya Elokim emet*, He is the living G-d." And if so, regarding the animal which has no intellect and yet lives, we come to the realization that he lives from G-dliness. Thus, the purpose of the human who is intellectual, is to arrive to this level of *chai;* that is, he should know and feel – the human who is intelligent can experience this – that he lives from G-d.

From the discourse, *Lema'an da'at* of the year *5690* (1930) from the Rebbe Rayatz *ztz'l*, in *Sefer Maamorim Kuntresim Aleph*, Page 168 (*Kuntres vov*):

"In general, the creation is divided into four categories: Mineral, vegetable, animal and human. The purpose of the mineral world is realized when it ascends beyond its level and it germinates fodder, etc. And the purpose of the vegetable world is fulfilled when it becomes included within the animal world, and the purpose of the animal world is to become included in the human. And the purpose of the human being is achieved as his spirit ascends, and becomes included in spiritual levels that are above him. [This happens] as he learns Torah, which is the wisdom and will of G-d, and the Torah and the Holy One blessed be He are one. And when man involves himself in the Torah, and delves carefully into matters in order to truly understand them, he unites with the wisdom and will of G-d with a tremendous unity, as written in the first section of Tanya, Chapter 5.

Now with this bond that unites man with Torah, he becomes connected and included in G-d's wisdom, whether he is involved in the revealed side of Torah, which is the essence of His wisdom and will, for thus He concluded in His wisdom that this particular object is kosher, and this one unfit…or whether he is involved in the inner dimensions of the Torah, which is knowledge and grasp of G-dliness. For, all matters and laws of the Torah as they appear in their physical condition, exist in their true state within the *sephirot* above and [are expressed] in spiritual matters. For example, take the *halacha* of "two who are holding on to a *talit*." Down in the physical world, this is a physical *talit* with two physical people. But, this *halacha* is learned as well in *gan eden*, where it is not appropriate to speak of anything physical at all. And the learning there takes place on the real, true level of the concept as it really exists, as our sages, such as the Rashbi and the *Ariz'l*, as well as our rabbis revealed in the inner dimensions of the soul, which is the inner aspect of His wisdom. And when man is involved in this, he becomes united with the inner wisdom of G-d, far above the unity of the revealed dimensions oft the Torah…"

xliv) Page 46 (Page 207 in the translation)

Note: "Noise of involvement in *avoda*...as written elsewhere"

See the discourse *Ve'eleh shemot* of the year *5675* (1915) of the Rebbe Rashab, Page 812 in the series *Besha'ah shehikdimu 5672* (1912), vol. 2

Page 819 (Ch. 398)

The subject is as follows; whether we are speaking of external or internal mindfulness (*chitzoniyut* or *pnimiyut hamochin*) - which in general correspond to the external and the internal elements of the heart - both are associated with the entire process of prayer, [beginning] with the *pesukei dezimra* ("songs of praise"), the blessings before the *kriat shema* and the *kriat shema* itself (which correspond to [the soul-levels of] *ruach* and *neshama*). The only difference is in their spiritual level. For it is known that the three sections of prayer mentioned above correspond to *ruach* ("wind"), *ra'ash* ("noise, commotion") and *aish* ("fire"), all of which are components of the *midot*, or spiritual emotions. *Ruach* applies to the *pesukei dezimra*, during which we arouse our emotions with great excitement through meditation upon the creation from nothing to something. In essence this is a process that goes beyond intellectual grasp, but its amazing origins arouse exhilaration in the heart. In general, this is but a transcendent excitement that does not penetrate the inner core of the soul, but remains external alone. For that reason, there is no goal ascribed to it, aside from spiritual ascent alone (just as the animal soul rises to a higher level, as explained in Ch. 382 and 392, so for the G-dly soul, there is only elevation and uplift, as the soul rises to a higher level).

And *ra'ash* applies to the blessings that we say before the *kriat shema*, as the *ofanim* (lower angels) and the holy *chayot* (higher angels) create a great tumult. This corresponds to our meditation on the subject of *kadosh* ("holiness"), as discussed in *Likutei Torah* in the second discourse beginning with the words *Ani HaShem Elokeichem* ("I am the Lord your G-d"). This tumult is the result of the amazing loftiness of the subject. It is produced as a result of the apparent newness of the concept under investigation. When a man sees something new that he never imagined, he becomes greatly excited, with a lot of commotion. Something to which he is already accustomed or which is already within his normal range of experience does not stimulate him at all. Only that which is outside of his ordinary experience and is new to him is capable of greatly exciting him. Like [*istarei belegina*], which is the result of the novelty of the situation. And similarly in the realm of spirituality, intellectual grasp of anything holy is novel regarding the creation, since the inner vitality and experience of any created being comes from a mere ray and reflection of G-dliness, while the infinite essence of G-d, may he be blessed, is holy and beyond. And therefore, [intellectual grasp] among created beings is a rarity, and causes much excitement and commotion. Part of the wonder of it is that it doesn't come into full intellectual grasp, since no thought can truly grasp Him. And this is further cause for excitement, since that which a person grasps, he internalizes and accepts in a settled manner, while that which he does not totally grasp, meaning that he may understand it, but not in totality, produces "noise" and tumult (and this as well is new and novel, since that which is not entirely understood is novel).

And therefore, the noise and commotion of the *ofanim* is greater than that of the *seraphim*, since their grasp is on a lesser level. They know of holiness, but they do not know what it is, and this is what produces a great amount of commotion. And nonetheless, this is a more internal feeling than is *ruach*, since at least they grasp how the infinite light is holy and removed from the worlds. And in particular, as they grasp the nature of the loftiness of G-d's infinite light, the resulting excitement, while noisy, nevertheless contains an element of inner vitality since it arrives via the intellect. And therefore the excitement includes a goal and endpoint – the desire to becomes subsumed and included in G-d's infinite light – all this because the excitement is internalized within...

Ch. 399 ...Now, regarding the three levels of *ruach* ("spirit" or "wind"), *ra'ash* ("noise" or "commotion") and *aish* ("fire"), the scripture says that they are not the *ruach* of *Havaya*, nor the *ra'ash* of *Havaya*, etc... The topic is as follows; *ruach* ("spirit" or "wind") is associated with the *pesukei dezimra*, and involves meditation upon the creation of the worlds, which came into being from the *ruach* or breath of His mouth, may He be blessed. Now, this is not the *ruach* of *Havaya*, but the *ruach* of *Elokim*, as known that from the name *Havaya* it was not possible to create. The creation took place using the name *Elokim*, as we see in the first verse of the Torah, "In the beginning, *Elokim* created." Only the final 'hey' of the name *Havaya* was associated with creation, as we see from the word, *behibaram* ("when they were creation," Gen 2:4) – which may be re-written, *be Hey baram* ("with the *hey* they were created"). The final *hey*, described in the Zohar as a "light letter that has no substance," is nothing more than a breath of external *ruach*.

And the *ruach* is followed by *ra'ash* ("noise" or "commotion") corresponding to the *yotzar ohr* – [the blessings preceding the *kriat shema*], which involves nullification of the angels and souls in the higher spiritual worlds. [This occurs] as we meditate upon the concept of *kadosh* ("holy"). This word *kadosh* (Hebrew letters *kuf-dalet-vav-shin*) contains the letter *vav*, indicating descent of a ray of spirituality from a higher transcendent level called *kodesh elyon* ("supernal holiness"), in order to bring together both immanent (*memalle*) spirituality and transcendent (*sovev*) G-dliness. The meditation is upon the holiness of the infinite light of G-d may He be blessed, how there is nothing as holy as *Havaya*, (as written in *Likutei Torah*, in the second discourse entitled *Tze'ena Ure'ena*). And yet, this [meditation] is does not lead to the *ra'ash* of *Havaya*, since it involves only the *vov-hey*, or final two letters of His name, and not the first two (*yud-hey*). And also, the G-dliness that descends with the *vov* remains *makif* [beyond us, not internalized], which is what is meant by *kadosh vov* – transcendent holiness that descends.

Jerusalem Connection is a non-profit organization
dedicated to Jewish outreach and education.
It was created with the blessing of the Lubavitcher Rebbe ztz'l in 1991,
and has since flourished in the Old City of Jerusalem.
It is frequented by Jewish university students, tourists and
new immigrants to Israel who seek spiritual guidance
and connection with the One Above,
and also instruction in the inner dimensions of Torah
(Chassidic and Kabbalistic literature).
It is located at Rechov HaMekubalim 3/5 in the Old City of Jerusalem.
For more information, visit the Jerusalem Connection website at
www.jerusalemconnection.org
or email jerconn@netvision.net.il

www.ingramcontent.com/pod-product-compliance
Lightning Source LLC
Chambersburg PA
CBHW080238170426
43192CB00014BA/2489